South-East Asia
on a shoestring

South-East Asia on a Shoestring
5th edition

Published by
Lonely Planet Publications
PO Box 88, South Yarra 3141, Australia
PO Box 2001A, Berkeley, CA 94702, USA

Printed by
Colorcraft, Hong Kong

Cover illustrations by
Anthony Jenkins

First Published
1975

This edition
1985

National Library of Australia
Cataloguing-in-publication entry

Wheeler, Tony, 1946-
South-East Asia on a Shoestring

5th ed.
ISBN 0 908086 67 9.

1.Asia, Southeastern — Description and travel — Guide-books. I. Title.

915.9'0453

Tony Wheeler was born in England but spent most of his younger days overseas due to his father's occupation with British Airways. Those years included a lengthy spell in Pakistan, a shorter period in the West Indies and all his high school years in the US. He returned to England to do a university degree in engineering, worked for a short time as an automotive design engineer, returned to university again and did an MBA then dropped out on the Asian overland trail with his wife Maureen. They've been travelling, writing and publishing guidebooks ever since, having set up Lonely Planet Publications in the mid-70s. Travelling for Tony and Maureen is now considerably enlivened by their daughter Tashi (who had visited four of the countries in this book before her third birthday) and son Kieran (who had visited two before he was one). The Wheelers spent 1984 and the first part of 1985 in Berkeley, California establishing the Lonely Planet office there but expect to be back in Australia in the second half of '85.

This Edition

It's more than 10 years now since Maureen and I started off on our first long trek around South-East Asia to produce the original edition of *South-East Asia on a Shoestring*. Along the way from that first 144 page edition to this much larger 5th edition it has shed a couple of countries (Portuguese Timor and Laos, in real detail at least), added several more (Hong Kong, Macau, Papua New Guinea and the Philippines) but always kept that familiar yellow cover!

Although it's physically impossible for me to get back to every single place in this book I always get back to some of them and there is always some place which I cover again in great depth. Equally important, Lonely Planet now has a string of regular researchers whose work I can trust and between us we do the most

thorough and comprehensive updating job possible. Since the previous edition I've been back to Burma, Hong Kong, Indonesia, Singapore and Thailand. My Hong Kong and Singapore visits were brief ones, but in Burma I did the complete loop once again and also managed to visit a couple of places I had not got to on any previous trip. I made two trips through Thailand, the first time concentrating on Bangkok (where the backpackers' accommodation 'centre' has made a complete shift across town) and Ayuthaya. The second trip I got up to the north to enjoy the cool air of Chiang Mai once again. In Indonesia I spent some time in Bali with Maureen and our two children, Tashi and Kieran.

That covers my own jaunts around the region. This book also enjoys the most thorough Lonely Planet investigation of

Indonesia yet when three researchers, all from our office in Melbourne, fanned out to cover the entire archipelago. Ginny Bruce covered Java, Mary Covernton (who had earlier worked with me on our Bali & Lombok book) covered Sumatra while Alan Samagalski trekked around all the other islands travellers are likely to get to including Kalimantan, Sulawesi, the Moluccas, Irian Jaya and all the important islands of Nusa Tenggara.

Apart from my own visits to Thailand, American Joe Cummings travelled throughout the kingdom to update his own *Thailand – a travel survival kit*. In Malaysia Canadian Mark Lightbody travelled around both the peninsula and north Borneo to update *Malaysia, Singapore & Brunei – a travel survival kit*. Mark also did a complete circuit of PNG for *Papua New Guinea – a travel survival kit*. This book also enjoys Jens Peter's research for *The Philippines – a travel survival kit*. That only leaves Hong Kong and Macau and after she had finished with Java, Ginny continued on to those currently topical city-states. So you see we managed to get back to everywhere there was to get back to!

Of course there are two other groups who also contributed to this book. One is the Lonely Planet 'gang' both at our office in Berkeley, California (where all the information and updates were assembled and edited) and at our office in Melbourne, Australia (where the actual assembly of the book took place). Thank you Elizabeth Kim, Sharon Rufus, Mary Covernton,

Ginny Bruce, Alan Samagalski, Michael Langley, Anne Logan, Graham Imeson, Fiona Boyes, Lindy Cameron, Todd Pierce, Marianne Poole and Pooh Bear.

The other group is 'our travellers' out there on the road who write to us with suggestions, corrections and additional information. Special thanks must also go to Paul Cummings of Orbitours to who initially supplied the information for the 'Other South-East Asia' section for the last edition and to the anonymous contributor who supplemented it for this one. Many travellers who wrote with suggestions on countries covered in this book have already been credited in recent editions of our Philippines, Malaysia-Singapore, Thailand, Burma and Papua New Guinea travel survival kits.

Many others who wrote to us are listed at the back of the book.

A Warning & a Request
Things change – prices go up, good places go bad, bad places go bankrupt and nothing stays the same. So if you find things better, worse, cheaper, more expensive, recently opened or long ago closed please don't blame me but please do write and tell me. The letters we get from 'our' travellers out there on the road are some of the nicest things about doing these guides for a living. As usual the best letters will be rewarded with a free copy of the next edition (or any other LP guide if you prefer) (and your information is good enough!).

Contents

Introduction

If I had to nominate one region of the world as my favourite for travelling, the one area I'd choose if I had to quit travelling everywhere else, I would have no second thoughts – South-East Asia. There is simply more variety here than almost any other region of the world. In food, religion, culture, South-East Asia has everything you could possibly ask for.

What's more, it's a great area for travel simply for the sake of travel. Sure the big international airlines cruise high overhead on their way to Singapore, Bangkok or Hong Kong, but you've not really experienced flying until you've been into a few of Papua New Guinea's 'third level' airstrips. When you get to the end of the runway you're either flying or falling, there's no third choice. If island hopping sounds like fun then you can't beat South-East Asia for opportunities in that field. The Philippines, for example, claim to have over 7000 islands and there are countless ships ploughing back and forth between them. In lots of places you can make island hopping even more adventurous; I'll always remember the time six of us chartered an Indonesian *prahu* to sail from Flores to Sumbawa via the island of Komodo to see the famous dragons. And spent four solid days pumping the bilge to keep that leaky bucket afloat.

Food is another great pleasure of South-East Asia. After my first long trip through the region I became a complete addict for tropical fruit, and thoughts of rambutans, mangosteens and salaks still make me glassy eyed! I must admit I'm still working on developing a taste for durians though. Singapore just has to be one of the world's food capitals; every time I fly there I seem to spend the last half hour of the flight thinking over where I'm going to eat each and every meal for the next few days.

Of course travelling and eating are not all there are to exploring a region, but if you want memorable scenes and unforgettable moments you'll certainly find those. The great Shwe Dagon Pagoda in Rangoon is still one of those 'magical' places where time seems to stand still and each visit reveals something new. Early mornings in Bali have a pastoral beauty words and even pictures simply cannot capture.

South-East Asia also has a healthy share of the world's most interesting volcanoes. Over the years I've stood on top of Mayon in the Philippines, the world's 'most perfect' volcano; gazed down on the three different-coloured crater-lakes of Keli Mutu in Flores, and watched the sun rise from the crater rim of Bromo in Java. Even if simply lying on beaches is more your thing, South-East Asia has plenty to offer. You can spend a lot of time wrestling with momentous decisions about whether Tioman, Phuket or Koh Samui is the most beautiful tropical island. In fact the more I think about it the more enthusiastic I am to go back again!

Facts about the Region

DOCUMENTS

There are two documents you have to have and a number worth considering. You must have a passport and health certificate. Make sure your passport is valid for a reasonably long period of time and has plenty of space for those rubber-stamp-happy Asians to do their bit. Some countries actually require that your passport is valid for a certain time when applying for visas. It could be embarrassing to run out of blank pages too – although in my experience it is generally fairly easy to get a new passport in Asia (I've had one in Jakarta, Maureen in Bangkok) so long as you haven't lost the old one. Some people (Americans for example) can simply have an extra concertina-section stuck in when their passport gets filled up. The second 'necessary' document is an International Health Certificate – see Vaccinations for more details.

If you plan to be driving abroad get an International Driving Permit from your local automobile association. Usual cost is around US$5. They are valid for one year only and make life much simpler, especially for hiring motorcycles in Bali. An International Youth Hostel card can be useful even if you don't intend to use hostels. Although many Asian hostels do not require that you be a YHA member they will often charge you less if you have a card.

Then there are student cards. The ISIC, International Student Identity Card, is a green and white card with your photograph on it, usually supplied in a clear plastic pouch. It can perform all sorts of wonders, particularly when it comes to airline tickets – so it's no wonder that there is a worldwide industry in fake student cards. Usual price for a fake card is around US$7.50 and Bangkok is a great centre for finding them – notices appear in all the relevant places! Of course some of the cards are of deplorably low quality, but airlines simply want to get you into their aircraft, even if it is with a student discount, they're not too worried about how pretty the card is. Many places now also stipulate a maximum age for student discounts.

Finally remember that 'student' is a very respectable thing to be and if your passport has a blank space for occupation you are much better off having 'student' there than something nasty like 'journalist' or 'photographer'.

Losing your passport is a real bummer, it can be made a little easier if somewhere else you've got a record of its number, issue date and a photocopy of your birth certificate. While you're compiling that info add the serial number of your travellers' cheques and US$50 or so as emergency cash – keep all that material totally separate from your passport, cheques and other cash.

VISAS

Visas remain my pet Asian hate. Visas are a stamp in your passport permitting you to enter the country in question and stay for a specified period of time. They're generally pure red tape and another means of gouging a few more dollars out of you. If you spend much time travelling around the region you'll waste a lot of time, money, effort and passport pages on them.

Several steps can make visas a little easier. As far as possible get your visas as you go along rather than all at once before you leave home. Two reasons – one, they often expire after x days, and two, it is often easier and very often cheaper to get them in neighbouring countries than far away. Shop around for your visas, you'll hear on the grapevine that city A is far better than city B for such and such a visa.

Finally there is the dreaded ticket-out

problem. For some reason several countries have this phobia that if you don't arrive clutching your departure ticket in your hand you'll never leave. This is a real hassle if you intend to depart by some unusual means for which the tickets can only be bought after you arrive! There are two possible answers. One is to get an mco, 'miscellaneous charges order', which is like an airline ticket but with no destination. Some places will accept this. Alternatively just get the cheapest ticket out and refund it later on – make sure it's the cheapest and safest; there are some airlines who part with refunds like Scrooge with his pennies.

Of course if you really are going to be departing as planned you've got no problems. Note that in places where renewing visas can be difficult (Indonesia in particular) a confirmed ticket out from the place you're trying to renew in will be much more acceptable. If you're in Bali a ticket out of Denpasar will stand you in much better stead than an undated one from Medan in north Sumatra.

If you hit a sticky visa problem, shop around. In some other city or country the situation may be better. See the section on visas under the individual countries in this book. Remember the most important rule: treat embassies, consulates and borders as formal occasions – dress up for them.

MONEY
Bring as much of this fine stuff as possible. Despite the ups and downs of international currencies over the past few years you're probably still best off with US dollars. The pound is nice to have in some places (Hong Kong, Malaysia, Singapore and most definitely in India), the Deutsche mark or the yen are well accepted everywhere, but when it comes down to day-in-day-out acceptability the dollar is the currency to carry. Of late it has also been unbelievably strong as well. It's particularly good in the Philippines and Thailand (where US influence is/has been strong) and in Indonesia where the US dollar often seems to enjoy a strange premium over the other currencies.

American Express or Thomas Cook travellers' cheques are probably the best to carry because of their 'instant replacement' policies. The main idea of carrying cheques rather than cash is the protection they offer from theft, but it doesn't do a lot of good if you have to go back home first to get the refund. Amex have offices in many major cities, you can be certain that your local bank won't have. Of course 'instant replacement' may not always be instantaneous, particularly if you look a little freaky, but overall most people seem to be pretty satisfied with the service. Keeping a record of the cheque numbers and the initial purchase details is vitally important. Without this you may well find that 'instant' is a very long time indeed. If you're going to really out-of-the-way places it may be worth taking a couple of different brands of travellers' cheques since banks may not always accept all varieties.

It is a good idea to take some cash with you. Often it is much easier to change just a few dollars (when leaving a country for example) in cash rather than cheques – and more economical. When banks are closed cash is also better. In countries where there is a black market cash is what's wanted, not travellers' cheques. And of course the odd dollar laid in the right place (the right hand) can perform wonders.

If you run out of cash, accidentally or deliberately, and need more, instruct your bank back home to send a draft to you (always assuming you've got some $ back home to send!). Specify the city and the bank – once I made the mistake of saying 'to your usual bank' and then spent a day trying to find out which was their 'usual bank'. If you don't know a bank then ask them to write to you and tell you where it is. It's probably a good idea to ask them anyway; I recently discovered that Lonely Planet's bank in the US had dealings with about 20 different banks in Hong Kong,

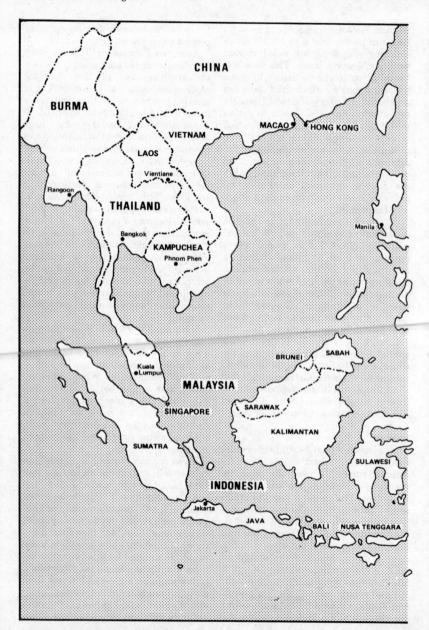

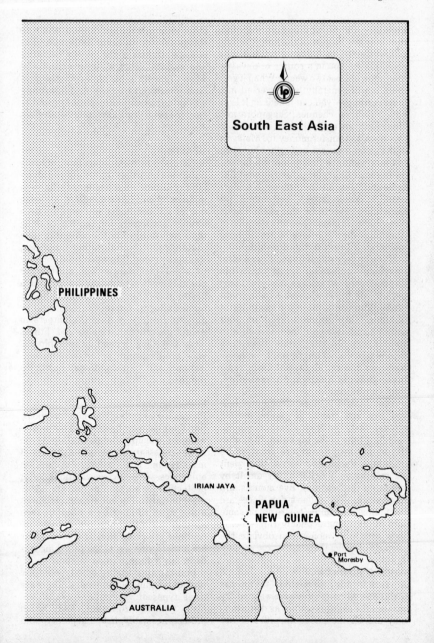

excluding the Hong Kong & Shanghai, probably the biggest of the lot!

Transferred by cable or telex money should reach you in a couple of days, by mail allow at least two weeks. When it gets there it will generally be converted into local currency – you can take it as it is or buy travellers' cheques. Singapore and Hong Kong are easily the best countries in this book to transfer money to. Malaysia and Thailand are not bad either but even Indonesia and the Philippines are far and away easier than places further west like India and Pakistan where money transfers seem to drop into a bottomless pit sometimes never to be seen again. Papua New Guinea is almost like an extension of Australia when it comes to transferring money so it's very straightforward.

If you're very sound financially an ideal travelling companion is an American Express card. It amuses me how many pack-toting freaks also have their credit cards! With one of these you can put a lot of things (like airline tickets) on your account and save carrying so much with you. If you run low, rather than have money transferred out to you from home base you can get an instant cash transfusion from any American Express office. Very convenient.

Your budget is dependent upon how you live and travel. If you're moving around fast, going to lots of places, spending time in the big cities, then your day-to-day living costs are going to be quite high. People who tell you they spent six months on a dollar a day did it by sitting on the beach for five months and three weeks. The dollar-a-day places are fast fading! Remember you're not on some sort of travelling economy run – being tight with your money can obviate the purpose of being there.

WHEN & HOW LONG?

Anytime for any time might be the answer to this one. Although there are wet and dry seasons the changes are not as distinct as they are on the subcontinent. Nor are there seasons when you can and cannot do things (as for trekking in Nepal). The climate sections of the various countries and regions detail what to expect and when to expect it, but anytime is the right time somewhere or other! And how long – why as long as you can manage. It would be easy to spend years exploring South-East Asia.

HEALTH

A British medical magazine actually published an article describing the 'overland syndrome' – a collection of afflictions suffered by many Asia travellers. Although one of its symptoms was said to be a strange propensity for eastern clothing the article finished on the reassuring note that this, along with the other symptoms, was easily cured. They don't tell you how to avoid that danger but most other possible medical problems are covered in health guides like *The Traveller's Health Guide* (Roger Lascelles, London) or *Staying Healthy in Asia* (Volunteers in Asia Publications). Health and fitness while travelling depend on two things – your pre-departure protection (immunisations) and your day-to-day health on the road.

Immunisations

Plan ahead for getting your immunisations. Smallpox has now been wiped out worldwide so smallpox immunization is no longer necessary. Cholera is a disease of insanitation and usually occurs in epidemics. Cholera vaccinations offer protection for six months and are highly recommended. The initial shot is followed a month or so later by a booster, then another booster every six months to continue the protection. If cholera shots are a sneak preview of the real thing it is definitely a disease to do without.

Immunization against both typhoid and tetanus is highly recommended. There are three types of vaccinations available – plain typhoid protection, TAB which protects against typhoid and paratyphoid

A and B, and TABT which provides the whole lot including protection against tetanus. TABT lasts for three years. If you've not had a recent polio booster it's not a bad idea to get one. Vaccination enthusiasts can also consider protection against typhus and plague but there is a limit!

Yellow fever shots, which last a nice round 10 years, are only necessary for Africa or Latin America. Then there's hepatitis and gamma-globulin shots. The period of immunity to hepatitis which gamma-globulin gives is relatively short and some people question just how efficacious it is, even suggesting that once its period of protection has finished you are more susceptible to the hep than before. Doctors say the latest gamma-globulin shots are better than before and also cause less reaction so you ought to have them. The best protection against the hep, as against most other diseases of insanitation, is to take care what and where you eat and to wash your hands frequently.

As proof of all these scratches, jabs and punctures you need an International Health Certificate to be signed and stamped by your doctor and local health authority. In some countries (Australia, the UK, many countries in Asia) immunisations are available from airport or government health centres. Travel agents or airline offices will tell you where.

Malaria

Malarial mosquitoes are rife in much of South-East Asia including the more remote parts of Malaysia, Thailand and the Philippines, much of Indonesia and, most important, Papua New Guinea. The malaria strain found in PNG is resistant to the normal malarial prophylactics so if you're going to PNG stress it to your doctor. Elsewhere protection consists of a weekly dose of chloroquine or daily paludrine – opinions differ on which is best amongst doctors and which is easiest to remember to take amongst travellers. I

was travelling once with somebody who did not take malarial tabs and he caught malaria in Flores. It's not a nice thing to have and what's worse it can recur years later. Avoid it. Further protection can be gained by keeping the little buggers at bay with mosquito nets or by burning mosquito coils.

Stomach Problems

Although stomach upsets are far less here common than further west, for example in India, they're still a good possibility. Often this can be due simply to a change of diet or a system unused to spicy food. Many times, however, contaminated food or water is the problem. There are two answers to upset stomachs. First avoid them by taking care in what you eat and drink – make sure food is well cooked and hasn't been sitting around. Make sure fresh food has been properly cleaned. And don't drink untreated water. Secondly if avoidance fails do something about it.

The simplest treatment is to do nothing. If your system can fight off the invaders naturally you'll probably build up some immunity. Stick to hot tea and try not to eat too much. If you do decide to resort to modern medicines don't do so too readily, don't overdo them and if you start a course of medicine follow it through to the end. There are various over-the-counter cures like the popular Lomotil. The name indicates that it 'lowers motility'; it simply slows your system down and lets it work things out. Plain codeine works as well and is cheaper. Antibiotics, on the other hand, actually go into battle for you but I have a suspicion that people who have the most stomach problems are the ones who resort too readily to antibiotics and other 'big guns'.

The word 'dysentery' is used far too lightly by many travellers. If you've just got loose movements you've got diarrhoea. If blood or pus are also present then you probably have amoebic dysentery which requires an anti-amoebic drug like metronidazole or flagyl. If on top of that you also have a fever then it's probably bacillary dysentery and you need an antibiotic like tetracycline or a sulfa drug. None of these drugs need the supervision of a doctor and are usually readily available.

Whether you just have travellers' diarrhoea or something worse the important thing is to keep your fluid intake up and avoid dehydration. Keep drinking.

Medical Kit

Carry a small, straightforward medical kit with any necessary medicines, band-aids, antiseptic, aspirin and a small thermometer. In Asia you'll usually find that if a medicine is available at all it will generally be available over the counter and the price will be much cheaper than in the west.

General Thoughts

Bring your spectacle prescription with you if you're shortsighted. If you need glasses you can get them made up very cheaply and efficiently in places like Singapore or Hong Kong where standards are high and costs are a small fraction of optical costs in the west. Get your teeth checked before you depart; dental problems in remote places are no joke. Rubber thongs are good protection against athletes' foot or other foot infections.

Take care with simple cuts and scratches – they can all-too-easily become infected. Make sure they're properly cleaned and kept that way. When the weather is very hot be careful to avoid dehydration. If your urine starts to turn dark yellow or orange or the need to urinate becomes very infrequent you should be drinking more. Avoid dogs and monkeys, rabies is a nasty thing to catch. If you should be so unfortunate as to get the dreaded hepatitis the only real cure is good food, no alcohol and rest.

If you need medical help your embassy or consulate can usually advise a good place to go. So can five-star hotels although they often recommend doctors with five-star prices. Don't forget to take out medical insurance; check if it will fly you home in a dire emergency.

Last, but far from least, don't be overly concerned with your health. In over 10 years of kicking around Asia I've had nothing more serious than a few stomach upsets. South-East Asia is generally a pleasantly healthy area to travel around, even Bali Belly is less common and less serious than its close relation from Delhi!

ACCOMMODATION

In most of South-East Asia accommodation is no problem; about the only time you might have difficulties is over Chinese New Year when finding a room can be a hassle in some places. In Indonesia cheap hotels are usually known as *losmen* – they're small, often family-run places. Elsewhere hotels are often Chinese run – spartan, noisy, but generally clean and well kept. Costs are very variable but in most of the region you can get a reasonable room for two from around US$2.50 to 5, more expensive in some of the big cities of course.

If you arrive in a country by air there is often an airport hotel booking desk although they often do not cover the lower strata of hotels. Some airports (like Bangkok's) are better than others (like Singapore's) for this game. Otherwise you'll generally find hotels clustered around the bus and train station areas – always good places to start hunting. Always check your room and the bathroom before you agree to take it. If the sheets don't look clean ask to have them changed right away.

If you think a hotel is too expensive ask if they have anything cheaper. Often they may try to steer you into more expensive rooms, may simply be trying it on a bit, or may even be open to a little bargaining. A very important point to remember in Chinese hotels is that a 'single' room usually has a double bed while a 'double' has two beds. A couple can always request a single room.

FOOD

Eat what you like when you want to would be my first advice, since in general food in South-East Asia is pretty healthy. A good rule of thumb is to glance at the restaurant or food stall and its proprietor – if it looks clean and he looks healthy then chances are the food will be OK too. In general there are two things to be careful about – water and fresh, uncooked food. Only in Singapore, Hong Kong and some other major cities can you drink water straight from the taps – elsewhere you should ensure that water is boiled or purified. It's no good avoiding the water if you then eat fruit or vegetables that have been washed in that unhealthy water. Ice can be a danger too; freezing things certainly doesn't kill germs. Cooked food that has been allowed to go cold can also be dangerous.

In general you should have few problems and in places like Singapore you can usually eat from any street stall with impunity. Of course you'll also find Coke and other hygienically pure western delights. McDonald's are spreading their tentacles through the region too.

Since the last edition two Danish travellers wrote at length of the economies to be made by preparing your own food. Their experience was that it wasn't to much weight to carry some cooking gear and a Camping Gaz cooker (replacement cylinders available in most places in the region) and that you could save a reasonable amount of money and still eat well.

Fruit

South-East Asian travel can be a special taste treat when it comes to fruit. Apart from all those mundane bananas, pineapples and coconuts there are a host of fruits that will do wonderful things for your taste buds. Fruit stalls are on hand all over to sell iced slices or segments of these fruits in season.

Rambutan A bright red fruit covered in soft, hairy spines – the name means hairy. Break it open to reveal a delicious, white, lychee-like fruit inside.

Salak Found chiefly in Indonesia the salak is immediately recognisable by its brown 'snakeskin' covering. Peel it off to reveal segments that taste like a cross between an apple and a walnut. Bali salaks are much nicer than any others.

Zurzat Also spelt sirsat sometimes called a white mango and known in the west as custard apple or soursop, a warty green skin covers a thirst quenching interior with a slight lemonish taste. They are ripe when they feel squishy.

Nangcur An enormous yellow-green fruit that can weigh over 20 kilo, inside are hundreds of individual bright yellow segments. Also called jackfruit the taste is distinctive and the texture slightly rubbery.

Jeruk The pomelo is a citrus fruit, larger than a grapefruit but with a sweeter, more orange-like taste. Jeruk often seems to refer to citrus fruit in general.

Mangosteen The small purple-brown mangosteen cracks open to reveal tasty white segments with a very fine flavour. Queen Victoria once offered a reward to anyone able to transport a mangosteen back to England while still edible.

Starfruit Called blimbing in Bali the name is obvious when you see a slice – it's star shaped; a cool, crispy, watery taste.

Durian The most infamous fruit of the region, the durian is a large green fruit with a hard spiny exterior. Crack it open to reveal – the biggest stink imaginable! Drains blocked up? No, it's just the durian season. If you can hold your nose you might actually learn to love them although one traveller felt that I should come right out with it and admit that durians 'look like shit, smell like shit and taste like shit. On the other hand,' he went on, 'you can try durian in a milder form by having a durian ice cream – which also smells like shit and tastes like shit but looks like ice cream.' You can't satisfy everybody!

Other Sawo looks like a potato and tastes like a pear. Jambu is pear shaped but has a radish-like crispy texture and a pink, shiny colour. Papaya or paw paw, well we should all know what they are. Bananas are pisang and pineapple are nanas in Indonesia.

PEOPLE

It's people that make travel – seeing things may be great, doing things may be exciting, but it's the people who'll stay with you. So make the most of them, go out of your way to meet people and to get to know them. It's the only way you'll really get to know the countries you visit. The same consideration applies to your fellow travellers. For perhaps obvious reasons a cross-section of travellers seems to be a whole lot more interesting than a similar slice of the general population. Apart from making friends you'll run into time and again over the years, travel also provides a lot of immediate benefits through the friends you make. You rarely travel alone for long, it always seems that somebody else is going the same direction as you and you soon end up as part of a group heading who knows where. Remember also that your fellow travellers are the best source of information on what lies ahead.

THEFT

I've made several trips through South-East Asia and not lost a thing – and one trip where every time I turned round something went missing. Theft is a problem; it's probably no more endemic than in most western countries but as a traveller you're often fairly open to be stolen from and when you do lose things it can be a real hassle. Most important things to guard are your passport, papers, tickets and money. It's best to always carry these next to your skin or in a sturdy leather pouch on your belt. I've got one of those that takes all those important items and the notebook from which I assemble this book. When I'm travelling it never leaves me.

You can further lessen the risks by being careful of snatch thieves in certain cities. Cameras or shoulder bags are great for these people. Be careful on buses and trains and even in hotels; don't leave valuables lying around in your room. A very useful anti-theft item is a small padlock – you can use it to double lock your room (there's often a latch for this purpose) or to tie your bag down to a train luggage rack. Be wary of your fellow travellers also, not all of them are scrupulously honest.

DOPE

With caution. There is, of course, lots of dope around the region and a little grass at Kuta Beach or Phuket is hardly likely to cause you much hassle but as soon as you start messing with heavier stuff or trying to export it they'll land on top of you. There are a hell of a lot of travellers languishing behind bars and more have found themselves inside looking out after they tried to bring stuff back home with them. Don't.

In Thailand the whole scene is fairly corrupt and once the right number of palms have been lined with the right amount of money you will probably find yourself 'out on bail' which means exit the country as quickly as possible. The right amount of money can easily run into the thousands of dollars. Indonesia can go that way or it can go the straight-behind-bars direction. In Malaysia it's into the clink with no questions asked while in Singapore drug offenders not only find themselves behind bars, they also get to try out Singapore's local form of corporal punishment – the rotan. And big drug importers to Singapore get the death penalty.

Unless you're keen on making lengthy, first-hand investigations of conditions in Asian jails don't try smuggling dope or mailing it out of the country. Even more important don't bother bringing it home with you. With the stamps you'll have on your passport you're guaranteed to be a subject of suspicion. I would have thought I had a fairly good reason for spending some time kicking around odd places, but when I get home to Melbourne the lovely customs guys always seem glad to see me, to usher me off to a private room and to go through everything with the fine tooth comb.

WHAT TO TAKE & HOW TO TAKE IT

As little as possible is the best policy – but not so little that you have to scrounge off other travellers, as some of the 'super lightweight' travellers do. It's very easy to find almost anything you need along the way and since you'll inevitably buy things as you go it's better to start with too little rather than too much.

A backpack is still the most popular carrying container as it is commodious and the only way to go if you have to do any walking. On the debit side a backpack is awkward to load on and off buses and trains, it doesn't offer too much protection for your valuables and some airlines may refuse to be responsible if the pack is damaged or broken into. Fortunately they no longer have the 'pack œ hippy' and 'hippy œ bad' connotation they used to be saddled with.

Recently combination backpack/shoulder bags have become available. The straps zip away inside the pack when not needed so you almost have the best of both worlds. It's not really suitable for long hiking trips but it's much easier to carry than a bag. Another alternative is a large, soft, zip bag with a wide shoulder strap so it can be carried with relative ease if necessary. In either case get some tabs sewn on so you can semi-thief-proof it with small padlocks. Forget suitcases.

Inside? You will, no doubt, be buying local clothes along the way (Levi jeans are cheaper in Singapore or Hong Kong than back home), wherever that might be, so start light. My list would include:

underwear & swimming gear
pair of jeans & a pair of shorts
a few T-shirts
sweater for cold nights
a pair of sneakers or shoes
sandals or thongs
lightweight jacket or raincoat
a dress-up set of clothes

Modesty rates highly in most Asian countries, especially for women. Wearing shorts away from the beach is often looked down upon as being rather 'low class'. On the non-clothing side I'd bring:

washing gear
medical & sewing kit
sunglasses

padlock
sleeping bag
sarong

The sleeping bag is only necessary if you're going to be roughing it, getting well off the beaten track, climbing mountains and the like. It can also double as a coat on cold days, a cushion on hard train-seats, a seat for long waits at bus or railway stations and a bed top-cover, since hotels rarely give you one. The sarong is equally useful since it can be everything from a bed sheet to a towel, a beach wrap, a dressing gown and even something to wear.

The padlock will lock your bag to a train or bus luggage rack and will also fortify your hotel room – which often locks with a latch in any case. Soap, toothpaste and so on are readily obtainable but well off the beaten track toilet paper can be impossible to find and tampons are also difficult to find away from the big cities.

Two final thoughts: The secret of successful packing is plastic bags or 'stuff bags' – It not only keeps things separate and clean but also dry. Airlines do lose bags from time to time – you've got much better chance of it not being yours if it is tagged with your name and address *inside* the bag as well as outside. Other tags can always fall off or be removed.

APPEARANCES & CONDUCT

If you want to have a smooth trip, how you look is very important. Throughout South-East Asia the official powers-that-be have a morbid hatred of 'hippies', 'freaks' and other similar low forms of life. When you arrive at embassies or consulates for visas, at the border to enter a country, or at docks or airports, you'll find life much simpler if you look neat and affluent. Particularly disliked are thongs, shorts, jeans (especially with patches on them), local attire, T-shirts – I could go on. It's always advisable to have one set of 'dress up' gear to wear for these formal occasions. If you're male have short hair.

Encounters with Asian officialdom are made much smoother if you keep repeating 'I must retain my cool' the more they annoy you! Temper usually has a counter-productive effect; they just want to show you who's boss – if you imply that you realise they are but that you still insist (calmly) on your rights you'll probably manage OK.

FILM & CAMERA

You'll run through plenty of film in South-East Asia, and in Singapore and Hong Kong it's fairly cheap, particularly if you buy it in bulk – say a dozen at a time. Elsewhere film is often readily available (Malaysia or Thailand for example), but rather more expensive than in the west. Cameras are also cheap in Singapore or Hong Kong where the choice of camera equipment is literally staggering. If you have any difficulties these are also the places to have your camera attended to.

Particular points to note when photographing in the region are to compensate for the intensity of the light – for a few hours before and after mid-day the height of the sun will tend to leave pictures very washed out. Try to photograph earlier or later in the day. On the other hand there are plenty of occasions when you'll want a flash, either for indoor shots or in jungle locations where the amount of light that filters through can be surprisingly low. When taking photographs of people make sure they don't mind. They generally don't but it's polite to check first.

MAIL

Poste Restantes (at almost any post office) are the best way of getting mail. American Express have client mail services but it's not usually worth the effort. If you've got some difinite contact point or know you will be at a certain hotel then use that. Very few embassies will hold mail for their people these days – they'll just forward it on to poste restante. When getting people to write to you ask them to leave plenty of time for mail to arrive and to print your name very clearly. Under-lining the surname also helps; remember in some countries the surname comes first so it's not surprising that so many 'missing' letters are just misfiled.

When sending mail from the less affluent countries always have the stamps franked before your eyes, otherwise they'll quite likely be nicked! Or use aerograms which are quite safe. For similar reasons I'd be distrustful of 'mail it home' packaging services. I've sent parcels home from South-East Asia on a few occasions and (touch wood) they've always arrived – slightly battered and a long time later. If it's something you value consider air freight. Enquire at the post office before you bring a parcel in, there may be special wrapping requirements or it may have to be inspected (in Indonesia) before you wrap it.

BUYING & SELLING

The selling things scene isn't what it used to be – in most cases you can find pretty much everything you have at home and cheaper to boot. Obvious exceptions are places like Burma where almost everything has its demand and its price. Nor is there much opportunity for picking up casual work in the region; you have to get up to North-East Asia before you get into the lucrative 'English lessons' racket. Since the last edition one traveller did write, however, saying how easily he got work (illegally of course) in Singapore as a (male) clothes model. Just have blue eyes.

Buying things is a different game but don't get carried away with the idea of making your fortune with the goodies you bring back home with you. The people who buy art and handicrafts to profitably resell in the west are usually experts and the Asian clothes you see for sale in the west are usually brought in as a full-time business, not some one-off trip.

There are plenty of things you'll want to buy just for their own sake and it's worth having a few ground rules to follow. First of all don't buy it unless you really want it. Secondly outside of the odd 'fixed price' store that really is fixed the name of the game is bargaining. Food in markets, handicrafts, even transport are things you may have to bargain for. The secrets of successful bargaining are to make a game of it, to make a first offer that is sufficiently low to allow both buyer and seller room to manoeuvre (but not so low as to be laughable) and to be good humoured about it. Accept that you're simply going to have to end up paying more money than the locals and remember that it's not a matter of life and death or personal honour!

FINAL THOUGHTS
Since the shoestring traveller seems to get a fair amount of flak from time to time I'd better outline my philosophy of what he/ she is not. They're not scrounges, penniless layabouts, permanently high or rip-off merchants. If I had to define my belief in travel it's that if you've been some place and stayed in the local Hilton you've not been there (sorry Conrad). Tourists stay in Hiltons, travellers don't. The traveller wants to see the country at ground level, to breathe it, experience it – live it. This usually requires two things the tourist can't provide – more time and less money. If you're going to really travel it's going to take longer and on a day-to-day basis cost less. So blend in, enjoy yourself, but most important make it easy for the travellers who are going to follow your footsteps.

Getting There

Step one is to get to Asia and these days with competition between the airlines as severe as it is there are plenty of opportunities to find cheap tickets to a variety of 'gateway' cities. You virtually have no choice apart from flying though – boat services are now limited and apart from odd routes (like hopping across from Thursday Island off the northern tip of Queensland to PNG on a fishing boat) the only regular shipping service runs between the port of Fremantle (near Perth, Western Australia) and Singapore.

The major Asian gateways for cheap flights are Singapore, Bangkok and Hong Kong. They are all good places to fly to and good places to fly from. Bangkok has long had a reputation as a bargain centre for cheap airline tickets, but first Singapore and then Penang joined it. Now Hong Kong is also a good place to shop around.

Cheap tickets are available in two distinct categories – official and unofficial. The official ones are advance purchase tickets, budget-fares, apex, super-apex or whatever other brand name the airlines care to tack on them in order to put, as it is so succinctly expressed, 'bums on seats'. The unofficial tickets are simply discounted tickets which the airlines release through selected travel agents. Don't look for discounted tickets straight from the airlines. They are only available through travel agents. Generally you can find discounted tickets at prices as low or lower than the apex, budget or whatever ticket plus there is no advance purchase requirement nor should there be any cancellation penalty although individual travel agents may institute their own cancellation charges. A little caution is necessary with discounted tickets – see below for more details.

FROM THE UK

Ticket discounting is a long established business in the UK and it's wide open – the various agents advertise their fares and there's nothing under the counter about it at all. To find out what is available and where to get it, pick up a copy of the giveaway newspaper *Australasian Express* or the weekly 'what's on' guide *Time Out*. Note, however, that discounted tickets are almost exclusively available in London – you won't find your friendly local travel agent offering exciting deals out in the country. The magazine *Business Traveller* also produces a regular survey listing and analysing what is available on air fares throughout the world. They even work out where better deals are available due to currency fluctuations.

The danger with discounted tickets in the UK is that some of the 'bucket shops', as ticket discounters are knowns, are more than a little shonky. Backstairs, over-the-shop travel agents sometimes tend to fold up and disappear after you've handed over the money and before they hand over the tickets. Always make sure you have tickets in hand before you give them the folding stuff. These days there are plenty of reputable, efficient discounters. A couple of excellent places to look are Trail Finders, 46 Earls Court Rd, London W8 and STA (Student Travel Australia) at 74 Old Brompton Rd, London W7.

Quoted one-way fares to South-East Asia include Bangkok for £190, Singapore £225, Jakarta £235, Denpasar (Bali) £285, Manila £225 and Hong Kong from around £230. London to the Australian east coast tickets are available with stopovers in South-East Asia from as low as £320 to around £400 for fairly straightforward tickets with just a few stops in Asia and/or South-East Asia. Fares are slightly less to Perth, rather more on to New Zealand.

On the continent Netherlands, Brussels and Antwerp are among the best places for buying airline tickets. WATS, de Keyserlei 44, Antwerp, Belgium, has been recommended.

FROM AUSTRALIA
In the past few years ticket discounting out of Australia has gone through quite an upheaval. First of all advance purchase fares came in, which reduced ticket prices to much more manageable levels. Then the government finally gave up on its feeble attempts to clamp down on travel agents and ticket discounting, once very much an under-the-counter operation, became much more open. It's still not as widely advertised and promoted as it is in the UK, but you can easily find travel agents with interesting ticketing possibilities on offer. Check with Student Travel Australia (STA) for starters. The advance purchase fares out of Australia are the usual benchmark to use when you go ticket shopping. You should be able to find tickets (though not to all places) through travel agents at the same price or lower than the official apex fares – with the advantage that you can take off tomorrow.

From Sydney the one-way and return apex fares (which vary from a low to a shoulder and then a peak season) cost A$506-612 one way, A$778-940 return to Singapore, A$591-714 one way, A$908-1100 return to Hong Kong, A$441-541 one way, A$680-832 return to Jakarta, A$502-608 one way, A$772-936 return to Manila, A$601-727 one way, A$924-1118 return to Bangkok and A$533-641 one way, A$820-986 return to Kuala Lumpur. Fares from Melbourne are in some cases slightly more expensive, while from Brisbane, Perth or Darwin a bit less if flights are available. Some travel agents will discount these prices, but only at their own expense, and not to any great degree.

Other possibilities out of Australia include the flights to PNG either from Sydney, Brisbane or Cairns. These are available both as straightforward economy tickets or as advance purchase tickets. Another possibility to consider is to fly from Melbourne to Nauru and on from there to the Philippines, Hong Kong or Japan. The tiny (but very rich) island nation of Nauru operates a small airline at a stupendous loss and has some interesting ticketing possibilities to the region – as well as to other Pacific nations.

FROM NORTH AMERICA
You can pick up interesting tickets from North American to South-East Asia, particularly from the US west coast or from Vancouver. In fact the intense competition between Asian airlines is resulting in ticket discounting operations very similar to the London bucket shops. To find cheap tickets simply scan the travel sections of the Sunday papers for likely looking agents – the *New York Times, San Francisco Chronicle-Examiner* and the *Los Angeles Times* are particularly good. The network of student travel offices known as Council Travel are particularly good and there are also offices of STA on the west coast.

Typical fares from the west coast include return fares like Bangkok US$840, Singapore US$930, Manila US$780 or Hong Kong US$650. One-way fares are a bit more than half.

Getting Around

FLYING AROUND ASIA
There are all sorts of ticket bargains around the region once you arrive in South-East Asia. These inter-Asia fares are widely available although Bangkok, Singapore, Penang and Hong Kong are the major ticket discounting centres. In Australia you can buy inter-Asia tickets as add-on fares to apex tickets. These cost pretty much the same as you would pay through agents in Asia.

A little caution is necessary when looking for tickets in Asia. First of all shop around, a wise move anywhere of course. Secondly don't believe everything you are told – ticket agents in Penang are very fond of telling people that tickets there are cheaper than in Bangkok or Singapore or whatever. In actual fact they are often pretty much the same price anywhere and if there is any difference it's likely to be in the favour of the originating city. You're unlikely to find a Bangkok-Kathmandu ticket cheaper in Penang than in Bangkok for example. Or a Penang-Hong Kong ticket cheaper in Singapore than in Penang.

Most important be very careful that you get what you want before handing over money and that the ticket is precisely what you pay for. We have had a lot of letters of late from people complaining that they were done by various agents. Favourite tricks include tickets with very limited periods of validity when you have been told they are valid year round. A variation on that is a ticket that you had been told could be used anytime in (say) the next 12 months only to find it is only usable for a much more restricted time. Or you could find a ticket is marked 'OK', indicating that you have a seat reservation, when no reservation has been made. Or even that an airline will not accept your ticket for a subsequent sector of your travels. Take care, but don't get too uptight about it,

I've bought quite a few tickets from quite a few agents in Asia and never had any problems whatsoever.

The chart opposite illustrates typical inter-Asia fares.

Airport Taxes Most airports in South-East Asia charge a departure tax so make sure you have that final necessary bit of local currency left. It's another time when a few cash dollars can come in useful.

OVERLANDING IN SOUTH-EAST ASIA
With all the water in the way 'overlanding' through South-East Asia seems to be a misnomer but if by overlanding you mean travelling from place to place by local transport with the minimum use of aircraft then South-East Asia offers enormous scope. First, of course, you have to get there but assuming you've made the first step from Australia, Europe, North America or wherever and you've arrived at the starting point of your travels, what's the next step?

Indonesia
There are two logical 'ends' to the Indonesian trip – Bali at one end and Medan in Sumatra at the other. The middle would have to be Jakarta and many people make their arrival in Indonesia here, at the nation's capital and largest city. The old Australian starting point used to be beyond Bali at the island of Timor, but with Indonesia's take-over of that ex-Portuguese colony there are no longer flights from Darwin in Australia and Timor is virtually off-limits.

So from Bali, after you've explored that magical island, the first stage is to hop on a bus to Surabaya, usually an overnight trip. It's worth stopping off on the way to Surabaya to climb the extraordinary volcano Mt Bromo. From Surabaya you continue to Yogyakarta, the cultural

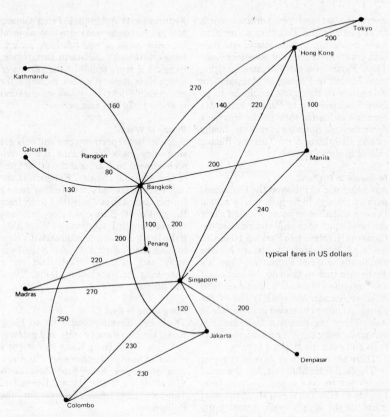

typical fares in US dollars

heartland of Java and Indonesia. Yogya is also the second of Indonesia's three major travellers' centres. The first is, of course, Bali and the third is Lake Toba in Sumatra. On from Yogya you can train or bus to Jakarta, although if you have time there are interesting stops en route at, for example, the Dieng Plateau, Pangandaran, Bandung and Bogor.

Jakarta is the first decision point. If your visa is running short, and unfortunately present Indonesian visa limitation make it virtually impossible to really explore the country in one bite, you have to leave. If you're in that situation then head to Singapore – either by air or by the

infamous Pelni ship *Tampomas*. From Singapore you can then re-enter Indonesia and start again. There's no need to go right back to Jakarta though. You can fly to Pekanbaru in Sumatra or head back to Tanjung Pinang, the Indonesian island south of Singapore where the *Tampomas* terminates, and go from there to Sumatra. If you weren't in visa problems back in Jakarta you could continue to Sumatra either by bus or train then by ferry and once again bus or train. The Sumatran trip is the hardest travel in Indonesia so many people opt instead for the regular ship from Jakarta to Padang. Or they fly.

After Padang the roads through Sumatra

aren't so bad and you continue north through delightful Bukittinggi, perhaps make a side trip to Nias Island and then take a well-earned rest at laid-back Lake Toba. Finally you exit Sumatra by flying from Medan to Penang in Malaysia. An alternative to this route would be to go from Singapore up to Penang and enter Sumatra at Medan then do the trip back down through Sumatra in reverse, finally exiting to Jakarta or to Tanjung Pinang and/or Singapore.

Malaysia & Thailand

Assuming you've followed the traditional path up through Indonesia, you're now in Penang and after enjoying yourself there can head south to the hill stations like the Cameron Highlands, to Pangkor Island, to modern Kuala Lumpur, to historic Melaka and finally arrive at Singapore. Then it's about turn time to head up the east coast and sample Malaysia's beaches and offshore islands. Malaysia is one of the easiest countries to travel in anywhere in Asia. There are excellent train and bus services, remarkably economical share-taxis and even the hitching is easy.

There are a variety of ways of crossing to Thailand from Malaysia, but the usual routes are to take a taxi or train from Penang to Hat Yai, if you're on the west coast, or to simply walk across from Rantau Panjang to Sungai Golok on the east coast. From Hat Yai, the major city in the south of Thailand, you can continue by bus to Phuket, the resort island with the superb beaches. Then continue north to Surat Thani and the equally beautiful island of Koh Samui where you can wrestle with the important question of whether Phuket or Koh Samui is the better place to get away from it all. Finally you reach hyper-active Bangkok and decide where to head next.

For most travellers that decision will be to head north to Chiang Mai, the second city of Thailand and another great travellers' centre. On the way you could pause to explore the ancient cities of Ayuthaya and Sukhothai. From Chiang Mai you can make treks into the colourful hill tribe areas or you can look back to Bangkok through the north-east region. Bangkok is more than just the sin city of South-East Asia, it's also a centre for cheap airline tickets so your next question is where to fly to – east or west.

Burma & West

Since (at last report) you can still only get seven-day visas for Burma it's a well orchestrated rush around the attractions of that unusual country. Rangoon is the only entry point and you can either make a Burma visit as an out-and-back foray from Bangkok or use Burma as a stepping stone between South-East Asia and West Asia. If the latter is your intention then it's time to pack *South-East Asia on a Shoestring* away and pick up *West Asia on a Shoestring* for Bangladesh, India, Nepal and beyond.

Hong Kong & East

The other direction could be to Hong Kong, the frenetic city state and gateway to China. From Hong Kong you've got a choice of heading further east – in which case you need *North-East Asia on a Shoestring* for China, Japan, Korea and Taiwan – or turning south for the Philippines.

The Philippines

Manila is overwhelmingly the gateway city to the Philippines, but from there you can head north to the rice terraces and beaches of north Luzon, south to the Mayon Volcano and other attractions of south Luzon. Or island hop off into the tightly clustered islands of the Visayas. Eventually you can hop back to Manila and decide where next – on to Australia or further afield. This could be quite a good loop through the region from Australia – Indonesia-Singapore-Malaysia-Thailand-Hong Kong-Philippines and finally back to Australia. But, of course, there are lots of other possibilities.

Papua New Guinea & Elsewhere

PNG is one obvious 'other' place. From Australia you can make the short flight from Cairns to Port Moresby and explore PNG on the way to Indonesia. It's a fascinating country with the drawback that it can be horrendously expensive. From Jayapura, the entry point to Indonesia from PNG, you can continue to the Moluccas (or Malukus, the historic spice islands) then Sulawesi and finally Bali or Java. Or cross to Kalimantan, the southern half of Borneo.

The northern Borneo states – Malaysia's Sabah and Sarawak and the independent kingdom of Brunei – are most easily visited from Singapore or Peninsular Malaysia since connections between north Borneo and Kalimantan are very tenuous; but it can be done. You can sometimes, and only with some effort, cross between Sabah and Mindanao, the southernmost island of the Philippines, but it's easier to fly from Sabah direct to Manila or Hong Kong.

TRANSPORT

If there are people in A and people in B, there will be transport between A and B. That's a simple rule which almost always seems to work; if you put your mind to it you can always find a way of getting from one place to another. Because South-East Asian countries are often separated by water you'll unavoidably have to spend more on transport than you would in other parts of Asia but some of these trips can be great experiences. There are not a lot of inter-country shipping services although those that are available are often very interesting.

Land transport in the region is generally great value. In Malaysia and Thailand, for example, trains and buses are both reasonably cheap and, certainly by the standards further west, absurdly comfortable. Usually public transport is far more convenient, frequent and interesting than in the west simply because far more people use it.

Of course you can hit the road with your own transport, but you really cannot go that far in South-East Asia. It's not like the Asia overland trip where you've got a whole continent to cross. You could always buy a motorcycle in Singapore, but once you've ridden it through Malaysia and Thailand you've come to the end of the road. Land borders to Burma are firmly shut so the idea of crossing Burma and heading across Asia to Europe is just a dream. The best you can do is to put it on the boat from Penang to Madras in India. Remember too that many places (including Thailand and Indonesia) require a carnet – an expensive customs document guaranteeing that you will later remove the vehicle from their country.

If you must have you own wheels it's better to hire them when necessary. Malaysia is just like most countries in the west when it comes to car hire and you can also hire cars in Thailand. Motorcycles can be hired in many places in Malaysia; in Phuket, Koh Samui, Pattaya and Chiang Mai in Thailand; and, of course, in Bali in Indonesia. More sensibly you can hire bicycles in many places including Bali, Penang, Chiang Mai and Pagan in Burma.

STUDENT TRAVEL

There are student travel offices in most South-East Asian capitals, most of them associated in some way with Student Travel Australia – the major force in student travel in the region. They're most useful for discounted air fares and are generally worth enquiring at if you want to fly somewhere. Other services they can provide include local tours and accommodation bookings. Usually the hotels they have deals with are somewhat up-market and even with discounts they're well above the usual budget travellers range. If you're a real honest-to-God student then they can also do student cards. Major student travel offices include:

Hong Kong
> Hong Kong Student Travel Bureau, 1024 Star House, Kowloon (tel 3-694847)

Indonesia
> Student Travel Australia, Jalan Wahid Hasyim 110 (tel 353748-9)

Malaysia
> Student Travel Australia, MSL Travel, 1st floor, South-East Asia Hotel, 69 Jalan Haji Hussein, Kuala Lumpur (tel 980961)

Philippines
> Ystaphil (Youth Student Travel Association of the Philippines), 1656 Taft Avenue, Manila (tel 50 0317)

Singapore
> Student Travel Australia, mezzanine floor, Ming Court Hotel, Tanglin Rd, Singapore (tel 734 7091)

Thailand
> Trad Travel Service, Viengtai Hotel, 42 Tanee Rd, Banglamphu, Bangkok (tel 28 15788)

YACHTS

With a little effort it's often possible to get yacht rides from various places in the region. Very often yacht owners are just travellers too and they often need another crew member or two. Willingness to give it a try is often more important than experience and often all it costs you is a contribution to the food kitty. Where to look – well anywhere that yachts pass through or in towns with western-style yacht clubs, try the clubs. Maureen and I managed a ride from Bali to Exmouth in Western Australia this way once. Since the past edition we've had letters from people who've manage to get rides from Singapore, Penang, Phuket and (like us) Benoa in Bali. Other popular yachting places include the main ports in Papua New Guinea and Hong Kong.

Brunei Darussalam

A comic-book little country, Brunei is blessed with a supply of that most prized of commodities – oil. It shows from the glossy public buildings of the capital, Bandar Seri Begawan, to the airport terminal large enough for a country 10 times Brunei's size, to the Sultan's fleet of Italian exoticars.

HISTORY

At one time Brunei was a considerable power in these parts. Under the fifth Sultan, Bolkiah (known as the 'singing admiral', for his love of music), Brunei's power extended throughout Borneo and into the Philippines. The arrival of the British, in the guise of Rajah Brooke, and their intention to wipe out piracy along the Borneo coast, a favourite Bruneian occupation, spelt the end of its power. Gradually the country was whittled away. The final absurdity was when it was forced to cede Limbang to Sarawak, separating the country into two halves. Then, in 1929, oil was discovered on the tiny bit of land left.

On that windfall Brunei basks with no income tax, pensions for all, magnificent and rather redundant public buildings, and what must be the highest per capita consumption of cars in South-East Asia. Car importers appear to be plentiful but repairers are in very short supply; the slightest dent is a ticket to one of Brunei's many scrapyards. The current Sultan is 28th in line. His father is still around, matches his son's sports cars with his own London taxi, and pragmatically kept the country out of the Malaysian confederation before abdicating. In 1984 Brunei, rather reluctantly, became independent of Britain. The Sultan celebrated by building himself a new US$350 million palace and renaming the country Brunei Darussalam.

FACTS

Brunei has a population of about 220,000 in an area of 5700 square km. The people are Malays, Chinese, Indians and around 25,000 Iban, Dusan and other tribespeople of the interior. Brunei is strictly Islamic – behave yourself! Apart from the capital and the oil town of Seria the country is mainly jungle. A little rubber is exported along with all the oil.

VISAS

Visas are not required for most western nationalities although some nationalities, like the Japanese, do need visas. British diplomatic missions handle external affairs for Brunei. Usually visitors are given a one-week stay permit on arrival but if you ask you will usually be given two weeks. The anti-hippy line of Singapore and Malaysia is closely followed by Brunei, but visitors are fairly few and far between so there are few hassles. Women travellers are said to be treated with some suspicion at the airport.

MONEY

A$1 = B$1.80
US$1 = B$2.20
£1 = B$2.50

Brunei dollars are roughly interchangeable with Singapore dollars. Malay dollars are worth a bit less and are not so popular!

CLIMATE

Uniformly warm year-round with quite heavy rainfall that peaks from October to January.

GETTING THERE

Air You can fly to Brunei from Singapore, Kuala Lumpur, Hong Kong and Darwin in Australia. British Airways have a weekly London-Australia flight that goes via Bandar Seri Begawan. There are also

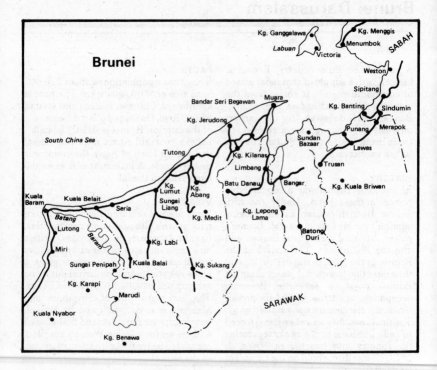

Brunei

South China Sea

Kuala Baram
Lutong
Miri
Kg. Karapi
Kuala Nyabor
Kg. Benawa
Batang
Baram
Kuala Belait
Seria
Sungai Penipah
Marudi
Kuala Balai
Kg. Labi
Kg. Sukang
Kg. Medit
Sungai Liang
Kg. Lumut
Kg. Abang
Tutong
Kg. Jerudong
Bandar Seri Begawan
Kg. Kilanas
Limbang
Batu Danau
Kg. Lepong Lama
Batong Duri
Bangar
Kg. Kuala Briwan
Trusan
Sundan Bazaar
Muara
Kg. Ganggalawa
Labuan
Victoria
Kg. Menggis
Menumbok
Weston
Sipitang
Kg. Banting
Punang
Merapok
Lawas
Sindumin
SABAH
SARAWAK

flights between Bandar Seri Begawan and Kota Kinabalu in Sabah, Kuching in Sarawak and other Sabah and Sarawak towns. There are no longer shipping services to Brunei from Singapore.

To/From Sabah Although there is no road connection between Brunei and Sabah there are several routes by water and land.

Via Limbang It's a half hour by private boat from BSB to Limbang, a town in the finger of Sarawak sandwiched between the two halves of Brunei. The boats leave according to demand and the fare is B$5. From Limbang you can continue by boat to Punang, still in Sarawak but on the other side of the smaller half of Brunei. From there share-taxis run to Lawas, see below.

Via Labuan Labuan is an island off the coast of Sabah. You can take a boat from Bandar Seri Begawan to Labuan, another from Labuan to Menumbok and from there minibuses and share-taxis run to Beaufort, Kota Kinabalu and other places in Sabah. BSB-Labuan boats cost B$12 and there are also very fast private boats which charge B$15 although they will generally try to ask B$20.

From Labuan to Menumbok there are several launches daily which cost M$7. They depart from the dock opposite the Hock Hua Bank, several blocks to the left after you clear Labuan immigration. It is intended that government car ferries will soon start operating this service. From Menumbok you can get to Beaufort by minibus or share-taxi for M$7 or 8. Although Labuan is a duty-free port and has historical importance as the place where Japanese forces in Borneo surrendered at the end of WW II, it's otherwise uninteresting and is a very expensive place to hang around in.

Via Lawas There are usually one or two launches daily to Lawas which cost B$15 and take about two hours. Most travellers take the one scheduled to leave at 11 am. In Lawas you can stay at the *Government Rest House* or the *Federal Hotel* but recently costs here have jumped dramatically to around M$30 a night. With luck you can continue straight on to Merapok, a 45-minute, M$4 trip along a serpentine maze of rivers. Sometimes the boat taking you to Lawas will hail a Lawas-Merapok boat and you can transfer from one boat to another and skip Lawas completely. The road from Kota Kinabalu and Beaufort now continues all the way to Lawas but traffic is still very light so making this trip by road is not easy yet.

From Merapok you have to find a ride to Sipitang, usually around M$2.50 per person for the half-hour journey. Sabah immigration is several hundred metres outside Merapok and is quite easy to miss. If you do zoom straight by you can usually complete the formalities later in Sipitang, Tenom or KK (but not Beaufort) although it's better to clear immigration at Merapok.

Should you arrive in Sipitang too late to continue straight through to Beaufort or KK there's a *Government Rest House* with rooms at M$12 per person. It's about a km from the centre towards Merapok. There's also a more basic and somewhat cheaper flea-pit in the centre of the village. Share-taxis depart for Beaufort every day around 7 to 8 am and cost M$7 per person. From Beaufort there is a variety of transport to KK or Tenom.

To/From Sarawak The only road out of Brunei is the one west to Sarawak. It's said the Brunei government purposely keeps this solitary road across the border in lousy condition to make any invasion more difficult. It's a B$4 bus trip to Seria, taking 1-1/2 to two hours. There are plenty of buses every day, departing from the station next to the central market at the back of the Brunei Hotel. From Seria to Kuala Belait there are again lots of buses; the fare is B$1 for the half-hour trip. It's very easy to hitch these first two stretches because there are so many cars. And so few hitch-hikers.

From Kuala Belait there are just four or five buses daily to Miri. They're operated by the Sharikat Berlima Belait bus company. The 2½ hour trip costs B$10 and involves several river crossings. Just out of Kuala Belait you reach the Belait River, where you have to get out of the bus for the crossing. The worst stretch of road (it's a private Shell Oil road) runs from here to the border but at low tide buses abandon the road and drive along the nice, smooth beach. After clearing immigration at the Sarawak border you change to a Sarawak bus and drive over more sandy, unsealed road to the Baram River. Here you again leave the bus and cross the river either on a slower free ferry or for M$1 by a faster motor boat. The bus people try to get you to take the motor boat to save queueing for the ferry. Once across the river you board the third bus, but all on the same ticket, for the short run on a sealed road to Miri.

LANGUAGE
Brunei has a mixture of languages, as in Malaysia and Singapore. English is widely spoken.

THINGS TO BUY
Oil? There's a preposterously large and grandiose handicraft centre along the waterfront from the town towards the museum. The craftwork is modern, nothing traditional at all, and it's all very expensive.

BANDAR SERI BEGAWAN
Outside of BSB, a pleasant town to spend a few days in, Brunei has little to offer. The excellent highway runs west to the oil town

of Seria before petering out into a dirt track near the Sarawak border. If you have not already made an upriver trip in Sarawak you can do so from Kuala Belait near the border. Eastwards there are no roads at all towards Sabah.

Thing to See

Omar Ali Saifuddin Mosque Named after the Sultan's father this impressive, gold-topped mosque floats in an artificial lagoon. Take the lift, shoeless, to the top of the minaret for a view over the town and the riverside kampong ayer or water village.

Kampong Ayer Boatmen will take you on a 'tour' through the kampong ayer in BSB for B$10 but it's more fun just to cross over for 50c and walk around the tightly packed houses on stilts. The people are very friendly. There's a museum in the main kampong, directly across from the customs wharf – ask the children, they'll tell you where it is. **Churchill Monument** Churchill in Brunei? There's an impressive monument and a fairly vapid Churchill museum. The small but well-equipped and imaginatively displayed aquarium in the same flashy complex is more interesting. Admission is 30c to the aquarium, which is open 9 am to 12 noon, 1.15 to 7 pm, daily except Monday.

Museum BSB is notoriously short of public transport so getting to the museum six km from town is difficult. It is big, new and shiny but its collection is now quite interesting with many displays relating to local culture. Check the extensive oil display with an amusing vignette showing local life with and without the 'benefits' oil brings. The museum is open Tuesday, Wednesday, Thursday, Saturday and Sunday from 9.30 am to 5 pm; Friday it's closed between 11.30 am and 2.30 pm; Monday closed all day. Buses run there infrequently and cost 50c. Taxis are B$6 but you can easily hitch or even walk. The tomb of the 'singing admiral', Sultan Bolkiah, is about a km on the town side of the museum.

Other There are plenty of beaches around BSB but Brunei is fairly strictly Muslim (more so than Malaysia) so discretion is all important. If you don't mind the odd leech you can make an interesting walk from Labi to the Rampayoh waterfall, via a longhouse on the way. In Tamburong district you can take a boat trip along a winding river and through mangrove swamps to Bangar, the main town with a single row of shop-houses and a Singapore military base. You can reach Limbang in Sarawak from here.

Places to Stay

Brunei's capital is a good town for a short stay if you can get into the youth centre or *Pusat Belia* (tel 23936). In typical Bruneian fashion they've built this huge and luxurious place – complete with gymnasium, swimming pool, library, canteen and two immense dormitories – and then do their best to stop anyone from using it. With charm, short hair, youth, student cards, persuasion and a YHA card you just might be allowed to use it! If you are it's quite possible that you'll have an entire dormitory to yourself. The Pusat Belia is a 'youth centre', not a 'youth hostel', so they really don't have to take you at all; it's intended to be used for visiting youth groups, not individual travellers. So don't push it too far or too hard or you may just make it more difficult for other travellers later on.

The BSB Pusat Belia is one of the continuing sagas of South-East Asian travel – there's always somebody who has yet another tale to tell about it. Once you've got in it costs B$10 total for the first three nights (quite long enough for BSB), then B$5 per night thereafter.

Should the Pusat Belia be totally unavailable (they tend to shut down for odd holidays) then the next best possibility is the *Capital Hostel* (tel 23561) directly behind it, where rooms are B$70/85 for singles/doubles. All rooms have air-con and a TV. Other hotels in BSB are still more expensive although the fairly recent

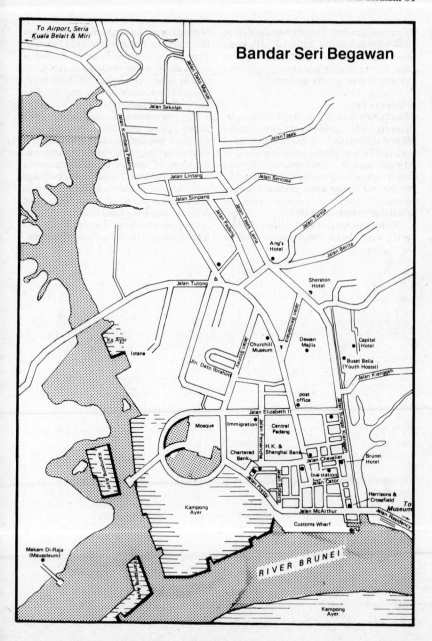

Bandar Seri Begawan

To Airport, Seria Kuala Belait & Miri

Jalan Dato Marsal

Jalan Sekolah

Jalan Tasek

Jalan Kumbang Pasing

Jalan Lintang

Jalan Sentosa

Jalan Simpang

Jalan Padang

Jalan Tasek Lama

Jalan Gereja

Ang's Hotel

Jalan Berita

Jalan Tutong

Jalan Bendahara

Sheraton Hotel

 Kg Ayer

Istana

Jalan Stoney

Churchill Museum

Dewan Majlis

Capital Hotel

Busat Belia (Youth Hostel)

Jln. Dato Ibrahim

Jalan Kianggeh

post office

Jalan Sungai Kianggeh

Jalan Elizabeth II

Mosque

Immigration

Jalan Pemancha

Central Padang

Chartered Bank

H.K. & Shanghai Bank

Jalan Chevalier

Brunei Hotel

bus station

Jalan Cator

Jalan Roberts

Jalan McArthur

Harrisons & Crossfield

To Museum

Kampong Ayer

Customs Wharf

Jalan Residency

Makam Di-Raja (Mausoleum)

Kampong Ayer

RIVER BRUNEI

Kampong Ayer

Jalan Mariji

National Inn (tel 21128) has singles at B$69-99, doubles at B$69-109. It's away from the town centre on Jalan Tutong, but they have a shuttle bus service into town as well as free airport transport.

Places to Eat

The hotels and *Pusat Belia* have restaurants with good food; the *Capital Hostel's* breakfast is particularly good value. The best place to eat, especially in the evenings, is at the food stalls down at the riverfront near the bridge. Looking out to the stilt village while you eat is a very pleasant experience. Various dishes are available from around B$2.

Along the main street, Jalan Sultan, you'll find cheap Muslim-style food at *Wisma Bahru*, Indian food at *Darassalam* and ice cream and snacks at *The Creamery*. The *Seri Indah* on Jalan McArthur is quick and popular, ditto the Indian *Chop Chuan Huat*. For a better, although much more expensive, meal try the Chinese *Lucky Restaurant*.

The government is supposedly strict about alcohol and Islam, and the non-Chinese population are officially not allowed to touch it. It's said that a request for a pot of 'special tea' will produce a teapot full of beer! Nevertheless beer and other alcohol is *much* cheaper in Brunei than in Sarawak or Sabah. *Sin Hup Leong*, on Jalan Roberts across from the cinema, is the place for a beer. Soft drinks are B$1 all over town, a bit more than in Malaysia.

Burma

Burma is one of the least western-influenced countries in the world – even China has Coke today. For the visitor Burma is a fascinating glimpse of a culturally unique country which for some time managed to get itself economically and materially right off the rails. It's only fairly recently that foreigners have been allowed once more to visit, Burma and although a visit involves a fair bit of red tape the effort is well worthwhile.

HISTORY

The Mons were the first recorded people in Burma and their influence extended into present-day Thailand. The Mons were pushed back when the Burmese, who now comprise two-thirds of the population, arrived from the north. King Anurudha came to the throne of Pagan in 1044 and with his conquest of the kingdom of Thaton in 1057 inaugurated the golden age of Burmese history. The spoils he brought back developed Pagan to fabled heights and resulted in the introduction of Buddhism and the Burmese alphabet. Today Burma is 90% Buddhist, although belief in nats, animal spirits, still persist.

Despite Anurudha's efforts, Burma had entered a period of decline by the 13th century, helped on its way by the vast amounts of money and effort squandered on making Pagan such an incredible monument to man's vanity. Kublai Khan hastened the decline by sacking Pagan in 1287, at that time said to contain 13,000 pagodas. For centuries after that Burmese history consisted of conflicts with kingdoms in neighbouring Siam and a series of petty tribal wars.

The coming of Europeans to the east had little influence on the Burmese who were too busy fighting to be interested in trade. Unfortunately for the Burmese their squabbles eventually encroached on the Raj in neighbouring Bengal and the British moved in to keep things quiet on their borders. In three moves in 1824, 1852 and 1883 the British took over all of Burma. They built railroads and under them Burma became the world's greatest rice exporter and developed large teak markets. Less commendably large numbers of Chinese and Indians came in with the British and exploited the commercially unsophisticated Burmese.

As in other South-East Asian countries, WW II was at first seen as a liberating godsend. An idea which the Japanese, as in Indonesia, soon dispelled. The wartime group of 'Thirty Comrades' was able to form a government after the war, with Aung San as their leader. In 1947 he was assassinated with most of his cabinet. Independence came in 1948 but uniting Burma proved to be a difficult task and continuing confrontations with breakaway tribes and Communist rebels still take place.

In 1962 General Ne Win led that most unusual event, a left-wing army takeover. Chucking out the government of U Nu, who languished in prison for four years, Ne Win set the country on the 'Burmese Way to Socialism'. It was a downhill path. Nationalising everything in sight, including retail shops, soon crippled the country, and the Burmese saw their naturally well-endowed economy stumbling as exports of everything plummeted.

Until recently Burma's sorry economy had not improved much under military rule. At least the official economy hadn't; the secondary economy, the black economy, had never been healthier. It's still said that the three major Burmese industries are rice, teak and smuggling but in many ways Burma does look materially better off than 10 years ago. For years things just fell apart, went out of stock or simply became unusable. Apart from ineffectual moves, like changing to driving on the right in contrast to all neighbouring countries and despite the fact that most cars are right-hand drive, nothing seemed to be done. Recently socialist ideals seem to have been tempered with a little realism.

The Burmese are a naturally happy-go-lucky people and despite riots in late '74 over the burial of former UN Secretary U Thant, a longtime Ne Win political foe, opposition appears very muted. You may hear stories of activists disappearing in the middle of the night, but one has an over-powering feeling that some sort of Burmese benevolent incompetence will keep things from getting too unpleasant. In late '81 Ne Win retired but the 'election' of his successor appeared to be very much a preordained choice. The fact that U Nu was allowed to return to Burma (where he now translates Buddhist scriptures) has been interpreted as a sign that the government would be taking a more open attitude in the future.

FACTS

Population No accurate census has been made for years but the population is around 33 million, made up of several Burmese racial groupings. There are still quite a few Indians and Chinese in Burma, but not many other foreigners.

Geography Burma has an area of 671,000 square km, sandwiched between Thailand and Bangladesh with India and China bordering on the north.

Economy Despite recent advances the Burmese economy is still weaker than it should be – which is kind of crazy because Burma has enormous potential both in agriculture and minerals. It's even got some oil! Rice is the mainstay of the economy, but the pre-war production levels have never been matched – by a long way. Socialism Burmese-style may have done harm to the economy, but it's done wonders for the black market. The country is so completely tied up with black market dealings that the whole thing would probably collapse without it.

Religion Burma is Buddhist from top to bottom, but there is also strong belief in *nats*, the animist spirits of the land.

INFO

There is a tourist information office on Sule Pagoda Rd in Rangoon, close to the central Sule Pagoda. The information it has to hand out is sparse and not very interesting, but they're friendly and helpful people. Anything to do with timetables and costs in places you are 'officially' permitted to visit they do have right to hand. There are Tourist Burma offices in all the main centres, but they sometimes give the feeling that their purpose is to hinder and bureaucraticise life rather than to be useful.

BOOKS

For much more information about travelling in Burma look for my guidebook *Burma – a travel survival kit*. Apa Productions have *Insight Guide Burma* in their series of glossy coffee-table guidebooks. George Orwell's *Burmese Days* is the book to read for a feel of British Burma. In Pagan or Rangoon before you head upcountry get a copy of *Guide to Pagan*, an invaluable introduction to the many temples, pagodas and ruins. *Golden Earth* by Norman Lewis (Eland Books) is a recently reprinted edition of a classic account of a visit to Burma soon after WW II.

Rangoon has quite a few bookshops, particularly along Bogyoke Aung San St opposite the Bogyoke Market where you can find some really interesting books. Also check the Pagan Bookshop at 100 37th St, quite close to the Strand Hotel.

VISAS

You can only get a 24-hour or seven-day visa and since a flight in and out within 24 hours is pretty crazy most people opt for the seven days. The long-awaited 15-day visa has been talked about for years and recently has been more heavily rumoured than ever, but seems no closer to reality. In Singapore the cost is S$15 but takes two days to get and requires tickets in and out. Bangkok is easier, where the cost is 100 bahts, no tickets necessary and it's even available the same day if you smile. Four photos are required and at the equivalent of around US$5 it's quite an expensive visa.

Although it is officially very important to ensure that you get out of Burma on the appointed day, the penalties for over-staying your visa are not severe so long as you have a good excuse. There have been instances of people overstaying their visas due to their train breaking down on the way back from Pagan – a far from unusual occurrence. Changed airline schedules also can add a day or two to your allotment and over the years more than a few people flying with Bangladesh Biman have enjoyed a whole extra week when the once-weekly flight has been cancelled. The secret is to get some official explanation for your over-stay. If your train back to Rangoon breaks down try to get a letter from the local stationmaster (where the train

collapses). To avoid last-minute hassles, however, make sure you get back to Rangoon with time to spare; leave the capital to the end rather than the beginning of your trip.

Rangoon is a good place to get visas for other countries. You can pay for them with your whisky kyats so they're very cheap and because the embassy officials know your time is limited they issue them very quickly. You can get Nepalese visas here in 15 minutes!

MONEY & COSTS

A$1 = 7.2 kyats
US$1 = 8.6 kyats
£1 = 10.2 kyats

The kyat (say chat) is divided into 100 pyas with a collection of confusing coins. Generally it's easiest to change money at Tourist Burma offices which are open longer hours than the banks.

The official exchange rates for travellers' cheques and cash (TCs are worth more

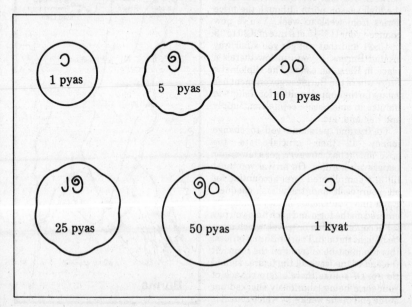

than cash) have little relation to reality. Unofficially cash is worth far more than the rates above. You can buy kyats in Singapore, Penang or Bangkok and illegally bring them in with you. Or you can illegally change US dollars on the black market – Rangoon is the best place and you can expect to get K16 to 20 to US$1, larger-denomination US dollar notes are preferred.

Either of these procedures has some element of risk but it's part of Burma's benevolent incompetence that there is a delightfully simple way round this impasse. At the airport when you depart for Rangoon invest in some duty frees – a carton of 555 cigarettes and a bottle of Johnny Walker Red Label whisky will cost you around US$15. If you can't get the preferred brands move down-market rather than up. No sooner have you left customs behind at Rangoon airport then people will leap forward offering to take them off your hands. For the two something between 300 and 400 kyats seems to be the high season norm although the price varies from week to week. You've now changed your US$15 at a rate of K20 to 25 to US$1 and that will get you a fair way around Burma. If you run low there's a place in Rangoon called The Diplomatic Store where the Burmese government has set up further opportunities for visitors to indulge in small-scale capitalism, supply and demand, etc.

To try and persuade you to change money at their official rate the government has, however, got a few minor paperwork hurdles. On arrival you must fill in a complicated form accounting for all your cash and travellers' cheques. Each time you change money it must be entered on the form and each time you pay for accommodation or travel, which must be bought through Tourist Burma offices, this too must be entered on the form. At the end of the week all the figures should tie up. Of course there's zero chance of your form being laboriously checked out at the end of the week – by which time it is

crumpled, dirty, crossed out, rewritten and totally confused anyway. Plus you'll find that accommodation or transport costs often don't get entered on your form – Tourist Burma is not everywhere. If you simply purchase a railway ticket at a station outside the Tourist Burma field of view you can be certain nobody is going to want to see your currency form. It's that benevolent incompetence at work again. Nevertheless you do have to change some money at official rates.

The main drag about all this is not the money, but the sheer amount of time you have to waste chasing Tourist Burma to their often out-of-the-way offices to pay

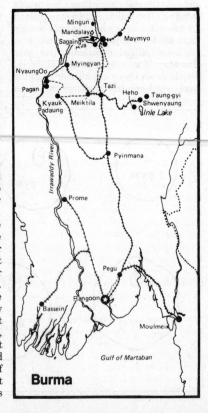

Burma

for hotels and transport which could much more conveniently be paid for at source.

CLIMATE

The rainy season lasts from mid-May until mid-October. For a few months from then, the weather is quite reasonable, in fact it is actually cool in Mandalay at night. From February it gets very hot before the rains arrive once more. The Burmese New Year in April, at the peak of the hot season, means much fun throwing water at all concerned. November through February are the best visiting months. Late December can be difficult as the number of visitors can exceed the transport and accommodation facilities' capacity.

FOOD

Food in Burma is basically curry and rice. You normally get two kinds of rather mild curry and a side plate of salad; unlimited quantities of soup and Chinese tea will be included in the price. It's straightforward, unexciting but quite good food. You will probably also see some less appetising Burmese cuisine. A popular favourite on the trains are crunchy grasshopper kebabs! Indian and Chinese food are also generally available; in fact you're far more likely to find restaurants run by Indians or Chinese than by Burmese.

Burmese soft drinks, usually around K3 or 4, are fairly safe and not always too bad, particularly if you dilute them with soda water or ice. One traveller wrote that 'You are amazingly kind about Burmese soft drinks. I encountered nobody who found them anything but appalling. The honourable exception is Vimto, a strange relic of British rule and usually obtainable only in the north of England'. His opinion was seriously devalued after my last trip when I sought out and tried a bottle of Vimto and found it disgusting!

A bottle of Mandalay Beer from the Peoples' Brewery and Distillery will cost around K16. It's a bit watery but not bad beer – expensive though, at the official rate of exchange. Burmese tea tastes fairly awful and also stains your tongue a lurid orange colour. Ice cream, in the more hygienic-looking ice cream parlours in Rangoon and Mandalay, seems to be OK and I managed to drink a lot of crushed sugar cane during one hot-season visit without any ill effect, but you should be careful. One cannot afford to be ill with the seven-day sprint to complete.

restaurant	sar thow syne
tea shop	la bet yea syne
bread	pow moh
toast	pow moh kin
butter	taw but
coffee	kaw pee
drinking water	thow ye
hot	ah poo
egg, boiled	kyet (chet), ou byoke
egg, fried	kyet (chet), ou chor
noodles	kaw swe
sugar	tha jar
tea	la bet ye
chicken	kyet (chet) that
fish	ngar
muton	seik that
soup	hin jo
rice (cooked)	ta min

GETTING THERE

Burma is purely a fly-in, fly-out situation. No ship arrivals are permitted for tourists and all roads are closed at the borders – except to smugglers of course. BAC's F28s fly to and from Bangkok every day of the week and also connect to Calcutta and Kathmandu. Thai International also fly Bangkok-Rangoon, Bangladesh Biman fly Bangkok-Rangoon-Dacca and Royal Nepal Airlines fly Kathmandu-Rangoon. Fares are a bit of a mixup due to the keen fare-cutting in Bangkok. Shopping around, with your student card handy, you should be able to fly Bangkok-Rangoon-Bangkok for around US$140, Bangkok-Rangoon-Calcutta for a similar price or Bangkok-Rangoon-Kathmandu for around US$180. Some travel agents in Bangkok will do a deal including your tickets and visa.

Aeroflot fly from Vietnam and Laos to Rangoon, then on to Moscow. Not many travellers are likely to use that route but some people have been entering Burma from Kunming in China with CAAC. If you're travelling around China this makes a very interesting way of continuing on to South-East Asia, rather than going back to Hong Kong and flying from there.

GETTING AROUND

Travel in Burma is not that easy. It's uncertain and often uncomfortable by whatever means of travel you choose.

Rail Apart from the daily Rangoon-Mandalay express (which is a special 'impress the tourists' service) the ordinary class trains are better forgotten – dirty, slow, unreliable and very dark at night due to the national shortage of light bulbs! Upper class travel (Burmese socialism or not) is generally better. Apart from on the main tourist routes you may find it impossible to buy railway tickets through Tourist Burma – and the station is not supposed to sell tickets to foreigners, who should get them from Tourist Burma! The answer is to ask somebody at the station to buy them for you although I must admit I've bought tickets at public stations and had no trouble at all.

Bus Road travel is not much used for longer trips – the exceptions would be between Inle Lake and Mandalay or Mandalay and Pagan. Burmese buses tend to be extremely crowded with people hanging out the sides, sitting on the roof and occupying every possible space inside. Recently, however, small Japanese pickup trucks have started to appear on Burmese roads in increasing numbers. With a couple of benches down each side they operate just like Indonesian *bemos* or Thai *songthaews*. They can be uncomfortable when crowded but groups of people can sometimes charter them quite economically – such as between Pagan and Inle Lake. Or even further afield.

Boat The boat trip downriver from Mandalay to Pagan is popular and you can also make other shorter trips from Mandalay or Rangoon. If you had the time you could continue the boat trip from Pagan right down the river to Rangoon – on your seven-day visa you'd be devoting the entire week to just that one trip!

Air Because of the short visa period travellers to Burma sometimes take to the air where normally they would be quite happy to travel by land. Flying can certainly save a lot of time and effort although all tickets must be bought through Tourist Burma with 'official' kyats. The problem with flying BAC is that you never know where you are. Schedules are fixed from day to day and you'll find it virtually impossible to be certain of any reservation. They'll tell you to arrive at the airport at noon for a 2 pm flight which may not leave until 4 pm, 5 pm, who knows. Very frustrating when time is so limited.

Recently they have started a 'tourists only' service around the Rangoon-Pagan-Mandalay-Inle-Rangoon loop each day but you still waste a lot of time and endure a lot of uncertainty before actually getting up in the air. If it's any consolation when it comes to a fight for seats foreigners have priority over Burmese! But then a foreigner will get bumped off a flight for a foreigner on a package tour. And you'll all get bumped off for a government official!

Note that BAC will not accept any tickets issued overseas for their flights. The best they will do is give you a refund against them, for purchase of their own tickets sector by sector through Burma.

GETTING AROUND

The impossibly crowded and delightfully ancient buses in Rangoon and Mandalay are very cheap and fairly convenient although you may well end up hanging out the side or off the back. Trishaws are also economic and unique since the passengers sit back to back – always negotiate the fare beforehand. Taxi-trucks are becoming more readily available throughout Burma. Some of them operate fixed routes, others can be hired like a taxi. There are also taxis in Rangoon and smaller three wheelers like an Indian *auto-rickshaw* or Thai *samlor*. Mandalay also has horse carts (tongas) which are somewhat more expensive than trishaws. You can hire bicycles in Pagan.

BURMA IN SEVEN DAYS

With a non-extendable seven days most people just try to rush around the Rangoon-Mandalay-Pagan-Rangoon loop. At surface level it is possible, but only just. With allowances for arrival and departure times on day 1 and 8 the schedule is:

Day 0
  Arrive, book Mandalay train tickets, see Rangoon
Day 1
  Train all day to Mandalay
Day 2
  See Mandalay
Day 3
  Bus or boat to Pagan, the bus is more expensive but gives you an extra afternoon in Pagan
Day 4
  See Pagan
Day 5
  Back to Rangoon via Thazi, arrive at night or travel overnight
Day 6
  Time to look around Rangoon, even make a day trip to Pegu
Day 7
  Depart

There are all sorts of alternative ways of spending your seven days. Just some possibilities include:

Alternative 1 Cut something out, some people miss Mandalay to have longer in Pagan, some deluded souls actually miss out on Pagan.

Alternative 2 Fly a sector, if you've already taken the train from Rangoon to Mandalay the Pagan-Rangoon flight will save you a lot of time and effort in repeating that train journey.

Alternative 3 If you get into Rangoon early enough on day 1 get the overnight train up to Mandalay and have an extra day to spare.

Alternative 4 Do it all backwards, Pagan first, Mandalay second. Doing this there's a fair chance that you'll find travel easier since most people all move round the circle in the same direction!

Alternative 6 Try to fit in other things – Inle Lake, Maymyo for example. Some people prefer Inle to Mandalay.

Whichever alternative you take I recommend you leave Rangoon for the end – arrive, get out up-country as quickly as possible. Ten to one you'll have plenty of time to see Rangoon at the end, even on the day you depart. If you're going to run into hassles getting back to the capital it's better to have time in hand. If you fly to Burma on a weekend the tourist office closes earlier – so unless you're on an early flight you have little chance of getting on the night train or even getting tickets for the train next morning.

BURMESE BUREAUCRACY

The government tries to keep tabs on you while you are in Burma in two ways. One is that they don't want you wandering off to touchy regions – that's part of the reason for the seven-day visa. With so little time to spare visitors have little incentive to get off the beaten track.

Secondly with so much difference between the official exchange rate and the real one they obviously want to stop you from spending 'black' money. To keep control on the money question they insist that much of your expenditure is made with Tourist Burma rather than with the railway station, airline, hotel or whatever. When you want a hotel (apart from the major ones which have Tourist Burma in the saddle anyway) you have to first trot around to the Tourist Burma office and pay for your room there. The amount spent is then entered on your currency exchange form. Similarly you have to buy any rail tickets, airline tickets and even the Mandalay-Pagan boat ticket from Tourist Burma.

Supposedly at the end they can tote up how much you have spent at the tourist offices and make sure it doesn't exceed the amount you've changed. In practice there is no way in the world they could do all that arithmetic on each and every tourist on departure so the only purpose it serves is to cause visitors a lot of wasted time and energy dragging around to Tourist Burma offices before they go to their hotel or depart for the station. It's a real annoyance to have to waste so much of your 168 precious hours going back and forth from the often inconveniently located tourist offices. Of course meals, souvenirs, drinks, buses, taxis and much other expenditure can still be made with any old kyats. All train, air and accommodation costs now include a 10% government tax – which accounts for the often strange prices quoted.

The restrictions on where visitors may go are also somewhat open to interpretation. Most visitors don't wander off the Rangoon-Mandalay-Pagan-Inle Lake circuit apart from short detours to Pegu, Syriam, Maymyo or the deserted cities around Mandalay. If you ask about going to other places the answer you'll get will probably be a firm 'no'. But if you simply set out to go there it's quite possible you'll manage it. Of course there are touchy areas (the north-east towards the Golden Triangle, north of Mandalay towards the China border) which are absolutely no go but lots of people manage to get to Kyaikto to see the balancing pagoda and even further to Thaton. A few have even managed Myohaung, and Bassein and Prome are quite easy to get to. If only we all had more time!

Caution in Burma Burma is a land of temples and your one-week visit begins to feel like a procession from one to another. The Burmese are very fussy about bare-footing it in the temple precincts. That means the steps from the very bottom of Mandalay Hill, the whole shop-lined arcade to the Shwe Dagon and even the ruins of Pagan. Carry your shoes.

THINGS TO BUY

There is nice lacquerware, particularly at Pagan. The black and gold items probably aren't as good quality as in Chiang Mai, but coloured items are much more alive. Look for flexibility in bowls or dishes and clarity of design. Opium weights are cheaper than in Thailand, but rather hard to find. Beautiful shoulder bags are made by the Shan tribes. Be very careful if you decide to buy gems. A lot of foolish travellers seem to buy fake gemstones. It's another of those fields you should dabble in only if you really know what is and what isn't although I must admit I bought a 'ruby' last trip and it turned out to really be one. Don't buy betel nut; several travellers have written of being talked into buying Burmese betel to re-sell at a profit in Bangladesh. Forget it!

If you want to sell things, virtually any western goods from radio batteries to cheap make-up have an amazing demand in Burma but they have to be name brands, not any old rubbish.

LANGUAGE

There are a wide variety of languages in Burma, but fortunately English is widely spoken. The Burmese alphabet is most unusual, it looks like a collection of interlocked circles. The following words are in Burmese, the main language.

good morning/afternoon/evening
   min ga la baa
thank you
   kyai (chay) zoo tin baa dai (day)
goodbye (I'm going)
   pyan dor mai (may)

excuse me
  kwin pyu baa
where is . . . ?
  beh mah lai (lay)
how much?
  bah lout lai (lay)?
too much
  myar dai (day)

Numbers

1	tit	၁
2	nit	၂
3	thone	၃
4	lay	၄
5	ngar	၅
6	chak	၆
7	kun nit	၇
8	shit	၈
9	co	၉
10	ta sair	၁၀
11	sair tit	၁၁
12	sair nit	၁၂
20	na sair	၂၀
30	thone sair	၃၀
100	ta yar	၁၀၀

RANGOON

The capital of Burma for less than one hundred years, Rangoon is 30 km upriver from the sea and has an air of seedy decay along with a great pagoda that is one of the real wonders of South-East Asia. A city of wide streets and spacious architecture, it looks run down, worn out and thoroughly neglected. The streets are lively at night with hordes of stalls selling delicious-looking food, piles of huge cigars and those western cigarettes you've just unloaded. Look for the tape recorder studios where young Burmese entertain themselves by adding Burmese words to western pop music. Recently electronic games have also become a Rangoon craze. Watch out for rats late at night!

Information & Orientation

The Tourist Burma office is right by the Sule Pagoda at the junction of Sule Pagoda Rd and Maha Bandoola St. Rangoon is a relatively simple city to find your way around – the centre is quite compact, the streets are laid out in a grid pattern and walking is no problem.

Things to See

Shwedagon Pagoda Dominating the entire city from its hilltop site, this is the most sacred Buddhist temple in Burma. Nearly 100 metres high, it is clearly visible from the air as you fly in or out of Rangoon. I saw it once as a tiny golden dot while flying over Burma to Kathmandu – magic! Visit it in the early morning or evening when the gold spire gleams in the sun and the temperature is cooler. Or see its shimmering reflection from across the Royal Lake at night. A European visitor in 1587 wrote of its 'wonderful bignesse and all gilded from foote to the toppe'.

Facts and figures – the site is over 2500 years old, there are over 8000 gold plates covering the pagoda, the top of the spire is encrusted with more than 5000 diamonds and 2000 other precious or semi-precious stones and the compound around the pagoda has 82 other buildings. It is this sheer mass of buildings that gives the place its awesome appeal.

In the north-west corner is a huge bell which the butter-fingered British managed to drop into the Rangoon River while carrying it off. Unable to recover it, they gave the bell back to the Burmese who refloated it by tying a vast number of lengths of bamboo to it. The Shwedagon has an equally impressive appearance at night when it glows gold against a velvet backdrop.

Sule Pagoda Also over 2000 years old and right in the centre of town the Sule Pagoda makes a fine spectacle at night; but everything palls after the Shwedagon.

Other There's a mirror maze in the stupa of the Bo-Ta-Taung temple. Rangoon has a fine morning market and the extensive Bogyoke Market is always worth a wander. Rangoon has an interesting museum but to the two upstairs floors are almost

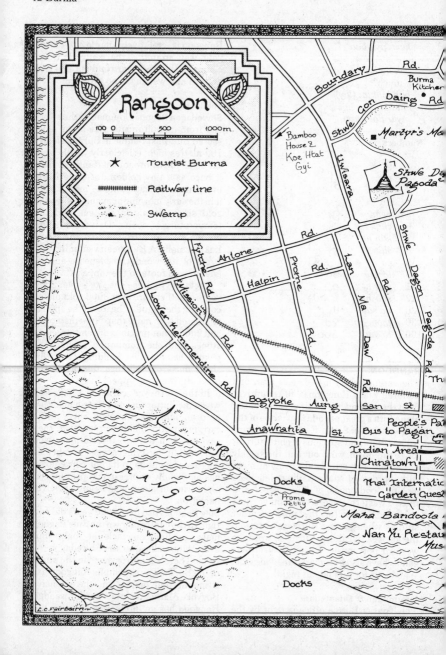

Rangoon

100 0 500 1000 m.

★ Tourist Burma

++++++++ Railway line

Swamp

Chauk Htat Gyi Pagoda

Ngu Htat Gyi Pagoda

Airport, and Mandalay

Bow Lane

To Mandalay

Natmauk

Bogyoke Aungsan Park

Royal Lake

Karaweik

Kandawgyi Hotel

Zoological Garden

Horticultural Garden

Upper Pazundaung Rd.

Sule Pagoda

Thaketa Bridge

Railway Station

Bogyoke Market

Docks

Dagon

Diplomatic Shop

PAZUNDAUNG CREEK

Sule Pagoda

Pansodan St.

Maha Bandoola St.

YWCA

YMCA

Syriam Jetty

Pazundaung Rd.

Thein Byu St.

Botataung Pagoda Rd.

Merchant St.

Lower

Strand Rd.

Botataung Pagoda

Mandalay Jetty

GPO
Strand Hotel
BAC Office

Monkey Point

R I V E R

hidden – if you can't find the obscure entry to the stairs you will have to leave the museum and re-enter next door! It's a pleasant stroll around the Royal Lake where you can visit the huge Karaweik non-floating restaurant. Rangoon has a zoo with a collection of Burmese animals and an elephant and snake charmer performance on Sundays.

Outside of town is the Kaba Aya, or World Peace, pagoda which was built in the mid-50s for the 2500th anniversary of Buddhism. The Martyrs' Mausoleum to Aung San and his comrades is close to the Shwedagon. The huge reclining Buddha at Chauk Htat Gyi is also close by and there are a couple of other gigantic Buddha figures in Rangoon. An interesting excursion from Rangoon can be made across the river to Syriam, where you can take a bus to Kyauktan with its small 'island pagoda' or take a longer river trip to Twante, two or three hours away.

Places to Stay

Shoestring travellers in Burma generally head for the *YMCA* which is reasonably central, reasonably priced, has pretty good food and is reasonably tatty. It is an excellent information source, however, both from your fellow travellers and from

the management. There is a basic dormitory but it's really only on if you have got a sleeping bag since the beds are just a wooden board – no mattress, no sheets or blankets and (probably most important) no mosquito nets. The men's dorm takes 25 people, the ladies' only four.

The singles and doubles are probably a bit better value. They start at K24/36 for singles/doubles with common bath and go up to K48, 54 or 60 depending on whether you share a bathroom between two rooms or have one to yourself. On the top floor there are somewhat dismal rooms for men only at K30 double or K39 triple. For K5 they will even make an advance reservation for you – and it works! On our first visit to Burma we were plagued by mosquitoes at the Y; they subsequently installed mosquito nets, then took them out again and provided meshed wire on the windows. Which keeps the air out and lets the insects in. They do have new fans though, and the toilets work.

If the YMCA is full, as it often is, there are a number of alternatives. Right next door to the Tourist Burma office on Sule Pagoda Rd is the *Garden Guest House*. It's a more modern establishment than the Y and when first opened was spotlessly clean. Unfortunately it already seems to

1 Peking Restaurant	21 Great Wall Restaurant
2 Sakantha Hotel	22 Nan Yu
3 Hotel de City	23 Mya Sabe Cafe
4 Moulmein Buses (Ramanya Bus)	24 Indian Embassy
5 Prome Buses	25 Customs House
6 Meiktila Buses (Road & Transport Corp.)	26 Bangladesh Biman Airways
7 Nila Briwane Shop	27 Nilarwin Cafe
8 Burma Pattisserie	28 Pagan Bookshop
9 Gold Cup Cafe	29 Palace Restaurant
10 Yatha Restaurant	30 Museum
11 Diplomatic Shop	31 Burma Airways
12 Thai International	32 Strand Hotel
13 Tourist Burma	33 Sarpay Beikman Library
14 Garden Guest House	34 Synagogue
15 Sule Pagoda	35 Australian Embassy
16 Dagon Hotel	36 British Embassy
17 Shwe Mya Bakery	37 Post Office
18 Bookstalls	38 Ruby Restaurant
19 Independence Monument	39 Sein Win Restaurant
20 US Embassy	40 YWCA
	41 YMCA
	42 City Hall & Library

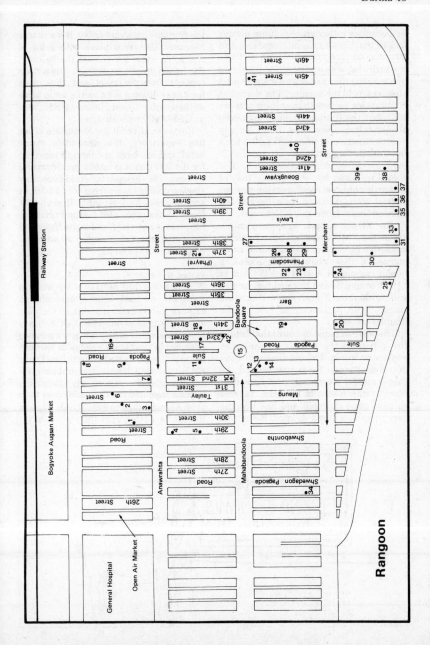

Rangoon

be becoming rather grubby. It has always lacked the Y's pleasant atmosphere, and its restaurant is nothing like the Y's. When I asked what was available for breakfast one morning the answer was 'soup'. And it closes early in the evening. The dorm has comfortable beds with mosquito nets for K22, but you'll probably need your own sleeping bag since they don't supply sheets. Rooms cost from US$3.50/6 for a fan-cooled single/double up to US$7/9.50 for an air-con single/double. The rooms are clean but very plain – they're just little cubicles, small, spartan and not special value. You can leave bags at the Garden Guest House for K1 per day.

The *YWCA* is open to women only – unlike the YMCA which is open to either sex although couples are supposed to be married if they share double rooms, a quaint custom for Asia. The YWCA is at 119 Brooking St and has just two singles and two doubles. Nightly cost is K24 in the singles (with bathroom) or K36 in the doubles (without).

There are a couple of hotels that bridge the gap from the hostels to the more expensive hotels. The old Orient at 256/260 Sule Pagoda Rd is now named the *Dagon* and for a time was a very pleasant place to stay. Recently, however, it seems to have gone downhill and has become very dilapidated and ill-kept. Rooms on the front are also very noisy. It's a shame because this was a place with a bit of character – nice views from the balcony, good food in the restaurant downstairs (upstairs from the street) and a fine place for a beer. Rooms are now the same price as the Garden Guest House – US$3.50/6 or US$7/9.50 with air-con.

If you can afford it the *Strand Hotel* is a fine experience. It's Rangoon's 'name hotel' and has bags of charm to make up for the fact that it is totally run down and decrepit. The cheapest fan-cooled economy singles/doubles start from US$11.50/14 and they're quite acceptable. Right by the Royal Lake the old Natural History Museum is now the *Kandawgyi Hotel* and has quite reasonable rooms, all with air-con, from US$15 to 21.

Places to Eat

With only a couple of days at the most in Rangoon you have little opportunity to explore the gourmet delights of socialist living Burmese-style. The *YMCA* has a pretty reasonable cafeteria where a number of separate food stalls engage in spirited but most un-Burmese competition. There are numerous Chinese and Indian restaurants around – particularly along Sule Pagoda road (try the *Chung Wah* at 162) or on Anawrahta St to west of Sule Pagoda Rd. At 84 37th Street the *Palace* has a

တိ ရ စ္ဆာန် များ ကို မ စား ၿခင်း ၁ ၃ ၀ ၄ . ၃ ၁ း ႀ က င္ နာ ပါ

BE KIND TO ANIMALS BY NOT EATING THEM

well-deserved reputation for the best Chinese food in Rangoon. It's a bit pricey but worth it. There are a number of Indian biriyani stalls along Anawrahta St, to the west of the Sule Pagoda Rd. Try the crowded (but snappy service) at the *Nila Briwane Shop* between 31st and 32nd Sts.

There are lots of places for a quick snack or a cold beer. You can get yoghurt (curd) or lassi (a delicious yoghurt drink) at the *Nilarwin Cold Drink Shop* at 377 Maha Bandoola Street about midway between the Y and the Sule Pagoda. If there's a single locale in Rangoon which serves as a travellers' meeting spot then the Nilarwin is it. *Yatha*, a white-fronted building within sight of the tourist office, is a good place for drinks and ice cream. The friendly owner speaks excellent English. You can get good baked goods at the *Shwe Mya Bakery* at 184/186 Sule Pagoda Rd.

In the evening a beer in the lounge of the *Strand* is a time-honoured pursuit. There's always a friendly crowd of people here to talk with. When the bar closes down the reception desk still has a cache of cold bottles behind the counter! The *Dagon* restaurant is another good place for a cold bottle of the Burmese amber fluid although the advent of television has kind of killed the place as far as being a restaurant goes – the staff are all too busy watching the box.

Moving upmarket, if you feel like trying the *Strand* then make it lobster – it's an incredible bargain even at the official exchange rate. It's worth the trip to 141 West Shwegondine St, just north of the Shwedagon Pagoda, to try the genuine Burmese food at the *Burma Kitchen*. It's a plain and straightforward restaurant, the food is very good and the prices quite reasonable. Count on around K30 per person. By the Royal Lake the *Karaweik* is as much a Rangoon tourist attraction as a restaurant but the food isn't bad. You can get a complete fixed-price meal for K30, and there are Burmese dance

performances here in the evening. If you just come to gawk there's a K1 admission price.

Getting Around

The generally agreed fare for a taxi between the airport and Rangoon is still K30, which it has been for years. You can also take a local bus although that entails getting out to the main road first, about a km away. On departure BAC provides a bus for its passengers but it departs so long before flight time that you may decide to sleep in and get a taxi if you have an early morning departure. On international departures there is a K15 airport tax.

You can get around Rangoon on the fairly comprehensive bus service or by trishaws, taxis or the small Mazda taxi-trucks. Some of these operate just like taxis, though they're cheaper. Others seem to run their own little bus routes with fares of a kyat or two.

PEGU

Eighty km from Rangoon on the Mandalay line, this city used to be a major seaport – but then the river changed course. This event, coupled with Pegu's destruction by a rival Burmese king in 1757, was the city's downfall.

Things to See

Shwemawdaw Pagoda The 'Great Golden God Pagoda' was rebuilt after an earthquake in 1930 and is nearly as high as the Shwedagon. Murals tell the sad story of the quake. Note the large chunk of the *hti* toppled by an earlier 1917 quake, embedded in the north-east corner of the pagoda.

Shwethalyaung This huge reclining Buddha image is over five metres larger than the one in Bangkok and claimed to be extremely life-like. There's a terrific signboard giving the dimensions of the figure's big toe and other vital information.

Other Pegu has a number of other attractions to visit. Beyond the Shwemawdaw is the Hintha Gone, a hilltop shrine guarded by mythical swans. On the Rangoon side of town the Kyaik Pun has three back-to-back sitting Buddhas – the fourth one has fallen down. Just before the Shwethalyaung is the Kalyani Sima 'hall of ordination' and a curious quartet of standing Buddha figures. Carry on beyond the Shwethalyaung and you soon come to the Mahazedi Pagoda, where you can climb to the top for a fine view over the surrounding country. The Shwegugale Pagoda, with 64 seated Buddha images, is a little beyond the Mahazedi.

Places to Stay & Eat
There's no official accommodation in Pegu although you can probably find a rest house near the station. There are a number of food stalls around the market place and some snack bars and restaurants near the station.

Getting There
There are plenty of buses and trains between Rangoon and Pegu but Tourist Burma are reluctant to sell train tickets to you and, therefore, so are the personnel at the railway station. Coming from Pegu, however, it's no problem at all to get tickets. If you plan to disembark at Pegu from the Mandalay-Rangoon Express there are two minor problems. First of all Tourist Burma are again reluctant to sell you a ticket to Pegu – no problem, just buy a Rangoon ticket; you only waste a couple of kyats. Secondly the overnight train does not stop in Pegu although the day train does. On my most recent trip to Burma I took the night train from Thazi and it went through the station so slowly that I simply hopped off the moving train. Don't try to visit Pegu on the way north to Mandalay; you may have trouble getting a seat on another train northbound. Coming south it's only another hour or two into Rangoon by train or bus.

As well as numerous trains there are also plenty of buses with fares around K5. They start from Rangoon as early as 5 or 6 am but avoid Pegu on weekends when it is very crowded with Burmese, as the excursion there from Rangoon is a popular one. If you want to splash out a bit get a group together and hire a huge old American taxi from near the Strand – ride there like a travelling Al Capone. Count on around K250 for the whole day, less if you care to pay in dollars.

Getting Around
The easiest way to explore Pegu is to hire a trishaw by the station and negotiate a rate to visit all the Pegu attractions.

MANDALAY
The last capital of Burma to fall to the British, Mandalay was founded comparatively recently in 1857. With a population of about one third of a million, it is Burma's second city as well as the country's cultural centre. Dry and dusty in the hot season, Mandalay is a sprawling town of dirt streets, trishaws and horse carts.

In 1981 a disastrous fire destroyed a great number of buildings along the riverside but did not affect any of Mandalay's sights. Although Mandalay is of some interest in itself the 'deserted cities' around Mandalay are probably even more worthwhile.

Information & Orientation
The Tourist Burma Office is in the Mandalay Hotel, a very long walk from the main part of town where most of the cheap hotels are located. Mandalay is laid out on an extremely straightforward grid pattern but it is very sprawling – distances in Mandalay are quite amazing.

Things to See
Royal Palace Contained within the enormous palace walls and moat, this amazing example of wooden architecture was completely burnt out during the closing

days of WW II. Some foundations and a model can be seen. To enter get permission from the sentry at the south gate.

Mandalay Hill An easy half-hour's barefoot climb up the sheltered steps brings you to a wide view over the palace, Mandalay and the pagoda-studded countryside.

Kuthodaw Pagoda 729 small temples each shelter a marble slab inscribed with Buddhist scriptures. The central pagoda makes it 730. Built by King Mindon around 1860, it is the world's biggest book. Don't confuse it with the Sandamuni Pagoda which is right in front of it and also has a large collection of inscribed slabs. The ruins of the Atumashi Kyaung, or 'incomparable monastery' are also close to the foot of Mandalay Hill.

Shwenandaw Kyaung Once a part of King Mindon's palace, this wooden building was moved to its present site and converted into a monastery after his death. This is the finest remaining example of traditional wooden Burmese architecture since all the other palace buildings were destroyed during the last war.

Kyauktawgyi The pagoda at the base of Mandalay Hill was another King Mindon construction. The marble Buddha is said to have taken 10,000 men 13 days to install in the temple.

Mahamuni Pagoda The 'Arakan Pagoda' stands to the south of town. It's noted for its venerated Buddha image which is thickly covered in goldleaf. Around the main pagoda are rooms containing a huge gong weighing five tonnes and statues of legendary warriors. Rubbing parts of their bodies is supposed to cure afflictions on corresponding parts of your own. Outside the pagoda are streets of Buddha image makers.

Other Zegyo Market in the centre of town comes alive at night. The Eindawya Pagoda and the Shwekyimyint Pagoda are also centrally located. The latter is older than Mandalay itself. Several of the town pagodas have amusing clockwork coin-in-the-slot displays. Mandalay's museum is tatty and waiting to be rehoused.

Places to Stay

Mandalay has a lot of hotels and rest houses in the bottom-end bracket but they're uniformly spartan and basic and Tourist Burma hardly encourages any improvement. Since you have to book them through the inconveniently placed tourist office in the Mandalay Hotel (or at the station if you arrive by train) you often find yourself simply 'assigned' to one particular hotel so there is little incentive to managers to improve their places. Worse still there are places in Mandalay which are not on the Tourist Burma approved list and are better than some of those that are. At the height of the tourist season Mandalay can get really packed out and you may simply have to stay at some of these unapproved places. The government-approved list of guest houses tends to vary a bit from year to year. Some places, like the Man San Dar Win, have always been on the list; others tend to come and go.

The shoestring hotels are all around the town-centre area, to the south-west of the palace. With the odd exception they charge an identical K18/30 for singles/doubles and all offer similar standards – bare little cubicles for rooms; narrow, hard beds, fortunately usually with mosquito nets. I'd say the *Aye Thaw Dar* was probably the best of the bunch – it's on 26th Rd (B Rd), but quite a distance from the Zegyo Market towards the Mingun pier on the river. There are some air-con rooms here and they are generally a bit bigger and more solid than the norm. The manager is helpful and knowledgeable and it's a friendly sort of place.

The *Man San Dar Win* (tel 23317) is at 177 31st Rd, between 81st and 80th Sts. It's also friendly and well kept; take your shoes off before going upstairs. Chinese tea is always available in this place. Opposite it is the *Man Shwe Myo*.

The *Mya Tha Mar* and the *Thi Dar* have nothing outside them (in our script) to indicate that they are actually guest houses although the Mya Tha Mar does at

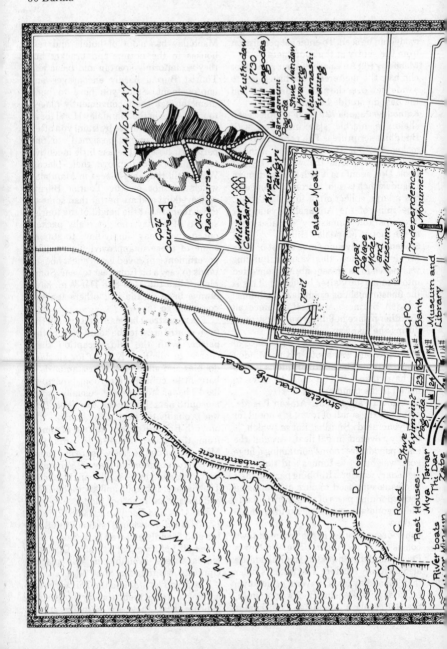

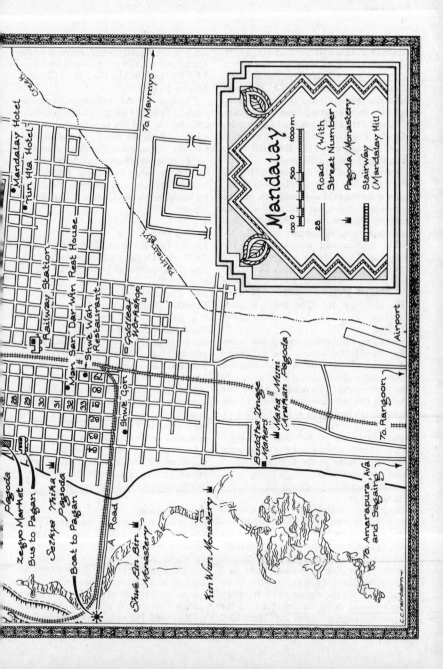

Mandalay

28	Road (With Street Number)
	Pagoda/Monastery
	Stairway (Mandalay Hill)

100 0   500   1000 m.

To Maymyo

To Rangoon

Airport

To Amarapura, Ava and Sagaing

Pagoda

Zegyo Market

Bus to Pagan

Sethya Thika Pagoda

Boat to Pagan

A Road

Shwe Kin Bin Monastery

Kin Wun Monastery

Buddha Image Makers

Maha Muni (Arakan Pagoda)

Shwe Gon

Man San Dar Win Rest House

Shwe Wah Restaurant

Goldleaf Workshop

Railway Station

Mandalay Hotel

Tun Hla Hotel

Pathettan Creek

28   29   30   31   32   33

81   80   79   78

82   83   84

L.C. rainbarrow

least look like one. It's quite pleasant although it shuts its door at 10 pm, by which time most of Mandalay has closed down anyway. It's on 25th Rd between 82nd and 83rd Sts. The Thi Dar isn't particularly friendly and since it's located right by the market on 26th Rd between 83rd and 84th Sts it tends to be a bit noisy at night. The *Zabe* (or Sabai) is on 84th St between 25th and 26th Rds and it's a rather gruff and grubby place.

Inconveniently far out on 35th Rd the *Shwe Gon Rest House* is a brick building, more solid than the real cheapies, but the rooms are still square little prison-like cubicles. Air-con, but without attached bathroom, singles/doubles are K24/48. Other bottom end places include the *Bandoola Guest House* on the corner of 26th Rd and 81st St, the *Man Ya Ta Nar* on the corner of 29th Rd and 82nd St and the *Man Myo Daw* on 80th St between 30th and 31st Rd. The latter is more expensive at US$4.50/6.50 for singles/doubles.

Bridging the bottom-to-top gap is the *Mya Mandalar*, behind the expensive Mandalay Hotel, a block back from the moat road and a couple of blocks towards the town centre. This used to be the Tun Hla but has now been taken over by the government and is not as good as before. Rooms cost US$6/7 and US$7/9.50 for singles/doubles, all with attached bathroom. There is a restaurant and a swimming pool here. None of the central cheapies have any place to eat.

Places to Eat

The grubby-looking little *Shwe Wah* on 80th St between 32nd and 33rd Rds is very popular for food – the quality of the food certainly outshines the surroundings. On 83rd St, between 26th and 25th Rds (close to the Zegyo Market) there is a cluster of pleasant places – try the *Mann Restaurant* for quite reasonable food and don't miss a delicious ice cream in the extremely popular *Nylon Ice Cream Bar*. Next door is the *Olympia Cafe*, good for light snacks at any time of day. Next door again is the equally popular *Orient* while not far away on 83rd St between 26th and 27th Rd the *Min Min* does good Chinese Muslim food.

There are a number of very economical food stalls beside the Zegyo Market along 26th Rd. On 29th Rd, particularly between 83rd and 84th Sts, you'll find a number of Chinese restaurants. Mandalay's myriad sugar cane crushers provide a thirst-quenching (and seemingly reasonably healthy) drink for just one kyat. Watch out for strawberries on sale near the market in season.

Getting There

Air Air fare Rangoon-Mandalay is now K439 including airport transport at each end. It takes about an hour by F-28 jet, 1½ hours by F-27.

Rail The daily express trains on the Rangoon-Mandalay route leave both ends at around 7 am and arrive 12 hours later. Night departure is at 6.45 pm. This tourist service is fairly uncrowded and admirably punctual but reserve your seat as early as possible. If you're going straight to Mandalay from Rangoon I'd advise heading immediately for Tourist Burma from the airport and getting a ticket for the next morning – even that night if you arrive early enough. Ticket sales stop at 6 pm, earlier on weekends. Ordinary class costs K44, upper class K110, a sleeper K138. Get an excellent chicken biriyani for lunch at one of the stations on the way – it will be neatly wrapped in a banana leaf.

Getting Around

A jeep into town costs a standard K20 or you can do it on a No 2 bus but Burma Airways now includes airport transport in their ticket price for tourists. Around town horse-drawn tongas and Burma's familiar back-to-back trishaws are the usual transport. A couple of people could hire a trishaw for the day to get around Mandalay for K50 or 60. Hiring a jeep for the day on a trip to Amarapura and Sagaing would be

K100 to 150. Count on K4 or 5 for a trishaw from the Mandalay Hotel (tourist office) to the town centre, K9 or 10 for a tonga from the centre down to the Irrawaddy.

Travelling around Mandalay by the impossibly crowded buses (worse during the rush hours) is actually quite fun, very friendly. Take a No 1 to the Maha Muni Pagoda, a 2 to the river end of B Rd (Mingun ferry departure point) or to the railway and airport in the other direction, 4 to Mandalay Hill from the clock tower, 5 to Mandalay Hill via the Mandalay Hotel, 8 via the Mahamuni and Amarapura to Ava – starts from the corner of 27th and 84th. Don't start walking around Mandalay without thinking three times (hard). Distances are great.

AROUND MANDALAY

Close to Mandalay are four 'deserted cities' which make interesting day trips from Mandalay. You can also visit Maymyo, further out and probably requiring an overnight stop.

Amarapura

Situated 11 km south of Mandalay, this was the capital of upper Burma for a brief period before Mandalay. Amongst the most interesting sights is the rickety U Bein's Bridge leading to the Kyauktawgyi Pagoda.

Sagaing

If you continue a little further beyond Amarapura you'll reach the Ava Bridge, the only bridge across the Irrawaddy. Built by the British, it was put out of action during WW II and not repaired until 1954. Crossing the bridge will bring you to Sagaing with its temple-studded hill. Sagaing's best-known pagoda is not on Sagaing Hill though; you must continue 10 km beyond Sagaing to reach the Kaunghmudaw Pagoda which is said to have been modelled on a well-endowed queen's perfect breast.

Ava

The ancient city of Ava, long a capital of upper Burma after the fall of Pagan, is on the Mandalay side of the Irrawaddy close to the Ava Bridge. To get to it take an 8 bus which runs right down to the Myitnge river which you must cross by a ferry or canoe. Or get off the Sagaing minibus at the Ava Bridge and stroll across the fields to the Myitnge River. There is very little left of Ava today apart from the Maha Aungmye Bonzan monastery and a crumbling 27-metre-high watch tower.

Mingun

The fourth of these old cities is Mingun, a pleasant 11 km upriver trip on the opposite bank from Mandalay. Get a riverboat from the bottom of 26th St. Cost is K2 and the trip takes anything from 45 minutes to two hours. The trip to Mingun is very pleasant and makes a very good introduction to Burmese river travel, particularly if you do not take the boat to Pagan.

Principal sights at Mingun are the huge ruined base of the Mingun Pagoda and the equally grandiose Mingun Bell. The pagoda would have been the largest in the world if it had been completed. The bell is said to be the largest uncracked bell in the world – there is a bigger one in Russia but it is badly cracked.

MAYMYO

If you've not got time to head downriver to Pagan then Maymyo may make an interesting substitute. It's an old British hill station just 60 km north of Mandalay and about 800 metres higher. Get there in a jeep (frequent departures from the market) or rather cheaper, but much slower, by train – it zig-zags its way up the hills. The chief pleasure of Maymyo is a stay at the old British bachelor's quarters *Candacraig*; you can read a delightful description of it in Paul Theroux's *Great Railway Bazaar*.

Places to Stay *Candacraig*, now officially known as the Maymyo Government Rest

House, was once the bachelor quarters of the Bombay Burma Trading Company. It was maintained and run by the late Mr Bernard until around his 90th birthday in exactly the way it was during the British era. Recently the edge has been taken off the colonial splendour but it is still a pleasant place to stay with rooms at K29/55 for singles/doubles. A roaring fire, a cold bottle of Mandalay beer and the 'English dinner' all add to the atmosphere. You can hire bicycles here to explore Maymyo.

Other places to stay include the *Thin Sabai*, the *Shwe Yema* and the *Ububahan*, all at K11/22, and the other Tourist Burma place, the *Nann Myaing* at the beginning of town. There is a variety of restaurants around the town centre including a couple of Chinese places reputed to have the best Chinese food in Burma.

Getting There From Mandalay you can take a jeep for K15. Jeeps depart from near the Zegyo Market and the trip takes about two to 2½ hours up, one to 1½ down. Chartering a whole jeep costs around K150. There is also a daily train but it's more for railway enthusiasts then straightforward transport – it takes four to five hours up the many switchbacks.

PAGAN

Pronounce it 'pah-garn' not 'pay-gan'. One of the true wonders of Asia, Pagan is an amazing deserted city of fabulous pagodas and temples on the banks of the Irrawaddy south of Mandalay. Pagan's period of grandeur started in 1057 when King Anawrahta conquered Thaton and brought back artists, craftsmen, monks and 30 elephant-loads of Buddhist scriptures.

Over the next two centuries an enormous number of magnificent buildings were erected but after Kublai Khan sacked the city in 1287 it was never rebuilt. The major earthquake in 1975 caused enormous damage but everything of importance has now been restored or reconstructed. Unhappily the plunderers who visit places like Pagan for western art collectors have also done their damage but it is definitely the place in Burma not to be missed. There is a museum near the Co-Op guest house and the Gawdawpalin Temple. The following are just a handful of the more interesting of Pagan's 5000 plus temples:

Information & Orientation Pagan is a tiny little village today, a mere suburb of nearby Nyaung-Oo. Buses depart from the latter and the Mandalay ferry docks there. The Pagan airport is also near Nyaung-Oo. Tourist Bureau has an office in the main street of Pagan. Without fail you should get a copy of the *Guide to Pagan* as an aid to exploring the ruins.

Things to See

Ananda This huge white temple was built in 1091 and houses four standing Buddhas and two sacred Buddha footprints. It's close to the Pagan village and one of the most important temples of all.

Thatbyinnyu The highest temple in Pagan with Buddha images in the upper storey and magnificent views from the top. Pagan has to be seen from above for proper appreciation.

Gawdawpalin Also close to the village of Pagan the Gawdawpalin looks like a slightly smaller Thatbyinnyu. Built between 1174 and 1211 this is the best place to be to catch the Irrawaddy at sunset. This temple was probably the most extensively damaged in the '75 quake but has now been rebuilt.

Mingalazedi One of the last temples completed before Kublai Khan's sack of the city. Fine terra cotta tiles can be seen around the base of the huge bell-shaped stupa.

Shwesandaw A cylindrical stupa on top of five ultra-steep terraces, good views from the top. In the shed beside the stupa is a 20-metre reclining Buddha.

Shwezigon This traditionally shaped gold pagoda was started by King Anawrahta and stands close to the village of Nyaung-Oo. The magnificent lions guarding the entrances are ruined by the arcades built between them.

Manuha In the village of Myinkaba this temple was built by King Manuha, the 'captive king'. The Buddhas are impossibly squeezed in their enclosures – an allegorical representation of the king's own discomfort with captivity. Excellent lacquerware workshops can be visited in the village.

Other Htiliminlo – the 'blessing of three worlds' was built in 1211 and has fine Buddhas on the ground and upper levels. It's beside the road from Pagan to Nyaung-Oo. In Pagan village the Pitakat Taik is the library built in 1058 to house those 30 elephant-loads of scriptures. Down towards the Irrawaddy the Mahabodhi is modelled after Indian-style temples. Further out from the centre the massive and brooding Dhammayangyi has superb views from its upper terraces and is said to have the finest brickwork in Pagan. Beyond the Dhammayangyi the Sulamani is another larger temple with interesting, though fairly recent, frescoes on its interior walls and fine views from the top.

Places to Stay

All Pagan's accommodation is close to the Tourist Burma office in Pagan village. The cheap places are K12/22 for singles/doubles and are spartan, straightforward but also friendly and quite livable. They include the very friendly and well-run *Sithu Guest House*, the *Burma Rest House* and the *Aung Thahaya*, both friendly and convenient. Others include the *Moe Moe*, the *Zar Nee* and the *Min Chan Myei*.

Slightly more expensive, the *Co-Operative* is directly behind the Gawdawpalin Temple and costs K16/22 and has a pleasant garden. Down towards the Irrawaddy the *Irra Inn* is a bit remote from the other places and a bit more expensive at US$2.50/3.50 or with bath US$3.50/77, but upstairs rooms have fine views

across the river and it's quite a pleasant place. The *Thiripyitsaya Hotel*, Pagan's deluxe place, is much more expensive.

Places to Eat

The *Nation Restaurant* on the main street of the village is probably the most popular travellers' hangout. There's excellent Chinese food at the *Co-Operative*. Try the *Thiripyitsaya* or the *Irra Inn* for a good cold beer; you can watch the sun set over the river from the Thiripyitsaya's verandah. A proper Burmese dinner at the Thiripyitsaya is a good K30 investment – eat as much as you like but bring your fire extinguisher, it's hot. There are several other restaurants along the main street of the village and other places in Nyaung-Oo.

Getting There – Mandalay-Pagan

Air The flight from Mandalay is brief and quite interesting and costs K121. Sit on the right out of Mandalay to see Sagaing as you leave and the Irrawaddy all the way.

Bus There's a bus to Pagan (or rather Nyaung-Oo) which departs at 4 am from near the Zegyo Market – supposedly daily but check first. The bus fare is K22 and it arrives at Nyaung-Oo at around 2 pm, after a few tea stops on the way. This does give you an extra afternoon in Pagan compared to the boat. Faster small pickup trucks are also beginning to appear on this route – count on around K40 to 45. From Nyaung-Oo to Pagan you can take a horse cart for something between K5 and 10, or grab a ride on the pickups which shuttle back and forth.

River At 5 am daily a riverboat departs for Pagan – the fare is K16 on deck or K31 in the cabins. Some people reckon the cabin (there's only one four-berth cabin) is worth extra, others don't. You can sleep on board the night before departure for free. Tourist Burma will look after your baggage during the day if you arrive in Mandalay in the morning and plan to take the boat straight out the next morning.

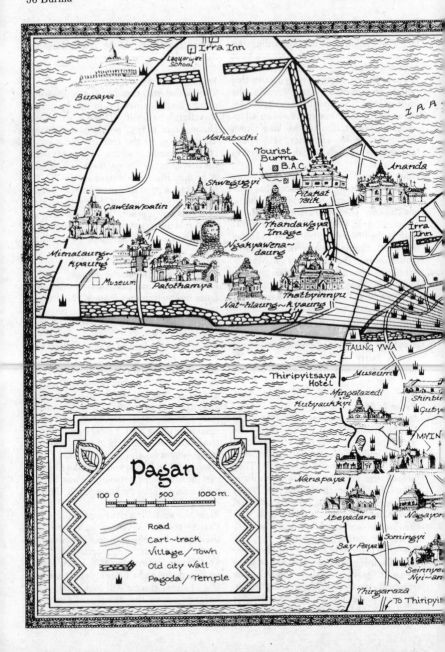

Irra Inn

Laquerware School

Bupaya

Mahabodhi

Tourist Burma
B.A.C.

Ananda

Shwegugyi

Pitahat Taik

Gawdawpatin

Thandawgya Image

Irra Inn

Mimalaung~kyaung

Nyahyawena~daung

☐ Museum

Patothamya

Thatbyinnyu

Nat~hlaung~kyaung

TAUNG YWA

Thiripyitsaya Hotel

Museum

Mingalazedi

Kubyaukkyi

Shinbin

Guby

MYIN

Nanapaya

Abeyadana

Nagayon

Somingyi

Say Paya

Seinnye Nyi~an

Thingaraza

To Thiripyit

Pagan

100   0   500   1000 m.

Road
Cart~track
Village / Town
Old city wall
Pagoda / Temple

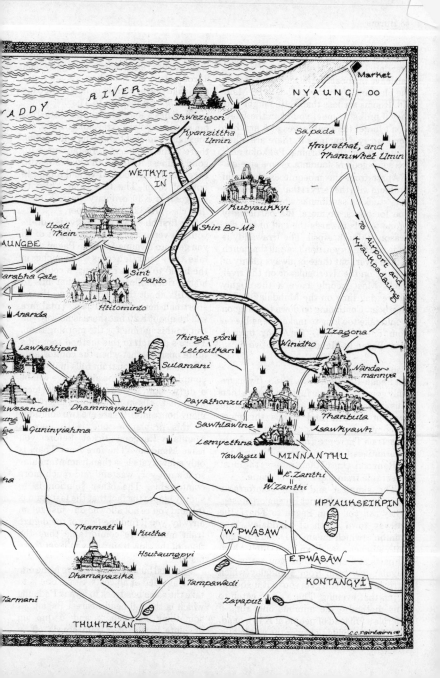

The ferry gets as far as Pakkoku on the first day, 13 km north of Nyaung-Oo. You can leave the boat for the night and stay in the pleasant *Myayatanar Inn*, 2288 Main Rd. Rooms are less than K10 a night and they'll probably meet you from the boat. Don't forget the boat leaves at 5 am, but don't worry if you miss it, there are other boats later in the morning. Pakkoku also has some good restaurants, even a cinema!

Apart from the mosquitoes the main problem with the ferry is that it sometimes gets stuck on sandbanks which can delay you for hours, or more. It's particularly prone to this towards the end of the dry season – March, April. The Irrawaddy is wide and flat so you don't see all that much off the river, but there is always plenty of activity on the riverbanks or on the river itself. Most people have a thoroughly interesting time on the Mandalay-Pagan riverboat. Continuing on down to Rangoon would take too long to make it feasible on your one-week visa. Travelling upriver from Pagan to Mandalay takes two days.

Pagan-Rangoon

Air Pagan-Rangoon costs K385. If you are only going to take one flight in Burma then this is the one which saves the maximum amount of time and avoids the most discomfort.

Bus-Train There are a number of bus-train alternatives for getting from Pagan back to Rangoon. One of them rates as the most miserable train trip I've ever made.

The simplest and most comfortable route is the one Tourist Burma organises. They run you from Pagan to Thazi, the railway town south of Mandalay, in a minibus (which means a Datsun pickup with a bench seat down each side!) which departs at 4 am. In Thazi you get on the regular day train from Mandalay which arrives at 8 am and gets you to Rangoon at 7 pm that evening. There's one catch to this method – the minibus only runs if there's a full load of people at K46 a head, or you're willing to charter the whole bus. Tourist Burma guarantee you a seat on the

train if you take their truck. There are also other similar vehicles around Pagan which a group of peopple can charter – you could then take the night train or make sidetrips to Mt Popa on the way to Thazi.

Thazi has a somewhat grubby little rest house where you can stay, unofficially. On the main road, just before the railway line, there's the *Wonderful* restaurant with good Chinese food and the *Red Star* with excellent Indian food – I've had dinner in both of them! The fare from Thazi to Rangoon is K36 ordinary class, K99 in first class, K132 with a sleeper.

The first bus-train alternative is a do-it-yourself version of the above. First of all you get into Nyaung-Oo from Pagan, then take a bus-truck (ie a truck with benches in the back) to Kyauk Padaung, a couple of hours' ride, followed by another bus to Meiktila about three hours away, then a short half-hour ride to Thazi. Total fare will be about K20 but there is no way you can do this in time for the morning train. There's a catch to this method too – it's quite possible that when the comfortable Mandalay-Rangoon train rolls in it will be completely full and the alternative will be a dirty, slow, crowded, miserable local train that rolls in many hours later (and many hours late). There are two solutions to this problem – one is to book a Mandalay-Rangoon ticket before you leave Mandalay. The fare from Thazi is only a few kyats less than from Mandalay so it's not very wasteful and much more comfortable. The other solution is to simply ignore the fact that the fast train is full and you're not allowed on – just get on anyway, you'll find the floor of the deluxe train much more comfortable than the floor of the slow train and you'll get there faster.

The final bus-train alternative is the one to be avoided at all costs. Stage one is to take the same bus-truck to Kyauk Padaung which is the rail head nearest Pagan. At something between 2 and 5 pm an absolute horror of a train crawls off to Rangoon, arriving something over 24 hours later. The fare is virtually the same as from Thazi and it's a dirty, uncomfortable, unlit, slow, crowded, tedious, unpleasant cattle train. Avoid it.

Getting Around
The ruins are fairly widespread, particularly if you want to get to some of the more remote ones. You can hire a horse cart for around K10 an hour, a jeep for around K30 an hour, less by the day or half day of course. You can also hire bicycles now from a number of shops along the main street of Pagan. They generally cost K2 an hour or K10 to 15 for a day. They're a very·pleasant way of getting around Pagan but check that the brakes and other vital functions are operating.

Mt Popa
Near Kyauk Padaung the monastery-topped hill of Mt Popa can be visited as a day-trip from Pagan or if you get a group together to charter a taxi-truck to Thazi or on to the Inle Lake a detour can be organised. It only takes 20 minutes or so to make the stiff climb to the top of the hill. This is a centre for worship of the *nats*.

INLE LAKE
Although it can be difficult to fit Inle, Pagan and Mandalay into your seven days it can be done and more and more people are doing it. The lake is extraordinarily beautiful and is famous for its leg rowers. This is also the best places to find yourself an attractive (and useful) Shan shoulder bag. To get out on the lake you need a group of people to charter a boat – K200 or 300 – or take the local boat to the village and back for K30 return. There's also an interesting temple in the village of Yaunghwe at the top of the lake.

There are several excursions you can make en route to the lake. The Thazi-Taunggyi road passes through Kalaw, a popular hill station during the British era. At Aungban you can turn off the main road and travel north to Pindaya where the Pindaya caves are packed with countless Buddha images, gathered there over the centuries.

Information & Orientation
There are four place names to remember in the lake area. First there's Heho, where the airport is located. Continue east from there and you reach Shwenyaung where the railway terminates and where you turn off the road, south to the lake. Continue further east and Taunggyi is the main town in the area. Actually at the northern end of the lake is Yaunghwe. Although buses and taxi-trucks normally go to Taunggyi there is no need for you to go there – you can save a couple of hours' travel by getting off at Shwenyaung and going straight to Yaunghwe. The main Tourist Burma office is in Taunggyi, however, and it's the only place to change money. The smaller Tourist Burma office at Yaunghwe only handles excursions on the lake.

Places to Stay
Although Taunggyi is the main centre in the area there is no need to stay there, or indeed to go there at all. At Yaunghwe, right by the lake, the *Inle Inn* has singles/doubles at K25/40 or at K60 with attached bathroom. A short stroll back towards the village is the simpler *Bamboo House* at K20/30.

Otherwise accommodation is concentrated at Taunggyi where the *Taunggyi Hotel* costs US$10.45/12.65. The rooms are modern with attached bathrooms and it's very pleasant. There is also a handful of similarly basic guest houses, much like the little boxes you find in Mandalay. They cost K25/40 and the *San Pya Guest* is probably the best of the bunch.

Places to Eat
Close to the lake in Yaunghwe the *Friendship Restaurant* is a popular little hangout with good food. The impecunious can find cheaper food in the market.

There's excellent food at the *Tha Pye* or

the *Lyan You*, both on the main street of Taunggyi. The *Academy Cafe*, close to the San Pya, is a friendly place for breakfast.

Getting There
You can reach Inle Lake from Rangoon, Mandalay or Pagan.

Air The airfare Rangoon-Heho is K340, Mandalay-Heho K132, Pagan-Heho K253. The Pagan flight goes via Mandalay.

Rail From Rangoon take the regular Mandalay train and disembark at Thazi, only an hour or so before Mandalay. From there you can take another train to Shwenyaung, near the lake. This is rather time consuming though, it's better to take a jeep from Thazi for K30, it takes six to eight hours. If you're heading back to Rangoon by this method note the possible problems in getting a seat on the train from Thazi if you've not pre-booked it.

Bus You can reach Taunggyi by bus from all three centres. From Rangoon you have to make a 16-hour bus trip, leaving at 3.30 am and arriving at 7.30 pm. The fare for this exhausting trip is K75. From or to Mandalay there are buses and taxi-trucks every morning. The buses leave around 4.30 or 5 am – the trip takes 10 to 12 hours. The Datsun taxi-trucks depart around 6 am and can get there by 1.30 pm. Costs range from around K45 to 60. It is now fairly feasible to combine Inle Lake with

Pagan because the Tourist Burma bus which operates from Nyaung-Oo (Pagan) to Thazi continues right on to Taunggyi, arriving there around 2.30 pm. From Taunggyi it departs at 5.30 am and reaches Pagan at around 3 pm. Or with a group you can charter a pickup truck for around K600 or 700. It's a long and fairly gruelling trip from Pagan to the lake in one day.

OTHER
It seems to be getting easier to visit some of the supposedly 'off-limits' places. You can quite easily get to Kyaiktiyo, the balancing pagoda, beyond Pegu. Buses depart regularly from Pegu since this is a popular pilgrimage spot. However, having got there you have a 10-km walk ascending about 1000 metres in altitude. It's not possible to get back to Pegu (or Rangoon) in the same day so come prepared to camp out – a sleeping bag is a wise thing to bring with you anywhere in the back-tracks of Burma.

Visiting the beach resort of Sandoway is an on-again, off-again possibility but Bassein is quite easy to get to. You can also visit Prome without too much trouble and the scattered ruins of the ancient city of Sri-Kshetra are nearby and definitely worth exploring. The answer to all these places is to ignore Tourist Burma and simply go!

Hong Kong

Precariously perched on the side of China, Hong Kong is a curious anomaly. It's an energetic paragon of the virtues of capitalism which nevertheless gets an unofficial blessing from the largest Communist country on earth – on which it is dependent for its very existence. The countdown to 1997, when Hong Kong is due to be handed back to the Peoples Republic, has made it an even more volatile and interesting enigma. To the visitor it has such a reputation as a shopping centre that almost everything else is forgotten – but actually it's a fascinating city-state with glimpses of rural China to be seen in the New Territories and on some of the relatively untouched islands.

HISTORY

Hong Kong must stand as one of the more successful rewards for dope running. The dope was opium and the runners were backed by the British government. European trade with China goes back over 400 years, but as the trade mushroomed during the 1700s the balance turned more and more against the Europeans – until they started to pump opium, grown in Bengal under the control of the British East India Company, into the country. Finally the Middle Kingdom grew tired of the barbarians and their 'foreign mud', as opium was known, and attempted to chuck the chief offenders, the British, out. But not too far out, as their money was still wanted, if not their opium. Unfortunately the war of words ended when, in true British fashion, the gunboats were sent in; there were only two of them, but they managed to fairly well demolish a Chinese fleet of 29 ships. The ensuing First Opium War went pretty much the same way and at its close the British were ceded the island of Hong Kong in 1842.

Following the Second Opium War in 1860, Britain took possession of the Kowloon peninsula, adding another 11 square km to the 75 square km of the island. Finally in 1898 a 99-year lease was granted on the 948 square km of the New Territories. What will happen after this lease ends on 1 July 1997 has been the subject of considerable speculation over recent years. Although Britain supposedly had possession of Hong Kong Island and the Kowloon peninsula for all eternity it was pretty clear that if they handed back everything else China would want that too. And in any case the Peoples Republic doesn't recognise any pre-1949 agreements.

In late 1984 an agreement was finally reached that China would take over lock, stock and barrel, but that Hong Kong's unique free enterprise situation would be maintained for at least 50 years. A tiny enclave of all-out capitalism within the Chinese empire. China has issued an invitation to Taiwan to return to the motherland under similar conditions. What Taiwan will decide remains to be seen.

The reality of the situation has always been, of course, that China could reclaim not only the New Territories, but all the rest of Hong Kong any time it wanted to. Hong Kong has survived so long already simply because it's useful. Conveniently situated, it acts as a funnel for Chinese goods to the west, western goods into China and as a source of foreign exchange and information without ever having to let the corrupting foreign influence across the borders. The upheavals during the Cultural Revolution, the Chinese-inspired riots that had the country in turmoil, and relaxed border controls that allowed a lemming-like crowd of Chinese to flood Hong Kong, all probably served as a flexing of the mainland muscles . . . . just to show where the power was.

Acting as an intermediary hasn't been Hong Kong's sole function. During the Korean war the Americans placed an embargo on Chinese goods, which threatened to strangle the colony economically. For survival it developed an extremely vigorous manufacturing, banking and insurance industry instead. Part of the reason for the boundless energy of Hong Kong is that it is a capitalist's dream: lax controls and a maximum tax rate of 18%. Fortunes could be made and were usually made fast because who knew what tomorrow would bring? On the other side of the coin the low taxes mean there is little money for even fairly basic social services. Hong Kong is in nowhere near the same league as Singapore when it comes to looking after its citizens.

Finally, in a form of poetic Chinese justice, that initial founding has rebounded and Hong Kong has a serious dope problem.

FACTS

Population When the Japanese left after WW II the population was not much over half a million. Today it has topped the five million mark, most of it squeezed on to Hong Kong Island, Kowloon and the bottom portion of the New Territories known as New Kowloon.

Economy Trade, both to the west and to China, and the flourishing duty free trade to tourists is still the cornerstone of the Hong Kong economy, but there are now other important elements. There is a thriving light-industry sector and Hong Kong is a major Asian banking and insurance centre. Despite the limited expected lifespan there's no shortage of

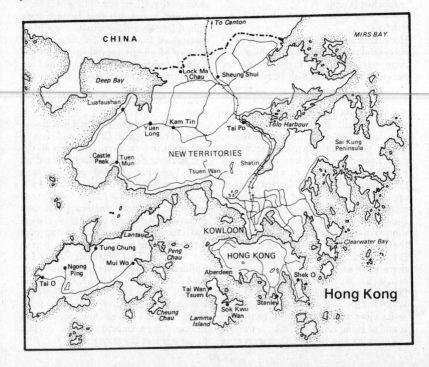

money for investments in huge projects like the tunnel connecting Hong Kong Island with Kowloon and the extensive new underground railway system. Commercial loans lasting beyond 1997 were negotiated in Hong Kong even prior to the 1984 agreement between Britain and China.

Geography The colony covers 1034 square km. Hong Kong Island is separated from Kowloon and the New Territories on the mainland by the 'Fragrant Harbour', which gave Hong Kong its name, and is claimed by many to be one of the most beautiful in the world. The New Territories includes not only the farmland up to the border, but also a scattering of islands, some of them still only sparsely populated.

INFO

The enterprising Hong Kong Tourist Association (HKTA) has desks at the airport, on the Kowloon side of the Star Ferry run, in the GPO next to the Hong Kong side of the Star Ferry run, and way up in the Connaught Centre in Central near the Star Ferry. The Kowloon office is open from 8 am to 6 pm Monday to Friday and public holidays; and from 8 am to 1 pm on Saturdays and Sundays. The Connaught Centre office is open the same hours except that it is closed on Sundays and public holidays. The GPO office is open 9 am to 6 pm Monday to Friday and from 9 am to 1 pm on Saturday. They have numerous brochures and booklets. Particularly useful are the pamphlets *Six Walks*, *Outlying Islands* and *Places of Interest by Public Transport*.

The Hong Kong Student Travel Bureau is in room 1020, Star House, Kowloon (tel 3-7213269) and also at 8/F Tai Sang Bank Building, 130-132 Des Voeux Rd in Central (tel 5-414841). They put out a useful little *Youth Travel Guide & City Map* and are an excellent source of information on China travel. They also supply competitively priced airline tickets if you're under 26. You can get vaccinations at the Port Health Authority on the Hong Kong side. A Typhoid inoculation costs HK$25.

The GPO with poste restante is beside the Star Ferry Landing in Hong Kong Central. Sometimes letters end up at the Kowloon post office on Middle Rd so check there too. Note that phone numbers are prefixed with 5 for Hong Kong Island, 3 for Kowloon and 0 for the New Territories. You do not dial the prefix when you are within the prefix area.

BOOKS

If you want more information on Hong Kong and on Canton in the Republic of China look for the Lonely Planet guidebook *Hong Kong, Macau & Canton*. If you're going further on into China then look for the Lonely Planet guides *North-East Asia on a Shoestring* or *China – a travel survival kit*.

Borrowed Place, Borrowed Time is the book to read on Hong Kong's birth and development. It was written by the late Richard Hughes, one of the real 'old China hands'. Novels to dip into include the readable (and highly dramatic) *Tai-pan* by James Clavell, which is (very) loosely based on the Jardine-Matheson organisation in its early days. Richard Mason's *The World of Suzie Wong* is also interesting – after all she was Hong Kong's best-known citizen.

Hong Kong has a number of good bookshops where you should be able to find the above books.

VISAS

For almost all non-Communist nationalities there are no visa requirements. British passport holders have no regulations applying to their length of stay. Commonwealth citizens and some other nationalities are permitted a two-month visa-free stay. If you need to stay longer check with any British consulate. If you're arriving in Hong Kong from Bangkok be prepared for a thorough going over by customs officers looking for drugs.

MONEY

A\$1 = HK\$5.6
US\$1 = HK\$7.8
£1 = HK\$8.7

Hong Kong's currency is pretty solid and freely importable and exportable. Exchange rates tend to vary so shop around a bit, the rate at the airport money changers is very bad, particularly on the arrival level. It's better on the departure level although still not comparable with downtown. Money changers in Kowloon are open seven days a week and give a far better rate than the airport. If you're changing large amounts with a money changer, bargain. Hong Kong is a good place for buying other currencies.

COSTS

Hong Kong is certainly not cheap – it's a result of the continuing economic boom and the ever-increasing cost of land in the colony. The rapid change in relations between the west and China has certainly fuelled Hong Kong's boom. You can still find dorm beds for around HK\$20 but it takes effort to find a double room for HK\$100 these days. Food is reasonably priced, transport is cheap and duty-free shopping is still a bargain (although HK's shopkeepers and assistants are often appallingly rude). The decline in value of the Hong Kong dollar over the past few years has also made life a little easier for visitors.

CLIMATE

Although it never gets really cold even in the middle of winter (January and February), Hong Kong is certainly colder than South-East Asia. If you're flying here in winter from Bangkok, Manila or Singapore, be prepared. In the summer it can get pretty hot and humid, especially in July and August. From June to October Hong Kong is occasionally hit by typhoons. Generally the spring and the late autumn are the most pleasant times of the year.

GETTING THERE

Hong Kong has one of the most spectacular harbours in the world so it's kind of a shame that there's not much of a chance of arriving by boat – unless you're rich, old and on a cruise liner. It may still be possible, since the occasional freight ship to or from Japan, the Philippines or Singapore may take passengers. The regular Singapore-Hong Kong passenger/ freight service has stopped so there are now no remaining regular services.

For most of us the normal arrival point will be Kai Tak airport – with its runway sticking out into the harbour from Kowloon it makes a pretty dramatic entrance. Departure tax has gone up to a sky-high HK\$100.

Hong Kong was once a difficult place to find cheap tickets to and even more difficult to find cheap tickets out, but now it's as freewheeling as anywhere. The London-Hong Kong route, once a British Airways monopoly, is now particularly hard-fought, but there are plenty of other cheap tickets, both under and over the counter.

From the UK From London, Apex tickets to Hong Kong with British Airways, British Caledonian or Cathay Pacific are £225, £240 or £290 one-way, double that for return, depending on the season. From travel agents in London you can probably find tickets slightly cheaper, depending on the season and demand. You can also find interesting tickets from the UK to Australia via Hong Kong for £400 or less. If you are going anywhere in the north-east Asian region (Japan, Korea, Taiwan, China) or to the Philippines or Sabah in Borneo then Hong Kong is the best gateway from Europe.

From Australia Advance purchase fares to Hong Kong from Sydney or Melbourne cost A\$591 one-way, A\$908 return in the low season. The high season is just a short period in December-January when fares go up to A\$714 and A\$1100. From Perth

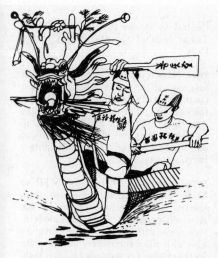

the equivalent low-season fares are A$498 and A$768. In the high season it's A$602 and A$928.

Shopping around will generally reveal somewhat cheaper fares than that through travel agents – discounts of 5 to 15% are possible although you may have to take a more circuitous route through the Philippines or Malaysia.

From the USA There are lots of cheap flights available out of the US west coast if you scan the Sunday travel pages of the *LA Times* or the *San Francisco Chronicle*. Return fares vary from around US$630 to 700. In the *NY Times* travel pages you'll find return fares around US$770 to 800.

From Asia Cheap fares to Hong Kong cost around US$100 from Bangkok, US$100 from Manila, US$200 from Singapore.

Getting Away Hong Kong has plenty of travel agents offering cheap tickets although fares available are only really good for flights originating in Hong Kong. The Hong Kong Student Travel Bureau, Room 1020, Star House, Tsimshatsui, Kowloon is one of the best places to try. There are many others, not all of them

100% reliable. Travellers have recommended Prestige Travel (tel 3-698271-4) at 63 Mody Rd, Kowloon and Phoenix Travel on Nathan Rd, Kowloon. One-way fares being quoted include London HK$2300, US west coast HK$1900, Melbourne HK$3400, Bangkok HK$650, Singapore HK$1300, Manila HK$700, Tokyo HK$1000.

GETTING AROUND

Hong Kong has an incredibly varied and frequent public transport system, but there are two warnings: before setting out to travel anywhere by bus ensure you have a good pocketful of small change – the exact fare must normally be deposited in the cashbox – nobody has change. The second warning is that on weekends everybody, plus his brother, his sister and his girlfriend sets out to go somewhere. Particularly on Sundays you must be prepared to take much longer getting anywhere, to pay more on certain ferries, and even to miss the odd overfull bus. Plus everybody (and his etc) will be taking photographs of everybody else so take care you don't appear in too many family portraits.

Airport Transport There are a variety of ways of getting to and from the airport. Easiest is a taxi – the fares to hotels are listed by the pickup point in the airport and to most places in the Tsimshatsui area of Kowloon. It should be in the HK$15 to 20 range but they can charge HK$1 extra for each bag. If you're crossing between Kowloon and Hong Kong Island, taxi drivers are entitled to charge an additional HK$20 to cover the toll on the Cross-Harbour Tunnel both ways.

Next most convenient and rather cheaper (especially if you're travelling solo) are the airport buses. A 201 runs regularly between the airport and the bus park near Kowloon Star Ferry terminal. It's easy walking distance from here to Chungking Mansions. The fare is HK$2.50 and this is a very convenient bus since it runs right from the airport terminal and there is plenty of room for your gear. A 200 bus does the same thing to Hong Kong Central, through the tunnel, for HK$4.

The cheapest way of all is to make your way out of the terminal and up to the public bus stop on the ramp where you can take a 5 or 9 bus to the Kowloon Star Ferry for about 60c. The 5 goes via Chatham St, the 9 goes down Nathan Rd, the spine of Tsimshatsui where you will find most of the hotels. Frankly to save about 30c Australian or US it's hardly worth the effort and I'd recommend either the 201 bus or, if there is a group of you, a taxi.

On departure there is a HK$100 airport tax. The airport restaurants have the usual inflated prices but if you just want a pre-departure Coke the bar upstairs may well be cheaper than the more basic-looking cafe downstairs.

Bus There are plenty of buses with fares starting at 70c and going up to HK$3.50 for the longest rides into the New Territories. The longest rides on Hong Kong Island cost HK$2.50 and it's HK$2.50 for the trip through the harbour tunnel. While most bus services stop at 11 pm or 12 midnight the 121 continues from 12.45 to 5 am, going through the tunnel every 15 minutes. Buses numbered 200 and up are fancier and more comfortable than the regular buses and also more expensive.

Minibus The small red-and-cream mini-buses supplement the regular bus services. they are a little more expensive (generally HK$2 to 6) and the prices often go up during the rush hour or in rainy weather! They generally don't run such regular routes but you can get on or off almost anywhere. If you know where you are going and where they are going you may well find them fast and convenient. Maxicabs are just like minibuses except they are green and cream and they do run regular routes. Two popular ones are from the carpark in front of the Star Ferry in

Central to Ocean Park or from HMS Tamar (east of the Star Ferry) to the Peak.

Tram There is just one tram line, but it is a long one – all the way from Kennedy Town (to the west of Central) to Shaukiwan (at the eastern end of the island) and it also runs right through the middle of Central. As well as being ridiculously picturesque and fun to travel on, the tram is quite a bargain at 60c for any distance.

MTR Opened in 1979-80 the MTR or Mass Transit Railway operates from Central across the harbour and up the Kowloon peninsula. This ultra-modern, high-speed subway system has been quite a hit with office commuters but the price for the system's convenience is fairly high. Fares vary from HK$2.50 to 4 one-way. The MTR Tourist Ticket, valid for HK$15 worth of travel, saves having to buy a ticket for each trip and it's useful if you're planning to make good use of the subway during your stay. Tickets are available from big hotels and the HKTA offices.

Railway The Kowloon-Canton railway runs right up to the border where visitors to China used to have to walk across the bridge and change trains. Now trains run right through to Canton. Apart from being one of the best ways of entering China it's also an excellent alternative to buses for getting into the New Territories.

Harbour Ferries The Star Ferry shuttles back and forth across the harbour every couple of minutes for a mere 50c (lower class) – a real travel bargain. If you want to cross between 2 and 6 am, while the Star Ferry takes a break, you can rent a sampan (walla walla).

There are other ferries making longer trips across the harbour – from Shaukiwan or the Jordan Rd terminal for example. The Jordan Rd to Wanchai ferry is pleasant for a longer look at the night lights and a visit to Wanchai, Suzie Wong land. You can also ferry to or from Hunghom (the other side of the railway station in Kowloon), Kwung Tong (an uninteresting area beyond the airport) or to North Point on Hong Kong Island (an interesting trip back through Causeway Bay and Wanchai). Out on the harbour there seems to be a nonstop procession of ferries ploughing back and forth.

Island Ferries The HKTA can supply you with a schedule for these ferries but there are so many of them that timings are bound to change. There are more services on Sundays and holidays when the fares also go up and the boats are very crowded. From Central most ferries go from the Outer Island Terminal between the Star Ferry and Macau Ferry terminals. Fares are generally between HK$1 and 4 on weekdays, by far the best time to get out to the islands. During the summer months there are also sightseeing services once a week around Hong Kong Island. It's quite a travel bargain.

Lantau Island Most services go via Peng Chau island to Silvermine Bay (Mui Wo). There are about 16 services a day plus four a day to Tai O on the other end of the island.
Cheung Chau About 17 a day, it takes about an hour.
Lamma Island There are separate services to Sok Kwu Wan and Yung Shue Wan, about 10 a day to each.
Tolo Harbour There are just a couple of services a day running out from Tai Po Hoi to Tap Mun (Grass Island) with lots of stops en route.
Inter-island There's a Cheung Chau-Chi Ma Wan-Silvermine Bay-Hei Ling Chau-Peng Chau boat several times a day, but it does not always stop at every point.
Other Places You can ferry from Castle Peak in the New Territories to Tung Chung on Lantau and, of course, there are lots of ferries to Macau.

Taxis Flagfall is HK$5 for the first two km and then it's 70c for each 250 metres. There's an additional charge of HK$1 for each bag. In the New Territories the costs are lower. If you're taking a taxi through the harbour tunnel, taxi drivers are entitled to charge an additional HK$20 to cover toll costs. All taxis have a translation card listing the 'Top 50 Destinations'. It's probably under the driver's sun visor. Beware of the pseudo taxis which look just like the red and silver ones, but have no sign on the roof. They do not have meters and any fare must be agreed in advance.

Rickshaws These are really only for photographs – would you want to ride in one? Since no new licences are being issued they are gradually disappearing. Count on HK$10-20 just to take a picture.

Bicycles Bike riding in Kowloon or Central would be suicidal, but in quiet areas of the New Territories or on the islands a bike can be quite a nice way of getting around. The bike rental places tend to run out early, though. Note that you can rent bicycles to take into China.

THINGS TO BUY
Oh yeah, shopping – some people do come to Hong Kong for that. Well, a lot of the same things apply as to Singapore – shop around, try and find out what the 'real' retail price is before you believe the discounts, make sure guarantees are international and – most important – don't go on a buying binge. It's very easy in Hong Kong to suddenly decide you need all sorts of consumer goods you don't really need at all. It's hard to say just how HK and Singapore really compare in price or choice – they're probably pretty similar. The HKTA has a shopping guide booklet which gives list prices and the approved shops.

For cameras, hi fi equipment and electrical items the touristy shops in the Tsimshatsui 'tourist ghetto' of Kowloon are probably the best, along with places in HK Central. On this sort of thing there isn't so much bargaining on the offered price – but more shopping around to start with. Make sure voltages are compatible and guarantees are OK. If buying film you get a better price buying in bulk, 10 or 12 rolls at a time. Don't tell anyone, but a lot of the record shops will record tapes for you, but play before you buy – the Chinese musical ear is not good. When buying equipment with accessories (like a camera with several lenses) compare total costs, not just the basic camera.

Hong Kong's reputation for made-to-measure clothes is not what it was – prices have escalated so they're no longer really cheap, and anyway who wears suits? Better to check out some of the ready-made places as HK is now getting very fashionable. Good jeans and denim, even suits in Wrangler shops. Trendy women's gear in Bang Bang.

Jade, ivory and antiques are more for the knowledgeable purchaser. Safety depends on buying from reputable dealers. Antique shops on Hollywood Rd (up from HK Central) are interesting to wander around. If you're into 'instant Woolworths oil paintings' there are plenty around Kowloon and very cheap. Glasses and contact lenses are cheap and well made. The HK Government Printers Office near the HK Star Ferry has good reproductions of some of the interesting prints in the HK History Museum.

Check out the China emporiums – all sorts of everyday items often of good quality at low prices. Chinese carpets are excellent value. Also have a look around Causeway Bay – it's less touristy and flash than Tsimshatsui in Kowloon or HK Central.

LANGUAGE

Cantonese is the Chinese dialect most spoken in Hong Kong. Although English is widely spoken and you're unlikely to have difficulty making yourself understood, it is not as widely used as in Singapore. A foreign devil (*gwai-lo*) will have trouble with Chinese because it's tonal – the meaning varies with the tone. But here are a few to have a go with:

how much? *gay doa cheen?*
too expensive *tie goo-why*
waiter, the bill *fo-kay, my don*
go away! *jaaw hoy!*

ORIENTATION

Hong Kong is conveniently divided into four parts. First there is Hong Kong Island, the original part of the colony on which stands Hong Kong Central, the 'city' of Hong Kong. A short ferry ride across the harbour from the island is the Kowloon peninsula which is also totally 'city'. These are the two parts which were not due to be handed back to China in 1997. The southern tip of the peninsula is Tsimshatsui, the tourist heart of Kowloon. Most of Hong Kong's hotels are either in Central or in Tsimshatsui.

Kai Tak airport is also in Kowloon, although its runway juts out into the harbour. Beyond Kowloon you move into the New Territories, the rural area that runs up to the Chinese border. The New Territories get progressively less rural each year as Kowloon sprawls further and further across its borders. The fourth part of Hong Kong is really just more of the New Territories (except for one small island) since the islands that dot the area to the west of Hong Kong Island are also part of the 1997 package. Largest of the islands is sparsely populated Lantau, much larger than Hong Kong Island itself. The islands are relatively undeveloped and in some ways the most surprising and enjoyable part of Hong Kong.

KOWLOON

Kowloon, the peninsula pointing out towards Hong Kong Island, is shops, hotels, night clubs and tourists. Nathan Rd, which runs through Kowloon like a spine, has plenty of all four. Some of the

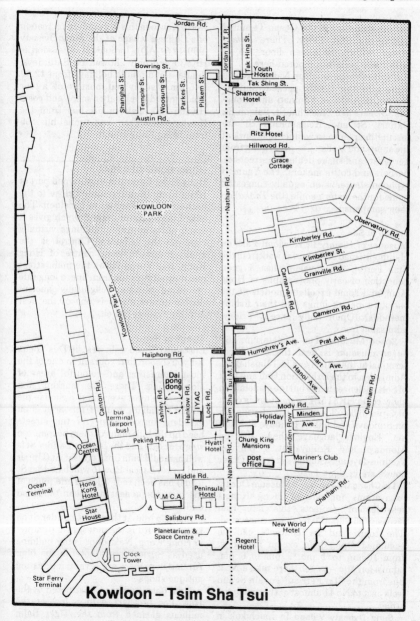

Kowloon – Tsim Sha Tsui

ritziest shops are in the Ocean Terminal beside the Star Ferry. There always seems to be one ocean liner full of millionaire geriatrics moored here.

If you continue north up Nathan Rd you come into the tightly packed Chinese residential areas of Yaumati and Mongkok. Streets like Shanghai St, Saigon St, Battery St and Reclamation St are fascinating places to wander and gawk at the shops and stalls .... everything from herbalists and snake dealers to streetside barbers and coffin makers. The Yaumati typhoon shelter is an equally congested home for the water people (the *Tanka*) on their sampans.

Things to See

Museum of History In Kowloon Park on Haiphong Road (10 minutes walk from the Star Ferry), the museum has a good collection of early photographs of Hong Kong and some excellent models of the various types of junks and their fishing methods. (Open daily except Friday, admission free.)

Space Museum The planetarium and space museum is near the Star Ferry terminal at the waterfront in Tsimshatsui. Admission to the Exhibition Hall and Hall of Solar Sciences is free but the planetarium show costs HK$15. The museum is open at 2 pm daily, closed on Tuesdays, open on Sundays and public holidays at 10.30 am. English language shows are on Mondays and Fridays at 4 pm, on Wednesdays and Sundays at 9 pm. Other shows are in Cantonese.

Lei Cheng Uk Tomb and Museum During excavations for one of Hong Kong's resettlement projects this late Han Dynasty (25-220 AD) tomb was uncovered. The tomb and its contents can be examined. Open daily, except Thursday, from 10 am to 1 pm, 2 pm to 6 pm, admission 10c – to get there take a No 2 bus from the Star Ferry to Tonkin St and walk east to No 41 almost at the end of the street.

Sung Dynasty Village In Laichikok in North Kowloon this is a modern recreation of a Chinese village of the Sung Dynasty (960-1279 AD). Individual admission is HK$30 and only allowed on Saturdays, Sundays and public holidays from 12.30 to 5 pm. Usually you must go on a tour which includes a meal or snack and costs HK$95-120. Take a 6A bus from the Kowloon Star Ferry or a tunnel bus 105 from Hong Kong Island.

HONG KONG CENTRAL

Hong Kong Central is only a small part of Hong Kong Island, crowded close to the harbour looking across to Kowloon. The island is steep and rugged which gives it much of its appeal – buildings virtually cling to the hillsides. Central is the banking and business centre of Hong Kong. Des Voeux Rd is the main street and down it runs the tram line; a long ride on Hong Kong's delightfully ancient double-decker trams is one of the best introductions to the city.

Things to See

Chinatown If you walk west up Des Voeux Rd you'll soon find yourself in one of the most interesting and colourful areas of Hong Kong. There are markets and streets for almost every kind of goods – the HKTA's walking tour of this area is an excellent introduction. As the streets head up the hills many of them become too steep for cars and the famous Ladder St is well named! Unfortunately Cat St (Upper and Lower Lascar Row to which Ladder St leads) has been redeveloped and much of the picturesqueness has been ploughed under.

Man Mo Miu At the top of Ladder St on Hollywood Rd is the oldest Miu (temple) in Hong Kong. Next door is the building used as Suzie Wong's hotel in the film. Around here there are several interesting antique shops.

Tiger Balm Gardens Constructed by the Haw Par brothers with a few of the millions gleaned from the Tiger Balm medicament, it is two hectares of Chinese imagination run wild. Admission is free and if you telephone 5-616211 beforehand you can also arrange to see the jade collection. An 11 bus will get you there from Central.

Causeway Bay East of Hong Kong Central, it's a less touristy shopping and amusement centre. Wander Jardine's Bazaar and Jardine's Crescent – busy shopping streets today but reminders that this was the area where the Jardine-Matheson company operated in its early days. The noonday gun, by the waterfront across from the Excelsior Hotel, is a continuing reminder of those pioneering days in Hong Kong's history.

Wanchai Between Causeway Bay and the HK Central is the girlie bar centre – full of topless bars but a pale shadow of its peak of activity during the Vietnam era and not very exciting to wander around.

The Peak Take the famous peak tram from Garden Rd, up behind the Hilton Hotel, to the top of Victoria Peak. As you climb higher up the hill the houses and apartment blocks get steadily flashier and more expensive. Don't just admire the view from the top – wander up Mt Austin Rd to the old Governor's Lodge (demolished by the Japanese during WW II) or take the more leisurely stroll around Lugard and Harlech Rds – together they make a complete circuit of the peak. You can walk right down to Aberdeen on the south side of the island or you can try the Old Peak Rd for a couple of km return trip to HK Central. The Peak Tram costs HK$4 to the top, but you can also get there by a 15 bus (HK$2.50) or a more frequent minibus from HMS Tamar. The peak is very crowded on weekends. It's worth repeating the peak trip at night – the illuminated view is something else.

Poor Man's Night Club In the evenings the cars depart from the car park by the Macau Ferry Terminal and the stalls and vendors move in. It's bright, noisy and good fun – an excellent place for a cheap meal while you watch the action.

Other There are pleasant walks and views in the Zoo and Botanical Gardens on Robinson Rd overlooking Hong Kong Central. This is a good place to come early in the morning to see people exercising by traditional Chinese shadow boxing. Entry is free to the Hong Kong Museum of Art in the City Hall (closed Thursdays) and the Flagstaff House Museum of Tea Ware on Cotton Tree Drive (closed Wednesdays). The Fung Ping Shan Museum in Hong Kong University (closed Sundays) is also free.

HONG KONG ISLAND

For less than HK$10 in fares you can make an interesting circumnavigation of Hong Kong Island. From the Central Bus Terminal, a stone's throw from the Star Ferry, a bus will transport you through the downtown business district, hustling Wanchai and bustling Causeway Bay to the Sai Wan Ho Ferry Pier at Shaukiwan. For the same price you can make the trip on one of the delightful old trams – just look for the one marked 'Shaukiwan' and hop off just before the end of the line. Alternatively you can take a bus directly to Aberdeen.

A second bus takes you up and over the central hills; look for the cemetery terraced up the hills off to your left. You'll also pass a popular rowboat-hiring spot before terminating at Stanley. Many Europeans working in Hong Kong live in Stanley which is a pleasant small fishing port with a nice beach and many junks anchored offshore. It's also a maximum security prison where it is said the inmates emerge more addicted to heroin than when they went in.

Another bus takes you along the coast, by beautiful Repulse Bay (stop off here if you wish) and Deep Water Bay, to the floating town of Aberdeen. There used to be 20,000 people living on the thousands of sampans that literally packed the harbour area, but most of them have been relocated on dry land. There will generally

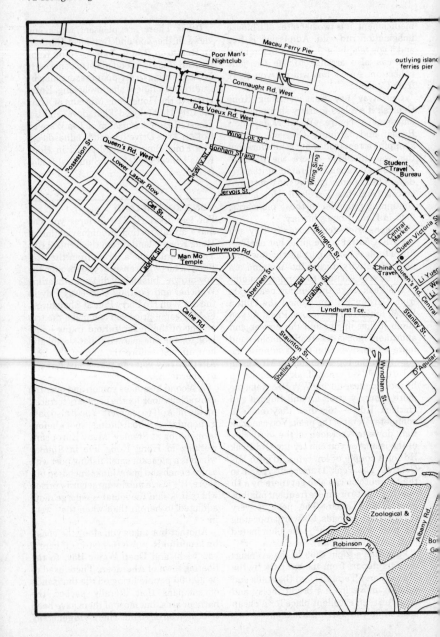

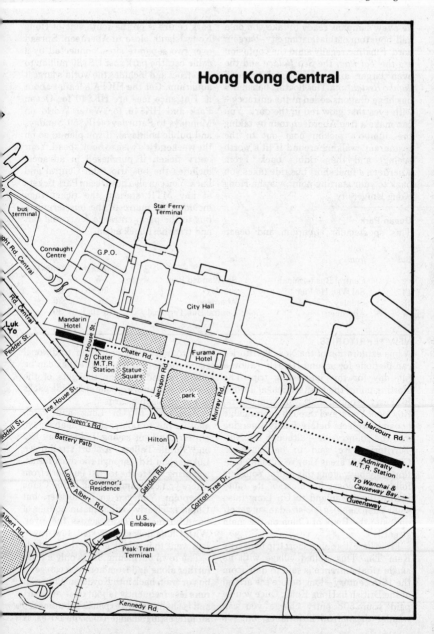

Hong Kong Central

bus terminal

Connaught Centre

Star Ferry Terminal

G.P.O.

City Hall

Light Rd Central

Rd Central

Luk Yo

Pedder St.

Mandarin Hotel

Ice House St.

Chater Rd.

Furama Hotel

Chater M.T.R. Station

Statue Square

Jackson Rd.

park

Murray Rd.

Harcourt Rd.

eddell St.

Ice House St.

Queen's Rd

Battery Path

Hilton

Admiralty M.T.R. Station

Lower Albert Rd.

Governor's Residence

Garden Rd.

Cotton Tree Dr.

To Wanchai & Causeway Bay

Queensway

Albert Rd.

U.S. Embassy

Peak Tram Terminal

Kennedy Rd.

be a few sampans ready to take you on a half-hour tour of this floating city – bargain hard. Floating regally amid the confusion are the *Tai Pak*, the *Sea Palace* and the even larger and appropriately named *Jumbo Restaurant*. This floating behemoth has huge dragons coiled at the entrance – with eyes that glow red in the dark. You can make a free Aberdeen tour by taking the Jumbo's pickup boat out to the restaurant, walking around it (it's worth seeing) and then riding back. From Aberdeen a final short bus ride takes you back to your starting point, via the Hong Kong University.

Ocean Park

This spectacular aquarium and ocean park centre is on the south side of Hong Kong Island, close to Aberdeen. Spread over two separate sites, connected by a cable car, the park cost US$80 million to construct and includes the world's largest aquarium. Get the HKTA's leaflet about it. Entrance fees are HK$40 for Ocean Park and HK$40 for Water World on Mondays to Saturdays (HK$50 Sundays and public holidays). If you plan to go on the weekend it's wise to book ahead. Your entry ticket, if purchased in advance, includes the bus trip from Central and back. You can also buy Ocean Park tickets at any MTR station, the ticket then includes the metro to the bus terminal, bus to the park, entrance fee, cable car, and transport back again.

Bus	from	to	every (mins)	trip (mins)
2	Central Bus terminal	Sai Wan Ho Pier	3-5	40
14	Sai Wan Ho Pier	Stanley	30-60	30
73	Stanley	Aberdeen	15	30
7	Aberdeen	Central Bus Terminal	5-10	30

NEW TERRITORIES

A bus exploration of the New Territories can be done for around HK$10 – allow a full day for this interesting trip. The starting point, the bus terminal at Jordan Rd Ferry, is only a short walk from central Kowloon. You travel through interminable housing projects before finally emerging into the countryside – although the New Territories are said to be 'unspoilt' Chinese rural areas they're actually continuously busy along this route. Your bus follows the coast for most of its route before turning inland to Un Long (also spelt Yuen Long), a fair-sized town; get off opposite the Bank of China on the main street.

From here it's only a short trip to nearby Kam Tin. This walled village with its single stout entrance is said to date from the 16th century – long before the arrival of the British in Hong Kong. Once you've paid your 50c entry charge you can wander the narrow little lanes, but it's very touristy. Old crones in traditional gear require payment before they can be photographed and the thoughts of the good chairman are on sale alongside packs of pin-up playing cards.

Backtrack to Un Long and catch another bus to Lokmachau – keep an eye out for the signs saying 'Lokmachau Rd' and 'Public Toilets'. A short stroll down Lokmachau Rd, through the duck farms, will bring you to the tourist bus park from where you can climb the hill to the China viewpoint. You can go no further, but China is clearly visible just a couple of hundred metres away across the river. With China now easy to visit, few travellers want to just look across the border!

The town of Sheung Shi is only a little further along and from here you can get a bus or train back into Kowloon. The train runs less frequently (about once an hour) and is slightly more expensive, but makes an interesting change from the buses. If you have time to spare, you can get off at Taipo, an interesting market town; or at the Chinese University, near to which you can hire boats and row yourself around; or Shatin, from where the fit and healthy can make the long climb up to the Temple of 10,000 Buddhas, Shatin Pagoda or Amah Rock.

Other There are countless other places to visit in the New Territories, some of them far less touristy. The Sai Kung Peninsula is probably the most unspoilt area of the New Territories – great for hiking and you can get from village to village on boats in the Tolo Harbour. At Castle Peak, on the road to Un Long, there are several interesting temples. Ditto at Tsuen Wan where there is a particularly good Taoist temple. Go to Lau Fau Shan on Deep Bay for its famous oysters. Plover Cove on Tolo Harbour is a cove that was dammed, drained and refilled with fresh water to make a reservoir!

Bus	from	to	every (mins)	trip (mins)
50	Jordan Road Ferry	Un Long	8	70
74/51	Un Long	Kam Tin	12	20 return (mins)
76	Un Long	Lokmachau	10	20
76	Lokmachau	Sheung Shi	10	15
70	Sheung Shi	Jordan Road Ferry	12-15	60

THE ISLANDS
There are over 200 islands dotting the waters around Hong Kong and if you have the time several are definitely worth visiting. Because they are part of the leased land, development has been relatively minor although some of them are almost commuter suburbs from Hong Kong and Kowloon. There are frequent ferries to the islands but they're very crowded on weekends.

Cheung Chau
This dumbbell-shaped island has become fairly popular for western residents who can't afford Hong Kong's sky-high rentals. It's a pleasant little place with a very Mediterranean air to it. Were it not for the Chinese signs and people, you might think you were in some tiny Greek island village.

The town sprawls across the narrow bar connecting the two ends of the island. You'll see junks being built on slips up from the beach and at the north end of the town the old Pak Tai temple built in 1783. At the southern tip of the island is the hideaway cave of notorious pirate Cheung Po Tsai. There are some pleasant beaches and each May the frantic Bun Festival, when seekers of good fortune scramble up a 20-metre-high tower of sugar buns to get the topmost (and luckiest) one.

Peng Chau
Another small island with a similarly Mediterranean-looking town and an old temple (Tin Hau – 1792). If you're going to Lantau it's worth stopping for a look around.

Lantau
The largest of the islands and most sparsely populated – it's almost twice the size of Hong Kong Island, but the population is only 20,000. It's definitely worth spending a couple of days here as there are some excellent walking trails and you can get a little feel for rural Chinese life in some relatively untouched parts of the island.

Mui Wo (Silvermine Bay) is the normal arrival point for ferries, but there's a more interesting way of getting there. Take a ferry from HK Central bound for Mui Wo, but get off at Peng Chau. A small sampan (it meets every ferry) will shuttle you across the narrow stretch of water to the island and if you follow the trail up the hill (fine views from the top), you'll soon see Silvermine Bay down below. On the descent you pass a deserted building that looks like it would make a fine little hotel – Balinese losmen style. There are some good cheap eating places just before you reach Mui Wo and you can get a cold drink right at the bottom of the hill as you arrive at the beach.

From Mui Wo if you have the time you can take a long (four to five hours) walk right across the island to Tung Chung. The trail passes through a whole series of relatively unspoilt settlements including Pak Mong, a very fine example of an old walled village. At Tung Chung there is a fort and ferries run from here to Castle Peak, from where you can bus into Kowloon.

An alternative is to start walking inland from Tung Chung – you follow a paved footpath up an interminable hill for a couple of hours finally passing through a tea plantation and arriving at the spectacularly ornate Po Lin (Precious Lotus) Monastery. It's a relatively recent construction and almost as much a tourist attraction as a religious centre. Just outside the monastery the construction of South East Asia's tallest statue of Buddha, at the cost of HK$20 million, has recently begun and will take take four to five years to complete. For HK$30 a head, including meals, you can spend the night here in dormitories, and the food is pretty tasteless. Next day you can take a bus back to Mui Wo and thus complete a fairly in-depth look at the island. It's a lot of walking to do in one day so if you intend to do the lot it might be better to leave the Peng Chau-Trappist Monastery-Mui Wo bit till day two and start off by going straight from HK Central to Mui Wo.

Lamma

Another fairly large island, this one is south-east of Hong Kong and is a good beach and swimming centre with some cheap restaurants. Ferries run to Yung Shue Wan or Sok Kwu Wan on the island.

BEACHES

Hong Kong has many excellent beaches both on the island, in the New Territories and on the outer islands. The HKTA *Beaches* brochure is a useful guide to where they are, what they've got and how to get to them. On HK Island, Repulse Bay is the best-known beach, but others worth checking out in the summer include Clear Water Bay, Big Wave Bay and Shek O. Best beaches in the New Territories are along the west coast beyond Castle Peak. Silvermine Bay on Lantau Island is probably the most beautiful of the outer island beaches but Cheung Chau and Lamma Island also have good beaches.

Places to Stay

The cost of accommodation is the major expense in visiting Hong Kong although you can still get by reasonably cheaply with a little effort. There are a number of youth hostels and similarly oriented places with dormitory accommodation; you can try the several YMCAs and YWCAs; or head for the guest houses which are clustered in Chungking Mansions.

There are several pointers to follow in looking for a reasonable place. First is that Hong Kong suffers an accommodation crush so it's worth writing ahead and trying to get a reservation, or be prepared to hunt around a bit. If anything this has worsened over the last year or two because hotel construction plans have been shelved while waiting for the 1997 question to be settled between the UK and China. Secondly, guest house prices are variable with supply and demand and also with the length of your stay. If you're in Hong Kong during a low-season period or you plan to stay for an extended time it's definitely worth bargaining over the price.

Almost all the cheap accommodation is on the Kowloon side. Over on Hong Kong Island the hotels are mainly big, expensive, 'international' places. You can, however, find some interesting cheaper places out on the islands (particularly Cheung Chau) or in the New Territories. At the airport the HKTA has a desk, but they generally only deal with the more expensive hotels for reservations. The Student Travel Bureau also has discount arrangements with a number of places, but reservations and payment must be made through their office.

Chungking Mansions Next door to the Holiday Inn and across the road from the Hyatt on Nathan Rd, right in the centre of the Tsimshatsui 'downtown' area of Kowloon is Chungking Mansions – the magic word for cheap accommodation in Hong Kong. Down at the bottom of this multi-storey block is Chungking Arcade, a rather drab shopping arcade. If you wander around you'll find a number of lifts labelled A through E and over the elevator doors are name plates for guest houses. There are lots of them and the standards vary widely. The best policy is to pick a block and try a few. In winter they'll be less crowded than in summer and at any time of year it's worth haggling over the price, particularly if you plan a longer stay. With effort you can find a double room for as low as HK$75. You pay a little more for rooms with extras like attached bathrooms.

Some of the places are 'short-time' specialists – if you get an odd response it's likely that the place generally rents rooms by the hour. Try another! Avoid walking down the steps of Chungking Mansions unless you want to get very depressed – they're extremely dirty and dismal. In between the guest houses are offices, private apartments, Indian 'club messes'

(actually open to anyone and with excellent Indian food), and lots of cottage industry – clothes making, semi-precious stone grinding – a regular hotbed of Chinese enterprise.

A block, at the front, is the block with the cream of the guest houses although you'll also find the *Travellers' Hostel* (tel 3-687710) on the 16th floor. It's a friendly, reasonably clean and well-run place and this is an excellent information source for China visits. Dorm beds are HK$20 and up (some fan-cooled, some air-con) while rooms cost from HK$80.

On the 3rd floor the *Lee Garden Guest House* is nice. *Chungking House* (tel 3-665362), on the 4th and 5th floors, has singles from around HK$130, doubles from HK$150. Rooms at the front have a view of the Hyatt Hotel, across the road, which is often 'better than television!'

B and D blocks are the other two main hunting grounds. There's not much in C or E block and in any case these places can generally be reached from D block. It's in B and D that you'll find the cheaper rooms too. Places to try include the *Crown* and *Astor* on floor 16, the *Shangrila* on 15, the *New Washington* on 13, the *Colombia* on 12 and the not-so-friendly *Hong Kong Guest House* on 11. D block places include *Lees Guest House* on the 16th, the *Boston* and the *Paris* on the 10th and the friendly *Princess* on 3 where clean rooms are available for HK$70.

E block has the *New Sheraton* on floor 3 and the *Hoover Guest House* on 9. A traveller recommended the *Welcome Guest House* on the 8th floor as being friendly and a good place to stay – dorm beds are HK$20, doubles HK$80.

Hostels There are other guest houses around although Chungking Mansions is the main centre. They're lumped in below with the cheaper hotels. Hong Kong has a number of hostel places (apart from the Travellers' Hostel in Chungking Mansions). They include the *International Youth Accommodation Centre* (tel 3-663419) on the 6th floor at 21A Lock Rd. It's a little bit anonymous but quite easy to find, directly behind the Hyatt hotel so it's only a block over from Chungking Mansions and Nathan Rd. It's another good information source and has dorm beds for HK$20. Cheaper rates are available for longer stays.

Or you can continue quite a distance down Nathan Rd and find the *Hong Kong Hostel* (tel 3-678952), also known as the Foreign Youth Service Centre, on the 11th floor at 230. It's directly across from the Shamrock Hotel and on the 9 or 201 bus route from the airport. Finding the hostel is a little difficult and once inside it's a bit noisy from the traffic on Nathan Rd, but once again it's a convenient and reasonably well-kept place with similar prices to the other hostels. The *Young Traveller's Service Centre* (tel 3-693369) at 24 Cameron Rd is another hostel to look for.

Apart from these unofficial youth hostels there are also a number of real YHA places. The YHA office (tel 5-700985 and 5 706222) is at Room 1408, Block A, Watson's Estate, 4-6 Watson Rd, North Point, Hong Kong Island. The hostels charge HK$8 a night for a dorm bed; they're closed between 10 am and 4 pm, lights-out is at 11 pm and you must be a YHA member to use them. If you're not already a member it costs HK$80 to join in HK. The hostels are usually located in remote areas and it's generally a good idea (or even required at some of the hostels) to book in advance.

Mau Wui Hall (tel 5-875715) on top of Mt Davis on Hong Kong Island is beautifully situated, very popular and the most centrally located of the YHA hostels. To get there take a 5B bus to the end of the line, walk back 100 metres and look for the YHA sign. You've then got a 20 to 30 minute climb up the hill! There are 112 beds here.

For more detailed information on finding these hostels contact the YHA. Other YHA hostels are:

Bradbury Hall (tel 3-282458), Chek Keng, Sai Kung Peninsula, New Territories. To get there take a 92 bus from Choi Hung Estate, then a 94 bus to Pak Tam Au, then walk to Chek Keng village. Or take the ferry from Ma Liu Shui, adjacent to the University Railway Station. It's a two hour trip to Chek Keng and the hostel is right at the pier.

Cambrai Lodge is at Nim Wan, Lau Fau Shan in the New Territories and is only open on weekends and holidays. Whichever route you take final access involves walking to Nim Wan village.

Jockey Club Mong Tung Wan Hostel (tel 5-9841389), Mong Tung Wan, Lantau Island. It's about 45 minutes walk from the junction of the Chi Ma Wan Rd and the temple along the footpath to Mong Tung Wan. Or you can get there by hiring a sampan from Cheung Chau to the Mong Tung Wan jetty – cost is about HK$40 for up to 10 passengers.

Pak Sha O Hostel (tel 3-282327), Pak Sha O, Sai Kung Peninsula, New Territories. You can get there by a 94 bus to Ko Tong village or a ferry to Lai Chi Chong from Ma Liu Shui.

Sze Lok Yuen (tel 0-988188), Tai Mo Shan, Tsuen Wan, New Territories. Get there by a 51M bus from the Tsuen Wan MTR station to Tai Mo Shan Rd from where it's a 45 minute walk.

S G Davis Hostel (tel 5-9857610), Ngong Ping, Lantau Island. The hostel is close to the Po Lin Monastery.

Wayfoong Hall (tel 0-6568323), Plover Cove, Ting Kok Rd, Tai, New Territories. There are a number of buses operating there or you can reach Tai Po by rail.

The Ys Right at the end of the Kowloon peninsula the *Salisbury Rd YMCA* (tel 3-692211) has a location which many of the big hotels in Hong Kong would give their right arm for. The view across the harbour from the rooftop cafeteria alone is worth a small fortune and if the YMCA ever decides to sell their block of land they'll have no shortage of bidders. There are a handful of dorm beds here for both men and women, but the cheapest rooms are only available for men. Otherwise singles run HK$85-180, doubles HK$100-220; still a bargain for the location. With its relatively low prices and very fine location it's hardly surprising that the YMCA is heavily booked. To ensure a room you need to book a month ahead enclosing the first night's costs. Write to PO Box 95096, TST Kowloon.

Also known as the 'Chinese Y', the *YMCA International House* (tel 3-319111) is further out from Kowloon at 23 Waterloo Rd. It's near the less touristy areas of Mongkok and Yaumati. This large and relatively modern place has 305 rooms. The cheapest rooms with shared bathrooms cost from HK$30 to 50, HK$40 for a second person. The cheapest singles are for men only. Regular rooms cost from HK$180 to 220. You can get there on a 1A or a 9 bus from the airport or a 7 or 7A from the Star Ferry. The Y has a western and Chinese restaurant, the latter does very good dim sum.

A little further up the road, and visible from Waterloo Rd although it is actually on Man Fuk Rd, is the *YWCA Anne Black Centre* (tel 3-7139211). It's just up a hill on the right, behind a Caltex petrol station. There are 165 rooms here, 104 of them are air-con. The cheapest rooms are for women only and start from around HK$90. More expensive rooms go from HK$100 up to HK$200.

Finally there's the *YWCA 'Headquarters Hostel'* (tel 5-223101) across on Hong Kong Island at 1 MacDonnell Rd. It's a smaller hostel and again the cheaper rooms are for women only; the doubles are for either sex. Singles are HK$50-110 or HK$170 with bath. Doubles are HK$80-130 or HK$170-190 with bath. To get there take a 200 airport bus to the Hilton and walk up the hill, or leave the bus at the Mandarin and take a taxi, or from the Star Ferry in Central take a 12A bus from beside the City Hall.

Cheap Hotels The *Washington Guest House* (tel 3-690177) is at 15A Austin Avenue in Kowloon. Rooms are all air-con and cost from around HK$120. At 223 Nathan Rd the *Shamrock Hotel* (tel 3-662271) is near the Jordan Rd MTR station. It's Chinese in decor despite its

Irish name and gets quite a few travellers. All rooms have TV, and student discounts are available through the Student Travel Bureau – otherwise you're looking at HK$200 to 300.

Others to try include *Green Jade House* (tel 3-677121) at 29-31 Chatham Rd in Kowloon or the *Ritz Hotel* (tel 3-672191 to 6) at 122 Austin Rd, a half block off Nathan Rd. Good set meals in the restaurant here. Back on Nathan Rd the *Chung Hing Hotel* (tel 3-887001) at 380 has singles at HK$185-210, doubles at HK$225-250. The rooms are bigger but not so nicely furnished as the Shamrock. The *King's Hotel* (tel 3-301281) at 473 is also reasonably priced. Or try the *Fuji Hotel* (tel 3-678111) at 140 Austin Rd, in the same price bracket.

Cheaper hotels on Hong Kong Island include the famous *Luk Kwok* (tel 5-270721) at 67 Gloucester Rd, Wanchai. This was Suzie Wong's hotel, the *Nam Kok*. It's big, old-fashioned, usually has room and it's really not a bad place to stay. Good doubles are nearly HK$300. Further down at 116-122 the *Harbour Hotel* (tel 5-748211) is also good. Or try the *Singapore Hotel* (tel 5-272721) at 41-49 Hennessey Rd, also in Wanchai.

At 22 Hennessey Rd on Hong Kong Island the *Soldiers & Sailors Methodist Hostel* has rooms from around HK$60 and you can book through the HKTA or get a discount through the Student Travel Bureau. It's clean, comfortable and even has a TV lounge with a library. The downstairs cafeteria does excellent value set meals. During the June-to-September summer vacations you may be able to stay in the student residential halls at *Hong Kong University* on Bonham Rd in Central. Phone 5-492927 for details; get there on a bus No 3 from the Connaught Centre.

Places to Eat
Surprisingly, Hong Kong is not a great place for cheap eating – in fact it's a real let down after a fantastic food trip like

Singapore. It's particularly surprising when you consider that Canton, the Mecca of Chinese cuisine, is just up the tracks a little distance. Part of the problem is that English is not so widely spoken in Hong Kong as in Singapore and cheap restaurants are hard to find and even more difficult to communicate with. You end up pointing a lot. Not that eating cheap in Hong Kong is any real problem – you simply find yourself eating more Big Macs than you might have expected. At the food stalls, called *dai pai dongs*, you can get very good noodles though; just point to whatever looks good and eat. A couple of dollars will fill you up.

Fast Food *McDonald's* has had quite an impact on Hong Kong and there are about a dozen of them scattered around so you're never too far from a burger, french fries and a shake. They're just like back home (wherever that might be), probably in part because many of the components are imported anyway. *Burger King* also operates here or you can try the local *Maxim's* chain – they're also a good place for breakfast, particularly the one in Ocean Terminal, Kowloon. The *White Stag* pub on Canton Rd, Kowloon (up from the Ocean Centre) does great hamburgers – a real meal.

Hong Kong is packed with handy little bakeries and at breakfast time an apple or orange and a fresh bread roll or pastry makes an appetising and very economical start to the day. If you're buying fruit off a street stall check the prices first – they tend to vary a lot from place to place (and customer to customer) and they're often quite seasonal. *Rikki's* on Carnarvon St is quite a good bakery. The *Crossroads Coffee Shop* on the second floor in the Ocean Terminal, Kowloon is another good place for breakfast. It's handy for the YMCA.

Set Meals Another economical way of eating in Hong Kong is at the many places offering excellent fixed-price set meals. You'll find them in some hotels and also in restaurant chains like the *ABCs*. There are ABCs at 580 and 719 Nathan Rd, 72A Waterloo 159 Sai Yee and 368 Prince Edwards, all in Kowloon. They're often bakery/restaurant combinations so you may have to find your way through the bakery part to get to the restaurant. The *Ritz Hotel* at 122 Austin Rd in Kowloon also has a fine five-course lunch which is great value. The 2nd floor *Ruby Bakery & Restaurant* on Carnarvon Rd in Kowloon is economical for Chinese and western dishes.

Yum Cha One of the most popular ways of lunching in Hong Kong is to yum cha or 'drink tea'. The name comes from the Chinese tea which is always consumed when eating dim sum. These Cantonese dim sum specialists are generally huge places with little ladies circulating with trays or trolleys of dim sums. You take your chances, pick plates of anything that looks appetising and when you've had enough the bill is toted up from the number of empty plates left on your table. They're pretty economical and often very crowded at lunchtime when the office workers pack in. So arrive early if you want a seat and if you want the full variety of dim sum. Flip your teapot lid over when you want the teapot refilled!

Yum cha restaurants can be a little difficult to locate since signs are rarely in English and they are often located upstairs. If you see a sign with dim sums illustrated on it you're getting close. Places to try can be found along Nathan Rd in Kowloon or Queens Rd in Central. A Hong Kong resident wrote that the best dim sum places are on the Central side. Some places to consider:

Hong Kong Island
Blue Heaven, 38 Queens Rd, Central
City Hall, top floor, Edinburgh Place, Central
Luk Yu Teahouse, 24 Stanley St, Central
Glorious, East Town Building, 41 Lockhart Rd, Wanchai

Some popular dim sum include:

har kau	淡水鮮蝦餃	shrimp dumpling
shiu mai	蟹黃乾蒸賣	meat dumpling
pai kwat	豉汁蒸排骨	steamed spare ribs
ngau yuk mai	乾蒸牛肉賣	steamed beef balls
tsing fun kuen	雞絲蒸粉卷	steamed shredded chicken
kai bao tsai	香菰雞飽仔	steamed chicken bun
cha siu bau	蠔油叉燒飽	steamed barbecued pork bun
tsing ngau yuk	荷葉蒸牛肉	steamed beef ball in lotus leaf
cha chun kuen	炸雞絲春卷	fried spring roll
wook kok	蜂巢香芋角	fried taro vegetable puff
ham sui kok	軟滑咸水角	fried dumplings
fun gwor	鳳城蒸粉果	steamed dumplings filled with vegetables & shrimps
daan tart	千層雞蛋撻	custard tart
ma tai go	炸馬蹄糕條	fried water chestnut sticks
ma lai go	欖仁馬拉糕	steamed sponge cake
ma yung bau	蛋黃蔴蓉飽	steamed sesame bun
yeh chup go	鮮奶椰汁糕	coconut pudding
shui tsung kau	雪耳水晶餃	white fungus sweet dumpling
chien tsang go	蛋黃千層糕	1000 layer sweet cake with egg yolk filling
tse chup go	炎滑蔗汁糕	sugar cane juice roll

State, 9th & 10th floor, Li Po Chun Chambers (opposite Macau Ferry Pier), Des Voeux Rd *New Neptune Restaurant*, Aberdeen

Kowloon

Gold Wheel, 172 Nathan Rd, Tsimshatsui
Kingsland, Miramar Hotel, 134 Nathan Rd, Tsimshatsui
Capital Restaurant, 2nd floor, Chungking Mansions, 40-44 Nathan Rd, Tsimshatsui (more expensive but big helpings!)
Golden Crown, 66 Nathan Rd, Tsimshatsui
Oceania, Shop 281, Ocean Terminal, Tsimshatsui

The *Luk Yu* in Central is very old and traditional; only Chinese is spoken and *gwailos* are suffered rather than welcomed! Travellers have recommended the *Asiana*, 23rd floor, Asia Building, Wanchai (opposite the police headquarters and near the Hennessey Rd post office). You should be able to get a more than filling dim sum meal for HK$25 or less. Yum cha is also a popular way of having a long, leisurely Sunday brunch.

Other Naturally there are plenty of straightforward Chinese (Cantonese) restaurants around. Even the simpler places will be able to produce a menu with English translation on request. For a splurge try the *Yung Kee* at 32 Wellington St in Central. It's a classy yum cha place in the afternoon but also has excellent Cantonese food. Dishes are generally in the HK$15 to 20 bracket. The roast goose is magnificent.

Of course the floating restaurants at Aberdeen are the places that come to mind for seafood but these days they are rather touristy and over-priced. The *Lei Yue Mun* area on Kowloon side is supposed to be one of the best places for seafood. Take the Shaukiwan ferry to Lei Yue Mun from Hong Kong and walk to the right for 10 minutes. Or if you are already in Kowloon take a 14 bus to Yau Tong and walk straight ahead. There's also good seafood on the islands and Laufaushan is said to be the place for oysters.

The *Poor Man's Night Club* near the Macau Ferry Wharf has Mongolian hot pot (also known as steamboat) where you have a plate full of goodies to cook for yourself over a burner and bowl on your table. In Causeway Bay *Food Street* is a new restaurant arcade with some cheapish places. It's a bit plastic but not too bad.

There are some really good vegetarian places around, like *Wishful Cottage* at 336-340 Lockhart Rd in Wanchai or the *Grace Cottage* at 20 Stanley Rd in Central. The latter is rather crowded since it also does good takeaways. For good Peking food at low cost try the strangely named *American* at 23 Lockhart Rd, Wanchai or the *New American* at 177 Wanchai Rd.

Chungking Mansions has some excellent places including the Indian and Pakistani 'messes' between floors. Try the *Sher-i-Punjab* on the 8th floor, D block; the *Karachi Mess* on the 3rd floor of E block; or the *New Madras* on the 16th floor of D block. There are no menus, just a blackboard showing what's on for the day.

Golden Bell at Hart Avenue in Kowloon has reasonably priced Vietnamese food. The *Salisbury Rd YMCA* has straightforward cafe food (eggs & chips and the like) in its splendid cafeteria. Try the rotating restaurant atop the *Furama Hotel* for a real splurge night – terrific views and a not-too-expensive buffet. At 184 Nathan Rd, Kowloon try *Cherikoff* for good American-style breakfasts. *Lindy's* at 57 Peking Rd, Kowloon does expensive New York deli-style giant sandwiches. The *Holiday Inn* on Nathan Rd in Kowloon offers an all-you-can-eat breakfast buffet for HK\$45. Over on Hong Kong Island the *Spaghetti House* does good spaghetti amongst other things. It's on Hennessey Rd, just down from the Soldiers & Sailors Guest House.

Nightlife

Apart from all the girlie bars, topless bars, hostess bars and god-knows-what-else bars Hong Kong also has lots of straightforward places where you can get a reasonably priced beer in pleasant surroundings. Many of them are English or Australian in their flavour. Try the popular *Ned Kelly's Last Stand* on Ashley Rd in Kowloon. Other places for a cold Fosters include the *Stoned Crow* in Minden Avenue, the nearby *Kangaroo Bar* in Hart Avenue or the *Waltzing Matilda Arms* in Cameron Rd – all Kowloon side. British-style places include the *Jockey Pub* in Swire House, Central and *Mad Dogs* on Wyndham Street. Back on Minden Avenue the *Blacksmith's Arms* is also OK.

If you want to spend more – well, you can lay out twice as much for a beer in the big hotel bars or head for the topless bars around Wanchai or Tsimshatsui. Still more expensive are the night clubs and discos. Or you can simply go up the Peak for a free view of the nightlife down below. Or head for a cinema where western films are likely to be heavily cut so they can show more films per day!

If you've ever wondered what year you were born in here's the chart – remember Chinese new year usually falls in February so January will be included in the year before.	snake	29	41	53	65	77
	horse	30	42	54	66	78
	sheep	31	43	55	67	79
	monkey	32	44	56	68	80
	cock	33	45	57	69	81
	dog	34	46	58	70	82
	pig	35	47	59	71	83
	rat	36	48	60	72	84
	ox	37	49	61	73	85
	tiger	38	50	62	74	86
	rabbit	39	51	63	75	87
	dragon	40	52	64	76	88

Indonesia

Indonesia is a long chain of tropical islands offering a mixture of cultures, people, scenery, prospects, problems and aspirations unmatched in South-East Asia. For the budget traveller Indonesia is a kaleidoscope of cheap food, adventurous travel and every sort of attraction – from the tropical paradise of Bali, the untouched wilderness of Sumatra, the historical monuments of Yogyakarta, with the unbelievable squalor of Jakarta thrown in to leaven the mix.

HISTORY

Powerful kingdoms began to appear in Java and Sumatra towards the end of the 7th century. The Budhhist Srivijaya empire ruled south Sumatra and much of the Malay peninsula for six centuries, whilst the Hindu Mataram kingdom presided over Java. The two developed side by side as both rivals and partners, and between them raised inspiring monuments like Borobudur.

The last important kingdom to remain Hindu was the Java-based Majapahit, founded in the 13th century. It reached its peak under the Prime Minister Gajah Madah, and though it is said to have ruled over a vast area of the archipelago it probably controlled only Java, Bali and the island of Madura off Java's north coast.

The spread of Islam into the archipelago spelt the end of the Majapahits as satellite kingdoms took on the new religion and declared themselves independent of the Majapahits. But unlike the fierce brand initially exported by the Arabs, the Islamic religion was considerably mellowed by the time of its arrival in Java. The Majapahits retreated to Bali in the 15th century to found a flourishing culture while Java split into separate sultanates.

By the 15th century a strong Muslim empire had developed with its centre at

Malacca (Melaka) on the Malay peninsula, but in 1511 it fell to the Portuguese and the period of European influence in the archipelago began. The Portuguese were soon displaced by the Dutch who began to take over Indonesia in the early 1600s. A British attempt to oust the Dutch in 1619 failed; Malacca fell to the Dutch in 1641 and by 1700 they dominated most of Indonesia by virtue of their supremacy at sea and control of the trade routes and some important ports. By the middle of the 18th century all of Java was under their control.

The Napoleonic wars led to a temporary British takeover between 1811-1816 in response to the French occupation of Holland, and Java came under the command of Sir Stamford Raffles. Indonesia was eventually handed back to the Dutch after the cessation of the wars in Europe, and an agreement made whereby the English evacuated their settlements in Indonesia in return for the Dutch moving out of India and the Malay peninsula. But whilst the Europeans may have settled their differences the Indonesians were of a different mind; for five years from 1825 onwards the Dutch had to put down a revolt led by the Javanese Prince Diponegoro. It was not until the early 20th century that the Dutch brought the whole of the archipelago – including Aceh and Bali – under control.

Although the Dutch rule was softened during this century, dissatisfaction still simmered and a strong nationalist movement – whose foremost leader was Sukarno – developed despite Dutch attempts to suppress it. The Japanese occupied the archipelago during World War II, and after their defeat the Dutch returned and tried to take back control of their old territories. For four bitter years – from 1945 until 1949 – the Indonesians fought an intermittent war with the Dutch,

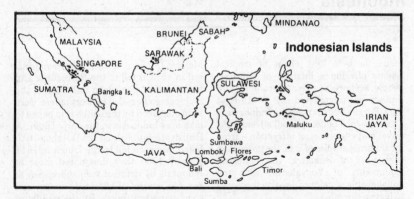

by the end of which the Dutch gave in and recognised Indonesia's independence.

Weakened by the long struggle and without the government structure bequeathed to British colonies, independence did not come easily. The first 10 years of independence saw the Indonesian politicians preoccupied with their own political games until, in 1957, President Sukarno put an end to the impasse by declaring 'Guided Democracy' and investing more power in himself. But Sukarno proved to be a less adept nation-builder than revolutionary leader. Grandiose building projects, the planned 'socialisation' of the economy and a senseless confrontation with Malaysia, led to internal dissension and a steady deterioration in the national economy.

As events came to a head there was an attempted coup in 1965 led by an officer of Sukarno's palace guard and several of Indonesia's top army generals were murdered. The coup was suppressed by the Indonesian army under the leadership of General Suharto; the reasons for the coup are unclear but it was passed off as an attempt by the Communists to sieze power and tens of thousands of Communists and suspected Communists and sympathisers were killed or imprisoned. Suharto eventually pushed Sukarno out of power and took over the presidency himself.

A stark contrast to the turbulent Sukarno years, things have – on the whole – been steadier under Suharto. The invasion of Portuguese Timor in 1975 stands as much to Australia's discredit as Indonesia's and it's surely no coincidence that Sideshow Kissinger and President Gerald Ford left Jakarta the day before the invasion. In recent years Indonesia has shown signs of coming to grips with its internal economic problems, with some of the worse excesses curbed. Large oil exports and other substantial natural resources seem to offer the promise of better days to come but graft and corruption are still very much a way of life and while some people get very rich the lot of the average Indonesian, particularly in parts of overcrowded Java, is very hard.

FACTS

Population Indonesia is the fifth most populous country in the world. The population is around 156 million and fully 60% are crammed into just 7% of the nation's land area – the island of Java. The people are of the Malay race although there are many different groupings and a vast number of local dialects.

Geography Indonesia occupies 1,475,000 square km scattered over about 13,700 islands. It is a far less compact mass of islands than the Philippines, the other island nation of the region. Indonesia stretches far north of the equator in Sumatra, Kalimantan and Sulawesi – all of which straddle it. Parts of Indonesia are still vast, barely-explored regions of dense jungle.

Economy Still basically a rural subsistence economy, Indonesia has vast mineral resources which are only now starting to be tapped. It also has oil although a truly Asian combination of inefficiency and corruption allowed the massive Pertamina oil conglomerate to go bankrupt in the 1970s! The fortunate combination of fertility and rainfall allows Indonesia to approach self-sufficiency in food production, but often the food potential isn't where the population is and every year the population gets larger.

Religion Nominally a Muslim nation there is actually an amazing diversity of religions and a commendable degree of religious tolerance. From the Dutch days pockets of Christianity still exist – the islands of Timor and Flores, the Lake Toba region of north Sumatra and the Tana Toraja area of Sulawesi for example. At one time Sumatra was predominantly Buddhist and Java predominantly Hindu – before Islam spread into the archipelago and took over from both. The last remnants of Hinduism retreated to Bali, where they remain to this day.

INFORMATION

The Indonesian tourist office is the poorest in South-East Asia in terms of useful information to visitors. They have nothing apart from the odd brochure and not even many offices around the country. The Indonesia National Tourist Organization does produce a *Calendar of Events* for the entire country and a useful *Indonesia Tourist Map* booklet which includes some good maps and helpful travel information. They're available from the Directorate General of Tourism office at Jalan Kramat Raya 81, Jakarta, and you should be able to get brochures on all tourist destinations here too. Some of the regional offices produce some local information or useful items like the festival calendar available from the office in

Denpasar, Bali. The Jakarta office in the Jakarta Theatre Building on Jalan Thamrin, next to the Sarinah department store, is fairly helpful. There are other regional offices, as in north Sumatra or in Yogyakarta, plus an excellent independent tourist office in Ubud, Bali. The usefulness of the individual tourist offices around Indonesia often depends on who works there – the representatives in Manado and Ujung Pandang, for example, both speak good English and are exceptionally friendly and helpful.

BOOKS

For detailed information on Bali and neighbouring Lombok look for the Lonely Planet guidebook, *Bali & Lombok – a travel survival kit*. Later in 1985 it will be joined by a very detailed new guidebook to the whole nation: *Indonesia – a travel survival kit*.

Other guidebooks to Indonesia include Bill Dalton's long-running *Indonesia Handbook*. The Apa Insight series of coffee table guidebooks include *Insight Bali*, *Insight Java* and *Insight Indonesia*. For an introduction to the country read *Indonesia* by Bruce Grant, *Indonesia since Sukarno* by Peter Polomka and *Suharto's Indonesia* by Hamish McDonald. The first two are available in Penguin paperbacks; the third was published by Fontana in 1980. *Sukarno – An Autobiography* as told to Cindy Adams captures the charisma and ego of the man.

The award-winning Australian novel *The Year of Living Dangerously* by Christopher Koch is an evocative reconstruction of life in Jakarta during the final chaotic months of the Sukarno period. *Twilight in Jakarta* by the Indonesian journalist, Mochtar Lubis, is an outspoken condemnation of political corruption and one of the best documents of life in the capital, particularly of Jakarta's lower depths – the prostitutes, becak drivers, and rural immigrants. Lubis has twice been imprisoned for his political convictions and the book goes on and off the ban list; at present the Oxford in Asia paperback is on sale in Jakarta. *Indonesia, Between Myth and Reality* by Lee Khoon Choy is an excellent compilation of some of the intriguing religious, social and mystical customs of Indonesia (published by Federal Publications, Singapore).

Time and *Newsweek* are readily available in Indonesia but are often bizarrely censored.

VISAS

The new visa system instituted in Indonesia in 1983 has caused considerable confusion for people not following the beaten tourist tracks. Basically the new system allows visitors from most western countries to enter Indonesia without a visa and be granted a two month stay on arrival.

This is a wonderful improvement compared to the previous visa situation in Indonesia but there is one major catch: it only applies if you both enter and leave Indonesia through certain recognised 'gateways'. In addition to that catch a number of travellers have discovered, to their cost, that many Indonesian diplomatic offices are blissfully unaware of this condition or have interpreted the regulations to mean that entry is only permitted through those 'no visa' gateways.

Neither belief is true – if you want to you can enter or leave Indonesia through an unrecognised gateway (such as Pontianak or Tarakan in Kalimantan or Jayapura in Irian Jaya) but you must obtain a visa before you arrive in Indonesia. Furthermore if you are in Indonesia with a visa then any extension beyond the first month will be subject to the expensive old 'landing tax' – 46,000 rp plus 3500 rp for something or other at last report.

The recognised 'no visa' entry points to Indonesia are:

Airports:
  Halim (Jakarta)
  Polonia (Medan – North Sumatra)
  Simpang Tiga (Pekanbaru – Sumatra)
  Tabing (Padang – West Sumatra)
  Patu Besar (Batam Island, Riau Archipelago near Singapore)
  Mokmer (Biak)
  Sam Ratu Langi (Manado – North Sulawesi)
  Patimura (Ambon)
  Ngurah Rai (Denpasar – Bali)

Seaports:
  Tanjung Priok (Jakarta)
  Tanjung Perak (Surabaya)
  Benoa (Bali)
  Padang Bai (Bali)
  Ambon (Ambon)
  Bitung (North Sulawesi)
  Belawan (Medan – North Sumatra)
  Batam (Batam Island, Riau Archipelago near Singapore)

The traveller who wrote to us having suffered the most inconvenience over this regulation had entered Indonesia at Jakarta and intended to exit from Jayapura to Wewak in Papua New Guinea. He had bought an Air Niugini ticket Jayapura-Wewak, got a PNG visa, checked with Garuda in Kuala Lumpur, checked with the Indonesian consulates in Bangkok and Singapore, had his Jayapura-Wewak ticket checked by immigration officials at Jakarta who still granted him a regular no visa entry permit. None of these offices appreciated that when he got to Jayapura he wouldn't be allowed to continue to PNG! That's what happened: at Sentani Airport in Jayapura they wouldn't allow him to leave and he had to trek back all the way to Bali and fly from there to Australia!

The two-month maximum period means many people have to rethink their travels through Indonesia – there's no way two months is going to get you from one end of Sumatra right down to Bali with any ease. One possibility is to start from north Sumatra and travel down to Palembang, then exit to Tanjung Pinang and Singapore. From there you can start with a fresh visa and continue to Java and Bali. Which still leaves Nusa Tenggara and the outer islands to worry about!

MONEY

A$1 = 900 rp
US$1 = 1062 rp
£1 = 1161 rp

Indonesia used to have a real banana republic currency but for many years it has been extremely stable – apart from sudden shifts like the late '78 50% devaluation. This caught everyone in Indonesia completely by surprise and made foreigners (who suddenly found everything was that much cheaper) very unpopular for a short time. Prices soon came back to a new stable level.

US dollars are easily the most widely accepted foreign currency and often have a far better exchange rate than other currencies, particularly outside Jakarta. If you're going to be in really remote regions carry sufficient cash with you as banks may be few and far between. Even those you do come across may only accept certain varieties of travellers' cheques – stick to the major companies. On the whole changing money and travellers' cheques is a lot easier than it was a few years ago – notably in the islands of Nusa Tenggara where there are now more banks changing more varieties of cash and cheques.

Exchange rates tend to vary a bit from bank to bank – shop around. Bank Bumi Daya gives the best rates all over Java according to one amateur banking expert. The rates also tend to vary between cities – Jakarta and Yogya seem to have better rates than Surabaya for example. In some remote regions the rate can be terrible – or there may be no banks at all!

As in many other Asian countries there is a permanent shortage of small change and torn or dirty bank notes are not wanted! If you get stuck with any don't cause hassles by complaining, just wait until you get to a big city or bank.

COSTS

Indonesian costs are very variable – absolutely equivalent places to stay can be four times as expensive in some places (like Irian Jaya) than in others (like Bali). So what it costs you depends on where you go. If you follow the well-beaten tourist track through Bali-Java-Sumatra you may well find Indonesia one of the cheapest places in the region – exceptions like Jakarta apart. Travellers' centres like Bali, Yogyakarta and Lake Toba are superbly good value. At one time Indonesia had the cheapest fuel prices in the region and it's still not bad (insofar as westerners are concerned) by international standards, averaging 320 to 400 rp a litre (around US$1.50 a gallon) so transport costs are also pleasantly low if you've got your own motorcycle to travel around on. Fuel prices are pretty much the same right throughout Indonesia and only in really remote places (like the interior of Irian Jaya) do prices skyrocket – in the Baliem Valley fuel is 800 rp per litre.

CLIMATE

Draped over the equator, it's hot year

round – hot and wet in the wet, hot and dry during the dry. But it can get very cold indeed in the mountains. The wet season generally starts later the further south-east you go. In north Sumatra the rain begins to fall in September, in Timor not until November. Sumatran seasons have been fairly described as the wet and the wetter. Wet seasons are roughly:

Sumatra	September to March
Java	October to April
Bali & south	November to May

The odd islands out are the Moluccas (Maluku Province) where seasons are the reverse – the dry season in the Moluccas is September to March; the wet is from the beginning of April to the end of August.

ACCOMMODATION

Look for *losmen* or *penginapan* or just say you want to *tidur* – 'sleep'. Losmen are usually very basic, rarely more than a bed and a small table; in compensation tea or coffee is usually provided gratis a couple of times a day. Washing facilities consist of a *mandi*, a large water tank from which you scoop water with a dipper. Climbing in the tank is very bad form! Prices in Indonesia vary considerably – Yogya and Bali are much cheaper than other places in the country. In Bali the austerity of the rooms is often balanced by pleasant gardens and courtyards. There are some really nice places around and finding rooms for US$2 a night is often quite possible, particularly in Bali and Yogya.

FOOD

A *rumah makan*, literally 'house to eat', is the equivalent of a restaurant – a *warung* or food stall is a supposedly less grand eating place, but the dividing line is hazy. In Bali where food is cheap the cost difference is minimal. In more expensive Java, food is often much cheaper in warungs. *Pasars* (markets) are good food sources, especially the *pasar malam* (night market).

Like the rest of Asia, Indonesian food is heavily based on rice. *Nasi goreng* is the national dish – fried rice, with an egg on top in deluxe versions. *Nasi campur*, rice with whatever is available, is a *warung* favourite, often served cold. The two other real Indonesian dishes are *gado gado* and *satay*. Gado gado is a fresh salad with prawn crackers and peanut sauce. It tends to vary a lot so if your first one isn't so special try again somewhere else. Satay are tiny kebabs served with another spicy peanut dip.

The Dutch feast, *rijstaffel* or rice table, consists of rice served with everything imaginable – for gargantuan appetites only. Some big hotels still do a passable imitation. Indonesians are keen snackers so you'll get plenty of *pisang goreng* (banana fritters), peanuts in palm sugar, or shredded coconut cookies.

Popular throughout Indonesia, although it originated in Padang in Sumatra, is Padang food. In a Padang restaurant a bowl of rice is plonked in front of you, followed by a whole collection of small bowls of vegetables, meat, fish and eggs. Eat what you want and your bill is added up from the number of empty bowls. In Sumatra, food can be hot enough to burn your fingers. Spicy hot that is. Did you expect knives and forks?

Drinking unboiled water is not recommended in Indonesia – and iced juice drinks can be good, but take care! Indonesian tea is fine and coffee is also good. Soft drinks are quite expensive compared to those in other Asian countries. Local beer is good – Bintang Baru is Heineken supervised, but moderately expensive. Bali Brem rice wine is super-potent; the more you drink the nicer it tastes. *Es Buah* or *es campur* is a strange concoction of fruit salad, jelly cubes, syrup, crushed rice and condensed milk. Tastes absolutely *enak*.

An Indonesian warning, however: this is the country in the region where the most travellers get the most stomach upsets, in some cases pretty serious ones. A lot of this is due to poor hygiene and contaminated drinking water. Take especial care with cold drinks – OK, the drink itself may be made from boiled water; but how about the *ice*? The same warning applies to seafood, which is particularly susceptible to contamination. If you aren't positive it is safe and, equally important, *fresh* – then leave it alone.

Food (*Makan*)

fried rice	*nasi goreng*
white rice	*nasi putih*
rice with odds & ends	*nasi campur*
fried noodles	*mie goreng*
noodle soup	*mie kuah*
soup	*soto*
fried vegies	*cap cai*
with crispy noodles	*tami*
sweet & sour omelette	*fu yung hai*
fish	*ikan*
chicken	*ayam*
egg	*telur*
pork	*babi*
frog	*kodok*
crab	*kepiting*
beef	*daging*
prawns	*udang*
potatoes	*kentang*
vegetables	*sayur*

Drink (*Minum*)

drinking water	*air minum*
orange juice	*air jeruk*
coffee	*kopi*
tea with sugar	*teh manis*
milk	*susu*
cordial	*stroop*

Additions

butter	*mentega*
sugar	*gula*
salt	*garam*
ice	*es*
hot peppers	*sambal*

Descriptions

sweet	*manis*
no sugar	*pahit*
hot hot	*panas*
hot spicy	*pedas*
cold	*dingin*
delicious	*enak*
special; usually means 'an egg on top'	*istemiwa*

GETTING THERE

Air Indonesia's two main international gateways are Denpasar in Bali and Jakarta in Java. Although Bali is far and away Indonesia's major tourist attraction the Indonesian government strictly limits the number of flights into Bali so from many destinations arriving passengers have to go to Jakarta and continue on from there by air or land. From Australia Qantas and Garuda both fly to Bali and Jakarta. Advance purchase one-way and round trip fares for the high and low seasons are:

		Bali	Jakarta
one way			
east coast	high	A$457	A$541
	low	A$373	A$441
Perth/	high	A$265	A$305
Darwin	low	A$215	A$250
return			
east coast	high	A$702	A$832
	low	A$574	A$680
Perth/	high	A$406	A$472
Darwin	low	A$332	A$386

From London fares to Jakarta are from around £240 one-way or £450 return. Cheap fares to Bali are very similar and you can get a London-Australia ticket with stopover in Bali (and Singapore or Colombo for that matter) for around £400. Good London agents to check with for cheap tickets include STA Travel on Old Brompton Rd and Trail Finders on Earls Court Rd. From the US west coast the cheapest fares would probably be through Hong Kong, Bangkok or Singapore with a flight on from there.

There are also a number of lesser international gateways to Indonesia from neighbouring Asian nations. From Papua New Guinea there is a once-weekly flight that hops across the border from Wewak to Jayapura. There is no land or sea crossing permitted between the two countries although it would be quite easy to do.

Between north Borneo (the Malaysian states of Sabah and Sarawak) there is a regular service between Pontianak and Kuching and between Tarakan and Tawau. The usual route into Indonesia from Singapore is Singapore-Jakarta on which there are all sorts of flights with all sorts of fares quoted around US$120. Other less well known services include Pekanbaru-Singapore, useful if you're doing the double-visa route through the country.

Probably the most popular of all the 'local hops' into Indonesia is the 20-minute leap over the Melaka Straits from Penang to Medan in Sumatra – fare is about US$50. Unfortunately there is no short hop route between the Philippines and Indonesia – Sulawesi and Mindanao look temptingly close.

Airport tax for international departures from Indonesia is 4000 rp.

Ship Surprisingly for an island country there are very limited opportunities to arrive there by sea. Apart from cruise ships and private yachts the only really feasible route is the Jakarta-Tanjung Pinang-Singapore service. See Jakarta and Singapore for more details.

Land Only two countries – Malaysia and Papua New Guinea – have land borders with Indonesia and it's not really possible to cross either border by land. Physically it's quite possible; officially it certainly isn't.

GETTING AROUND
Air Indonesia has an amazing variety of airlines and aircraft, so getting around the country by air can still be quite an experience in our dull jumbo age. They fly to some pretty amazing places too. Check fares before you go if you've got a definite route, though – it may well be cheaper to get your tickets in advance.

The major airline is Garuda, named after the mythical man-bird vehicle of the Hindu god Vishnu and a hero of the Ramayana. Garuda operates all the long-distance international connections and has an extensive domestic network using DC9s, F28s and Airbuses. Within the country their operations are supposedly more reliable and (dare I say it) safer than the other airlines. Note that domestic fares in Indonesia are not identical among the different carriers – Garuda's will usually be somewhat more expensive.

The second-string airline is Merpati but it has now been taken over by Garuda and its services integrated into Garuda's. Merpati operates a mind-boggling collection of aircraft, but the intention is that they should run the services to remote and out-of-the-way locations and not compete directly with Garuda on the major routes. Other airlines, and there are quite a few, include Bouraq, Mandala and Sempati. Bouraq has services mainly to Kalimantan and Sulawesi and interesting international connections Pontianak-Singapore and Tarakan-Tawau (Malaysia).

Last, but very far from least, there's Zamrud. Based in Denpasar, Bali, it is the phoenix of all phoenixes since Zamrud regularly goes under due to cash shortages or aircraft crack-ups, only to reappear a year or so later as if nothing had ever happened. Their fleet of admirably beat-up DC3s stumble around the Nusa Tenggara islands and their chief pilot is an Asian travellers' legend. If you get an opportunity to fly Zamrud take it. Where else does one find an airline where the passengers get to vote on which route to take? As of our last edition they were up again; at present they're down.

Airport tax on domestic flights varies from 800 to 1500 rp and should be included on your ticket.

Rail There is a pretty good railway service running from end to end of Java – in the east it connects with the ferry to Bali, in the west with the ferry to Sumatra. There's a bit of rail into Sumatra but most of that vast island is reserved for the incredible buses. Trains vary – there are slow, miserable, cheap ones and fast, comfortable, expensive ones, not to mention ones in between. So check out what you're getting before you hand your rupiah over.

Some major towns (Jakarta and Surabaya in particular) also have several stations so check where you'll be going to and from as well. Student discounts are generally available but tend to vary too, from about 10% to 25%.

Bus There is an extensive bus network in Java – they're not very fast on the crowded daytime roads but at night the drivers really put their foot down. Safety – wazzat?? On certain routes where there is no rail competition or for shorter runs the bus services are very useful. These include Denpasar-Surabaya and Bandung-Jakarta.

In Sumatra, the bus is just about all there is – the rail line only runs as far as Palembang. Travelling through Sumatra in the brightly illustrated and amazingly uncomfortable buses is one of those experiences where at the end you think, 'my God, I've done it, but never again.' Even here there's progress, however; the roads are being improved and more modern buses are being introduced.

Ship Indonesia is an island nation so ships are important; if you're going to really explore you'll have to use them. Pelni are the biggest shipper with services almost everywhere – and often pretty miserable ships! Pelni does have some regular timetabled shipping connections – notably the modern liners *Kambuna* and *Kerinci* and the older *Tampomas* which do loops out of Java around Sulawesi, Kalimantan and Sumatra, stopping at various ports depending on the ship. Many of the smaller islands are now connected by fairly regular shipping – like the three-times weekly Sumbawa to Flores ferry which also drops in at Komodo Island once a week.

Often though getting a boat is generally a matter of hanging loose until something comes by. Check with the shipping companies, the harbour office, anyone else you can think of. When the ship arrives it's usually better to negotiate your fare on board rather than buy tickets from the office in advance, big centres like Jakarta and Surabaya apart. If you're travelling deck class unroll your sleeping bag on the deck and make yourself comfortable. Travelling deck class during the wet season can be an extremely uncomfortable experience. Either get one person in your party to take a cabin or discuss renting one of the crew's cabin (it's a popular way for the crew to make a little extra). Bring some food of your own.

It's also possible to make some more unusual sea trips. The old Makassar schooners still sail the Indonesian waters and it's possible to travel on them – from Sulawesi to other islands, particularly Java and Nusa Tenggara.

Some general advice from other travellers regarding ship travel through the archipelago includes: 'Unless it's really wet I reckon deck class is as good as cabin but get as high in the ship as possible. Privacy and security are major considerations. If you want fresh air in your cabin you get a lot of Indonesian faces too. If you keep your ultra-valuables on you an official will give you somewhere to stick your pack. Cabins get very hot, windows often don't help. Rats and cockroaches do not abound on the higher decks'.

Another suggestion is, 'If you're travelling in a cabin take 1st class – very little more than 2nd class, but you get reasonable food, a private cabin and your own private collection of cockroaches and mice!'

And a final thought: 'Definitely a once-only experience!'

Local Transport There's an enormous variety of local transport in Indonesia. This includes the ubiquitous *bemo* – a tiny pickup truck with two rows of seats down the sides. Bemos usually run standard routes like buses and depart when full but can also be chartered like a taxi. A step up from the bemo is the small minibus known either as an *opelet* or a *colt* – since they are often Mitsubishi Colts. They operate services much like buses.

Then there's the *becak* or bicycle-rickshaw – they're just the same as in so many other Asian countries, but are only found in towns and cities – but in central Jakarta, they're banned except for late at night. There are none in Bali. The *bajaj*, a three-wheeler powered by a noisy two-stroke engine, is only found in Jakarta. In quieter towns you may find *andongs* and *dokars* – horse or pony carts with two wheels (dokars) or four (andongs).

In Bali and Yogya you can hire bicycles or motorcycles. You can also hire drive-yourself cars in Jakarta and Bali. Then there are all sorts of oddities: you can hire horses in some places; many towns have taxis of course (they even use their meters in Jakarta); near the old harbour in Jakarta there is even a bicycle-taxi service where you ride on the rear carrier!

LANGUAGE
Although there are a vast number of local languages and dialects in the country, bahasa Indonesia, which is all but identical to Malay, is being actively promoted as the one national language. Like any language, Indonesian has its simplified colloquial form and its more developed literate language. For the visitor who wants to pick up enough to get by in the common language, *pasar* or 'market Indonesian' is very easy to learn. It's rated as one of the simplest languages in the world as there are no tenses, no genders and often one word can convey the meaning of a whole sentence. There are often no plurals or it is only necessary to say the word twice – child is *anak*, children are *anak anak* or *anak 2*. Book – *buku*, books – *buku 2*. It can also be delightfully poetic with words like sun – *mata hari* derived from eye – *mata*, day – *hari*, so the sun is literally the eye of the day.

Indonesia Phrasebook is the first of Lonely Planet's Language Survival Kits. It's a pocket-size introduction to the language intended to make getting by in bahasa as easy as possible.

Civilities
thank you
terima kasih
(very much)
(banyak)
please
silakan
good morning
selamat pagi
good day
selamat siang
good afternoon/evening
selamat sore
good night
selamat malam
goodbye (to person staying)
selamat tinggal
goodbye (to person going)
selamat jalan
sorry
ma'af
excuse me
permisi
how are you
apa kabar?

Questions
what is this?
apa ini?
how much (money)?
berapa (harga)?
expensive
mahal
what is your name?
siapa nama saudara?
my name is . . .
nama saya . . . .
how many km?
berapa kilometres?

where is?
dimana ada?
to where?
kemana?

Travelling

ticket	*karcis*
bus	*bis*
train	*kereta-api*
ship	*kapal*

Numbers

1	*satu*
2	*dua*
3	*tiga*
4	*empat*
5	*lima*
6	*enam*
7	*tujuh*
8	*delapan*
9	*sembilan*
10	*sepuluh*
12	*duabelas*
20	*duapuluh*
21	*duapuluh satu*
30	*tigapuluh*
53	*limapuluh tiga*
100	*seratus*
1000	*seribu*
½	*setengah (say 'stinger')*

Time

when?	*kapan*
tomorrow/yesterday	*besok/kemarin*
week/year	*minggu/tahun*
hour	*jam*
what time?	*jam berapa*
how long?	*berapa jam*
rubber time	*jam karet*
7 o'clock	*jam tujuh*

Days of the Week

Monday	*Hari Senen*
Tuesday	*Hari Selasa*
Wednesday	*Hari Rabu*
Thursday	*Hari Kamis*
Friday	*Hari Jumat*
Saturday	*Hari Sabtu*
Sunday	*Hari Minggu*

Useful Words & Phrases

I want to go to . . .
saya mau ke . . . .
bank
bank
street
jalan
Post Office
Kantor Pos
stamp
perangko
envelope
amplop
immigration
immigrasi
how much for . . . ?
berapa harga . . . . ?
one night?
satu malam?
one person?
satu orang?
sleep
tidur
bed
tempat tidukamar
bathroom
kamar mandi
toilet
WC ('way say'), kamar kecil
soap
sabun
toothpaste
pasta gigi
mosquito coil
ombat nyamok
I don't understand
saya tidak mengerti
this/that
ini/itu
big/small
besar/kecil
here
disini
stop
berhenti
another
satu lagi
no, not, negative
tidak

shop
  toko, kedai
open/closed
  buka/tutup
see
  lihat
good, very nice
  bagus (« big smile)
no good
  tidak baik
all right, good, fine
  baik
finished
  habis
dirty
  kotor

THINGS TO BUY
There are so many regional crafts and arts in Indonesia that they're dealt with under the separate regional sections. For an overview of the whole gamut of Indonesian crafts pay a visit to the Sarinah department store or Ancol's Pasar Seni in Jakarta. They've got items from all over the archipelago and while you may not find all the most interesting products you'll certainly see enough for a good introduction to what is available.

Java

Indonesia's most populous island, Java presents vivid contrasts of wealth and squalor, majestic open country and crowded filthy cities, quiet rural scenes and hustling modern traffic. For the traveller it has everything from live volcanoes to inspiring thousand-year-old monuments.

Java is a long, narrow island and it can be conveniently divided into three sections – West Java, Central Java and East Java. The western region, also known as Sunda, is particularly strongly Islamic and it is here that you will find the capital, Jakarta. Other important historic centres of the Sunda region were Banten, Bandung and Cirebon. For visitors today the most important places other than Jakarta are Bogor and Bandung. This is an area noted for its wooden *wayang golek* puppets.

Central Java is the most 'Indonesian' part of Indonesia and the centre for much of the island's early culture. Here the great Buddhist and Hindu dynasties that constructed the immense Borobudur temple and the complex of temples at Prambanan had their centre. Later, the rise of Islam carried sultans to power and the palaces or *kratons* at Yogyakarta and Solo (Surakarta) can be visited. This is a region for dance drama (*wayang orang*), *gamelan* orchestras and shadow puppet performances (*wayang kulit*).

Finally there is East Java or Java Timur, the area most likely to be rushed through by travellers in their haste to get to Bali. The major city here is the important port of Surabaya and, although East Java's attractions include the ruins at Trowulan and around Malang, the main interest in the region is natural rather than man-made – the many hill stations and the superb Mt Bromo volcano.

Most travellers going through Java follow the well-worn route Jakarta-Bogor-Bandung-Yogyakarta-Solo-Surabaya-Bali with short diversions or day trips from points along that route. Many only stop at Jakarta and Yogya! There are also a number of major towns along the north coast, but they attract few visitors.

GETTING THERE

You can get to Java by a number of means and from a variety of directions. The basic places from which people come to Java are Sumatra (either by the Padang-Jakarta shipping service or the short trip from Panjang in Sumatra to Merak in Java – see Sumatra for full details), or at the other end of the island they take the very short ferry trip to or from Bali between Banyuwangi and Gilimanuk – see Bali for full details. Or they might fly or ship to the outer islands like Sulawesi, Kalimantan, the Moluccas or Irian Jaya. Or they could arrive from Singapore or further afield.

Air Jakarta is another good place for shopping around for airline tickets, although not in the same class as Singapore. See the 'Getting There' section for Jakarta for information. For details of air fares from Australia or Europe to Indonesia see the introductory section on getting to South-East Asia. From Australia fares go pretty much by the book, principally because Bali is such an important holiday destination for Australians, From Europe, on the other hand, Garuda are active fare cutters and you can find all sorts of interesting tickets either simply to Jakarta or all the way to Australia, with stop-overs in Indonesia. The other popular entry point to Jakarta is from Singapore and you'll find a variety of ticket prices quoted from there.

Sea There are, of course, shipping services from other Indonesian islands, but there is only one international connection to Java – and even that isn't a real international connection, since it goes to the island of Tanjung Pinang near Singapore. The renowned Pelni ship *KM Tampomas*, however, no longer operates the round-trip Jakarta-Tanjung Pinang-Medan-Jakarta route and, at time of writing, there

is no regular shipping service on this route. The Pelni ship *Bogowonto* has been operating from Jakarta to Tanjung Pinang (and possibly Medan) when not in service for transmigration, and one traveller has written to say that a new Pelni service will be starting soon. It's worth checking with the Pelni office in Jakarta in any case because it's a reasonably good way of getting from Jakarta to Singapore. It's a very roundabout way of getting from Singapore to Jakarta since you have to go all the way up to Medan first and then backtrack.

The trip takes about 36 hours from Tanjung Priok, the Jakarta port, to Tanjung Pinang. Be on the watch for pickpockets arriving or departing Tanjung Priok. They work overtime during this congested stampede. Fares between Jakarta and Tanjung Pinang go from around US$20 (20,000 rp) for deck class to about US$30 (30,000 rp) for a 3rd-class cabin or about US$40 for a better cabin with aircon. Tanjung Pinang is still part of Indonesia and from here you take a 21,000 rp hydrofoil to Batam to clear Indonesian immigration and on from there to Singapore. There's an additional 1000 rp port charge at Tanjung Pinang. There's also a slower ferry service between Tanjung Pinang and Singapore which takes five or six hours instead of the faster 2½ hour service. Take care in Tanjung Pinang coming from Singapore; there are various 'travel agents' in cahoots with losmen owners who will try to ensure that you miss the boat (or give up because it's 'full') so that you'll stay in Tanjung Pinang. See Singapore for more details on this shipping route.

The alternative from Jakarta is to go round the docks at the old harbour of Sunda Kelapa and check with the harbour master (Kantor Syahbandar), the different shipping companies there, and the men working on the Makassar schooners too. Pulau Indah, for example, has a cargo boat from Sunda Kelapa to Tanjung Pinang once a month – it costs around 25,000 rp but it does take three days!

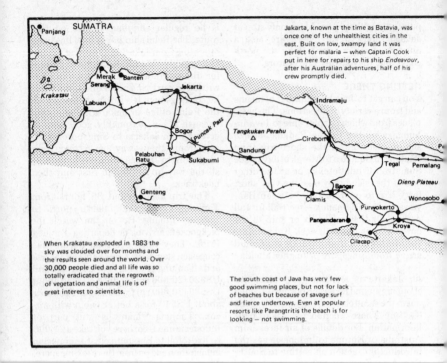

SUMATRA

Panjang

Krakatau

Merak
Serang
Banten
Labuan
Jakarta
Indramaju
Bogor
Puncak Pass
Tangkukan Perahu
Cirebon
Pelabuhan
Ratu
Sukabumi
Bandung
Tegal
Pemalang
Genteng
Ciamis
Bangar
Dieng Plateau
Wonosobo
Purwokerto
Pangandaran
Kroya
Cilacap

Jakarta, known at the time as Batavia, was once one of the unhealthiest cities in the east. Built on low, swampy land it was perfect for malaria – when Captain Cook put in here for repairs to his ship *Endeavour*, after his Australian adventures, half of his crew promptly died.

When Krakatau exploded in 1883 the sky was clouded over for months and the results seen around the world. Over 30,000 people died and all life was so totally eradicated that the regrowth of vegetation and animal life is of great interest to scientists.

The south coast of Java has very few good swimming places, but not for lack of beaches but because of savage surf and fierce undertows. Even at popular resorts like Parangtritis the beach is for looking – not swimming.

The old *Tampomas* was famed all along the Asian travel circuit for its supreme grottiness and high discomfort rating. Pelni ships are rarely anything special, but if you travel deck class what can you expect? Deck class includes nothing – you have to provide your own sleeping bag, even your own plate and eating utensils if you want to eat the *Tampomas'* infamous rice-and-a-fish-head food. Toilet facilities are nothing to write home about either. It's a wise idea to bring some food with you and drinks too, since they tend to be expensive on board. One advantage the *Tampomas* does have is the 'nightclub' that operates at night; anyone is welcome (not just cabin class passengers) and beers are reasonably priced.

If, on the other hand, you fork out for a cabin you can travel in reasonable comfort especially in the better cabins – which are only marginally more expensive than the most basic ones. Four-berth cabins utilise the same lousy toilet facilities as deck class. Note that cabins tend to be booked out some time ahead, but for deck class you simply turn up and buy your ticket on the boat. Whatever you say about travelling with Pelni lines it's certainly not a trip people forget. And usually not in a bad way – 'that Pelni ship, boy what a ride,' they'll say years later. You can be sure nobody is going to say that about flying. If being comfortable is really important to you, you can always stay home.

GETTING AROUND

Air There's no real need to fly around Java unless you're in a real hurry or have money to burn – there's so much readily available transport at ground level. If you do decide to take to the air you will get some spectacular views of Java's many mountains and volcanoes. Flying Garuda, fares include Jakarta-Yogyakarta 52300 rp, Jakarta-Surabaya 7600 rp (Merpati 63500 rp), Jakarta-Denpasar 90600 rp (Merpati 77000 rp), Yogyakarta-Surabaya 25500

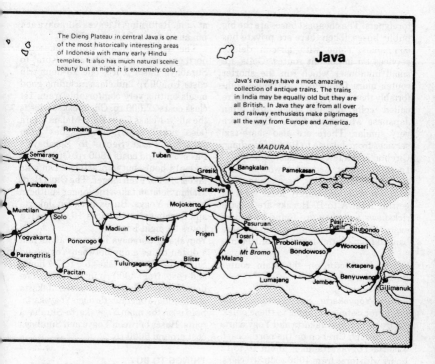

The Dieng Plateau in central Java is one of the most historically interesting areas of Indonesia with many early Hindu temples. It also has much natural scenic beauty but at night it is extremely cold.

Java

Java's railways have a most amazing collection of antique trains. The trains in India may be equally old but they are all British. In Java they are from all over and railway enthusiasts make pilgrimages all the way from Europe and America.

rp, Yogyakarta-Denpasar 48900 rp, Surabaya-Denpasar 36900 rp (Merpati 31400 rp).

Rail Choose your trains for comfort, speed and destination. There are cheap slow trains, reasonably cheap fast trains, very expensive expresses and squalid all-3rd-class cattle trains – a wide variety. Schedules change with reasonable frequency and although departures may be on-the-second, arrivals will be late for most services, very late for some of them. In Jakarta and Surabaya in particular there are several stations, some of them far more convenient than others. Bear this in mind when choosing your trains. Student discounts are generally available, but not for the expensive Bima and Mutiara night expresses. Try going straight to the station master for speedier tickets and also for any tickets at all when

officially the train is booked right out. Remember, once again, that fares for the same journey and in the same class will vary widely from train to train.

Bus Daytime bus travel is kind of slow and nerve-wracking. It would probably be just as bad for your nerves at night (if you were awake), but at least travel is much faster. Although buses run all over Java you're generally better off taking trains for the long hauls and using buses on the shorter trips. In some places there are particularly good reasons for going by bus, as on the Jakarta-Bandung trip over the Puncak Pass.

As with trains there can be quite a variance in fares and a variety of bus types. Where the fare isn't ticketed or fixed it's wise to check the fare with other passengers – colt and oplet drivers are the worst culprits for doubling fares for foreigners. The cheapest buses are the big public buses. Then there are private bus companies, some with air-con deluxe services on important routes. Colts are small minibuses which run the shorter routes more frequently and more comfortably than the big public buses. They're called colts because they are often Japanese Mitsubishi Colts. Oplets are very similar. There are also share-taxi services from Jakarta to Bogor, Bandung, Cirebon and a few other destinations.

Local Transport Around towns in Java there are buses, bemos, becaks and some very peculiar and purely local ways of getting from A to B. Becaks are bicycle rickshaws and they are found in almost every town of any size in Java, but they are banned from central Jakarta until 10 pm.

Sector by sector on the main routes through Java:

Jakarta-Yogyakarta See Bandung and Bogor for details on travel to these cities. All trains between Jakarta and Yogyakarta pass through Cirebon on the north coast. Jakarta-Yogyakarta takes about 10 to 12 hours with fares from 4000 rp in 3rd class, 8000 rp in 2nd. The fast Bima Express costs from 20,000 rp in 2nd including meals. It departs Jakarta (Kota) at 4 pm and arrives in Yogya at 1.08 am then continues on to Surabaya. In the other direction it leaves Surabaya at 4 pm, goes through Yogya at 9.28 pm and arrives Jakarta at 7 am the next morning. At the other end of the train luxury scale is the all-3rd-class Gaya Baru Malam Selatan which costs 4900 rp; it also continues from Yogya to Surabaya. By bus it costs from 5500 rp to Yogyakarta and takes about 14 hours.

Jakarta-Surabaya Trains between Jakarta and Surabaya either take the shorter northern route via Semarang or the longer southern route via Yogyakarta. The most expensive train is the deluxe Bima Express, via Yogya, which departs Jakarta (Kota) at 4 pm and arrives in Surabaya (Gubeng) at 7 am. Returning, it leaves Surabaya at 4 pm and arrives Jakarta at 7 am.

The deluxe Mutiara Utara takes the northern route from Jakarta Kota to Surabaya Pasar Turi. The 15-hour trip costs 15,500 rp 2nd class including good meals on this very comfortable train; 1st class costs 22,000 rp. Cheapest service is the all-3rd-class Gaya Baru Malam Utara (also north coast), which goes from Jakarta's Pasar Senen to Surabaya's Pasar Turi and costs 6800 rp. Officially it takes 14 hours but in practice it can take 22, 24 or even longer. The Gaya Baru Malam Selatan takes the longer southern route via Yogya. Buses between Jakarta and Surabaya cost around 10,000 rp (15 hours by night bus).

Yogyakarta-Surabaya There are about half a dozen trains a day between Yogya and Surabaya. The trip takes 5½ to 7½ hours and costs from 3000 rp in 3rd class. The deluxe Bima Express between Jakarta and Surabaya operates through Yogyakarta. Solo is on the main Yogyakarta-Surabaya route. Buses between Yogya and Surabaya cost around 6000 rp.

THINGS TO BUY

Yogya is the place in Java where your money deserves to be spent, but it's worth checking out the Sarinah department store in Jakarta. The third floor of Sarinah, on Jalan Thamrin, is devoted to handicrafts from all over the country. It can be a little variable – you might not be able to find certain items that really interest you or you might find one area badly represented – but overall it's a great place to look for an overall view of Indonesian crafts. The art market, Pasar Seni, at Ancol in Jakarta is also worth a visit.

Batik The art of batik making is one of Indonesia's best known crafts and it has been a Yogya speciality since who knows when. In my opinion Yogya is still the best place to look for batik. Batik is the craft of producing designs on material by covering part of it with wax then dyeing it. When the wax is scraped or melted off an undyed patch is left. Repeated waxing and dyeing can produce colourful and complex designs. Batik pieces can be made by a hand-blocked process known as *batik cap* in which a copper stamp is used to apply the wax – or they can be hand drawn, *batik tulis*, using a wax-filled pen known as a *canting*.

Batik can be bought as pieces of material, cushion covers, T-shirts, dresses, dinner sets and as batik 'paintings'. An easy check for basic quality is simply to turn it over to ensure the design is of equal colour strength on both sides of the material – that it really is batik and not just printed material. In Yogya you can buy batik in shops, in the market or from the many galleries. See Yogyakarta for much more information on batik there.

Other Crafts In Yogyakarta, silverwork can be found in the Kota Gede area. Wayang puppets can be found all over Yogya but wayang golek puppets are more frequently found in the West Java area around Bandung and Bogor. Kebayas, those flimsy lace jackets, are now a little old hat as a fashion but you can find lots of them in Yogya along with other popular western clothing. At Prambanan and Borobudur look for bamboo whistling tops; they make great presents for children. Leatherwork in Yogya is cheap but the quality is not always high. Very good lampshades and other cane craft can be found in Yogya but they're an incredible hassle to transport. Solo, near Yogya, is also a major centre for batik – it's much less touristy so prices are often lower. Music cassettes are of dubious quality but remarkably cheap around 1500 rp. In Surabaya there is something of a free port policy, but it is nothing like Singapore.

JAKARTA
An often squalid and dirty city that many travellers try to give a miss (you should have seen it 15 years ago, say the old

hands!), Jakarta actually has a lot to offer. Apart from a few interesting museums and a collection of terrible public monuments, Jakarta has some fine old Dutch architecture and is the most impressive reminder of the age of sailing ships to be seen anywhere in the world. The Dutch took Jakarta and renamed it Batavia back in 1619. The part of town known as Kota is the old Dutch town. Jakarta is very sprawling: it's 25 km from the docks to the suburb of Kebayoran.

The Jakarta rush hour is a positively enthralling sight if you stand in Jalan Thamrin and watch the Honda-powered maniacs swing through that series of roundabouts as if there was a pot of gold waiting for the first one to Merdeka Square. When they installed traffic lights in Jakarta they threatened to issue policemen with stones to hurl at drivers and motorcyclists who neglected to obey them.

'Jakarta is not as bad as your opening paragraph suggests,' wrote one traveller who found the Merdeka Square 'impressive', the 'dancing fountain' (complete with lights and music, every night at 10 pm) in the park nearby 'really beautiful' and the 'big dipper' in the amusement park 'fantastic.' Another traveller noted that he got lots of interesting offers from the local hookers who ply their trade along the way to the fountain. 'Must be the symbolism of that huge phallus,' he decided.

Information & Orientation
Sukarno's towering Merdeka square monument (Monas) serves as an excellent landmark for Jakarta – you can always get your bearings from it. North of the monument is the older part of Jakarta including the old Dutch town, then the waterfront and the old harbour area known as Sunda Kelapa. The modern harbour, Tanjung Priok, is several km along the coast to the east. The more modern part of Jakarta is to the south of the monument.

Jalan Thamrin, which runs to the west of the monument, is the main north-south street of the new city and along Jalan Thamrin you'll find the big hotels, big banks and the Sarinah department store.

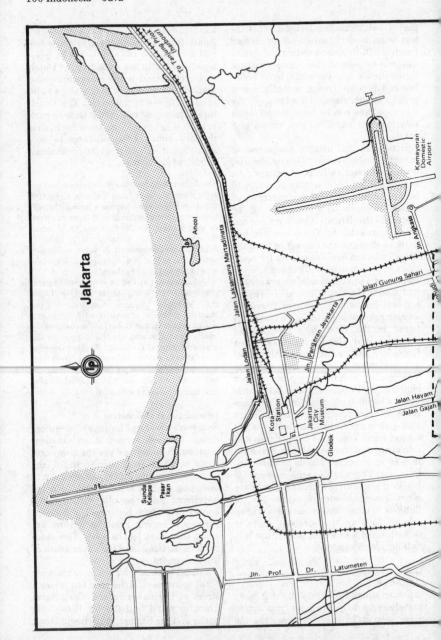

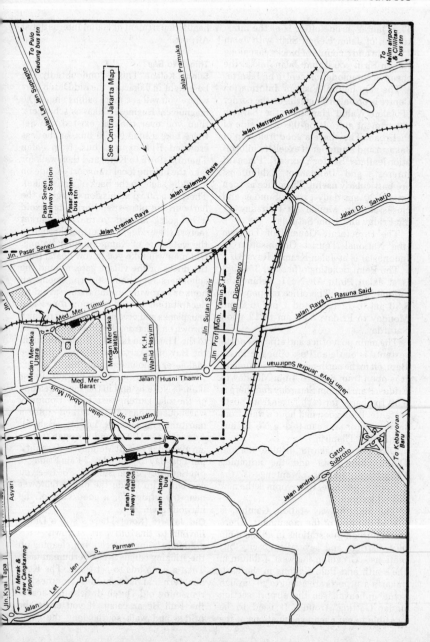

The Qantas airline office is at the intersection of Jalan Kebon Sirih with Jalan Thamrin and a couple of blocks east along Kebon Sirih you'll find Jalan Jaksa, the cheap accommodation centre of Jakarta.

The very helpful Visitors' Information Centre is on Jalan Thamrin, on the corner of Jalan Wahid Hasyim – the Sarinah department store is on the other side of that road. They have a good free map of Jakarta and a number of excellent information leaflets: 'See for Yourself', 'Places of Interest', and 'Permanent Exhibitions' are particularly useful. The office is open from 8.30 am daily except Sunday and closes at 3 pm Monday to Thursday, 11 am Friday and 1 pm Saturday.

The Directorate General of Tourism (the National Tourist Organisation of Indonesia) is at Jalan Kramat Raya 81.

The Pelni ticketing office (tel 358398) is at Jalan Pintu Air No 1, behind the Istiqlal Mosque. The office is open from 8.30 am to 12 noon and 1 pm to 2 pm Monday to Friday; 8.30 am to 12 noon Saturday.

The main post office and efficient poste restante is on Jalan Pos, opposite Pasar Baru, off to the north-east of the monument. It is open from 8 am to 4 pm Monday to Friday, 8 am to 1 pm Saturday and there is a 50 rp charge for each letter from poste restante. It's a good half hour's walk from the centre or you can take a No 12 bus from Jalan Thamrin.

Districts of Jakarta include the old Dutch town Kota and the adjoining Chinatown, Glodok. Menteng is the foreigners' enclave, Kebayoran is the new suburban area.

The main railway station, Gambir, is just to the east of the monument. There are suburban bus stations in all the main city districts and several inter-city bus stations – Grogol in the west, Cililitan in the south and Pulo Gadung in the east. Jakarta's airports are about to go through some upheaval, see the airport section under Getting Around. It used to be possible to get cheap vaccinations at the health department at Halim International Airport.

Things to See
Sunda Kelapa This is undoubtedly the best sight in Jakarta – the old Dutch port where you will see more sailing ships, the magnificent Buginese Makassar schooners, than you ever thought existed. To get there take a blue No 70 bus, or the less crowded P11 express bus, from Jalan Thamrin down to Kota, and then walk (or take the unique local transport – a ride on a 'kiddie seat' on the back of a pushbike). There is a 50 rp admission charge to the harbour, but ultra-spendthrifts can avoid it by going around to the fish market (across the bridge) and cutting through to the watergate of Kampong Luar Batang. Old men will take you in row boats, from the docks or the village gate, around the schooners for about 300 rp. Spend an hour or so rowing around them – avoiding decapitation by the mooring ropes and gangplanks and occasionally having rubbish thrown on you from the ships. If you go out to the Thousand Islands (Pulau Seribu) in the Bay of Jakarta you will probably see Makassar schooners under sail.

The early-morning fish market, Pasar Ikan, is close by and in the same area one of the old Dutch East India Company warehouses has been turned into a maritime museum (Museum Bahari). Admission is 100 rp and it's open from 9 am every day except Monday; it closes at 2 pm Tuesday to Thursday, 11 am Friday, 1 pm Saturday, 2 pm Sunday. For free you can climb up inside the old watchtower near the bridge for a good view of the harbour area.

Old Jakarta (Kota) There's still a Dutch flavour to this old part of town – it's gradually being restored, but cleaning up the stinking canals is a superhuman task. Take a Kota bus to get there. The Kota bus terminal is right next to the last remaining old Dutch drawbridge across the Kali Besar canal. If you cross the bridge and walk south along the canal you'll pass two early 18th century houses – the Toko Merah or 'Red Shop', which is the office of PT Dharma Niaga, and a large yellow house now used by the Chartered Bank. Cross the canal again and you can cut through to the Taman Fatahillah square.

Standing on the open cobbled square is the old City Hall which houses the Old Batavia Museum (also known as the Sejarah Jakarta Museum). There are some interesting exhibits of Dutch colonial life and the building itself, dating from 1710, is impressive. The City Hall was also the main prison compound of Batavia – in the basement there are cells and 'water-prisons' where often more than 300 people were kept. Admission to the museum is 100 rp. It opens at 9 am every day except Monday and closes at 2 pm Tuesday to Thursday, 11 am Friday, 1 pm Saturday, and 3 pm Sunday.

The old Portuguese canon (Si Jagur or 'Mr Fertility'), opposite the museum, was believed by women to be a cure for barrenness because of its strange clenched fist (a symbol of fertility on Java) and Latin inscription ('Ex me ipsa renata sum' – 'Out of myself I was reborn'). Women used to offer flowers to the canon and sit on top of it before it was moved to the safety of a museum for a few years to stop this ritual.

Across the square, on Jalan Pintu Besar Utara, the Wayang Museum has an excellent display of puppets not only from Indonesia but also China, Malaysia, India and Kampuchea. Wayang golek or kulit performances are put on every Sunday between 10 am and 1.30 pm. In the Balai Seni Rupa and Museum Keramik, on the east side of the square, there's a small gallery of modern Indonesian paintings and a collection of ceramics. (Opening hours and admissions are the same as the Old Batavia Museum.)

Nearby at Jalan Pangeran Jayakarta 1 is the 1695 Gereja Sion, the oldest remaining church in Jakarta. It was built outside the old city walls for the 'black Portuguese' who were brought to Batavia as slaves and given their freedom if they joined the Dutch Reformed Church. Glodok was the old Chinatown of Batavia. It is now a centre of trade, banking and entertainment but, behind the new Glodok shopping plazas, the lanes off Jalan Pancoran are still crammed with narrow crooked houses, small shops, temples and market stalls.

Monuments Inspired tastelessness best describes the plentiful supply of monuments Sukarno left to Jakarta – all in the Russian 'heroes of socialism' style. The giant column in Merdeka Square (Sukarno's last erection) is, according to a tourist brochure, 'constructed entirely of Italian marbles'. It costs 1250 rp (500 rp for students) to go to the top (9 am to 4.30 pm) and 300 rp (100 rp for students) to get into the National History Museum, which is 'so atrocious it shouldn't be missed' according to one traveller. 'Quite interesting' according to another, who felt it gave a good rundown on Indonesia's history. The lines to get up the monument are lengthy: tourists on the weekend, schoolkids on the weekdays.

All the other monuments have acquired descriptive nicknames – like the gentleman holding the flaming dish who is known as 'the mad waiter'. To the north of Merdeka square is the gleaming white Presidential Palace; to the north-east is the vast Istiqlal Mosque, the largest mosque in South-East Asia. The Jakarta Fair is held at the square from early June to mid-July. There are plans for holding wayang kulit and wayang goleck performances outdoors in the Jakarta Fair area on the second and fourth Saturdays of each month so it's worth checking with the Tourist office. They're to be all-night performances from 9 pm and admission about 300 to 500 rp.

Indonesian National Museum Situated on the west side of Merdeka Square this is one of the most interesting museums in South-East Asia. It has excellent displays of pottery and porcelain, a huge ethnic

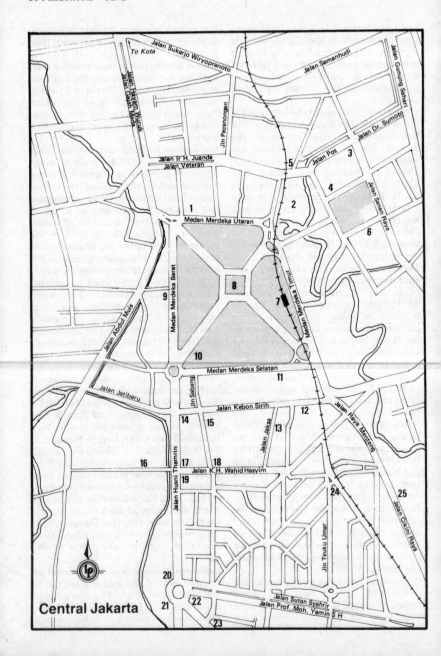

Central Jakarta

map of Indonesia and an equally big relief map on which you can pick out all those volcanoes you have climbed. Admission to the museum is 50 rp and it's open from 8.30 daily except Monday, to 2.30 pm Tuesday to Thursday, 11 am on Friday, 1.30 pm on Saturday, 2.30 pm on Sunday. On Sundays the treasure room is also open. There are worthwhile free guided tours in English on Tuesday, Wednesday and Thursday at 9.30 am. Gamelan performances are held between 9.30 and 10.30 am every Sunday.

Textile Museum This excellent museum is in an old Dutch colonial house on Jalan Satsuit Tubun, west of the National Museum past a huge daily market. It has a large collection of fabrics from all over Indonesia plus looms, batik-making tools and so on. Opening hours are like those of the other Jakarta museums and admission is 100 rp.

Taman Mini-Indonesia This is another of those 'the whole country in one park' collections which every South-East Asian country seems to be acquiring. It's near the Halim airport – take a bus No 408 or P11 express to Cililitan and then a metro-mini T55 (marked 'Mini-Indonesia') to the park entrance. It's open from 9 am to 5 pm daily (houses close at 4 pm); admission is 300 rp and the exhibits include 27 traditional houses for the 27 provinces of Indonesia and a lagoon 'map' where you

can row around the islands of Indonesia. Allow 1½ hours to get there and three hours to look around. It's pretty good value. On Sunday mornings there are free cultural performances in most regional houses and a monthly calendar of various events is available at the Visitor's Information Centre.

Taman Impian Jaya Ancol 'Dreamland' is on the bayfront between Kota and Tanjung Priok harbour. This huge amusement complex has an oceanarium and an amazing swimming pool complex with wave making facilities (800 rp, open 7 am to 9 pm). Pasar Seni – the art market – has an exhibition gallery, numerous small shops and sidewalk cafes, and is also worth a visit. Admission to the park is 300 rp but avoid it on weekends when it's crowded – and more expensive. Take a bus to Kota and then a No 64 or 65 bus or a minibus M15.

Taman Ismail Marzuki TIM is the Jakarta cultural centre, with all kinds of cultural performances – western as well as Indonesian. Here you can see everything from Balinese dancing to poetry readings; movies to gamelan concerts; a batik exhibition or the planetarium. Events are listed in the TIM monthly program and in the daily Jakarta Post. A No 34 bus from Jalan Thamrin for Megaria/Rawamangun will get you to TIM at Jalan Cikini Raya 73.

1 Presidential Palace	14 Qantas
2 Istiqlal Mosque	15 Natrabu Restaurant
3 Post Office	16 Wisma Ise
4 Cathedral	17 Information Office
5 Pelni Ticketing	18 Bali International Hotel
6 Borobudur Hotel	19 Sarinah Department Store
7 Gambir Station	20 Australian Embassy
8 Merdeka Monument	21 Hotel Indonesia
9 National Museum	22 British Embassy
10 Taman Ria Amusement Park	23 Thai Embassy
11 US Embassy	24 Immigration Department
12 Pondok Sudibjo	25 TIM Cultural Centre
13 Wisma Delima (Jalan Jaksa)	

Thousand Islands Pulau Seribu start only a few km out in the Bay of Jakarta. Some of them are virtually deserted and have fine beaches; some are crowded out, particularly on weekends. From Pasar Ikan it's four hours to Pulau Panggang and you can reach other islands from there. There are also daily boats to some islands, or boats can be hired, from the Marina at Ancol. It's a one hour boat trip (15 km) from the Marina to Pulau Bidadari and you can reach other islands from there; a boat leaves at 10.30 am and returns 3 or 4 pm, 6000 rp return. The Pulau Putri islands, 75 km out, are being developed as Jakarta's 'tropical paradise' resort. You can get information about the Pulau Seribu Paradise resort from their office in the Jakarta Theatre Building on Jalan Wahid Hasyim.

Other The Jakarta Ragunan Zoo, in the Pasar Minggu district south of the city, has Komodo dragons, orang-utans and other interesting Indonesian wildlife. The Sarinah department store with its fine handicrafts section is always worth a wander. There are also antique market stalls along Jalan Surabaya and at Jalan Pramuka there is a bird market. At 8.15 pm every evening except Monday and Thursday wayang orang can be seen at the Bharata Theatre, Jalan Kalilio 15 near Pasar Senen. Ketoprak performances take place here on Monday and Thursday evenings.

The Ganesha Society has weekly films or lectures about Indonesia at Erasmus Huis by the Dutch Embassy, south of the centre, for 1000 rp. The National Museum has their schedule, or ask the volunteer guides there – they are another Ganesha Society project.

If you want to get away from Jakarta for a few days try Carita Beach on the west coast of Java. The *Carita Krakatau Beach Hotel* has some hostel accommodation and you can get a hostel card from the Visitors' Information Centre which is good for a 25% discount on your first night. It's a three to four hour bus trip to

Labuan for Carita and buses go regularly from the Grogol station – see the section on the 'West Coast' for more information.

Places to Stay

Jakarta's cheap accommodation centre is Jalan Jaksa, a small street very centrally located in the newer part of Jakarta. It runs between Jalan Kebon Sirih and Jalan Wahid Hasyim, a few blocks over from Jakarta's main drag – Jalan Thamrin.

Jakarta's most popular resting place is *Wisma Delima* at Jalan Jaksa 5; in fact simply asking for 'Jalan Jaksa' will get you to Wisma Delima. If it looks a little chaotic at first glance you'll soon realise that is exactly how it is all the time – well, what can you expect – demand always exceeds supply. Despite the pressure it's a friendly place and a great contact point. Dormitory beds are 1500 rp (1250 rp if you're a YHA member), or there are rooms from 2500 to 5000 rp. The Lawalatas, who run number 5, are unfailingly helpful and calm in the face of non-stop demand for space they simply do not have. You can also get food and cold drinks here, breakfast is 750 rp and other meals 1500 rp or more. These are excellent value for Jakarta although they take a while to prepare. Not everybody seems to like number 5, but before you decide it's not good value it's worth contemplating just how much everything else in Jakarta costs – it's an expensive city.

There are a number of other places along and close to Jalan Jaksa which act as overflow points or alternatives. At No 17, *Hotel Nick* has dorm beds and rooms at 3000 and 4000 rp. It's run by helpful (chess crazy) people and food is available although it's quite expensive. At No 27 the old Wisma Esther has just been redecorated and reopened as the *Djody Hostel*. Dormitory beds cost 2500 rp, or there are rooms for 5000 rp and 6000 rp with fan. It has showers, and there are open sitting areas at front and back. *Number 40* has singles for 2500 rp, doubles for 4500 rp. At No 32-34 there's the higher-class *Hotel*

Karya with rooms from 11,000 rp for a double with fan and bathroom, including breakfast. There are more expensive rooms with air-con and hot and cold water.

At No 35 on Kebon Sirih Barat Dalam, running west off Jalan Jaksa, is the fairly new *Borneo Hostel* (tel 32 0095). It's got a 2000 rp dorm and rooms from 7000 rp and seems to get mixed reports – some people think it's a useful addition to the cheap hotel scene, others that it's unfriendly and expensive. At No 1 on the same lane the *Wim Homestay* (tel 32 7725) is a spacious family home with half a dozen extra rooms upstairs for guests. Singles cost 3500 rp and doubles 5000 rp, and you can also get breakfast for 750 rp. It's clean and friendly with a small patio garden downstairs and a balcony with chairs.

On Gang 1, a small connecting alley between Jalan Jaksa and Jalan Kebon Sirih Timur Dalam (east off Jalan Jaksa), there are two new and popular places. The *Kresna* at No 175 has only five rooms for guests but they're very accommodating and they'll shift the family if they're full. Doubles cost 5000 rp and it's a friendly place, recommended by a long-term stayer. Across the road at No 173 the small *Bloem Steen* has three rooms for 4000 and 5000 rp, good showers and there is a nice garden terrace. Food and drinks are available at reasonable prices.

Continue along Jalan Kebon Sirih, slightly beyond Jalan Jaksa, and behind the travel agent at 23 you'll find the very pleasant little *Pondok Sudibjo*. Built around a courtyard it's almost like a Balinese losmen and delightfully quiet for Jakarta. There are doubles for 6000 rp, one triple for 7000 rp, including breakfast.

Jalan Kebon Sirih is at one end of Jalan Jaksa; Jalan Wahid Hasyim is at the other. Walk back towards Jalan Thamrin to the *Bali International Hotel* at Jalan Wahid Hasyim 116. It's a largish and rather ugly hotel but has dormitory beds for 5000 rp and non air-con rooms from 7000 rp.

Keep walking along Jalan Wahid Hasyim across Jalan Thamrin and at No 168 you'll come to the *Wisma Ise Guest House* (tel 333463). It's pretty plain, but fair value for Jakarta with rooms at 5000/6000 rp for singles/doubles. Breakfast here also costs 750 rp. It's clean and friendly and there's a pleasant balcony/bar at the back where you can look out over quite a bit of Jakarta.

Places to Eat

Food in Jakarta tends to be expensive if it's any good. Jalan Jaksa's meals are one of the best deals going and apart from the accommodation places themselves on that street there is also *Angies* at No 16 – just a few tables in the front garden but it's popular and the food is good and cheap. At night the car park of Sarinah turns into a food market, lots of stalls set up around the central area of the city and there are plenty of places in old Jakarta too. Jalan Kebon Sirih and Wahid Hasyim have a collection of food stalls but check them first as some are of dubious cleanliness.

On the corner of Jalan Jaksa, the *Senayan Satay House* at Jalan Kebon Sirih 31A serves good Indonesian food and prices are very reasonable, most meals around 1,000 to 2,000 rp. Jalan Haji Agus Salim, about midway between Jalan Jaksa and Jalan Thamrin, has a string of fairly good places including the popular *Natrabu Restaurant* which specialises in Padang food. The cheaper *Budi Bundo* also serves good Padang food. The shiny, Japanese-run *Modern Bakery* at 25/27 is clean and reasonably priced and has ice creams and cheap drinks. Across the road there's a sort of Indonesian imitation of McDonald's; the milkshakes are good. Down a little alley off the road at Jalan Haji Agus Salim 30 the *Paradiso 2001* is a new vegetarian restaurant with good food and a claim that they're 'a restaurant for men of the future'. Women and children of the future can eat there too.

The *Mini Indah Restaurant* does good

cap cai – turn left out of Jalan Jaksa on Jalan K H Wahid Hasyim and it's at the multi-road junction. At No 212 on the same road the *Pasar Raya* is a Padang restaurant with cheap and quite good food and at No 49 there's a tiny garden warung serving nasi gudeg and very cheap beer.

Continuing down to Jalan Thamrin the *Jakarta Cafeteria* in the same building as the tourist office and the telephone office is not bad. The Sarinah department store on Jalan Thamrin has an excellent (though expensive) bakery downstairs. The *Sari Bunga* at 131A Jalan Wahid Hasyim, the other side of Thamrin near the Wisma Ise, has been recommended – good cheap

Javanese food and ice juices. The *Gumarang Restaurant* by the harbour entrance has good Padang food and cheap beer.

At the entrance to the cinema on Medan Merdeka Selatan you can get a good, filling meal for just 200 or 300 rps from the guys who sell fried food hot from the wok there. On Jalan Pecanongan there are night market food stalls with good Chinese and seafood. Jalan Pecanongan, about three km from Jalan Jaksa past the Merdeka Monument, runs north-to-south between Jalan Juanda and Jalan Batutulis, directly north of the monument. In the same area the *Jun Njan* at Jalan Batu

Ceper 69 specialises in seafood and delicious fried squid in oyster sauce for 4000 rp; it's not cheap but a great place for splashing out (closed Monday). There's also a night market (Pasar Boplo), north of the GPO, for good warung food. Jalan Mangga Besar, off Jalan Hayam Wuruk in the north, is another night market area.

You'll find plenty of Chinese restaurants in Glodok and a wide variety of food in the Pasar Senen shopping centre, a km east of the monument – but daytime only. The Blok M shopping centre, way down Jalan Thamrin, also has a wide variety of places to eat. Good American icecream here at Swensen's.

Finally if you want to give your taste buds a real treat there are plenty of expensive places to eat in and around the 'international' hotels. It's worth laying out the 5000 rp for the 80-dish smorgasbord at *Vic's Viking Restaurant* on Jalan Thamrin between the Hotel Indonesia and Kartika Plaza. The *Mitra* roof-garden restaurant on Jalan Kebon Sirih also does a good smorgasbord for 4000 rp. The *Omar Khayam* at Jalan Antara 5-7, near the GPO, serves an Indian buffet lunch for 6000 rp.

Getting There

See the introductory Getting Around Java section for details of Jakarta-Yogyakarta and Jakarta-Surabaya transport.

Air The domestic airline offices are dotted around the city. Garuda (tel 333408) has a branch office conveniently located in the Wisma Nusantara building on Jalan Thamrin. Mandala (tel 368107) is at Jalan Veteran I/No 34, en route to the Pelni office. Merpati (tel 413608) is at Jalan Angkasa 2, Bouraq (tel 625150) at Jalan Angkasa 1; both near Kemayoran airport.

In the Pasar Baru district there are travel agents who will discount domestic airline tickets – particularly Merpati and Mandala tickets. For flights to Nusa Tenggara, Sulawesi, Sumatra or Bali you can get as much as 25% discount. There are plenty of agents around; try Mitra Kercana Tour & Travel Service (tel 349699, 361366), Jalan Pintu Air 20A, near the Pelni office.

For international flights Kaliman Travel (tel 330101) in the President Hotel on Jalan Thamrin is a good place for cheap tickets and offer a discount on some airline tickets if you pay in cash. They're open from 8 am to 6 pm daily, but close at 2 pm on Sunday. Other agents worth checking are Vayatour (tel 336640) next door to Kaliman, and Pacto Ltd (tel 320309) at Jalan Cikini Raya 24. Fares being quoted include Singapore US$160 (return), Bangkok US$290, Kuala Lumpur US$145, Hong Kong US$332, Sydney US$446, US West Coast US$650, Bombay US$430, London US$610. The agent for AUS (Australian Union of Students) is Travair Buana (tel 371479) in the Hotel Sabang, Jalan Haji Agus Salim. As from September 1984 any student with an international student card can pay an AUS fare which is cheaper than the normal 25% student discount on airline tickets and cheaper than fares listed above.

Train Jakarta has a number of train stations, the most convenient of which is Gambir, beside the Merdeka Square. Pasar Senen is further south and Kota is in the old city area in the north. Tanah Abang is off to the west of the square and trains to Merak, for the ferry to Sumatra, go from here; there is a train in the early morning and another late afternoon. From Gambir trains to Bogor depart every hour and take 1½ hours at a cost of about 350 rp which can be faster than by bus. There are four daily Parahiyangan trains to Bandung; the trip takes about 3½ hours and it's a comfortable train, 4500 rp in second class.

Bus There are also a number of bus stations. There are city bus stations in all main districts of Jakarta and buses radiate out from them to the suburban inter-city stations. Buses to towns around Jakarta go from the Cililitan suburban station out towards Halim airport. Buses from here include Bogor (500 rp), Puncak, Sukabumi, Pelabuhan Ratu and Bandung (1700 rp). Buses to the east operate from the Pulo Gadung station; the bus to Cirebon costs 2200 rp, night buses to Yogya cost from 5500 rp. Buses for Merak depart every 10 minutes or so and go from the Grogol bus station in the north-west.

Taxis There are fast and convenient, but rather more expensive, inter-city taxis and minibuses to Bandung. They will pick you up and drop you off at your hotel. Parahiangan (tel 325539 in Jakarta) is at Jalan Wahid Hasyim 13. '4848' (tel 348048) is at Jalan Prapatan 34. Fares start at 7000 rp and taxis depart as soon as they have five passengers.

Getting Around

Airport Airport tax is 4000 rp on international flights; it varies up to 2000 rp on domestic ones. Jakarta's airport picture is scheduled to undergo some major upheavals during 1985. The old Kemayoran domestic airport, very centrally located, is scheduled to be closed. It was only used for a very limited number of flights in any case. The present Halim International Airport will also be phased out of the airline picture, replaced by the new Cenkareng International Airport which will handle all international and domestic flights.

The new airport is 20 km west of the centre. A new road is being built to link it to the city and a bus service between the airport and Gambir is planned. From the old Halim airport (16 km from the centre) a taxi into town would cost around 3500 rp – taxis are metered but make sure the meter is switched on. Or, from the entrance gate, you could take a pale blue Trans-Halim minibus to Cililitan (200 rp) and then a No 408 or P11 bus to Jalan Thamrin (150 rp). Jakarta buses, though, are all hopelessly crowded and getting on board with a backpack would be nearly impossible.

The Wisma Delima losmen on Jalan Jaksa has been operating a good-value minibus service to Halim (and to Tanjung Priok harbour) and will probably do so to Cenkareng. The minibus takes eight passengers and, to Halim or Tanjung Priok, costs 4000 rp for one to three people and an extra 1000 rp for each additional person.

Tanjung Priok Harbour The Pelni ships all use Pelabuhan (dock) No 1 – it's two km from the dock, past the Pelni office, to the Tanjung Priok bus station. From Tanjung Priok take a No 64 bus or pale blue minibus M15 to Kota and from there a No 70 bus to Sarinah store on Jalan Thamrin. Tanjung Priok is 20 km from the centre of the city so allow at least an hour to get there. A taxi will cost around 3000 rp.

Bus The regular big city buses charge a fixed 150 rp and the express Patas buses, which are usually less crowded, charge 250 rp. The central Banteng station has been replaced by a new Pasar Senen station, not far away, off to the east side of Merdeka Square. Take a No 10 bus from Pasar Senen to Sarinah department store on Jalan Thamrin for Jalan Jaksa. There are a number of other stations for suburban and inter-city buses, like the Cililitan suburban station or the Grogol and Pulo Gadung bus stations. The regular bus service is supplemented by orange metro-minis (minibuses) which cost 150 rp and, in a few areas, pale blue microlet buses which cost 200 rp.

If you arrive in Jakarta at the Cililitan bus station a No 408 or P11 express bus will take you down Jalan Thamrin and if you get off at the Sarinah Department store it's only a short stroll to Jalan Jaksa. From the Pulo Gadung bus station a No 59 bus will take you to Sarinah's on Jalan Thamrin – from Kota station a No 70 bus or the P11 will get you there. From Grogol take a No 16 bus. Buses all have their ultimate destination on the front.

Beware of pickpockets on Jakarta buses – they're great bag slashers too.

Train Stations There are several train stations in Jakarta. Most convenient is the

Gambir Station, right beside the Merdeka Square on the east side. It's within walking distance of Jalan Jaksa (staggering if your gear is heavy). Walking may be necessary since the taxi and bajaj drivers who meet the trains here are a mercenary lot of bastards; it's better to take a metered taxi rather than argue with them. Kota Station, for the Bima and Mutiara night trains, is in the old part of town. Allow plenty of time to get there during the rush hour – a metered taxi would be about 1500 rp from Jalan Jaksa. Other stations are Pasar Senen off to the south-east of Jalan Jaksa and Tanah Abang directly to the west of Merdeka square. Trains for Merak and Sumatra depart from Tanah Abang.

Other Transport Taxis in Jakarta have real working meters; just make sure they aren't 'broken' before you get in and check they get switched on. Bajajs are nothing less than Indian auto-rickshaws, three wheelers that carry two passengers (three at a squeeze) and are powered by noisy two-stroke engines. You can get most places for 300 to 600 rp but bajajs are not allowed along Jalan Thamrin. Becaks (bicycle rickshaws) are only allowed into the city centre after 10 pm, most trips cost from 200 to 500 rp. Jakarta also has some weird and wonderful means of getting around – like the 'Morris' bemos that run mainly down Jalan Gajah Madah and are all old English Morris vans. And near the Pasar Ikan in Kota there are the push bikes with a padded carrier on the back.

MERAK

This is the port at the western end of Java for the ferry crossing to Sumatra. It's a small place and the bus and train station are within easy walking distance of each other. The ferry to Panjang leaves at 11 am and 11 pm from the dock near the train station and takes four to six hours. It costs from 1300 rp in third class. Ferries to Bakauheni depart every hour from the dock near the bus station and the trip takes 1½ hours, from 750 rp in third class.

Refer to the 'Getting There' section in Sumatra for greater detail.

Places to Stay

If you have to spend the night in Merak there are a couple of reasonable losmen just across the railway line, opposite the bus station, on Jalan Florida. The *Hotel Anda* has single rooms for 4000 rp, doubles 6000 rp. The *Hotel Robinson* is right next door.

Getting There

Buses for Merak depart roughly every 10 minutes – between 3 am and 12 pm – from the Grogol bus station in Jakarta and take about 3½ hours, 1200 rp. Trains leave at 6.15 am and 5 pm from the Tanah Abang railway station. The day train is faster and links up with the daytime ferry service to Panjang.

From Merak it's a short trip to Carita Beach (Pantai Carita), just north of Labuan on the west coast. Take the Jakarta bus to Cilegon and from there a colt along the coast road to Carita.

BANTEN

En route to Merak from Jakarta you pass through Serang, the turn off point for the historic town of Banten where the first haggard Dutchmen to set foot on Java arrived in 1596. In the 16th and 17th centuries the town was the centre of a great and wealthy sultanate but it's hardly a splendid city now. There's not a lot to see around this small coastal village but Banten has an interesting mosque, *Mesjid Agung*, and a great white lighthouse of a minaret which was designed by a Chinese Muslim in the early 17th century. The old palaces are now in ruins and the Dutch Speelwijk fortress, built in 1682, is equally ruined.

WEST COAST

There are good beaches along the west coast south of Merak at Anyer, Karang Bolong and Carita. Anyer has a luxury beach motel but the 'rustic style' *Carita*

Krakatau Beach Hotel, further south near Labuan, does have a few hostel rooms for 3000 rp single, 4000 rp double. The hotel hostel card, available from the Visitors' Information Centre in Jakarta, is good for a 25% discount on your first night. The hotel restaurant is not cheap – eg a bowl of soup costs 1500 rp and a nasi goreng will set you back 2200 rp – but there are a couple of simple (very) warungs close by.

This is a good base for visits to the Krakatau Islands in the Sunda Strait, about 50 km from Carita and Labuan, and to the Ujong Kulon Nature Reserve. Boat hire is expensive, and difficult during the wet season, but if you're interested in either place ask to see the hotel's video documentary about Krakatau's explosion and its effects on the west coast – it's free!

Carita is a pleasant place if you want to get away from Jakarta for a few days but it's close enough to the capital for it to get fairly crowded at weekends. Buses go hourly from the Grogol station – look for signs 'Jakarta-Labuan'; the trip takes about three to four hours and the fare is 1700 rp. From Labuan a colt will take you the seven km to the hotel at Carita Beach (Pantai Carita) for 250 rp.

BOGOR

The Kebun Raya are huge botanical gardens 60 km outside Jakarta. They were founded in 1817 by Sir Stamford Raffles during the British interregnum, and have a huge collection of tropical plants. A monument to Raffles' wife, Olivia, is near the main entrance to the gardens. The Presidential Palace, built by the Dutch and much favoured by Sukarno although Suharto has ignored it, stands beside the gardens and deer graze on the palace lawns. The gardens are a popular place on the weekends for young guys and girls from Jakarta to flirt safe from parental eyes. Admission to the gardens is a fairly hefty 800 rp – its cheaper on Sundays but the crowds are too heavy for comfort. Bogor also has a good zoological museum

with a blue whale skeleton and other interesting exhibits.

Information

Bogor's Visitor's Information Centre is at Jalan Ir H Juanda 38, west of the gardens. At number 9 on the same street, next to the garden gates, is the headquarters of the PPA (Perlindungan dan Pengawetan Alam) – the official body for administration of all of Indonesia's wildlife reserves.

Places to Stay

Bogor is not a great place for losmen so many people visit the gardens from Jakarta. A good alternative to Bogor's dreary losmen is the *Kopo Hostel* at Cisarua which is cheap and pleasant – see 'Around Bogor'.

Only about five minutes walk from the train station is *Losmen Damai* at Jalan Mayor Oking 28, which is a bit drab and grubby (well, the rooms are OK, but the toilets are terrible) and costs from 3500 rp for a double. Or over the railway tracks and the river, away from the gardens, *Penginapan Pasundan* is at Jalan Mantarena 19, close behind Jalan Veteran. It's more expensive but hardly any better – doubles with bathroom cost from 6000 rp. The *Wisma Teladan* at Jalan Sawojajar 3A, a short walk from the train station along Jalan Dewi Sartika, is similarly priced but much more pleasant.

Other places are quite a bit more expensive – the *Hotel Salak* is at Jalan Ir H Juanda 8 and costs from 11,000 rp. It's opposite the palace and has a variety of singles and doubles with and without bath. It's a big and rather run-down place but the staff are very friendly. Or there's the *Elsana Transit Hotel* (seems to define Bogor) at Jalan Sawojajar 36, which is not as pleasant as the Salak and even eore expensive – roods start from around 14,000 rp.

Places to Eat

Try the *Lautan Bakery & Restaurant* or

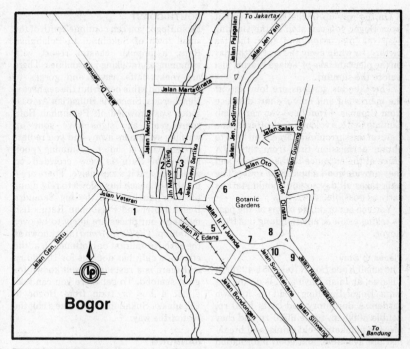

Bogor

1 Penginapan
2 Losmen Damai
3 Railway Station
4 Bemo Station
5 Tourist Office
6 Presidential Palace
7 Garden Entrance &
  Zoological Museum
8 Orchid House
9 Bus Station

the *Bogor Permai Coffee House* restaurants for good food, both on Jalan Jen Sudirman near Jalan Sawojajar. The *Hotel Salak* has a pleasant restauraft with an extensive menu but it's probably best to stick to nasi goreng. There's lots of good fruit available in the Pasar Bogor (market) where you'll also find a range of food stalls. Behind the bus station there are a number of cheap warungs serving good food.

Getting There

Trains operate to and from Jakarta hourly and cost 400 rp. The trip takes about 1½ hours which can be slightly faster than by bus. Buses for Bogor (500 rp) depart from the Cililitan bus station in Jakarta. Take a Jalan Jagorawi bus which goes via the expressway and is a fair bit faster and only marginally more expensive than the buses which go via Cibinong.

AROUND BOGOR

At Cibodas, just over the Puncak Pass, there is a cooler, high altitude extension of the Bogor botanical gardens. There are tea plantations and a number of small resort towns on the way up and over the beautiful Puncak Pass between Bogor and Bandung. You can make pleasant walks from Tugu and Cisarua on the Bogor side of the pass or Cibodas and Cipanas on the other side.

On the way up to the Puncak summit from Bogor you can stop at the Gunung Mas tea plantation and tour the tea factory, or while away the rest of the day on the pleasant lake of Telaga Warna, just before the summit.

The Cibodas gardens are four km off the main road and only a short distance from Cipanas. From here you can climb Gunung Gede, a volcano peak offering fine views of the surrounding area. You have to obtain permission first from the PPA office at the entrance to the gardens and they provide good maps of the route. The walk takes all day so you should start as early as possible.

You can get up to the towns on the pass by taking a colt or any Bandung bus from Bogor.

Places to Stay

The small *Kopo Hostel* (tel 0251-4296) in Cisarua, at Jalan Raya 502, is on the the main Bogor-Bandung road in its own garden. A dormitory bed costs 1500 rp, double 5000 rp, triple 6000 rp and they provide blankets. Cold drinks and breakfast are available, and good information on the area. The hostel is open from 7 am to 10 pm and from Bogor it's about ¾ hour by bus or colt (300 rp). Ask for the Cisarua Petrol Station *Pompa Bensin Cisarua* –the hostel is right next door.

Also in Cisarua, the *Chalet Bali International* is affiliated with the Bali International in Jakarta and has dormitory beds for 3500 rp – rooms from 10,000 rp.

In Cibulan the *Hotel Cibulan* is an old-world Dutch hotel – run-down but friendly. Rooms cost from around 5000 rp; they're more expensive on weekends when people from Jakarta flock up here to escape the heat.

The new *Pondok Pemuda Cibodas* near the Cibodas PPA office is comfortable and friendly and has dormitory beds for 3750 rp, doubles for 7500 rp. Or in the village, 500 metres down the hill, you can stay with Muhamed Saleh Abdullah for 500 to 1000 rp.

SOUTH COAST

From Bogor you can continue south of the small town of Sukabumi to Pelabuhan Ratu, a popular coastal resort with swimming and walking possibilities. There are rocky cliffs, caves and gorges to explore and a fine beach but the sea here is treacherous. Since the Bulgarian Ambassador was drowned off Pelabuhan Ratu some years ago signs have gone up warning swimmers away, and you're best off enjoying a hotel swimming pool. Pelabuhan Ratu is very crowded on weekends and it's expensive. There are a number of beach bungalows to rent along the four km between the big Samudra Beach Hotel and Pelabuhan Ratu's fish market – but prices are likely to be over 10,000 rp. The *Bayu Armta* (also known as the Fish Restaurant or Hoffman's), at the edge of a cliff, has doubles for 10,000 rp and there is a restaurant well known for good seafood. To get there you can take either a bus or train from Bogor to Cibadak or Sukabumi, then take a colt the rest of the way.

BANDUNG

The capital of West Java and third largest city in Indonesia, Bandung's chief claim to fame is that it was the site for the first (and so far only) Afro-Asian conference back in 1955. Third World leaders from all over converged on Bandung and not much seems to have happened since. Due to its 750-metre altitude the climate in Bandung is fairly cool and comfortable. Treat it as a short stop between Yogya and Jakarta – it's worth a brief pause to visit the nearby volcano Tangkuban Perahu and from Bandung it's a good idea to take the bus to Bogor in order to see the beautiful Puncak Pass. Bandung is a big university town and students tend to monopolise the cheaper losmen.

There's a helpful Visitor's Information Centre on the corner of the main square on Jalan Asia Afrika, and the West Java Regional Tourist office is on Jalan Braga in the Gedung Merdeka building.

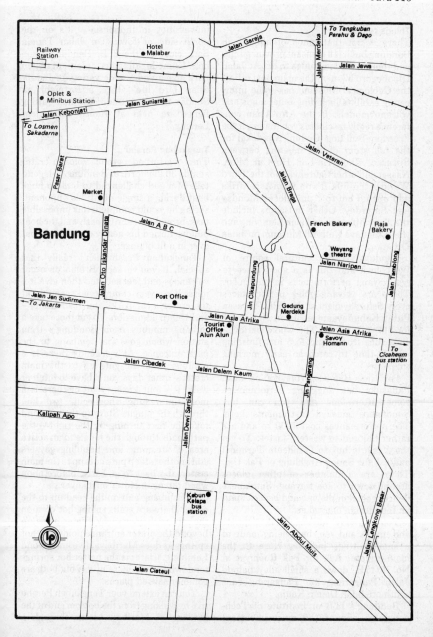

Things to See

There is not that much of interest in Bandung but it is a pleasant provincial city and there are a few things to do. At Jalan Diponegoro 57, near the main post office, the Geological Museum has some interesting exhibits including relief maps and volcano models. If the Afro-Asian conference really fascinates you then visit the Freedom Building (Gedung Merdeka) for the full story of the meeting between Sukarno, Chou En-Lai, Ho Chi Minh, Nasser and other figureheads of the Third World of the '50s. It's on Jalan Asia Afrika and open 8 am to 1 pm, closed Monday and Saturday. Other museums include the Army Museum on Jalan Lembong and the West Java Cultural Museum on Jalan Ottista.

Bandung is the cultural centre of West Java and this is a good place to see wayang performances in particular. There are wayang golek performances every Saturday night at the YPK (Yayasan Pusat Kebudayaan) at Jalan Naripan 7 for 500 to 700 rp. The whole performance runs from 9 pm to 5 am, finishing just in time to catch an early morning train out!

Pak Ujo's Bamboo Workshop on Jalan Padasuka has angklung performances some afternoons and you can buy Sundanese musical instruments here. The performances cost 3000 rp and are rather tailored to western tastes. To get there take a bus to Cicaheum Terminal and ask for Saung Angklung or Pak Ujo. There are a number of other places around town to see wayang, Sundanese dance, gamelan playing and *pencak silat*, an Indonesian martial art.

You can buy wayang golek puppets and masks and see them being made at a small cottage industry close to the main square. Ask for Pak Roehiyat at No 78/17B, down a small alley behind Jalan Pangarang 22. Pangarang runs south off Jalan Dalem Kaum.

Bandung's ITB or Institute of Technology is one of the most important universities in Indonesia – it's on the north side of town. On Jalan Taman Sari, close to the ITB, Bandung's zoo has Komodo dragons, pleasant open park space and a wide variety of Indonesian bird life. Once a fortnight on Sunday mornings traditional ram-butting fights are held at Ranca Buni near Ledeng.

Tangkuban Perahu

The 'overturned perahu' volcano crater stands 30 km north of Bandung. A legend tells of a god challenged to build a huge boat during a single night; his opponent, seeing he would complete this impossible task, brought the sun up early and the boat builder turned his nearly completed boat over in a fit of anger.

Tangkuban Perahu isn't really that special. If you've seen Bromo or other volcanoes and feel satiated then give it a miss. It's a very commercial scene up at the crater – car parks and restaurants – and 150 rp admission. To get there take a Subang minibus from Bandung's train station which goes via Lembang to the park entrance. At weekends there is a minibus from the gate up to the main crater – other days you'll have to hitch or walk. It's four km by road or there is a more interesting short cut, two km, through the jungle. Start up the road and take the first turning on the right – the path leads through the jungle to an active area of steaming and bubbling geysers and another steep path cuts up to the main crater. It's best to go early, before noon when the main crater mists over.

In Lembang and on the road up to the crater there are stalls selling hot corn on the cob, a delicious snack. Ciater, a few km beyond the crater entrance point, has hot springs as does Maribaya, five km beyond Lembang. Ciater is the better hot springs for a swim on a cold, rainy day but both are commercialised places.

You can extend your Tangkuban Perahu trip by walking from the bottom end of the gardens at Maribaya down through a brilliant river gorge (there's a good track) to Dago where you can eat at the *Dago Tea House* at sunset. Allow about two hours for the walk to Dago. It's a good spot to watch the city light up. After a nasi goreng you can then get back into town for 125 rp by Honda. You can also travel straight out to the tea house by taking a Dago Honda from the train station in Bandung.

Places to Stay

Bandung is not a great place for cheaper hotels. *Losmen Sakadarna*, near the railway station and the centre of town, is quite good though with singles for 3000 rp, doubles for 4000 rp and there is a balcony with chairs. It's very friendly and they have maps and useful information on the Bandung area. From the station turn right along Jalan Kebonjati and you'll find it at 50/7B, down a small alley beside the big Hotel Melati. The *Surabaya Hotel* is near the Sakadarna at Jalan Kebonjati 71; singles cost 2300 rp, doubles 4500 rp.

Hotel Malabar at Jalan Kebun Jukut 3, just over the railway pass, has rooms from 4000 rp. It's not great value even though it's fairly clean (if a little dark) – but not bad for Bandung. Other hotels in the station area are more expensive – like the *Hotel Sahara* on Jalan Oto Iskandar Dinata and the *Hotel Guntur* on the same street, both just around the corner from the Malabar.

The *Wisma Remaja*, in a government youth centre at Jalan Merdeka 64, has dormitory beds for 2250 rp, doubles for 4500 rp and a reasonably priced cafe. It's a 20 minute walk from the railway station or take a Dago minibus and ask for the youth centre, *Gelanggang Generasi Muda Bandung*. The *Hotel Mawar* at Jalan Pangarang 14 is right in the centre of town near the main square and a short walk from the Kebun Kelapa bus station. It's quite good and has singles for 4000 rp and doubles for 4500 rp. The *Pangarang Sari Hotel* close by at No 3 has rooms with bathroom for 7000 rp, including breakfast.

Places to Eat

Restaurant food tends to be expensive but on Jalan Cikapundung Barat, directly across Asia-Afrika from the Visitor's Information Centre, there is a very appetising night market. One traveller recommended trying roti bakar here – a whole loaf sliced horizontally and spread with peanut butter and condensed milk. It sounds terrible, although he reported it to be 'delicious and filling'.

On Jalan Tamblong the *Rasa Bakery* sells very good ice cream and a wild assortment of expensive but irresistible cakes. The *French Bakery*, on nearby Jalan Braga, is also good. Or you could invest in a coffee or a drink at the genteel *Savoy Homman* on Jalan Asia-Afrika – it's an old colonial hotel and a superb example of the Art Deco period.

At the Tambuo restaurant, beside the mosque on the central square on Asia-Afrika, you'll find excellent Padang food upstairs. Or try the *Warung Nasi Mudju* on Jalan Dewi Sartika just south of the square for delicious Sundanese food, which is a combination of Javanese and Sumatran cooking styles. An assortment of dishes – steamed chicken in bamboo leaf, ginger spiced fish, meat, tempe, salad – is put in front of you and you pay for whatever you have with your rice. Sundanese food, like Padang, is eaten with the fingers – but you can use a knife and fork if you really want to cop out! At Jalan Asia-Afrika 113 the *Galaya Pub & Restaurant* is a quiet, pleasant place, although a little more expensive. The self-service section specialises in Sundanese dishes. Also on Asia-Afrika, close to the tourist office, the *Mitra* has a great all-you-can-eat buffet for 3000 rp. The little 'Cantien' next door has decent food.

The *Rose Flower* at Jalan Jen Achmad Yani 32 (this street turns into Jalan Asia-Afrika 150 metres away) has terrific Chinese food although it's rather expensive. You really need a large group to sample the variety of dishes. Or there's the *Queen Restaurant* at Jalan Dalem Kaum 79 and at Jalan Merdeka 17 the *Rumah Makan Vanda Sari* also has good, though pricey, Chinese food.

Restaurant Karjan on Jalan Pasir Kaliki, north over the railway pass, has good satay. *Restaurant Sakadarna* at Jalan Kebonjati 34 is cheap for Bandung, food is good and you can get a western-style breakfast. *Tizi's*, in a lovely garden setting out towards Dago at Jalan Kidang Pananjung 3, has a good reputation for Indonesian and European food.

Getting There

There are four daily services by the Parahiyangan trains between Jakarta and Bandung which take 3½ hours and cost from 4500 rp in second class. Three trains operate between Yogya and Bandung and the fare varies, from 3200 rp in the 3rd class slower train. Buses cost around 1700 rp to Cililitan station in Jakarta, from 5000 rp to Yogya. The bus station for Jakarta, Kebun Kelapa on Jalan Dewi Sartika, is quite central but for Yogya and other places to the east it's a 45-minute, 100 rp trip by city bus to the Cicaheum station out of town. City bus No 1 operates along Jalan Asia-Afrika to Cicaheum. Bogor is 3½ hours and 1200 rp away by bus.

Getting Around

Bandung has a fairly good city bus service using Indian Tata buses. Bus No 1 runs from east to west right down Asia-Afrika to Cicaheum. There are also plenty of bemos, Hondas and Daihatsus; for most destinations they depart from the terminal outside the railway station. Count on 125 rp for a bemo ride, only 100 rp for the city buses. There are a phenomenal number of becaks in Bandung – it's said that many Jakarta becak riders pedalled off to Bandung after they were banned from the centre of Jakarta.

GARUT

This pleasant town is between Bandung and Banjar. There are popular air panas (hot springs) just five km north of Garut at Cipanas village, Tarogong. From Garut you can climb Gunung Papandayan while east towards Banjar is Gunung Galunggung, a volcano which exploded dramatically a few years back. You can get to Galunggung by motorcycle from Tasikmalaya for 800 rp although the locals will think you nuts to want to climb it.

Places to Stay

The *Hotel National* is neither very cheap nor very friendly.

PANGANDARAN

This south coast resort is one of the few places on the south Java coast where it is safe to swim, due to a coral reef that cuts the surf and dangerous undertows. It's more or less centrally located between Yogyakarta and Bandung and Banjar, on the Yogya-Bandung road, is where you turn off. Pangandaran has beautiful broad beaches and a headland reserve with many monkeys and buffalo. There's a small 100 rp entry charge to the reserve. Avoid the weekends and holidays – at Christmas and after Ramadan in particular – when it gets very crowded but at other times this is a very peaceful and relaxing place to take a break from travel. There's good snorkelling off the white beach.

Places to Stay & Eat

Pangandaran has really grown and there are now lots of good cheap places to stay. Popular places include *Losmen Mini I* with rooms from 2500 rp including breakfast; more expensive rooms are big and have attached mandi. *Losmen Mini II*, off the main road, is cheaper and good value. There are two rooms in the house from 2000 rp single, rooms in a bamboo hut from 1500 rp, and free tea and coffee. *Losmen Laut Biru* has small rooms from 1500 rp, large rooms from 2000 to 3500 rp, and free tea and coffee. It's a good place with friendly people.

Losmen Samudra has rooms at 2000/2500 rp including free tea and it's run by

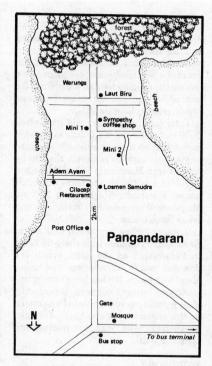

Map labels:
forest
Warungs
Laut Biru
beach
Mini 1
Sympathy coffee shop
beach
Mini 2
Adem Ayam
Losmen Samudra
Cilacap Restaurant
Post Office
2km
Pangandaran
Gate
Mosque
N
Bus stop
To bus terminal

Getting There

From Jakarta you can bus directly from Cililitan station to Banjar, via Bogor and Bandung. From Bandung you can also approach Banjar by rail – it takes about five hours from Bandung. There's a pleasant losmen across the railway lines from the Banjar station, and cheap restaurants near the bus station. The final stretch from Banjar, by bus or colt, takes about two hours and costs 700 rp. You then have to walk a couple of km or take a becak from the bus stop to the main tourist area of Pangandaran. Continuing to Yogya, or coming from Yogya, it's six to eight hours by train and nine hours by bus Banjar-Yogya.

An interesting alternative route from Yogya is to take an early morning train to Kroya. The trip takes about four to six hours and costs around 2000 rp. From there take a colt to Sleko, the port of Cilacap – about an hour's ride. Or get the 7 am minibus from the Kartika Travel Agent on Jalan Sosrowijayan in Yogya. It costs 3500 rp and will drop you right at the port in time for the last ferry around 12 am. You can also approach Cilacap from Dieng by taking a bus from Wonosobo. Early in the morning you may well have to change buses at Purwokerto. The trip takes about six hours and, with luck, you may get to Cilacap on time. It's a three-to-four hour boat trip for around 800 rp from Cilacap to Kalipucang, about 17 km from Pangandaran. It's a fascinating trip, across inland sea, from village to village. At Kalipucang it's a 500 metre walk to the main road and a half-hour, 200 rp bus ride to Pangandaran. Take a becak into Pangandaran from the bus stop. It's a long day's travel costing about three or four thousand rp in total. If you arrive in Cilacap too late to get a boat there are several losmen. *Losmen Lima* and *Losmen Bahagia* are near the ferry. *Losmen Tiga*, at Jalan Mayor Sutoyo 61, is central and about one km from the train station. It's comfortable and friendly and single rooms cost from 2000 rp.

friendly people. *Adem Ayam* is a good cheap losmen with rooms at 2000 and 2500 rp including breakfast, complete with sea breezes and views.

Most of the eating places along the main road have an English menu and serve some western-style dishes. Across the road from Laut Biru there are a number of small warungs serving good cheap food. Or you could try the *Sympathy Coffee Shop* (the best fruit salads here) or the *Restaurant Cilacap*. The Cilacap is slightly more expensive but the food is good, they always have fresh fish and delicious fruit juices in the evenings. The warungs do great fried fish (ikan goreng) and they'll cook fresh seafood if you order it during the day. You can also buy fresh fish and get it cooked and served up for dinner in your losmen.

DIENG PLATEAU

About 130 km from Yogya this 2000-metre high plateau has a number of interesting temples, some beautiful scenery, good walks and (at night) freezing temperatures. Come prepared for the night-time cold and Dieng's pretty unexciting losmen and food and you'll probably find it a very interesting place.

Dieng is the collapsed remains of an ancient crater. In the centre, where it is very swampy, there is a group of five Hindu-Buddhist temples. These temples are thought to be the oldest in Java, pre-dating Borobudur and Prambanan. There are a number of other temples scattered around. Candi Bima to the south is particularly fine but, like all too many places in Indonesia, has been defaced by graffitists.

The road forks at Bima. The right fork goes on to a sulphur-smelling area with frantically bubbling mud ponds. The left fork goes to placid Lake Warna with Semar Cave, an old meditation spot. The energetic can walk to many other places around, including the highest village in Java.

The kiosk next to Losmen Bu Jono, as you enter Dieng, sells hand drawn maps of the area but you can ignore them and get a free map at the tourist office almost next door.

Places to Stay

Bring a sleeping bag or be prepared to shiver. The Losmen Bu Jono is the only reasonable place in town. It has small, airy rooms for 1500 rp single and 2000 rp double, blankets and freezing mandi water. Good value in Dieng. Food is available at Bu Jono's or there's a very friendly warung, Sederhana, close by on the road to the mushroom factory. A spicy nasi goreng or noodles costs only 200 rp. The very unspecial Hotel Dieng Plateau, on the main road beside the tourist office, has rooms from 1000 rp and supplies blankets.

Getting There

From Yogya take a bus or colt to Magelang and another to Wonosobo. Yogya to Wonosobo takes at least three hours. From the Wonosobo market place it's a colt up the winding road to the plateau for around 500 rp. The trip takes 1½ hours uphill, only an hour downhill.

Total fare from Yogya will be around 2000 rp by bus and it's quite easy to visit Borobudur on the way although you need to start out early to complete the trip by night. Yogya-Muntilan is 300 rp, Muntilan-Borobudur is 150 rp and takes about 1½ hours. Borobudur-Magelang is 250 rp, Magelang-Wonosobo 800 rp by colt and takes three hours.

If you're feeling fit you can walk out to Bawang and continue from there by bemo to Pekalongan on the north coast. It's downhill nearly all the way and takes about four hours. If it has been raining this route can be very slippery. If you start early from Dieng you can be in Pekalongan in the afternoon. It's a quiet, friendly, hassle-free town with interesting and colourful batik.

WONOSOBO

This is a pleasant place en route to the Dieng Plateau or as a break between Bandung and Yogya. The Wonosobo bus station is about a km out of town.

Places to Stay

Losmen Jawa Tengah, on Jalan Jen A Yani next to the market and colt terminal for Dieng, is a good, clean place with rooms from 4000 rp. Others include the Losmen Widuri at nearby Jalan Tanggung 20 with rooms for 1500 rp or the more comfortable Hotel Petra, 200 metres down from the Jawa Tengah at Jalan A Yani 81, with rooms from 1750 rp.

Restaurant Asia and the Dieng Restaurant, on Jalan Kawedanan almost opposite the Jawa Tengah, both have good food. At the Dieng, Mr Agus has maps and photographs and lots of interesting tales about the plateau. Or you can eat well and cheaply at the *Rumah Makan Klenyer*, in the small grocery shop next to the Petra.

YOGYAKARTA

The most popular city in Indonesia, Yogya is easy going, economical and offers plenty to see for the budget traveller. Long a centre of power, the kingdom of Mataram extended control as far as Sumatra and Bali over one thousand years ago. The final Hindu-Buddhist kingdom of the Majapahits also controlled this area until the arrival of Islam and the second kingdom of Mataram drove them to Bali.

The coming of the Dutch resulted in the kingdom being split into sultanates. From 1825 to 1830 the great Indonesian hero, Prince Diponegoro, led a bitter revolt against the Dutch which was finally resolved when he was captured by a rather nasty trick. Invited to discuss truce negotiations the unsuspecting Diponegoro was captured and exiled to Sulawesi. In this century Yogya was again a centre of resistance to the Dutch and after WW II was the capital of the revolution until eventual independence from Holland was achieved.

Information & Orientation

There's a tourist information office at Jalan Malioboro 16, open from 8 am to 8.30 pm Monday to Saturday. They have good free maps of the city and can give you all the latest information on cultural performances in Yogya. Finding your way around Yogya is pretty easy. Jalan Malioboro is the main road and runs straight down from the railway station to the Kraton at the far end. Most of the restaurants and shops are along this street and most of the cheap accommodation places are just off it, near the railway line.

Although Yogyakarta is now spelt with a Y (not Jogjakarta) it's still pronounced with a J. Asking for Yogya will get you blank stares. Yogya is plagued with thieves – break-into-your-room thieves, snatch-your-bag thieves, steal-your-bicycle thieves, pick-your-pocket thieves. Take care.

Things to See

Kraton The huge palace of the Sultan of Yogya, founded in 1756, is actually a city within the city. Over 20,000 people live within its walls. The palace is guarded by elderly gentlemen in traditional costume and a guide shows you around its sumptuous pavilions and halls. The 300 rp admission includes the guide. It's open daily from 8.30 am to 12.30 pm, but only to 11.30 am on Fridays and Saturdays, and it's closed on national and kraton holidays. The inner court, with its 'male' and 'female' stairways to the entrance, has two small museums and a pavilion where you can see gamelan playing on Mondays and Wednesdays from 10.30 am to 12 noon or classical dancing on Sundays from 10.30 am to 12.30.

Taman Sari The 'Fragrant Garden', a water palace, was a complex of canals, pools and palaces built within the Kraton between 1758 and 1765. Damaged first by Diponegoro's Java War and then further by an earthquake, today it's a mass of ruins, crowded with small houses and batik galleries. Parts are being restored but not very well. Admission is 100 rp to the restored area. On the edge of the site is an interesting bird market.

Museum Sono-Budoyo Close to the kraton, on the north-west corner of the square, the museum has some excellent exhibits including palace furnishings, jewellery, bronze statues and wayang puppets. It is open from 8 am daily except Monday and closes at 1.30 pm Tuesday to Thursday, 10.30 am Friday and 11.30 am at the weekend. Admission is only 20 rp and it's well worth a visit.

Monumen Diponegoro This is a reconstruction of Prince Diponegoro's residence, destroyed by the Dutch in 1825. The hole in the wall where the prince escaped is still there. It's four km out of Yogya – No 2 bus

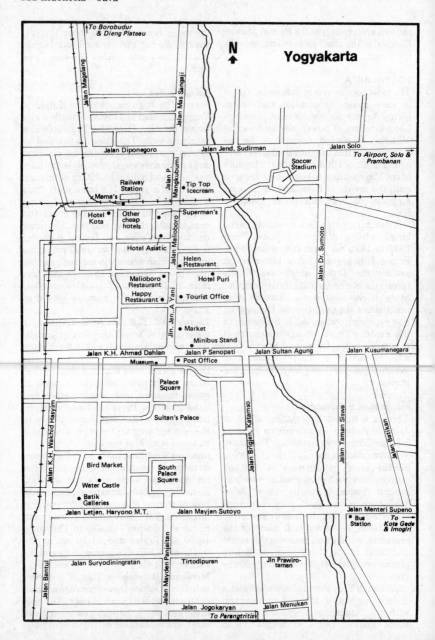

N

Yogyakarta

To Borobudur & Dieng Plateau

Jalan Magelang

Jalan Mas Sangaji

Jalan Diponegoro

Jalan Jend. Sudirman

Jalan Solo

To Airport, Solo & Prambanan

Soccer Stadium

Jalan P. Mangkubumi

Railway Station

Tip Top Icecream

Mama's

Superman's

Hotel Kota

Other cheap hotels

Jalan Malioboro

Jalan Dr. Sumoto

Hotel Asiatic

Helen Restaurant

Hotel Puri

Malioboro Restaurant

Happy Restaurant

Jln. Jen. A. Yani

Tourist Office

Market

Minibus Stand

Jalan K.H. Ahmad Dahlan

Jalan P Senopati

Jalan Sultan Agung

Jalan Kusumanegara

Museum

Post Office

Palace Square

Jalan Brigjen. Katamso

Jalan Taman Siswa

Sultan's Palace

Jalan Batikan

Bird Market

South Palace Square

Water Castle

Batik Galleries

Jalan K.H. Wakhid Hasyim

Jalan Letjen. Haryono M.T.

Jalan Mayjen Sutoyo

Jalan Menteri Supeno

Bus Station

To Kota Gede & Imogiri

Jalan Bantul

Jalan Suryodiningratan

Jalan Mayden Panjaitan

Tirtodipuran

Jln Prawiro-taman

Jalan Jogokaryan

Jalan Menukan

To Parangtritis

along Jalan Mataram will get you there, No 1 bus will get you back to Jalan Malioboro.

Performances Classical dancing and gamelan rehearsals in the Kraton are mentioned above. Wayang kulit (leather shadow puppets) can be seen at several places around Yogya on virtually every night of the week. On every second Saturday there is an all-night wayang kulit performance at Sasono Hinggil in the south palace square. Tickets cost from 300 rp.

Wayang golek (wooden puppet) plays are also performed frequently. There is a Nitour performance, from 10 am to noon every day except Sunday, which also has a useful handout explaining the history of the wayang and the Ramayana story. The Nitour puppet plays are at Jalan KHA Dahlan 71 and tickets cost 600 rp.

The great Ramayana ballet performance at Prambanan takes place over the full moon nights from May to October, but there are also evening performances at theatres in the city from Monday to Thursday. There were nightly performances at the People's Park but the theatre is undergoing renovations at present.

Batik & Batik Classes See the introductory section on Things to Buy for more information on batik. Batik cloth is sold all over Yogya but the Terang Bulan shop, before the market as you walk south on Jalan Malioboro, will give you a good idea of what is available. Prices are fixed but very reasonable and quality is reliable. For batik art in Yogya there are a great number of galleries to visit. Top of the scale is Amri Yahya's flash gallery at Jalan Gampingan 67 – his beautiful modern batiks can cost over US$1000 and there are a number of beautiful, and even more expensive, oil paintings on display. Nearby on the same street is ASRI (Academy of Fine Arts) which is open to visitors in the mornings Monday to Saturday. Carry on up Jalan Wates (the extension of Jalan KHA Dahlan) and you'll come to other interesting – but more reasonably priced –

places. Another good place for top-quality, but expensive, batik is Kuswadji's in the north square near the kraton. Or there's Bambang Utoro, to the east of town off Jalan Kusumanegara, the continuation of Jalan Senopati. There are also a number of batik workshops and galleries along Jalan Tirtodipuran and Prawirotaman in the south of Yogya.

Affandi, Indonesia's internationally best-known painter, has an interesting modern gallery about five km out of Yogya on the Solo road and a short distance before the Ambarrukmo Palace Hotel. Paintings are for sale but the gallery is also a permanent museum displaying the works of Affandi, his daughter Kartika and other artists. It's open from 9 am to 4 pm.

The water palace is the site for most of the cheaper galleries but the great percentage of them are very poor quality and very 'me-too' in their style. Look carefully and be very selective if you're buying there. The best of these galleries is undoubtedly Mr Lod E A's, where a number of the better, younger batik artists are given a go. You'll certainly find the most original water palace work here. The Astuti Batik Gallery has some interesting surrealist work and just outside the water palace the Adhi Busano Studio also has some interesting batik although the style has been fairly stagnant now for some years.

Some batik artists only draw the outline and then have teams of women fill in the intricate details. This certainly enables them to churn out pictures in great numbers! When shopping around in the water palace take great care not to be led into the galleries by the teams of touts who follow you around – you'll end up paying commission on anything you buy. Yogya is positively crawling with would-be batik salesmen.

If you want to have a go at batik yourself there are lots of batik courses and classes in Yogya. Many of the teachers are just self-proclaimed 'experts' out to make some easy money so before investing time and money it's a good idea to ask around among other travellers who may have just completed a course. The Intensive Batik Course of Hadjir Digdodarmojo seems to get a generally high approval rating although some people have also reported it as being rather mechanical and dull. It's on the left of the water palace main entrance at Taman Kp 3/177 and there are three or five-day courses from 2 to 6 pm daily. Mr Topps at the Lucy Gallery in Gang I (near Superman's) has also been recommended. Tulus Warsito, at Jalan Wates 31, runs various courses from one day (3500 rp) to three weeks (50,000 rp) – expensive but recommended by the Batik Research Centre.

The Yogya government-run Batik Research Centre (tel 2557) at Jalan Kusumanegara 2 has been closed for renovation but it may be open again to visitors later in 1985. It's an interesting place to visit – they explain the batik process in detail and have some unusual batiks on display and for sale. It's a little expensive but the quality is high. The centre did run a very comprehensive four-week batik-making course for foreigners and are likely to do so again.

Other Kota Gede is the silverwork centre of Yogya and the grave of Senopati, the first king of Mataram, can also be seen here. The Ambarrukmo Palace is in the grounds of the Ambarrukmo Palace Hotel, 11 km out of Yogya on the Solo road. It's another interesting example of Javanese palace architecture. The Yogyakarta Craft Centre, opposite the hotel, is promoted by the government and has a good display of reasonably priced, high-quality crafts. If the heat in Yogya gets too much you can use the swimming pool at the luxurious Hotel Ambarrukmo, or the Hotel Mutiara in the centre of town, for 1500 rp.

Places to Stay

Although Yogya is no longer Indonesia's bargain basement for accommodation, it's still remarkably good value and offers a superb choice of places to stay. It's certainly the best city in Java for places to stay and places to eat. Most of the cheap hotels can be found along Jalan Pasar Kembang, parallel to and immediately south of the railway line, and along Jalan Sosrowijayan, a block south again. Connecting the two and just a couple of doors down from the main street of Yogya (Jalan Malioboro) is the narrow alleyway known as Gang Sosrowijayan. Here you'll find more real cheapies and one of Yogya's most popular eating places. There are more places to stay in other small gangs in this area.

At the end of Jalan Pasar Kembang it changes names to Jalan Gandekan Lor and at number 79 you'll find the spotlessly clean and highly efficient *Losmen Kota*. There are pleasant open lounges and the only real drawback to its corner location is that the front rooms are kind of noisy. Doubles cost 4500 rp and larger rooms from 5500 rp. They now require a hefty deposit of 7500 rp from each person and, although the general consensus is that it's a well-run and pleasant place, some people find it a bit over-officious and even too security conscious. 'Full', some travellers report, may simply mean that the owner doesn't like the looks of you!

Back along Jalan Pasar Kembang towards Malioboro there are numerous cheapies including the *Mataram* at 61 (private mandi and toilet) with rooms around 3500 rp. At 49 there's the *Nusantara* ('swarming with cockroaches,' reported one traveller, 'and not your small rubbish either – the twitching five cm jobs'). Then there's the *Rachmat* ('very ordinary, nothing much wrong with it but there are better places around') at 5000 rp and the similarly priced *Shinta*. The *Asia-Africa* has a whole variety of rooms from 3000 rp to more expensive rooms with private mandi at 6000 rp and above. There's an attractive garden at the back. At 17A the *Ratna* is slightly flashier with good doubles including private mandi and toilet for 7700 rp, cheaper without. It's set back from the road and pleasantly quiet.

Gang Sosrowijayan I, that little connecting alley, has some very low-cost places but make sure your room is secure – Yogyakarta is notorious for theft of all types including the straight-from-your-room variety. *Losmen Beta* is clean, small, noisy and fairly commercial (but popular) with rooms from 1000 rp. If you stay here they give you a 25% discount on tickets for shows at the Arjuna Plaza Hotel. A bit further along the gang are the *Rama* and *Jogja*, two adjoining losmen with rooms around 2500 rp. *Superman's Losmen* is clean and cheap at 1000 to 3000 rp. Others include the *Bu Purwo* with rooms from 1000 rp, the *Losmen Lucy* from 1500 rp, the *Home Sweet Home*.

On Gang Sosrowijayan II, the next alley back, is the clean, modern, good-value and very popular *Hotel Bagus*. It's built around a central courtyard, run by a veritable classroom of children and rooms with fan cost from 1750 rp. Free tea three times a day. The *Jaya Losmen* in the same gang is also good. The *Gandhi*, opposite the Jaya in its own garden, has come in for some recent recommendations. Rooms are clean and cost 1500 to 2500 rp. Others in this area worth trying include the *Losmen Setia* and the *Utar Pension Inn*.

On Jalan Sosrowijayan, between Gang I and Malioboro, is the security conscious *Aziatic* – at night the doors are locked and there are stout bars on the windows. 'As secure as Pentridge,' (Pentridge is a major Australian jail!) wrote one obviously impressed Australian visitor. It's also clean, cool and comfortable, has big beds in the 3000 rp doubles (no singles) and a wide central hallway where you can sit and chat. They also rent bicycles and have a good restaurant in the back. Across the road the *Indonesia* has a pleasant courtyard and some cheap and basic singles from 2000 rp and a variety of doubles. At Jalan Sosrowijayan 1/192 the *Losmen Wisma Wijaya* has plain but clean singles/doubles at 2000/3000 rp with a small

breakfast. The management is very friendly and informative. Round the back of the Aziatic is the cheapest losmen in town – *Losmen Lima* has rooms from 750 rp.

Cross Malioboro and follow the alley down beside the Helen Restaurant. You'll soon come to the extremely well-kept and very quiet *Puri* with rooms from 3500 rp and free tea or coffee in the mornings and evenings. A personal favourite, this one. The nearby *Hotel Intan* is similarly priced and also good value and the *Hotel Prambanan* has rooms from 4000 rp.

There are a number of nice somewhat upmarket places south of the Kraton and well away from the centre. They often send touts to intercept travellers at the station. You get a free bemo ride there and if you don't like the place you only have to say no. One traveller recommended a 10,000 rp splurge at the *Duta Guest House*, at Jalan Prawirotaman 20, where there are also four economy rooms at 3500/5000 rp including breakfast. Major attraction here is the swimming pool. The *Metro Guest House* on the same road has doubles with bathroom at 8000 rp including breakfast. There's a nice garden. In this same area another traveller recommended the *Rose*. Becaks into town from this area cost 400 to 500 rp. The more central *Peti Mas*, at Jalan Dagen 39 off Malioboro, has doubles with bathroom from 12,000 rp and a nice garden with a restaurant area. The big old Dutch-built *Garuda Hotel* on Malioboro is another splurge place – a superb old building.

Places to Eat
There is as wide a variety of eating places as losmen in Yogya. Two of them have earned a permanent niche in the travellers' bottleneck department – everybody seems to pay a visit to either Mama's or Superman's. You'll find *Superman's* on Gang Sosrowijayan I. It's very popular at breakfast time and has good music so it's a good place to while away a rainy afternoon. If there is a catch, it's that it's too popular with Javanese (and foreign) trendies.

On Jalan Pasar Kembang, beside the railway line, there is a whole host of popular warungs, but *Mama's* is definitely the number one warung. Evening time is when it comes into full swing with good food and great salad. It's always crowded and may even be getting a little too popular. *Bu Sis* is a small restaurant just down from Superman's and is popular for snacks. *Anna's* has recently opened on Gang II and is already popular. *Lovina Tavern*, in a cul-de-sac off Jalan Sosrowijayan between Gang I and II, has been recommended for its good atmosphere and music and you can sit outside here.

There are a number of places along Malioboro but several of them seem to have taken a sharp tumble in standards over the years. They all specialise in giving you a menu and a notepad to write your order on and many of them have Time and other magazines available for you to catch up on world events while you're eating. The long-popular *Helen* is one place that seems to have suffered a marked decline in standards.

At Jalan Malioboro 87 the *Malioboro* is still popular with good food in clean surroundings. The *Shinta*, across from the Helen, is a little expensive but has some of the best iced juice in Indonesia. Further down towards the Kraton the *Happy* has had its ups and downs over the years. On the corner of Jalan Suryatmajan and Malioboro, a side street leads into the unusual *Legian Restaurant* with slightly expensive prices, but it is a little quieter and free from petrol and diesel fumes. At 97 Malioboro the new *Mirama* is clean and friendly with good food. Late at night, after 9 pm, food stalls replace the souvenirs on Jalan Malioboro and you can take a seat on the woven mats along the pavement. Most of them serve the speciality of Yogya, nasi gudeg (rice with young jackfruit cooked in coconut milk) – a good meal with a glass of hot orange juice for about 300 rp.

Jalan Malioboro changes names across the railway line and becomes Jalan Mangkubumi. There are some excellent Nasi Padang places here, including the *Sinar Budi* and the *Wiena*, which make a change from all the pseudo-western travellers' delights found elsewhere in Yogya. A bit further along at number 28 is the *Tip Top* with excellent ice cream and cakes. On Jalan Jen Sudirman the *Holland Bakery* and *Chitty 2 Bang 2* (Chitty Chitty Bang Bang) are next to the President Movie Theatre. Even better ice cream and cakes, reports a recent visitor.

Getting There

See the introductory Getting Around Java section for details of Jakarta-Yogya and Surabaya-Yogya travel.

Trains Unlike Jakarta and Surabaya there is only one station in Yogya and it is very conveniently located in the centre of town. Solo is on the main Yoga-Surabaya railway line, only about an hour out of Yogya.

Buses The new bus station is four km from the centre. There are a number of ticket agents along Jalan Sosrowijayan selling tickets for the various bus companies and in some cases running their own services too. The bus company offices are mainly along Jalan Mangkabumi, the extension of Jalan Malioboro across the railway lines. Colts for Solo can be caught as they run up Jalan Mataram, a block over from Malioboro. Fares from Yogya include Jakarta from 5500 rp, Bandung from 5000 rp, Surabaya 6000 rp (night bus) and 3500 rp (day), Denpasar around 9000 rp or 11,000 rp by the super-duper-deluxe bus (which isn't worth it). Solo costs 600 rp by public bus or 1300 rp by minibus, door to door.

Getting Around

You can hire pushbikes and motorcycles by the day or week in Yogya but lock them up ultra-securely. Theft is a big business in Yogya. Becaks cost around 100 rp a km and there are plenty of them. If you're touring the batik galleries it can be a good idea to hire a becak for a round trip. There are also horse-drawn andongs around town. Local colts and oplets go from the bus station next to the shopping centre on Jalan Senopati.

'Bis Kotas' are bright orange minibuses operating on eight set routes around the city for a flat 125 rp fare. There are route maps for reference in the information centre. From the bus station a No 2 bus will drop you on Jalan Mataram, a block over from Malioboro. A No 1 bus from Jalan Malioboro will get you out to the bus station, about 20 minutes from the centre.

A taxi to or from Yogya airport will be about 4500 rp but if you stroll out to the main road, only 200 metres from the terminal, you can get any Solo colt coming by for about 200 rp into Yogya (Yogya's to the left). From Yogya you can catch a colt bound for Solo, via the Ambarrukmo Hotel and Prambanan, from Jalan Mataram.

The bus for Borobudur runs along Jalan Magelang to the north and No 5 city bus will drop you at the bus stop there. The Aziatic and the Indonesia hotels, and Losmen Beta run day-trips to Borobudur and the Dieng Plateau for about 8500 rp which includes snacks and admission.

The Kartika Travel Agent on Jalan Sosrowijayan organises trips to climb Merapi from Selo in time for sunrise, for 15,000 rp per person for a minimum of four people.

AROUND YOGYAKARTA

There are a whole series of places to visit around Yogyakarta. Best known, of course, are the great temple complex of Prambanan and the huge Buddhist centre at Borobudur, but there are a number of others worth a visit. Although most of them are day-trips from Yogya there are some places in which you can also stay.

Prambanan

The biggest Hindu temple complex in Java, Prambanan is 17 km from Yogya on the Solo road. Of the original group the outer compound contains the ruins of 224 temples, only two of which have been restored. Eight minor and eight main temples stand in the central court. The largest of these, the Shiva temple, has been restored and others are being reconstructed. The 50-metre-high temple bears 42 scenes from the Ramayana. The statue of Shiva stands in the central chamber and statues of the goddess Durga, Shiva's elephant-headed son Ganesh, and Agastya the teacher stand in the other chapels of the upper part of the temple. The Shiva temple is flanked by the Vishnu and Brahma temples, the latter carrying further scenes from the Ramayana. In the small central temple oposite the Shiva temple stands a fine statue of the bull Nandi, Shiva's mount.

Built in the 9th century AD, possibly 50 years or so later than Borobudur, Prambanan was abandoned soon after its completion when its builders moved east. Many of the temples had collapsed by the last century and not until 1937 was reconstruction first attempted. Other temple ruins can be found close to Prambanan and on the road back to Yogya. Don't miss the Ramayana dance which is performed here on the full moon nights from May to October each year.

To get to Prambanan take a Solo bus or colt from Yogya. There is a 100 rp admission charge to the temple complex plus a 100 rp camera charge. It's open from 6 am to 6 pm and the temples are at their best in the early evening light or early morning when it's quiet.

Borobudur

Ranking with Pagan and Angkor Wat as one of the greatest South-East Asian Buddhist monuments, Borobudur is a huge construction covering a hill, 40 km from Yogya. With the decline of Buddhism Borobudur was abandoned and only rediscovered in 1814 while Raffles governed Java.

The temple consists of six square bases

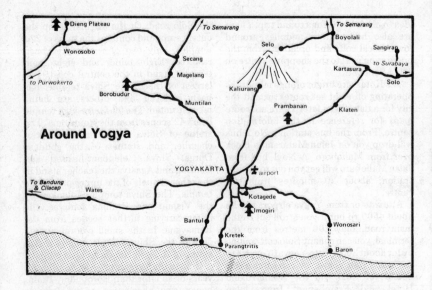

Around Yogya

topped by three circular ones and was constructed contemporaneously with Prambanan in the early half of the 9th century AD. Over the centuries the supporting hill became waterlogged and the whole immense stone mass started to subside at a variety of angles. A US$12 million restoration project is now more or less completed.

Nearly 1500 panels on the terraces illustrate Buddhist teachings and tales while over 400 Buddha images sit in chambers on the terraces. On the upper circular terraces latticed stupas contain 72 more Buddha images.

The Mendut temple, three km east of Borobudur, has a magnificent statue of Buddha seated with two disciples. He is three metres high and sits with both feet on the ground, rather than in the usual lotus position. It is believed that this image was originally intended to top Borobudur but proved impossible to raise to the summit.

To get to Borobudur take a bus to Muntilan and another on to the site. It's a two km walk from the bus stop or a 200 rp

becak ride to the temple where there is a 100 rp admission charge. If you're stopping off at Borobudur en route to somewhere else you must leave your bags in a hut at the entrance where they will be looked after – it's free. The Mendut temple costs another 100 rp. The bus from Muntilan passes first Mendut and then the smaller Pawon temple en route to Borobudur so if you don't feel like walking you can use the bus, for 50 rp, to hop from one temple to the next.

Kaliurang

A pleasant mountain resort on the slopes of volcanically active Mt Merapi, 26 km from Yogya and only 500 rp by colt. Kaliurang is an interesting alternative to the better-known trip to the Dieng Plateau. There are great views of the mountains, lovely bushwalks, waterfalls and a rather chilly swimming pool. It's pleasant to feel the crisp mountain air after the sweaty heat of the plains. To climb Mt Merapi takes about eight hours there and back for experienced walkers and more like 15 hours for less experienced climbers.

Starting at about 3 am to get the sunrise. Merapi is a difficult climb from Kaliurang (easier from Selo to the north of the volcano) and it's worth contacting the owner of Vogels for information and advice. It's only a one hour climb to the volcano observation point from where you can watch Merapi when it's in action.

Places to Stay This is basically a local resort but you can get rooms for 2000 rp in the delightful *Vogels*. A number of travellers have written to recommend this little place. You can also eat at Vogels and the food is excellent value. 'We were dining in candlelight while the rain poured down (as it does every afternoon),' reported one visitor, 'when the staff put on a crackling Bing Crosby record from the '40s – we briefly floated out of Indonesia!' The *Penginapan Garuda* has rooms for 2000 rp and the *Losmen Kumala* with rooms with shower for 3000 rp has also been recommended.

Parangtritis

Best known of the beaches south of Yogya, Parangtritis is 27 km away. Cheap accommodation and food are available and although the currents and undertows are reputed to be dangerous here several travellers have written to say that swimming is quite possible. Perhaps it's seasonal. You can swim in freshwater pools, the *Pemandian* at the base of the hill, however. This is a centre for worship of Queen Lara Kidul, the Goddess of the South Sea. A Sultan of Yogya is supposed to have taken her as his wife. Parangtritis has 'lovely sand dunes and terrible magic mushrooms,' reported one traveller. Avoid Fridays and the weekends when Parangtritis is very crowded.

Places to Stay There are plenty of more or less similar losmen along the main street in this Yogya beach resort. Prices are low but facilities are limited and a bit unhealthy. Away from the main street, the *Penginapan Parang Endong* has simple

rooms for 2000 rp and a good swimming pool.

Getting There From Yogya it's 350 rp from the bus station, or 400 rp by colt from the station on Jalan Senopati – and a bumpy one hour trip over one of the worst roads in Java! The last bus back to Yogya leaves at 6 pm.

Imogiri

The Royal Cemetery of the sultans of Mataram, 20 km from Yogya, sits high on a hillside at the top of 345 steps. Imogiri is a sacred site and many local people visit to pay their respects at the royal graves, at the tomb of the great Sultan Agung in particular. It's an interesting place to visit but you are expected to follow the strict etiquette of the kraton rules. Visitors must sign the ubiquitous 'Visitor's Book', pay a small donation and hire traditional Javanese dress before entering the graveyard. Men have to wear sarong, women have to be bare shouldered and wear kain and kebayan. Follow everyone else and you'll know what to do. They don't seem to mind you entering the tomb of Sultan Agung, although it could be a problem if you're tall – it's a matter of crawling inside and keeping on your knees. Cameras are not allowed in the graveyard. Imogiri is open on Monday from 10.30 am to noon and on Friday from 1.30 pm to 4 pm.

SOLO (Surakarta or Sala)

Situated between Yogya and Surabaya, Solo was for a time the capital of the Mataram kingdom. The sultanate had shifted its capital several times from Kota Gede to Plered and then to Kartasura. The court of Kartasura was devastated by fighting in 1742 and the capital was moved east to the small village of Sala on the Bengawan Solo river. It's a relatively quiet, easy-going and hassle-free town with two royal palaces to visit where you can tour the pavilions and museums. Solo is also a good source of high-quality batik. The helpful tourist office at Jalan Slamet

Riyadi 235 has a useful Solo guide map and a great many leaflets, including free booklets on Candi Sukuh and Sangiran.

Kratons The Susuhunan of Mataram, Pakubuwono II, finally moved from Kartasura into his new palace – the Kraton Surakarta – in 1745. The museum here is particularly interesting, especially with one of the English-speaking guides, and exhibits include three Dutch carriages which have been used for weddings. The oldest, named Kiyai Grudo, was used by the Susuhunan for his stately entry into the new capital. The giant pop-eyed figurehead with hairy whiskers once graced the royal perahu which at one time was able to navigate the Solo river all the way to the north coast. Admission is 600 rp, cheaper for students, and it's open every day except Friday from 9 am to 12.30 pm.

The minor kraton, Puro Mangkunegaran, was founded in 1757 by a dissident prince Raden Mas Said. The museum, in the main hall of the palace behind the pavilion, has some unusual exhibits – including an extraordinary gold genital cover. It's also worth having a look at the wayang kulit puppets in the palace shop. They're made at the kraton by the resident dalang and prices are reasonable for some very fine work. The palace is open the same hours as the Surakarta, but it closes at 11.30 am on Friday and it is closed on Sunday. At the pavilion you can see dance practise sessions on Wednesday mornings from 9.30 am or gamelan on Saturday mornings.

Radya Pustaka Museum This small museum, next to the tourist office on Jalan Slamet Riyadi, has good exhibits of gamelan instruments and wayang puppets. Admission to the museum is 100 rp and it is open from 8 am to 12.15 pm, closed Mondays.

Performances You can see wayang orang performances every evening except Sunday at the Sriwedari amusement park theatres on Slamet Riyadi. The costumes are stunning and the seats are cheap: 225 rp for the cheapest, only 250 rp for quite good ones. Other cultural performances are sometimes held at the RRI, the local radio broadcasting station and the tourist office will have details. Dance and gamelan rehearsals can be seen at the Sasono Mulyo building, near the Kraton Surakarta, every afternoon except Sunday between 2 and 4 pm.

Batik Solo is a batik centre rivalling Yogya but with a totally individual style. Many people find it better value for batik and handicrafts than Yogya, quite possibly because it attracts far fewer tourists. There are hundreds of stalls at Pasar Klewer with cheap batik, or try the numerous shops for more sophisticated work. Batik Semar is one good place and you can see the batik being made. The Trisne Batik and Artshop has some fine traditional batik tulis and other crafts.

There is also a good antiques market on Jalan Diponegoro. Look for old batik 'cap' stamps here; they're much cheaper than in Yogya but check that they are not damaged.

Other You can use the swimming pool at the Kusuma Sahid Prince Hotel for 1000 rp a day.

Places to Stay

Pat Mawardi's Homestay (tel 3106) at Kemlayan Kidul 11, a small alley near Jalan Yos Sudarso and Jalan Secoyudan, is friendly and great value. Singles cost from 2000 rp and doubles 3000 rp and there is a quiet courtyard with tables and chairs. Free tea and drinking water, breakfast is available for 1000 rp and you can buy coffee and soft drinks. It's also known as 'The Westerners'.

The *Hotel Kota* still seems to be reasonably popular despite higher prices and reports of a slide in standards. It's a double-storey place built around a large open courtyard. Rooms cost from 3500 rp and it's at Jalan Slamet Riyadi 113, only a 100 metres from the centre of town.

Close by on Jalan Achmad Dahlan are a

Solo — Surakarta

number of places in the same price range – including the open and airy *Hotel Central*, a clean and pleasant place in the old 'grand' style with singles/doubles for 3000 and 3500 rp. There's some good art deco woodwork and you get coffee in the morning, tea in the afternoon. Street rooms can be a bit noisy but you have a great view of the town, the sunset and Merapi volcano. On this same street you'll also find the *Islam*, *Seneng* and *Hotel Keprabon*. The *Losmen Timur*, down a small alley alongside the Hotel Central, has singles for 2000 rp but it's pretty dismal. At Jalan Imam Bonjol 44 the *Hotel Mawar Melati* is clean and has rooms from 3000 rp including tea twice a day.

There is a cluster of losmen, offering various prices, near the central railway station, Solo Balapan. Jalan Pasar Nongko is close to the station and has several places including the *Wismantara* at 53 with rooms for 5000 rp surrounding a somewhat gloomy courtyard. The *Kondang Asri* at 86 has singles at 3000 rp, friendly people, good music (even if it is too loud sometimes) and even free tea (sometimes).

Further out from the centre the more expensive *Hotel Putri Ayu* at Jalan Slamet Riyadi 293 has good doubles, from 10,000 rp with bathroom, including breakfast.

Places to Eat

There are countless warungs and rumah makans including several serving Padang food. Along Jalan Teuku Umar there is an excellent night market and fresh milk, known as susu sagar or minuman sehat (healthy drink), is available from some of the warungs – hot or cold or with honey. Nasi gudeg is popular but the speciality of Solo is *nasi liwet*, rice with chicken and coconut milk. Other local specialities to try at night are the small rice puddings served up on a crispy pancake with banana, chocolate or jackfruit on top – best eaten when they're piping hot.

The *New Holland Bakery*, near the Garuda office on Jalan Slamet Riyadi, has a bewildering array of baked goods and delicious savoury martabak rolls for 400 rp. The *Toko Tiga Enam* bakery at Jalan Gatot Subroto 36 is also good and cheaper. There are several good Chinese places in Solo, such as the *Jakarta* close to the centre and *Adem Ayam* further out at Jalan Slamet Riyadi 296. At number 262 on the same street, just a short way up from the entertainment park, the *Mataram* has excellent Chinese food at very reasonable prices. The Chinese *Centrum* at Jalan Kratonan 151, close to the Westerners, is a small and busy place with good atmosphere – it closes at 8 pm. *Taman Sari* at Jalan Gatot Sibroto 42C has good fruit juices and cheap noodle dishes. The *Bu Mari* warung, on the same street, does great nasi gudeg and chicken curry.

Getting There & Getting Around

Solo is on the main Yogya-Surabaya rail and road route. It's around 3000 rp for a public bus Surabaya-Solo and takes six hours. The 3rd class train Surabaya-Solo costs 2000 rp, 1500 rp with student discount, and takes five hours. Yogya is only an hour or so away by bus and costs 600 rp by public bus, 1300 rp by minibus door-to-door. To Blitar it's 2500 rp and takes about six hours. To Malang takes about nine hours and costs 3200 rp by bus. They leave frequently in the morning between 7 and 9 am.

The main bus station is about three km from the centre, 500 rp by becak. For buses to Semarang, Prambanan and Yogya it's cheaper to take the double decker to Kartasura and catch a bus from there. A becak from the railway station into the centre is around 300 rp. The minibus station is by the Kraton on the opposite side to the batik market.

The city double decker bus runs between Kartasura in the west and Palur in the east right along Jalan Slamet Riyadi, and costs a flat fare of 125 rp. Bicycles can be hired from the Westerners for 600 rp a day.

AROUND SOLO

Sangiran

Prehistoric 'Java Man' was discovered at Sangiran, 15 km north of Solo, and there is a small museum with fossil exhibits including some amazing 'mammoth' bones and tusks. They are still finding things and if you wander up the road past the museum a bit and have a look in some of the exposed banks you may find shells or fossil bones and crabs.

Candi Sukuh & Tawangmangu

Candi Sukuh is a primitive-style temple on the slopes of Mt Lawu, 36 km east of Solo. It dates from the 15th or 16th century and has a curious Inca-like look. The tourist office in Solo has a leaflet about the place. To get there take the double decker to Tertomoyo, then a Tawangmangu bus to Karangpandan for 300 rp, and from Karangpandan catch a minibus to Candi Sukuh for 250 rp. On market days the minibus stops right beside the temple but other days it's a couple of km uphill walk to the site. It is about 1½ hours travelling by bus in total but it's worth it for the views are superb and the place has a lot of atmosphere.

Tawangmangu, a mountain resort about 1½ hour's ride out of Solo, has an impressive waterfall (the *Grojogan Sewu*) where you can take a dip in the very chilly pool. You can catch a bus from Karangpandan but it's possible to walk to Tawangmangu from Candi Sukuh. It's a very pleasant 2½ hour walk along well-worn cobble-stoned paths and from Tawangmangu you can bus back to Solo for around 400 rp. Some people find the walk more interesting than Tawangmangu or Candi Sukuh.

Places to Stay In Tawangmangu you can stay at the *Pak Amat Losmen* which has a garden. The rooms, from 5000 rp, are each individual little houses with bathrooms and verandah. Further up the hill the *Losmen Pondok Garuda* next to the mosque has a variety of rooms with and without bathroom from 5000 rp, some with a good view over the valley. On the main street Jalan Lawu, about a km up from the bus station, *Wisma Lawu* has doubles at around 6000 rp. Good food in the warungs further up the hill.

SEMARANG

This north coast port is the capital of central Java. It's about 120 km north of Yogya and about two-thirds of the way from Jakarta to Surabaya. Even though it's an important port there are no deep water berthing facilities and boats have to anchor out in the mouth of the Kali Baru River and transfer their cargo to shore by lighter.

Information

There is a Semarang tourist office in the Wisma Pancasila building on Simpang Lima, the town square. The office is open from 8 am to 2 pm from Monday to Thursday, to 11 am on Friday and 1 pm on Saturday. There is also a Central Java tourist office, Kantor Dinas Pariwisata, at Jalan Pemuda 171. It's open the same hours as the Semarang tourist office but closes an hour earlier Monday to Thursday and Saturday.

Things to See

The Sam Po Kong Temple, in the southwest of the city, is dedicated to Admiral Cheng Ho – the famous Muslim eunuch of the Ming dynasty who led several expeditions from China to Java and other parts of South-East Asia in the early 15th century. He is particularly revered in Melaka in Malaysia and the Chinese temple in Semarang is the largest in Indonesia, honoured by both Chinese Buddhists and Muslims. It's better known as Gedong Batu (stone building) and is in the form of a huge cave. To get there take a Daihatsu from terminal Baru in the centre of town to Karang Ayu and another from there to Gedong Batu. The temple is about half an hour's drive from the city centre.

There isn't a great deal to do or see in Semarang itself except for a sprinkling of old buildings from the Dutch colonial era. On Jalan Let Jen Suprapto, south of Tawang railway station, there's the 1753 Gereja Blenduk church with its huge dome and baroque organ. Behind Poncol railway station there is the ruin of an old Dutch East India Company fort and there are numerous old warehouses around Tawang. The Thay Kak Sie Temple is on Gang Lombok, off Jalan Pekojan in Semarang's old Chinatown. Semarang also has an interesting day market, Pasar Johar, on the square at the top of Jalan Pemuda.

Every evening there are wayang orang performances at the Ngesti Pandowo Theatre at Jalan Pemuda 116. Performances start at 7 pm and tickets cost from 500 rp. Or take a city bus out to Gombel, the 'new town' on the hills to the south, and have a drink at the Sky Garden Hotel from where there is a fine view of the city and ships at sea. To get there take a bus down Jalan Pemuda bound for Jatingalen and ask for Gombel Hill, which is just past the hotel. If you're really stuck for something to do you could always visit the Tjap Djapo herbal medicines factory. Their adverts use a squad of dwarves! 'I tried a Jamu Sekhot,' reported one traveller, 'which, according to the packet, "increases health and vitality in men, curing impotence and bringing you to a happy family".' 'Unfortunately,' he went on to report, 'it didn't help and tastes like shit.'

Places to Stay

The *Hotel Jaya* at Jalan Let Jen Haryono 85, about a km south of the bus station, has comfortable rooms with fan from 4500 rp, 7000 rp with bathroom, including breakfast. There's a string of places along Jalan Imam Bonjol. The *Hotel Poncol* at No 60, near the Poncol railway station, is cheap (rooms from 3000 rp) but grubby and noisy. Close by the more comfortable *Losmen Ardjuna* at No 51 has rooms for 5000 rp including breakfast. The *Losmen Rahayu* at No 35 has rooms for 6000 rp with fan, 8000 rp with bathroom, including breakfast.

The *Losmen Singapore* at Jalan Imam Bonjol 12, near Pasar Johar and more central, has singles for 4000 rp and doubles for 6000 rp including breakfast. Right across the street, the *Hotel Oewa-Asia* is a former colonial hotel. It's a friendly, comfortable place with doubles from 6500 rp including breakfast; more expensive rooms with bathroom and fan or air-con. *Hotel Agung* is within walking distance of the bus station but better to take a becak – it is another colonial relic and the reasonably clean rooms are good value.

Places to Eat

The *Toko Oen* on Jalan Pemuda, a short walk from the Pasar, is a wonderfully genteel old place. It's not cheap but well worth a visit; the food is good and they have a terrific selection of exotic ice creams. Restaurants along Jalan Gajah Mada include the reasonably priced *Gajah Mada* at No 43 for good Chinese and seafood. On Gang Lombok, off Jalan Pekojan in Chinatown, there are good Chinese eating places too. At Pasar Ya'ik, the night market next to Pasar Johar, there are plenty of cheap foodstalls. The *Hotel Dibya Puri* restaurant, on Jalan Pemuda, serves good European and Indonesian food and their set Indonesian meal, complete with fruit and coffee, for 3000 rp is good value.

Getting There & Getting Around

Semarang is on the main Jakarta-Surabaya train route and can also be reached from those towns by bus. Tawang is the main railway station in Semarang. The Jurnatan bus station is close to Tawang and fairly central on Jalan Let Jen Haryono. Most bus ticket agents are near the bus station along the same street. From Yogya it takes about 3½ hours by bus for around 1000 rp. There are also regular bus services from Solo. Semarang to Surabaya by public bus costs 4500 rp, from 5000 rp by night bus and takes about eight hours. Buses to Jakarata cost from around 5000 rp but it's better to take the train. The night buses arrive at ungodly hours at the remote Pulo Gadung bus station.

You can get around town by fixed-price city bus or by Daihatsu minivan at a fixed cost of 100 rp. Daihatsus depart from terminal Baru, on Jalan H A Salim behind Pasar Johar.

OTHER NORTH COAST PLACES

Cirebon, about midway between Jakarta and Semarang, is the other major town on the north coast. Visit the Kesepuhan and Kanoman kratons there, the Sunyaragi rock palace and the batik village of Trusmi. There are a number of cheap places to stay along Jalan Siliwangi, the main street from the railway station, including the *Hotel Islam* with rooms for 2000 rp. The *Hotel Asia*, with rooms from 4500 rp including breakfast, is excellent value for the money. It's a clean and friendly place on Jalan Kalibaru Selatan, along the canal near the market on the main street.

Between Solo or Yogya and Semarang you can stop at Bandungan to see the Gedung Songo ('nine buildings' in Javanese), a collection of small but beautifully sited Hindu temples on the slopes of Mt Ungaran. The town of Ambarawa, on the main central route, is the turn off point for Bandungan and anyone who's fascinated by railway engines will enjoy the Ambarawa Railway Museum.

The collection of 20 or so railway engines at the old depot includes a 1902 cog locomotive, still in working order. From Ambarawa to Bandungan it's half an hour by colt, and from the market place (also worth a visit) in Bandungan you have to get another colt about six km to the actual site. To visit all the temples it could take up to six hours, or you can go on horseback. Places to stay in Bandungan include the cheap *Riani I* and *Penginapan Sri Rejeki*, and the more expensive *Madya Hillview Inn*. Avoid weekends when Bandungan gets very crowded.

SURABAYA

A big, busy and not particularly interesting city, the capital of East Java is a major port and the second largest city in Indonesia. For most people it's just a short stop between Central Java and Bali although it is probably the most 'Indonesian' of all the large cities. People who do find Surabaya interesting, and to be fair quite a few people do, generally enjoy the Indonesian atmosphere of the place. If you do have to hang around for a while, waiting for a ship to Sulawesi or Kalimantan for example, there are a few things to do.

Information

The East Java Regional Tourist Office is on Jalan Pemuda, just down from the Bamboe Denn. The office is open from 7 am daily except Sunday, and closes at 2 pm Monday to Thursday, 11 am Friday and 1 pm Saturday.

The Pelni ticketing office (tel 21694) is at Jalan Pahlawan 20 and open from 8 am to 4 pm (closed over lunch, 12 noon to 1 pm) Monday to Friday, 8 am to 1 pm Saturday. The front ticket counter is chaotic but you can go straight round to the back office where the staff are more helpful – speak to Mr Kris Nanlohy (Sales) or Mr Marto, the Manager.

We've had a couple of reports from people who have been befriended in Surabaya, have then been given drugged coffee and woken up later to find their valuables gone – take care.

Things to See

Zoo The Surabaya zoo is reputed to be the largest in South-East Asia. It is quite well laid out and has a couple of big Komodo dragons – who seem to spend half the time fast asleep. Admission is 350 rp and it costs 100 rp more for the aquarium (worth it) or the nocturama. The zoo is only a short ride, by city bus No 2 or bemo V, from Jalan Jen Sudirman in the centre of town.

Other Close to the centre is the THR amusement park, open in the evenings. Plenty of Makassar schooners can be seen at the Kali Mas wharf. The Bamboe Denn, see below, offers a free morning walking tour of the city. There is a swimming pool at the Garden Hotel next door to the Denn, or try the Hotel Simpang.

Places to Stay

If you're staying in this busy port town – and most people do at least overnight here between Yogya and Bali – there's really only one place. The *Bamboe Denn* (tel 40333) is almost a Surabaya institution and is always packed out with travellers. Dorm beds are 1000 rp, and rooms cost from 2000 rp. Although it's a little airless the Denn is clean and friendly. There's lots of travel information, a snack bar and it's conveniently central – the Gubeng train station is only a couple of minutes' walk down Jalan Pemuda. If becak drivers haven't heard of the Denn ask for the *Hotel Transito* (its other name) or for the big (and expensive) Garden Hotel, right next door. The Denn is at Jalan Pemuda 19, almost at the junction with Jalan Jen Sudirman. You may well get roped into a little English conversation with Indonesian students at the language school also run from the Denn – perhaps it helps to keep the costs down.

Other cheap hotels (and there aren't many) tend to be dismal. There are a number of places in the Gubeng Station

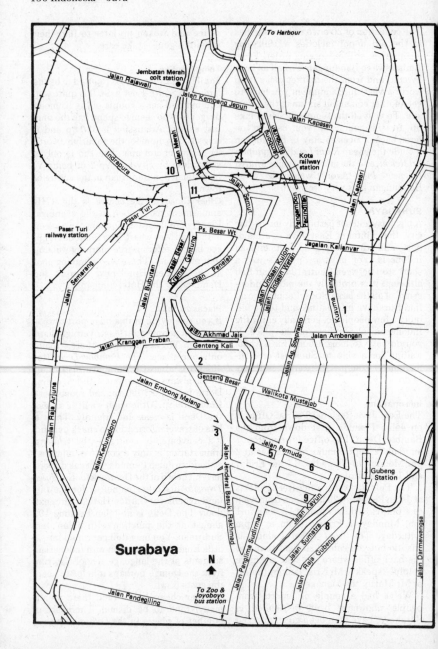

Surabaya

area such as the *Hotel Gubeng* on Jalan Sumatra, only 100 metres from the station. *Hotel Carmen*, between Gubeng and the Denn, is reasonably priced but a bit dirty, and the *Hotel Kayoon* round the corner on Jalan Kayoon is similar. Further down Jalan Sumatra from the station you'll find *Wisma Ganesha* at 34A – believe the number, there's no sign. It has some pleasant rooms, from 5000 rp including breakfast, if you want something better than the Denn.

Near the Kota Station on Jalan Bongkaran there's the *Merdeka I* at number 6, and the cheaper *Merdeka II* at number 14 with rooms for 5000 rp. The *Hotel Paviljoen*, an old colonial place at Jalan Genteng Besar 94, has reasonable rooms from 6000 rp.

Places to Eat

Food seems painfully expensive compared to Bali or Yogya but it can be very good. There are some good places close to the Denn like *Depot Tiga* (a grocery shop with no name) on Jalan Jen Sudirman, next to the cinema. One visitor raved that their 'es buah buah susu surpassed all es campurs and for that matter all other taste treats in South-East Asia'!

On the same street, but a few doors down, you'll find the *Michiko*. The buffet at the more expensive *Chez Rose* next door is worth a splurge. Or there's the cheap *Warung Kosgoro* on Jalan Pemuda across from the Denn. For cheap eating you can also patronise the stalls around the Gubeng Station or off Jalan Tunjungan, and there are night markets near the

flower market on Jalan Kayoon and on Jalan Pandegiling. Opposite the Bamboe Denn the *Granada Modern Bakery* is good for breakfast and cakes. Around the corner from the Denn you can have an expensive ice cream at the *Zangrandi* and watch the wealthy Surabayans roll up in their Mercedes and Volvos.

Getting There

See the introductory Getting Around section for Java for details on Jakarta-Surabaya and Yogyakarta-Surabaya transport.

Trains Trains from Jakarta, taking the northern route via Semarang, arrive at the Pasar Turi station. Trains taking the southern route via Yogya, and trains from Banyuwangi and Malang, arrive at Gubeng and carry on to Kota. The Gubeng station is much more convenient for the Bamboe Denn and other central places than Kota or Pasar Turi. Apart from services to the main cities there is a 3rd class evening train to Malang for 800 rp (from Malang the train leaves at the crack of dawn) and a morning and night train to Banyuwangi for the ferry to Bali. Through to Denpasar the train fare is 4600 to 5300 rp inclusive of the ferry to Bali and a bus to Denpasar.

Buses Public buses in Surabaya go from the Joyoboyo bus station – most night buses depart from the Bratang station to the east of Joyoboyo. The Elteha bus company has an office at Joyoboyo and at Jalan Sumatra 73; their night bus to Denpasar costs 5500 rp. There are also a number of private bus stands on Jalan B Rachmat but take care – they are very keen on overcharging. To Solo and Yogya by night bus the fares range from 5000 rp, to Jakarta from 9000 rp, and to Denpasar from 5500 rp. See Bali for more details on Surabaya-Denpasar transport.

Boats From Surabaya the most frequently made boat trips are to Kalimantan and Sulawesi. Apart from regular Pelni services to these islands – the *Tampomas*, *Kambuna* and the new *Rinjani* – Pelni also operate cargo ships to various desnations which sometimes take passengers. There are no regular timetables or fixed fares but you can get up-to-date information from the Pelni office (tel 293347) at Tanjung Perak harbour – ask for Mr Rifai. For information on other cargo boats try the Harbour Master, Mr Mawikere, at Kalimas Baru 194, Tanjung Perak.

Getting Around

Becaks are useful for local transport and there are plenty of them around town. Bemos are labelled A, B or K and all charge a standard 150 rp. City buses charge a fixed 125 rp fare. Gubeng Station is within easy walking distance of the Bamboe Denn and other losmen in that vicinity. From Joyoboyo bus station a bemo M or V will drop you on or near Jalan Pemuda. The ferry to Madura is 225 rp and you take a city bus or K bemo to the harbour. Buses also go directly from Joyoboyo to towns on Madura, eg Joyoboyo-Sumenep costs 2250 rp. The Surabaya airport is 15 km out and it's an expensive trip by taxi for around 7000 rp.

MADURA

Only half an hour from Surabaya by ferry, the relatively untouristed island of Madura has many fine beaches and beautiful remote countryside. Coming up from Bali, Madura is also accessible by daily ferry from Panarukan, a few km north of Situbondo, to Kalianget on the island's eastern tip – so you could make a trip through Madura and exit from Kamal to Surabaya. Madura is a flat and rugged island, much of it dry and sometimes barren, and it's a contrast to Java in both the general landscape and lifestyle of the people. Cattle raising is important rather than rice growing. The production of salt is another major industry – much of Indonesia's supply comes from the vast salt tracts around Kalianget in the east.

During the dry season, particularly August and September, Madura is famed for its colourful bull races, the *kerapan sapi*, which climax with the finals held at Pamekasan. The bulls are harnessed in pairs, two teams compete at a time and they're raced across a 120-metre course in a special stadium. Races don't last long; the best time recorded is nine seconds over 100 metres which is faster than man's world track record. Bull races for tourists are sometimes staged at the Bangkalan stadium. The East Java tourist board can supply details of where and when the bull races will be held.

Apart from beaches and the bull races, there are a number of interesting places to visit dotted around the island. Near the village of Arasbaya, on the west coast, is Air Mata – 'Water of the Eye' or 'Tears' – where the old royal cemetery of the Cakraningrat family is perched on the edge of a small ravine, with beautiful views along the river valley and across the terraced hills. To get there from Kamal take a colt for Arasbaya (28 km north) and ask for the turn off to Air Mata; from there it's a four km walk inland.

Along the south coast road to Pamekasan, 100 km east of Kamal, there are fields of immaculately-groomed cattle, small fishing villages and a sea of rainbow-coloured perahus. Camplong, about 15 km short of Pamekasan, has a fine sweeping beach and calm water. From Pamekasan, the capital of Madura, you can visit the strange natural fire resources of Api Abadi (Eternal Fire), where 'fire spouts out of the earth'. Sumenep is an old and attractive town, 53 km north-east of Pamekasan in the more isolated hills of the interior. See Sumenep's 18th century mosque, the kraton and its small but interesting museum of royal family possessions. Asta Tinggi, the royal cemetery, is only about three km from the town centre.

At Salopeng, 21 km from Sumenep and near the fishing village of Ambunten on the north coast, there are great yellow sand dunes, palm trees, and rough seas. The beach at Lombang, 30 km from Sumenep, is supposed to be even more beautiful but less easily accessible – there are no roads and the local people ride their bicycles along the sands.

Not everybody is entranced with Madura – it has 'unfriendly people and it's a boring place, don't go alone,' said one traveller. But another thought it was very interesting and that 'the local girls are incredibly sensual, it's not surprising that so many migrate to the red light district of Surabaya. I must confess', added this Madura fan, 'to really enjoying Surabaya – but no one else seems to so I guess I am just weird!'

Places to Stay In Pamekasan, you could try the *Hotel Garuda*, at Jalan Masegit near the town square, with singles/doubles from 1650 to 3300 rp. Or there's the *Trunojoyo* round the corner on Jalan Trunojoyo, or the cheaper *Losmen Bahagia*. They're all in the centre of town and a 200 rp becak ride from the bus station.

Sumenep, to the east of Pamekasan, is more interesting than Pamekasan and a good base for visiting remoter parts of the island. *Losmen Wijaya I and II* are good with rooms from 5500 rp, or try the cheaper *Losmen Damai* or *Losmen Matahari* near the town square.

Getting There
It's only half an hour by ferry from Surabaya to Kamal, the harbour town in Madura, and from there you can take a bus or colt to other main towns. From Kamal it's a bumpy two or three-hour bus trip to Pamekasan, the island's capital. Bangkalan is only about half an hour from the ferry terminal. There is a ferry from Panarukan to Kalianget at 1 pm, from Kalianget to Panarukan at 7 am.

AROUND SURABAYA
Gresik
25 km from Surabaya is the tomb of the Muslim saint credited with introducing Islam to Java in the 13th century.

Trowulan
Scattered around Trowulan, near Mojokerto, 60 km from Surabaya on the Surabaya-Solo road, are the remains of the ancient Majapahit kingdom. The Majapahits were the final Hindu kingdom to rule on Java until the advance of the Muslims drove them out to Bali in the early 1500s. The Trowulan museum has a large map indicating the locations of the temples *candis*, tombs, and graves. The museum is open from 7 am daily except Mondays, and closes at 2 pm Tuesday to Thursday and Sunday, 11 am Friday and 12.30 pm Saturday.

Some of the temple remains are very impressive in their shattered grandeur and a few of the sites are within walking distance of the museum. If you're en route to somewhere else, you can leave your gear at the office. Or you can hire a becak – a three to four hour trip costs about 5000 rp and the ride along the country lanes is easily as good as the temples themselves. A bus from Surabaya (600 rp) will drop you right at the museum on the main road; it's another 1000 rp on to Madiun.

Pandaan
The open air Candra Wilwatikta theatre at Pandaan, 40 km south of Surabaya on the road to Malang, is the site of the East Java classical ballet festival held during the dry season on the first and third Saturday nights of the months May to October.

Mountain Resorts
Tretes and Prigen have a network of footpaths and trails and many waterfalls. I wouldn't recommend it for a special trip but if you have to kill time in Surabaya this is a good place to escape to. On the other side of the same mountain, the similar resorts of Selecta and Batu are easily accessible from Malang. Selecta has an excellent swimming pool and Songgoriti, near Batu, is a spa town with relaxing hot sulphur baths. Others are Tosari and Wendit which has a lake where you can swim and also lots of monkeys.

Places to Stay There are lots of cottages or individual rooms available in Tretes and

Prigen, just below Tretes – somebody will find you a place although this is principally a local resort where few foreigners are seen. Prices are not too cheap and go up towards the sky. There are some good and cheap places to eat around the market. The story is similar in Batu and Selecta.

Pasir Putih

Some distance east of Probolinggo on the Surabaya-Banyuwangi, Pasir Putih is East Java's main coastal resort and it can be mobbed at weekends. The name means 'white beach' but the sand is more grey-black than white! No matter – there's clear water, pleasant swimming and lots of picturesque outrigger boats – but compared to Lovina Beach, only a few hours away on Bali, it's no big deal.

Places to Stay There are a number of hotels jammed between the highway and

the beach. Next door to the *Oriental Restaurant* the *Wisma Bhayangkara* has doubles facing the highway from 3000 rp; rooms facing the beach, with private mandi, cost from 4200 rp.

Situbondo

Only a short distance on the Banyuwangi side of Pasir Putih there are several places to stay in this reasonably large town.

Places to Stay The *Hotel Asia* is on the main road and quite pleasant. The *Losmen Sarworini* is near the railway station or there's the *Hotel Situbondo*.

MOUNT BROMO

This fantastic, and still far from extinct, volcano is easy to fit in between Bali and Surabaya. The usual jumping-off point for Bromo is the town of Probolinggo on the main Surabaya-Banyuwangi road. From there you have to get to Ngadisari, high on the slopes of an ancient volcano. At Ngadisari you have to sign the visitors' book, pay 100 rp and think about a place to stay. You can stay with one of the villagers in Ngadisari or you can continue up the very steep final three km to Cemoro Lawang at the rim of the crater – hoping for a ride if you're on foot. There's a slightly expensive hotel at Cemoro Lawang but the advantage of staying up here is that you've got a shorter and easier walk in the morning. On Bromo, as at so many other mountains, it's being there for the sunrise which is all-important!

As at Mt Batur in Bali, Bromo is a crater within a crater. The outer one is vast and across to Bromo and nearby Mt Batok is a scene of utter desolation. Get up at 4 am, or earlier for an easy stroll across, if you're staying at the top (the hotel will wake you up) and just follow the path down into the crater and the white markers across the lava sand to Bromo. Take a torch or the descent in the dark can be fairly dodgey. There is no need for a guide or horses although if you want to ride across it costs about 5000 rp. By the time you've crossed the lava plain and started to climb up Bromo (246 steps, one traveller reported) it should be fairly light. From the top you'll get an unreal view of the sun sailing up over the outer crater. Bromo continuously pours out some very smelly white smoke – New Zealanders will find it familiar!

A number of travellers have made additional suggestions about the Bromo trip – almost all noting that it's definitely worthwhile. In the wet season the dawn and the clouds are likely to arrive simultaneously so at that time of year you might just as well stay in bed and stroll across later in the day when it's much warmer. In January or February there's a big annual festival and at that time of year getting up the mountain involves fighting your way through the crowds. One visitor even suggested that if you're really crazy you could climb right down inside the crater. Another nutcase suggested climbing it at night while it's erupting, adding that it 'scares the shit out of you'!

As an alternative to returning to Probolinggo you can walk right around Bromo across the lava plain and climb up over the opposite edge to Ngadas. You can walk down from village to village until you eventually get a ride into Malang. It entails six or seven hours of walking, so start early in order to get to Malang by evening.

Places to Stay

Mt Bromo There are now lots of places to stay in Ngadisari although the quality varies a lot and security is not always so great. Prices vary from around 2000 rp, less for really basic rooms and much higher if you arrive too late to hunt around. At Cemoro Lawang the *Hotel Bromo Permai* has comfortable dorm beds for 1800 rp (1500 rp for students or YHA) but rooms are rather expensive, from 5400 rp to 8400 rp double with bathroom. The hotel has a bar and restaurant – food here is also fairly pricey but they're quite substantial meals. It's warm and a good place for an early breakfast before setting out to Bromo. At night it's very cold at the top (it is in Ngadisari too) but staying up here does save an hour or so of pre-dawn walking! At the village of *Lawang Sair*, 300 metres below the hotel, you can stay with Mbuk Artini for 1000 rp, good food too.

Probolinggo This town is a useful midpoint between Surabaya and Banyuwangi as well as being the jumping-off point for Mt Bromo. There are hotels and some cheap restaurants along the main street, Jalan Raja P Sudirman, within 10 minutes walk of the bus station. The *Hotel Bromo Permai II*, right opposite the bus station, is a good source of information on Bromo and transport for Bali. At the other end of the street, on a corner, you'll find the imposing *Hotel Victoria*, with basic doubles for 2750 rp and rooms with bathroom and fan from 11,000 rp. Tea on arrival and breakfast are thrown in too. And 'a never-ending cassette tape playing 'Aulde Lang Syne' in Indonesian,' warned one visitor! *Hotel Ratna* at Jalan Raja P Sudirman 94 is also good with rooms from 3000 rp, from 7500 rp with bathroom and fan, including breakfast. *Hotel Kamayoran*, almost pposite the Victoria, is cheap but also Orather dirty.

Getting There

Probolinggo is a 1000 rp bus ride from the Joyoboyo bus station in Surabaya. There are several departures an hour and the trip takes 2½ to 3½ hours. Coming from Bali it's around 2000 rp to Probolinggo from Banyuwangi and takes about six hours. The bus from Malang costs 950 rp and takes two hours.

Colts from Probolinggo to Ngadisari, for Bromo, run roughly from 7 am to 7 pm. The colt station is only about 300 metres from the bus station and from there it's a 1000 rp, 1½ to two hour colt ride to Ngadisari. From Probolinggo it's 28 km to Sukapura and another 14 km from there to Ngadisari.

MALANG

Malang is a big country town on the 'back route' between Yogyakarta and Banyuwangi. The countryside on this run is particularly beautiful and Malang is a pleasant city with just enough altitude to take the edge off the heat. It gets few western visitors although it has good parks and trees and a large central market. For an interesting trip in this area take a train from Solo to Jombang, then colts to Blimbing, Kandangan, Batu and finally Malang. There is a direct bus from Malang to Probolinggo.

There are a number of high mountains around Malang including Gunung Semeru, the highest point in Java at 3678 metres. It takes three or four days to climb to the top and back and it is a real climb, not an easy walk. The hill resort of Selecta (see Around Surabaya) is just 16 km north-west of Malang; take a colt to Batu and from there another colt will drop you right at the Selecta swimming pool.

Malang has some excellent ruins. A good day trip is the circle to Candi Singosari (right in Singosari, 500 metres from the main Malang-Surabaya road), then east to Candi Jago at Tumpang, and then to Candi Kidal in the small village of Kidal. Finally you can circle back south to Malang via Tajinan. First take a bemo (125 rp) to the colt terminal at Blimbing, and from Blimbing there are colts all the way with a total fare of about 1000 rp.

Places to Stay

There are lots of places to stay and some excellent cheap eating places. The Surabaya *Bamboe Denn* now has a branch hostel (tel 24859) at Jalan Semeru 35, which is only about 10 minutes' walk from the bus or railway station. Ignore the becak jockeys who say it's three km away. It's very cheap and has dorm beds for just 1000 rp – you'll probably get roped into more English conversation lessons too! If it seems to be locked up ring the bell inside the gate. Only two minutes from the bus station the *Hotel Helios* on Jalan Pattimura has a very pleasant garden and rooms for 4000 rp including breakfast. The *Hotel Montana* at Jalan Kahuripan 8 has rooms from 3000 rp but it's a bit airless and dingy.

Hotel Aloha at Jalan Gajah Mada 7 is nice but expensive; doubles with bathroom cost 10,000 rp including breakfast. *Hotel Pelangi*, a very large yellow building right on the town square, is also quite good although expensive.

Hotel Santosa is central at Jalan H A Salim 24, just off the main square, and has basic but clean rooms with a private mandi from 4600 rp for a double. The *Hotel Malang* on Jalan K H Zainul Arifin, off Jalan H A Salim, is also central but rather noisy. The doubles have monster beds. Better value is the pleasantly old-fashioned *Hotel Malinda*, also on Zainul Arifin, with rooms with private mandi from 5500 rp for two to 8500 rp for four – and ceilings that must be seven metres high!

Places to Eat

Amongst the good places to eat is *Toko Oen* on the town square, but it's rather expensive. *Rumah Makan Padang Minang Jaya* at Jalan Basuki Rachmat 111 has terrific Padang food, or try *Depot Pangsit Mie Gadjah Mada* on Jalan Pasar Besar for good cheap noodles. Malang also has an excellent cheap night market, Pasar Senggol, along Jalan Majapahit by the river.

Getting There

Buses to or from Solo take about nine hours and cost 3300 rp, around 6000 rp by night bus. To and from Surabaya buses leave regularly and take around 2½ hours, about 800 rp. The train from Surabaya takes about three hours and costs 800 rp, 3rd class only. The bus to Probolinggo takes about two hours. Buses to or from Banyuwangi cost around 2900 rp and take about nine hours. Night buses to Bali cost from 5750 rp. Bali Indah has an office on Jalan Pattimura, and Pemudi Express at Jalan Basuki Rachmat 1 operates night buses to Bali and other destinations.

OTHER PLACES IN EAST JAVA

Although there are no particular attractions to drag you there, schedules or just the urge to be somewhere different might take you to Banyuwangi, the ferry departure point for Bali; to Madiun, a small town between Surabaya and Solo; as well as to Malang.

Another interesting trip is to take a bus from Malang to Bondowoso and on from there to Gempol, a tiny village in a coffee growing area. You can spend the night there and climb the nearby small but beautiful volcano Ijen in the morning. There's a house near the top where you can leave your gear, retrieve it on the way down and continue walking until you reach a road to Banyuwangi.

Madiun

There is a group of cheap hotels clustered on the Surabaya side of town. The *Hotel Madiun* and *Hotel Raya* are similarly priced; the *Hotel 7777* is a little cheaper.

Blitar

Blitar is a small town on the Malang-Kediri road. The very beautiful Panataran temple complex is 10 km north of Blitar and can be reached by motorbike or an expensive and infrequent colt service. On the way out to Panataran you can visit Sukarno's elaborate grave.

The *Hotel Sri Lestari*, about 10 minutes' walk from the bus station on the main street Jalan Merdeka, has rooms for 3000 rp and more expensive rooms with bathroom. It's a friendly place: cheap meals for 500 rp are available at the family kitchen and the owner will arrange a motorbike for the trip to Panataran. The *Penginapan Sentosa*, with singles at 3000 rp, is a rather dirty place but right by the bus station.

Banyuwangi

The actual ferry departure point for Bali is a few km from the town at Ketapang. In Banyuwangi you could try the *Hotel Anda* on Jalan Basuki Rachmat, five minutes' walk from the bus terminal for Ketapang. Rooms cost 2000 rp. The *Hotel Selamet* is right next to the railway station and has singles/doubles for 2000/3000 rp. The *Hotel Baru* on Jalan Pattimura, also close to the railway station, is friendly and good value with big airy rooms from 2000 rp, from 3500 rp with bathroom, including breakfast. Next door there's an excellent warung run by the family.

In the centre of town, about 15 minutes' walk from the railway station, the *Hotel Baru Raya* at Jalan Dr Sutomo 32 has reasonable, cheap rooms from 1000 rp for a single. The *Simpang Lima* by the junction on Jalan Jaksa Agung is more expensive and rather musty and run-down.

Bali

Bali is a tropical island so picturesque and immaculate it could easily be a painted backdrop. Bali is shatteringly beautiful countryside, gleaming white beaches, warm blue waters and friendly people who don't just have a culture but actually live it. In Bali every night is a festival and even a funeral is a joyous occasion.

A curious mixture of position and events account for Bali's relative isolation from Indonesian history and religion and the vitality of its culture. Gajah Mada, chief minister of the Majapahit kingdom, ruled Bali from 1343 with his capital at Gelgel near Klungkung. At that time Muslim power was on the rise in Java and the final flight of the Majapahits to Bali in 1478, with their entire entourage of scholars, artists and intelligentsia was the starting point for Bali's extraordinary cultural activity.

CULTURE – RELIGION

Balinese life centres around religion from birth to death. Their temples are open, cheerful places and there are thousands of them. Every village must have at least three. The *pura desa* is the town temple where official functions involving the whole village are held. The *pura puseh* is the temple to honour the village founders. The *pura dalem* is the temple of the dead, dedicated to the spirits of the afterlife. There can also be temples to certain deities or temples to the spirits of agriculture, lakes and mountains. Every rice paddy needs a small *subak* temple and every compound requires a family temple. In the morning offerings have to be made to Bali's prolific spirits – on high shelves for the good ones, casually placed on the ground for the baddies.

Temple festivals are splashes of colour. They can be held for all sorts of reasons but the most common are the *odalans* or temple birthdays. Held every 210 days (the Balinese year) the festival can last for days. There will be cockfights, processions and offerings in the daytime. The temples are decorated with flowers, umbrellas, streamers and a feast of food offerings. Sensibly the gods can stuff themselves on the spirit and essence of the food; the mere substance is taken home and eaten afterwards. At night it is like a country fair with food stalls, gambling and things for sale. Later there are dances, *wayang kulits* and fun till dawn. There is always one on somewhere, so don't miss it.

Remember that religion is an important part of Balinese life and be respectful in the temples. Dress neatly and always wear a temple scarf around the waist – pick one up in the market quite cheaply. Also remember it is very bad manners to put yourself on a higher level than the village elders; don't stand on walls to get a better view or take photographs. Women are not supposed to enter temples during their periods. But you don't have to hang a notice round your neck saying 'unclean, unclean'.

Even funerals are fun in Bali, with crowds of people and brilliantly decorated towers. A cremation is a release of the soul so that it can go to its afterlife, and therefore is a cause for celebration. To confuse the soul, the funeral tower containing the body is bounced, shaken, spun, twirled, splashed and run all the way from the deceased's home to the cremation field. The guests and spectators sprint along behind. If the soul isn't sufficiently confused it might find its way back home, which would be annoying. A funeral is an expensive business so bodies are often buried for months or even years till the cremation can be afforded. Alternatively people will wait for a big funeral that they can join in.

Behaviour

Wherever you go in Bali or elsewhere in Indonesia remember that what goes down in Kuta does not go down so well anywhere else. Kuta is a little enclave where the most outrageous behaviour is tolerated, even found amusing. Elsewhere in the country that won't be the case and dressing or acting as you can in Kuta is not going to do you or any of the travellers who follow you any good whatsoever. If all that Bali means to you is Kuta and all that Kuta means is Surf City then to my mind you might as well stay home.

BALINESE DANCES

Although dances are now as often performed for tourists as for temple festivals, with a little luck you will see plenty for free. The best known and most 'touristed' are the Kechak or monkey dance, the Ramayana, the Barong-Rangda or kris dance and the Legong. They are performed regularly at Kuta Beach, Ubud and other centres from 1000 to 3000 rp for a ticket. The Ramayana Ballet is also performed at Prambanan in Java.

Unfortunately there's been a trend of late to present shortened tourist versions of the dances and convenient little combinations of the most popular dances. Half a Kechak and a bit of a kris dance is not the way they should be seen. Fortunately if you're in Bali for long (and away from Kuta) there's a very good chance that you'll get to see a good performance, one not put on exclusively for tourists.

Kechak The most exciting and visually spectacular of the dances, the Kechak tells a tale from the Ramayana of the capture of Sita by Rawana and her subsequent rescue by the monkey army. The excitement is provided by the circle of men who provide fantastically coordinated movements and the hypnotic 'Chak Chak Chak' noise which imitates monkeys – they're called kechak in Indonesia for that reason.

Barong-Rangda or Kris Dance This well-known trance dance tells a tale of good, in the shape of the lion-like Barong, in conflict with evil, the witch Rangda. The high point of the dance comes when the Barong's supporters attack Rangda, but her magic turns their knives – the famous *kris* – against themselves. The Barong in turn applies his magic to prevent their krises from wounding them. The 'every morning at 10 am' performances tend to be a little artificial, but when the dancers really do go into a trance it's hard not to believe it!

Legong The most graceful and feminine of the Balinese dances, this is performed by very young girls. The Legong Kraton, or Legong of the Palace, tells a story of a little bird warning the king of impending doom if he insists on going to war. The king

ignores the warning and is killed. The tiny figures in their dazzling costumes are exquisitely graceful.

Ramayana This is one of the best known and beloved legends in Asia. A Hindu epic comparable to *the Odyssey* or *The Iliad*, it is the inspiration behind many carvings, wayangs and dances. The dance begins many years after Prince Rama, his wife Sita and brother Laksamana have been banished, unjustly, to the forest. Rawana, King of the Demons, devises a scheme to kidnap the beautiful Sita. He succeeds in luring Rama and his brother away, leaving Sita alone, and then carries her off. After a long, weary search, Rama enlists the help of Hanuman, the white monkey general. Hanuman finds Sita and then helps Rama defeat the Demon King and retrieve his wife. In Balinese dancing, animals and clowns are allowed to improvise and they are usually extremely funny; a good Hanuman can create an unforgettable role. The Kechak is another version of the Ramayana.

MUSIC
Gamelan The traditional Balinese orchestra is almost entirely based on percussion instruments. They are a brilliant visual as well as aural sensation and accompany dances, processions, puppet plays and every other facet of Balinese life. You can get cassette tapes of gamelan performances.

OTHER ENTERTAINMENT
Wayang Kulit Shadow puppet plays are a traditional form of entertainment, not only in Bali, but in Java, Malaysia and parts of Thailand. A late-night, all-night activity, they can be rather tiresome to the westerner who cannot understand the language, but try to see at least part of one. The *dalang* is not just a puppet master, he also has to tell the story, be all the characters' voices, supply the rhythmic beat to the action, and direct the gamelan accompaniment. Since performances commonly last all night he also needs endurance.

The leather puppets are seen as shadows on the screen, the male part of the audience sits behind the screen with the dalang.

Other traditional entertainments include cockfights – to the death – which go on all over the island, particularly at festivals. Dogfights are less traditional entertainment, but there are certainly plenty of them.

INFO

The 'Bandung' tourist office on the main street past the square in Denpasar is helpful and has a festival calendar for Bali's many festivals. It's open from 7 am daily except Mondays and closes at 11 am on Friday, 1 pm on Saturday and Sunday, 2 pm on other days. There's an excellent privately-run tourist information service in Ubud which puts a lot of effort into preserving the 'real' Bali from the depradations of the surf-booze-motorcycle crowds.

The main post office in Denpasar with poste restante service is inconveniently far out from the centre, sort of halfway between Denpasar and Sanur by the back route. You're better off using the convenient little post office in Kuta or the one in Ubud. There's a 50 rp charge for each letter.

There's an American Express office in Sanur. If you're having money transferred to Bali the Bank Ekspor-Impor at Jalan Gajah Mada 87 in Denpasar is probably the best. The immigration office (Kantor Immigrasi) is at Jalan Diponegoro 222 in the south of Denpasar, get there on a Sanglah bemo – and make sure you're togged up in your best.

Warning Bali suffers from a surfeit of pickpockets these days – they're particularly prevalent on bemos. The usual routine is this: somebody starts a conversation with you, distracting you while his accomplice steals your wallet, purse or whatever. Bemos tend to be pretty tightly packed so it's no problem. A painting, large parcel, basket or the like can also serve as a cover for such activities.

Other forms of theft are prevalent, particularly at Kuta where losmen rooms are very often not at all secure. Don't leave valuables in your room and beware of people who wander in and out of losmen; keep your room locked if you're not actually in it. There have been mugging incidents down some of the less frequented *gangs* (alleys) at night. Many travellers leave their airline tickets or other valuables in safe deposit boxes which are to be found at many money changers and other such places around Kuta.

Remember that if you get your passport stolen in Bali it's Jakarta where all the embassies are located. Fortunately for Australians, after years of procrastination, the Australian government has finally been established a diplomatic office at Jalan Raya Sanur 146 at Sanur Beach. Just as well because lots of Australians seem to strike trouble in Bali. There's also a US consular agent at Sanur.

Almost every tourist attraction in Bali takes an entrance charge now and lots of them chase you for 'donations' too. One writer noted that donation books at temples indicated that most people seemed to make donations of 500, 1000 or even 2000 rp! More likely you can read that as 50, 100 or even 200 rp – with an extra zero added later.

GETTING THERE

Air See the introductory section on Getting There for Indonesia as a whole for details of air fares. The travel agents at Kuta Beach sell cheap tickets to Australia, Europe and other cities in Asia. Reconfirming tickets in Bali is a real bore. Agents at Kuta Beach charge 500 rp to make Garuda reservations or reconfirmations and these arrangements don't necessarily get made. The Garuda office in Denpasar is at Jalan Melati 61 and can be very crowded and time-consuming too. There are smaller Garuda offices at the Kuta Beach Hotel and at the Bali Beach

Inter-Continental at Sanur, where you'll also find a Garuda office.

Bali-Java

Air You can fly from Denpasar to Surabaya, Yogyakarta or Jakarta in Java. The flight to Ujung Pandang from Denpasar is cheaper than from Surabaya or other towns in Java. There is also various flights from Denpasar to the islands of Nusa Tenggara.

Bus There are morning and evening departures for the trip to Surabaya in Java – with improvements to the roads and the introduction of Mercedes buses it is now a faster trip than in the past. So much so that if you're doing it overnight look for a later evening departure or you'll get into Surabaya at a ridiculously early hour in the morning. They drive like madmen! You can get buses from various depots in Denpasar or direct from Kuta beach – there are a lot of companies making the trip so just shop around for a convenient departure time. Make sure it's a modern, comfortable Mercedes bus and not one of the few remaining old bangers. Cost is in the 5000 to 6000 rp bracket, more with air-con. The fare may include a usually rather lousy meal at the midpoint of the trip.

You can also get a bus straight through to Yogya for around 11,000 rp (air-con) or 9000 rp (non air-con) or even to Jakarta. You would have to have amazing endurance! Buses also run from Singaraja on the north coast to Surabaya for a little less than the Denpasar buses. The Bali-Java ferry is included in all the ticket prices. Gita, Bali, Damri, Elteha, Jawa Indah, Bali Mas and Bali Express are some of the bus companies.

Do-it-yourself You can forget the straight-through bus and do it in stages if you want to stop at Mt Bromo on the way to Surabaya. Straight-through buses will drop you off in Probolinggo or you can take a local bus to Gilimanuk, a bemo from the bus station to the ferry terminal, take the ferry across to Java and then bus or train from there. The ferry costs 425 rp but there are also small landing craft which cost anything from 175 to 275 rp. The crossing only takes about 15 minutes, but the town of Banyuwangi, to which the ferry supposedly runs, is actually a couple of km south of the ferry dock. Banyuwangi is the railhead for this end of Java. Buses, however, go straight from the ferry terminal so you don't need to go into town.

Train The train ticket office in Denpasar is by the Immigrasi, but you can also buy train tickets from agents at Kuta beach or from Mutiara Express at Jalan Diponegoro 172 in Denpasar. They have train tickets to Surabaya and Yogya at prices a bit lower than the buses – they include a minibus from Denpasar to Gilimanuk, the ferry across to Java and transport from there to the station.

Bali-Nusa Tenggara

Air There are flights east to the various islands of Nusa Tenggara with Garuda, Merpati and Zamrud. If they've managed to yet again get back in the air Denpasar is the hub for Zamrud's network around the islands and they're likely to be cheaper (and more interesting) than the others. They even fly to the ex-Portuguese half of Timor but you've got little chance of being allowed to buy a ticket! See the Nusa Tenggara section for more details. Zamrud is at Jalan Wahidin 1.

Boat That overlander's dream of a cheap and regular ship service to Darwin in north Australia remains a dream but if you skip down to Benoa harbour you'll find there are all sorts of yachts anchored there and it's no great feat to hitch a ride to somewhere far away. Maureen and I got a ride to Western Australia once and several travellers have written to us recently to express their surprise at how easy it can be to hitch a yacht ride.

If you've got the visa time, island hopping through the Nusa Tenggara islands is great fun but these days it's just an out-and-back adventure from Bali as

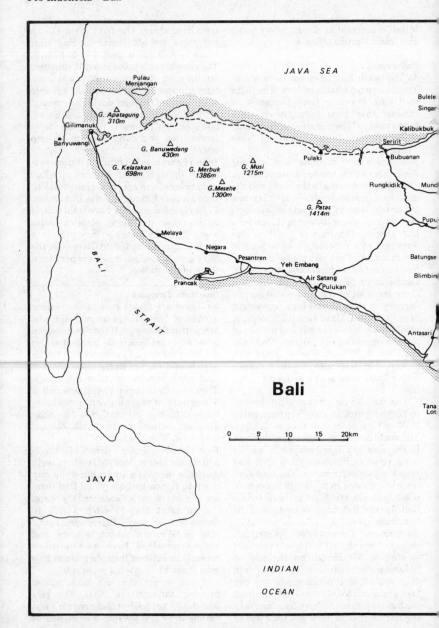

JAVA SEA

Bulele

Singar

Kalibukbuk

Pulau
Menjangan

G. Apatagung
310m

Gilimanuk

Banyuwangi

Seririt

Pulaki

Bubuanan

G. Banuwedang
430m

G. Kelatakan
698m

G. Merbuk
1386m

G. Musi
1215m

Rungkidik

Mund

G.Mesehe
1300m

G. Patas
1414m

Pupu

Melaya

Negara

Pesantren

Yeh Embang

Batungse

Prancak

Air Satang

Pulukan

Blimbin

BALI STRAIT

Antasari

Bali

0   5   10   15   20km

JAVA

Tana
Lot

INDIAN

OCEAN

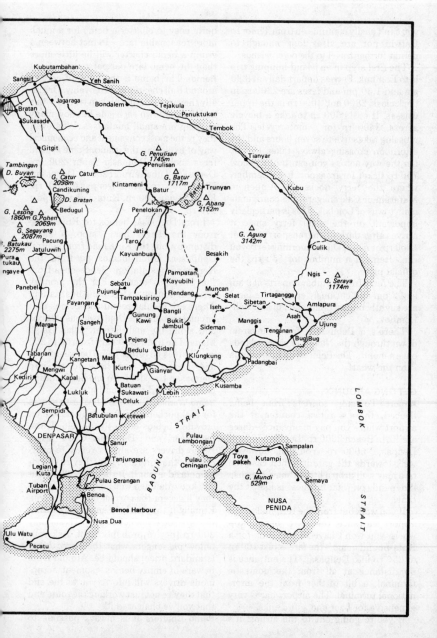

you can't easily continue on from Timor to Darwin nor are visas long enough to permit further travel to the outer islands.

The first step in an island-hopping trip is to Lombok. Ferries depart daily at 8.30 am and 1.30 pm and fares are 2300 rp in deck class, 2800 and 4000 rp in the upper classes. It costs 600 rp to take a bicycle across, 3400 rp for a motorcycle. The crossing takes five to seven hours and the afternoon crossing always takes longer. On the way across you can buy a yellow 750 rp ticket for transport from Lembar, where the ferry docks, to Ampenan, Mataram or Cakranegara, the contiguous main towns of Lombok. This is particularly important on the night ferry since it arrives after dark when transport can cost 1000 rp or more. On the morning ferry you can often get a minibus for 550 rp, the official price.

The ferry from Lembar departs at 9 am and 2 pm and curiously enough the fares are slightly higher Lombok-Bali and Bali-Lombok.

There's a Pelni ship from Singaraja down through the Nusa Tenggara islands once a month. The Pelni office in Singaraja is on the wharf.

GETTING AROUND

Airport To stop tourists from being fleeced, there's a taxi counter at the airport where you pay in advance – fares are Kuta Beach 2300 rp, Legian 3500 rp, Denpasar 5000 rp. You can, however, walk towards the gate in which case the fare may well drop a little – 'may' because it depends on what business is like at the time!

If you walk out from the terminal to the airport entrance there's a bemo stop where you won't have to wait long for a Kuta-bound bemo – the fare is just 100 rp or 250 rp into Denpasar. The entrance is no distance at all from the domestic terminal, a bit further from the international terminal. The airport bar is very expensive for beer and soft drinks.

If you're going out to the airport it's quite easy to charter a bemo for a much more reasonable fare – in fact between a group a bemo charter will be little more than the bemo fare per person.

Bemos The bemo is the basis of getting around Bali cheaply and enjoyably. Originally they were all tiny pickup trucks with a bench seat down each side but now many of them are small minibuses. Whatever, they're the most convenient and economical way of exploring the island. Some typical fares include Denpasar-Sanur 200 rp, Denpasar-Tuban airport 250 rp, Denpasar-Ubud 300 rp, Kuta-Denpasar 150 rp, Kuta-Legian 100 rp, Kuta-Tuban airport 150 rp.

From Denpasar bemos for Kuta leave from the Tegal bemo stop, a short distance along the Kuta road from central Denpasar. Ubud bemos go from the Kereneng bus station, Benoa ones from the Suci bus station. For the monkey forest at Sangeh go to Ubung bus station. There are regular round-trip bemos that circulate around the Denpasar bus stations and along the main street, Jalan Gajah Mada. The fixed fares vary from 50 to 200 rp. There is no direct bemo between Kuta and Denpasar. You have to go into Denpasar, transfer from one bemo station to another and then continue.

Bemo Warning Bemos are favourite haunts for pickpockets. Be especially careful on crowded bemos or on the popular Kuta-Denpasar and Denpasar-Ubud trips. Bemo drivers are always ready to overcharge the unwary but they're good-humoured about it. If they ask 200 rp but you know damned well it should be 100 rp they'll accept the correct fare with a grin. Equally if they make a huge protest that the fare you thought was 150 rp is actually 200 rp they're probably right. Ask your fellow passengers what the *harga biasa* (standard price) should be. Around Kuta beware of empty bemos – some unscrupulous drivers will inform you at the end that they're not just working the route and that you've chartered it!

Bemo Charters It is always possible to

charter bemos and between a few people the cost can be little more than the regular bemo fares and much more convenient. If, for example, you wanted to go from Kuta Beach to Ubud you'd have to take one bemo to the Tegal station in Denpasar, transfer from Tegal to Kereneng and then take another bemo from there to Ubud. A chartered bemo for this trip would cost 4000 to 5000 rp, only US$4 or 5 and you get door to door service. The trip between Kuta and Sanur costs about 2000 rp which between four people is about the same as the regular fare and is much more convenient than the roundabout route via Denpasar. You can also charter bemos by the day. The cost depends on where you want to go but around 20,000 rp is a good figure to work on. This is less than hiring a car and involves you in no paperwork, no insurance problems – you don't even pay for the gas. As a rule of thumb for chartering bemos, count on around 15 rp per km or about 12 times the regular fare – since a bemo will customarily carry about 12 passengers.

Buses Denpasar has a number of bus stations. Suci handles mainly local traffic and some of the Surabaya buses. Kereneng is for the east and north-east. Ubung is for the west and north-west. Bali's big, old buses have virtually disappeared in favour of minibuses which are much more comfortable and also more frequent. Some typical minibus fares from Denpasar include Klungkung 600 rp, Amlapura 1200 rp, Padangbai 800 rp, Kintimani 1200 rp (all from Kereneng), Gilimanuk 2000 rp, Singaraja 1250 rp (all from Ubung). From Singaraja it costs 900 rp to Gilimanuk, 700 rp to Kintimani. Where buses are still available they'll be cheaper.

Motorcycles Driving yourself around Bali on a motorcycle is a pleasant and convenient way of seeing the island – but there are several big BUTS. Biggest is don't plan to learn how to ride in Bali – motorcycling is a risky activity at the best of times; when you add all the unique Asian hazards as well, Bali is no place for a beginner. They'll let you out on the road even though you may have never straddled a bike before – don't consider it unless you're a reasonably experienced rider. BUT number two is that bikes are a miniature ecological disaster for Bali – there are thousands of them and they're horribly noisy as well as unsafe.

On the plus side, getting around Bali is often a matter of moving along until you see something happening, then stopping – there's always a procession, festival, funeral or something happening. A bike is ideal for this sort of travel. You can stop whenever and wherever you choose. So if you can ride and you decide to bike it here are the rules of the game:

First of all get an international driving permit, endorsed for motorcycles, before you depart. Otherwise you're involved in all sorts of bureaucratic hassles. Getting a Balinese licence is simply a matter of riding a few metres without falling off, but it's expensive (3500 rp) and time-consuming (allow at least four hours) and you're then required to get special Balinese insurance which is also expensive. The police do occasional roadside licence checks, especially between Kuta and Denpasar. Virtually every tourist attraction in Bali also has a motorcycle parking charge.

Before accepting a bike to rent make sure it's in good shape – there are some awful old nails about. If you're hiring for longer periods expect to pay less than on a day or short-term rate. Shop around; the local members of the Kuta Hell's Angels chapter (100 cc division) will often be cheaper than the more reputable bike shops but equally their bikes will not be so special. Typically you can expect to pay 2500 to 3000 rp a day. A newish 125 cc in good condition might cost you 4000 rp a day. If you only want a bike for one day you might have to pay as much as 5000 or even 6000 rp. Most important of all, ride sensibly. You don't want to come home from Bali in a box. A 100 cc bike is really all you need to explore Bali; there's no hurry after all. Try to preserve a little of Bali and a lot of yourself.

Pushbikes There are also plenty of places that hire bicycles now and if you can stand the traffic (or get off the main roads and avoid it) this can be a really peaceful way of doing the island. The uphill bits can be real killers – put your bike on a bus in those situations.

Jeeps Bali is starting to develop a rent-a-car business, mainly with open VW-based 'jeeps' or the little Japanese mini-jeeps. They cost from around US$30 a day and between a group they can be no more expensive than motorcycles – and a whole lot safer. But they tend to make you even more remote from the people and if you just want four wheels for a day you can charter a bemo even cheaper.

Tours If time is short there are some pretty good tours available from agents in Kuta. They can be especially good value for getting to places like Besakih where public transport is somewhat problematical. Standard day tours cost from around US$5, longer tours are multiples of that, often staying at regular losmen.

Round the Island Just driving is probably the nicest way to see Bali but if time's short you can make an interesting round-the-island circuit in about a week – either by motorcycle or public transport. A possible route from Kuta would be day 1 to Amlapura – 125 km; day 2 Amlapura to Penelokan – 125 km; day 3 on Lake Trunyan; day 4 Penelokan to Singaraja – 90 km; day 5 Lovina beach; day 6 Singaraja back to Kuta – 140 km. That's rushing it and your starting and finishing point could just as well be Singaraja as Kuta!

THINGS TO BUY

Only lay out your money for one thing (apart from accommodation and food of course) on your first day in Bali – and that's a Balinese massage. Women come round to your losmen and for around 1000 rp prove you have dozens of muscles you never knew existed. You'll end up feeling like a new person and smelling as pretty as a flower.

The trouble with Bali's much-vaunted handicrafts is that there are just too many. A wood carving that looks very fine on your first day at Kuta looks pretty awful by the time you've been shown the first thousand. A lot of stuff is churned out for the undiscerning and over wealthy tourist. Do your little bit to preserve the good things by avoiding the mundane and the overpriced. Look around, develop a feel for workmanship, before you consider making any purchase. Worse even than the local tendency to mass produce the elements of Balinese art that westerners seem to like is a new tendency to actually mass produce some of the worst elements of western art. It's a sad sight to see Balinese painters turning out real-imitation-Woolworths oil paintings. If some idiots didn't buy them they wouldn't do it.

Having complained about the bad side let me add that some of the nice things are really nice. We've got a few things from Bali around the house which we like today every bit as much as we did on the day we bought them. Look for:

Woodcarving Mas and Ubud are the centre and shops there have a good selection of the awful, the reasonable and the good. Personally I prefer the painted carvings to the lookalike ebony ones – a little shoal of painted fish swim near the roof of our bathroom in Australia. Many other birds, fish and owls can also be readily found. Balinese masks can be very good but there are an awful lot of churned out, run-of-the-mill Rangdas. Look around a lot before buying anything and always keep an eye open for the odd exciting piece which seems to pop up without warning. Last trip to Bali we found a delightful wooden bell which only cost a couple of dollars.

Paintings Look around the Ubud museum and art centre to get a feel. Compare their 'young artist' paintings, the technicoloured, primitive, rural scenes, with the churned-out junk around Ubud to see what is going wrong. The four styles you see most often are 'young artist'; the older, less bright rural and legendary scenes; 'Klungkung' style pictorial paintings and the Balinese calendars. Just as with the woodwork there's a lot of garbage but every now and then you come across a painting that stands out from all the rest.

Silver & Gold Work Lots of workshops at Celuk and Kuta Beach produce mainly filigree work. I don't have much of a feel for jewellery so I can't make any recommendations, but if you ask around among your fellow travellers you're certain to get recommendations and suggestions.

Clothes Get clothes made up cheaply at Kuta – as in India there's now a major industry making clothes for shops in the west and a steady trickle, often the 'seconds', finds its way on to the local market. Clothes you'll find everywhere from South Yarra and Double Bay in Australia to Berkeley or LA with price tags from $40 to $100 can often be found in Kuta for $4 to 10. Woven sarongs are very good but the batik is not so special – look for that in Yogya.

Stone Statues Want to transport a stone Balinese statue home? It'll scare hell out of the neighbours' dwarves – this is one art form that hasn't been corrupted, as it's too heavy for the tourists to buy. Actually Balinese stone is surprisingly light (and somewhat fragile) and between a couple of people, if you've come to Bali without too much gear, it's quite possible to bring a stone statue home in your baggage! We've got a temple door guardian in our back garden; they cost US$20 in Bali.

Other You'll find carved coconut shells and bone work around Tampaksiring. Temple umbrellas are found all over the place but particularly at Klungkung. Little rice paper umbrellas are also a useful buy. How about musical instruments? Wayang kulit shadow puppets?

The government art centre, Sanngraha Kriya Asta (closed Mondays) is just outside of Denpasar towards Ubud and has a very representative selection with reasonable (and fixed) prices. Maureen and I bought a big wooden owl here once, hollowed out to make a bell. It's one of our favourite possessions.

KUTA & LEGIAN

For most budget travellers, Kuta is the first taste of Bali and for too many of them it's all they ever see of Bali. Kuta may be good fun and quite a scene, but Bali it most certainly is not. If you want to get any taste of Bali then you've got to get up into the hills where the tourist impact is not so great.

Still, we all hit Kuta to start with so you might as well enjoy it. Basically Kuta beach is just that, a strip of pretty pleasant palm-backed beach with some fairly fine surf (and tricky undercurrents that take away a few swimmers every year) plus the most spectacular sunsets you could ask for . . . . and particularly spectacular for the crowds of onlookers who are already eight miles high with a little help from some local mushrooms. Back of the beach a network of little roads and alleys (known as *gangs*) run to the biggest collection of small hotels (known as losmen), rest-aurants, bars, food stalls (known as warungs) and shops you could possibly imagine. With so many places to work your way around it's hardly surprising that many people just get stuck there semi-permanently.

Legian is the next beach down from Kuta and 10 years ago, when Legian first began to develop as an accommodation and food centre in its own right, it was totally separate. Today Kuta and Legian have spread to meet each other and it's impossible to tell where one ends and the other begins. Unhappily all this rampant development has taken its toll. Kuta and Legian are nowhere near as relaxed and laid back as they used to be and old hands who first visited Bali in the late '60s or early '70s will find Kuta a rather sad and

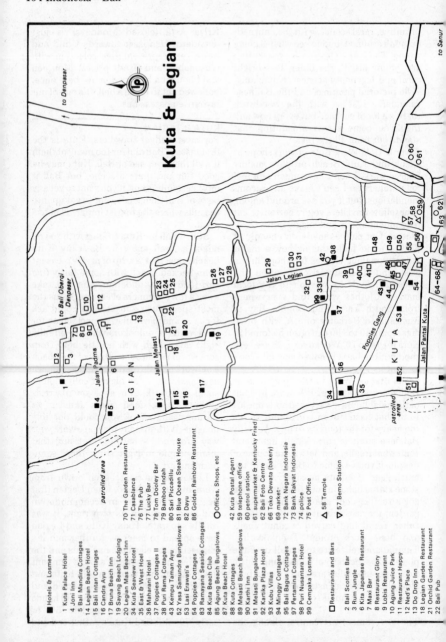

Kuta & Legian

to Denpasar

to Bali Oberai,
Denpasar

to Sanur

Jalan Legian

Jalan Padma

Jalan Melasti

Jalan Pantai Kuta

LEGIAN

KUTA

Poppies Gang

patrolled area

patrolled area

■ Hotels & Losmen

1 Kuta Palace Hotel
4 Joni Inn
5 Bali Mandira Cottages
14 Legian Beach Hotel
15 Bali Intan Cottages
16 Candra Ayu
17 Bruna Beach Inn
19 Sayang Beach Lodging
20 Legian Mas Beach Inn
34 Kuta Seaview Hotel
36 East & West Hotel
36 Maharani Hotel
37 Poppies Cottages II
38 Puri Rama Cottages
43 Kempu Taman Ayu
52 Yasa Samundra Bungalows
53 Lasi Erawati's
54 Poppies Cottages
83 Ramayana Seaside Cottages
84 Kuta Beach Club
85 Agung Beach Bungalows
87 Kuta Beach Hotel
88 Kuta Cottages
89 Melasti Beach Bungalows
90 Karthi Inn
91 Melasti Bungalows
92 Kartika Plaza Hotel
93 Kubu Villas
94 Mingay Cottages
95 Bali Bagus Cottages
97 Pertamina Cottages
98 Puri Nusantara Hotel
99 Cempaka Losmen

□ Restaurants and Bars

2 Bali Scotties Bar
3 Rum Jungle
6 Kita Japanese Restaurant
7 Maxi Bar
8 Restaurant Glory
9 Lobis Restaurant
10 Agung Juice Park
11 Restaurant Happy
12 Ned's Place
13 Do Drop Inn
18 Legian Garden Restaurant
21 Orchid Garden Restaurant
22 Bali Pub

70 The Garden Restaurant
71 Casablanca
76 The Pub
77 Lucky Bar
78 Tom Dooley Bar
79 Bamboo Indah
80 Sari Piccadilu
81 Blue Ocean Steak House
82 Dayu
86 Golden Rainbow Restaurant

○ Offices, Shops, etc

42 Kuta Postal Agent
59 telephone office
60 petrol station
61 supermarket & Kentucky Fried
62 Bali Foto Centre
66 Toko Dewata (bakery)
69 market-
72 Bank Negara Indonesia
73 Bank Rakyat Indonesia
74 police
75 Post Office

△ 58 Temple

▽ 57 Bemo Station

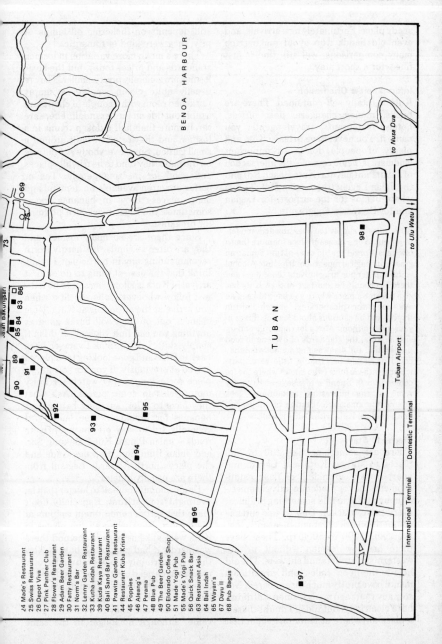

24 Made's Restaurant
25 Swiss Restaurant
26 Depot Viva
27 Pink Panther Club
28 Flower's Restaurant
29 Adam Beer Garden
30 Fatty Restaurant
31 Norm's Bar
32 Lenny Garden Restaurant
33 Kutha Indah Restaurant
39 Kuda Kaya Restaurant
40 Bali Sand Bar Restaurant
41 Prawita Garden Restaurant
44 Restaurant Kuba Krisna
45 Poppies
46 Aleang's
47 Perama
48 Blue Pub
49 The Beer Garden
50 Eldorado Coffee Shop
51 Made Yogi Pub
55 Made's Yogi Pub
56 Quick Snack Bar
63 Restaurant Asia
64 Bali Indah
65 Wayan's
67 Dayu II
68 Pub Bagus

seedy place. Fortunately new arrivals, and even old hands who avoid making too many comparisons, will still find it just fine – for a short stay.

Information & Orientation

Kuta is totally self-contained. There are banks, money changers, post offices, hotels, restaurants, travel agents, you name it. You never have to leave Kuta and plenty of people don't. An important landmark is 'bemo corner' – the intersection of Jalan Pantai Kuta (Kuta Beach Rd) and the Jalan Legian (the Legian Rd). This is where bemos for the airport, for Legian and for Denpasar congregate.

Kuta today is simply too overcrowded, too jet-in-jet-out to be a pleasant place for more than a few days. Forget the old tales of fine Sumatran grass and magical mushroom trips too. Alcohol is the number one drug at Kuta these days and there's certainly no shortage of that. Kuta has also become a place where you have to keep an eye open for pickpockets, snatch-and-run thieves and be cautious about leaving things in your losmen room. Also a lot of people end up sick at Kuta; the standards of hygiene in food preparation and dishwashing are not what they could or should be. Take a little care, particularly with ice juice (who knows where the ice comes from?). Spend a few days at Kuta, try some of the interesting restaurants, look around the amazing collection of shops, but don't confuse Kuta with Bali – it isn't.

Places to Stay

There are something like 200 to 300 places to stay at Kuta and Legian and apart from a sprinkling of flash establishments they're predominantly cheapies – although you can find something in almost every price bracket. Due to this intense competition prices remain pleasantly low, averaging 3000 to 6000 rp. These days there are few losmen without private western-style toilets and showers. The old hole-in-the-floor toilet and traditional mandi have pretty much disappeared. Not so many years ago many losmen still didn't have electricity, but today I doubt there's a place anywhere at Kuta or Legian that

still depends on flickering oil lamps. A pity, they were kind of romantic.

There's much more variation in losmen standards and prices today, but the basic losmen are generally pretty similar. They're usually quite clean; you get a simply furnished room with a couple of chairs and a table outside on the verandah. There are rarely more than half a dozen rooms in a losmen and they're often built around a small garden. Since everybody sits outside on the patio they tend to be friendly places and good for meeting people. Tea or coffee are often available on demand and many places throw in bananas too – sometimes you'll get black rice pudding for breakfast.

Since there are so many losmen and they are often so similar it's hardly worth recommending any in particular. I really think that the easiest thing to do on first arrival at Kuta is allow yourself to be led – just follow whoever grabs you first when you arrive at the airport or at Kuta. Nine chances out of 10 it will be as good as anything you can find yourself. If it isn't, simply shift. I don't think I've ever been back to Kuta and gone looking for a place I stayed at previously. If you are selecting a place for a longer stay watch for noisy motorcycles in some places. Ask what they have to offer; anything better than bananas for breakfast? free laundry? I generally try to stay off the main Kuta roads – Jalan Pantai Kuta, Bakung Sari and Jalan Buni Sari. Poppies Gang and the places north (towards Legian) from there are usually quieter.

Don't commit yourself to longer than an overnight stay at first. Especially don't make that sort of commitment to touts at the airport. Back when all the places in Kuta were alike as peas in the pod there was hardly a bad one in the bunch. Now there are certainly a few drab and grotty places which need only to be considered in an emergency. Overall, though, you can hardly lose at Kuta – there are just so many places and they're generally good value, although no longer in the same league as Ubud or Singaraja on the north coast.

If you do want something a little 'higher class' there are also lots of places from around US$15 to 25 a night. These include the very beautiful *Poppies Cottages*, just across from Poppies Restaurant. Even the bathrooms here have their own little internal garden. In Legian the *Bruna Beach Inn*, close to the beach about a hundred metres on the Kuta side of Jalan Melasti, has a variety of rooms from standard losmen-style for US$6 to pleasant bungalows for US$16.

Places to Eat

Kuta has as many restaurants and warungs as it has places to stay, and their popularity rises and falls in tune with the food fads. Nearly all the restaurants provide pseudo-western food – closely related to what you'll find all along the overland trail, but nice for all that. Perennial favourites include fruit salad (with so many delicious tropical fruits that's a natural for Bali), ice juice (take one or more varieties of fruit, a large cup of shaved ice and feed the whole lot through a blender to produce the most delicious drink imaginable), and anything else you can dream up from hamburgers or jaffles to spaghetti or tacos. Mexican food is still a current kick at Kuta. The Balinese artistic flair comes through in beautiful garden settings and often equally artistically arranged food.

For sheer pleasant ambience you still can't beat *Poppies*. Way back in the early Kuta days Jenik's was a very popular warung – with a western partner Jenik opened Poppies with the biggest and most attractive garden setting at Kuta. Lots of trees, pools, statues, cane furniture and food that, while it is a little more expensive than elsewhere, is not too bad. Combine that with a reputation for cleanliness that even attracts the Sanur Beach tourists and Poppies can't fail. Find it down Poppies Gang, it's equally nice at lunchtime. Some people have written to say that

it's somewhat artificial and pricey, but I still think it's a place you should try at Kuta.

A little beyond Poppies is *Lasi Erawati's*, a popular breakfast place. There are plenty of other possibilities around Kuta, particularly along Jalan Pantai Kuta, Jalan Bakung Sari and right along the Legian road. Starting from bemo corner there's the antiseptic looking *Quick Snack Bar*, right on the corner. It's good for snacks, breakfast or for great yoghurt. Going down Jalan Pantai Kuta there's the long-running *Made's Warung*, an open-front place that's been popular for over 10 years now. Further down is *Lenny's*, popular for its seafood dishes.

Along Jalan Buni Sari, which connects bemo corner with Jalan Bakung Sari, there are more long-term survivors like the *Bali Indah, Wayan's* or *Dayu II*. Here too you'll find several of Kuta's bars, something that simply didn't exist in the Kuta of 10 or 12 years ago. Back then marijuana or magic mushrooms were the drug of choice, not alcohol! *The Pub* is the flashiest, cleanest and most expensive of these bars; it's really quite pleasant although the sight of some of its drunken customers is not always so edifying.

Or you can head along the Legian road towards Legian. These days it's dotted with restaurants all along its length, but unfortunately the traffic down this quite narrow road is so heavy that places close to the road are not always pleasant to eat in. Close to bemo corner is *Perama* and, right next door, *Aleangs*, where the yoghurt is very good indeed – try it with muesli and honey. A little further along *Lenny's Garden Restaurant* is very good, particularly for seafood, although it's certainly not cheap with dishes in the 3000 to 6000 rp range!

Continuing towards Legian *Depot Viva* is an open-roofed place with surprisingly good Indonesian and Chinese food despite its bare, basic and grubby appearance. The prices are pleasantly basic too. A little further along the *Swiss Restaurant* is ideal for homesick German-speakers and the food makes a pleasant change from rice and noodles. Next door is *Made's Restaurant* with good steaks and banana fritters.

Beyond Jalan Melasti but before Jalan Padma is the *Dew Drop Inn*, one of the first Legian restaurants and still going strong. Ditto for the *Agung Juice Park*, a little further up the road. On the corner of Jalan Padma is *Restaurant Happy* while halfway down is the Japanese *Kita Restaurant*.

That's only a skim-the-surface glance at Kuta and Legian's eating possibilities. There are far more to try. If you stayed there for a month and ate breakfast, lunch and dinner at a different place every time you'd hardly begin to explore them. Keep your ears open and you'll hear plenty of recommendations of what's currently popular, or what should be avoided. The cheapest food around Kuta or Legian? Try the night market.

SANUR

Sanur beach is the jet-setter's Kuta – the beach is not so good and there are no sunset spectaculars but the water is calmer if you're not a big-surf fan. These days, however, Sanur is much calmer and more peaceful than Kuta. In many ways it's a more pleasant place to stay. Sanur was one of the places favoured by western artists during their pre-war discovery of the island. The former home of the Belgian artist Le Mayeur, who lived here from 1932 to 1958, can still be visited, squeezed beside the Bali Beach Hotel. Sanur is also a centre for kite flying and the local *banjars'* big kites take a half dozen men to launch and look quite capable of bringing down a 747!

Places to Stay

The 'international' Bali hotels are all along Sanur beach but there are a few medium-priced places although nothing down towards the Kuta level. *Pura Taman Agung* is a very pleasant place with a pretty garden and rooms from 10,000 to 15,000 rp. It's on the main road through Sanur. On Jalan Segara, right next to the Segara Village Hotel, the *Tourist Beach Inn* is one of the most economical places at Sanur with rooms at 8000/10,000 rp for singles/doubles.

Places to Eat

There are lots of restaurants too and although many of these flashier places are quite expensive there are also many restaurants right out of the Kuta mould plus a scattering of local warungs with dirt-cheap prices.

BENOA & THE SOUTH
Ulu Watu

Right at the southern tip of the island, beyond the airport from Kuta, is Ulu Watu where a temple teeters on a sheer 100-metre drop from the cliff face to the blue water below. A little north of Ulu Watu (there's a clearly marked path about two km long) is Pantai Suluban – this is the local surfing Mecca and probably the best known surfing spot in Bali.

Nusa Dua

Also down at the south end of the island is Nusa Dua (two islands) which is slated to be the site for Bali's next 'tourist development' – a sort of Sanur Mark II. It's situated well away from the rest of Bali since this area is dry and relatively sparsely populated. After considerable development delays, the first hotels are now open but it's strictly up market. There's said to be good surfing too although I've never seen anybody surfing there.

Benoa

Across the bay mouth from Benoa, the harbour for Denpasar, turtles are caught at the village of Benoa. They're raised on the nearby island of Serangan. Benoa is the major port for the south of Bali and the centre for visiting yachts. If you ask around it's often possible to get a crew position.

DENPASAR

Ten years ago, which seems to be a throw-away cliche for too many things about Bali, Denpasar was a pleasant, quiet little town. Today it's a cacophony of motor-cycles, a polluted disaster area of bemos and buses. Not at all a pleasant place to stay. Still Denpasar, the capital of Bali, does have a very good museum founded by the Dutch in 1932 (although it closes at 11 am on weekdays, 1 pm on weekends, and all day on Monday; entry is just 10 rp) plus there's an art gallery and a lot of shops.

Places to Stay

With all the noise and confusion there is very little reason to stay in Denpasar and few people do these days. It's a shame since it means even fewer people escape from speedy Kuta. If you do decide to try Denpasar there's one losmen which has managed to remain popular and pleasant despite everything. The *Two Brothers' Inn* is friendly, well run and has singles/doubles at 2500/3500 rp. Find it about 50 metres off the main Kuta road, just far enough to be relatively quiet and peaceful. It's within easy walking distance of the centre only a short distance south of the Tegal (Kuta) bemo station.

The other popular budget hotel of the old days, *Adi Yasa*, also continues but is no longer busy and bustling with life. It's at Jalan Nakula 11 and has a bar and restaurant. Doubles are 5000 rp or 8500 rp with attached bathroom.

The youth hostel connected *Hotel Wisma Taruna* is at Jalan Gedung 17, a little distance from the centre, but convenient for the Kereneng bus station. It's very basic, strictly for those on a tight budget, with beds at 1750 rp or 1500 rp if you have a YHA card.

Places to Eat

Many of Denpasar's more popular rest-aurants have also shut their doors over the years. Among those that still soldier on are the long-running *Delicious Restaurant* on Jalan Kartini, good for Chinese food. Ditto the spartan but expensive *Atoom Baru* on Jalan Gajah Mada. Across the road the *Hong Kong Restaurant* has Chinese and Indonesian food and cafeteria-style self-service.

UBUD

In the hills north of Denpasar, Ubud is the calm and peaceful cultural centre of Bali. It's far too pleasant to be properly appreciated in just a day visit so plan on at least a few days there. Visit the beautifully landscaped art gallery (200 rp) with its display of top-quality Balinese paintings. It's a sad comparison between the quality here and the stuff churned out for the shops in Ubud and elsewhere.

Ubud has had some foreign artists in residence too – like Hans Snel and the Spanish artist Blanco whose superbly ostentatious castle (entry 200 rp) is just beyond the river bridge. Walk through the rice paddies from Canderi's to the small monkey forest with its temple. In fact when you're in Ubud – walk, walk, walk. It's a wonderful place for walking and every stroll will take you somewhere picturesque and interesting. Down the road from Ubud the village of Peliatan has a famous dance troupe and there are dances in and around Ubud virtually every night.

Ubud is also a very good centre for visiting many attractions in the vicinity. There's far more to see around Ubud than around Kuta. One of the nicest things about Ubud is the locally organised tourist centre where they're making a real effort to preserve the 'real Bali' in Ubud, and prevent it from becoming another Kuta.

Places to Stay

Ubud is probably the most popular place for a long-term stay. Up here in the hills it's much cooler and quieter than down on the coast and it's the ideal place to develop a feel for Balinese art and culture. There are lots of losmen in Ubud so

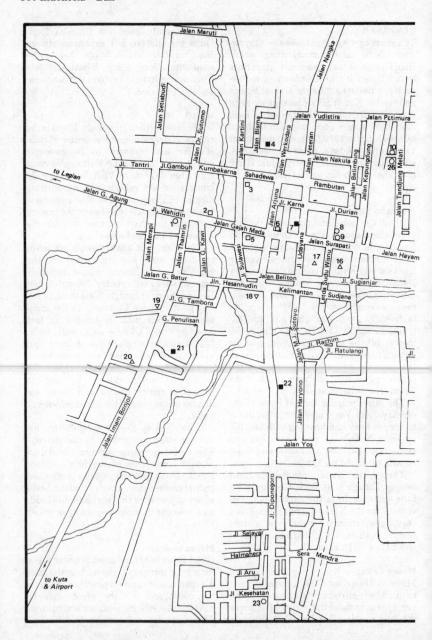

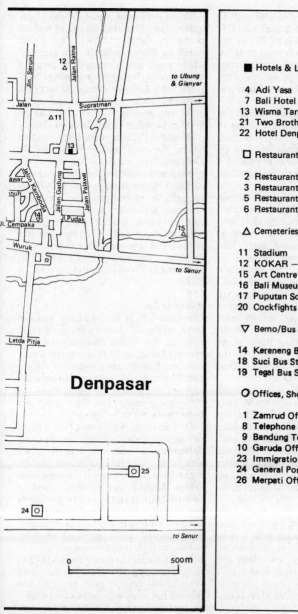

Denpasar

■ Hotels & Losmen

4 Adi Yasa
7 Bali Hotel
13 Wisma Taruna — YHA
21 Two Brothers Losmen
22 Hotel Denpasar

□ Restaurant & Bars

2 Restaurant Atoom Baru
3 Restaurant Delicious
5 Restaurant Gajah Mada
6 Restaurant Puri Selera

△ Cemeteries, Temples, Museum etc.

11 Stadium
12 KOKAR — art School
15 Art Centre
16 Bali Museum
17 Puputan Square
20 Cockfights

▽ Bemo/Bus Stations

14 Kereneng Bus Station
18 Suci Bus Station
19 Tegal Bus Station

O Offices, Shops etc.

1 Zamrud Office
8 Telephone & telegram Office
9 Bandung Tourist Office
10 Garuda Office
23 Immigration Office
24 General Post Office
26 Merpati Office

finding a place to suit is no trouble at all. In fact the town has had a real spate of losmen construction of late. Prices are generally somewhat lower than at Kuta. Simple doubles with attached mandi start at around 2500 rp and go up to around 12,000 rp for the flashiest bottom-end places.

There are lots of places along the Monkey Forest road from the centre of town including one of Ubud's original travellers' haunts, *Canderi's*. Unfortunately it's not as popular or as good as it was in the old days. Rooms start at 2500 rp.

Popular places along this road include *Igna Accommodation, Ibu Rai* or *Sari Nadi*, off towards the rice paddies with rooms with bathroom at 3000 rp. Next door is the very pleasant and clean *Okawati's Homestay* with doubles at 10,000 and 12,000 rp. This place is a definite notch up from the regular losmen.

Further down the road is the clean and well-kept *Frog Pond Inn* with doubles at 5000 rp. Or the popular, though more expensive, *Ubud Inn* with rooms in the 8000 to 12,000 rp bracket. Right at the bottom, almost in the forest, is the secluded and peaceful *Monkey Forest Hideaway*.

Starting back from the main road and going down the road opposite the Monkey Forest road you'll find the *Suci Inn* directly opposite Okawati's ever-popular warung. This is a straightforward losmen-style place with simple rooms with bathroom at 3000 rp includes for the price black rice pudding for breakfast. Next door is the old *Hotel Ubud*, one of the oldest hotels in the village.

Other places along the main road include *Geria Taman Sari* with straightforward losmen-style rooms at 2500 rp or *Losmen Mustika* at 3000 rp for doubles. *Agung Pension* is fairly new, clean and friendly. Or on the post office road there's the reasonably priced *Budi Losmen*. *Suartha Pension*, at 2500/3500 rp, is also excellent value.

There are lots of places around Ubud, either in neighbouring villages or just out in the rice paddies. Take the steep path uphill by Blanco's house, for example. There you'll find a pretty little group of homestays including the appealing *Kardi*. Right behind Blanco's house, *Arjuna's Inn* has been recommended as a comfortable place with good atmosphere. Doubles are 5000 rp including an excellent breakfast.

Or on the Peliatan road, at the junction where the road bends sharply left to Denpasar, you can follow the sign to the popular and attractive *Sari Homestay* with pleasant singles/doubles at 1600/2500 rp, right by the rice paddies. *Puri Agung Homestay* is also very good. Like Kuta you can just look around until you find something that suits. Wherever you stay in the Ubud area remember to bring your earplugs – the anjings here are terrible; dogfights in Ubud are notorious even for Bali.

Places to Eat

Ubud has lots of places to eat, many of them very good. Just off the main road, opposite Puri Ubud, *Okawati's* is a long-running Ubud institution and still a very pleasant, friendly and economical place to eat. The music alternates from classical western to Balinese to Dylan while the Bali-style porridge and the yoghurt are taste treats not to be missed.

Or walk down the Monkey Forest Road (a long walk on a dark night) to the *Ubud Restaurant*, a quiet and peaceful place with some authentic Balinese dishes. Right down the main road at the suspension bridge *Murni's* has excellent food, a beautiful setting and some interesting arts and crafts for sale. All in all it's worth the extra cost for their delicious nasi campur, satay served on a personal charcoal holder, or their delicious cakes.

Back towards the centre there's the *Ery Restaurant* opposite the museum. *Ari's Warung* has terrific gado gado. Or the relaxed but more expensive *Lotus Cafe* – oh, that cheesecake. Also far from cheap –

count on 10,000 rp for a complete meal for two – is *Han Snel's Garden Restaurant* with a beautiful garden setting, superb food and impeccable service.

Enough of this high living. If the shoestring is thin there are plenty of warungs and cheaper restaurants around where you can eat economically and well. Finally Ubud offers a fine opportunity to try real Balinese food in a real Balinese setting. Ketut Suartana, the young man who runs the *Suci Inn*, will organise a Balinese feast at his parents' home (just up the road) for small groups. The cost is around 4000 rp per person and includes a whole series of Balinese dishes rarely seen in restaurants, all washed down with Bali Brem rice wine. You'll get plenty of chances to learn about Balinese life during the meal too. Fun, delicious and recommended.

AROUND UBUD
Denpasar to Ubud
The first few km out of Denpasar on the Ubud and Klungkung road is gallery alley. Stop at the government-run fixed-price store for a window shop. First village reached is Batubulan, the stone carving centre. Lots of apprentices chipping away at blocks of stone, impressively big lumps when they're packed in straw ready for shipping. Next up is Celuk, the silver-work centre where again you're welcome to stop and wander the workshops. The turn-off to Ubud is soon after Celuk. Before Ubud you pass through Mas, which means 'gold' in Indonesian, but is actually the wood carving centre.

Close to Ubud
Bedulu, on the road up to Tampaksiring from the main Denpasar-Klungkung road, was the centre of a powerful dynasty for two centuries. A short stroll through the rice paddies from the Ubud turn-off at Bedulu takes you to Yeh Pulu with its carved bas relief discovered in 1925. A km along towards Ubud is Goa Gajah, the elephant cave, discovered at much the

same time as Yeh Pulu and believed to have been a Buddhist hermitage. The bathing place in front with the female-shaped fountains was only unearthed in 1954.

A km north of the turn-off at Pejeng, the Pura Penataran Sasih Temple has a huge bronze drum said to be two thousand years old. A legend tells of it falling to earth as the 'moon of Pejeng'.

Gunung Kawi & Tampaksiring
Gunung Kawi, a group of burial towers, stands in the rice paddies to the right of the road shortly before Tampaksiring. They're one of the best sights in Bali, impressive both for their sheer size and their setting.

In the shadow of Sukarno's palace at Tampaksiring is the holy spring of Tirta Empul. An inscription dates the spring from 926 AD. There are fine carvings and Garudas on the courtyard buildings. As at Gunung Kawi there is an admission charge and you will have to wear a temple scarf to enter the temple.

Getting Around
From Ubud you can cover these places by bemo and on foot. Take a bemo right up to Tampaksiring as any walking from there on will be downhill. It's only a km or two back downhill to Gunung Kawi. You can follow the path beside the river and come out right in Gunung Kawi. From there you can take bemos back down to Pejeng, Bedulu, Goa Gajah and on to Ubud. Pejeng to the Bedulu turn-off is only about a km and from there it's a half km or so to Yeh Pulu and a similar distance to Goa Gajah. Alternatively from Pejeng you can cut across country directly to Ubud.

EAST BALI
Continuing beyond the turn-off to Ubud the Denpasar-Klungkung road takes you to Kutri where there is a temple dominated by a large banyan tree in the courtyard. A long flight of steps leads to a hilltop statue. Gianyar is a weaving centre. Visit

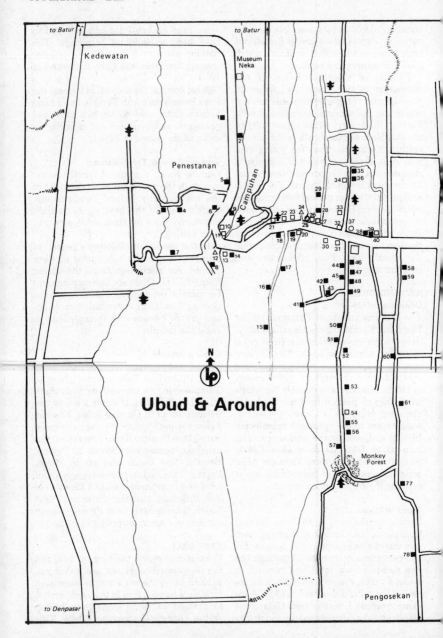

Ubud & Around

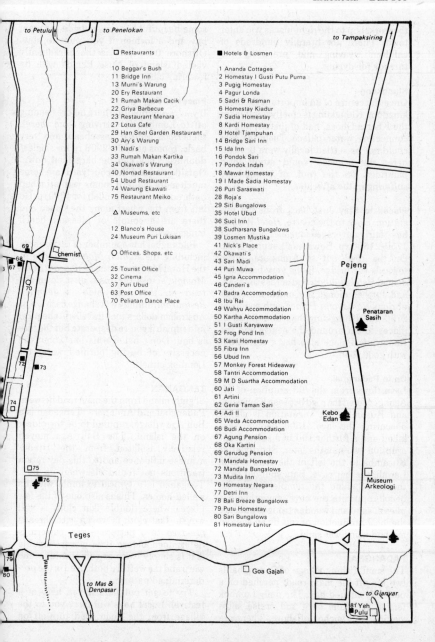

to Petulu | to Penelokan | to Tampaksiring

□ Restaurants

10 Beggar's Bush
11 Bridge Inn
13 Murni's Warung
20 Ery Restaurant
21 Rumah Makan Cacik
22 Griya Barbecue
23 Restaurant Menara
27 Lotus Cafe
29 Han Snel Garden Restaurant
30 Ary's Warung
31 Nadi's
33 Rumah Makan Kartika
34 Okawati's Warung
40 Nomad Restaurant
54 Ubud Restaurant
74 Warung Ekawati
75 Restaurant Meiko

△ Museums, etc

12 Blanco's House
24 Museum Puri Lukisan

O Offices, Shops, etc

25 Tourist Office
32 Cinema
37 Puri Ubud
63 Post Office
70 Peliatan Dance Place

■ Hotels & Losmen

1 Ananda Cottages
2 Homestay I Gusti Putu Purna
3 Pugig Homestay
4 Pagur Londa
5 Sadri & Rasman
6 Homestay Kiadur
7 Sadia Homestay
8 Kardi Homestay
9 Hotel Tjampuhan
14 Bridge Sari Inn
15 Ida Inn
16 Pondok Sari
17 Pondok Indah
18 Mawar Homestay
19 I Made Sadia Homestay
26 Puri Saraswati
28 Roja's
29 Siti Bungalows
35 Hotel Ubud
36 Suci Inn
38 Sudharsana Bungalows
39 Losmen Mustika
41 Nick's Place
42 Okawati's
43 Sari Madi
44 Puri Muwa
45 Igna Accommodation
46 Canderi's
47 Badra Accommodation
48 Ibu Rai
49 Wahyu Accommodation
50 Kartha Accommodation
51 I Gusti Karyawaw
52 Frog Pond Inn
53 Karsi Homestay
55 Fibra Inn
56 Ubud Inn
57 Monkey Forest Hideaway
58 Tantri Accommodation
59 M D Suartha Accommodation
60 Jati
61 Artini
62 Geria Taman Sari
64 Adi II
65 Weda Accommodation
66 Budi Accommodation
67 Agung Pension
68 Oka Kartini
69 Gerudug Pension
71 Mandala Homestay
72 Mandala Bungalows
73 Mudita Inn
76 Homestay Negara
77 Detri Inn
78 Bali Breeze Bungalows
79 Putu Homestay
80 Sari Bungalows
81 Homestay Lantur

Pejeng

Penataran Sasih

Kebo Edan

Museum Arkeologi

Teges

to Mas & Denpasar

Goa Gajah

to Gianyar

81 Yeh Pulu

the workshop to the right just as you enter town. There are literally hundreds of children weaving and preparing the threads for dyeing.

Klungkung

Once the centre of an important Balinese kingdom, Klungkung is chiefly notable for the Kherta Ghosa, hall of justice, and its connecting water palace. Disputes that could not be settled locally were brought here; the accused could study lurid paintings, on the roof, of wrongdoers suffering in the afterlife.

Places to Stay Just back from the bus station, close to the centre, *Hotel Wishnu* has fairly average singles/doubles at 1750/21500 rp. Beware of peeping toms. On the road out to Amlapura, down towards the bridge, is the very basic and dismal *Hotel Sudihati* and across the road, and further along, the much more salubrious *Ramayana Palace* with rooms at 2750 rp. Klungkung has a number of places to eat around the centre and the Ramayana Palace also has a restaurant with good food.

On to Padangbai

Lava flows from the '63 eruption of Mt Agung covered the road between Klungkung and Kusamba but vegetation is slowly obscuring the lava. 1500 people were killed and a further 100 in a subsequent eruption two months later. Shortly after Kusamba to the left of the road is Goa Lawah, the bat cave. Bats spill out from the cave behind the temple. Along the beach, opposite the cave, smoothed-out piles of sand and wooden troughs indicate the local production of salt by an age-old method using wet sand.

PADANGBAI

The small fishing village of Padangbai is two km off the main road, perched on a perfectly shaped bay. The daily Lombok ferries run from here and cruise ships visiting Bali anchor offshore. There are some beautiful beaches outside the main bay and a losmen if you want to stay. Offshore from here is the infrequently visited island of Nusa Penida with its towering cliff.

Places to Stay

If you're overnighting here before heading off to Lombok (or arriving from there), then *Hotel Madya* has cheap, and very basic, rooms at 1500/2000 rp for singles/doubles. They can be bargained down. Outside, around the courtyard, are some much more modern rooms with attached bathrooms and a verandah for 4000 rp. Go left from the wharf along the beach and there are a couple of pleasant beach bungalows.

Padangbai has a number of restaurants including the *Rumah Makan Candra* at the Hotel Madya and the *Restaurant Suda Mampir* across the road. Just down the road on the same side is *Johnny's Restaurant*. Johnny will change cash US or Australian dollars (not travellers' cheques) into rupiah if you're desperate but the rate is bad. Don't believe his line about the necessity of buying purified water for Lombok either!

TENGANAN

Slightly inland from the main road between Padangbai and Amlapura, Tenganan is a Bali Aga village, reputed to be the oldest on the island. The Bali Aga stayed relatively isolated from the Hindu-avanese influence and to this day retain traditions not found elsewhere in Bali. Tenganan is a typical example with its walled homes. This is also one of the few places where double ikat cloth is still woven. Ikat cloth is woven with threads *pre-dyed* to a pattern – the pattern is determined before it is woven. Double ikat is simply twice as complicated – the warp and the weft are both dyed in the pre-determined pattern.

Try to get out here if you hear of a festival. Local boys will ferry you to the village from the main road turn-off on their motorcycles for 150 rp. The walk is not very interesting. The village has become a bit commercialised with a few souvenir shops but it is still a fascinating place.

CANDIDASA

Near Bug Bug (between Padangbai and Amlapura) the beach at Candidasa has suddenly become popular. There's a nice white-sand beach and around the cliffs towards Amlapura a black-sand one.

Places to Stay & Eat

The *Candidasa Beach Inn* is one of the new places which has sprung up here. Beautiful and peaceful bungalows on the beach cost 3000 rp including breakfast. *Losmen Lila Berata* is also good at 1500/3000 rp including breakfast. There are some good places to eat here, especially for fish.

AMLAPURA

Amlapura (or Karangasem as it is sometimes called) is an attractive little town with a fine old palace – interesting for its tooth filing pavilion. The area around the temple in Amlapura is very soothing – plain little houses with courtyards, fountains and small gardens. The old Raja of Karangasem was very fond of water and all of his buildings made use of it. Tirtagangga (see below) was one of his palaces and if you continue through Amlapura down towards the seashore you'll come to the ruins of his Ujung Palace. This palace was built in 1921 and for some reason has suffered much additional damage in the past 10 years. It's about three or four km out of town.

Over the bridge to the right, just beyond Ujung, a road leads down to the sea and a fishing village. You can get out to Ujung by bemo and there is an admission charge to the palace gardens. The town's name was changed from Karangasem after the '63 eruption, to get rid of any influences which might provoke a similar occurrence in the future.

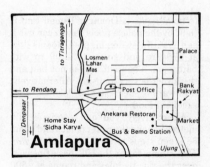

Places to Stay

Amlapura has a couple of places to stay but most travellers prefer to continue to Tirtagangga or Homestay Lila, a short distance down the road towards Rendang. In Amlapura the *Lahar Mas Inn* is on your left just as you enter town and has doubles with bathroom at 3750 rp including breakfast. It's a pleasant place with friendly people. The price is the same across the road and a little further along at the *Homestay Sidha Karya*.

You can eat at the usual collection of warungs or try the *Anekarsa Restoran* by the bus stand. Amlapura tends to shut up early so don't wait too long for your evening meal.

TIRTAGANGGA

A couple of km before Amlapura turn inland to see the old Tirtagangga bathing place (admission 100 rp) – actually it's not so old; it was built in 1947 but it's a delightful place with a losmen situated right by the bathing pool. The rice terraces around Tirtagangga are particularly picturesque.

Tirtagangga is about five or six km (take a bemo) off the main road, on the road that runs around the north-east coast, and a little beyond a village. The road beyond Tirtagangga around the east coast to Singaraja used to be rough going, but it's been upgraded and is now quite OK.

Places to Stay

The delightful *Water Palace Losmen*

(official name is Dhangin Taman Inn) is right by the palace pools so you can use it as a beautiful swimming pool. Rooms start at 2750 rp and go up to 4000 rp with bathroom. The food here is not bad and the owner is very amusing. Alternatively, the warung nearest the losmen does excellent food.

Alternatively you can continue 300 metres beyond the water palace and climb 68 steep steps to the *Kusama Jaya Inn*. The 'Homestay on the Hill' has a fine view over the rice paddies and rooms at 2500 and 3000 rp. The new *Taman Sari Inn* has doubles at 3500 rp including a banana and tea for breakfast.

AMLAPURA TO RENDANG
At Amlapura you can either head north around the coast to Singaraja or double back towards Denpasar. Doubling back you can take an alternative route to Klungkung, higher up the slopes of Gunung Agung. This road runs through some pretty countryside and it's a quiet, less visited route than the relatively busy Amlapura-Denpasar road. While it is a fine way to go with your own transport, it can be very time-consuming by bemo.

The road runs through salak country, particularly at Rendang, so in season pause to buy some of that most delicious fruit from a roadside stall. A short detour to Iseh is worth making to see the house where German artist Walter Spies once lived: magnificent views of Mt Agung from there. Later the Swiss painter Theo Meier lived in the same house.

From Rendang you can turn uphill to Besakih, downhill to Klungkung or cut across on a minor road to Bangli.

Places to Stay
Just three km along the Rendang (or Bebandem) road from the Amlapura junction is the pretty and secluded little *Homestay Lila*. There are individual bungalows with singles/doubles at 1750/2750 rp including breakfast – no electricity but it's a fine place to relax.

Further along, 11 km beyond Bebandem, you can turn off to the *Putung Bungalows* right at the top of the ridge. From here the land drops clear away to the coast, far below. You can see ships anchored off Padangbai and across to Nusa Penida. There are 'losmen class' rooms at 3500/5500 rp and two-storey bungalows for 10,000 rp.

BANGLI
Bangli is halfway up the slope to Penelokan. You can reach it from the main Denpasar-Amlapura road near Gianyar, from Ubud via Tampaksiring (although this means going a considerable distance further uphill and then doubling back) or by a very pretty small road that cuts across just below Rendang.

Bangli has the fine Pura Ke'hen temple with a massive banyan tree in the first courtyard. Look for the old Chinese plates set into the inner courtyard walls. Just down from the temple is a little-used art centre; admire the fine gate inside. Just below Bangli on the Gianyar road there's a fine temple of the dead, Pura Dalem Penunggekan, with some particularly gruesome sculpture panels along the front.

Places to Stay
The *Artha Sastra Inn* is a former palace residence and is still run by the grandson of the last king of Bangli. There are 10 rooms, a couple of them with private bath. Costs are around 3500 rp for a double. It's a pleasant, friendly place and conveniently central.

The alternative is the youth hostel connected to *Losmen Dharmaputra*, a short distance up the road. It's a fair bit cheaper with rooms at 1250/1750 rp but rather basic. Bangli has a good night market virtually opposite the Artha Sastra Inn and there are some great warungs here but they all close early. One catch in Bangli – the dogs are even worse than Ubud.

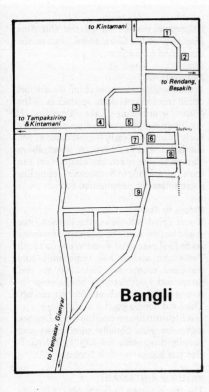

1 Pura Kehen
2 Art Centre
3 Homestay Dharmaputra
4 Post Office
5 Cinema
6 Artha Sastra Inn
7 Bus Stop
8 Market
9 Telephone Office

Bangli

stay if you wanted to climb Gunung Agung from Besakih and would like to make an early-morning start.

Getting There
There are regular bemos from Klungkung to the temple. If you go with your own wheels take the left fork about a km before the temple. This brings you to a car park close to the entrance. The right fork leaves you with a long walk up the main entrance road from the car park.

WEST BALI
There are a number of places of interest to the west of Denpasar which make interesting day trips although few people pause when heading further west towards Gilimanuk, the ferry port for Java. If you're travelling this way from Kuta or Legian with your own transport you can avoid Denpasar by simply following the Legian road which eventually meets the main road out of Denpasar at Sempidi.

Tanah Lot
Spectacularly balanced on a rocky islet which is connected to shore at low tide, Tanah Lot is probably the best known and most photographed temple in Bali. Particularly at sunset time. It's also horrifically touristy. You can get there by bemo but beware of missing the last one back and being forced into an expensive charter. If you come with your own wheels avoid the crush by visiting Tanah Lot early in the day.

BESAKIH
Nearly a thousand metres up the side of mighty Gunung Agung, this is Bali's most important temple. It's big, majestically located and very well kept. It's not only the 'mother temple', it's also the mother of Balinese financial efforts. You pay to park, pay to enter, pay to rent a scarf, brave all the souvenir sellers – and at this point you may well find most of the temple is closed for the day!

Places to Stay
About five km below Besakih is the *Arca Valley Inn* with 2250 rp doubles and a restaurant. It would be a good place to

Mengwi

In Mengwi there's a beautiful royal water palace and temple while right across the wide moat there's a most unusual arts centre which appears to get very little use and to be a bit of a white elephant. Near Mengwi is the memorial to Balinese forces which put up a futile resistance to the Dutch in 1946, intent on reclaiming the island following the departure of the Japanese.

Sangeh

Continue on from Mengwi to the monkey forest of Sangeh but watch out; they're greedy little devils who don't take no for an answer. If you bring peanuts to feed them, keep a tight grip on them; the monkeys will tear a bag right out of your hands. Sangeh can also be reached from Denpasar or Ubud.

Further West

Further west, Rambut Siwi is a beautiful temple perched high on a cliff top. At Negara, bullock races are held between July and October each year. Gilimanuk is the terminus for ferries to and from Banyuwangi on Java.

The North Coast

If you take the north coast Singaraja road to Gilimanuk you pass the coastal temple of Pulaki with its many monkeys. Off the north-west corner of Bali is Pulau Menjangan which has a superb coral reef. The area around Terima has recently been made a national park. There's a 500 rp entry charge to the park and boats can be hired for 1500 rp an hour. There's also a 25 km coastal track between Terima and Gilimanuk. Accommodation and some food are available in at the park although, at present, it's rather spartan and fairly expensive.

Places to Stay

There are a number of losmen in Negara such as the *Hotel Ana*, which has rooms from around 2500 rp. If you get stuck in Gilimanuk you could try the *Gili Sari Homestay* or *Kartika Candra*, both on the main road to the port.

PENELOKAN

From Bangli or Tampaksiring it's a short uphill trip to Penelokan, on the rim of the crater overlooking Lake Trunyan. If you're on a motorcycle be prepared for a fairly dramatic drop in temperature as you climb up to Penelokan. A short sharp shower as you reach the cloud level can have you arriving in Penelokan feeling like a candidate for pneumonia!

Places to Stay

If you could sell views, the losmen here would be five-star. The *Lakeview Homestay* is the first place you come to as you reach Penelokan and it has impossibly tiny standard rooms at 1250/2500 rp and rather more comfortable bungalow-style rooms with bathroom at 3000 rp and up. The food here is good if a bit pricey.

A little further around the rim is *Losmen Gunawan* with equally good views and equally tiny rooms for 1250/1750 rp. It also has bungalow-style rooms.

BATUR & KINTAMANI

The market town of Kintamani is further round the crater rim and Mt Batur, which you can climb from either centre, is within the larger volcanic crater. Batur is between Penelokan and Kintamani. When the original Batur and its temple, down in the crater, were engulfed by Mt Batur in the 1926 eruption the temple was rebuilt on its present site at Batur. Like many other Balinese temples the site is far more impressive than the temple itself.

Just beyond Kintamani is Penulisan, the site of the highest temple in Bali. It's a steep climb up from the road and offers a fine view right down to the north coast. It's a sad sign of progress, but the new gods have established their temple right beside it: the Bali TV relay station towers over the temple.

Places to Stay

There are a number of losmen along the main street of this volcano rim town, but they don't have the spectacular setting of Penelokan and most of them are rather drab and dismal.

They include, starting from the Penelokan end, the basic *Losmen Superman's* at 1750/2500 rp. Then the plain *Losmen Batur Sari* at 1750/3500 rp and the drab but cheap *Losmen Lingga Giri* at 1250/1750 rp. The food here is, however, quite good, so it's a popular gathering place in the evenings. Then there's the slightly better *Hotel Miranda* from 1250 – 3000 rp.

Beyond the main 'centre' of town is the somewhat brighter and airier *Losmen Kencana* at 1750/3000 rp, and a km or so off the road towards the crater is the reasonably comfortable *Hotel Puri Astini* at 2250/3000 rp which has excellent (though slow) food and is a good starting point for climbing Mt Batur.

LAKE BATUR & MT BATUR

Although it's one of the most visually spectacular places in Bali and you can have a very interesting and enjoyable time here, many people have found Penelokan and the lake the site for some unpleasant hassles. Having hired a boat to go across the lake, their boatman was quite liable to decide to renegotiate halfway across. Meanwhile their motorcycle was being stripped back in Kedisan, the lakeside village. It got so bad that the government eventually stepped in and the boat prices are now government controlled and there's a boat office and a safe car park.

When the morning mists clear, go down the switchback road to the lake; a bemo costs 150 rp. From Kedisan you can take a boat across the lake to Trunyan and Tirtha and back for 7000 to 9000 rp, depending on how many stops you make. This is the cost for a whole boat, big enough for about 12 people. If you can't form an impromptu group try tagging on to one of the many Indonesian tourist groups. Don't consider paddling yourself across in a hired dugout – it's farther than it looks and the lake can get very choppy.

From Kedisan you can walk around the lakeside to Trunyan in an hour or two and from there hire a boat across to Tirtha, the site for the hot springs. Or you can follow the rough road across the lava flow to Tirtha and and take a boat across to Trunyan from there.

Trunyan is a rather dull Bali Aga village and has a temple with a huge statue, which they will probably not let you see. They don't seem to mind your having a look at their cemetery a little further around – the dead are laid out in bamboo cages to decompose. The cemetery is another boat trip; the path ends in Trunyan. Straight across the lake is the small settlement of Tirtha with its hot springs or 'air panas'.

From Tirtha, or directly from Kedisan, or from Kintamani you can climb Mt Batur. It's probably quicker straight up from Tirtha at the lakeside but it's more interesting to take one route up and another down. The way to the top is clear as day; there's no need for a guide, but Made from the hot springs or flute-playing Gede from Kintamani are popular companions. It's possible to walk right around the rim of Mt Batur or even descend into the crater and climb out up the other side. Climbing up, spending a reasonable amount of time on the top and descending by a different route can all be done in four or five hours. On the well-beaten path up from Kedisan, enterprising locals have soft drinks for sale on the honour system. From Kintamani it takes about an hour's steep climb down the outer rim, half an hour across the very fertile and intensively cultivated crater bottom and it's a 1½ hour climb to the top. Mt Batur is still active; it last erupted in 1963.

Places to Stay

There are several places to stay at Tirtha. *Hotel Wisma Tirta Yatra* is right by the lake (part of it has actually sunk into the lake). Further round the lake is another small losmen. Or there's *Losmen Mountain View* which is straightforward, plain and ordinary at 1750 rp a double. There's also the flashier *Balai Seni Toyabungkah Art Centre* with good doubles at 10,000 rp.

The warung just above the hot springs has the usual warung food at the usual cheap prices. The art centre has surprisingly good food at commensurately higher prices.

While you're staying at Tirtha join half the village (women at one end, men at the other) for a sunset bath in the hot springs. Very relaxing after climbing the volcano.

BEDUGUL
The alternative route from the south to the north goes via Bedugul then drops down to Singaraja on the north coast. Beside calm and peaceful Lake Bedugul is the picturesquely sited Candi Kuning temple. Bedugul itself is about three km south of the temple. If you're just going to the temple tell the bemo driver you want Candi Kluning. It's a pleasant hike around the lake which is also good for swimming. There's a big flower market at Candi Kluning on Sundays. It costs 100 rp to go down to the lakeside by the losmen, further round the lake.

West of the road down from Bedugul to Mengwi is Mt Batukau with the remote temple of Pura Luhur perched on its slopes. At Baturiti, near the Denpasar 40 km sign, the unsurfaced road will take you through Penebel and up to this tranquil temple.

Still further west there's another little-used road which winds up from the south to the north coast. There's pretty scenery along this interesting alternative to the two busier routes through the mountains, via Penelokan-Kintamani or via Bedugul.

Places to Stay
There's one place to stay by a bend in the road just before you reach the lake plus a cluster right down by the lakeside – the turn-off is also over on the Denpasar side. They're all pretty standard losmen-style;

Hadi Rahajo up by the main road, *Penginapan Raksa Gangga* down by the lake.

SINGARAJA
Singaraja is Bali's principal north coast town and an important port. Until the advent of air travel this was the usual arrival point for Bali's infrequent international visitors. Freight ships from Java and other Indonesian islands still call in.

Places to Stay
There are plenty of places to stay and eat in Singaraja but few people bother – the attractions of the north coast beach strip, only 10 km away, are too great. If you do want to stay here then the *Hotel Sentral* or the *Hotel Cendrawasih*, side by side just on the Gilimanuk side of the centre, are fairly cheap at 3500 rp for doubles.

Other low-priced central hotels include the *Hotel Merta Yadnja*, right on the main intersection so likely to be very noisy, and the *Hotel Ratna* at Jalan Iman Bonjol 33, also on a noisy street. There are many other hotels including some more expensive places with prices up to 10,000 rp.

Places to Eat
There are a batch of small eating places in the Mumbul Market on Jalan Jen Achmad Yani including the popular Chinese *Restaurant Gandhi*.

Getting There
Minibuses from Denpasar cost around 1250 rp. There are bus services direct from Singaraja to Surabaya for 5100 rp.

SINGARAJA BEACHES
There's a whole string of popular beaches to the west of Singaraja. They're nowhere near as developed as Kuta and Sanur, nor is the beach itself as good, nor is there any surf. In exchange you get some good coral reef, generally clear water and an easygoing, peaceful atmosphere. Most importantly you don't get the constant buy-buy-buy barrage put up by Kuta's shops and

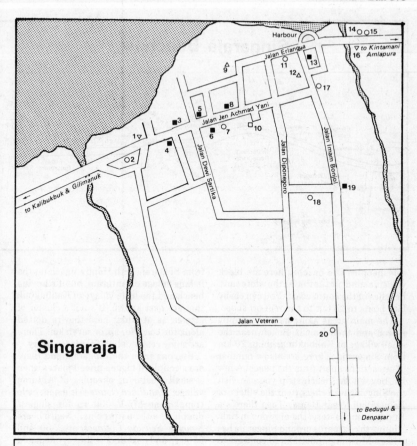

Singaraja

■ Hotels & Losmen	14 Bank Dagang Negara
3 Hotel Saka Bundu	15 cinema
4 Hotel Gekarsari	17 post office
5 Hotel Garuda	18 Telephone & Telegraph Office
8 Hotel Sentral & Hotel Cendrawasih	20 Gedung Kirtya — Historical Library
13 Losmen Ratna	
19 Hotel Sedana Yoga	△ Cemeteries, Temples, Museums, Etc.
	9 mosque
□ Restaurants & Bars	12 mosque
10 Restaurant Gandhi	
	▽ Bemo / Bus Stations
O Offices, Shops, Etc.	1 bus station — Kalibukbuk,
2 petrol station	Gilimanuk, Denpasar
7 Garuda office	16 bus station — Kintamani, Amlapura
11 Bank Bumi Daya	

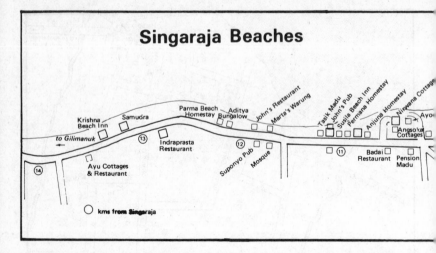

Singaraja Beaches

salespeople. The beaches here are black volcanic sand, not as fine as the white sand beaches of the south coast. You can easily hire boats to go out to the reef off shore.

The main areas along here are Happy Beach and then Lovina Beach near the small village of Kalibukbuk, about 10 km from Singaraja. There are also a number of attractions apart from the beach. A few km beyond the beach strip you can visit the Singsing waterfalls, near the village of Labuanhaji. Near Banjar Tega there's a Buddhist monastery, the only one in Bali. The north coast area around Singaraja has a large Muslim population, in contrast to the overwhelming Hinduism of most of the rest of the island.

Bemos run regularly along the beach strip from Singaraja for 150 to 200 rp. If you're continuing from here to Java there are regular bus services between Singaraja and Gilimanuk or Surabaya.

Places to Stay & Eat

It's really another symptom of the get-away-from-Kuta urge – first people shifted down the road to Legian. When that didn't work they moved right up to the north coast beaches west of Singaraja. The north coast beaches start about six km

from Singaraja with Happy Beach (at the fishing village of Anturan), but it's Lovina beach and the little village of Kalibukbuk that are best known. It's not a cluster of losmen as at Kuta; here they're dotted along the coast for six or seven km. There are some really delightful places to try.

Starting from the Singaraja end there are a couple of higher-priced places, then a small cluster of cheapies at Anturan village. *Mandhara Cottages* is a neat little complex at 1750/3000 rp for singles/doubles with bathrooms. Nearby are *Simon's Seaside Cottages* at 2500 and 3500 rp and next door is the very neat and clean little *Agung Homestay* complex with similar prices. Their more expensive rooms are interesting two-storey places and the food at Agung has a very good reputation.

Continuing along from Anturan the *Lila Cita* is simple, friendly and popular with rooms at 2000 and 2500 rp and a location as close to the beach as you could get. Also by the beach is the *Kalibukbuk Beach Inn* with rooms with bath at 3500 rp while just back from it is the pleasant *Banyualit Beach Inn*.

Just beyond the 10 km marker is the village of Kalibukbuk itself where you'll

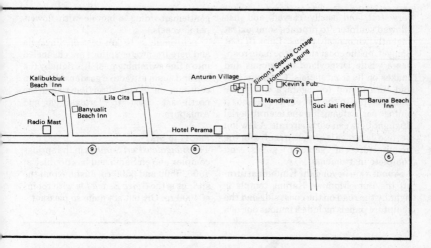

Kalibukbuk
Beach Inn

Lila Cita

Banyualit
Beach Inn

Radio Mast

Anturan Village

Simon's Seaside Cottage

Homestay Agung

Kevin's Pub

Mandhara

Hotel Perama

Suci Jati Reef

Baruna Beach
Inn

⑨ ⑧ ⑦ ⑥

find *Ayodya Accommodation*, a traditional old Balinese house with rooms at 2400 rp. Travellers have described it as 'Gothama's stately home – taking in guests', but unfortunately the increasingly heavy traffic roaring by on the main road outside has rather spoilt the peace and quiet of this otherwise quite delightful place. If you take the small road almost beside Ayodya down to the beach you'll come to *Ayodya II*, close to the beach.

A little further along the beach is the large *Nirwana Cottages* complex; the turn-off is just beyond the 11 km marker or you can walk to them from Ayodya II. Rooms start at the standard base price of 1750 rp. There are larger rooms at 5000 rp and some superb double-storey bungalows at 10,000 rp, ideal for families. Nirwana also has a very good beachfront restaurant. Right behind Nirwana, *Angsoka Cottages* with rooms at 2500 rp is excellent value.

Back on the main road is what is probably the most popular eating place on the beach strip, the *Badai Restaurant*. This is one of those places where the conversation never stops and you always seem to meet somebody who has just come from somewhere interesting. Across the road there's a new two-storey *Nirwana*

Restaurant with good food at regular sort of prices. More losmen along here include a cluster of places including the *Arjuna Homestay* with the cheapest prices on the beach strip and other standard places like the *Permata Cottages* or the *Mangalla Homestay*. Be careful with your valuables at the latter. Then there's *Tasik Madu*, a pleasant and friendly place with rooms at 2500 rp and fancier bungalows at 5000 rp. Finally you come to *Aditya Homestay* with some rooms right by the beach, and almost at the 14 km marker there's the basic (no electricity), cheap (1000 to 1250 rp) and very friendly *Krishna Beach Inn*. There are plenty of others scattered in between.

There are also a number of other eating places among this cluster of losmen near Kalibukbuk. They include cheap warungs like *Marta's* or *John's Restaurant* or, right across the road, the *Suponyo Pub* along with some larger restaurants like the *Indraprasta Restaurant* or the *Ayu Restaurant*.

EAST OF SINGARAJA

There are a number of places of interest just to the east of Singaraja. The local sandstone used in temple construction is very soft and easily carved and has allowed sculptors to produce some extravagantly whimsical scenes. Pura Beji at Sangsit, on the coast side of the main road, has a whole Disneyland of demons and snakes on its front panels. Continue east and turn inland to Jagaraga where the small temple to the left of the road has a vintage car, a steamship and even an aerial dogfight between early aircraft. A few km beyond Jagaraga is Sawan, a centre for the manufacture of gamelan gongs and complete instruments.

About a km beyond the Kintamani turn-off the Pura Maduwe Karang temple is right by the road on the coast side and the sculpture panels include a famous one of a gentleman riding a bicycle with flower-petal wheels.

Yeh Sanih is 15 km east of Singaraja and here freshwater springs are channeled into a fine swimming pool. It's right by the sea and set in attractive gardens. You can continue on in this direction round the north-east coast to Tirtagangga and Amlapura.

Places to Stay

The *Bungalow Puri Sanih* is in the springs complex at Yeh Sanih and has doubles at 4500, 5500 and 6500 rp. Just beyond the springs is the *Ginza Beach Inn* with rooms at 4000 rp, OK but not quite so pleasant.

Sumatra

Indonesia's 'new frontier', Sumatra, has vast wealth in natural resources but is comparatively unpopulated and undeveloped. It offers wild jungle scenery, the Bukit Barisan or 'marching mountains' do just that right down the west coast and there are a diverse collection of highly individual cultures and peoples. In 1958 Sumatra tried to break away from the rest of Indonesia in the abortive Sumatran rebellion. Today major resettlement projects from Java are being undertaken.

GETTING THERE

You can approach Sumatra from a number of directions and by a number of means. The most conventional route though is to fly in from Penang to Medan, travel down through the island on those famous Sumatran buses, then either take the ship from Padang to Jakarta or continue right down through Palembang to Panjang and take the ferry across from Panjang to Merak in Java. Or, of course, do that trip in reverse. Another variation is the Tanjung Pinang-Medan boat trip.

There are also a number of flights from Tanjung Pinang and Batam Island to various places in mainland Sumatra and to Jakarta. Costs from Tanjung Pinang to Jakarta via Garuda is 90,600 rp, or it's 46,700 to Padang, 53,800 to Pekanbaru.

Penang-Medan This is the easiest way into or out of Sumatra and since most of Sumatra's attractions are up at the northern end of the island many people visit Sumatra coming and going by this flight. It only takes 20 minutes to make the short hop across the Melaka Straits with either MAS or Garuda. The flight costs M$109, 50,600 rp or US$48 – take care if you're buying this ticket in Australia, many agents and airlines seem to quote far more than that. This is a very popular flight to satisfy the 'ticket out' requirement of Indonesian visas. If you're getting it for that purpose and suspect you may not use the ticket in the end and you will want to refund it then buy an MAS ticket rather than a Garuda one. Garuda don't part with refunds too readily. There is still no ferry service between Penang and Medan, but it seems certain to happen soon. Negotiations between the countries are well underway, so it would be worth checking out.

Singapore-Medan Garuda has a daily flight out of Singapore for S$251 or 119,200 rp, which takes about 55 minutes. After customs and visa checks, make your way to the information office and pick up a map, then go to the taxi desk and get them to book your trip into town. This way you'll pay 2700 rp for the short trip into the city, still steep but not the ripoff 4000 rp or more they'll slug you if you organise a taxi yourself. Becaks are banned from the airport grounds, but if you go out to the road you should have no trouble getting one. The cost of a becak ride into Medan is 700 rp, but 1000's likely.

Tanjung Pinang-Pekanbaru Tanjung Pinang is an Indonesian island a few hours south of Singapore and easily accessible by launch. There is no direct service between Singapore and Tanjung Pinang, but there are no problems in getting there. All boats now go via Batam Island, where you must clear customs and obtain a visa before travelling on to Tanjung Pinang. The customs shed is a few hundred metres from the pier and provided you have a ticket out of Indonesia you should have no hassles.

Two boats depart Finger Point Pier in Singapore on Mondays through Fridays at 8 am and at 2.30 pm and there is one serivce a day on Saturdays and Sundays. Cost is 7500 rp and most launches are fast and comfortable with aircraft-type seats and video movies. The earlier service is slower, cheaper and you have only a slim chance of catching a boat on to Pekanbaru

or Medan on the same day if you don't wish to stay overnight in Tanjung Pinang. But the chances of departing Tanjung Pinang by boat on the same day are not very likely anyway, so it doesn't matter much. Many of the slower boats call themselves 'express', so make sure your ticket is for the fast boat if that's what you asked for. If you catch the hydrofoil which runs between Batam and Singapore it costs from 18,500 and 21,000 rp and only takes about half an hour in air-conditioned luxury. Between Batam and Tanjung Pinang it costs 4500 rp and takes about four hours on the small local boats. The boats leave frequently and although it's a slow trip, it is usually not crowded. You can get tickets through travel agents or German-Asian Travels, but it's cheaper to buy them at Finger Point Pier. The address for German Asian Travels is Room 1303/4, 13th floor, Straits Trading building, 9 Battery Rd, Singapore 1 – telephone 915116 or 915117.

The journey between Tanjung Pinang and Pekanbaru takes at least 40 hours – sometimes 48 hours depending on the size of the boat – and costs a minimum of 12,350 rp deck class and 16,825 rp for a cabin. But it's quite likely – depending on the size of the boat – your cabin may simply be a few planks tacked together to form a platform and raised about a metre off the deck, so check carefully before you commit yourself or you could find yourself in for a tedious and uncomfortable ride.

Buying an onward ticket to Batam from Tanjung Pinang can be confusing if you want to go straight through to Singapore. There are at least two services a day – one around 10 am, another about 2 pm, the *MV Auto Batam-Batam* which has air-con, TV and video – from Monday to Saturday. In addition there are various local craft you can get to Batam on for the same price as the others. It *is* possible to get tickets on the boats or from the quayside office – 4000 rp for Europeans, cheaper for the locals – but you may be given the run around. There are numerous stalls on the

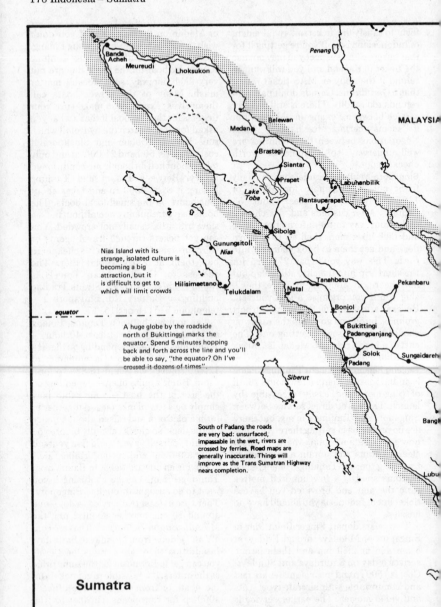

Bande Acheh
Meureudi
Lhoksukon
Penang
Medan
Belewan
Brastagi
Siantar
Prapat
Lake Toba
Labuhanbilik
Rantauparapat
Sibolga
MALAYSIA

Gunungsitoli
Nias

Nias Island with its strange, isolated culture is becoming a big attraction, but it is difficult to get to which will limit crowds

Hilisimaetano
Telukdalam
Natal
Tanahbatu
Pekanbaru

Bonjol

equator

A huge globe by the roadside north of Bukittinggi marks the equator. Spend 5 minutes hopping back and forth across the line and you'll be able to say, "the equator? Oh I've crossed it dozens of times".

Bukittingi
Padangpanjang

Solok
Sungaidareh

Padang

Siberut

South of Padang the roads are very bad: unsurfaced, impassable in the wet, rivers are crossed by ferries. Road maps are generally inaccurate. Things will improve as the Trans Sumatran Highway nears completion.

Bang

Lubu

Sumatra

SINGAPORE

SARAWAK

Kuching

Tanjun Pinang

A Pelni ship departs from
Tanjun Pinang for Jakarta
every week – arrive early
or risk a week's wait

equator

KALIMANTAN
(BORNEO)

Bangku

Jambi

esi

Mentok   Pangkalpinang

angan   Gresik

Tanjungpandan

Palembang

Belitung

Perabumlih

Martapura

Kotabumi

Krui   Panjang

Merak

Krakatau

JAVA

pier advertising ticket sales to Singapore, but they don't – won't or can't – make a direct transaction. They will send someone off to pick up a ticket for you. This is usually OK but can sometimes be a bit dodgy as you may never set eyes on a ticket or see your money again. If you have any trouble and want to be certain of getting a ticket, go to Toko Osaka, Jalan Merdeka 57, Tanjung Pinang (telephone 21829, contact Raymond Chin) or to Rustami's Homestay, Jalan Rimbajaya 80A, Depan Pemancar RR1.

Foreigners are charged 1000 rp departure tax instead of the regular 100 rp that locals pay. But no matter how loudly you complain, you can't avoid it.

Tanjung Pinang-Medan There is a boat every week from Tanjung Pinang to Medan for 26,000 rp departing Wednesdays at 10 am, arriving at the port of Belawas on Thursday morning. But don't rely on getting to Sumatra this way, the service is not altogether predictable. See Java or Singapore for more information.

Jakarta-Padang There's a weekly shipping service between these cities. And the good news is that Pelni has a mega-luxurious boat on this run, *KM Kerinci*, with hot and cold showers and air-con. It leaves Tanjung Priok in Jakarta every Saturday at 9 pm and arrives in Padang about 33 hours later at around 6 am. There are four classes plus deck class and prices are 39,200 rp for first class, 33,000 rp in second, 30,200 rp for third and 24,800 rp in fourth. Deck class is 22,500 rp, but it's better to pay the extra money to get a cabin. Taking this trip will save you heaps of rupiah on the flight from Jakarta to Padang (100,000 rp). You also get a fine view of Krakatoa, the famous volcanic island between Java and Sumatra.

Meals are provided three times a day, but it's the usual story of rice, rice and more rice. Take fruit and anything else you like to supplement your diet.

There are lots of Pelni outlets in Jakarta but they only sell deck class. If you want to buy a cabin ticket you have to go to the main Pelni Office at Jalan Pintu Air 1 – telephone 358398.

Merak-Panjang There are ferries departing every day from Merak at the western end of Java to Panjang at the eastern end of Sumatra. There are two services a day at 11 am and 11 pm from the dock near the train station. The trip is about six hours, but if you catch the night boat it might take a little longer because it may have to hang around until dawn before docking. Cost of the tickets in first, second and third classes respectively are 3700 rp, 2600 rp and 1300 rp.

There are two Sumatran ferry terminals in Panjang, the old one (the railway ferry) right in town and a roll-on roll-off (RoRo to shipping enthusiasts) which docks at Strengsen, about five km east of the Panjang terminal. To get to Merak from Jakarta you can travel by train or bus. Buses depart from the Grogol bus station approximately every 10 minutes between 3 am and 12 pm, cost 1200 rp and take about 3½ hours. Trains leave at 6.15 am and 5 pm from the Tanah Abang railway station. The morning train is faster and connects with the daytime ferry service.

Ferries to Bakauheni, the easternmost tip of Sumatra, depart every hour from the dock near the bus station and it is a 1½ hour trip. Prices are 1650 rp first class, 1300 rp second and 750 rp in third.

Other There are various interesting and/or easy possibilities for getting to or from Sumatra. From Pekanbaru you can fly to Singapore for S$172. Pekanbaru is a bit of a hole, but easily accessible to/from Bukittinggi. You can also fly from Pekanbaru to Tanjung Pinang for 32,400 rp or from Palembang to Tanjung Pinang for 53,800 rp. Ships also operate from Tanjung Pinang to Pekanbaru, up the Siak River, from Monday to Saturday for 12,350 rp deck class. There are occasional boats between Port Kelang (the port for Kuala Lumpur in Malaysia) and Dunia in Sumatra. Or a semi-regular charter service between Melaka and Pekanbaru. And, of course, you can fly from Jakarta to

Sumatra. Jakarta-Palembang is 54,500 rp, Jakarta-Pekanbaru is 101,600, Jakarta-Jambi is 71,000 rp, Jakarta-Padang is 100,0000 rp.

GETTING AROUND

Once you've arrived in Sumatra bus is the way to travel. It's hard going and distances are long but the Trans-Sumatran Highway has made a huge improvement to speed and pleasure. Nonetheless, travelling around Sumatra by bus can be grindingly slow, diabolically uncomfortable and thoroughly exhausting, particularly during the wet season when bridges are washed away and the roads develop huge potholes. Another improvement has been the introduction of more modern buses and minibuses. Sumatran buses have always been works of art, but as works of engineering they've been built for strength without a single thought for comfort.

The old-fashioned Sumatran buses were based on Japanese or American truck chassis fitted with locally-made bodies then painted up as mobile works of art that only an Afghan truck could rival. They were supremely uncomfortable and the seats were hard and far too small for most average sized westerners. Furthermore the drivers were madmen, people who flew down shocking roads, sustained and kept awake by prodigious amounts of fiery Padang food. From Palembang to Padang the road runs through as good a jungle as you're likely to find – you always expected to see those elusive Sumatran tigers, although wild boars and monkeys were probably the nearest you'd get to them. Rivers were, and are, muddy, wide, winding facsimiles of the Amazon. All the way from Palembang to Padang the road was dirt and during the wet winches had to be used to get you through. Today many of the bridges destroyed during the Sumatran rebellion of 1958 have been replaced and the Trans-Sumatran Highway is almost complete, which makes things much easier. Modern Mercedes buses also help (although it's unlikely that Mercedes ever imagined they could contain so many seats) but don't think that simply sealing the roads will take all the adventure out of Sumatran travel – as one traveller experienced it:

We took the new Mercedes bus from Bukittinggi to Prapat. If they are really better than the old ones (hard seats, no legroom, non-waterproof windows) then I must come from a new generation of softies. One window across the aisle from us was simply not there and since the pane could not be slid across to cover a window space twice its size we had the comical situation, when the rain came down, of two Sumatrans shouting blue murder at each other, tugging the window in opposite directions in an attempt to keep dry. After this, a landslide, three breakdowns and a collapsed bridge the 18 hour journey took 26.

Another madman travelled through Sumatra during the wet season and told how rain could turn hard work into real torture:

The trip involves sheer physical hardship and you need to be mentally prepared. Buses were taking five to seven days to reach Bukittinggi (from Palembang). Very little rest is possible when moving and also when stopped as the bus and other vehicles have to be pushed and the ground is wet and muddy. None of the new buses appear to have winches which means plenty of hold ups. Anyone doing Sumatra in the wet without unlimited time should fly Palembang-Padang.

So if travelling through Sumatra by bus be prepared. It's hard work and if you haven't got the endurance of a marathon runner, you need to give yourself time off to recover. Don't expect to be able to cover the whole island by bus if you are pressed for time. You need the whole two months of your entry permit. Avoid seats at the very back where the bouncing is multiplied. And in rough weather look for a bus with a winch! Sector by sector through Sumatra:

Panjang-Palembang From Panjang you can take a bus or train to Palembang. You can also get buses from Strengsen (the other ferry terminal) but the bus touts there are amazingly voracious and it's probably easier to escape to the relative sanity of Panjang. You can get buses from here all the way to Bukittinggi or even Medan although most people will prefer to travel sector by sector. ANS is probably the best of the various Sumatran bus companies. You can take the train from Panjang to Palembang and even further to Lubuklinggau from where you can continue by bus to Bengkulu or Padang. Coming from Panjang you can save a little money, but no time, on this route by de-training at Parembulih, between Panjang and Palembang, where the line branches off to Lubuklinggau. You save no time because your train continues on into Palembang, two hours away, then about turns and comes back to pick you up at Parembulih. You can buy cheap pineapples while you wait. From Lubuklinggau you can continue on to Bengkulu where there are sometimes ships to Padang. The road to Padang is gradually being improved.

Palembang-Padang This takes about two days if the going is easy, *jam karet* or rubber time during the wet season. Fares on this sector are very fluid – they depend on what the trip is expected to be like. Count on perhaps 13,000 rp for Palembang-Padang, perhaps 15,000 rp for Panjang-Padang. The ANS bus station is near the Asiana Hotel in Palembang. The road from Lubuklinggau – the end of the railway line north – to Padang, which runs along the eastern side of the mountains, has been upgraded and is now one of the best and most scenic in Sumatra. The Bengkulu-Lubuklinggau road is fairly good, all sealed but with some potholes and slow. Lubuklinggau-Maurarupit is sealed but there are a few potholes and it can be slow-going. Maurarupit-Bangko is generally good and the last 75 km excellent. Bangko-Muarabungo is generally good apart from a few bad patches. Muarabungo-Bukittinggi and beyond is excellent. Apart from these 'usual' routes there are also some unusual ones. From Jambi, if you are willing to hang around,

you might get a river boat up to Sungaidareh. This is a good possibility for the wet season but it is better, of course, for the downstream trip.

Padang-Prapat Most people make one or more stops on this sector – either Bukittinggi and/or Sibolga. The roads are paved on this sector, but it is still a long, tough trip. Between Padang and Bukittinggi the road is excellent and very beautiful, but from Bukittinggi on it's the pits. It's only a few hours to Bukittinggi (950 rp) from here, although the delightful old steam trains that used to operate on this route have now been stopped. Freight trains still do operate and you can probably get a ride if you're a train enthusiast. Bukittinggi-Prapat is about 20 hours, but can take up to 30 or more hours. It costs between 5000 rp and 6500 rp for this section, and it's wiser to pay more for the extra comfort. Sibolga is a particularly popular stopping point for the boats across to Nias. From Bukittinggi all the way to Medan would cost around 8500 rp.

Prapat-Medan There are now comfortable (well, relatively) new Mercedes buses as well as the old bangers on this route. The fare is around 2000 rp although it can be rather less from Prapat to Medan than vice versa – it's a question of how many commissions have to be paid. The trip can now be done in only 3-1/2 hours as the road has been upgraded fairly recently, but it can still take five or six. On the journey from Prapat to Brastagi you can avoid Medan by taking three buses via Siantar and Kabanjahe.

Fly Of course it's possible to fly around Sumatra and save a lot of time and trouble. Fares include Palembang-Jambi 29,200 rp, Palembang-Padang 63,700 rp, Padang-Palembang 64,850, Medan-Padang 63,600 rp and Medan-Palembang 105,000 rp, Medan-Banda Aceh 53,800 rp, Bengkulu-Jambi 65,900 rp, Jambi-Bengkulu 65,900, Bengkulu-Palembang 36,700 and Pekanbaru-Padang 28,100.

The fares quoted above are all Garuda.

Check out Merpati and Mandala, they often fly the same routes at cheaper prices.

RIAU ARCHIPELAGO

South of Singapore scattered across the South China Sea like confetti are the islands of the Riau Archipelago. There are more than 3000 islands in the archipelago, but only about a third of them are inhabited. They can be divided roughly into two groups, one bunched close to the coast of Sumatra, the second lot nearer to Singapore and the administrative district of Riau (Kabupaten Kepulauan Riau). The main islands in the first group consist of Bengkalis, Rupat, Padang, Tebingtinggi, Rangsang, Lalang, Mendol, Penyalai, Serapung, Muda, Kijang, Pucung and Katemun. The second can be broken down into seven sub-groups comprising the Karimun islands, the Riau islands – after which the archipelago is named – the Lingga-Singkep lot, the Tambelan, Anambas, North Natuna and Serasan groups.

It's still explorer territory, adventure land, much of it unexploited and unspoilt, but it's also one of the richest areas in Indonesia due to its oil and tin exports.

Other

The main local festival in the Riau is the Sea Sacrifice performed on Pulau Sarasan held during the second month of the Islamic calendar. The islanders hang packets of sticky rice on trees near the beach, then cut logs from the forest which they cart down to the beach, load into canoes and drop into deep sea to appease the gods of the ocean and protect themselves from drowning. Apart from this they celebrate the principal festivals on the Islamic calendar.

Warning Mosquitoes are rife in these islands. It would be wise to take both kinds of anti-malaria tablets, chloroquine and pyrimethane-sulfadoxine and make sure you have plenty of repellent.

TANJUNG PINANG

Almost in spitting distance of Singapore is Pulau Batam, an official entry point to Indonesia and a handy gateway to or from Singapore. A little further on is Pulau Bintan where the biggest town in the archipelago, Tanjung Pinang, is situated. It's almost pancake flat except for a couple of peaks Gunung Bintan Besar and Gunung Kijang.

Tanjung Pinang is where most travellers – using this route in or out of Indonesia – stop over. The majority of people only hang around for twenty-four hours or so waiting for boat connections, but if you have the time or need a rest from travelling, Tanjung Pinang is a good base for exploring other islands in the group and has a few interesting sights of its own. It's one of those quaint, Indonesian towns which literally has a 'floating' population. Apart from its varied and various visitors, there is a constant stream of boats and sampans sailing between the islands and upriver and there's an old wooden section of the town that juts out over the sea on stilts. Tanjung Pinang has an aura of prosperity and growth. It seems to be sprouting with new buildings – public and private – like rice shoots in a paddy field – and – wonder of wonders – it's clean. With its lush parks and gardens, it's a relaxing and, in its own way, rather cosmopolitan place to be. Tanjung Pinang has a reputation for shady deals and theft which has been exaggerated beyond reality, but you would be wise to take notice of the *awas copet* signs – beware of pickpockets – and not be too naive and trusting.

Information & Orientation

The main tourist office for the Province of Riau is in Pekanbaru, so if you're thinking about staying on the islands for a while write to Badan Pengembangan Pariwisata Daerah, Kantor Gubernur Riau, TK 1, Pekanbaru, Riau, Indonesia for information well in advance. The best map of Riau is at the Kandil Riau Museum. Other maps are hard to find, but if you go into the Netra

Service Jaya, at the harbour there is a map of Tanjung Pinang on the wall and the people there are very helpful.

The main street Jalan Merdeka leads to the markets. Goods are not cheap here but you can get the usual 'el cheapo' cassettes and treat yourself to some Cadbury's chocolate. You'll find it in the shop next to the money changer, Oriki.

You can get good exchange rates for US$, A$ and other currencies at the Bank Dagang Negara. Oriki Money Changer on Jalan Merdeka offers good rates for US$ but not for other currencies. There are no banks on Daik and Lingga islands.

The Post Office is on Jalan Merdeka, not far from the harbour. It's open from 9 am to 4 pm on Mondays to Thursdays, from 9 am to 11 am on Fridays and from 9 am to 1 pm on Saturdays.

Things to Do & See

There are fine opportunities for diving and snorkelling most of the year except from November to March when the monsoon is blowing. Several beautiful beaches with milk-white sand and shiny sapphire seas, but the best of them – Berakit, Teluk Dalam, Pantai Trikora – are on the east coast and there's no public transport there. Access is by motorbike over roads that are mostly in atrocious condition. Occasionally they are in reasonable repair and it is possible to charter a taxi to get to the beaches, but it's an expensive way to get around.

You can climb Gunung Bintang Besar (348 metres), if you're feeling sufficiently energetic. It's a fair way out of Tanjung Pinang by road or boat and takes about two hours to climb.

Tanjung Pinang is a good place to stroll around. For a peaceful hour or two wander down to the old harbour of Pejantan 11 or for colour and movement the market is worth a visit. There is a Chinese temple right in town and another across the harbour by sampan in Senggarang – and a mosque. Or you could charter a sampan to take you up Sanke River through the

mangroves to see the Chinese Temple with its graphically gory murals on the trials and tortures of going to hell. Be prepared to bargain hard with the boatman. Nearby you can see the ruins of ancient Sea Dayak capitals.

Only 200 rp by ojek from the city centre is the Riau Kandil Museum which has a vast collection of old guns, ships, ceramics, charts, antique brassware and other exhibits from the Riau kingdom.

Tanjung Pinang has two red-light districts at the villages of Batu Duabelas and Batu Enambelas – no prizes for guessing that they are respectively 12 km and 16 km out of town. A trip to one of these village seems to be a regular and popular after-dark activity with the local lads, judging by the amount of traffic heading in that direction. More salubrious nightlife amounts to wandering around town or taking yourself off to one of the two cinemas, the Mutiara or the Gembira.

Other You can make excursions to other islands like Pulau Mapor, Pulau Terkulai where the lighthouse keeper lives in solitary splendour – the trip out to the latter takes about 20 minutes and you have to charter a sampan to get you there because there's not much boat traffic to or from the island – or to nearby Pulau Penyengat, once the capital of Riau – see below for more information on Pulau Penyengat.

Places to Stay & Eat

The term *losmen* is not widely used in these parts; look for the sign *penginapan* for budget accommodation. What you'll get is basic accommodation but it's clean. There are quite a few hotels in Tanjung Pinang, but most are expensive costing 10,000 rp a double: Highly recommended is *Rustami's Homestay*, which is 2000 rp per person including tea. It's in a quiet street near the museum and is a very relaxing and friendly place to stay. Mr Rustami knows a lot about both Tanjung Pinang and the Province of Riau: he is also very helpful about organising onward travel. You had better check around locally to make sure it's still operating, because although it's only been opened a short time we've heard that the family has moved to mainland Sumatra. If it is still open head for Jalan Rimbajaya 80, Depan Pemancar RRI, a 100 rp fare by ojek or 200 rp by oplet from Jalan Merdeka. Get off at the junction of Jalan Bakarbatu and Jalan Rimbajaya.

One of the cheaper homestays is *Penginapan Sondang* on Jalan Josuf Khahar for 6000 rp a double. Other places along this street are the luxury hotel *Sempurna Jaya*, the expensive *Wisma Riau* and the slightly more modest *Sempurna Inn* which has rooms from 8250 rp.

There's a fairly new place – no name, but not difficult to find – not far from the harbour. Ask for 'Rommell' at the wharf – he's usually there. If you can't find him turn right at the end of the dock, then left about 300 metres further on, two houses past the police department is a large white house. It's clean and airy and costs 2000 rp a single.

Avoid getting mixed up with Ahmody, who has a homestay at Jalan Pelantar Datuk 10; there are claims he's into a con trick with a couple of travel agents, which results in travellers having to stay overnight at his losmen because they've 'missed' the last boat out or it's 'full'. What's more his losmen was described as 'revoltingly smelly'.

There are a few other cheap homestays along Jalan Bintan at around 2000 rp per person and a couple of others between the Bank Dagang Negara and the Chinese temple. Otherwise you can stay with a local family for between 1500 to 2000 rp per person. There's no problem about finding this kind of accommodation as it's more than likely you will be approached by someone as soon as you get off the boat.

Eat at the night markets where there is a variety of Indonesian, Chinese and seafood available. Stalls outside the coffee shops have good value food during the day. The coffee is excellent here and is served in cups rather than glasses like it is in most parts of Indonesia.

There's good, cheap Padang food at the little warung on the corner of Jalan Rimbajay and Jalan Bakarbatu. A basic meal of rice, fish, curried egg etc from most warungs will cost around 1000 rp or a little more. Elsewhere food is expensive.

Getting Around

The only two bus services in Tanjung Pinang operate to Kijang and Tanjung Uban. The main method of transport is the ojek – public motorcycle. You can distinguish them from privately-owned motorbikes by the small yellow reflector on the front left-hand side. The fare is 100 rp around town, 200 rp for short trips or 1000 to 1500 rp an hour for longer trips. There are also oplets, the standard fare being 200 rp. Otherwise it's shanks pony.

Various kinds of boats – from rowboats and sampans to largish ships – is the way to island hop or go upriver. The following is a list of boats, prices, times and schedules to some destinations out of Tanjung Pinang.

	rupiah	
Penyenget	300 to 500	daily by sampan
Batam	4500	daily
Moro	4000	daily
Dabo (Singkep)	9500	Friday, Tuesday
Pulau Karimun		regular ferry
Pekanbaru	12,350	daily
Selatpanjang	16,500	daily
Tanjungbatu	5500	daily
Belawan (Medan)	26,000	Wednesday

Getting There & Away

A regular ferry service connects Singapore and Sumatra via Batam and Tanjung Pinang – see the Getting There section on Sumatra above for more details. Most launches are fast, clean and comfortable with aircraft-type seats and video facilities. Don't forget to get your passport stamped with an entry permit and clear customs at Batam Island, otherwise you will have to turn around and go back again. On from Tanjung Pinang there is a weekly service on Wednesdays – not particularly reliable – to Medan.

In early 1985 regular shipping connections between Tanjung Priok, Jakarta and Tanjung Pinang were still not being offered but there was lots of talk of a service between the two places starting soon. Check with the Harbour Master to see what the state of play is at the time. Alternatively, you can get a flight from Jakarta to Pangalpinang (Bangka, Singkep Island) at 11 am every day for 42,000 rp and take a boat from there – see Getting Around above. Kijang airport is on the south-eastern tip of Bintan Island about 17 km from Tanjung Pinang. A taxi will cost you 5000 rp or more or you can take an ojek for 1500 to 2000 rp.

There are also boats to Pekanbaru for 12,350 rp deck class, tickets are sold on the quay. It's a typical Indonesian boat with cramped conditions and abysmal food but the journey up-river is really superb. 'Tolerance of Boney M tapes is a necessity', one traveller warned, while another advised that if faced with a choice of boats it's better to choose the grotty, old one which is less crowded (not my experience but . . .) and gets there in the same time. All of them make numerous stops at small ports along the way and there is plenty of time to visit the markets and buy fresh food – a necessity as the usual nosh on these boats is one bowl of boiled rice a day with a smidgeon of dry salt fish in chilli sauce and a cup of coffee if you're lucky. This trip takes at least 40 hours and can take up to 48 hours. From Pekanbaru – the pits of a place – it's only a few hours by bus to Bukittinggi.

Air There are daily flights between Tanjung Pinang and Jakarta (90,600 rp via Garuda, 77,500 rp via Sempati or Merpati), Pekanbaru (46,700 via Garuda, 40,000 via Sempati), Palembang (via Sempati for 46,000 rp) and Singapore, the latter being a rather elusive service run by SMAC – Sabang-Merauke Air Charter. On Wednesdays and Saturdays there are flights to Medan by Sempati for 78,500 rp while on Fridays there's a flight to Tanjungbalai via SMAC for 26,700 rp and also to Bangka on Singkep Island for 46,000 rp with Sempati.

OTHER ISLANDS
Pulau Penyenget
A tiny island – less than 2½ square km – that you could walk around in a few hours, once capital of the kingdom and pervaded with history. After 1721 the island played an important political and cultural role in the history of the Riau as one of the two seats of government. It is believed to have been given to Sultan Raja Riau-Lingga VI in 1805 by his brother-in-law Sultan Mahmud Lingga-Riau IV as a wedding present. The place is littered with reminders of its past; there are ruins and graveyards wherever you walk.

When you arrive at the island you'll see a road close to where the sampan lands. Turn right and head off to the north-east – most of the kampungs are along the shoreline but the ruins of the old palace of Raja Ali and the tombs and graveyards of Raja Jaafar and Raja Ali are slightly further inland. All the main sites are marked with small plaques and inscriptions. Particularly spectacular is the sulphur-coloured mosque with its forest of domes – 13 of them – pillars and minarets. Housed here is a library which contains hundreds of tomes on history, culture, law, languages and religions including five hand written and illustrated copies of the Koran.

Get there by boat from the main pier at Tanjung Pinang. Tell officials where you're going and you won't have to pay the US$1 harbour tax. The boats leave from halfway along the pier and the cost is 300 to 500 rp each way. Don't be tricked into chartering to Penyengat as there are always boats sailing over there.

Singkep

The headquarters of Riau tin and Timah mining companies, it is the third largest island in the archipelago and has a big ethnic Chinese population. Few outsiders visit here, but it's a handy stopover point on the Singapore-Tanjung Pinang-Singkep-Pangkalpinang-Palembang run and has most of the services of a much larger place. The main town, Dabo, shaded by lush trees and gardens, clusters around a central park. Nearby, on the road to Sungeibuluh a big mosque dominates the skyline. There are microbuses or becaks for getting around, but they're expensive and you can walk to most places.

Information Bank Dagang Negara will change US$ and A$ for quite good rates. The Post Office is on Jalan Pahlawan and there is also an overseas telephone office about three km out of town on the road to Sungeibuluh.

The fish and vegetable markets down near the harbour are interesting to wander around and among the best places in town to buy fresh, cheap food. Jalan Pasar Lamar is a good browsing and shopping area and if you need any snorkelling equipment try Toko Aneka Tekni on Jalan Merdeka.

Every Saturday night at Taman Seni classical Malay theatre is performed. The acting is very stylised and ritualistic and the costumes are so elaborate and ornate Liberace's glitter outfits are cheap tat by comparison. Admission is 200 rp for a brilliant night out. There are also a couple of cinemas, Mandala and Jalaria.

Not far out of town is a white sand beach, fringed with palms, Batu Bedau, a good way to spend a relaxing few hours. There are a couple of others nearby called Sergang and Jago. You get fine views if you walk to the top of the hill past the residential district of Bukit Asem.

Places to Stay & Eat Try the *Penginapan Sri Indah* on Jalan Perusahaan which costs 6000 rp a single, 8000 rp a double and 10,000 rp for a room with three beds. Coffee is included in the price, it's spotlessly clean and has a comfortable sitting-room. Or if you want to indulge yourself you could stay at *Wisma Timah* for 17,500 a room.

Eat at the markets behing Penginapan Sri Indah or try any of the warungs on Jalan Pasar Lama and Jalan Merdeka. Bakmie and warungs pop up all over the place at night. If you want a drink check out the bar at Wisma Timah.

Getting There & Getting Away The boat trip from Tanjung Pinang takes about 11 hours, crosses the equator and passes several shimmering islands on the way. The *KM Hentry* is a fairly new ship, built of teak, and departs from Tanjung Pinang on Mondays, Wednesdays and Fridays. From Dabo, it departs for Tanjung Pinang on Tuesdays, Thursdays and Saturdays. Cost of the fare is 8200 rp and this includes one meal. You'll find the agent P T Cuaca Terang, at Jalan Lorong Merdeka 1V, in Tanjung Pinang (telephone 21906) or at Jalan Pramuka 63 in Dabo. If you want to get to Jakarta you may be to get a ride on one of the cargo boats – like the Intisari 111 – which transport timber from here. It's a long shot but you never know your luck.

There are flights to Tanjung Pinang on Tuesdays and Saturdays for 36,000 rp. There are also flights to Jakarta twice-weekly – Wednesdays and Saturdays – for 65,000 rp.

PANJANG

An arrival port for ferries from Java and not much else. Most of the losmen are lousy value too. Try the *Losmen Kastari* if you want to stay here.

PALEMBANG

Built along the River Musi and only 50 km upstream from the sea, Palembang was forced into the 20th century rather abruptly because of its strategic position. When Sumatra's oil fields were discovered and opened early in the century, Palembang quickly became the main export outlet for south Sumatra. Today Palembang is a heavily industrial city – it also has tin mines and a petro-chemical refinery – the capital of south Sumatra and a rather dull place to visit. But a thousand years ago it was centre of the highly developed civilisation of Srivijaya from which much of its art and culture are inherited. Unfortunately, there are few relics from this period remaining – no sculpture, monuments or architecture of note – nor is there much of interest from the early 18th century when Palembang was an Islamic kingdom. Most of the buildings of the latter era were destroyed in battles with the Dutch, the last of which occurred in 1811.

Coming into Palembang from the south you pass plantations of rubber, coffee, pepper and pineapples. In complete contrast are the smokestacks of the Sungai Gerong refinery and the petro-chemical complex at Plaju which give the landscape a kind of futuristic look, particularly at night.

The city is split in half by the River Musi and sprawls along both banks. The two halves of the city are connected by the Ampera bridge, only built in the mid-60s. A hodge podge of wooden houses standing – like storks – on stilts crowd both banks, but the south side, known as Ulu, is where the majority of people live. The 'better half' Ilir is on the north bank is where you'll find most of the government offices, shops, the wealthy residential district and access to the quickest way to skip town Talang Betutu, the airport.

If you get up early you'll catch the floating market, which operates like an extension of the main market. But there are usually people selling all kinds of stuff – food, household gear and clothing – from boats most of the day. Other things to see are the Grand Mosque – near the bridge –

built by Sultan Mahmud Badaruddin in the 18th century, the graves of the sultans and their families – these are are fairly neglected and much like other cemeteries – or hire a boat and take a look the Chinese temple on Kemaro Island. It's near the junction of the Musi, Oghan and Komering rivers. About a 100 years old, its architectural design and ornamentation could only be Chinese and statues of dragons and monkeys guard the entrance. You can also take a boat up to the refinery, Sungai Gerong if you're interested. To hire a motorboat there and back costs around 10,000 rp between six people. The boat terminal is right by the bridge.

Places to Stay
Walk down Jalan Jen Surdiman from the bus stop and you will come to *Hotel Asiana* at 45E, by the traffic lights. Rooms are 4000 rp for singles and it's reasonably clean and not as noisy as it might be because it's high up. The *Lusyana Hotel*, on the corner by the Asiana, is similarly priced. From the Asiana turn right into Jalan Lematang and you'll find the *Aman* at 453. A couple of hundred metres further on at Jalan Segaran 207C is the new, upgraded *Segaran*. None of them standout as being any better than another. There are some other cheap places across the river where the train comes into town. For example *Losmen Semeru*, five minutes walk from the station over the bridge, at Jalan Ogan I Ulu Darat 6, costs 2500 rp a single.

Places to Eat
You can find good Chinese food on Jalan Sajangan, close to the hotels and parallel to the main road. There are no particularly memorable restaurants but the one on the corner of Jalan Lematang and Jalan Jawa is OK. Nice bakeries on Jalan Mailain, which connects Jalan Sajangan with the main road. The food at the railway station is all right too.

Getting Around & Away

The Kertepati railway station is about eight km out of Palembang across two rivers, get there by bemo from the town centre bus station for 200 rp.

You can catch a ferry to Bangalincur for 7000 rp three times a week on Saturdays, Mondays and Wednesdays. It's a slow, soporific trip departing Palembang at around 2 pm and arriving Bangalincur around 5 am the following day. The river cuts through dense jungle, noisy with the chatter of monkeys, past villages of river houses on stilts and basking crocodiles. At dusk giant fruit bats swoop about in big mobs. When you arrive there is an oplet waiting at the wharf to take you to Jambi for 200 rp, but you may have to hang about until light before it will set off. If you start walking, you can see more of the jungle and will probably be able to catch a ride further down the road for less.

Garuda offers regular flights out of Palembang to Denpasar for 145,100 rp, Jakarta for 54,500 rp and within Sumatra to Jambi for 29,200, Medan 105,000 and Padang 63,700.

JAMBI

There's nothing much to be said for this unexciting riverine town – it's just there.

Places to Stay

The cheaper places are generally drab and unpleasant and the more expensive ones are . . . more expensive. Try the *Mustika* on the Padang and Palembang side of town or the *Mutiara*, slightly closer to the town centre. In the centre itself the *Sumateri* and the *Jelita* are cheaper but very unfriendly. *Hotel Makmar* at Jalan Cut Nyak Dien 14 is altogether more pleasant but also more expensive. Of course Padang food is what you find to eat and there are lots of stalls selling slices of chilled fruit, particularly delicious pineapple.

BENGKULU (BENCOOLEN)

This was Raffles' foot in the door to Indonesia and his Fort Marlborough is still there. The British traded it with the Dutch, giving them hegemony over Sumatra, in exchange for the Malay coast port of Melaka.

The bus station at Bengkulu is a few km from town and the bemo (they call thems taxis) drivers insist that there are no public buses and demand that you charter one of them for 2000 rp. There is a public bemo which costs 100 rp, but it's almost impossible to find. If you approach any of the locals or bureaucrats to confirm this story they stick together.

Places to Stay

Penginapan Aman is very comfortable and friendly; it's run by a particularly helpful woman, who has singles/doubles from 1500/3000 rp. There's a snack bar here too. On Jalan Indah there is also the *Wisma Pemuda. Restaurant Miasra* has good but rather expensive food – 2000 rp for fried prawns. As usual if you want a cold beer you have to put ice in it. The satay man outside the Aman makes excellent satays.

KERINCI

Kerinci is a mountain valley accessible by bus from either Jambi or Padang – the road from Padang is most beautiful and also a better road. It's a rich, green area with two very dominating features – Gunung Kerinci, the highest mountain in the Sumatra-Sunda island chain and Danau Kerinci (lake) at the other end of the valley. Sungai Penuh is the largest town with some 200 small villages in the area. Its matrinlineal social structure is similar to that found in west Sumatra.

Things to Do & See

In Sungai Penuh there is a large, pagoda-style mosque which is said to be over 400 years old. You need permission to go inside – it has large carved beams and old Dutch tiles. Dusun Sungai Tetung is nationally renowned for its basket weaving. All over the area that are stone carvings which have not really been carefully investigated. Locals have a legend of a great kingdom here long ago. The carvings are very different from those of the Mojopahit or Srivijaya areas. It's easy to find a cheap guide for day trips from Sungai Penuh.

Tours around the lake are good – start at Jujun or Keluru (20 km from Sungai Penuh and half a km apart). Make sure to ask to see Batu Gong. About 40 km out of Sungai Penuh on the way to Gunung Kerinci there is a tea plantation called Kayo Aro, worth going to see if you've never been over one before. There are hot springs nearby – too hot for swimming in the main pool, but you can get a private room with a hot mandi for 100 rp per person.

Watch for tigers, there are said to be many still around. If you are lucky you might catch a magic dance or a Pincuk Silat performance, a fantastical experience where swords are swung around like something out of Ali Baba or that scene in *Raiders of the Lost Ark*. Don't mention the word 'communist' – this was the last area to fall to the Dutch in 1902, the Japanese had a hard time and in Sukarno's time it was a strong communist area – and we know what happened then.

Places to Stay & Eat

The *Mata Hari Losmen* is cheap and clean. For a taste treat try *dending batokok*, a speciality of the region – strips of beef smoked and grilled over a fire. One of the best restaurants in Sungai Penuh is the *Minang Soto*, which has good Padang food and is cheap and clean.

PADANG

This is the centre of the matrilineal Minangkabau area where the eldest female is the boss and property is inherited through the female line. Beautiful examples of the high-peaked Minangkabau houses can be seen on the pastorally tranquil road down to Padang from Solok. As you start the final descent down to Padang there are spectacular sweeping views along the coast.

Information

The Tourist Information Office is at Jalan Khatib Sulaiman. It's a fair way out of the city centre, difficult to get to – catch a bemo or hire a dokar – and closes at 2 pm. But if you do get out there the staff are very helpful and several can speak fairly good English. The Garuda office (tel 23431) is on Jalan Sudirman on the other side of town and it closes at 4 pm. There's an agent in the Cendrawasih Hotel on Jalan Pemuda. Merpati (tel 21303) is on Jalan Ratulangi and Mandala (tel 21979) on Jalan Pemuda.

If you're intending to catch the *Kerinci* to Java the Pelni office (tel 22109) is on Jalan Tanjung Priok, Teluk Bayur. If you arrive by air it's a lot cheaper to walk out to the road and catch a bus for 100 rp to the downtown market area, than to take a taxi, which will rip you off. It's only a couple of hundred metres to the road and buses to Padang and to Bukittinggi go past the airport regularly. Catch an orange bus marked Bis Kota if you're heading for Padang, but there's no need to go into town at all if you're on your way to Bukittinggi. The bus station in the city centre is on Jalan Pemuda and the oplet terminal on Jalan M H Yamin. You'll find the Post Office at Jalan B Azizchan 7. Bank Negara Indonesia 46 is on Jalan Dobi.

Padang is a good place to get a visa extension if you need one. The Immigration Office (tel 21294) is in Jalan Pahlawan.

Things to Do & See

Padang itself does not have much to offer apart from Padang food, although you can see the rusting remains of Dutch ships, sunk by the Japanese at the time they entered WW II, in the harbour.

In the centre of town – just down the road from the bus station – is the new museum on Jalan Diponengoro, built in the Minangkabau tradition with two rice

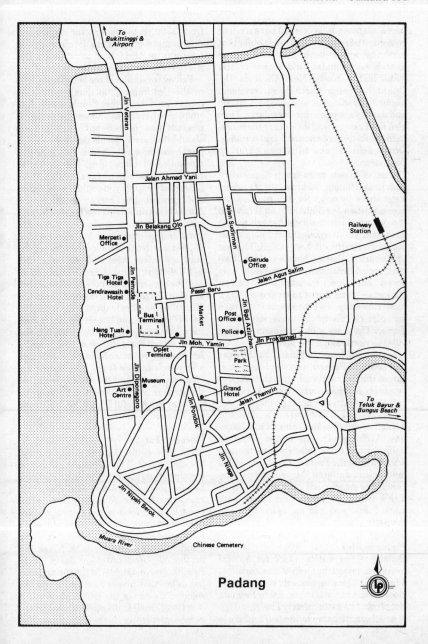

Padang

barns out front. It has a small but excellent collection of antiques and other objects of historical and cultural interest from all over West Sumatra, and a particularly good textile room. Next to it is the Cultural Centre where local, regional, national, traditional and modern music and dances are performed regularly. They also hold poetry readings, stage plays and hold exhibitions of paintings and carvings. Open daily 9 am to 2 pm, 100 rp admission.

One of those palm-fringed, postcard beaches is Bungus, 22 km south of Padang – get there by oplet for 350 rp. You can hire a prahau for 3000 rp, you'll have to row yourself but the local fisherboy who goes with you to navigate will help. Row out to the nearby offshore island. The last oplet back to Padang leaves at dusk. Two other good beaches are Pasir Putih, only seven km from Padang and Taman Nirwana, 12 km out of town and a 150 rp oplet ride away. To get to Pasir Putih take an oplet or bus to the university at Air Tawar. There are some interesting fishing villages north along the beach.

If you get a bemo to Muaro, on the river just south of Padang, you can take a boat across the river and walk up to the Chinese cemetery overlooking the town. A km walk will take you to the fishing village of Air Manis and at low tide you can wade out to a small island or take a sampan to a larger one. A clump of stone in the village is believed to be the final form of the son who, back in the mists of time, denied his mother and suffered this ignomious fate. Climb the nearby hill for a good view of Teluk Bayur, Padang's port. Then walk back there and get an oplet into the town.

Places to Stay
Padang is not a good place for accommodation, especially clean accommodation. The cheap places are mainly conveniently close to the bus station on Jalan Pemuda but tend to be rather noisy. The *Tiga Tiga* is at 33 (as its name indicates) and costs

from 3500 rp to 6500 rp for singles and doubles. It also has dorm accommodation for 1000 rp. And lots of mosquitoes. But it's been slicked up slightly recently.

Prices are similar at the *Olo* at number 2 or the *Cendrawasih* at number 27. One report said that the Cendrawasih had some cheaper rooms and was better value than the other places – but added that you should 'beware of locals perving through peepholes in walls. And it has rats and possibly bed bugs.' And that is better value!? The *Hotel Sriwijaya* at Jalan Alang Lawar is 150 rp, or you could try the *Adina* and around the corner from it the *Darlia Hotel* on Jalan Jawa Dalam. Rooms start from 8000 rp at the *Grand Hotel*, a dank and gloomy place at Jalan Pondok 84, not worth the money. In its favour the staff are informative and the restaurant has delicious Chinese and Padang food. And the once reasonably cheap *Machudums*, at Jalan Hiligoo 43 near the bemo stand, is fairly flash and has leapt in price to 12,000 rp, with air-con and hot water. But it does have some economy rooms with fan and share mandi for 4500 rp a double and a few 'transit' room with fan, private mandi and porch for 6500 rp. The rooms are clean and large and the staff friendly. At the springs (Air Manis) near Padang you can stay at cheerful Mr Chili-Chili's, and yes his food is hot!

Places to Eat
What else would you eat in Padang but Padang food? The *Simpang*, the first restaurant you come to from Jalan Pemuda, has ice juice drinks and first-class vegetable martabaks. Another places to get good Padang food is the *Pagi-Sore*. For delicious but more up-market Indonesian food treat yourself at *Kings* on Jalan Pondok, the *Phoenix* on Jalan Niaga 138 or the *Sky Restaurant* on Jalan Imam Bonjol. The restaurant in the *Grand Hotel* has delicious Chinese food and if you like seafood try one of the crab dishes.

A lot of small stalls operate around the bemo/oplet station in the morning, selling pancakes and appetising little coconut-rice waffles. They aren't very good at cooking food from other regions of Indonesia, so stick to the local speciality.

PADANG TO BUKITTINGGI

Around Padang Panjang bull fights – nothing like those in Spain, no bloodshed, not even the bulls get hurt – are held every Tuesday afternoon around 5 pm in the village of Kota Baru. The fight is known as *adu sapi* and involves two water buffaloes or Karibau of roughly the same size and weight locking horns under the watchful eyes of their respective owners. Most of the fun is in watching the locals make their bets. Once the fight starts it continues until one of the bulls breaks away and runs out of the ring – which usually results in two bulls chasing each other around and the on-lookers running in every direction arms and legs going in all directions and having the time of their lives. Worth a look, admission is 250 rp. To get there take a bus or a bemo from Bukittinggi to Kota Baru for 200 rp, check out the Tuesday market there (small but nice selection of embroidered scarfs and sarongs with the gold threads woven in). Follow the crowd down heaps of steps and along a path through an exquisite paddy field until you get to the arena.

The market on Monday in Padang Panjang is also worth visiting. Not as big as Bukittinggi but just as exciting and lots of good taste treats. You can get a bus from Bukittinggi (the ones that go to Padang) to Padang Panjang for 200 rp.

Even though the passenger train no longer runs between Padang and Bukittinggi there is still an ancient Dutch steam engine that hauls coal up and down the tracks. It is possible to hitch a free ride on the engine for a short distance if you're there when the train is going by. There's no written schedule but the station masters usually know what time the train will come by. A good short trip can be made between Kota Baru and Padang Panjang. There is also a passenger train that runs between Solok and Padang Panjang – but again the schedule varies – usually it goes when the train is full!

BUKITTINGGI

This cool, easy-going mountain town is one of the most popular in Sumatra. It's a spectacular drive north of Padang. About 45 km before Bukittinggi, on the road via Padang Panjang, you pass the village of Batu Sangkar. Turn off the road towards the village of Pagaruyung (four km distance) and you'll see many Minangkabau houses. Along the roadside are stone tablets inscribed in Sanskrit.

Bukittinggi is often called Kota Jam Gadang – the Big Ben Town – because of the clock tower that overlooks the large market square and is also known as Tri Arga, meaning the town of three mountains. It is 930 metres above sea level and the three mountains it is encircled by are Mts Merapi, Singgalang and Sago.

Information

The Tourist Office is on Jalan Jen A Yani between Murni's Hotel and the Coffee House. They have several leaflets and brochures on West Sumatra but not much in the way of maps. They also organise a tour of Bukittinggi and surrounding villages. It's an all-day trip, costs 5000 rp per person and is a good way to see a lot of country, which would be difficult to get to otherwise. Much the same kind of tour to almost exactly the same places and for the same price is run out of the Coffee House, so competition for custom is fierce. With a group of five or six people it is cheaper to hire a minibus for a day and go where you want.

Be careful of organising on-going travel through the Coffee House because you may get a right royal run-around. One traveller booked Bukittinggi-Prapat direct via express ALS bus through an agent at the Coffee House and it took an hour careering round the township in a bemo before he got to the bus terminal. When he finally arrived there he was met by the guy

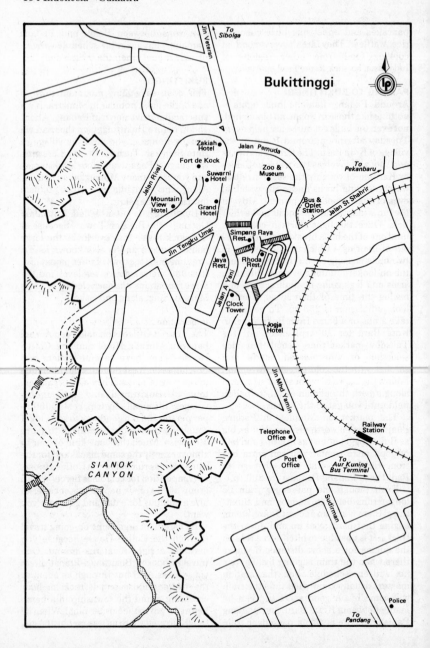

who had organised his ticket and ushered to a good seat on an unusually empty bus, hardly believing his good fortune. His well-being was shattered when he discovered that the most 'expressive' thing about the bus was his language when he realised he was heading for the northeast coast and Medan. After 22 hours of travelling, crawling through villages and stopping every few minutes to pick up passengers, he was dumped off at Tebing-tinggi at 7 am, and had to pay an additional 1100 rp and spend several more hours waiting around, then catch another bus before he eventually reached his destination. The moral is get yourself down to the terminal and organise your own trip, it's easier in the long run. On the subject of travel agents, officially there are four of them in Bukittinggi – Maju Indosari, Jalan Pasar Atas, Dymens Tour & Travel, Jalan Nawawi 3, Yani Vaelleyrama, Jalan A Yani and Anta Japuik, also on Jalan A Yani.

The Bank Negara Indonesia 1946 is at the top of Jalan Jen A Yani opposite the clock tower. Exchange rates are not as good here as they are in Medan or Padang.

If you're arriving in Bukittinggi from Prapat make sure you get off the bus near the start of Jalan Jen A Yani before it turns the corner into Jalan Pemuda. It will save you a 100 rp bemo ride from the terminal, which is a few km out of town.

There are several interesting antique shops worth browsing around. Near the clock tower on Jalan Jen A Yani is the Aladdin Art & Antique Shop and not far up the road is another one, which is just called the Antique Shop. On Jalan Minangkabau are the Haji Mokhtar Is and Toko Mas & Antiques. There are some fine samples of antique cloth and weaving in most of these shops, particularly at the Aladdin. The bookshop at Jalan A Yani 2, Pustaka Pahlawan has a limited selection of books in other languages – English, German and French – if you want something to read.

Things to Do & See

The market is on Wednesdays and Saturdays and well worth checking out. It's a big market, crammed with stalls of fruit and vegetable, clothing and craftware.

On a hill top site right in the centre of town is Taman Bundokanduag, a museum and zoo. The museum, which was built in 1935 during the Dutch rule by J Manedelau, 'Controleur' of the district, is a superb example of Minangkabau architecture with its two rice barns out front. It is the oldest museum in the province and has a good collection of Minangkabau historical and cultural exhibits. There is a 100 rp admission fee. By contrast the adjoining zoo (200 rp admission) is a depressing place with sadly neglected, moth-eaten looking animals kept captive in appalling conditions. But if you are interested in Sumatra's native animals you can see a *Buceros rhinoceros*, honey bears and tigers here.

Not much remains of Bukittinggi's old Fort de Kock, built during the Padri Wars (1821-1837) by the Dutch, except the defence moat and a few cannons, but it provides fine views over the town and surrounding countryside from an adjoining hill. Panorama Park, on the southern edge of the town, is part of a deep canyon that cuts right into Bukittinggi. There is a path through the canyon, Ngarai Sianok, to the other side and on to the village of Kota Gadang. Turn left at the bottom of the road just before the canyon and keep going. Don't cross the bridge there. Kota Gadang is noted for its silverwork, which though exquisite is limited in range. It is about 12 km from Bukittinggi.

There are several other villages around Bukittinggi which are still producing traditional crafts, one of the more interesting being Pandai Sikat, 13 km away, a centre for weavings and wood carving.

Other Beneath the town itself are hundreds of metres of winding channels built by the Japanese during World War II as a defence strategy and an escape route. You can walk through them with a guide if you're interested.

Fifteen km east of Bukittinggi is Ngalau Kamanga, the scene of active resistance against the Dutch in the 19th and early 20th centuries. The story goes that the villagers used a local cave – 1500 metres long – as a hideout from the Dutch, conducting effective guerrilla attacks in the surrounding country from this base. The cave is dripping with stalactites and stalagmites and has a small, clear lake. Get to it from Ngalau Kamanga by oplet for 250 rp.

There is a Rafflesia sanctuary about 15 km north of town, a sign at the village of Batang Palupuh indicates the path. Rafflesia are giant, cabbage-sized flowers named after Sir Stamford Guess Who of Singapore fame. The Rafflesia bloom between August and December. Further north on the way to Sibolga a large globe stands in a rice paddy beside the road, indicating the position of the equator.

Check out the horse racing on Sunday on the way to Sibolga. Definitely not the Grand National or the Melbourne Cup but lots of fun.

Around Bukittinggi

There are quite a few places of interest around Bukittinggi. Get a map of the area from the Jaya Restaurant.

Lake Maninjau About 30 km south-west of the town is Lawang Top and directly below it, Lake Maninjau. The final descent to the lake involves covering 12 km with 44 numbered hairpin bends, quite a terrifying trip. You can bus there direct from Bukittinggi or get off at Matur, climb to Lawang for the view and then walk down to the lake, which takes a couple of hours if you're fit, much longer if you're not. If you miss the last bus you either have to charter a bemo back – which could be expensive – or spend the night there. The choice of accommodation is limited to the *Maninjau Indah* which has three grades of rooms ranging from those

with communal mandi, no fan and no view at 5000 rp to rooms with a view, tinted windows, air panas, fan and plastic chandelier for 15,000 rp or the *Coffee House Losmen* for 1000 rp. Rooms at the latter are clean, quiet, peaceful and small. The food is plentiful, but the choice is limited. It's run by a friendly ex-cop, whose one peculiar foible is that he likes collecting passport photos of his guests – he'd be delighted to add yours to his ID lineup.

Lake Maninjau is warmer than Toba and is an extremely beautiful crater lake. You can zip around it by speedboat or water scooter if you wish.

Places to Stay

Bukittinggi has a lot of losmen although they seem to open, close, change names and decline in standards with alarming regularity. Many of them smell musty and look much grimmer than they are. Most are between 1000 and 1500 rp for one and 2000 and 3000 rp for a couple. On Jalan Jen A Yani the new *Wisma Tiga Balai* is one of the better ones and costs 2500 rp a double. In the same street is the *Nirwana* which is 3000 rp a double and the management is downright inhospitable. Down the road is the *Grand Hotel*, once one of the most popular places in town but now rather run down and dirty, although some travellers still report that it is not too bad. Near the Nirwana is *Murni's*, which is 2000 rp a double. It's neat and clean – good mandis and loos – the people are friendly, the worst aspect being the noise. Also on Jalan Jen A Yani not far from the Mona Lisa Restaurant is the *Hotel Gangga* which has – wonder of wonders a washing machine and an iron! Neither works brilliantly, but it makes a change from hand washing and creased clothes. You also get free tea and coffee at the Gangga.

Up on the road to Fort de Kock – Jalan Yos Sudarso 3 – there is the very relaxing *Mountain View Guest House*, although it's rather more expensive at 5000 rp for the cheapest rooms. But they're spacious, have their own mandis and a small outdoor area with good views of the mountains. Other rooms run from 7000 to 9000 rp. At Jalan Benteng 1 there's the comfortable *Benteng Hotel* with its antique furniture, TV and great view of the fort and township. There are a few cheap rooms at 3000 rp a single or double with common mandi, but the regular price is 12,500 rp. Next door is *Suwarni's Guest House*. It's rather quieter up on this small hill than in town but don't let that delude you into thinking that everything's sweet with this place. Several letters have warned that it can be rather isolated and unpleasant at this guest house and you should not be too trusting. Make sure you take great care of your possessions. The cost of accommodation is 1000 rp per person.

Other places include the *Singgalang Hotel*, next door to the Grand and the *Jogja*, down in the lower part of town.

Places to Eat

The *Coffee House* between the Grand and Murni's on Jalan Jen A Yani seems to have gained a cult following with travellers. But although the food is OK and it's a travellers' hangout, this place exudes a feeling of smug self-satisfaction. It's over-rated and altogether too western.

The best place to eat in town is the *Roda*, in the Pasar Atas building, particularly for Padang food. Try their delicious vegetable martabaks and the dadhi campur – a mixture of oats, coconut, avocado, banana, molasses and buffalo yoghurt. *Saida's Yoghurt Place*, also in the Pasar Atas building, is another restaurant which offers this local speciality as does the warung across from the Roda. There are lots of street sellers and food stalls in Bukittinggi too.

There's also the Chinese *Mona Lisa* restaurant (excellent, although a bit pricey) but most places here are Padang specialists. *Simpang Raya*, in the top part of town, across from the Gloria Cinema,

specialises in Minangkabau food including fried eels, caught in the rice paddies. Near there is the *Kedai Kopi Sianok*, the place to sample the local sweet sarikaya – custard on top of bread or rice – tastes better than it sounds. Next door to the Hotel Benteng is the *Rumah Makan Famili*, which has delicious Padang food and great views to help you digest it by.

At Jalan Tengku Umar 10A is a small private restaurant run by a Chinese man known as Mac and his daughter which gets big raves.

PEKANBARU

This is a grubby oil town, with a sleazy port and an airport which will cost you 5000 rp to get away from because taxis are the only method of public transport. It's simply somewhere to pass through either on the way to or from Singapore via Tanjun Pinang and Batam. Catch a boat down river the day you arrive in Pekanbaru if you're on your way to Singapore or get a bus straight out if you're heading for Bukittinggi. The journey to Bukittinggi takes about six hours and will cost 2500 rp. You can change money at the airport, the Bank Negara Indonesia 1946 at Jalan Sudirman 63 or at Toko Firmas, Jalan Sudirman 27. There is no tourist office as such, the local government department handles this service. Find it in the Governor's Office on Jalan Sudirman. The Pelni office and various other shipping agencies are in Jalan M Yatim, close to the harbour, which makes it easy to organise onward travel to Singapore. If you have to stay overnight there are numerous losmen around the bus terminal on Jalan Nangka. One of the better places to stay in this area is the *Hotel Linda*, which is reasonably clean and costs 5000 rp for one and 7500 rp for a double. If you're departing by boat there are a couple of rundown and depressing hotels on Jalan M Yatim, with little to recommend them except that their proximity to the port. The best you can say about the *Nirmala* at 11 is that it's only a few hundred metres from the river and that the manager, Aris, is very helpful and can speak some English. Other places to try in Pekanbaru are the *Hotel Cempaka* on Jalan H Wahid Hasyim, the *Hotel Dharma Utama* on Jalan Sisingamangaraja or the *Hotel Tun Teja* on the same road. On average, the cost for a night is 3500 rp for a single and 7000 rp a double.

SIBOLGA

There's no attraction to bring you to this rather dirty and drab little port, except as an overnight stop between Bukittinggi and Prapat or a setting off point to Nias. There is a regular service between Sibolga and Teluk Dalam in Nias, most days except Sundays depending on weather, departing 9 pm and arriving around 9 am. Two boats ply this route but you'd be wise to take the larger one, which has two decks, if you can as the crossing can be rough. The smaller one is a cramped, uncomfortable cargo boat, which tends to treat passengers like cargo as well. The fare is 5000 rp, sometimes 6000 rp. There are also daily boats between Sibolga and Gunung Sitoli in the north of Nias for 5000 rp.

Sibolga is north of Bukittinggi, where the road turns inland to Prapat and Lake Toba. The descent into Sibolga – approaching from Prapat – is very beautiful, particularly at sunset, the harbour itself is attractive and there are some good beaches nearby.

Places to Stay

The losmen in the central area are generally dirty and/or unfriendly. They include the *Hotel Sudi Mampir*, the *Murni Indah* and the *Subur*, all with doubles at around 3000 rp. *Hotel Indah Sari* is slightly more expensive but at least it's reasonable – they also have rooms with air-con and attached bathrooms. Opposite the Indah is the *Maturi*, not much to write home about but OK for a night and cheap at 1000 rp a single. Off to the north of town, and near the immigration office, the *Hotel Taman Nauli* is much nicer – rooms

have attached bathrooms and and a balcony – but it's also much more expensive, prices start from 6000 rp. To compensate for Sibolga's other drawbacks there are some good restaurants and an ice cream place on the corner across from the cinema.

NIAS

The island of Nias is off the west coast of North Sumatra and can be reached by boat from Sibolga or by air from Medan. It's interesting for its traditional villages, unique customs and fine beaches. Roads around Nias are rotten but the two most interesting towns in the south of the island are fairly close together. Teluk Dalam is the port and main town in the south, Gunung Sitoli the main town in the north and the only place on the island where you can cash travellers' cheques. Make sure you take enough cash with you because the exchange rates here are grim.

There are various good, easy jungle treks in the south, most of which follow stone tracks. Try to get hold of a map or copy the one in the Teluk Dalam police office.

Outbreaks of malaria are not uncommon on this island, but because chloroquine has been widely used for many years in South-East Asia certain malarial strains are resistant to this drug and it is no longer enough to safeguard you. Nias is one of the regions where the chloroquine resistant drug, pyrimethane-sulfadoxine, is recommended as a backup. Brand names on the market are Fansidar, Faladar, Antemal and Methipox. It is advisable to avoid taking pyrimethane-sulfadoxine if you are pregnant as it may cause birth defects. Women planning to become pregnant within 12 months of travelling should be aware that it may remain in the system for some time after the last dose has been taken.

Bawamataluo (Sunhill) Situated 14 km from Teluk Dalam the last part of the trip involves climbing 480 stone steps! Here

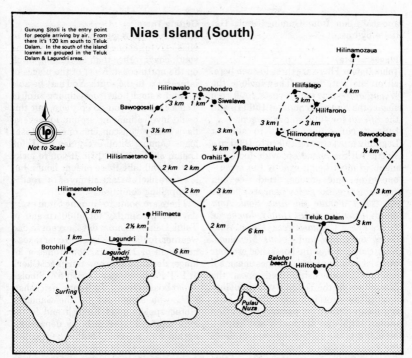

Gunung Sitoli is the entry point for people arriving by air. From there it's 120 km south to Teluk Dalam. In the south of the island losmen are grouped in the Teluk Dalam & Lagundri areas.

Nias Island (South)

Not to Scale

Hilinamozaua

Hilinawalo Onohondro 3 km 1 km Siwalawa

Hilifalego 2 km 4 km

Bawogosali Hilifarono

3½ km 3 km 3 km 3 km

3 km Hilimondregeraya

½ km Bawomataluo Bawodobara

Hilisimaetano Orahili ½ km

2 km 2 km

2 km 3 km 3 km

Hilimaenamolo

3 km Hilimaeta 2 km Teluk Dalam 3 km

2½ km 6 km

1 km Lagundri

Botohili Lagundri 6 km Baloho beach Hilitobara

beach

Surfing Pulau Nuza

---

one can see the high-roofed traditional houses and the fine 'palace' of the tribal chief. In front of this building are stone tables where dead bodies were once left to decay. Traditional war dances may be performed by young, unmarried males, who decorate themselves with feathers. Bawamataluo is now very touristed and prices for statues or for watching the dances are exorbitant. Many of the villagers will pose for photographs – annoying in itself – then demand 100 rp for doing it and get quite aggro if you don't hand over the money. Despite these quibbles it's well worth exploring

Hilisimaetano This larger – there are 140 traditional houses here – but newer village is 16 km from Teluk Dalam. Stone jumping is performed here most Saturdays – once a form of war training, the jumpers had to leap over a two metre high heap of stones surmounted by pointed sticks. These days the sticks are left off.

Lagundi A perfect horseshoe bay about 12 km from the harbour, this is a much more attractive place to stay than Teluk Dalam. Lagundi is a hangout for surfies, which has heaps of losmen all very similar in price and style. Most are clustered together at the far end of the horseshoe where the waves roll in across the reef. There's not much to do here except surf, swim and walk, but it's a great place for basking in the sun. Bring books, cards and chess sets etc to keep yourself amused when you tire of the beach. The turn off to Lagundi is about six km along the road to Hillisimaetano.

Gunung Sitoli Superficially a dump, but not as bad as it first seems. There are several nice walks near town and some *rumah adat* uphill from Hilimbawodesolo about 14 km from Gunung Sitoli. Get there by bus.

Places to Stay

Teluk Dalam There are three losmen here, all on the waterfront. They include the *Wisma Jamburae* which costs 2000 rp a single, the *Sabar Menanti* at 1500 rp and the *Effendi* for 4000 rp per person.

Lagundi Numerous places to stay at Lagundi, most costing 750 rp to 1000 rp a single. All the losmen provide food, the menu in most being exactly the same – omelettes, mie goreng, fried rice and vegetables, gado gado, pancakes, chips etc. They include the *Ama Soni, Ama Shady, Friendly, Rufus, Happy, Jamburae 1, 11, 111, 1V, Sea Breeze, Purba, Ama Gumi, Immanuel* and *Tolong Menolong*. Near the centre of the horseshoe are four other losmen, two fairly new ones unnamed, and two more established ones, the *Limadona* and the *Yanty*. If you're not into surfing the Yanti is a good place to stay. It's cheap – 500 rp per person – the losmen owner, Mr Milyar is friendly and helpful. He also acts as a guide so knows a lot about the area and speaks good English.

Gunung Sitoli Accommodation in this town is expensive, dirty and depressing. Far and away the best place to stay is the *Wisma Soliga* which is on the main road into the township. It's clean, spacious and the food – Chinese dishes – is tasty and there's lots of it. Cost is 6000 rp, but if you bargain hard you can get it down to 3000 rp. Perhaps the biggest disadvantage of this losmen is that it is two km out of town, but it's not far to walk and it's a lot more relaxing than staying elsewhere. In the centre of town is the *Hotel Gomo*, which is 7500 rp for a room that's grubby and dark, but does have its own mandi. Others include the *Ketilang Hotel* for 2000 rp a single, the *Wisata Hotel* at 7000 rp and the *Tenang* which has dorm accommodation for 1000 rp – best to avoid the latter unless you're skint.

Getting There

Boats run out regularly from Sibolga to Nias – try to get one to Teluk Dalam on the south coast rather than to Gunung Sitoli on the north coast. Most of the places of interest are in the south. You may be able to catch a small boat from Gunung Sitoli to Teluk Dalam if you do go there, but this could involve hanging around for several days before you can line one up. Buses leave Gunung Sitoli every day for Teluk Dalam and cost 4000 rp. If you're lucky the trip will take three or four hours, but it's more likely to take all day as the road is in appalling condition.

There are boats to Gunung Sitoli every day except Sunday for 5000 rp and to Teluk Dalam on most days, except in bad weather, for 6000 rp. The trip over takes a minimum of 12 hours, sometimes a lot longer depending on how things go! Check at P T Perlani, Jalan Letjen 57, Sibolga about boats. Or look for Benny, a rickshaw rider who hangs out by the Samudra Hotel, speaks good English and is the local unofficial expert on boats, departures, agents and so on. Another guy called Rickie also seeks out westerners on buses and is extremely skilful at eliciting a high price for his services without hassling. Undoubtedly one or the other or both is bound to catch up with you. There are daily flights from Medan by Smac departing at 8 am and costing 60,000 rp one-way. The only airport in Nias is 19 km from Gunung Sitoli and it will cost you 2500 rp to be dropped into town. There's talk of one being built at Teluk Dalam, but no visible sign of an airport so far. To get around you can rent bicycles, catch buses, walk or the locals will give you pillion rides on their motorbikes for a price.

PRAPAT

On the shores of Lake Toba this is the arrival and departure point for Samosir Island, the ferries operate across to the island from here and the buses for Medan to the north and Bukittinggi to the south depart from here. There's no reason to stay here though, unless you arrive at an inconvenient time for getting straight across to the island. Look in at the expensive Prapat Hotel, they sometimes put on performances of Batak singing or other local culture for tour groups. Prapat is also a good place to get Batak handicrafts like lime containers, leather, batik or wood carvings. Twenty-five km from Prapat is the village of Labuhan Garaga which is well worth a visit if you are interested in buying Batak blankets. They're not cheap – the price range is from 25,000 rp to 60,000 rp or more for good quality samples – but they are attractive and practical buys.

At Jalan Josep Sinaga 19 there is a Batak Cultural Centre where performances of dance and music are held on Saturday nights. Admission is 1000 rp.

Places to Stay
There are a number of rather nice places to stay in Prapat. The *Pago Pago Inn* is on the road close to the harbour – it's airy, has clean rooms and there are fine views across the lake. Doubles are 4000 rp. Right on the waterfront is the *Guerning* for 2000 rp or try the *Sudi Mampir* on the main road through town, which is similarly priced but not as appealing. Another losmen on the main road is the *Singgalang* which is good, clean and comfortable with an excellent restaurant down below, but it's more expensive. Not far from the Singgalang is the *Atsari* at 1000 rp a single. But don't plan on spending more than a night here because it's dirty, noisy and the rooms are like cells. *Andilo Travel* has accommodation for 2000 rp. Or there's the somewhat classier *Solu Jaya* on Jalan Sirikki which has almost luxurious rooms for 6000 rp a double.

Places to Eat
There are lots of eating places in Prapat, some rather pricey. Avoid the ones right by the harbour where the food is not so good. You can get cheap nasi ikan at the place next to Andilo's. The *Hong Kong Restaurant*, right across from the Pago Pago, has excellent Chinese food. Good Padang food in Prapat too.

LAKE TOBA
Samosir Island in beautiful Lake Toba has become much more commercial and pushy over the years but it's still a delightfully laid back, relaxed, easy-living place. The lake is dead centre in north Sumatra, 174 km south of Medan. It's high up (800 metres), big (almost two square km) and deep (450 metres).

Prapat on the shore of the lake is the principal town of the area, a popular resort for Medan with many hotels, restaurants, beaches and amusements but the real interest starts nine km from Prapat on Samosir Island.

Samosir is a centre for the likeable Batak people and you can see plenty of their high-peaked Batak houses in Tomok, the main village. Greet people with a hearty 'horas'! The island is very beautiful, very simple (no electricity) and the deep green lake invites swimming. Christian tombs (the Bataks are mainly Christian) are scattered in the fields and a high plateau rises up behind the narrow lakeside strip.

Information
Change money before you get to Lake Toba – exchange rates in Prapat or on Samosir are very bad. Beware of dope busts although one traveller reckoned that if the seller was allowed into the losmen he was probably OK. Not far from the stone chairs at Ambarita is the Golden Tourist Information Centre. It's only a small place, but the guy who runs it knows the island well and can speak some English.

Motorcycles and minibuses now run between Tomok and Ambarita daily and between Ambarita and Simanindo, but the service between the latter is more random. There is no specific time schedule but services are more frequent in the morning. Don't count on finding any

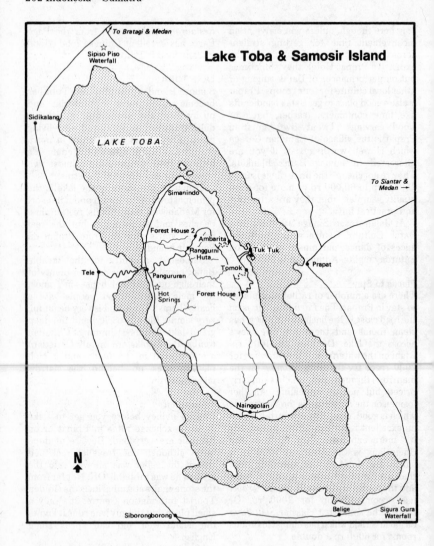

Lake Toba & Samosir Island

public transport after 3 pm. If you're stuck you can charter a minibus, but you'll pay heaps. To ride pillion on a motorbike from Simanindo to Tuk Tuk will cost you 4500 rp or it's 9000 rp by long boat with outboard motor. There is also a daily bus service from Pangururan to Brastagi and Medan. Buses run several times a week from Ranggurni Huta to Pangururan for 700 rp and continue to Simanindo for an additional 500 rp. They leave Ranggurni Huta at 6 am. For the same price minibuses ply between Pangururan and Simanindo regularly in the mornings and less frequently or reliably after noon. Apart from that you can hire a motorbike for 10,000 rp a day, less if you bargain hard.

Tomok If you follow the road away from the lakefront and the souvenir stalls in the village you will come to the tomb of King Sidabatu, one of the last animist kings before the arrival of Christianity. Although Tomok is the main village and has several places to stay, Tuk Tuk, a few km away, is where all the losmen are concentrated. There are heaps of losmen to choose from, so if you get a bummer first off you can take yourself off to another without any effort. The grassy plateau behind Tuk Tuk is soothing to the spirit – very peaceful.

Ambarita A few km the other side of the Tuk Tuk peninsula from Tomok, Ambarita has a group of stone chairs where important matters and disputes were once settled. Until the arrival of Christianity about 250 years ago, serious wrongdoers were led to a further group of stone furnishings in an adjoining courtyard and despatched from this world by application of an axe to the back of the neck. The villagers will tell you they were then chopped up and consumed, but it's probably just stories for the tourists.

If you climb the mountain from Ambarita take the path to the right, the other is very difficult. When you reach the top watch out for wild bull buffaloes, they are aggressive and dangerous. From here there is a path that leads down to Simanindo, but it's hard going at the end. After following the plantation as far as it goes, the path cuts off at right angles and forces its way through tall undergrowth to the lakeside. Once you get there, the water is crystal clear for swimming – very soothing and refreshing.

Simanindo & Pangururan On the northern tip of the island Simanindo has a fine old adat house once used by a Batak king. The road around the island is rather bad, but there is another choice, taking the weekly (Sundays) round-the-island boat tour. At Pangururan the island is only divided from the mainland by a canal. You can travel by bus from here to Brastagi but the road to Sidikalang is extremely bad.

There are relaxing hot springs five km beyond Pangururan. If you can get 12 people together you can hire a boat to go to the hot springs for the day for about 3000 rp per person.

Across the Island The hardy can walk right on up and over the island from Tomok in a day's hard walking. It's 13 km from Tomok to Pasanggrahan (Forest House 1) where you can stay if you wish. Then a further 16 km down to Forest House 2 – you can short cut to here from Ambarita. From here to Ranggurni Huta, almost in the centre of the island, is only four km and then it's 17 km down to Pangururan.

Places to Stay

These days Samosir is a real freak centre with dozens of places to stay and eat – just like a Kathmandu or a Kuta Beach. It's not as easy-going or carefree as it used to be but most people still find it good fun and pleasantly relaxed. A great place to rest up if you've just suffered the rigours of long days travelling on Sumatran buses from Padang or further south. Or to prepare yourself for that trip if you've only just arrived from Medan!

The two most central places to stay are Tomok and Tuk Tuk, although you can get accommodation elsewhere. Tomok is the main village and the place where most of the boats run to and from. It's busier and doesn't offer the variety in accommodation and places to eat that Tuk Tuk does. Tuk Tuk is on the tip of the little peninsula, a pleasant one-hour, five-km walk from Tomok. Here there is dormitory-style accommodation and rooms. Either way in many of the places you may have to use the lake as a mandi. Standard costs on Samosir are 750 rp per person, 1500 rp for a double; this is standard price.

The one real exception is *Carolinas* at Tuk Tuk. Individual rooms in small Batak-style houses cost from 2500 rp a night, complete with bathroom and electricity at night. The views over the lake from rooms with large windows are superb. It also has a balcony smothered in brilliant purple bougainvillea that overlooks a concrete patio and two diving boards. The lake is very clean and clear here and the food delicious. However, in the past couple of years travellers have been reporting that Carolinas is not as good as it was and is no longer so much better than every other losmen on Samosir.

Other places include *Krista's Lodge*, half a km from the main part of the island towards Carolinas and, according to some reports, a bit damp. It also has a reputation for things going missing, so don't leave anything important lying around if you stay there. One of our readers complained that he walked to the other side of the island, paying for his room at Krista's the night he spent away, only to discover on his return that the padlock had been broken, his luggage and belongings removed and the room re-let to other people. The famous *Pepy* has her own place, a nice, spacious building on the way to Carolinas. *Rudi's* gets almost universal raves as does *Bernard's*. *Karidin's* is one of the best losmen in Tuk Tuk – clean and friendly, but it's cheaper to eat elswhere. It's so close to the lake you can dive straight in from the top floor of your batak house if you've got the guts for it.

Timbul, on its own neat little peninsula between Tuk Tuk and Ambarita, consists of a number of separate little Batak houses and has great charm. The main drawback with Timbul is food; it's expensive, nowhere near as tasty as what's available in Tuk Tuk and the nearest restaurants are two km away. *Doman*, towards Ambarita, has also been recommended. *Abadi's*, a Batak house right on the edge of the lake, has had glowing reports for its accommodation – a small room costs 500 rp, a bigger one with own bathroom 1000 rp and a batak house 1500 rp – friendliness and food, particularly the guacomole, tacos, tapioca, fruit salad and coconut cookies. *Tony's* has also received raves. Rooms here have their own bathroom and are spotlessly clean. They also cost 1000 rp a single , 1500 rp for two. Try the vegetable tacos while you're here. *Lekjon's* has also been recommended for both accommodation and food.

Sosor Galung is a little village between Tomok and Tuk Tuk which is sometimes known as 'little Tuk Tuk'. Places here include *Romlan's* and the pricier *Mata Hari* which has great views and a good restaurant. *Gordon's* is 1½ km out of Ambarita towards Tuk Tuk. The position is good – right on the waterfront – but it's a bit isolated. The rooms here are OK with own mandi, but the beds are like slabs of concrete. You could do your kidneys a damage just lying on them. The food is expensive and not very appetising. One of our readers has complained bitterly of the threatening tactics used when he was challenged about why his food bill was so small and admitted to eating elsewhere. He was told without mincing of words that if he continued this practice the welcome mat would no longer be out. The story continues that when he and several others left the next morning one of them was accused of stealing a blanket. My own experience was nowhere near so dramatic, but there are better places to stay on this island. *Rohandy's* is also at Ambarita but not particularly good. Great atmosphere and fine food at *Rosita's*, it's at Tuk Tuk and just in front there's a little island you can swim to. *Judita's* is very friendly and conveniently situated for the lake. If you arrive at Samosir late in the evening it's easiest just to be led somewhere – you can always move next day.

Round at Pangururan, on the other side of the island, Mr Richard Barat's Kedai Kopi is close to the wharf and 'he's a friendly guy with a maniac laugh'. Worth trying if you want to stay there.

Places to Eat

Food at Samosir can be superb although it is very much inclined towards the standard 'travellers' menu'. Fantastic salads, enormous nightly smorgasbords at a number of places and superb fruit salad (pisang susu) are the popular features. The Samosir smorgasbord achieved its heights at *Bernard's* when *Pepy* was the power in the kitchen – no doubt it's down at her place where the best food is now. In general the food is very good everywhere, though. Try papaya alatoral filled with pineapple, banana, nuts, avocado, cucumber and topped with grated coconut and honey at *Antonius* which, according to one letter, has the best food in Tuk Tuk.

Getting There

It is often a five or six hour bus trip between Medan and Prapat but with improvements to the road and newer Mercedes buses it can now be done in a hair-raising 3½ hours. The fare is 2000 rp but sometimes it costs more Medan-Prapat than Prapat-Medan – possibly because of touts to be paid off. We have been warned that there is a scam operating between Prapat and Brastagi by some bus companies. They will sell you a ticket for a 'direct bus' to Brastagi for 1800 or 2000 rp but – surprise, surprise – there is nothing direct about this trip. You have to change buses twice, once at Siantar, the second time at Kabanjahe. Then you discover that the ticket between Kabanjahe and Brastagi is not valid because it's a different bus company, so you're up for another 1400 rp.

Tickets for the journey between Bukittinggi and Prapat can vary from 5000 rp to 6500 rp. It's usually wiser to pay more for a better bus because it's a long, long trip – about 18 hours is the most optimistic estimate, often a lot longer.

Boats operate between Prapat and Samosir on an irregular but reasonably frequent schedule. Make sure you get dropped off at Tuk Tuk and not at Timbul, Ambarita or anywhere you don't want to be. The fare is 500 rp, but they'll probably try you on for 1000 rp. Saturday is market day and you can get to and from the island for only 250 rp. The trip across takes about half an hour, except when the weather is bad when it could take as long as two hours. Once a week, on Sundays, there is a round the island boat trip with stops at the hot springs – it costs 3000 rp.

At Lake Toba (and also Medan for that matter) a lot of people have had travel hassles so beware of travel agents, booking offices and even just 'helpful' people. Amongst the problems people have come across have been purchasing bus tickets only to find the bus goes half-way, no reservations have been made or a deluxe bus turns out to be an old banger. Others have paid to have flight reservations made out of Medan and discovered that no reservations have been made or else they have been made for a non-existent flight. Lots of other problems also crop up so beware of booking agents – try and do things directly with bus companies or airline offices. Nany at Andilo Travel in Prapat is very helpful for information on accommodation, places to eat and booking you through to where you want to go.

BRASTAGI

On the back road from Medan to Lake Toba, 68 km from the city, is Brastagi, a centre of the Karo tribes. Their traditional 'horned' roof houses can be seen in surrounding villages. On the way there from Lake Toba, near the northern end of the lake, is the impressive Si Piso-Piso waterfall. The marquisha, a passionfruit variety, is grown only here and in Sulawesi and makes a very popular drink.

From Brastagi you can climb Gunung Sibayak, a 2094 metre high volcano and have a soak in the hot springs on the way back. Wear good walking boots because the path is wet and slippery all year round. The walk takes about six hours there and back and if you're staying at the Ginsata or the Wisma Sibayak you should be able to get hold of a map from Messrs Bullshit or Pelawi. There's quite a lot of good walking in this area.

Kotacane is interesting but not recommended for solo-women since it suffers from a touch of the Muslim heavies. Surya Dewa, next door, is better. Ketambe, 35 km away, about three hours by jeep, is good orang-utan country. Gunung Sinabung, a 2451 metre volcano, is also in this area. If you're interested in architecture take a bus 12 km south of Brastagi to Kabanjahe from where you can walk four km to the primitive village of Lingga. The design of these houses with their horn-shaped roofs has remained unchanged for centuries. Most of the ones in Lingga are reputed to be well over 250 years old and even more interesting is the fact that not a single nail was used in their construction. You'll also find Karo Batak houses in nearby Barusjahe. Twenty-four km from Kabanjahe and only about 300 metres from the road are the Si Piso-Piso falls.

Places to Stay & Eat

There are plenty of cheap places to stay in Brastagi but *Wisma Sibayak* gets particular recommendations from travellers. There's a dorm at 1500 rp or rooms from 3000 rp. A couple of criticisms are that the place isn't as clean as it could be – the mandis and loos being particularly foul and fetid – and that there are peepholes in strategic places. If you stay there the manager, Mr Pelawi, is helpful and informative about the locality. He teaches English in the local school and will arrange for visitors to stay in Ajijahe, a traditional village 10 km from Brastagi and to go to local Karo-Batak weddings. They can also tell you about visiting the orang-utan rehabilitation centre. But Mr Pelawi also has a competitor in town who operates out of the *Ginsata Hotel* at Jalan Veteran 79. He calls himself Mr Bullshit and a very apt name it is as he talks all the time and a lot of what he says is crap. But he also knows heaps about the area, is good company and can speak excellent English. The

Ginsata costs 2000 rp a double with attached mandi and is OK except that it's rather grubby and the smell wafting up the stairwell from the public loo below is extremely potent.

Other good places include the *Bungalow Trimurty* and *Wisma Dieng*. The latter costs 3000 rp a double with sitting room and is run by a nice old woman. Any amount of free tea and hot water is available. *Hotel Puspat* is rather run down and *Bukit Kubu Hotel* is luxurious and, would you believe, expensive. Good Chinese food at the *Terang Rumah Makan* on Jalan Veteran and at the *Ora et Lahore*, which is mega cheap for breakfast. You can also get cheap and tasty food from the stall in front of the billiard hall on Jalan Masjid. Or try the Budi Jaya, also on Jalan Veteran. Buy your own food from the fruit and vegetable market in the square on Jalan Veteran or check out the local market several hundred metres further down the road on the opposite side. Delicious cakes made from rice flour, palm sugar coconut and steamed in bamboo cylinders are available from a stall outside the market after dark for 100 rp for four.

SIANTAR

Try the *Hotel Delima* at this town between Prapat and Medan if you have to stop for some reason. You'll find it at Jalan Thamrin 131.

BINJEI

North of Brastagi and on the road from Medan to Bukit Lawang, Binjei is handy for all three locations. You can get there from Medan, just 22 km away, by minibus or share taxi from the Juwita Shopping Centre on Jalan Surabaya.

Stay at *Cafe de Malioboro Garden Restaurant & Guest House* (great name!) has accommodation in an old Dutch house at Jalan Ksatria 1 for 3000 rp a double. It's a friendly, relaxing place and a nice old building, but you need plenty of insect repellant and mosquito coils.

BUKIT LAWANG

Eighty km from Medan near Bukit Lawang is an orang-utan rehabilitation centre where these extraordinarily fascinting creatures are retrained to survive in the wild after a period of captivity. It's a steep half hour walk to the reserve along the Bohorok River, then across by a boat. You are supposed to go with a project officer – in fact you will be told that you are not allowed into the reserve without a guide and that their fee is 1000 rp an hour – but it's simple to find your own way. The trail is easy to pick up and follow and the guides are not very informative if you do go with them. Try to visit this centre if you have the time. Apart from the attraction of the apes, the country around here is wild and enchanting and with its dense jungle, clear, fast flowing river and splashy waterfalls it is a soothing and instantly refreshing place to wander through. If you secretly fantasise about being Jane or Tarzan, this is the perfect place to swing through the trees beating your chest, emitting primitive cries and swoony sighs, whatever your mood dictates.

Only 50 visitors at a time are allowed into the reserve, so avoid Sundays when there are lots of day-trippers from Medan, particularly if you're doing your Tarzan act and don't want to feel a complete fool. If you go in the morning you also avoid possible conflict with afternoon tour groups. Permits to visit the reserve are available from the PPA Rest House in Bukit Lawang or from Dinas PPA (Kantor Kehutanan), Jalan Singamangarata, Km 55, Medan. It's better to get a permit in Medan if possible because it's valid for three days whereas a permit issued in Bukit Lawang is only valid for 24 hours and costs the same, 2000 rp. It will take you about half a day to arrange your permit. The orang-utan feeding times are posted in the rest house. At present they are from 8 am to 9 am and from 3.30 pm to 4.30 pm. Maximum viewing time is 50 minutes.

While you're in this district ask around to see whether you can find someone to show you the rubber processing plant that's nearby.

Places to Stay

There is one small *PPA Rest House* outside of the reserve which has room for five while another within the reserve sleeps eight. The cost is between 1500 and 2500 rp per person a night and the accommodation is fairly spartan; no water – you bathe in the river – and no electricity. They will prepare meals for you at the rest house but at an outrageous price. The food at the small warung next door to the rest house is very good and fairly cheap. Otherwise bring your own supplies.

Getting There
The road to Bukit Lawang is fairly terrible, it takes four to five hours by bus from Medan. You can also get to Bukit Lawang from Brastagi. Buses depart at regular intervals throughout the day from the station in Jalan Sei Wampa in Medan, so there are no problems in getting there or from 9.30 am along Jalan Veteran in Brastagi. In Bukit Lawang they leave at 5.30 am from outside Pasangrahan – tell them the night before and they will wake you up.

MEDAN
The capital of North Sumatra and the main entry point for the country, Medan is not most peoples' favourite Indonesian city. The strongest images of this place are battalions of belching becaks belting towards you and the pungent attack of their noxious fumes. I got to like the din, sweat and squalor of Medan, but apart from some good antique shops, a mosque, a museum, a palace and lots of people, it has little else to offer although there are still remnants of the old Dutch planter aristocracy.

Information
The Medan Tourist Office or Kantor Wilayah Pariwisata Sumatera Utara is at Jalan Palang Merah 66 and has maps and information. There is also an information centre at the arrival terminal at Polonia International airport, which has a map of the city, a few brochures and not much else. Medan is famous for the hassles it puts travellers through. Amongst the problems you can expect are predatory

transport organisers – everybody from bus ticket offices to taxi drivers will try to overcharge you. Then there's the airline ticket business – countless travellers have arrived at Medan airport to find that, confirmed ticket or not, their seat on the flight to Penang has disappeared. Finally, the cops are getting into the drug bust business so be careful with that fine Sumatran dope you've brought with you. All in all Medan is an excellent introduction if you're just arriving in Indonesia or a great goodbye if you're about to leave.

The MAS office (tel 519333) is in the Hotel Danau Toba International, Jalan Imam Bonjol 17, Merpati (tel 28880) at Jalan Brigjen Katamso 41, Smac (tel 516617) at Jalan Imam Bonjol 59 and Garuda (tel 25700, 25702, 25809) on Jalan Lt Jen Suprapto (tel 25703). For shipping information go to the Pelni office (tel 251000, 25190) at Jalan Sugiono 5.

The best exchange rates in Sumatra are obtainable from the Bank Negara Indonesia 1946 (tel 22333) at Jalan Pemuda 12 but the service is excruciatingly slow. Every head in the bank turns to watch as you walk by and all business grinds to a halt while they assess what nationality you are. Expect waits of about 45 minutes the first time around. You'll find the General Post Office (tel 25945, 23612) on Jalan Bukit Barisan.

Things to Do & See
The Great Mosque or Masjid Raya is on Jalan Sisingamangaraja while the Istana Maimoon or Maimoon Palace is nearby on Jalan Katamso. The large and lovely mosque dates from 1906 and the palace from 1888, they were both built by the Sultan of Deli and the palace has recently been renovated.

Diagonally opposite the Danau Toba International Hotel on Jalan H Zainul Arifin 8 is the Museum Bukit Barisan. This is a military museum which has an extensive collection of weapons and memorabilia from World War II, the War

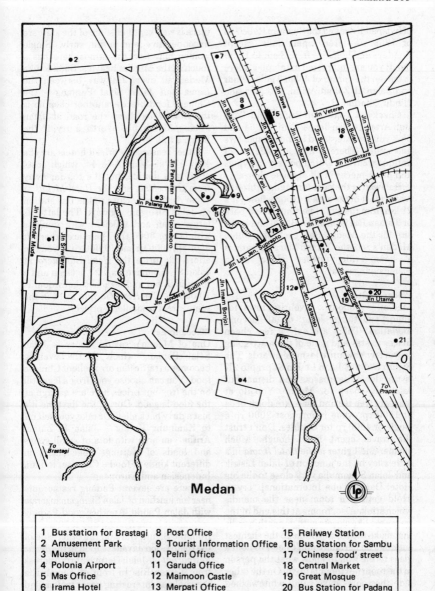

Medan

1 Bus station for Brastagi
2 Amusement Park
3 Museum
4 Polonia Airport
5 Mas Office
6 Irama Hotel
7 Immigration Office
8 Post Office
9 Tourist Information Office
10 Pelni Office
11 Garuda Office
12 Maimoon Castle
13 Merpati Office
14 Padang food
15 Railway Station
16 Bus Station for Sambu
17 'Chinese food' street
18 Central Market
19 Great Mosque
20 Bus Station for Padang
21 Bus Station for Prapat

of Independence and the Sumatra Rebellion of 1958. It's free, open daily except Sundays and holidays from 8 am to 12.30 pm. If you are interested in temples, there is one on the corner of Jalan Teuku Umar and Jalan H Zainul Arifin, the Parisada Hindu Dharma.

Check out Toko Asli, Rufino and Toko Bali Arts at Jalan Jen A Yani, 62, 64 and 68 if you are interested in Indonesian arts and crafts. There is a good selection of antique weaving, Dutch pottery, carvings and other pieces in all of these shops.

Belawan is the port for Medan through which most of the area's exports flow – it's 28 km from the city. The amusement park or Taman Ria is on Jalan Binjai and is the site for the Medan Fair each May-June. Medan's zoo, the Taman Margasawata, is a bemo ride further along Jalan Sisingamangaraja.

Places to Stay
Medan is nobody's favourite town for almost anything, least of all accommodation. There are only a few cheap places to stay and none of them are going to win any 'favourite losmen' awards. The *Sigura Gura* at Jalan Lt Jen Suprapto 2K is run down, depressing and dismal but relatively cheap for Medan. You do at least get free tea and there are dorm beds at 1500 rp, while rooms cost 2000 rp a single or 4000 rp for doubles. Don't trust the travel agent here though. Much cleaner and lighter is the *Hotel Irama* in a little alley by the junction of Jalan Listrik and Jalan Sukamulia very close to the big Hotel Danau Toba International. Try to avoid getting a room near the mandis which stink. Also, rooms at this end of the Irama are like closets with paper thin walls that make them susceptible to the slightest sound. You certainly don't need to hold a glass to the wall to know what the person in the room nextdoor is up to. On the other side the rooms have solid, whitewashed walls and, though still small, are much quieter. The Irama costs 2500 rp for one, 3000 rp for two and 4500 rp for three. The

place is well kept but some of the staff are uncooperative and a bit surly. Single women may find the atmosphere has a touch of the Muslim heavies. Sounds like Medan all over? Halfway between the Irama and Jalan Selat Panjang – the Chinese food place – another cheapie is the *Hotel Rion* down the road at Jalan Palang Merah 5b. Worth a try if the Irama's full.

Other reasonably priced hotels are the *Way Yat* at Jalan Asia 44, which costs 4000 rp a double, but it's too far away from the centre, and the *Hotel Melati* at Jalan Amaluin 6, close to the bus station on Jalan Sisingamangaraja. The latter is large, clean and efficient with doubles with fan for 5000 rp. There are others at 3500 rp, 8000 rp and 10,000 rp. If you can afford the price the *Hotel Sumatera* at Jalan Sisingamangaraja 21 is clean and a room with fan and attached bathroom is 10,000 rp. The *Hotel Garuda* at 18 in the same street is similarly priced.

Places to Eat
One of Medan's saving graces is Jalan Selat Panjang which in the evening becomes a traffic jam of excellent Chinese food. You can choose your frog's legs still on the frog but prices here are as high as the food is good. During the daytime it's just a dirty back alley. Or take yourself off to Kampung Keling – Jalan· H Zainul Arifin – an area with lots of small gangs and loads of warungs specialising in different kinds of food – Chinese, Indian, Indonesian and European.

There are several Padang restaurants near the junction of Jalan Sisingamangaraja with Jalan Pandu. Another good Padang restaurant is the *Remaja* about 50 metres from the Sigura Gura on the other side of the road. Good Javanese food in the *Jenar Restaurant* on Jalan Gatot Subroto across from Taman Ria. In front of Taman Ria they hold an interesting pasar malam and there are several superb bakeries along Jalan Pandu as well as the *Cold Store Ice Cream Centre*.

Excellent if expensive food and ice cream is available at the *Batik Restaurant* on Jalan Pemuda 14-C. The *Tip Top Restaurant* at Jalan Jen A Yani 92 is one of those restaurants which continues to be consistently good. Sit outside under the verandah shrouded in the poisonous vapours of the becaks and watch the passers-by or go inside where the ears are assailed by non-stop music, mostly western and almost all 50s schalmz. Whichever, the food is delicious and cheap and it's not only a travellers' venue, it's also where the local rich kids meet. Nearby is *Lyn's Restaurant* where the Medan business people and expatriates eat. It's dim and cool, almost sophisticated and expensive. The menu is predominantly western – rump steak, chicken rosemary, chateaubriand, spaghetti vongole and the like – and they actually ask you if you like your steak done rare, medium or well done. Worth checking out for a drink if nothing else.

Getting There & Getting Around

You can get to Medan from outside Sumatra by two methods – flights from Penang and Singapore or the Pelni ship from Tanjun Pinang. See the introductory Sumatra Getting There section for more details. There is no longer any boat service between Medan and Penang. From Medan most people go by bus to Prapat – see Prapat and Lake Toba for more details.

Arriving in Medan, or for that matter leaving Medan by aircraft, is always a business fraught with hassles. As soon as you get off the plane you will be rushed at by mobs of men in yellow overalls swarming like wasps to take over your luggage. If you make the mistake of letting them handle it expect to hand over 500 rp minimum per piece. Taxi drivers will look for 4500 rp from the airport into the city. Go straight to the taxi counter inside the terminal and let them organise your lift. You'll get a chit with a number and the price on it and all you have to do is wait

until your number is called. That way, though you're still paying through the nose, you won't be ripped off as much as you will if you try to arrange a lift yourself. Becak riders will want 1500 rp, but you will have to walk out to the road before you see one as they're not allowed inside the airport grounds. You can knock the price down to 700 rp for one and 1000 rp for two – it's only a couple of km from the airport into the town. Becak riders usually take you straight to one of the bus stations for Prapat and since they often get a commission for delivering you they're generally happy to bargain a bit on price. It's probably why buses are more expensive Medan-Prapat than Prapat-Medan. If you take a becak to the airport on your departure the rider will drop you some distance from the gates. A minibus to the terminal is laid on from here but you must bargain hard or you'll find your paying another 2000 rp for the privilege of not walking several hundred metres. Bemos run to Belawan, the port for Medan. From Medan get buses to Brastagi from Jalan Iskandar Mudah, 900 rp.

BANDA ACEH

Fiercely independent and devoutly Islamic, Aceh was once a powerful state in its own right and later held out against the Dutch longer than almost anywhere else in the archipelago. In recognition of this, today it is designated as a Special Territory by the Indonesian government, which gives it the freedom to pursue its own religious, cultural and educational policies and has also benefitted from various development programmes. Still the most staunchly Muslim part of the country, Aceh is run under Islamic law. Despite their rigid religious conservatism, the Acehnese are friendly and helpful people, particularly the students, most of whom have a good grasp of English, which they like using.

The capital of Aceh, Banda Aceh, is right at the northern tip of Sumatra and the centre of town is marked by an imposing five domed mosque.

Information

The government tourist office in Banda Aceh is on Jalan Teuku Aries (tel 21377), but it seems to be closed most of the time. There is also a travel agent, Pt Krueng Wayla Ltd, at Jalan Sri Ratu Safiatuddin 3, (tel 22066, 23506). They're mainly set up for package tours, booking flights home for the expatriate community and arranging travel within Sumatra, but they're interested in expanding the business to individuals and will advise you on how to get around, where to go, what to do etc if you're stuck. They've got a few brochures and pamphlets on Banda Aceh – no maps – but most are in Indonesian.

The Bank Negara Indonesia 1946 is on Jalan Merduati and the Post Office on Jalan Kuta Alam, one block from Simpang Tiga. Setui Bus Terminal on Jalan T Umar is where road transport departs for Medan and for Meulaboh or Tapaktuan. You can get smaller buses from the mosque area next to the old railroad station if you want to stop off at places like Sigli and Lhok Seumawe along the Medan road. Also near the mosque in front of the Bank Dagang Negara on Jalan Diponegoro large, fairly modern Damri buses depart for Darussalam, Lho'Nga and Blang Bintang.

Boats leave every day from the old port of Uleh-Leh at 2 pm and arrive at the Island of Weh (Sabang) about three or four hours later. Uleh-Leh is five km from the centre of town, and the cost over to the island is 2500 rp one-way. More streamlined boats depart for Sabang at 10 am daily from the new port of Krueng Raya and take around two hours. The problem is Krueng Raya is 35 km from the city and you have to be up very early to get there in time to catch the ferry. The fare to Sabang from Kreung Raya is 3500 rp one-way. To fly it costs 21,500 rp in a nine-seater plane from Banda Aceh to Sabang.

Banda Aceh is a dry area for alcohol so if you're hanging out for a drink, you will have to bring some with you, travel over to Sabang where there are no such restrictions,

drop into the Canadian club in Banda Aceh itself or check out the expatriate community at Lho'Nga.

Things to Do & See

The mosque is worth a visit. With it's stark white walls and licorice black domes, this stunningly beautiful building is like an oasis in the dust and fumes of central Banda Aceh. Ask the keeper to let you climb the staircase to one of the minarets so you can get a good view over the city. For a contrast in architectural styles go and see Gunongan on Jalan Teuku Umar, near the clock tower. This 'stately pleasure dome' was apparently built for the wife of a 17th century sultan – a Malaysian princess – as a private playground and bathing place. The building itself is a series of frosty peaks with narrow stairways and a walkway leading to hummocks which are supposed to represent the hills of her native land so she could take an evening stroll, a liberty not permitted in Banda Aceh in that era. But it looks like the concotion of a confectioner given carte blanche to create the tizziest wedding cake his imagination could come up with. Directly across from the Gunongan is a low vaulted-gate in the traditional *Pintu Aceh* style, which gave access to the sultan's palace and was supposed to have been used by royalty only. Nearby is the cemetery for more than 2000 Dutch soldiers who fell in battle against Acehnese. The entrance is about 250 metres from the clock tower on the road to Uleh-leh.

Banda Aceh has a large museum with exhibits of weapons, household furnishings, ceremonial costumes, every day clothing, gold jewellery, books on three floors. At Jalan Yakapeh 12, it's open from Tuesday to Thursday from 8.30 am to 2 pm and Fridays and Saturday between 8.30 am and noon. In the same compound is the Rumah Aceh, a fine example of traditional architecture, built without nails and held together with cord or pegs. It's open from Tuesday to Saturday between 4 pm and 6 pm and contains more Acehnese artifacts and war memorabilia. In front of the Rumah Aceh is a large cast-iron bell, which was given to the Acehnese by the Chinese Emperor in the 1st century AD.

You can make trips from Banda Aceh to Lho-Nga beach, 12 km from the city, or take a ferry to Sabang Island, just off the coast – see Information for details on cost. One of the attractions of this small island on the western rim of Indonesia – particularly for the local people – is that it's a duty free port. It also has lots of attractive, palm fringed beaches. You need your passport to show to immigration authorities. The township of Sabang is 12 km from the harbour, get an oplet there for 500 rp or a taxi for 5000 rp. In front of Toko Sahabar on Jalan Perdgangan is the taxi station. Ask here for motorcycle and boat hire.

Places to Stay
Accommodation in Banda Aceh is relatively expensive and not particularly good. If you head for Jalan Jen A Yani there are several hotels in a cluster. Among them are the *Hotel Medan* at 9 which has doubles with attached mandi for 8000 rp and the *Perapat* at 11 for 5500 rp. On nearby Jalan Khairil Anwar are the *Hotel Palembang* at 8 and the *Hotel Masda* at 10-12 with rooms ranging from 3000 rp to 13000 rp. Other places to try are the rather run down and depressing *Hotel Lading* at Jalan Nasional 9 with accommodation that starts at 4000 rp a single and 8000 rp a double or the *Rasa Sayang* at Jalan Cut Meutia 34E for between 5000 and 7000 rp.

Opposite the mosque at Jalan Muhammed Jam is the colonial *Hotel Aceh* with singles for 5000 rp minimum and doubles at 9000 rp minimum. Popular among the expatriates is another old colonial hotel the *Seulawah* at Jalan Nyak Adam Kamil 1V, but it's quite a way from the town centre. Near the market at Jalan Muhammad Jam 1 is the *Yusri*, which is fairly modern and has rooms with air-con and attached mandis for between 8000 rp and 12,000 rp a double.

Sabang There are several places to stay in Sabang, none of them cheap. The *Sabang Hill Hotel* has a good view of the bay but unless you have transport it's too far from town. Right in the centre are two losmen *Pulau Jaya* and *Raja Wali* with accommodation from 3000 rp a single and 5000 rp a double. There is also the *Sabang Guest House* at 9000 rp a double and the *Hotel Sabang Marauke*.

Places to Eat
Jalan Jen A Yani is a good place to start looking for food. If you take a stroll down it during the day you'll come across the *Gembira* at 36, the *Happy* at 40, *Dian* at 44 and the *Restoran Tropicana* at 90-92. The latter has good *mie bakso daging* for 1000 rp, *gado gado* for 600 rp and *ayam goreng* for 750 rp. At night this street and several off it are hopping with food stalls and warungs. It's a busy, noisy and colourful scene and the food is cheap, fresh, delicious – if you choose carefully – and has lots of variety. Smother yourself with insect repellent before you go out at night because the mossies come out in droves. At 3 Khairil Anwar is the *Satyva Modern Bakery*, which not only has lots of different kinds of mouth-watering cakes and breads but also more substantial dishes.

For Padang food try the *Sinar Surya* on Jalan Sri Ratu Safiatuddin 10 or there's the *Aroma* on Jalan Cut Nyak Dien has an excellent Chinese menu. There is lots of different kinds of cheap food available around the Pasar Aceh or market area.

Sabang There are numerous coffee places in the village, but the best places to have dinner are the *Pin Sun*, a small Chinese restaurant off Jalan Perdagangan, or the *Sedap* and the *Selecta*, right on Jalan Perdgangan.

Getting There
If the road is dry it's a 12- to 15-hour trip from Medan. Air-con buses cost 7500 rp one-way – try Kurnia – but you can get there in less comfortable buses for 1000

rp less. The road is in good condition and takes you through numerous villages, mountains, rice fields and rolling country.

The flight from Medan takes less than an hour and costs 44,000 rp by Smac and 55,200 rp by Garuda plus tax. Both airlines have two flights daily.

Nusa Tenggara

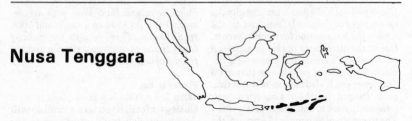

Nusa Tenggara refers to the string of islands which start, east of Java, with Bali and end with Timor. At one time they were governed as a group but now are split into three areas – Bali by itself; Lombok and Sumbawa with a regional capital at Mataram in Lombok; and Flores, Sumba and Timor with a regional capital at Kupang in Timor.

Some of the most spectacular attractions of Indonesia can be found in this string of islands – the dragons of Komodo, the immense stone tombs of Sumba and the coloured volcanic lakes of Keli Mutu on Flores. Culturally each island is distinctive although less accessible than those of Bali or Tanatoraja in Sulawesi.

All of these islands are underdeveloped from every point of view, including the tourist industry. Whilst a steady stream of people pass through the islands, there's nothing like the tourist hordes you find in Bali or Java. In one way this is an advantage because the reaction of the local people is generally more natural, but it does create one headache – you are constantly the centre of attraction. It's no problem at all to generate an entourage of over 100 children in any small village in Flores, or in the more remote parts of Lombok.

If you don't mind this constant attention then travelling in Nusa Tenggara is fairly easy going; people are very friendly, and there's been a great deal of improvement over the last few years – there are more surfaced roads, regular ferries between most of the islands, more losmen, more flights, and more regular road transport. Previously an awful lot of travel in Nusa Tenggara was just plain awful – you'd end up spending a lot of time hanging around in dreary ports waiting for boats, or shaking your bones loose in trucks attempting to traverse roads constructed out of large trenches. Much of Nusa Tenggara is still like that – but on the whole the main attractions are now fairly easy to get to. Just stick to the main routes, avoid travelling in the wet season when some of the roads turn to mud and holes, and you shouldn't have any trouble. You probably need a month to get a good look around the whole chain.

Language It's absolutely essential to learn some Indonesian if you're going to travel through Nusa Tenggara. A lot of people here know a few phrases of English, but never enough to have a conversation – those who speak reasonable English are few and very far between. Bahasa Indonesia is a simple enough language that learning enough to get by on is rather like learning to eat with chopsticks – when there's nothing else available you just have to.

Money & Costs The islands of Nusa Tenggara are marginally more expensive for food, accommodation and transport than they are in Bali and Java, and you don't get such good value for money. However, by any standards costs are still low. It's probably wise to allow for a couple of flights – particularly if you want to go to Timor and/or Sumba – and for getting back to Bali or Java, rather than being forced to backtrack all the way through the islands by road and ferry.

There are fewer places in Nusa Tenggara to change money than in Bali and Java – but even that situation has improved over the past few years. There will generally be at least one bank in each of the main towns which will change major foreign currencies and also the travellers' cheques of the larger companies. You can change cash and travellers' cheques in Cakranegara in Lombok; in Sumbawa Besar and Bima in Sumbawa; in Ruteng and Ende in Flores; Kupang in Timor; and Waingapu in Sumba. The Bank Negara Indonesia in Sumbawa Besar will, for example, change Thomas Cook, American Express and Bank of America travellers' cheques in a number of foreign currencies, and will also change cash – stick to American or Australian dollars, Deutsche marks, pounds sterling, or Netherlands florin and you should be OK. If in doubt take American dollars – they're the most widely accepted foreign currency throughout Indonesia.

GETTING AROUND

Most of the islands are now connected by regular ships and ferries making a loop through the islands out of Bali and back fairly easy. You can even charter sailing boats or small motor boats for short hops at fairly reasonable prices – the standard means of getting to Komodo is to charter a boat in Labuhanbajo on the west coast of Flores. Sometimes the Bugis Makassar schooners find their way right down into Nusa Tenggara – so if you want a really different way of getting to Sulawesi . . . !

Merpati handle the bulk of flights in this group of islands. Bouraq also have a number of flights between Bali and Lombok, Sumbawa, Timor and Sumba. Garuda flies between Bali and Lombok and Timor. Whilst flights out of Nusa Tenggara may terminate in Bali, these will often connect with flights to other parts of the country on the same day. Merpati, for example, will pick you up in Kupang in Timor at 7 am and land you on Tarakan on the east coast of Kalimantan in the afternoon.

Aside from the usual hazards of motor-cycling in Asia, this is the ideal way to see Nusa Tenggara. If you want to travel by motorcycle in Nusa Tenggara then its probably best to use your own bike – or hire one in Bali or Java. It's difficult to hire

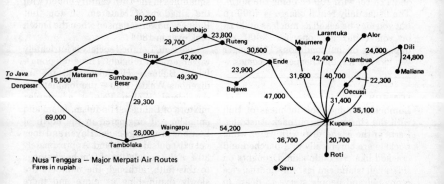

Nusa Tenggara – Major Merpati Air Routes
Fares in rupiah

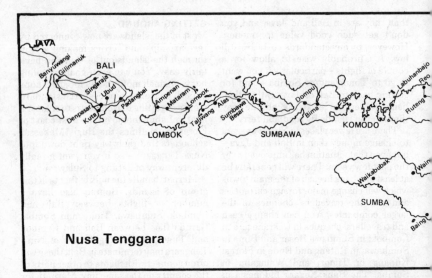

Nusa Tenggara

a motorcycle in Nusa Tenggara; in Lombok for example there are motorcycle hire places in the main centres but not as many as there are in Bali, and they are not easy to find – you won't see the 'motorbike for hire' signs stuck up all over the place that you do in Bali so you'll have to ask around. However, there are individual owners who rent out their bikes and a couple of specialist places in Ampenan and Mataram. Most motorbikes for rent are between 90 and 125 cc, with 100 cc being the norm. The usual daily rental charge is 4000 rp but you may be asked as much as 6000 rp or you could get one for 3000 rp, depending on its condition. The longer you hire one for, the cheaper it becomes.

LOMBOK

Lombok combines the lushness of Bali with the starkness of outback Australia. Parts of the island drip with water while pockets are chronically dry, parched and cracked like crocodile skin. Droughts on this small island can last for months, rice crops fail and people starve to death in their thousands. The people too reflect these extremes; many are outgoing and friendly, others shy and withdrawn.

About 10% of the population is Balinese, the rest mainly Sasaks. Balinese influence dates from a series of battles with the King of Sumbawa in 1723 to 1750. The Balinese aided the Lombok overlord Datu Selaparang. As a reward they were allowed to settle on Lombok but the poor Datu was killed dead in battle and his Balinese allies took over. A series of local squabbles in the 19th century ended with the kingdom of Mataram on top, but Balinese power collapsed when the Dutch took over in 1894.

Like Bali, Lombok society is intricately woven around religion. Three religions – Islam, Balinese Hinduism and the indigenous Wektu Telu – predominate on the island. Wektu Telu is a complex mixture of Balinese Hinduism, Islam and animism – it originated in the north of Lombok in a village called Bayan and does not exist outside the island. Approximately 30% of the population of Lombok belongs to this faith, although the numbers are slowly diminishing as more and more young people turn to Islam.

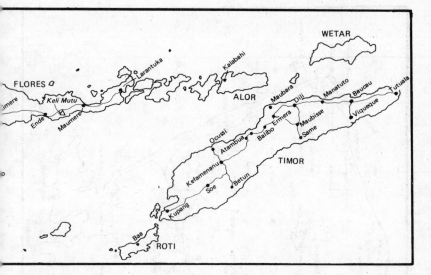

GETTING THERE

Air There are various flights to Mataram, the capital of Lombok, with Garuda, Merpati and Bouraq, generally routed through Denpasar. Flights include Denpasar to Mataram with Merpati for 15,500 rp; from Jakarta via Garuda for 103,500 rp, from Surabaya 47,700 rp, from Yogyakarta 64,400 rp. Bouraq also has several flights per week from various cities in Java to Mataram via Denpasar, and their fares are generally a bit less than Garudas. From Mataram there are also flight connections with other parts of Nusa Tenggara. These include the Merpati flight to Sumbawa Besar for 24,700 rp; with Bouraq to Bima for 40,700 rp.

Sea There's a twice daily ferry service at 8.30 am and 1.30 pm from the small port of Padangbai, east of Denpasar, Bali. The ferry office in Padangbai is opposite the Hotel Madya. Three classes are available on the ferry – I (Utama) tickets are 4000 rp, II (Ekonomi) is 2800 rp, III (Deck) is 2300 rp. Plus a 25 rp ticket charge in each case and an additional 75 rp departure tax. You can also take motorcycles along

with you – costs 3400 rp. The ferry docks at Lembar, south of Ampenan, in Lombok. Food, soft drinks, coffee, tea and cigarettes are available on board from the small bars in both 1st and 2nd classes or from the numerous hawkers who hang around the wharf until the ferry leaves. The trip takes a minimum of five hours, often up to seven, and the afternoon ferry is always slower than the morning one.

On the way across buy a yellow ticket for 750 rp from officials who tour the ferry from time to time or from the steward behind the bar to ensure transport to Ampenan, Mataram or Cakranegara. If you're arriving on the afternoon ferry after dark this is particularly important because if you're lucky enough to get any transport at all you'll pay over 1000 rp. Officially the fare from Lembar to Cakranegara is 500 rp and if you're arriving in daylight on the morning ferry it may be worth taking the risk of not buying a ticket – there's more transport around then. You could find yourself stranded if you try this at night. For details on the return journey from Lembar to Padangbai, see the section on Lembar below.

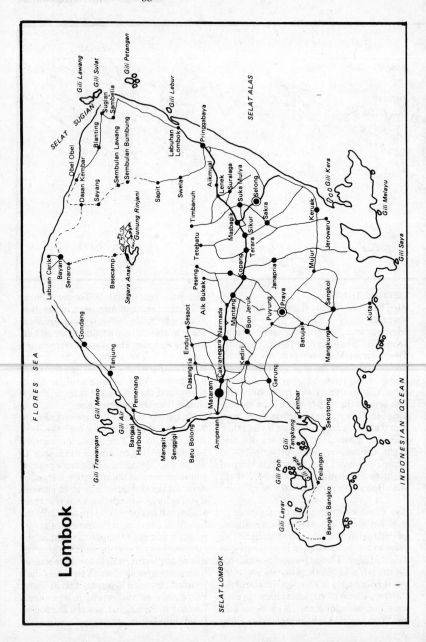

Lombok

There are daily passenger ferries from Lombok to Sumbawa Island – for details see the section on Labuhan Lombok below.

GETTING AROUND

There are several bemo terminals on Lombok including one at Cakranegara and another at Ampenan, but the main station is at Sweta, a couple of km out of Cakranegara. Here buses, microbuses, bemos and colts depart for various points all over the island. Public transport is generally restricted to main routes, which means that if you want to explore places that are off the beaten track you have to walk or hire a *dokar* (horse cart), motor-bike or charter a bemo or colt. The situation may improve radically in the near future as the government has instituted an ambitious road improvement scheme as part of a long-term plan of putting Lombok on the tourist map.

AMPENAN

Once the main port of Lombok, Ampenan is not much more than a small dirty, dusty fishing harbour, though cattle are still exported through here to Java, Hong Kong and Singapore. Today, Ampenan is the eastern end of Ampenan-Mataram-Cakranegara – the three towns run into each other and it's not clear where one ends and the next begins. Whilst the town isn't much to look at, Ampenan is not a bad spot to base yourself in Lombok with plenty of choice in accommodation, a couple of places of interest nearby, lots of transport, and various tourist facilities.

There's an interesting museum on Jalan Banjar Tiler Negara – well worth browsing around if you have a couple of free hours. On the beach, a few km north of Ampenan, is the Balinese temple complex of Pura Segara and near here are the remnants of a Muslim cemetery and an old Chinese cemetery. Gunung Pengsong is a hill nine km south of Ampenan – noted for its views, temple, and tame monkeys. About eight km from Ampenan is Batu

Bolong which is a large rock with a hole in it – not terribly interesting in itself, but from here you get a fantastic view across Lombok Strait to Bali and Gunung Agung – and particularly good sunsets.

Information

The main tourist office on Lombok, the Kantor Dinas Pariwisata Daerah (tel 21866, 21730), is in Ampenan at Jalan Langko 70 on the left hand side heading towards Mataram, almost diagonally opposite the post office. No one speaks English here and it's hard to get across what you want, but it's worth investigating: they have a map of Ampenan, Mataram and Cakranegara here as well as a couple of pamphlets in English with information on sights, customs, addresses, maps, etc. They're also very friendly and are delighted to get visitors.

The Bank Umum Nasional (tel 21626) is at Jalan Pabean 47-49, but it will only change American cash and American dollar travellers' cheques. The post office in Ampenan is on Jalan Langko, and is open between 8 am and 2 pm; don't expect speedy service or delivery – it's pretty unreliable.

Places to Stay

Losmen Wisma Triguna (tel 21705) is relatively new and is set back off Jalan Koperasi, a little over a km out of central Ampenan. The rooms here are spacious and have an attached mandi and lavatory. Singles for 2500 rp, doubles for 3500 rp. One of the advantages of this losmen is the owner, Mr Batu Bara – appears to be well known in a number of places on Lombok, can speak English and is very willing to advise you on what to do and see, how to get there and approximately how much it will cost. He will also help you organise the haul up Rinjani if you want to go there.

Closer to town on the same road – Jalan Koperasi 65 – is *Losmen Horas* (tel 21695), also owned by Mr Batu Bara. Singles for 1250 rp, doubles 1750 rp. It's one of the cheapest places to stay, but the

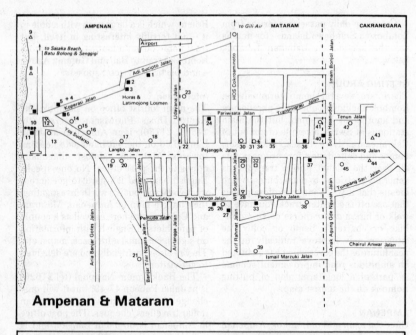

Ampenan & Mataram

■ Hotels & Losmen	19 Ampenan Post & Telegram Offices
1 Wisma Trijuna Losmen	20 Police Station
2 Horas Losmen	21 Museum
3 Latimojong Losmen	22 Bank Indonesia
5 Losmen Lombok	23 Immigration Office
6 Hotel Zahir	26 Rita Tours
7 Losmen Pabean	29 Governor's House
11 Hotel Tiga Mas	30 Governor's Office
24 Hotel Kertayoga	31 Ferry Office
25 Hotel Cemaka	39 Mataram Post Office (Post Restante)
27 Hotel Kamboja	41 Motorcycle Rent
33 Losmen Rinjani	42 Selamet Riady
35 Hotel Kertayoga	45 Cakra Market
36 Hotel Selaparang	
37 Hotel Mataram	△ Cemeteries, Temples, Museums etc.
40 Hotel Pusaka	8 Chinese Cemetery
	9 Moslem Cemetery
□ Restaurants & Bars	43 Mayura Water Palace
10 Rumah Makan	44 Meru Temple
(Mulia, Setia, Pabean, Tjirebon)	
	▽ Bemo, Bus Stations
O Offices, Shops etc.	12 Ampenan Bemo Station
13 Ampenan Market	28 Mataram Bemo Station
14 Merpati Office	
15 Customa Office	+ Hospitals
16 Garuda Office	4 St Antonius Hospital
17 Tourist Office	34 General Hospital
18 Bank Negara Indonesia 1946	38 Moslim Hospital

rooms here are small and dark, and it's close to a mosque. However if you like waking up at 5 to the sound of clapped out speakers and just want somewhere to crash, this is it. The same goes for the *Latimojong* which is two doors up the road at number 64. Singles 1250 rp, doubles l750 rp and triples 2500 rp.

A hop, skip and a jump from the town centre – still on the same road at number l2 – is the *Hotel Zahir* (tel 22403) with singles ranging from 2500 to 4000 rp, and doubles around 4000 to 5000 rp. Directly opposite the *Hotel Zahir* is the *Losmen Lombok* (tel 22049) which has singles for 1250 rp and doubles for 1750 rp.

Right in the centre of town is *Hotel Tiga Mas* (tel 23211) on the Kampung Melayu Tengah; singles 1250 rp, doubles 1750 rp. The big disadvantage with this place is that it's next door to a mosque and very noisy.

Another possibility is *Losmen Pabean* (tel 21758) at Jalan Pabean l46. Clean, pleasant rooms with attached mandi costs 2500 rp a single and 3500 rp a double. It's almost directly opposite most of the rumah makans and it is a travellers' hangout. The street names in Ampenan can be somewhat confusing – Jalan Pabean is also known as Jalan Yos Sudarso at certain points.

Places to Eat

There are two Indonesian and two Chinese restaurants across the road from the Losmen Pabean on Jalan Pabean. Both the Indonesian rumah makan, the *Mulia* and *Setia*, are cheaper than the Chinese ones, but the food is not as sustaining or as delicious. The Chinese restaurants, *Pabean* and *Tjirebon* have more variety and they also serve beer here. Their meat ball soup at 400 rp is very filling – and if you want to lash out the crab and asparagus soup is superb. In the Tjirebon there's fried crab and tomato at 1500 rp. A fish in sweet and sour sauce costs between 5000 rp and 7500 rp – but with rice and salad as extras is it large enough for two. Also try the the

Rumah Makan Arafat which has Indonesian food – not much variety – but cheap and good. It's on the left-hand side heading down Jalan Pabean towards the bemo terminal.

MATARAM

The administrative capital of Lombok and Sumbawa Islands, Mataram is surprising for the amount of money that's been poured into some quite unexpectedly impressive public buildings – like those along Jalan Pejanggik – the Bank of Indonesia, the new post office, the Governor's office and residence to name a few. The Lombok elite spends its lifestyle in palatial western-design houses on the outskirts of Mataram. The main square, Lampangan Mataram, is bounded by Jalan Pejanggik and Jalan Cempaka. Art exhibitions, theatre, dance and *wayang kulit* (shadow puppet) performances are held in the square.

Information

Lombok's *Kantor Imigrasi* (Immigration Office) is on Jalan Udayana, the road out to the airport. They're a friendly and co-operative bunch here.

Bank Negara Indonesia l946 (tel 21046), on Jalan Langko, will change foreign cash and travellers cheques. The bank shuts at noon – although sign indicates 3.30 pm.

The imposing Mataram Post Office is on the outskirts of town on Jalan Ismail Marzuki – there doesn't appear to be any regular public transport out here so you may have to charter a bemo or a dokkar in Mataram – and make sure they wait for you or you'll have a long walk back.

The airline offices are all located on Jalan Langsat – Merpati (tel 21037) Jalan Langsat 1; Garuda (tel 23762) Jalan Yos Sudarso 6; Bouraq (tel 227670 & 23235) is located in the Hotel Selaparang on Jalan Selaparang.

Places to Stay

There's a variety of accommodation in Mataram. At Jalan WR Supratman 10 is the pleasant and cheap *Hotel Kamboja* (tel 22211) with singles from 1250 to 4000 rp. *Losmen Rinjani* (tel 21633) on Jalan Cempaka is similarly priced as is *Hotel Mareje* (tel 21711) at Jalan Pariwisata 3.

Good value is the *Hotel Kertayoga* (tel 21775) at Jalan Selaparang 82. Singles with fan, attached mandi and breakfast (one egg, two slices of bread, and coffee) from 8000 rp, and doubles from around 12,000 rp.

The *Hotel Handika* on Jalan Panca Usaha, has rooms from 4000 rp, 8000 rp with fan, to 12,000 rp with air-con.

Also try the *Hotel Tenang* on Jalan Rumah Sakit Islam. Rooms here for 4000 and 5000 rp, and more expensive ones with air-con. The manager, Gusti Merti, speaks English and positively hangs out for travellers – whilst you may not agree with many of his views, you rarely find a local person on Lombok with a reasonable command of English.

Places to Eat

In the Mataram shopping centre on Jalan Penjanggik, several hundred metres down the road from the Governor's residence on the same side, there are two restaurants. The *Taliwang* offers local dishes, while the more expensive *Garden House Restaurant* has both Indonesian and Chinese food – and the best ice cream in west Nusa Tenggara. Not only that, but the chef here, Christine, studied cooking in New South Wales, Australia for several months, can speak English and is helpful about what to see and do.

For local food, try the *Seka Bajang* on Jalan Pancawarga and the *Paradiso* at Jalan Angsoka 3. Also try the *Taruka* on Jalan Selaparang. The *Restaurant Ken Dedes) on Jalan Rumah Sakit Islam has both Chinese and Indonesian food.*

CAKRANEGARA

Formerly the old capital, now the main commercial centre of Lombok, Cakra is one of those proverbial third-world colour-and-movement places. Cakra has a thriving Chinese community and many Balinese live here. It's also a centre for craftwork and is particularly well known for its basketware and weaving. Check out the bazaar (Pusaka) and watch the silver and goldsmiths at work. You may also be able to find some of the idiosyncratic clay animal figures and ceramics produced on Lombok.

Things to See

Weaving Factories One of the last weaving factories still operating is the *Selamet Riady* on Jalan Ukirkawi, where women weave delicate gold and silver thread sarongs and exquisite ikats on looms that look like they haven't altered since the Majapahit dynasty. A bemo will drop you within a few metres of the factory and you're welcome to wander around. The factory is open from 7.30 am.

Mayura Water Palace Built in 1744 and once part of the Royal Court of the former Balinese kingdom in Lombok, this structure is dominated by a large artificial lake. In the centre of the lake is an open-sided hall connected to the shoreline by a raised foothpath. The hall was used both as a court of justice and a meeting place for the Hindu lords who once ruled Lombok. Hard to imagine that less than a century ago this was where the Dutch General Van Ham (commanding a force sent to help the Sasaks in their rebellion against the Balinese) was killed in a surprise attack spearheaded by one of the Balinese princes in 1894 – after which the Dutch sent in the big guns and made short work of the Balinese.

Pura Meru Directly opposite the Mayura and just off the main road, is the Pura Meru – the largest temple on Lombok. It was built in 1720 under the patronage of a Balinese prince as an attempt to unite all the small kingdoms on Lombok. Though rather neglected looking now, it was built as a symbol of the universe and is dedicated to the Hindu trinity of Brahma, Vishnu and Shiva.

Gunung Pengsong About nine km from

Cakra is another Balinese temple, Gunung Pengsong – as the name suggests, built on top of a hill and with magnificent views overlooking the towns below. Try to get there early in the morning before the clouds envelop Mt Rinjani.

Places to Stay

There are several places to stay in Cakra – all pretty cheap. The *Hotel Ratih* (tel 21096) is on Jalan Selaparang with singles from 3000 to 5000 rp, and doubles from around 4000 to 8000 rp.

The *Hotel Pusaka* (tel 23119) is at Jalan S Hasanudin 23 – 40 rooms with singles ranging from 2500 to 5500 rp (the later with fan and attached bath), and doubles from 3500 to 6500 rp. There's also a canteen for snacks and drinks.

Close to the *Hotel Pusaka* is the *Losmen Merpati* at Jalan S Hasanudin 17. Singles 2500 rp, doubles 5000 rp.

Losmen Cakrajaya (tel 23480) on Jalan Tenun has 12 rooms with singles starting from 4000 rp and doubles from around 5000 or 5500 rp.

The *Losmen Tangguh* (tel 21822) on Jalan Koak-Koak is good value with singles for 2500 rp and doubles for 3000 rp, with attached mandi.

Places to Eat

Food in Cakra is generally more expensive than in Ampenan, and cheapest eats come from the warungs which are dotted around the place. There are also a couple of rumah makans along Jalan Selaparang – the *Asia* and *Harum* both have Chinese food. The *Istimewa* and *Hari Ini* offer local dishes. The *Friendship* has a Chinese and Indonesian menu.

Try the *Srikaya* on Jalan Merpati for soto ayam (chicken soup) and gado gado. On Jalan Rajawali the *Taliwang* and *Kurnia* have local dishes including soto ayam. The *Setuju* on Jalan Miru offers a range of Indonesian dishes. On Jalan Hasanuddin the *Rumah Makan Madya* has Indonesian food and the *Restaurant Minang* does regional dishes.

SWETA

Not far from Cakra is Sweta – the central transport terminal of Lombok. This is where you catch bemos, buses and microbuses to other parts of the island. A local bemo from Mataram to the Sweta terminal will cost you 75 rp. If in doubt about fares there is a sign up on the bus station office listing them. Sweta is also the site of the largest market on the island, including a bird market.

NARMADA

About 10 km east of Cakra, on the main east-west road crossing Lombok, is this hill and lake laid out as a miniature replica of the summit of Mt Rinjani and its crater lake. It was constructed by King Anak Agung Gede Karangasem of Mataram in 1805, when he was no longer able to climb Rinjani to make his offerings to the gods – the temple is still used today and is dedicated to Lord Shiva. It's a nice place to spend a few hours, but *don't* go there on weekends since it's overrun by the hordes.

A few km north of Narmada is Lingsar which is a large temple complex said to have been built in 1714. The temple combines the Bali-Hindu and Islam-Wektu Telu religions in one temple complex. East of Lingsar, is Suranadi which is one of the holiest temples on Lombok – noted for its ornate Balinese carvings.

Getting There

There are frequent bemos from Sweta to Narmada, costing around 75 to 100 rp – the gardens are across the road from the bemo terminal. Entry to Narmada is 50 rp for adults. Right at the Narmada bemo terminal is the local market and a number of warungs offering soto ayam and other dishes.

At Narmada catch another bemo to Lingsar for the same price and walk the short distance from here to the temple complex. You can see the temple from the road – can't miss it. There is a large square in front of the temple complex, with a couple of warungs to the right before you enter the main area and a small stall closer to the temple where you can buy snacks and hard-boiled eggs to feed to the holy eels which inhabit the pool in the Wektu Telu Temple. If the temple is locked ask at one of the warungs for a key.

SUKARARE

A small village just 25 km south of Mataram on the Kediri/Puyung road, this is one of the traditional weaving centres of Lombok. Nearly every house in Sukarare has an old wooden handloom on which the women weave the complicated and difficult patterns – some so intricate that they take one person three months to complete and involve weaving the hand-dyed threads in four separate directions. The women of this village specialise in highly decorative cloth interwoven with gold or silver threads. On the main street you'll see the sarongs slung out on display. For cheapest prices buy direct from the women.

In Sukarare stay with the kepala desa or make a day trip. You could also check with the woman who runs the warung – she sometimes puts people up for the night (and has a fine selection of cloth for sale). Take a bemo from Sweta to Puyung for 250 rp, then hire a dokar for 100 rp for the two km ride from Puyung to Sukarare.

LEMBAR

One of the two main ports of Lombok, 22 km south of Ampenan, this is where the ferries from Bali dock. There are regular buses and bemos for 500 rp from Sweta to Lembar during the day.

From Lembar to Padangbai ferries depart twice daily at 9 am and 2 pm. Buy your tickets at the wharf on the day. Bus and bemo drivers drop you off almost directly in front of the office. There's a canteen here where you can buy snacks and drinks while waiting to catch the ferry. Lembar has no overnight accommodation, nor does it have any rumah makan. Fares from Lombok to Bali are slightly more expensive than Bali to Lombok. 1st class

from Lombok costs 4150 rp, 2nd class 2950 rp.

LABUHAN LOMBOK

Labuhan Lombok, on the east coast of the island, is the port where you catch the ferry to Sumbawa Island. Not an unpleasant place by any means, a mixed bag of concrete houses, thatch shacks, stilt bungalows – the people are friendly, but there's little to do. Climb the hill on the right-hand side of the harbour and watch the boats travelling between here and Sumbawa. If you walk about four km north from Labuhan Lombok towards Sembalia there is a reservoir and fishing village – the children either run away in fear or surround you and touch your white skin to see if it feels the same as brown.

Places to Stay

There is only one place to stay in Labuhan Lombok – a hole called the *Losmen Sudimampir*. Without a doubt the worst place I have stayed in in the entire archipelago – in fact, when I was there they'd closed off some of the rooms because the rotting roof was threatening to collapse. Dead spiders dangle from dusty cobwebs in the toilet, and you lie in bed at night in your scungy room contemplating the size and nature of the creature that's going to fall on you from the tattered ceiling – the sort of place that's makes you wonder why you ever left Bali. For this the owner, who is actually quite an amiable fellow, charges 2000 rp a single and 3000 rp a double. The losmen is only a 10 minute walk from the bemo station.

Places to Eat

There are a couple of warungs around the bemo station, but they're all restricted to nasi campur, ayam goreng and the like – and rather poor at that. The *Rumah Makan Hidayat* across the road from the bemo station is a friendly place. You can buy a fish at the market and get it cooked at a warung.

Getting There

There are regular bemos and colts from Sweta for 800 rp to 900 rp and the trip takes a bit less than two hours. If you can't face staying at the Losmen Sudimampir then spend the night in Ampenan or Cakra and catch a bus early in the morning from there – you'll need to be on the road at 5.30 am at the latest if you're intending to head for Sumbawa Island. If you're staying at Losmen Horas in Ampenan then Mr Batubara will arrange for a bus to pick you up at the losmen at around 4.30 am – this should get you to Labuhan Lombok by 8 am, in plenty of time for the ferry. The cost is 1000 rp per person.

Ferries from Labuhan Lombok to Sumbawa

Ferries from Labuhan Lombok to Labuhan Alas on Sumbawa Island depart from a pier about one km from the bemo station. It's not far to walk if you've got little to carry – alternatively a dokar will cost you about 100 rp per person.

There are at least two ferries per day to Sumbawa, departing Labuhan Lombok at 8 am and 9 am, and there may be another at 10 am depending on the season. The fare is 1825 rp. You can also transport motorcycles on the ferry – cost is 2500 rp. Buy your ticket on the day of departure from the ticket office near the pier. The trip to Sumbawa takes about 3½ to four hours.

There are a couple of stalls at the pier where you can buy biscuits, bananas, and one or two warungs serving nasi campur. Guys come on board the boat selling fried rice wrapped in banana leaves and hard boiled eggs. Take a water bottle with you – it's a bloody hot ride! The ferry is a floating pile of closely compacted humanity – could be a good idea to get down to the dock early to get a seat – or bring a hat for sun protection and stretch out on the roof.

When you arrive in Labuhan Alas there will be lots of buses waiting at the pier to load passengers. Direct buses to Sumbawa Besar for around 1250 rp, to Bima for 5000 rp, and there'll probably be others heading in the Taliwang direction. The road is surfaced all the way across Sumbawa now, and the trip from Labuhan Alas to Sumbawa Besar takes 1¾ hrs. It's a good idea to agree on the price beforehand as they may try and rip you off.

KOTARAJA & LOYOK

Basketware from Lombok has such a fine reputation in the archipelago that many Balinese make special trips to Lombok to buy the stuff up, take it back to beautiful Bali and flog it off at inflated prices to foreigners. Kotaraja and Loyok villages in eastern Lombok are noted for their craftwork, particularly their basketware and plaited mats. Aside from that you may also come across exquisitely intricate metal jewellery as well as vases, caskets and other decorative objects in Kotaraja. Loyok is just a tiny village a few km from Kotaraja.

Getting There

Kotaraja is 32 km from Sweta – a day trip from the capital – but getting there involves a couple of bemo changes. Take a bemo to Narmada for 100 rp. From there take another bemo to Pomotong for 300 rp. From Pomotong you can either get a dokar to Kotaraja or wait for another bemo. The latter are cheaper than dokars, but not as plentiful. If you don't like bemo changes then you should be able to get a direct bus from Sweta to Pomotong.

To get to Loyok, you can get a bemo from Pomotong to take you as far as the turnoff to the village and then either walk the rest of the way or get a dokar for 100 rp per person. If you're setting out from Kotaraja for Loyok you've got the same options – either take a dokar or walk.

GILI TRAWANGAN

Off the north-west coast of Lombok are three small coral atolls – Gili Air, Gili Trawangan and Gili Meno – with superb, white sandy beaches, clear water, coral reefs, brilliantly coloured fish – and the best skin diving and snorkelling on Lombok. The best of the three islands is Gili Trawangan. There are no shops on Gili Trawangan so bring anything you need with you. Pak Majid, who runs the sole losmen here, has one snorkel, one mask and a set of fins which he lends to guests – but it would be a good idea to try and get hold of some before you get here. You can buy snorkel, mask and fins in Ampenan or hire them from Bouraq Airlines in that city (at US$2 per day).

Places to Stay

There is only one losmen on Gili Trawangan but it's a real winner. Run by Pak Majid and his Javanese wife, Suparmi, it's a simple house, set on stilts, with a spacious verandah that offers pleasant views of the island, sea and Gili Meno. You can eat out here or in a rather dim room inside. The losmen has seven rooms – each just big enough for two people – though additional space inside can be converted to temporary rooms. Suparmi cooks up delicious meals – you get three per day, more food than you can possibly eat – coffee and a never-ending supply of tea. They've also got a small collection of paperbacks here, mostly in English or German.

Getting There

To get to these islands take a bus from Sweta to Pemenang for 300 rp – 25 km and takes one to 1½ hours – quite a scenic trip past numerous small villages and through lush, green forest with monkeys by the side of the road. Once you reach Pemenang you can either take a dokar for 100 rp per person the short distance to Bangsal Harbour or walk. You can't get lost as it's straight down the road and only two km away at the most.

If you're going to Gili Trawangan try to get to Bangsal Harbour soon before 10 am. You may have to wait for a couple of hours or so, but it's a pleasant place to while away some time – there are some shaded warungs with good food and coffee. It may seem a rather ridiculous precaution to get to Bangsal Harbour so early, but there's only one boat per day to Gili Trawangan and while it usually doesn't go before noon it has been known to leave shortly after 10 am – it depends on the tide and the time of year.

The trip out to Gili Trawangan takes just over an hour and the cost there and back is added to your bill at Pak Majid's. It works out at about 1250 rp per person. So don't pay the boatman there and then, and if you've decided on going to Gili Trawangan don't be hassled by other boatmen to go to Gili Air (which is the chief tourist island of the group). There are plenty of boats out to Gili Air throughout the day which take about 20 minutes to half an hour and cost 500 rp one-way. You can, of course, always charter a boat to Gili Trawangan but this will cost you an arm and a leg.

MOUNT RINJANI

Both the Balinese and the local Sasak people revere Rinjani. To the Balinese it is equal to their own Gunung Agung, a seat of the gods, and many Balinese make a pilgrimage here each year. Full moon is the favourite time for the Sasaks to pay their respects and cure their ailments by bathing in the hot springs. Try to avoid going there then or you'll be sorry. Rinjani is the highest mountain in Lombok, the second highest in Indonesia – 3726 metres. The mountain is actually an active volcano – though the last eruption was in 1901 – and has a huge half-moon crater, a large slime-green lake and a number of steaming hot springs.

There are at least two ways of climbing Mt Rinjani. The first, and apparently the easier route, is via the villages of Bayan, Batu Koq and Senaro in the north. The other is from the east, starting at Sapit. You should not attempt to tackle this climb during the wet season as it's far too dangerous then. You need three clear days to do it – up and back down again – and probably at least another day to recover.

Whilst Rinjani is a pretty place and worth a visit if you're spending a fair amount of time on Lombok, its probably not worth it if you've got only a limited amount of time in Nusa Tenggara. For the full story on scaling Rinjani see Lonely Planet's *Bali & Lombok* book.

Other places to check out on or in the vicinity of Rinjani include the village of Bayan which is the birthplace of the Wektu Telu religion. The village of Senaro, high up in the foothills around Rinjani, about nine km from Bayan, is traditional and seems unchanged since it emerged from the primaeval age – it was less than a decade ago that the people here saw their first white man, and not many years before that that they started having regular contact with people in the surrounding area. On the eastern slopes of Rinjani are the Sasak villages of Sembalun Bumbung and Sembalun Lawang – they're five km apart and if you're feeling energetic you can walk to these villages from Bayan in a day.

Getting There

The village of Bayan is the main jumping off point for the climb up Mt Rinjani. Several buses daily from Sweta, the first leaving around 9 am. The fare is 1000 rp and it takes about three hours. The last bus back to Sweta departs Bayan around 6 pm. In Bayan stay with the kepala desa for around 1650 rp per person per night, including two meals, or 5000 rp for three people, accommodation and meals. There are a couple of warungs in Bayan, one being on the road to Senaro just off to the right – fried chicken and rice for just 1500 rp.

SUMBAWA

The earliest known kingdoms in west Nusa Tenggara were the comparatively small kingdoms of the Sasaks in Lombok, the Sumbawans in west Sumbawa and the Bimans and Dompuese in east Sumbawa. These people were animists and their communities agricultural. Today, Sumbawa is a strongly Muslim island although there are just a few traces left of the old sultanates of Sumbawa and Bima which date from the early 18th century.

Whilst there's not a great deal to see in Sumbawa, if you're there at the right time and in the right place – on holidays and festivals – you might see traditional Lombok or Sumbawan fighting. Sumbawan style is a sort of bare-fist boxing, palms bound in symbolic rice stalks – see it in east Bali too. Lombok style is called Peresehan and is a more violent affair involving leather-covered shields and bamboo poles. Most matches seem to end in draws. Water buffalo races take place at one festival, but their not exactly the Grand National.

GETTING THERE

There are flights on Merpati and Bouraq between Denpasar and Sumbawa Besar and Bima. Merpati flights from Sumbawa Besar include Denpasar 38,400 rp – with same-day connections to Jakarta and Surabaya. Flights from Bima to Denpasar cost 58,200 rp with connections to Jakarta and Surabaya.

Merpati also has various connections from Bima to other parts of Nusa Tenggara; these include Mataram 40,700 rp; Labuhanbajo 29,700 rp; Ruteng 42,600 rp; Ende 39,700 rp; Kupang 91,400 rp; Tambolaka 29,300 rp; Waingapu 42,400 rp; and from Sumbawa Besar to Mataram for 24,700 rp. Bouraq flies from Bima to Mataram and Denpasar with connections to Jakarta, Bandung and Surabaya.

For details of the daily ferry from Lombok to Sumbawa see the section Labuhan Lombok in the Lombok section. For details of the regular ferry from Sumbawa to Komodo and Flores see the section on Pelabuhan Sape below. There are irregular ships from Bima to various destinations – Ujung Pandang in Sulawesi and Dili in East Timor being two possibilities – but it's a case of waiting around the port and seeing what's available.

LABUHAN ALAS

Labuhan Alas is the port on the west coast of Sumbawa where you catch the ferry to Lombok. It's located in a pretty little bay and is not much more more than a dock and a small village. A Sulawesi fishing village clusters offshore on stilts.

There are daily ferries to Labuhan Lombok departing Labuhan Alas at 8 and 9 am – and there may be a third boat at 10 am depending on the season. Adult fare is 1975 rp. Taking a motorcycle on the ferry costs 2500 rp. Buy your ticket from the ticket office at the start of the pier where the buses pull in. There are a couple of stalls here selling biscuits and sweets and kids selling oranges and fried bananas. When you arrive in Labuhan Lombok there'll be buses waiting to pick up passengers and take them to various destinations around Lombok.

If you arrive in Labuhan Alas on the ferry from Labuhan Lombok there will be buses waiting at the pier to load on passengers. Direct buses to Sumbawa Besar (1250 rp, 1¾ hrs), to Bima (5000 rp), and there should be buses to Taliwang (1000 rp, 1¼ hrs).

SUMBAWA BESAR

The chief town of Sumbawa, Sumbawa Besar is a scrunched-up collection of concrete block houses, thatch-roofed and woven-mat-walled stilt bungalows, shacks clinging to the sides of the hills with paths leading up to them made of small boulders. The people here are very friendly and the place has a distinctly 'Asian' feel about it, with numerous dokars rattling down the streets, and Muslim men flooding out of the mosques after mid-day prayer.

The chief attractions are the Dakam Laka – the Sultan's Palace – an interesting wooden, barn-like building, set on stilts, with a sloping walkway leading up to the first floor. The Pura Agung Girinatha is a Hindu temple near the intersection of Jalan Yos Sudarso and Jalan Setiabudi, containing a few statues and one large, squat lingam.

Information

The Bank Negara Indonesia (tel 21936) is at Jalan Kartini 10. It's open Monday to Saturday from 7.30 am to 11.30 am. They'll change travellers' cheques from larger companies like Thomas Cook, American Express and Bank of America, and will also change cash – so long as its major foreign currencies like American dollars, Australian dollars, pounds sterling, Deutsche marks, or Netherlands florin.

The post office is located out past the airport, but there are fairly regular bemos out here for 100 rp. There is a large map of Sumbawa Island on the wall of the restaurant in the Hotel Tambora. It shows the roads (surfaced and unsurfaced), trails, towns and villages – worth checking out. The Merpati office is at Jalan Hasanuddin 80.

Places to Stay

Central Sumbawa Besar is a compact place and there's a cluster of losmen just five minutes' walk from the bus terminal, lined along Jalan Hasanuddin. Walk down Jalan Kaboja, which is opposite the bus station, to get to Jalan Hasanuddin. All these hotels are within range of the 5 am wake-up call from the mosque – experience indigenous culture at its loudest.

Probably the best of these hotels is the Losmen Suci (tel 21589) with rooms situated around an attractive courtyard and garden – keeps out much of the traffic noise. Singles 2250 rp, doubles 3250 rp, and rooms have fans and attached mandi and toilet – and they're clean.

The Losmen Dewi (tel 21170) has a very friendly manager, and much of the traffic noise is held at bay. Singles and doubles are 2500 rp with attached mandi and toilet (rooms are clean but the bathrooms could be cleaner).

The Losmen Saudara (tel 21528) has been recommended – I stayed there one night and found it pretty horrendous both from traffic and internal assaults on the eardrums (not to mention the mosque). Apart from that, it's clean and good value

– ideal for deaf people. For rooms without mandi and toilet, singles are 1500 rp, doubles 2200 rp; rooms with attached mandi and toilet are 2000 rp a single, 3000 rp a double and 4000 rp a triple.

The *Losmen Tunas* (tel 21212) is a rather non-descript place. Singles 1500 rp, doubles 2500 rp – OK but nothing to rave about.

Back up the road and right next to the bus terminal is the *Losmen Indra* (tel 21878) which is 2500 rp a single or double – probably very noisy during the day, but at night the bus terminal dies and it should be fairly quiet.

The best hotel in Sumbawa Besar is the *Hotel Tambora* (tel 21555), a 15-minute walk from the bus terminal (or take a dokar for about 75 rps per person). Singles from 4000 rp and doubles from 5000 rp with attached mandi.

Places to Eat

The *Rumah Makan Surabaya* is a minute's walk from the bus terminal and serves cheap dishes like nasi campur and nasi goreng for around 500 to 600 rp – they close early, like 5.30 pm. On Jalan Wahiddin the *Rumah Makan Anda* stays open somewhat later and has similar prices, standards and food. The *Hotel Tambora* has a pleasant restaurant set in a garden and a rather more varied menu with dishes in the 1000 to 1500 rp mark – like curried prawns. There are numerous night-time sate stalls along Jalan Wahiddin, near the junction with Jalan Merdeka

Getting There

The long-distance bus terminal is on Jalan Diponegoro and fares are posted up on the window of the office. Some fares from Sumbawa Besar are: to Empang 1400 rp; Dompu 2800 rp; Bima 3800 rp; Alas 1000 rp; Taliwang 1700 rp. The bus ride to Bima is a seven hour journey (including a half hour lunch break) and the road is now surfaced the whole way.

Getting Around

Sumbawa Besar is very small – you can walk around much of it with ease (except to more distant places like the post office). The bus terminal is pretty much the centre of town, and there is also a combined bemo and dokar station at the junction of Jalan Setiabudi and Jalan Urip Sumohaojo – 50 rp by dokar between the two. Bemos seem to operate on a flat rate of 100 rp per person – from central Sumbawa Besar to the airport, post office or to Labuhan Sumbawa the bemo fare is 100 rp.

BIMA-RABA

This is Sumbawa's main port and the major centre at the eastern end of the island. It's really just a stop on the way through Sumbawa, and there's nothing much to see or do here. Apart from the usual 'hello misters' some of the kids have learnt to say 'I love you'. The only notable attraction of Bima is the large former sultan's palace now used as a college. The night market is worth a wander – posters for sale include fab Sting and the Police rubbing shoulders with posters of President Suharto.

Information

The Bank Negara Indonesia will change major travellers' cheques and major foreign currencies like American and Australian dollars, and Deutsche German marks.

The post office is on Jalan Kampung Salama, which is out in the suburbs, way past the palace. Approximate opening hours are Monday to Thursday 8 am to 12 noon, Friday 8 to 11 am, Saturday 8 am to 12 noon. Closed on Sundays. Take a dokar out there.

Merpati is at Jalan Bioskop 17, behind the Losman Lila Graha. Bouraq (tel 780) is on Jalan Sudirman 234. Pelni (tel 224) is at the port of Bima on Jalan Pelabuhan 27 – take a dokar there for 100 rp.

Places to Stay

Like Sumbawa Besar, Bima is pretty compact and the losmen are all grouped together in the middle of town in the vicinity of the palace.

The best place to stay in Bima is the *Losmen Lila Graha* (tel 740) on Jalan Belakang Bioskop. It's the one saving grace of the town. Nice and clean, singles are 3300 rp, doubles 4400 rp. Doubles with attached mandi and toilet for 5500 rp. The losmen is a 10 minute walk from the central bus station, or you can take a dokar for 50 rp per person.

The *Losmen Kartini* on Jalan Sultan Kaharuddin is a large, dingy place. Spartan rooms go at 3600 a single and 7000 rp a double, but you could try bargaining them down.

The *Losmen Vivi* (te 411) is on the corner of Jalan Soekarno Hatte and Jalan Sultan Hasanuddin. Singles and doubles for 2000 rp – but they're not too friendly and I don't think they'll take you.

Apparently the cheap *Losmen Komodo* (tel 70) is still a going concern and is supposed to be located next to the Sultan's Palace.

Places to Eat

There are quite a few warungs and rumah makan around, but the choice is restricted to nasi ayam or nasi campur or nasi campur or nasi campur. Some places have more extensive menus but what's on the menu is not always what they've got.

The *Rumah Makan Nirwana* is one of the better places and is located on Jalan Belakang Bioskop near the Losmen Lila Graha. Have them make up a 'telur dadar udang' which is a shrimp omlette. It's not on the menu but they will make it for you – makes a tasty change and will cost around 1500 rp.

There's a couple of places on Jalan Martadinata including the *Rumah Makan Minang* with good curried chicken at 1300 rp; just down the road and worth a shot is the *Rumah Makan Surabaya*. The people working here are very friendly. The

Rumah Makan Anda has a fairly extensive menu – cap cai at 1250 rp, udang 2000 rp – could be worth a try. There are various cheap little warungs around the centre of town and the night market has some foodstalls serving interesting sweets and snacks.

Getting Around

Buses to destinations west of Bima depart from Bima's central bus station, just 10 minutes or so walk from the centre of town. Some fares: Bima to Dompu 900 rp; Sumbawa Besar 4000 rp; Labuhan Alas 5000 rp.

For buses to the east, you have to go up to Kumbe Station in Raba. There are frequent bemos up here for 100 rp per person – pick them up from around Jalan Sultan Hasanuddin in Bima – they go through central Bima before heading off to Raba. Buses to Sape – from where you catch the ferry to Flores and Komodo – depart from Kumbe.

SAPE

Sape is a pleasant enough little town. The ferry to Komodo and Flores leaves from Pelabuhan Sape which is just down the road from Sape. If you have to wait for it then Sape is probably a better place to wait than Bima.

Places to Stay & Eat

Losmen Give seems to be the only place to stay in Sape – it's basic but OK – singles 1500 rp, doubles 2500 rp. Take a dokar there from the bus station for 50 rp (but you'll probably have to pay 100 rp).

As for eating, the choice is between bad and bad. The two eating houses of Sape are the *Rumah Makan Seta Kawan* and next to it the *Rumah Makan Kita* – memorable for the two worst variations of nasi campur I had in all Indonesia! Much better to stock up on what's available in the market and local shops, or even bring some food with you from Bima.

Getting There

Buses go from the Kumbe bus station in Bima-Raba. The trip takes two hours and costs 650 rp. It seems that the earliest buses to Sape depart Kumbe station at around 7.30 am – there may be earlier ones on Mondays, Wednesdays and Saturdays to connect you with the ferry to Flores island, but don't count on it.

Ferries to Komodo & Flores Island Ferries for Komodo and Flores depart from Pelabuhan Sape – take a dokar from Sape for 150 to 200 rp per person. Pelabuhan Sape is nothing more than one street leading down to the dock, lined by stilt houses. The chief hobby here is building anything from a canoe to a galleon beside your house – apparently these are Sulawesi people here. The ferry schedule is:

Pelabuhan Sape-Komodo-Labuhanbajo departs Pelabuhan Sape at 8 am every Saturday.
Pelabuhan Sape-Labuhanbajo departs Pelabuhan Sape at 9 am every Monday and Wednesday.
Labuhanbajo-Komodo-Pelabuhan Sape departs Labuhanbajo at 8 am every Sunday.
Labuhanbajo-Pelabuhan Sape departs Labuhanbajo at 9 am every Tuesday and Thursday.

Passenger Fares There are two classes on the boat; Economy and Deck Class (except for price, I'm not too sure what the difference is – but I think the Economy Class means sitting under the canopy on the upper deck, whilst the plebs sunbake on the uncovered lower deck). Buy your ticket on the day of departure from the ticket office at the wharf. Fares between Sape and Labuhanbajo, and between Sape and Komodo are the same (travelling in either direction).

You also have to pay 75 rp at the wharf entrance for an additional ticket (no idea what this is for – probably a harbour tax), and 100 rp to the boatmen to paddle you out to the ship in a canoe. You can take a motorcycle across on the ferry; Sape-Labuhanbajo and Sape-Komodo is 6300 rp, and Labuhanbajo-Komodo is 2300 rp. The crossing takes about 12 hours.

	S to L S to K	L to K
economy		
adult	7100 rp	2350 rp
child	3600	1200 rp
deck		
adult	5600 rp	1850 rp
child	2900 rp	1000 rp

** S = Sape
** L = Labuhanbajo
** K = Komodo

KOMODO

A hilly, dry, desolate island neatly sandwiched between Flores and Sumbawa, Komodo's big attraction is lizards – four metre, 150 kilo lizards, appropriately known as the Komodo dragons. June to September – in the dry season – is the best time to see the dragons as there are more of them out looking for food then. They are carnivores and a goat is the recommended *makan bwaya* – dragon food. Normally the dragons eat the deer and wild pig which are found on the island. The only village on the island is Kampung Komodo – a fishing village situated on the eastern coast of the island and worth a look in. Also on the coast and a half-hour walk north of the village is Loh Liang, the site of the PPA tourist camp.

Permits You get your permit for Komodo on the island itself, at the PPA camp at Loh Liang. Permits cost 1000 rp per person. PPA is the Indonesian government organisation responsible for managing the country's nature reserves and national parks.

Dragon Spotting

The most accessible place to see the dragons has been set up like a little theatre. The PPA guides will take you to a dried up river bed about a half hour's walk from Loh Liang. A clearing has been made here overlooking the creek; the goat has its throat cut by one of the PPA people, and is then dangled by a rope from a tree that overhangs the river bed. There'll probably be some of the lizards already there since this is now an established feeding spot, but more will come – we saw about seven of the monsters in all – and I mean *monsters*!

The PPA people insist that you have a goat – they won't show you the way to the viewing site without one, though they don't insist that you buy the goat from them. A guide and goat porter will cost you a total of 7500 rp, according to their list of rates. The advantage of having the guide is that you don't have to be the one to kill the goat! Exactly why you have to have a goat is not clear but the PPA guys insist that they can't allow the dragons to be fed with anything that might be harmful to them – which is fair enough since it's their job to protect the reptiles – so there's no point buying a large dried fish in the village or in Labuhanbajo as an offering. We bought a small goat from one of the villagers in Kampung Komodo for 20,000 rp – and next day, accompanied by a guide and porter, went off to see the dragons. The guys at PPA were asking 30,000 rp to get a large goat for us from the village, or 25,000 rp for a small goat. Alternatively

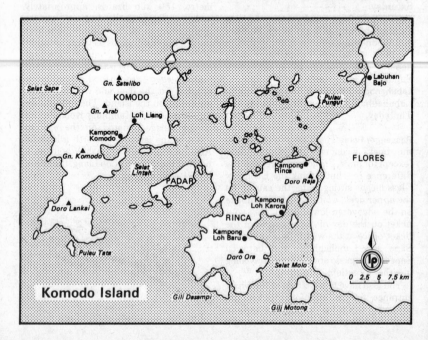

Komodo Island

buy a goat in Labuhanbajo (maybe 20,000 rp) and bring it over to Komodo with you.

Around the Island

Other things to do on Komodo include climbing up the hills at the rear of Kampung Komodo for a sweeping view across Komodo village and the other islands in the region.

If you go trekking around the island – or climbing Mt Arab for example – be warned that this place is bloody hot! If you really want to trek into the uplands on the island then make sure you're the sort of person who runs up and down a volcano before breakfast every morning. The PPA will provide you with a guide. Sights around the island include wild deer and large, poisonous (though not deadly) spiders – I ran into one of their webs stretched right across a track – as tough as plastic thread and harbouring an ugly monster.

As for swimming – the PPA guys say that the sea snakes only come out at night, and that you'll only attract sharks if you cut yourself on the coral and bleed. Land snakes are supposed to infest the island – signs around the PPA camp warn you to wear trousers and shoes and to watch for snakes. Wild pigs are commonly seen, often close to the camp – you'll also see them on the beach in front of the tourist camp early in the morning. The Komodo dragons occasionally wander into the PPA camp, but they avoid the kampung because there are too many people. If you want to go snorkelling bring your own equipment – PPA *may* have a snorkel and mask for hire.

Places to Stay & Eat

The PPA has established a large camp at Loh Liang, a half hour's walk from Kampung Komodo. The losmen here is a collection of *large*, spacious, clean wooden cabins on stilts; the cabins have partitioned compartments, each with a single bed and a curtain you can draw across each for privacy. These cost 3000 rp per night and

each cabin can accomodate about 10 people. Each cabin includes a lockable room with two beds costing 4000 rp each. Each hut has two mandis (including toilet) and cleanliness really depends on how recently the huts were last occupied. One cabin is made up entirely of double rooms. Electricity goes on from 6 until 10 pm – produced by a noisy generator down near the camp office. Once that goes off there's almost total silence.

Bring your own food! All the PPA can provide on the island is some rice, noodles, tea and sometimes some boiled vegetables. They have no oil to fry anything here. These guys have to live on this diet full time! You can buy dried fish in Labuhanbajo (1500 rp for a big one), as well as biscuits, canned milk, bananas (250 rp for a bunch of 15 or so) and papayas. There was no canned meat or canned fruit on sale in Labuhanbajo and so if you want these you should buy them in Sape or in Ruteng (depending on which way you're travelling). For other food, try in Kampung Komodo – you should be able to buy fish, eggs, or perhaps get them to kill and cook a chicken for you (chickens cost around 2000 rp each).

Getting There

You can get to Komodo on the regular ferry that runs between Labuhanbajo in Flores, Komodo and Pelabuhan Sape on Sumbawa. For full details of fares and schedules, see Pelabuhan Sape in the Sumbawa section of this book. There are also tours to Komodo from Bali – the usual length is of three days and two nights – look around the travel agents in Kuta. A common method of getting to Komodo is by chartering a motor boat in Labuhanbajo, a port on the western coast of Flores – see the section below on Labuhanbajo for details.

FLORES

One of the most beautiful islands in Indonesia, the backbone of Flores is an astounding string of active and extinct volcanoes. The name is Portuguese for 'flower' – the Portuguese being the first Europeans to colonise the island; they eventually sold it to the Dutch. The most notable feature of Flores is Catholicism – 95% of the population is Catholic and the church dominates every tiny village – only in the ports are there any number of Muslims.

GETTING THERE

Merpati and Bouraq have flights from Java and Denpasar to various places in Flores. Bouraq flights include Denpasar-Maumere for 80,200 rp, and Surabaya-Maumere via Denpasar for 107,800 rp. Merpati flights include Denpasar to Ende for 91,400 rp, and Denpasar-Labuhanbajo 87,900 rp.

Merpati also has flights between Flores and other parts of Nusa Tenggara including Bima to Labuhanbajo 29,700 rp; Bima to Ruteng 42,600 rp; Bima to Bajawa 49,300 rp; Ende to Kupang 47,000 rp; Maumere to Kupang 31,600 rp. Bouraq flies Maumere to Kupang for 31,600 rp.

Occasionally there are boats from Ende across to Waingapu in Sumba as well as the usual visits by cargo ships to the main ports of Labuhanbajo, Reo, Maumere, Larantuka, Ende and Mborong. There are also regular passenger ships from Larantuka, the main port on the eastern side of Flores, to Kupang in Timor and regular passenger ships from Larantuka to the islands immediately to the east of Flores – see the relevant sections below for details. And of course the regular ferry from Labuhanbajo over to Sumbawa Island via Komodo – for details see Pelabuhan Sape in the Sumbawa section.

GETTING AROUND

The transport situation in Flores has improved greatly over the last few years. Some stretches of road are being surfaced and there are daily buses or trucks between the main centres; at least during the dry season. The time *not* to go to Flores is during the wet season when the unmade roads (such as Labuhanbajo to Ruteng) become impossible! Vehicles get bogged and a trip that might take hours in the dry season can take days. In some cases you can avoid this problem by taking boats around the coast – such as the irregular boats that ply the water from Labuhanbajo to Reo, and from there take a truck up the rather better road to Ruteng.

Merpati has flights between various centres on Flores including Ende to Ruteng 30,500 rp; Labuhanbajo to Ruteng 23,800 rp; Bajawa to Ende 23,900 rp. These may be worth considering if you end up on the island during the wet season – but some spectacular stretches of terrain – like Ruteng to Bajawa and Bajawa to Ende – really have to be seen from the road!

LABUHANBAJO

This fishing village lies at the extreme western end of Flores and is the jumping off point for Komodo. If you've got a few days to while away then Labuhanbajo is a pleasant enough village to do it in – a pretty place with a harbour sheltered by several small islands. Apparently there's a sea garden in the vicinity of Labuhanbajo or off one of the nearby islands – could be worth bringing a mask and snorkel.

Information

There is a small bank in Labuhanbajo but it doesn't change travellers' cheques or foreign money. There *might* be a branch of the Bank Rakyat Indonesia opened in Labuhanbajo with money changing facilities by the time this edition is out.

The harbour master's office is just near the ferry dock. The PPA office is a two minute walk from the Losman Mutiara. They don't have any printed information except one or two out-of-date tourist leaflets. Nevertheless, things could improve and they may be worth dropping in on.

Merpati has its office on the road out to the airstrip. Walk down the main road to the south end of the town and then take the turnoff road to the airstrip. You'll eventually come to the *Kios Berkatusaka* on the left – the Merpati office is a little further up from here on the right. Your guess is as good as mine when it's open. The airstrip is a clearing a half hour's walk along the stony road past the Merpati office – you might be able to hitch in a jeep.

Places to Stay & Eat

There are a couple of places to stay in Labuhanbajo. The best of these is a relatively new place called the *Wisma Bajo*. Very clean and rooms have attached mandi and toilet. The price depends on what you look like, whether the competition across the road is full, and the relative position of the sun and the moon. I was offered a single room for 3000 rp and a double for 5000 rp (including breakfast). But normally you could pay up to 10,000/12,000 rp for singles/doubles; meals are usually 2500 rp each.

Across the road from the Wisma Bajo is the *Losmen Mutiara* which has been around for years. It's a decent little place with singles around 2000 rp, doubles around 4000 rp. Three meals per day will cost an additional 3000 rp per person. Otherwise pay for meals separately – quite decent food here. The only problem with this place is the owner, Leo, can be a major pain – hang on to your wallet, or he'll go through it like a plague of locusts!

There's also the *Komodo Jaya Losmen* near to the ferry jetty. Five rooms with bunk beds – 4000 rp per day with meals, and 3000 rp per day without meals – good food, friendly, clean place.

Getting There

For details of fares and schedules of the Flores-Komodo-Sumbawa ferry – which docks at Labuhanbajo – see Pelabuhan Sape in the Sumbawa section of this book. From time to time there are also occasional boats between Labuhanbajo and Maumere and Ende.

There are irregular trucks and jeeps along the track between Labuhanbajo and Ruteng – the fare is 3000 rp. *Don't* try this in the wet – you will definitely get bogged and could end up taking two days to make it to Ruteng! Get a seat in front of the rear axle – or risk wrecking the shock absorbers in your back! As an alternative to struggling up the road to Ruteng, consider taking one of the irregular but frequent boats from Reo on the northern coast of Flores. Buses and trucks use a rather better road between Reo and Ruteng. The boat fare from Labuhanbajo to Reo is 2000 rp (2500 rp if you buy from the harbour master).

Boats from Labuhanbajo to Komodo Island

Apart from the regular ferry, you can also charter small boats to take you over to Komodo Island. How much you pay depends on who you approach. Let's say you want to go over there, spend a night, and return the following day (which is enough time to see the dragons) then you'd probably be looking at about 20,000 rp to charter a boat for a roundtrip – if you go straight to a boatman. If you ask the harbour master to find you a boat he'll want 25,000 rp; Leo at the Losmen Mutiara and the owner of the Wisma Bajo were asking 35,000 rp! Sailing times will probably depend on the time of year and the tides. We got one letter from some people who did Komodo as a day-trip, departing Labuhanbajo at 3 am! The crossing takes about four or five hours.

If you want to stay more than one night on the island then you'll have to work out the price with the person you hire the boat from. You should also agree upon a price for the *boat* regardless of how many people are making the trip – so if extra people turn up you can spread the cost around. Otherwise, make an agreement that the cost of the boat is for a particular number of people and that each extra person will be charged a fixed amount – you should make things very clear to avoid argument. We got one letter from a traveller quoting 50,000 to 70,000 rp to charter a boat from Labuhanbajo to Komodo and back as the norm (for five people) – that sort of price is ridiculous!

RUTENG

Another stop on the way through Flores. For spectacular views of the hills and valleys to the north – rice padddies, terraced slopes and distant pools of clouds – there is a hill to the north of Ruteng which you should climb in the early morning; head down the road leading to Reo and about 10 minutes from the Wisma Agung you will come to a small bridge across a stream – turn right and head up the track immediately after the bridge to get to the top of the hill.

Information

The Bank Rakyat Indonesia will change foreign cash (like US and Australian dollars) and major travellers' cheques so long as they're in US dollars. The bank is open Monday to Friday 7.30 am-12 noon, and on Saturdays 7.30 to 11 am The post office is at Jalan Baruk 6. Merpati (tel 147) is located on Jalan Pertiwi 15 (tel 147) – they have a bus which will take you to the airport for 1000 rp per person.

Places to Stay

The *Wisma Agung* (tel 80) at Jalan Wae Cos 10, is the best place to stay with singles from 4000 rp and doubles from 5500 rp. The *Losmen Karya* is a decent little place but it always seems to be 'full' – they don't really want foreigners; singles 3000 rp, doubles 4000 rp. The *Wisma Sindha* is much the same standard as the Agung, but more expensive; doubles only for 6000 rp and 8500 rp.

Places to Eat

The *Rumah Makan Agung* run by the Wisma Agung is a pleasant place at the back of the Toko Agung in the middle of town. The Wisma Agung will also send out to the Rumah Makan Agung if you'd prefer to eat at the hotel. The *Rumah Makan Indonesia* is at the bus station – the menu is limited but servings are large and it's decent food, cheaper than the Rumah Makan Agung – less than 1000 rp will get you a very filling meal of rice, egg, fried chicken, roast meat, green vegetables and a bowl of stewed meat.

Also try the *Rumah Makan Dahlia* at the bus station and the string of little warungs by the adjacent market including the *Warung Suka Damai*, *Warung Sudimanpir* and *Warung Tungku-Mose*.

Getting There

Buses and trucks depart from the station next to the market and do the usual picking-up rounds about town. To get out of Ruteng get to the station early – around 7 am. Either front up at the bus station or catch one roaming around the streets, or else buy a ticket beforehand at one of the agents – these are usually shops in central Ruteng like the Toko Orion which charge you an additional 500 rp on top of the normal fare.

Trucks to Reo are 1000 rp, or occasional buses for 1250 rp. It takes only four hours to get down to Reo and you should be able to get a truck in the early afternoon. From Reo you can take a boat to Labuhanbajo – see the Reo section for more details. There are trucks going to Labuhanbajo from Ruteng but avoid this road in the wet.

Buses to Bajawa are 3000 rp and take about 6½ to seven hours; to Ende is 4000 rp and about 12 hours. These depart around 8 to 9 am. The road from Ruteng to Bajawa makes the strip of bitumen from Sumbawa Besar to Bima look like an eight-lane freeway. In parts you'd think they built this track by pushing a truck through the jungle leaving two tyre marks for the others to follow. Only when you get out onto the coast and start climbing into the hills that hug the southern coastline do you start getting views of the string of active and extinct volcanoes that run along the southern coastline – they're at their most spectacular coming into Bajawa in the early evening.

REO

On an estuary a little distance up from the sea, Reo is just an oversized village. Focal point of Reo is the large Catholic mission in the middle of the town.

Places to Stay & Eat

The *Losmen Telukbayur* (tel 17) at Jalan Mesjit 8 is a decent little two-storey place. Singles/doubles are 3000/6000 rp. The toilets and mandis could be cleaner but the rooms themselves are OK. The top floor rooms are probably best if you want to avoid the herds of staring kids. The losmen has its own warung.

Getting There

Daily trucks operate between Reo and Ruteng – the ride takes four hours and costs 1000 rp. The whole route might be surfaced by the time this edition is out. If you're coming in on the boat from Labuhanbajo there may be a bus or truck waiting at the dock to take people up to Ruteng. There's also a bus run by the Toko Garuda Mas in Reo; tickets are 1250 rp.

Look around the river for small boats going to Labuhanbajo – these seem to be fairly regular and cost 2000 rp per person. For boats to Maumere or further afield you may have to go to the port of Kedindi which is five km away from Reo.

BAJAWA

A little town nestled in the hills, coming in on the road from Ruteng you'll get a spectacular view of the great volcanic Mt Inerie – a spectacular sight in the setting sun. Nearby is Mt Wolobobor – an extinct volcano with the top half shaved off.

Apart from the spectacular scenery on the way into Bajawa, the main attraction of the area are the traditional houses and odd *ngadhu*. You can see a *ngadhu* in Bajawa at the end of Jalan Satsuitubu – it's basically a carved pole supporting a conical shaped thatched roof – looks like a large umbrella. A short distance out of Bajawa on the road to Ende you'll see four *ngadhu* lined up in a row in a village. The *ngadhu* appear to play some sort of role in ancestor worship, and are also kept to guard against sickness descending upon the village. They also play a role in preserving fertility – both human and agricultural – a sort of all-round 'tree of life'. Day-trip to the village of Soa to visit the Sunday afternoon market.

Information

Tickets for Merpati flights are available from the agent in a shop next to Bajawa market – the shop is diagonally across from the bus station – you'll see the sign on the 2nd floor.

Places to Stay & Eat

The *Wisma Johnni* on Jalan Ahmad Yani is a decent little place and has a friendly manager. Singles for 2500 rp, doubles for 3500 rp; for rooms with attached mandi and toilet a single is 3500 rp and a double is 7000 rp. Eat at the *Rumah Makan Beringin* on Jalan Busuki Ruhmat – not much to choose from but there's nothing else around. Stock up on fruit at the market.

Getting There

Many buses between Bajawa and Ende – the fare is 3000 rp, the road is fairly good and the trip takes six hours. Do the trip during the day, since you pass by the spectacular volcanic Mt Alaboba, and travel through a region of deep valleys and rolling hills. Heading in the other direction, transport west to Ruteng is the same problem as getting out of Ruteng – wake up early to catch a bus or truck. Fares are listed on a large sign at the Bajawa bus terminal. Bajawa to Ruteng is 3000 rp.

ENDE

The capital of Flores is a dull and dusty town – it's easy to see why the Dutch exiled Sukarno here in the 1930s. The revolting beach improves as you walk west from the town centre. Whilst the town isn't much it may be worth coming here to check out the weaving – Ende has its own distinctive style, and examples of Jopu, Nggela and Wolonjita weaving can also be found in the main street market near the waterfront.

Information

The Bank Rakyat Indonesia on Jalan Jend Sudirman will change various types of foreign cash but will only change US and Australian dollar travellers' cheques of major companies like American Express and Thomas Cook. Merpati is on Jalan Nangka, a 15 minute walk from the airstrip. There are frequent bemos which will drop you off at the intersection next to the airstrip, then you have to walk.

Places to Stay

Ende has a number of places to stay in, though few of them are particularly good.

Losmen Ikhlas is on Jalan Wolowona which is the road out to the airstrip. It's very basic, but clean and singles/doubles are 1000/2000 rp. Friendly people here.

Losmen Makmur, also on Jalan Wolowona, is basic but OK – mandis and toilets could be cleaner. Beds have mosquito nets and it costs 2000 rp per room (rooms have three beds each). It's quite good but right next to a mosque.

Backing onto the bay *Losmen Karya* (tel 8) at Jalan Pelabuhan 20 is a bit of a hole in the wall but will probably do for a night or two. Rooms on the ground floor are OK, but avoid the ones on the top floor which are full of cobwebs. Toilets and mandis in this losmen are somewhat slimy. Singles 2000 rp, doubles 4000 rp.

Losmen Hamansyus, on a small street running off Jalan Soekarno, down near the waterfront is an OK place. Downstairs rooms are bearable – just. Upstairs rooms are somewhat better. But wherever you are the noise is utterly horrendous! Normally it's quieter after 11 pm, but then starts again with a wakeup call from the mosque around 5 am. Try to avoid this losmen if you can, unless you're deaf.

Singles 2000 rp, doubles 5000 rp. They also serve food here including nasi campur at 600 rp and ayam goreng at 500 rp.

Wisma Dui Putra is on par with Wisma Wisata, but centrally located. It's a nice place run by the same family that runs the Depot Ende. Rooms from 7500 rp, plus 10% tax. *Wisma Wisata* (tel 368) at Jalan Kelimutu 68 is the best hotel in Ende. Worth the money but a long way out (bemos use this route so there's no trouble with transport except at night). Singles 8000 rp, doubles 10,000 rp – carpeted rooms with attached mandi and toilet and well worth the money.

Losmen Solafide at Jalan Onekore 2 is a bit out of the way but would certainly be quieter than staying in town! A variety of rooms here with two to four beds each, some with attached mandi and toilet, from 3300 rp and up.

Hotel Flores at Jalan Jen Sudirman 18 looks like it's in the first stages of becoming an archaeological dig. A real dump from the outside – could have been a former warehouse by the looks of things. But not too bad inside. Singles are 2500 rp, doubles 5000 rp.

Places to Eat

There are many warungs set up in the evening around the market serving satay, rice and boiled vegetables. Apart from that, the eating establishments of Ende are just bare rooms with bright lights – though they do have pretty good food. Try the *Rumah Makan Terminal* which is a clean, pleasant place right next to the bus and bemo terminal. Extensive menu, a bit expensive but excellent food. The *Rumah Makan Padang Indah* on Jalan Hatta has friendly staff and is a bit cheaper than the Rumah Makan Terminal, but there's not much to choose from.

Getting There

Frequent and regular buses go from Ende to Mone for 850 rp, to Maumere 3000 rp, to Bajawa 3000 rp, to Wolowaru 1100 rp. Other possibilities from Ende include boats to Labuhanbajo and to Waingapu on Sumba Island – ask around the harbour near the bus and bemo station.

Getting Around

Bemos fares around town are a flat 100 rp. The bemo terminal to the airport is 100 rp. Pelabuhan Ipi is one of the ports of Ende and is about 2½ km from the town. To get to Pelabuhan Ipi you can catch one of the frequent bemos to the junction of Jalan Wolowona and the road leading to Ipi – fare is 100 rp. From that junction the pier is a 15-minute walk. There may be bemos all the way to Ipi in the early morning to take people to the boat, but this is not a regular route.

KELI MUTU

This extinct volcano is the most fantastic sight in Nusa Tenggara if not all of Indonesia. The crater has three lakes – the largest is bright light blue, next to it a deep aqua green, and a bit further away a deep maroon lake. Chemicals in the soil account for this weird colour scheme. Best time to see Keli Mutu is in the early morning as clouds settle down later on and you need strong sunlight to bring out the colour in the maroon lake. If you get a really bad day – or if you get to the top too late in the day – the clouds will have covered the lakes and you won't be able to see anything at all!

Getting There

In Ende you can charter a bemo to take you to the top of Keli Mutu and back – but you'd be looking at 30,000 or 35,000 rp for the round-trip. To hire a bemo ask around the bus station, ask the drivers – its not hard to get a bemo, just hard to get one at a good price. It takes two hours to drive from Ende to the top of Keli Mutu.

You could also take a regular bus from Ende; get off at the turnoff just a km before you get to the village of Mone. The walk to the top will take three hours from here. Leave your bag in the seismologists' hut at the base of the mountain – a short walk from the main road.

Probably the easiest way of doing it is to walk – base yourself in Mone and head off – I was advised to leave Mone at around 2 am so I'd be up on the mountain top by 5 am not long before the sun came up, and some time before the clouds start rolling over. The road is surfaced all the way – you can walk it easily in the dark, but it's probably a good idea to have a torch (flashlight). There's only a short stretch right at the top which is not surfaced – just rocks and gravel. Some people have found motorcyclists in Mone and paid them 5000 rp to take them up to the top and back. If you go up on your own motorcycle watch for potholes and stray animals tied to the side of the road, often stretching their leash across it. Another possibility is to hire a horse in one of the villages on the way up to the top (one village is near the seismologists' hut and the other is further up the mountain). The walk from Mone to the top of Keli Mutu takes right on three hours. The road is not steep, just endless and wearisome. Entrance fee to the mountain is 100 rp per person, which you pay at the PPA post halfway up. There is one great advantage of walking up Keli Mutu – the mountain is by no means heavily touristed and if you walk up (as opposed to being driven up in a bemo along with how many other Indonesians decide to come along for the ride), you'll probably have the whole mountain to yourself!

MONE

Mone is a little village and mission on the Ende-Maumere road and at the base of Mount Keli Mutu. About one km out of Mone on the Ende side is the turn-off road leading to the top of Keli Mutu (a sign hangs over the start of the road – you can't miss it) – it's a 15 minute walk from Mone to the start of this road.

Places to Stay

The *Wisma Kelimutu* is next to Mone's large church and is run by the church. It's very basic – just rooms with cots (blankets provided) – but it's clean and quite comfortable. Best of all, it's quiet! Singles for 3000 rp, doubles 6000 rp. They will also serve you three meals a day for an extra 2000 rp per person – rice, noodles, fish, vegetables and tea – and eggs for breakfast.

Getting There

Mone lies on the Maumere-Ende road. The first buses to Maumere start coming through Mone around 9 am or 10 am. Mone to Maumere costs 1500 rp and takes about 4½ hours including a half hour break for lunch in Wolowaru. Buses to Ende come through Mone around 12 noon; Ende to Mone is about 2½ hour's by bus. Mone to Wolowaru is a half hour drive.

WOLOWARU

Wolowaru is an oversized village 12 km from Mone on the road to Maumere. From Wolowaru a road leads off to the villages of Jopu, Wolonjita and Nggela. As you come into Wolowaru from Ende, note the complex of five traditional houses, the *rumah adat*, distinguished by their high sloping roofs.

Places to Stay & Eat

There's one losmen in Wolowaru, the *Losmen Setia* which is an OK place. Singles 2000 rp, doubles 4000 rp. There are three cheap rumah makan here; the *Jawa Timur*, the *Bethania* and the *Selera Kita*.

Getting There

There are a couple of buses based in Wolowaru running to Maumere and to Ende. Some of the shops in the vicinity of the losmen act as agents. The Rumah Makan Bethania for example is agent for a Maumere-Ende bus; also try the Toko Sinar Jaya. Fares are Wolwaru-Ende 1000 rp, Wolowaru-Maumere 2000 rp, Wolowaru-Mone 250 rp.

Otherwise hang around the Ende-Maumere road and wait for a bus coming through in the direction you want to go. You should be able to get one either to Maumere or to Ende around midday – but don't expect anything in the late afternoon or in the evening.

WOLONJITA, JOPU & NGGELA

Beautiful and intricately woven sarongs and shawls can be found in these and other small villages. It's an interesting and pleasant walk from Wolowaru to these villages – so long as you avoid walking in the heat of the day. The volcano-studded skyline is beautiful and near Nggela, which is perched on a clifftop, there are fine views of the ocean. Wolonjita has similar sarongs to Nggela but doesn't have Nggela's fine views. Nggela also has a number of traditional houses in the village.

The chief attraction of Nggela is the stunning weaving – all hand done and still using natural dyes. You'll have to bargain hard; for one large sarong the starting price was 100,000 rp – you should be able to knock it down to half that amount. A shawl could be picked up for around 20,000 to 25,000 rp. Nggela sarongs are also sold in the market at Ende.

Jopu weaving has taken a plunge in the last few years. They no longer use natural dyes and the designs are not so intricate as they used to be – once upon a time you used to get soft pastel oranges and yellows, but now the yellows are egg yolk-bright and the cloth is splotched with garish red or bright red borders. Jopu sarongs are sold in the market at Wolowaru but there seems to be lots of junk around.

Getting There

There is a rough road leading all the way from Ende to Nggela via Wolowaru, Jopu and Wolonjita. There are irregular vehicles from Ende to Nggela (for 1500 rp) and you may also be able to hitch a ride on a truck – otherwise walk from Wolowaru. At Wolowaru there is a dirt road which leads off to Jopu four km away, and to Wolonjita which is a further four km. From Wolonjita there is also a dirt track leading downhill and across the paddy fields to Nggela – a 50-minute walk. You can easily get from Wolowaru to Nggela and back in a day, even if you have to walk both stretches.

There is a daily boat from Pelabuhan Ipi in Ende to Nggela leaving at 8 am – the trip takes two hours and the fare is 500 rp. Buy your ticket on the boat.

MAUMERE

Maumere is a port on the north-east coast and a stopover on the way through to Ende or to Larantuka. Wander down to the large church near the Losmen Bogor, which has an interesting series of pictures here adorning the walls illustrating the crucifixion of a very Indonesian-looking Jesus – God is not always a white man. Behind the church is an interesting old cemetery. Maumere market is in the middle of town and is worth some photographs. You'll also find the heavy Maumere blankets on sale here – ask the old women. Worth checking out is the village of Sika which has its own distinctive style of weaving; a bus from Maumere is 500 rp and takes one hour.

About 24 km from Maumere is Ladelero. This is a major Catholic seminary from where many of those Florinese priests are ordained. The chief attraction is the museum, run by Father Piet Petu, a Florinese. The museum has been going for around 20 years – and over the past few years Piet Petu has built up a collection of ikat weaving from Sikka, Jopu and other parts of Flores – you'll see examples here of design and natural dyes that are either rare or extinct. The museum also has an interesting collection of artifacts from all over Indonesia including ceremonial swords from Kalimantan, statues from Irian Jaya, Chinese and western imported porcelein. Buses to Ladalero from Maumere cost 200 rp and take 15 minutes.

Information

Bouraq (tel 167) has its office in Losmen Beng Goan. Merpati (tel 242) is on Jalan Ahmad Yani, a 10 minute walk from Losmen Bengoan. The Pelni office is across the road from Losmen Bogor.

Places to Stay & Eat

Losmen Beng Goan (tel 247) on Jalan Pasar Baru across from the market is a good place and fairly quiet. Singles from 3000 rp and doubles from 5000 rp. Beds have mosquito nets and the hotel also has a laundry service.

Losmen Bogor is a good place – one street up from the shoreline and across the bridge on the road leading up to the large cathedral. Singles and doubles are the same price at 4400 rp.

Wisma Flora Jaya is a good place with friendly people, but could be rather noisy and it's expensive for what you get. Singles/doubles are from 5000/10,000 rp. Close by on the same street is *Losmen Maiwali* with large rooms; singles 3500 rp, doubles 7000 rp.

There are lots of small rumah makan around the perimeter of the market – just look around until you find something you like.

Getting There

Buses between Maumere and Larantuka cost 3500 rp and take about five hours. Buses to Ende are 3000 rp. Trucks do the trip from Maumere direct to Wolojita on occasion. Buses and bemos leave from around the perimeter of the market. Maumere airport is three km out of town, on a street leading off the Maumere-Larantuka road.

Ships sail between Maumere and Ujung Pandang and Surabaya from time to time. Occasionally, boats go to other parts of Flores – like Reo and Labuhanbajo. Try around the harbour area due north of the Losmen Benggoan.

LARANTUKA

This little port nestles at the base of a high hill at the eastern end of Flores; from here you can see Solor and Adonara Islands across the narrow strait. There's not a great deal to see here; outside the Church of Kepala Maria is an old Portugeuse cannon and bell – both painted a ghastly silver.

Information

The post office is a long way out, past the main market. Take a bemo from the centre of town opposite the main wharf along Jalan Niaga and Jalan Pasar – 100 rp to the post office. The approximate opening hours are Monday to Thursday 8 am to 2 pm, Friday 8 to 11 am, Saturday 8 am to 12.30 pm.

Jalan Niaga is the main street, running along the waterfront. The Merpati office is diagonally opposite the large church on the street running parallel to Jalan Niaga. They provide a taxi which will take you the 10 km to the airport for 1500 rp per person.

For information on boats out of Larantuka go to the harbour master's office on Jalan Niaga. Boats leave from the wharf just near the harbour master's office. Also ask around the pier and at the Pelni office on Jalan Niaga. Passenger boats depart almost just about every day from Larantuka to the islands of Lembata, Adonara and Solor, and there are boats twice a week to Kupang in Timor.

Places to Stay & Eat

Losmen Rullies is one of the friendliest and convivial places I've stayed in Indonesia. Singles 2750 rp, doubles twice that.

Hotel Tresna looks better from the outside than it actually is. Basic, but clean and relatively new. Singles 3000 rp, doubles 6000 rp.

Wisma Kartika is a rather seedy looking place, but if the Tresna or the Rullies are full or you want something cheaper then it's OK – could get a lot of street noise though. Singles 2000 rp, doubles 4000 rp.

For food try the *Depot Nirwana* on the main street. Apart from that there's a nameless warung just down from the Wisma Kartika, but all they seem to have is fried and curried chicken and it's surprisingly expensive.

Getting There

Buses between Maumere and Larantuka cost 3000 rp. If you're coming in on the boat from Lembata or one of the other islands there'll probably be buses waiting to take passengers to Maumere. There are twice weekly boats between Larantuka and Kupang in Timor – see the section on Kupang below for details.

LEMBATA

The terrain of Lembata Island is strongly reminiscent of Australia – the palm trees of the coast giving way to gum trees in the hills. Lewoleba is the main town. Lamalera, on the south coast, is a whaling village. The villagers still uses small row boats and the hand-thrown harpoon to hunt these creatures.

Places to Stay & Eat

The only place to stay in Lewoleba is an OK losmen called the *Penginapan Rejeki*; singles for 2500 rp, doubles 5000 rp. There's a large map of Lembata on the wall in the front of the losmen. Meals at the losmen are excellent – three meals a day here will cost an extra 1000 rp per person – and you get rice, fish, meat, vegetables, squid and egg. The manager will fix you up with a guide if you want one to go hiking. You can safely leave your excess baggage with the manager. At Lamalera you should be able to stay with the missionary – or ask the kepala desa for somewhere to stay.

Getting Around

The easiest way to get to Lamalera is on the regular boat from Lewoleba, each Monday. Or, you can walk from Lewoleba to Lamalera. There are two roads – the long one and the short one. For the short one you head out of Lewoleba and ask directions for the nearby village of

Namaweke. If you simply ask for the road to Lamalera you could end up being directed along the main road which follows a wide circular route around the island. It takes about six or seven hours to walk to Lamalera from Lewoleba along the short route.

Getting There
Boats to Lewoleba depart daily from Larantuka at 8 am – fare is 1500 rp. The trip takes about 4½ hours including a 45 minute stop to load and unload passengers at Waiwerang. Boats from Lewoleba to Larantuka depart every day except Mondays at 7 am.

SUMBA
This dry island is one of the most interesting in the Nusa Tenggara group and is noted for the large decorated stone tombs in the graveyards found here. Sumba is also famous for its *ikat* blankets with their interesting motifs – including skulls hanging from trees, horse riders, crocodiles, dragons, lions, chickens, monkeys and deer.

GETTING THERE
Flights operate from Bali, Timor, Flores and Sumbawa to the main centres of Waikabubak and Waingapu. Merpati flights include Waingapu to Tambaloka (the airport of Waikabubak) for 26,000 rp; Bima 42,400 rp; Kupang 54,200 rp; Ende 32,800 rp; Denpasar 74,600 rp. Bouraq flights include Waingapu to Denpasar 74,600 rp; Kupang 54,200 rp; Surabaya 89,000 rp.

The Pelni ship *KM Baruna Fajar* sails from Waingapu to Sabu (on Sawu Island) to Kupang (on Timor) about once every two weeks. Waingapu to Kupang is 10,700 rp and Waingapu to Sabu is 6,150 rp. There are occasional ships between Waingapu and Ende.

GETTING AROUND
Waingapu and Waikabubak are the two main centres on the island. There are generally a couple of buses per day between Waingapu and Waikabubak; the fare is 2500 rp. The trip takes about 6½ hours, including a half hour stop for munchies. Try to book a day or two in advance – the hotels will usually book you a ticket or go to one of the bus agents. There are generally regular bemos to villages in the vicinity of these two towns. Merpati flies between Waingapu and Tambaloka (the airport of Waikabubak) for 26,000 rp.

WAINGAPU
There's nothing much to do in Waingapu, but it has some reasonable hotels and restaurants and is a good place for day-tripping to the interesting villages in the surrounding area where the blankets are made and where the stone tombs can be found.

Most blankets are blue, red and white – the pastel oranges and browns are only occasionally seen. There's a band of almost incredibly persistent middle-men working the streets of Waingapu with sacks full of blankets. They lay siege to your hotel, hanging around all day and half the night; every blanket is the 'Number One' blanket; artificial dyes are used to make instant 'antique' blankets; and asking prices are exorbitant although they will bargain. If you want a good blanket then *wait* – they'll eventually bring out the better stuff.

Information
The Bank Rakyat Indonesia in Waingapu will change American and Australian travellers' cheques and will change various types of cash.

Merpati (tel 180) is at Jalan Mutawai 20. Bouraq (tel 21820) is at Jalan Yos Sudarso 49. Pelni is located at the port of Waingapu – take a bemo there for 150 rp – goes straight past the office.

Places to Stay
Probably the best place is *Hotel Elim* (tel

32) at Jalan Ahmad Yani 55 – run by a Chinese man and his charming wife, who speaks some English. Rooms start from 4500 rp. *Hotel Surabaya* (tel 125) at Jalan Eltari 2, is an OK place but a bit overpriced – and it's too near the mosque. Bargain your room rate – the manager changes his prices day to day. Singles from 4500 rp and doubles from 7000 rp.

Hotel Sandlewood (tel 117) on Jalan Matawai is a good place. The owner speaks some English. Most of the rooms are expensive (though worth the money) but there are some available from 4000/6000 rp for singles/doubles.

You can also check out *Losmen Lima Saudara.*

Places to Eat

Possibilities are pretty much restricted to the hotels unless you want to go down to the area near the port. The *Hotel Surabaya* has a fairly extensive menu; cap cai for 1250 rp, udang for 1500 rp, nasi goreng istemiwa for 1000 rp. The *Hotel Sandlewood* has a fairly extensive menu – and like the accommodation is slightly up market – fried young pigeon at 2500 rp; fried frog in butter at 2000 rp. The *Hotel Elim* also provides evening meals.

Getting Around

Bemos from the town centre to the airport cost 100 rp, from the town centre to the port 150 rp. A taxi from the airport to the town centre costs 2500 rp.

AROUND WAINGAPU
Rende

Rende village is the sight of several traditional-style buffalo horn adorned Sumba houses and a number of massive carved stone graves. You're charged 500 rp as a sort of 'admission fee' to the village. Take an early morning bus from Waingapu – these buses go at around 7 am. If you miss this bus, then take a colt to Melolo for 1000 rp (takes two hours) and then walk from Melolo to Rende – seven km and about 1½ hours – take a water bottle!

Umabara

Umabara has several traditional Sumba houses and tombs. A few minutes' walk down the track from Umabara is the village of Pau, which also has a number of traditional houses. Umabara is a half hour walk from the village of Melolo, which is split by a river and the road to Umabara leads off from the Waingapu side. Have the colt driver drop you off at the start of this road.

Kaliuda

One of the ikat weaving centres of the area, though the place where most of the weaving is done is just before the village itself. To get to Kaliuda take an early morning bus heading in the Kaliuda direction from Waingapu (departure is around 7 am); you can then spend about two hours looking around Kaliuda before taking the same bus back to Waingapu – the bus will probably be packed as it comes back through Kaliuda on it's way to Waingapu – you have to insist on being picked up.

WAIKABUBAK

Waikabubak is a neat little town full of old graves carved with buffalo-horn motifs and many traditional houses. One of the attractions of western Sumba are the mock battles held near Waikabubak each year. At the village of Lamboya traditional Sumba horseback mock battles are held every year during February; the village is 20 km from Waikabubak. At Wanokaka the battles are held in March. At Rua Beach, 30 km south of Waikabubak, the 'pasola' festival is held in March – a kind of jousting match on horseback, rather dangerous.

Information

The agent for Merpati is in the centre of town, on Jalan Ahmad Yani. Waikabubak's airstrip is at Tambaloka. The Merpati taxi will take you there for 1500 rp per person – it's the only reliable way of getting out here to get your flight.

Places to Stay & Eat

Losmen Pelita is basic but clean – singles for 2500 rp, doubles 5000 rp. Meals cost an additional 2500 rp per person, per day.

Wisma Rakuta is a pleasant place with large rooms with big double beds and with attached mandi and toilet; singles 7500 rp and doubles 12,500 rp. The manager speaks some English and is good for information – he's also an amateur photographer and has some good photos of the yearly mock battles held on the island.

Rumah Makan Bandung specialises in soto ayam to the exclusion of everything else – there doesn't seem to be any other eating places around, not even warungs.

AROUND WAIKABUBAK
Anakalang

Twenty km from Waikabubak is the village of Anakalang with its large graveyard. Anakalang is also the site of the *Purung Takadonga* – a mass marriage festival held once every two years. In 1984 it was held on 21 June – but the actual date is determined by the full moon and it's different each time. There are regular bemos from Waikabubak to Anakalang – the trip takes about one hour and costs 500 rp.

Prai Bokul

Almost opposite the Anakalang graveyard is the road leading to the village of Prai Bokul, an hour's walk away. In Prai Bokul you'll find the *Umbu Sawola* tomb – a structure carved out of a single piece of rock and then mounted on supports. The slab cost 4,000,000 rp and took three months to carve; 250 buffalo were sacrificed. The base of the stone is about five metres long, four metres wide and a bit less than a metre thick.

TIMOR

The first Europeans to land in Timor were the Portuguese in the early 16th century. The Dutch occupied Kupang in the middle of the 17th century and after a lengthy conflict the Portuguese finally withdrew to the eastern half of the island in the middle of the 18th. When Indonesia became independent in 1949 the Dutch half of Timor became part of the new republic, but the Portuguese were still left holding the eastern half.

On 25 April 1974 there was a military coup in Portugal and the new government set about discarding the Portuguese colonial empire; within a few weeks of the coup three major political parties had been formed in East Timor. A brief civil war between the rival parties Fretilin and UDT – after the UDT attempted to sieze power in August 1975 – saw Fretilin come out on top. However, a number of top generals in the Indonesian army opposed the formation of an independent East Timor and on 7 December 1975 Indonesia launched a full-scale invasion of the former colony – hardly a coincidence that this happened just one day after US Secretary of State Henry Kissinger had cleared out of Indonesia after a brief visit – presumably having put the good world-keeping seal of appproval on the invasion.

By all accounts the Indonesian invasion was brutal; Fretilin fought a guerrilla war with marked success in the first two or three years – but after that began to weaken considerably. Nevertheless the war continues to this day, though just how many Fretilin guerrillas remain is unknown. The number of East Timorese killed in the fighting, or through starvation or disease due to disruption of food and medical supplies, has become a tug of war in itself – no one has really been in a position to take a body count but figures of 100,000 or more East Timorese dead would not be unreasonable.

GETTING THERE

Kupang, the capital of Timor, is well connected by air with other parts of Indonesia – both Garuda, Merpati and Bouraq fly to the city. Garuda flights to

Kupang include Denpasar 92,600 rp; Jakarta 182,000 rp; Surabaya 124,000 rp; Yogyakarta 141,500 rp. Merpati has various connections from Kupang to other parts of Nusa Tenggara including Maumere 31,600 rp; Larantuka 42,400 rp; Waingapu 54,200 rp; Bajawa 55,300 rp.

There are twice-weekly ships between Larantuka in Flores and Kupang. The fare is 7500 rp and the trip takes 14 hours. These ships go Larantuka-Kupang-Waiwerang-Larantuka. The mission ship *Ratu Rosari* is still plying the water on it's three week run from Kupang to Surabaya via Larantuka and other islands in Nusa Tenggara – you may be able to get a passage on board this ship if you're in the right port at the right time.

The Pelni ship *KM Baruna Fajar* sails from Waingapu to Sabu (on Sawu Island) to Kupang (on Timor) about once every two weeks. Waingapu to Kupang is 10,700 rp and Waingapu to Sabu is 6150 rp.

GETTING AROUND

There's no telling how long it will be before you'll be able to travel freely in Timor again. At the moment most of the island is off limits to foreigners, with the exception of places close to Kupang like Soe. For most other places you require a permit (a *surat jalan*) from the military command in Kupang (see the Kupang section for details). Places like Dili and Atambua require a permit, which they won't give you. Nevertheless, when I was in Timor I got on a bus at the Kupang bus terminal which was bound for Atambua – no hassles, no checks, no roadblocks, no nothing. However, on reaching Atambua I was taken by the guy at the losmen to register with the police and the military. The latter said I had to have a surat jalan from Kupang, and since I didn't have one they put me back that same night on the bus to Kupang.

The war in East Timor has also benefitted your arse; the road from Kupang to Atambua via Soe and Kefamenanu (and I understand all the way to Dili) is now well-surfaced all the way. Once upon a time the roads in Timor were really rotten, and it was odds on whether the Portuguese half was more or less neglected than the Indonesian half prior to the invasion. In the eastern half of the island they had a regular bus (well, they called them buses) services between Bacau and Dili. From Dili on towards the western (Indonesian) half of the island the roads got progressively worse and transport more difficult to find. In the wet the unbridged rivers were completely impassable by vehicles and you had to do some walking. Once you'd crossed into the Indonesian half things improved but only a very little – the roads were still impossibly rough bone-shakers and it was a very long day's bus ride between Atambua and Kupang.

Bus Buses out of Kupang depart from the Kupang Bus Station to various destinations around western Timor, including Atambua on the old border. The Laguna Inn and the large Fuji film shop across the road from the bus station, are agents for the night bus 'Horus' which runs from Kupang to Atambua every second day. It departs Kupang at 9 pm and the trip takes seven hours, costing 5000 rp. Other buses to Atambua depart from the bus terminal around 7 am – then do a tedious 1½ to two hours doing the picking up · rounds – Kupang to Soe is 1500 rp, and Kupang to Atambua is 4500 rp. Kupang to Atambua should take around eight to nine hours – including a meal stop and an hour or so doing the picking up round.

Air Merpati has flights from Kupang to various parts of Timor including Dili 34,700 rp; Baucau 62,600 rp; Occusi 31,400 rp. Also flights from Kupang to the island of Roti south of Timor for 20,700 rp; and Kupang to Sawu Island for 36,700 rp.

Boat Boats depart from Kupang Harbour at least every second day for the Termanu Oelaba at Bau on Roti Island. The fare is around 6000 rp and you buy your ticket on the boat on the day of departure – go down and ask a couple of days before when the boat will leave.

KUPANG

Kupang is the biggest town on the island and capital of the southern group of Nusa Tenggara islands. If you've been on the other islands of Nusa Tenggara for any length of time then Kupang comes as something of a shock – compared to the sedate little towns of Flores or Sumbawa, this is a booming metropolis. It's not a bad place to hang around — Captain Bligh did, following his misadventure on the Bounty.

Information

The Bank Dagang Indonesia down near the waterfront on Jalan Soekarno will change cash and travellers' cheques. The Bank Rakyat Indonesia, also on Jalan Soekarno, does not change travellers' cheques but will change some foreign cash.

The post office is also on Jalan Soekarno, diagonally across the road from the Bank Rakyat Indonesia.

For permits to travel elsewhere in Timor, you have to go to the Komando Daerah Militer – XVI Udayana at Komando Resor Militer – 161/Wirasakti. This place is a five minute walk up the road which splits off from the junction of Jalan Soekarno and Jalan Jendral Urip Sumahardjo – the junction is near the enormous Bank Indonesia building. Some places in West Timor you can visit without a permit – like Soe. For Atambua, Dili and Oecusi you require a permit and they won't give you one.

Bouraq (tel 21820) is at Jalan Sumatera 27. Garuda (tel 22088) is supposed to be located on Jalan Kosasih – if you can find it! There are a couple of Garuda agents around though, like the Gajahmada Travel Service (tel 22522 and 22622) in the Wisma Susi. The Mission Aviation Fellowship has an office in the airport terminal. Merpati (tel 21121, 21961 and 22654) is at Jalan Soekarno 15 – right next to the Kupang Bus Terminal.

Pelni is at Jalan Pahlawan 5. The Harbour Master's Office is at the harbour at Jalan Yos Soedarso 23 – open Monday to Thursday 8 am to 1 pm, Friday 8 am to 10.30 pm and Saturday 8 am to 12 noon.

Places to Stay

Accommodation in Kupang is some of the more expensive in Nusa Tenggara, and there's not a great deal at the bottom end to choose from.

The *Wisma Nusantara* (tel 21147) is at Jalan Tim Tim 8 – basic but OK. Somewhat out of the centre, but not too inconveniently so – you can walk in or take a bemo for 100 rp. Singles 4000 rp, doubles 8000 rp (with attached mandi and toilet).

The *Hotel Adian Natardas*, which is just back from Jalan Jendral Urip Sumarhardjo (near the junction with Jalan Soekarno), is a decent place and the rooms even have bathtubs! But it's overpriced and the buildings are already starting to look shoddy. Singles 7500 rp, doubles 15,000 rp.

The *Laguna Inn* (tel 21559, 21384) on Jalan Gunung Kelimutu is around the corner from the *Natardas*. It's an OK place and should be fairly quiet – but very basic. Singles and doubles (with fan and attached mandi and toilet) are 8000 rp.

The *Wisma Susi* (tel 22172) at Jalan Sumatera 37 is OK but nothing special. Singles from 4500 rp and doubles from 6500 rp.

Places to Eat

Try the Chinese-run snack shop next to the *Losmen Nusantara*; the *Rumah Makan Mirasa* is 10 minutes further down the road and is run by a friendly fellow. More interesting though are some of the places down on the waterfront – like the *Rumah Makan Pantain Karang* and next door the *Restaurant Karana Mas* on Jalan Siliwangi, near the corner with Jalan Soekarno.

Getting Around

Kupang's chief bus and bemo terminal is on the corner of Jalan Soekarno and Jalan Siliwangi – down on the waterfront.

A bemo from Eltari Airport to the centre of Kupang is 150 rp. Bemos may wait outside the terminal building, otherwise just walk out under the 'Selamat Datang' sign 100 metres to the main road leading to the city, and wait there. There's good food and decent sized servings of local delicacies.

Kupang Harbour is about seven km from the Bus Terminal. A bemo from the bus terminal will take you straight to the harbour for 150 rp, and drop you off right at the harbour master's office at Jalan Yos Soedarso 23.

SOE

Soe is a dull sprawl of wooden and corrugated-tin-roofed houses – but it would be worth taking a day trip up here to get a look at the western Timorese countryside. There are frequent bemos and buses to Soe from Kupang terminal – they leave from around 7 or 7.30 am and the trip takes about 2½ to three hours – coming back it could take three or four hours, depending on the slackness of the driver.

KEFAMANANU

A forgettable (and a forgotten) place – just a through town on the way to East Timor. If you stop here there is at least one losmen, the Losmen Setangkai, which also has a warung.

ATAMBUA & ATAPUPA

The major town and port at the eastern end of the originally Indonesian half of the island. When travel in East Timor was still possible, nearby Atapupa was the first town inside the Indonesian half and a good place for finding boats to travel to the other islands.

There are a couple of places to stay in Atambua – two of which date back as far as the 1975 edition of South East Asia on a Shoestring. One of these is the Wisma Sahabat at Jalan Merdeka 7 – basic but clean, and fairly friendly people. Singles for 3300 rp, doubles 6600 rp, Meals are an additional 900 rp, per day per person. Nearby is the Wisma Liurai. The other place mentioned in the old guide is the Losmen ABC, which is still a going concern. Eat at the Rumah Makan Sinar Kasih which is a five minute walk from the Wisma Sahabat – quite a long menu and decent sized helpings at decent prices. There are also a couple of warungs of unknown quality in the vicinity of the Wisma Sahabat.

DILI

The old capital of the Portuguese half of the island was a pleasantly lazy place in pre-invasion days. From here you could sidetrip to Same, a spectacular trip south. Ermera was a coffee growing centre on the road towards the Indonesian half. On the coast beyond Dili there was an old Dutch fort in the town of Maubara. Back in the pre-invasion days Dili had a range of hotels but the travellers headed en-masse for the open fronted hut on the beach where you could unroll your sleeping bag and stay forever for a first night charge of about a dollar. A wooden sign over the front correctly identified it as the Hippie Hilton!

BAUCAU

The second largest town on the Portuguese half, Baucau was the site of the international airport and was a charmingly rundown old colonial town. The altitude makes it pleasantly cool and the beaches, five km sharply downhill from the town, are breathtakingly beautiful. An interesting sidetrip from Baucau is to Tutuala on the eastern tip of the island. This village has interesting houses built on stilts, plus spectacular views out to sea. There is an old Portuguese fort at Laga, a town on the coast en route to Tutuala. Another sidetrip is down to Viequeque close to the south coast. On the way you pass Venilale with Japanese WW II bunkers outside the town. Apart from Dili and Baucau the only accommodation at this end of the island used to consist of the odd Portuguese guest house or 'pousada' and cheap hotels in Ermera and Maliana.

Kalimantan

The southern two-thirds of the island of Borneo, Kalimantan is a vast, jungle-covered, undeveloped wilderness. Apart from the area around Pontianak and the region from Samarinda to Banjarmasin there are few roads. The boats and ferries are the chief form of long-distance transport on the numerous rivers and waterways , although there are also plenty of flight connections. Some of the coastal cities have their own remarkable attractions – like the canals of Banjarmasin and the fiery orange sunsets over Pontianak – but on the whole, other than as a diversion between Sulawesi and Java, it is the native Dayak tribes of the inland areas that are the main reason for coming to Kalimantan.

GETTING THERE

Air Bouraq, Merpati and Garuda all fly into Kalimantan and there are lots of flights from other parts of Indonesia. Garuda flights include Jakarta-Banjarmasin for 100,000 rp, Jakarta-Pontianak 81,400, Jakarta-Balikpapan 128,200 rp, Ujung Pandang-Banjarmasin 145,600 rp. There are some interesting flight connections available – Garuda will fly you from Kupang in Timor to Tarakan on the east coast of Kalimantan same day; Bouraq will fly you from Ternate in the Moluccas to Balikpapan same day.

Ship There are shipping connections with Java and with Sulawesi, both via Pelni and other shipping companies. The Pelni ships *KM Tampomas* and *KM Kambuna* pull into various ports on the east Kalimantan coast, on their loops out of Java around Kalimantan and Sulawesi. Deck class fares on the *KM Tampomas* from Balikpapan are: Palu 11,700 rp; Toli Toli 15,300 rp; Tarakan 18,500 rp; Ujung Pandang 15,400 rp; Surabaya 21,900 rp. Next up the class IIB fares (which gives you a shared cabin) cost only slightly more than deck class.

Pelni's *KM Ilosangi* does a Pontianak-Jakarta trip once every 10 days, and takes two days and two nights. Deck class is 17,200 rp and includes food – no cabins available other than those you may be able to rent off the crew.

There are also regular ships between the ports on the east coast of Kalimantan to Pare Pare and Palu in Sulawesi. There are also regular passenger ships (about twice a week) between Surabaya and Banjarmasin – see the Banjarmasin section for details. Mahakan Shipping, Jalan Kali Besar Timur 111 in Jakarta, may be worth trying for more information on other ships to Kalimantan.

Leaving Indonesia from Kalimantan

It may be possible to enter and exit Indonesia through Kalimantan – but don't count on anything – and that applies to both air, sea and land crossings. If you try to enter Indonesia via Kalimantan you'll have to get an Indonesian visa beforehand as the entry points into Kalimantan do not issue tourist passes on arrival.

Merpati has a weekly flight from Pontianak to Kuching in Sarawak in East

Malaysia – the fare is 56,000 rp. Bouraq flies from Tarakan to Tawau in Sabah. There are daily longboats (long, narrow passenger boats powered by a couple of outboard motors) from Tarakan to Nunukan (7500 rp), and from Nunukan there are daily boats to Tawau (12,500 rp) – tickets from CV Tam Bersaudara on Jalan Pasar Lingkas in Tarakan.

Bouraq also has the occasional charter flight from Kalimantan to Singapore; Banjarmasin to Singapore (via Pontianak) 193,200 rp; Balikpapan to Singapore (via Pontianak) 155,000 rp. However since Pontianak, Balikpapan and Banjarmasin are not official exit points for foreign tourists don't expect to be able to leave this way. Union Oil has an air transportation service office at the airport at Balikpapan; they charter planes for direct flights from Balikpapan to Singapore – never know, you may be able to get on board . . .

GETTING AROUND

There are roads in the area around Pontianak and in the region from Banjarmasin to Balikpapan and Samarinda. Coastal shipping along the eastern coast of the province is also fairly easy to pick up. Going up river by boat into some of the Dayak regions is now relatively easy from Samarinda, but the further you go or the more off the track you go the more time you'll need. Small boats, ferries and speedboats use the rivers between some of the major towns and cities – for example there are daily ferries and speedboats between Banjarmasin and Palangkaraya, and longboats between Tarakan and Berau, and Tarakan and Nunukan.

There are flights into the interior with the regular airline companies (Merpati carries the bulk of the traffic) and there are also many flights with DAS (Dirgantara Air Service). Other possibilities include the planes run by the oil companies and the missionaries – if you're in the right place at the right time and ask the right person you might pick up a ride.

PONTIANAK

An interesting river city only 10 km from the equator, situated on the banks of the Kapuas River. It's a suprisingly large city, with a giant indoor sports stadium and a couple of big girder bridges spanning the river. Like Banjarmasin, it really needs to be seen from the canals, which criss-cross the whole city. Or walk over the bridge from Jalan Gajah Mada for a sweeping view of the river and the houses, and brilliant orange sunsets that make Bali sunsets look pathetic!

The city has a high proportion of Chinese, and there are many Chinese-owned shops around here selling porcelain and Chinese vases and amphoras, and gold and jewellery. From Pontianak take a trip northwards along the coast to Pasir Panjang, a lovely stretch of beach with clean, white sand and calm water, just back from the Pontianak-Singkawang road. Take a Singkawang-bound colt from Pontianak's Siantan Terminal – 2000 rp and the trip takes about 2½ hours along a nicely surfaced road used by lunatic colt drivers trying to break land, water and air speed records all at once.

Information

The main part of the city is on the southern side of the Kapuas River, in the region surrounding the Kapuas bemo terminal. In this vicinity you'll find several markets, a couple of hotels, airline offices, Pelni, banks, etc. From opposite the Kapuas terminal there are many small motorboats and a vehicle ferry to the opposite side of the river to Pasar Lintang, which is the site of Terminal Sintian, the main long-distance bus station.

DAS (tel 583) is at Jalan Gajah Mada 67. Merpati (tel 2332) is at Jalan Ir H Juanda 50A. Bouraq (tel 4011) is at Jalan Ir H Juanda 6. Sempati Airlines is at Jalan Sisingamangaraja 145. Garuda is at Jalan Rohadi Usman 8A and is open Monday to Friday 8 am to 4 pm, Saturday 8 am to 1 pm, Sundays and holiday 9 am to 12 noon. Pelni is on Jalan Pak Kasih on the southern bank of the river. For other ships inquire at the entrance to the port adjacent to the Pelni office.

Places to Stay

Accommodation in Pontianak is expensive – it always has been – but this has worsened over the last few years due to the disappearance of the cheaper places.

Backing onto the river opposite the Kapuas terminal is the *Hotel Wijaya Kusuma* (tel 2547) at Jalan Musi 51-53. It has singles for 7500 rp. It's a good hotel – largish rooms with fans and very clean with sweeping views across the river. But try and pick your room – avoid those facing the noisy street and get as far away as possible from the booming TV set. There's a Chinese nightclub downstairs, open every night until 12 – woefully soppy Chinese and Indonesian pop songs.

Not far away is the *Fatimah Guest House* (tel 2250) at Jalan Fatimah 5 – a pleasant place though quite basic. Singles are 8000 rp and doubles 12,000 rp and the rooms have a small attached mandi and toilet. Take a Gajah Mada bemo to get here.

A short distance west of the centre along the river is the *Pontianak City Hotel* (tel 2495) at Jalan Pak Kasih 44 which has singles and doubles from 13,200 rp, and for 17,500 and 19,500 rp with air-con. There's a large map of Pontianak in the foyer.

Places to Eat

The best places to eat are the warungs – of which there are untold numbers in this city. Good ones at the Kapuas Terminal – udang galah, ayam goreng, mixed vegetables, nasi putih for around 1500 rp. Try the night warungs on Jalan Pasar Sudirman for satay kambing (goat satay), and steaming plates of rice noodles, kepiting (crab), udang, ikan, vegetables – fried in a wok for 1000 rp. There are more foodstalls along Jalan Asahan. For thick fruit juices, try the place across the road from the Pontianak Theatre on Jalan

Pattimura – the iced avocado juice here is so thick it's like eating ice cream.

Getting Around

There are two main bemo stations in the middle of the city – the Kapuas terminal near the waterfront, and the other on Jalan Sisingamangaraja. Taxis for hire from alongside the Garuda office. Becaks aplenty – the drivers overcharge but they don't prey on you and they're not too difficult to bargain with.

Outboard motorboats depart from the Pasar Daging adjacent to the Kapuas bemo terminal and cross the river to the Pasar Lintang and Terminal Sintian – 100 rp per person. There is also a car and passenger ferry a short walk from the Pasar Daging which will take you over to Pasar Lintang – 100 rp per person.

There is a counter at the airport where you buy tickets for taxis into town – 4800 rp. Alternatively walk down the road in front of the terminal building – this brings you to the main road in Pontianak and from here you should be able to get a colt. The airport to the Kapuas terminal is a half-hour drive.

TARAKAN

Just a stepping stone to other places – it's an island town close to the Sabah border and was the site of bloody fighting between Australians and Japanese at the end of WW II. Unless you're really enthused about Japanese blockhouses, or want to try exiting Indonesia to Sabah, there's really no point coming to Tarakan. It's not a bad town (though one letter described it as a 'dump' which I thought was unfair) – just dull. Perhaps the most interesting thing I saw here was a house with old Japanese artillery shells painted silver and standing like garden gnomes on the front lawn. For details on getting to Malaysia from Tarakan see the section on 'Getting There' above.

Information

The Bank Dagang Negara on Jalan Yos

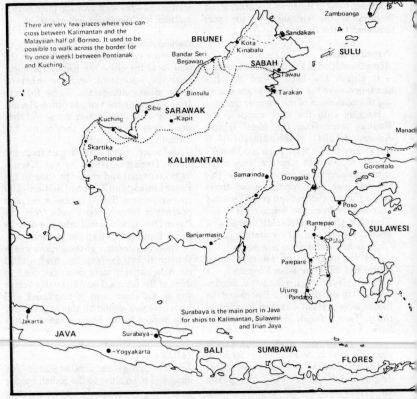

There are very few places where you can cross between Kalimantan and the Malaysian half of Borneo. It used to be possible to walk across the border (or fly once a week) between Pontianak and Kuching.

Surabaya is the main port in Java for ships to Kalimantan, Sulawesi and Irian Jaya

Sudarso will change some US dollar travellers' cheques and US, Malaysian and Singapore dollars cash.

Merpati (tel 568) is at Jalan Jendrel Yos Sudarso 48. Bouraq (tel 21148, 21216) is on Jalan Jendrel Sudirman. Pelni is located at the port – take a colt from the city centre almost to the end of Jalan Yos Sudarso.

Places to Stay
Theres a whole lineup of cheap and middle-range losmen and hotels along Jalan Jend Sudirman (also known as Jalan Kampung Bugis). These include the *Losmen Jakarta* (tel 21919) at No 112 which has little boxes for rooms but is otherwise quite a reasonable place to stay. At 1500 rp a single and 3000 rp a double you really can't complain. Experience the indigenous native way of life by filling your mandi with a hand-pump.

The *Barito Hotel* (tel 435) at Jalan Jen Sudirman 133, is a decent and relatively new place – basic but clean. Singles 4400 rp and doubles 5500 rp. The *Losmen Herlina* is basic but habitable – but avoid the dark, dismal downstairs rooms. Singles 3000 rp, doubles 4500 rp. The *Orchid Hotel* is OK, though the mandis could be cleaner. Singles 5500 rp, doubles 10,000 rp.

Furthur along the *Wisata Hotel* (tel 21245) on Jalan Jen Sudirman near the

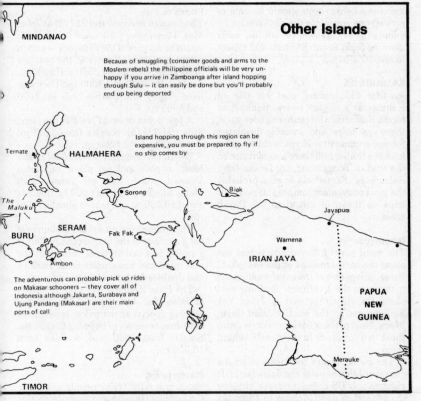

Other Islands

Because of smuggling (consumer goods and arms to the Moslem rebels) the Philippine officials will be very unhappy if you arrive in ZAMBOANGA after island hopping through Sulu – it can easily be done but you'll probably end up being deported

Island hopping through this region can be expensive, you must be prepared to fly if no ship comes by

The adventurous can probably pick up rides on Makasar schooners – they cover all of Indonesia although Jakarta, Surabaya and Ujung Pandang (Makasar) are their main ports of call

MINDANAO

Ternate HALMAHERA

The Maluku

Sorong Biak

BURU SERAM Fak Fak Jayapura

Ambon Wamena

IRIAN JAYA PAPUA NEW GUINEA

TIMOR Merauke

junction with Jalan Mulawarman, is a basic but pleasant place. Rooms at the rear are very quiet. Singles at 6000 rp, doubles at 9000 rp.

Around the corner the *Penginapan Alam Indah* (tel 19) on Jalan Yos Sudarso is very basic but quite good – singles 5000 rp and doubles 10,000 rp.

Places to Eat
There are various places to choose from on Jalan Jen Sudirman and Jalan Yos Sudarso. The *Rumah Makan Cahaya* on Jalan Jen Sudirman (across from the Losmen Jakarta) is memorable for the picture of the Mitsubishi Zero fighter plane on the wall; menu includes cumi

cumi (octopus) goreng at 2000 rp, cap cai goreng at 1500 rp, nasi goreng 1250 rp. There are cheap warungs at the juncture of Jalan Jen Sudirman and Jalan Sudarso – and stalls selling imported apples and oranges at 400 rp each! Best thing to do is just look around these streets until you find a restaurant with a price range to suit.

Getting Around
Transport around town is by colt – 125 rp flat rate gets you just about anywhere. From the airport buy tickets for taxis at the taxi counter in the airport terminal – it's 2500 rp to the city. Or walk down the airport turn-off road to the main road and

wait for a bemo – you should be able to pick up one going into the city (200 rp, 10 minute drive). If you've got an early morning flight to catch you should expect to charter a bemo.

SAMARINDA

Another old trading port on one of Kalimantan's mighty rivers. Balikpapan for oil, Samarinda for timber so once again there's a large and suitably insulated foreign community. If you want to get a look at a timber mill there's a giant one on the road to Tenggarong, not far out from Samarinda. Samarinda is also probably the most convenient jumping off point for trips up the river inland to the Dayak areas.

Information

The main part of Samarinda is laid out along the northern bank of the Mahakam River. The centre of town is the enormous mosque on the riverfront. Running east along the riverfront east is Jalan Yos Sudarso and to the west is Jalan Gajah Mada. Most of the offices and hotels are in these two streets or in the streets behind them.

The Bank Negara Indonesia is on the corner of Jalan Sebatik and Jalan Batur. It changes only US dollar travellers' cheques or cash and its open Monday to Thursday 8 am to 12.30 pm, Friday 1.30 to 4.30 pm, and Saturday 8 am to 11.30 pm

Merpati (tel 22624, 23895, 22965) is at Jalan Jen Sudirman 57. Bouraq is supposed to be at Jalan Mulawarman 12 – but they appear to have upped and moved – there are several Bouraq agents around like PT Angkasa Express at Jalan Awang Long 12/59.

For ships out of Samarinda try Pelni at Jalan Yos Sudarso 40/56. Also inquire nearby at the Terminal Penumpang Kapal Laut Samarinda, the Direktorat Jen Perhubungan Laut – both on Jalan Yos Sudarso and at the various shipping offices along the same street.

Places to Stay

The *Losmen Hidayah* (tel 21712) at Jalan Mas Temenggung 20 near the mosque would be my pick of the cheapies – spartan rooms but clean. Rooms at the rear are fairly quiet. Singles for 2500 and 3000 rp, doubles for 5000 and 6000 rp. They also have singles with double beds for 4000 and 5000 rp.

A few doors down at No 4 is the *Hotel Aida* (tel 22572). Singles from 3500 rp, and doubles from 7000 rp.

Worth checking out is the *Hotel Diana Mas*; a good-looking place on Jalan Veteran, which runs off Jalan Gajah Mada. Singles for about 6000 rp, doubles about 10,000 rp and triples about 13,000 rp.

The *Holiday Inn* on Jalan Pelabuhan is *not* a member of the famous chain. This is a rather less ostentatious version of the real thing and has singles from 9000 rp and doubles from 11,000 rp.

The *Hotel Andhika* (tel 22358, 23507) at Jalan Haji Agus Salim 37 is OK but nothing special at the price. It seems to have an over supply of booming televisions. Singles from 7000 and doubles from 10,000 rp.

Places to Eat

Samarinda is fruit city – people sit outside the Losmen Hidayah and along Jalan Mas Tenggarong carving giant nangka into manageable segments. A zurzat will cost you 500 rp and there are also pineapples, bananas and salaks in abundance. The other gastronomic wonder is *udang galah* – giant river prawns which you'll find in the local warungs.

There are many warungs in the evening along Jalan Niaga Selatan and in the vicinity of Losmen Hidayah. Try the *Restaurant Ramayana* on the corner of Jalan Yos Sudarso and Jalan Niaga Timor for good chicken curry at 2000 rp. The *Restaurant Gumarang* on the corner of Jalan Veteran and Jalan Jen Sudirman is highly recommended, especially for the freshly-squeezed fruit juices.

Getting Around

The long distance bus station is at Seberang on the southern side of the Mahakan River from the main part of town. To get there take a longboat from the pier at Pasar Pagi on Jalan Gajah Mada for 200 rp. It only takes a few minutes to make the crossing and they also have boats that take motorcycles across. The bus station is immediately behind the boat dock on the other side. From Seberang Station there are many buses to Tenggarong (800 rp) and to Balikpapan (1600 rp, two hours).

The airport is quite literally *in* the suburbs. You might think you're hard up when a freeway gets slapped down over your nature strip, but how many people have Twin Otters landing in their backyards? There is a taxi counter in the airport building – it's 3500 rp into the centre of town. Or, just walk out of the terminal down Jalan Pipit to Jalan Serindit and catch a public colt for 200 rp into the city. Getting out to the airport is the main problem – you should be able to catch a colt heading this way from the corner of Jalan Khalid and Jalan Panglima Batur – but beware of getting into empty colts unless you want to charter (or end up chartering) it.

UP THE MAHAKAM RIVER

Samarinda is probably the best jumping off point for visits to the Dayak tribes inland. Some of these are easily reached on the regular longboats that use the Mahakam River from Samarinda. The longboat dock in Samarinda is on Jalan Gajah Mada, opposite the large Bank Rakyat Indonesia and General Post Office. A good source of information about the Dayak areas is Adi Soepratno at the tourist office in Tenggarong – he speaks good English and is very friendly and helpful.

TENGGARONG

Situated 39 km beyond Samarinda, this little riverside town is noted for its sultan's palace, built by the Dutch in 1936 and now used as a museum. It's a somewhat unusual structure, constructed in the Leggo block-style of the period but it has some interesting exhibits. The palace is closed on Mondays; open Tuesday to Thursday 7.30 am to 2.30 pm, Friday 7.30 to 11 am, Saturday 7.30 am to 1.30 pm, Sundays and holidays 8 am to 2.30 pm. Admission is 100 rp.

Places to Stay & Eat

There are two places to stay down at the waterfront right on the boat dock. The *Penginapan Zaranah I* (tel 148) has singles for 2500 rp and doubles for 5000 rp. The *Warung & Penginapan Anda* (tel 78) has singles for 3000 rp and doubles for 5000 rp. There are a couple of rumah makans and warungs around the vicinity of the market and the boat dock, but nothing memorable.

Getting There

Colts to Tenggarong leave from Samarinda's Semperang bus station, across the river from the main part of Samarinda. The trip takes an hour, costs 800 rp and the colt pulls into the Petugas Terminal on the outskirts of Tenggarong. From here you have to get a 'taxi kota' which is another colt into the centre of Tenggarong for 200 rp. Guys with motorcycles will also take you in for 300 rp. The city taxis run between 7 am and 6 pm. It takes about 10 minutes to get from Terminal Petugas to Pasar Tepian Pandan, where you get off for the boat dock, palace and tourist office. Alternatively take a boat from Samarinda to Tenggarong from the pier in front of the mosque.

BALIKPAPAN

Apart from the clean, comfortable and highly insulated Pertamina, Union Oil and Total residential areas, Balikpapan consists of grubby backstreets and ravaged footpaths, both overrun by rampaging Hondas and Yamahas – a real culture contrast. The district north of the oil refinery, bounded by Jalan Randan Utara and Jalan Pandanwanyi is completely built on stilts over the muddy isthmus, and is connected by uneven lurching wooden walkways between the houses. The huge oil refinery dominates the city and when you fly into the place you'll see stray tankers and offshore oil rigs.

Information

A good landmark is the enormous Hotel Benakutai on Jalan Antasari near the shorefront, which is roughly the centre of town. Heading east from Jalan Antasari along the shorefront is the airport road; heading west along the shorefront is Kelandasan which runs into Jalan A Yani. Heading north Jalan Antasari merges into Jalan Sutuyo, Jalan Parman and Jalan Panjaitan, at the end of which is the Rapak Bus Terminal. Most of the hotels and offices can be found on these two streets.

The Bank Negara Indonesia on Jalan Antasari will change major travellers' cheques like American Express and Barclays, and various cash currencies. The bank is open Monday to Friday 8 am to 12 noon and 1.30 to 3 pm, Saturday 8 to 11 am. The branch office in the terminal of Seppingan Airport will also change money and travellers' cheques

There is a post office on Jalan A Yani open Mondays to Friday 8 am to 6 pm and on Saturdays, Sundays and holidays 8 am to 5 pm. The airport post office is open Mondays to Thursdays 8 am to 2 pm, Fridays 8 to 11 am, Saturdays 8 am to 1 pm, Sundays and holidays 8 am to 12 noon. The immigration office is on the corner of Jalan A Yani and Jalan Sudirman. For large and excellent maps of Balikpapan (1500 rp) go to the Cempaka Raya Agency on Kelandasan Ulu.

Merpati is near the Pasar Baru on the road leading out to the airport and is open Monday to Thursdays 8 am to 3 pm, and Fridays to Sundays 8 am to 12 noon. Bouraq (tel 21107, 21087) has an office in the enormous Hotel Benakutai on Jalan Antasari. Garuda is diagonally opposite the Hotel Benakutai. Pelni (tel 22187) is on Jalan Yos Sudarso.

Places to Stay

There's not much cheap accommodation in Balikpapan and what there is is usually taken over by resident Indonesians. Best bet is probably the *Penginapan Royal* not far from the Pasar Baru, at the beginning of the road to the airport and near the junction with Jalan Antasari. Basic but clean and it's a good location. Rooms at the back should be quiet, but avoid those in the front facing the main street. Singles 3500 rp and doubles 7000 rp. Also try the similar *Penginapan Fajar* (tel 22096), more or less diagonally across the road.

Worth trying is the *Hotel Sederhana* on Kelandasan Ulu – looks like a decent place and has recently had a new extension added. Singles 5400 rp, doubles 6600.

There's a string of places on Jalan Panjaitan. *Hotel Aida* (tel 21006) is clean and has singles from 6000 rp and doubles from 10,000 rp. Close by the *Hotel Murni* has singles/doubles for 6000/12,000 rp and looks like a decent place – but get a room at the back away from the main street. On the same street the *Penginapan Mama* looks OK but always seems to be full – doubles and singles for 3000 rp.

Other accommodation available is middle-range or up-market. On Jalan Panjaitan there's the *Hotel Tirta Plaza* (tel 22324, 22132) which has singles with fan and attached mandi/toilet for 10,000 rp and doubles from 13,000 rp. Fairly basic and probably noisy. The *Hotel Gajah Mada* (tel 21046) at Jalan Gajah Mada 108 looks pretty up-market with big beds and attached bathroom. Singles from 12,000 rp and doubles from 16,000 rp.

The *Hotel Kam Tim* on Jalan Mangonsidi is OK – singles and doubles for 12,500 rp. It's in the north-west of the city opposite the dock from where longboats and speedboats depart for Balikpapan's bus terminal on the other side of the water. Colts from the Rapak Terminal will take you straight to the hotel.

Places to Eat

One thing that Balikpapan has got to recommend it is good seafood masakan Padang places – although it tends to be expensive. Try the *Restaurant Masakan Padang Simpang Raya* next to the Hotel Murni. Similarly priced is the *Restaurant Salero Minang* at Jalan Gajah Mada 12B. Much the same price is the *Restaurant Sinar Minang* on Jalan Pangeran Antasari, marginally better than the Selaro Minang and also serves up udang galah. More unusual (for the decor) is the *Restaurant Roda Baru* near the Penginapan Royal – eat amidst a rockery featuring a kitsch collection of plaster storks and lit by a chandelier. Cheapest eats at the numerous warungs and food trolleys along Jalan Dondong near the Hotel Benakutai during the evening.

Getting Around

Jeep taxis – they look a bit like colts – cost 200 to 300 rp to get you anywhere around town. The chief station is the Rapak bus and bemo terminal at the end of Jalan Panjaitan – the jeep taxis do a circular route around the main streets. Guys also hang around the Rapak terminal with their motorcycles and will take you pillion-passenger anywhere you want to go.

Seppingan Airport is a fast 15-minute drive from Pasar Baru along a surfaced road. A taxi from the airport to town is around 4500 rp. In town you may be able to charter a jeep taxi for less – I got one from the Pasar Baru at the start of the airport road for just 2500 rp. Taxi seems to be the only way of getting out to the airport – it's right off the normal jeep taxi runs.

Buses to Samarinda (1600 rp) depart from the Rapak terminal. Buses to Banjarmasin (9200 rp) depart from the terminal on the opposite side of the harbour to the city – to get to this terminal take a colt from the Rapak bus station to the pier on Jalan Mangunsidi. From here take a speedboat to the other side. Cost is 1000 rp per person or around 3000 rp to charter and it takes 10 minutes. Alternatively, get a motorised longboat for 450 rp which takes 25 minutes. The bus terminal is immediately behind where the boats land.

There are various ships out of Balikpapan – for more details see 'Getting There' at the start of this section. For other ships to Surabaya try PT Ling Jaya Shipping (tel 21577) at Jalan Yos Sudarso 40 and PT Sudi Jaya Agung (tel 21956) at Jalan Pelabuhan 39. For ships across to Pare Pare in sulawesi go to PT Nurlina; the office is on the pier where you catch speedboats or longboats to the bus terminal on the other side of the harbour. Departures just about every day – the trip takes 20 hours and costs 17,500 rp.

BANJARMASIN

One of the most stunning cities in Indonesia , criss-crossed by canals lined with stilt houses, and buildings tacked on to the top of a bundle of floating logs lashed together. To look properly you have to see it from waterlevel – otherwise it appears to be like any other Indonesian city. Hire someone to paddle you round in a canoe – 1000 or 2000 rp for an hour or two should be more than enough – ask around the wharf near the junction of Jalan Lambung Mangkarat and Jalan Pasar Baru.

Check out the fortune-tellers and medicine men who inhabit the footpaths outside the Banjarmasin Theatre nearby. I'm still wondering about a guy who sat there tapping three inch nails into his nostrils at right angles to his face – followed by some fire-breathing before launching into a long spiel about the path to sexual prowess through the medicine he was flogging. As he spoke the nails gradually slipped out of his face.

In the middle of Banjarmasin is the Mesjid Raya Sabilal Muhtadin, a giant modern-art mosque with a copper-coloured flying-saucer-shaped dome and minarets with lids and spires sprouting out of an untidy lawn.

Information

Although Banjarmasin is a big place, almost everything you'll need is packed into a very small area in the region of the Pasar Baru, with several cheaper hotels along Jalan Ahmad Yani on the opposite side of the river.

The Bank Expor Impor Indonesia on Jalan Lambung Mangkurat will only change US dollar cash and travellers' cheques.

Garuda (tel 4023, 3885) is at Jalan Hasanuddin 11A. It's open Monday to Thursday 7 am to 4 pm, Fridays 7 am to 12 noon and 2 to 4 pm, Saturdays 7 am to 1 pm, Sundays and holidays 9 am to 12 noon. Bouraq (tel 4206, 3249) is at Jalan Lambung Mangkurat 40D. DAS (tel 2902) is across the road from Garuda at Jalan Hasanuddin No 6 Blok 4. Merpati (tel 4433, 4307) is at Jalan Suprapto 5A.

Places to Stay

At the lower end of the price scale, try the *Losmen Halidah* at Jalan Haryono 51. There's a friendly manager and the place looks quite good with singles/doubles at 2500/4500 rp and a good and cheap rumah makan attached.

Very central is the *Losmen Abang Amet* on Jalan Penatu – singles and doubles for 4000 rp. The place seems fine, the people are friendly but the hotel is always full.

Other than that there's not much cheap accommodation around. Some of the cheap places don't take foreigners, so you're left with medium-priced hotels – all pretty much alike really. The *Hotel Anda* on Jalan Suprapto has singles for 7000 rp and doubles for 12,000 rp. On the same street the *Rita City Hotel* (tel 2423, 4785) has singles from 13,500 rp and doubles from 18,500 rp – plus 20% service charge and tax – quite plain for the price.

The *Hotel Sabrina* (tel 4442, 4721) at Jalan Bank Rakyat 21 has singles for 7000 rp and doubles for 8500 rp with fan. A similar standard to the Sabrina but a bit more expensive are the *Banua Hotel* at Jalan Katsamo 8 and the *Perdana Hotel* at Jalan Katsamo 3.

There are a couple of OK places on the other side of the river from the Pasar Baru. These include the *Hotel Rahmat* on Jalan A Yani – basic but OK rooms. It's a sizeable place and the manager is friendly – singles from about 4000 rp and doubles from about 6600 rp. Close by on the same street the *Hotel Kuripan* has singles for 5000 rp and doubles for 7500 rp. Next door and about the same price and standard is the *Hotel Madiyati* (tel 3282).

Places to Eat

There's a whole string of cheap warungs and rumah makans along Jalan Veteran – places like the *Rumah Makan Sari Wangi* at No 70, the *Es Campur Flamingo* across the road, the *Rumah Makan Sari Rasa* a few doors up and lots of others the whole way along. At night there are many interesting warungs along Jalan Pasar Baru and Jalan Niaga in the area south of Jalan Samudra.

One of the better restaurants – though expensive by shoestring standards – is the *Restaurant Blue Ocean* on Jalan Hasanuddin. Its got a fairly varied menu and makes a change from the usual nasi goreng: fried chicken ball and mushrooms (ayam ca jamur) for 3500 rp; sweet and sour omelette with crab (fu yung hai) for 3500 rp; pork dishes for 3500 to 5000 rp; crab dishes for 3500 to 5000 rp; fried beef with oyster sauce or veggies for 3500 rp; fried pigeon for 3500 rp.

Getting Around

The central bemo station is at the Pasar Baru on Jalan Pasar Baru and from here you get bemos to various destinations around town. These include the KM 6 Terminal from where buses to Banjarbaru, Matapura and Balikpapan depart. The bemo fare from Pasar Baru to KM 6 is 150 rp. Buses and colts depart frequently from KM 6 for Matapura and Banjarbaru, and there are daily buses to Balikpapan (10,000 rp).

Banjarmasin becak drivers aren't predatory but they do ask hefty prices and are hard to bargain with – the *bajaj* drivers work in much the same way. Guys with motorcycles around Pasar Baru and KM 6 will take you wherever you want to go. If you're travelling light this is a good way to get out to the airport.

The airport is 26 km out of town on the road to Banjarbaru. To get there take a bemo from Pasar Baru to the KM 6 terminal, and then catch a Matapura-bound colt – get off at the branch road leading to the airport and walk the short distance to the airport. Alternatively a taxi all the way to the airport will cost you 6000 rp – get one from the cluster that hangs out near the Garuda office. From the airport to the city buy a taxi ticket at the counter in the airport terminal. Alternatively, walk out the airport building, through the car park, past the post office and the MIG aircraft, turn left and walk down to the Banjarmasin-Matapura Highway. From here you can pick up one of the Banjarmasin-Matapura colts into Banjarmasin.

There are regular ships (usually two per week) from Banjarmasin to Surabaya leaving from Pelabuhan Trisakti. To get there take a bemo from Pasar Baru for 150 rp, which will take you straight past the harbour master's office. Ticket agents for the ships are opposite the harbour master's office. Tickets are around 15,000 rp to 20,000 rp depending on which agent you go to. Agents for ships to Surabaya can also be found on Jalan Lambung Mangkarat, near the junction with Jalan Pasar Baru.

MATAPURA

Drop down to Matapura for a look at the market – a photographer's paradise on a good day – lots of colourfully-dressed Banjarmasin women. The market is behind the Matapura bus station; a few minutes' walk diagonally across the adjacent playing field is a diamond-polishing factory and shop – ask for the *Penggosokan Intan Tradisional KAYU TANGI*. You can get colts to Matapura from the KM 6 terminal in Banjarmasin for 500 rp. The trip takes about 45 minutes along a good surfaced road.

BANJARBARU

This town on the road from Banjarmasin to Matapura, has an interesting museum with a collection of Banjar and Dayak artifacts, and statues excavated from ancient Hindu temples in Kalimantan. The museum is open to the public on Saturdays and Sundays from 8.30 am to 2 pm – its really worth seeing but if you can't make it on one of those days go anyway – there'll probably be someone who'll open the place up and show you around.

CEMPAKA

Cempaka is 43 km from Banjarmasin. There's a creek bed here with people up to their necks in water panning for gold. Bemos from Matapura are infrequent (also enquire at the KM 6 terminal in Banjarmasin if there are any colts going direct to Cempaka). Or charter a bemo from Matapura bus station for 3000 rp-round trip with a brief stop at the creek.

Sulawesi

Sulawesi has rapidly become a very well known part of Indonesia due principally to the interesting Tanatoraja area in the south-western leg of this strangely-shaped island. Few visitors to Sulawesi get further than the southern area – travel is difficult or time consuming to the other areas, although it's getting easier with improvements in the roads and additional air transport. The Minhasa area of the northern limb of the island is interesting and there are some stunning coral reefs off the coast of Manado, the chief city of the region. But for most people Sulawesi is simply an Ujung Pandang-Tanatoraja loop.

GETTING THERE

Air There are air connections to various Sulawesi cities, chiefly to the capital of Ujung Pandang. Garuda, Merpati, Mandala and Bouraq all fly to Sulawesi. Most visitors either make Ujung Pandang a stepping stone between Java and/or Bali and the Moluccas and/or Irian Jaya. Alternatively you can make an out and back trip from Java or Bali – save a little cash if you're travelling Bali-Java and visiting Sulawesi too by flying Denpasar-Ujung Pandang-Surabaya.

Because of its central location there are all sorts of possibilities available with flights from Ujung Pandang to other parts of Sulawesi and to the other provinces of Indonesia. Flying Garuda, fares to Ujung Pandang include Denpasar 63,600 rp; Surabaya 85,800 rp; Jakarta 136,300 rp; Ambon 93,000 rp; Biak 179,600 rp; Jayapura 233,300 rp. Bouraq has flights from Ujung Pandang to central and northern Sulawesi and to Kalimantan and the Moluccas, including Balikpapan 89,200 rp; Gorontalo 97,600 rp; Manado 84,700 rp; Palu 49,200 rp; Pontianak 182,900 rp; Samarinda 116,600 rp; Tarakan 151,800 rp and Ternate 123,700 rp.

Ship There are Pelni ships to Ujung Pandang and other Sulawesi ports from eastern and western Indonesia. Chief amongst these ships are the new liners *Kerinci* and *Kambuna*, and the older *Tampomas* which pull into Ujung Pandang on their circuits out of Java. Depending on the ship you're on there are various stops including ports in Java, Sulawesi, Kalimantan and Sumatra.

Fares to Ujung Pandang on the *Tampomas* are;

from	I	IIA	IIB	Deck
Balikpapan	28,000	22,500	18,500	15,500
Pantoloan	30,000	24,000	20,000	16,500
Toli Toli	31,000	27,000	23,000	21,000
Tarakan	41,000	36,000	30,000	28,000
Surabaya	31,000	29,000	25,500	21,000

From Surabaya it's a day or two to Ujung Pandang and several days more round to Bitung (the port of Manado), with several stops in between. Because road transport in Sulawesi is still poor the coastal connections tend to be crowded. It's also possible to get across from Kalimantan to Sulawesi, with regular passenger ships from various east Kalimantan ports to Pare Pare, Donggala and Palu. Heading east, Pelni fares from Ujung Pandang start at about 23,000 rp to Ambon and 54,000 rp to Jayapura.

When looking for ships in any of the

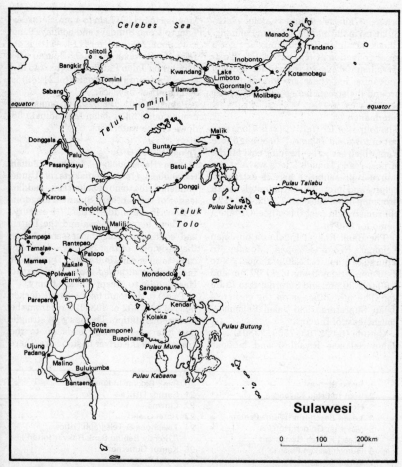

Sulawesi

Celebes Sea

Manado
Tolitoli
Bangkir
Inobonto
Tomini
Kwandang
Tandano
Sabang
Lake
Limboto
Kotamobagu
Dongkalan
Tilamuta
Gorontalo
Molibagu
equator   equator

Teluk Tomini

Malik
Donggala
Bunta
Palu
Batui
Pasangkayu
Poso
Donggi
Karosa
Pulau Taliabu
Pendolo
Pulau Salue
Teluk Tolo
Wotu
Malili
Sampaga
Rantepao
Tamalae
Palopo
Mamasa
Makale
Polewali
Enrekang
Mondeodo
Parepare
Sanggaona
Kendar
Kolaka
Pulau Butung
Bone (Watampone)
Buapinang
Pulau Muna
Ujung Padang
Malino
Bulukumba
Pulau Kabaena
Bantaeng

0   100   200km

ports check with the Pelni office first, and then check around the other shipping agents and around the ports. A really interesting trip would be by Makassar schooner – ask at Paotere harbour in Ujung Pandang or in Java at Surabya or Jakarta. Travellers also occasionally find them going to Nusa Tenggara. Fares are totally open to bargaining of course.

UJUNG PANDANG

The capital of Sulawesi province is also its foremost, grottiest, noisiest, dirtiest city. The Muslim Bugis are now the dominant group in Ujung Pandang, and the city is best known as the home of their magnificent prahus that trade extensively through the Indonesian archipelago. You can see some of these prahus at the Paotere harbour, a short becak ride north from the city centre, though they are no where as impressive as the awesome line up at the Pasar Ikan in Jakarta.

Other peculiarities include the brilliantly

ornate Chinese temples along Jalan Sulawesi in the middle of Ujung Pandang. Check out Jalan Sombu Opu – it's got a great collection of jewellery shops. Toko Kerajinam at No 20 is good for touristy souvenirs and there are lots of people around the streets here selling old coins.

Information

The tourist office (tel 21142) is a long way out of town, on Jalan A Pangerang Petta Rani which is a street heading east off the airport road. Though a long way out the tourist representative here is extremely helpful and informative – definitely worth dropping in on. Buses 301, 302, 303 (125 rp) run straight past this office. Or take a bemo for 200 rp.

The Bank Rakyat Indonesia on Jalan Selamat Riyadi is open Monday to Thursday 8 am to 12.30 pm and 1.30 to 2.30 pm, Friday 8 am to 11.30 pm and 1.30 to 2.30 pm, and Saturday 8 to 11.30 am. The post office is on the corner of Jalan Supratman and Jalan Selamat – southe-east of the fort.

Garuda (tel 22705, 7350, 22804) is at Jalan Selamat Riyadi 6 and is open Monday to Friday 7 am to 4 pm, Saturday 7 am to 1 pm, Sundays and holidays 9 am to 12 noon. Merpati (tel 4114, 4118) is on Jalan G Bawakareng 109. Bouraq (tel 5906) is on Jalan Pattimura 5 (next to the Hotel Pattimura). Mandala (tel 21289) is at Jalan Irian Jaya 2F.

Pelni (tel 7961, 7963) is in an unmarked, orange building at Jalan Martadinata 38 down on the waterfront.

Things to See & Do

Makam Hasanuddin – Tomb of Sultan Hasanuddin On the outskirts of Ujung Pandang is the tomb of Sultan Hasanuddin, leader of the southern Sulawesi kingdom of Gowa in the middle of the 17th century. Conflicts between Gowa and the Dutch had continued almost incessantly since the early part of that century – this only came to an end in 1660 when a Dutch East Indies fleet attacked Gowa and forced Hasanuddin to accept a peace treaty.

To get to the tomb take a double decker bus No 301, 302 or 303 (125 rp) from the central bus station. The bus goes straight past the street which leads up to the graves – ask the driver to stop here (there

1	Bemo Station	20	Bank Rakyat Indonesia
2	Boat to Palau Kayangan	21	Garuda Office
3	Hotel Benteng	22	Cinema
4	Losari Beach Inn (Wisma Pantai)	23	Hotel Grand
5	Makassar Golden Hotel & Losari French Restaurant	24	Telephone & Telegraph Office (Directly Behind Bank Rakyat Indon.)
6	Rumah Makan Fajar	25	Kantor Gubernor
7	Wisma Linggarjati	26	Hotel Purnama
8	Clare Bundt Orchid Garden	27	Bouraq
9	Hotel Victoria	28	Rumah Makan Pattimura
10	Restaurant Asia Bahru	29	Cinema
11	Big Mosque	30	Sports Field
12	Hotel Aman	31	Mandala
13	Merpati Office	32	PT Sutras Raya
14	Hotel Ramayana	33	Rumah Makan Malabar
15	Liman Express	34	Liman Express Head Office
16	Harapan Supermarket & Department Store	35	Hotel Sentral
17	Marannu City Hotel	36	THR Amusement Park
18	Entrance to Fort Rotterdam	37	Diponegoro Monument
19	Post Office	38	Schooner Harbour

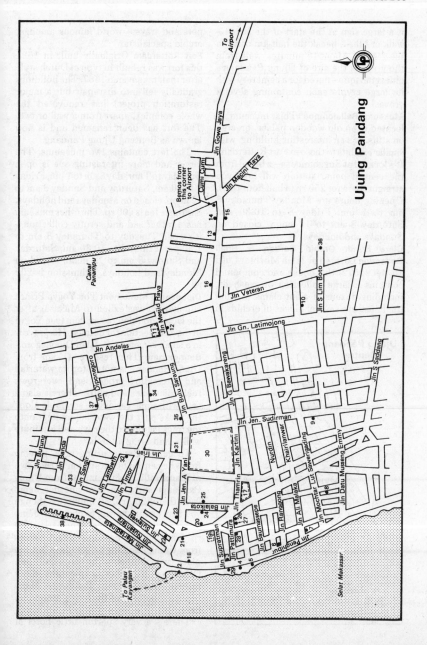

is a large sign at the start of the street – walk or take a becak the half km or so to the graves). About 15 minutes' walk from the grave is the site of Ujung Pandang's oldest mosque – noted for a cemetery with its large crypts each containing several graves.

Museum Ballalompoa This museum is located in an old wooden palace, erected on stilts. It's an interesting building, with similar exhibits to those in Fort Rotterdam. It's located at Suggominasa – a bemo from the central bemo station will take you straight there for 250 rp (a half hour ride). Opening hours are Monday-Thursday 8 am to 1 pm, Friday 8 to 10.30 am, Saturday 8 am to 12 noon, closed on Sundays and holidays.

Clara Bundt Orchid Garden & Shell Collection Located at Jalan Mochtar Lufti 15 (tel 22572) this house and compound contains a large collection of seashells, including dozens of giant clams. Behind the house are several blocks of orchids in pots and trays – world famous amongst orchid specialists.

Fort Rotterdam Originally built in 1634 this fort was rebuilt in typical Dutch style after their takeover in 1667. The buildings gradually fell into disrepair but a major restoration project has renovated the whole complex, apart from a wall or two. The fort has been renamed and is now known as Benteng Ujung Pandang.

The fort contains two museums. The larger and more interesting one is open Tuesday to Thursday 8 am to 1 pm, Friday 8 to 10 am, Saturday and Sunday 8 am to 12 noon, closed on Mondays and holidays. Entrance fee is 200 rp. The other museum has a rather sad and scruffy collection – it's open Tuesday to Thursday 8 am to 1.30 pm, Friday 8 to 10.30 am, Saturday and Sunday 8 am to 12 noon, closed on Monday and holidays. Admission is 200 rp.

Diponegoro Monument The Yogya Prince Diponegoro was exiled to Makasar after the Dutch double-crossed him (see Yogya in the Java section for details). His grave is in a small cemetery on Jalan Diponegoro.

Bantimurung This reserve 41 km from Ujung Pandang is noted for its waterfall and interesting eroded and overgrown rocky pinnacles and cliffs. There's also a cave with some carvings – scramble along the rocks past the waterfall and get onto the track leading to the cave – a 15-minute walk – and bring a torch.

To get to Bantimurung take a bemo from the central bemo station to the town of Maros (400 rp, 30 minutes from Ujung Pandang) and then take another bemo from there (200 rp, 30 minutes – though you may end up having to charter a bemo on a weekday). Entrance to the park is 300 rp. There might be some direct bemos from Ujung Pandang on Sundays but the place will probably be crowded out. Otherwise it makes a pleasant day's retreat from Ujung Pandang. Many beautiful butterflies fluttering around up here.

There's a very spartan little hotel at

Ujung Pandang
(Centre)

Jln Butung
Jln Sarrapo
Jln Banda
Jln Sangir
Jln Lembeh
Jln Timor
Jln Bali
Jln Sumbeh
Jln Serui Sama
Jln Marladinata
Jln Nigaera
Jln Sulawesi
Jln Jenderal A Yani

1 Hotel Nusantara	7 Chinese Temple
2 Restaurant at No. 185	8 Chinese Temple
3 Steak House Depot	9 Cinema (Theatre DKM)
4 Chinese Temple (No. 172)	10 Rumah Makan Malabar
5 Hotel Murah	11 Rumah Makan Empang
6 Chinese Temple	12 Schooner Dock

Bantimurumg – the *Wisma Bantimurung* with singles and doubles for 5000 rp. Lots of little shops around here sell soft drinks.

Places to Stay

Not a bad place, and close to the centre the *Wisma Linggarjati* on Jalan Ali Malaka has small but clean rooms with big double beds – but get a room back from the street. Singles and doubles for 7500 rp (with attached mandi and toilet).

Probably the best place to stay in Ujung Pandang is the *Hotel Ramayana* (tel 22165, 4153) on Jalan G Bawakaraeng, but avoid eating here since the food is hideously expensive. Take a bemo from the centre for 100 rp. Singles and doubles from 7000 rp.

The *Hotel Purnama* (tel 3830) at Jalan Pattimura 3-3A. Singles 6000 rp, doubles 9000 rp, extra bed an additional 2000 rp. Not a bad place – basic but clean – upstairs rooms are OK.

Further out the *Hotel Oriental* on Jalan Wr Mongisidi has singles and doubles for 5000 rp – nice clean rooms with attached mandi and toilet. Pots of tea at night (sometimes) and tea with condensed milk and fresh bread for breakfast are included in the price of the room. There are some good warungs in a street nearby, just ask at the hotel for directions.

The *Hotel Nusantara* at Jalan Sarappo 103 has singles for 2500 rp and doubles for 4500 rp (or if the singles are full and you're on your own they'll give you a double for 3000 rp). Rooms are sweat boxes – partitioned off from each other by masonite walls with the top enclosed by wire mesh. Hot and noisy, and grubby mandis too – a one-night-stand job at the most. Whilst it's a good central location, it's a bit like living in an anthill. Diagonally across the road is the similar *Hotel Murah* which has singles for 2500 rp, doubles for 5000 rp.

The *Benteng Hotel* on Jalan Supratman is a grubby place, though some rooms may be in better condition than others. Singles

6000 rp, doubles 8400 rp (with attached mandi and toilet).

The *Hotel Aman* is on Jalan Mesjid Raya across the road from the large mosque in the middle of Ujung Pandang. Singles for 3500 rp and doubles for 7000 rp. Clean rooms, but the mandi and toilets are a bit grubby – still better than the *Nusantara*. Generally it seems OK g,ood location – but avoid the front rooms as they face a horrendously busy street. It may be 'full' depending on whom you talk to.

The *Hotel Sentral* at Jalan Bulusaraung 7 is basic, noisy but clean. Singles/doubles are 4000/6000 rp and you could give it a shot, although it often seems to be 'full'.

Places to Eat

There are a couple of good seafood restaurants around Ujung Pandang serving ikan bakar (barbecued fish) and cumi cumi bakar (barbecued octopus) amongst other sea-going organisms.

Jalan Sulawesi is a good hunting ground for restaurants – notable is the little Chinese warung at Jalan Sulawesi 185. Also notable the *Steak House Depot* at No 178 though they have nothing resembling a steak. The *Rumah Makan Malabar* at No 290 advertises itself as a specialist in Indian food – what you get is a simple Indian curry, roti and rice here for around 2500 rp – which makes a slight change from Indonesian. Also worth trying are the dozens of night-time food trolleys that stretch along the waterfront south of the big Hotel Makassar on Jalan Pasar Ikan.

The *Asia Bahru Restaurant* near the corner of Jalan Latimojong and Jalan G Sala is a pleasant place to eat – and when you order a big fish you get a *big* fish! Dishes between 1500 and 3000 rp. Also try the *Rumah Makan Emping* at Jalan Siau 7 down by the harbour. Check out the warungs around the THR Amusement Park for a slab of ikan bakar with cucumber, peanut sauce and rice.

Getting Around

The main bemo station is at the northern end of Jalan Cokroaminoto, and from here you can get bemos to various destinations around Ujung Pandang.

Double decker buses (Nos 301, 302, 303) run from in front of the main bemo station, down Jalan Cokroaminoto and Jalan Sudirman, along Jalan G Bawakaraeng and past the Ramayana Hotel. They then turn along the airport road, and down Jalan A Pangerang Petta Rani. This has the tourist office and is the jumping off point for the tomb of Sultan Hasanuddin. There are bus stops in the city, but further along you just wave the bus down.

For short trips there are becaks – you really need them since Ujung Pandang is too big to do much walking. From the Hotel Ramayana to the waterfront 500 rp; from the bemo station to Fort Rotterdam 300 rp. Becak drivers tend to ask ridiculous fares – like 2000 rp for a simple 200 rp trip – though they bring the price down fast when you walk away. They're fearless drivers with your life in the frontline – getting into the traffic or cutting across streets during peak hour is a truly terrifying experience!

Bemos to Ujung Pandang's Hasanuddin airport (22 km out of town) go from the bemo station to the large intersection a few minutes walk east of the Hotel Ramayana, and then to the airport. They might detour to the airport, or just put you off at the start of the side-road leading to it – a few minutes walk. A taxi from the airport to the centre (buy your ticket at the taxi counter in the terminal) is 6000 rp. Or wander outside where you may find jeeps for around 5000 rp. Or walk down the road directly in front of the airport terminal to the main road leading to Ujung Pandang. This is a short walk – if you take a becak don't pay more than 100 rp. From there pick up a bemo to the city (300 rp) – these terminate at the main bemo station. There are several good cheap rumah makans out front and to the side of the airport terminal.

PARE PARE

A bustling seaport – a mini Ujung Pandang – but without the obnoxious traffic. For the most part though it's just a place to hang around for a boat to Kalimantan or to northern Sulawesi – more details below.

Places to Stay

The *Hotel Gandaria* (tel 98) at Jalan Bau Massepe 171 has singles and doubles (with attached toilet and shower) from 7500 rp – excellent value. A large detailed street map of Pare Pare hangs on the wall in the foyer of this hotel – photostat maps of Pare Pare can be bought just down the road from the *Gandaria* at the Toko ABC at Jalan Bau Massepe 183.

The *Tanty Hotel* on Jalan Hasanuddin is OK, basic but clean. The only problem is the belching television set in the foyer! Singles and doubles 7500 rp – but if you're prepared to pay that much you may as well go to the Gandaria and get your money's worth.

The *Hotel Siswa* (tel 21374) at Jalan Baso Daeng Patompo 30 is a great rambling run-down place. Rooms are thinly partitioned but should be OK for a night or two although the toilets and mandis could be cleaner! Singles from 2000 rp, doubles from 4000 rp. The hotel is only a 15 to 20 minute walk from the bus station.

A few doors from the Gandaria is the *Losmen Murni* at Jalan Bau Massepe 175 – a warehouse with boxes. Singles 2500 rp and doubles 5000 rp, but they probably won't take you. The losmen is only five minutes walk from the bus station.

The *Penginapan Palanro* and the *Penginapan AM* (tel 21801) are in the same building on Jalan Bau Meassepe – similar to the *Losmen Murah* with partitioned-off little boxes. Singles 2500 rp and doubles 5000 rp.

Places to Eat

The *Restaurant Sempurna* on Jalan Bau Massepe is a nice, clean place and pretty good value. Most dishes from the extensive menu are 1500 to 2500 rp – lots of seafood. The *Warung Sedap* is an ikan bakar specialist on Jalan Baso Daeng Patompo. There are various little warungs in the vicinity of the Hotel Siswa along Jalan Bau Massepe.

Getting There

Bus Regular buses from Ujung Pandang to Rantepao in Tanatoraja pass through Pare Pare. The best of these is usually reckoned to be Liman Express (tel 5851) which has an office on Jalan Laiya in Ujung Pandang. The Hotel Marlin on Jalan G Bawakaraeng (opposite the Ramayana Hotel) is an agent for this bus. The fare from Ujung Pandang to Pare Pare is 2500 rp.

In Pare Pare the bus companies have their ticket offices at the bus station. Buses from Pare Pare to Ujung Pandang 2000 rp; Rantepao 2500 rp; Palopo 3000 rp; Bone via Sengkang 1000 rp.

Ship The main reason to come to Pare Pare is to catch a boat to the east coast of Kalimantan (daily boats to one port or another) or to Donggala and Toli Toli in Sulawesi. There are ships around three times a week from Pare Pare to Donggala (20,000 rp – a two day trip) and Toli Toli (25,000 rp – a three day trip) in northern Sulawesi. For tickets and info try PT Bukit Harapanjaya (tel 21975) at Jalan Usahawan 51.

Pelni (tel 21017) is at Jalan Andicammi 130. The harbour master's office is on the waterfront on Jalan Andicammi, and several shipping companies have their offices here. Fares from Pare Pare to Kalimantan ports include Nunukan 30,000 to 40,000 rp; Tarakan 35,000 rp; Samarinda 22,500 rp to 25,000 rp; Balikpapan 20,000 to 25,000 rp.

There are plenty of other agents – they're easy enough to find – look around the bus station, at the harbour and along the main streets near the waterfront.

TANATORAJA

The Toraja Land area (also known as Tanatoraja or Tator) is about 320 km north of Ujung Pandang, a high mountainous area with beautiful scenery and a fascinating culture. The Torajas are now Christianised but they still retain strong animist traditions with traditional and complicated death ritual.

The first thing that strikes you in Toraja are the traditional Toraja houses, shaped like buffalo horns (an animal of great mythic and economic importance to the Torajas) with the roof rearing up at front and rear – similar to the Batak houses of Lake Toba in Sumatra. The houses are always aligned north-south with small rice barns facing them. There are a number of villages in the region still composed entirely of these traditional houses but most have corrugated tin roofs, and some have been built in strategic locations purely for the benefit of foreign tourists. The beams and supports of the Torajan houses are cut so that they all neatly slot together – and the whole house is painted (and carved on the older houses) with chicken and buffalo motifs – often buffalo skulls are used as decoration.

The burial customs of the Torajas are unique. Like the Balinese they generally have two funerals, one immediately after the death and the elaborate second funeral after sufficient time has elapsed to make the complex preparations and raise the necessary cash. Because they believe you can take it with you the dead generally go well equipped to their graves. Since this led to grave plundering the Torajas started to secrete their dead in caves (of which there are plenty around) or hack niches out of the rocks. The coffins go deep inside and sitting in balconies on rock faces you can see the tau tau – life size carved wooden effigies of the dead.

Makale (the capital) and Rantepao (the largest town) are the two main centres of Tana Toraja. There's a good road between them but elsewhere the roads are terrible – walking is a nice way of getting around.

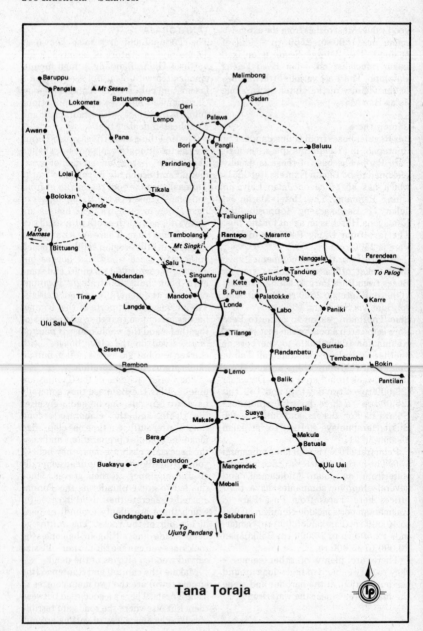

Tana Toraja

All the places to see are scattered around the lush green countryside around Rantepao – you've got to get out and explore.

Ask if there are any funeral ceremonies coming up while you're here. – they are worth seeing! The more important the deceased the more buffaloes that must be sacrificed – one for a commoner, four, eight, 12 or 24 as you move up the social scale. Pigs are also sacrificed. Animals ain't cheap either – a young buffalo is worth 175,000 rp and a medium sized one around 1,500,000 rp – size, fatness, solid black colour and good horns all push the price up; a large pig is worth about 85,000 rp.

The middle of the year – from around May onwards at the end of the rice harvest – is ceremony time in Tanatoraja; including funerals, house and harvest ceremonies – all of which may involve feasting and dancing, often buffalo fighting and the Torajan 'sisemba' fighting where the combatants kick each other.

Various people around Rantepao will take you to various ceremonies for a bargainable price. It's a good way of finding out what's going on – and if they speak enough English or if you speak enough Indonesian you can get some explaination of what's happening. You don't have to search hard for these guides – they'll find you. Often if you head off to these ceremonies on your own someone eventually hooks onto you and you're invited to sit down. Bring some cigarettes to offer around. There may be ceremonies or particular days in a ceremony where outsiders are not wanted – otherwise they all seem to be open to spectators.

Recently, government buildings and hotels have been built in traditional Torajan style, but they are not aligned north-south as tradition demands. The kids (and adults) demanding candy ('gula gula mister') can get on your nerves in Tanatoraja – and they can be bloody persistent about it too.

Shopping

Tana Toraja is the craft centre of Sulawesi. Look for interesting wood carving particularly panels carved like the decorations on traditional houses. They are always in the four colours: black, white, yellow and brown. You can get bamboo containers with designs carved and burnt on them – we keep spaghetti in a long one! Fabrics and sarongs are available in the villages or at shops in Rantepao.

RANTEPAO

A not very interesting town, but not a bad place to hang around and use as a base for tripping to the local sights. In Rantepao itself there's not much to do, though the main market and weekly cattle and pig market are interesting.

Information

The Bank Rakyat Indonesia is on the main street of Rantepao and is open Monday to Friday 7.30 am to 12 noon, and Saturday 7.30 to 11 am. They change cash and travellers' cheques but rates are lower than in Ujung Pandang. The authorised money changer in Rantepao gives slightly better rates than the bank and is faster – and will change both cash and travellers' cheques. Bring heaps of small change to Rantepao – no one seems to have it, not even the bank or the post office!

The post office is across from the Bank Rakyat Indonesia. It's open Monday to Thursday 8 am to 2 pm, Friday 8 to 11 am, and Saturday 8 am to 12.30 pm, Sunday closed. It also has poste restante.

Pelni has two agents in Rantepao – CV Antarissa Raya at Jalan Taman Bahagia 92 and another on Jalan Pahlawan near the corner with Jalan Sesean.

Places to Stay

Rantepao has a good selection of cheap hotels – good value, clean and usually comfortable. Quite a suprise after the dismal lot in Ujung Pandang. There are numerous places around, and the list below is just a sample of what's available.

One of the more favoured places with low-budget travellers is *Wisma Monika* on Jalan Ratulangi with singles for 2000 rp and doubles for 3500 rp (with mandi and toilet). It's an older, slightly tatty place, run by friendly people, and it's off the main streets and quiet.

Losmen Flora (tel 28) at Jalan Sesean 25 has friendly people, basic but clean and cheap. The only disadvantage is the early morning wake-up calls from the mosque across the road – and whatever you do don't take a front room because the street below is really noisy. Singles 2000 rp, doubles 4000 rp.

There are several other hotels on the road running off from the Jalan Sesan and Jalan Pahlawan intersection, like the *Hotel Marlin*. Highly recommended is the *Wisma Rosa* which has singles for 1500 rp and doubles for 3000 rp – with attached mandi. It's off next to the paddies just 10 minutes walk out of the centre, and should be quiet at night. Other places around Rantepao include the *Hotel Indra* (tel 97) at Jalan Pasar 63. The place is done out in a sort of traditional Tanatoraja-house style and rather nice. Singles 4500 rp, doubles 7000 rp.

The *Hotel Barita* at Jalan Pasar 55 is a bunker-style concrete block – but has good rooms with carpet, attached bathroom with real bathtubs! Single 5000 rp, doubles 6000 rp.

The *Wisma Nangala* (tel 91) at Jalan Taman Bahagia 81 has singles and doubles for 5000 rp – with attached bathroom. A good place to stay.

The *Hotel Victoria* at the corner of Jalan Sesean and Jalan Pahlawan has singles for 2000 rp and doubles for 4000 rp (with mandi). Rooms have attached bathroom and it's good value.

A bit north of the town centre is the *Wisma Surya* – clean and quiet and only 3500 rp a double – and even that's negotiable – plus you get morning and afternoon tea.

Places to Eat

Check out the market in the middle of Rantepao for local food – including bamboo tubes full of *tuak* (palm wine). At night try tuak in the warungs beside the market place. Tuak is tapped in the morning, carried into town in long bamboo containers (frothing at the top), left to ferment all day and drunk at night. It comes in a variety of strengths – from the colour of lemonade to the stronger orange or red.

If you tire of the kids asking for candy (kascis gula gula) indulge your own sweet tooth around Rantepao market. Try *wadi bandung*, a sweet rice-and-grated-coconut confection wrapped in paper. Or a *kajang goreng* – an almost oversweet concoction of peanuts and treacle (hard) wrapped in a dry palm leaf. Or a *baje*, a sticky rice-and-molasses mixture rolled in a dry palm leaf like a Christmas cracker. Going out to the ceremonies is a good chance to try black rice and pig and buffalo meat roasted in bamboo tubes over an open fire.

There are various restaurants, rumah makan and warungs around Rantepao. Good value is the *Kios Gembira* at Jalan Pembangunan 44 – a big nasi campur for 750 rp.

There are a couple of places with the 'Dodeng' title, but the original one is the *Chez Dodeng* just near the corner of Jalan Sesean and Jalan Pahlawan. It's run by a friendly guy named Bitty who speaks some English. He serves excellent food and drink, including a sort of ginger punch called *sarraba* which has almost the same effect as being hit on the head with a buffalo.

There are a couple of places around the back of the market including the *Kios Dodeng* and the *Rumah Makan Dodeng* on Jalan Pembangunan – good value and friendly people. There are also some cheap warungs and coffee/tuak places on the same street. For fantastic pork Torajan-style, local red rice (nasi merah) and tuak, try the *Warung Roma* on Jalan Pasar, just off the traffic circle on Jalan

Palahwan – its also got buffalo (kerbau) meat with peppers, all very cheap. The *Warung Ujung Pandang*, near the Liman Express Office, has a good nasi campur, kerbau curry, and excellent satay and is also very cheap aswell.

Getting There

Ujung Pandang to Rantepao For most people the next stop after Ujung Pandang is Tanatoraja. The road to Rantepao, the main town of Tanatoraja is now surfaced, and there are several companies running daily colts and buses there. The best of these is usually reckoned to be Liman Express (tel 5851) whose office is on Jalan Laiya in Ujung Pandang. The Hotel Marlin on Jalan G Bawakaraeng (opposite the Ramayana Hotel) is an agent for this bus. Bus fares from Ujung Pandang to Rantepao are 4000 rp on the night bus and 3500 rp on the day bus. Try and get a ticket a day in advance. The trip takes about nine hours – running via Pare Pare – including one or two brief stops at warungs.

Rantepao to Ujung Pandang There are various agents around with buses and colts down to Ujung Pandang via Pare Pare, and to Bone. Liman Express has its main office in the Hotel Marlin – daily departures to Ujung Pandang at 7 am (3500 rp) and 7 pm (4000 rp) – takes about nine to 10 hours from Rantepao to Ujung Pandang, but depends on how long you have to endure the picking-up round

Rantepao to Poso & Palu There are buses heading north from Rantepao through central Sulawesi to Poso and Palu. Ticket agents for these buses are located at the main intersection of Jalan Pasar and Jalan Taman Bahagia opposite the market – colts to Poso for 17,500 rp and to Palu for around 25,000 rp. For more information on the trip see the section below on central Sulawesi.

Getting Around

Central Rantepao is very small and easy to walk around. There are numerous becaks mobbed around the main intersection, but you probably won't have much use for them. Colts and bemos go to various destinations in the surrounding region – try to have the correct money since small change is scarce.

The roads to Makale, Palopo and Kete Kesu are all right, but the rest are awful. Some are constructed out of compacted boulders – you don't get stuck but your joints are shaken to pieces. Other roads, particularly in the wet, are real horror-show! Like the Rantepao to Sadan road which is only 13 km but takes an hour in the wet (if you don't get bogged).

Walking is easily the most comfortable means of travel although naturally somewhat slow. It should be possible to find a motorcycle for rent in Rantepao – ask in the restaurants and hotels – but allow two days' recovery after one day's riding! Alternatively a group could hire a jeep or charter a bemo for a day. Bemos run almost continuously from Rantepao to Makale and you can get off at the signs for Londa or Lemo and walk. There are also frequent bemos heading out towards Palopo for the sights in that direction. Bemos on the roads north of Rantepao aren't so frequent except on market days.

MAKALE

There's nothing really to Makale – though some people stay here just to be away from slightly larger and heavily-touristed Rantepao.

Places to Stay

There are a couple of places to choose from – all pretty similar but generally clean and basic. *Losmen Indra* (tel 43) at Jalan Merdeka 7 (also known as Jalan Jendral Sudirman) has singles for 3500 rp and doubles for 5000 rp. *Losmen Merry* on Jalan Pahlawan has singles for 3000 rp, doubles 6000 rp (without mandi). *Losmen Martha* on Jalan Pongtiku has friendly people – singles/doubles with attached mandi are 2500/5000. *Losmen Litha* on

Jalan Nusantara has paper thin walls and there's only a framework partition at the top. Singles 2500 rp and doubles 5000 rp.

Places to Eat

Not much around. Try the *Warung Maspul*, the *Kios Ermita* and the *Kios Asra* – none of them terribly exciting, but cheap.

Getting There

Frequent colts operate from Rantepao – the trip takes about 30 to 45 minutes depending on the number of stops for passengers and the fare is 350 rp. You can catch buses and colts direct from Makale to various destinations in Sulawesi. Ask the agents in the shops around central Makale – same destinations and prices as from Rantepao. Liman Express is at Jalan Ichwan 6.

AROUND RANTEPAO

The following places (distance in km from Rantepao) are all within fairly easy reach on day trips, but if you want to you can make longer trips staying overnight in villages as you go. If you do this don't exploit the Torajan hospitality – make sure you pay your share. Guides aren't necessary but if you want one they're easy to find – 3000 to 5000 rp per day seems to be the going rate; more for extended trips. It's better without a guide – the Torajans are friendly and used to tourists so they rarely bother you, and it's great to get out on your own in the beautiful countryside which surrounds Rantepao.

Karasbik (one km)

Situated on the outskirts of Rantepao, just off the road leading to Makale. The traditional-style houses here are arranged in a square, and apparently the complex was erected a couple of years ago for a single funeral.

Singki (one km)

A small hill just outside Rantepao – climb to the top for a panoramic view over the surrounding area.

Kete Kesu (six km)

Situated just off the main road south of Rantepao this is a traditional village with a reputation for wood carving. On the cliff face behind the village are some cave graves. There are also some very old hanging graves here – the rotting coffins are suspended from an overhang. The houses at Kete Kesu are decorated with more tourist souvenirs than you've probably ever seen . . . .

Sullukang

Just past Kete Kesu and off to the side of the main road is this village where there's a derelict shack on a rocky outcrop containing several derelict tau tau – almost buried under the foliage. There's also a *rante* here – large stone slabs planted in the ground – one of them about four metres high.

Londa (six km)

Two km off the Rantepao-Makale road, this is a very extensive burial cave, with a number of coffins containing bones and skulls. Kids hang around outside with oil lamps – 1000 rp (you could try bargaining but they're not very amenable to it) to guide you around. Unless you've got a strong torch you really do need a guide with a lamp.

Tilanga (11 km)

A natural cold water pool – there are several cold and hot springs in the Toraja area, and this one is very pretty. It's an attractive walk along the muddy trails and through the rice paddies from Lemo to Tilanga – but keep asking people directions along the way.

Lemo (11 km)

This is probably the most interesting burial area in Tanatoraja. The sheer rock face has a whole series of balconies carved out for the tau tau. The biggest balcony has a dozen figures – like spectators at a sports event. One tall tau tau stands on a slightly depressed section of floor so he can fit in. It's a good idea to go early in the morning so you get the sun on the rows of figures – by 9 am their heads are in the shadows. A bemo from Rantepao will drop you off at the road leading up to Lemo – a 15-minute walk.

Siguntu (seven km)
Another traditional village situated on a slight rise off to the west of the main road. It makes a pleasant walk from Rantepao via Singki to Siguntu and on to the main road at Alang Alang near the Londa burial site.

Marante (six km)
A very fine traditional village only a few metres off the road to Palopo.

Nanggala (16 km)
In the same direction – and rather further off the Palopo road – is this traditional village with a particularly grandiose traditional house with a whole fleet – 14 in all – of rice barns. Bemos from Rantepao take you straight there for 300 rp – or they might just drop you off on the main road and then it's a 1½ km walk.

Palawa (nine km)
A traditional village to the north of Rantepao.

Sadan (13 km)
A weaving centre, further out in the same direction. Bemos go there from Rantepao along a shocking road. The women here have a sort of tourist market where they sell their weaving.

Lokomata (23 km)
More caves graves, beautiful scenery.

Batutumonga (23 km)
A good viewpoint form where you can see a large part of Tanatoraja. Bemos go up here occasionally.

Others
Pangli (seven km) – house graves; Bori – funeral ceremony site; Pangala (35 km) – traditional village; Mt Sesean (25 km) – highest point in Tanatoraja.

THROUGH CENTRAL SULAWESI
A road bears eastwards from Rantepao to Soroako on the shores of Lake Matana in central Sulawesi. Mid-way along this road is the village of Wotu and just after Wotu another road cuts its way due north to Pendolo on the southern bank of Lake Poso.

The original track from Wotu was cut during WW II by the Japanese using Indonesian labour – there is a monument to the Indonesians at the top of the mountain pass at Perbatasan. Further roadwork has turned the track into a road of sorts and it is now possible to go all the way from Rantepao to Pendolo by colt.

Most of the Wotu to Pendolo road is literally cut through thick jungle and it's absolutely impassable two paces off the side. The road is abominable – constructed of rocks, gravel, mud, holes and more mud – colts have to be pushed out of metre-deep trenches. It took my vehicle 27 hours to get from Rantepao as far as Pendolo – bogged five times, three stops for food (two at warungs on the Rantepao-Wotu road and the other on the Wotu-Pendolo road), three stops to register with the police, one stop to sleep, two stops to repair the colt . . .

You cross Lake Poso on outriggers powered by an outboard motor. As a consolation prize the road from Tentena (on the northern side of the lake) to Poso is well surfaced. You can transport motorcycles on the Pendolo-Tentena boats – lashed to the side.

Some people actually walk from Wotu to Pendolo – 'Don't let anyone talk you into it,' wrote one traveller, 'unless you're crazy or run up and down a volcano every day before breakfast'. If you do walk it then get good, solid, high walking boots that give plenty of support to the ankles –

running shoes are a mistake. Carry a light pack – the road becomes a river after a shower. There's one warung about midway from Wotu to Pendolo and another about 30 km out of Pendolo – the colts pull into these for a rest stop. The sun is blistering hot and the air humid and steamy. When it rains it really rains. At night you sleep with 15 cm spiders that run away after you've stood on them and plenty of 10 cm long cockroaches. At night the jungle comes alive, the noise is indescribable – whatever is out there is in great number! You can try sleeping in-between flicking away the creepy-crawlies. Two guys I met in Manado tried hitching from Mangkutana (north of Wotu) to Pendolo – unaware of how bad the road was. It took them two days – including a 25 km walking stretch. And it pissed down with rain! One compensation for the hard work are the butterflies in this region – some as big as your hand and they'll flutter down and land on your finger.

An alternative to all this is to take the bus from Rantepao to Soroako (5000 rp along a very good road) and then fly with Merpati to Poso (32,800 rp) – but there only seems to be one flight per week.

PENDOLO

An overgrown village on the southern shores of Lake Poso. The fare on the outrigger across to Tentena on the northern side of the lake is 1500 rp. There are three places to stay in Pendolo, all close to the shorefront on Jalan Pelabuhan. The *Penginapan Sederhana* has singles for 1500 rp and doubles for 3000 rp – nice, clean, and friendly. The *Penginapan Danau Poso* is diagonally across from the Sederhana and of a similar standard – singles 1500 rp and doubles 3000 rp. The *Rumah Makan Cahaya Bone* has beds to crash on. As for eating, there's that and a few warungs along Jalan Pelabuhan.

TENTENA

Similar to Pendolo. There are at least three places to stay. The *Penginapan* *Wisata Remaja* and the *Hotel/Restaurant Puse Lemba* are both near the waterfront. Further away is the *Wisma Tiberias*.

POSO

Although it's the main town on the northern coast of central Sulawesi there's not much to be said about this town. It's fairly dull though not an unpleasant place.

Information

Merpati (tel 368) is on Jalan Yos Sudarso. The harbour master's Office (tel 444, 446) is at Jalan Pattimura 3 by the harbour. Pelni is nearby on the same street.

Places to Stay

Hotel Nels on Jalan Yos Sudarso is a good place with singles/doubles at 3500/7000 rp. On Jalan Hiji Agus Salim the *Hotel Kalimantan* is a decent place at 3000/4000 rp.

A few minutes' walk up the road at the corner of Jalan Haji Agus Salim and Jalan Iman Bonjol is the *Penginapan Sulawesi* which has singles for 1500 rp. The rooms are very basic little cubicles, but the place is clean and the people friendly.

Other hotels to check out are the *Penginapan Delie* and the *Penginapan Sederhana*, both on Jalan Haji Agus Salim.

Getting There

Depending on which direction you're heading, Poso is where you start from or end up at after the ride through central Sulawesi. There are road connections west to Palu and south to Tentena where you first catch a boat and then a bus to Rantepao in Tanatoraja. There are also passenger boats between Poso and northern Sulawesi.

To Palu There are regular colts and minibuses to Palu. Try the Merennu Express office at the Penginapan Sulawesi – 5500 rp to Palu. Other bus companies have their offices at the bus terminal or around the large Pasar Sentral across the river. The road from Poso to Palu isn't bad though the streams that the bus has to ford would be rivers in the wet season. A straight through trip takes about seven to nine hours and you pass by transmigrated Balinese villages complete with gamelan orchestras and stone temples.

To Tanatoraja There are regular buses from Poso to Tentena – costs 1500 rp. Then cross Lake Poso on an outrigger for 1500 rp (these depart Tentena around 9 am) to Pendolo. In Pendolo on the other side of the lake, wait for a colt going through to Rantepao in Tanatoraja – should cost around 15,000 rp. Or look around in Poso for bus companies making the trip straight through.

To northern Sulawesi There are ships departing for Gorontalo from Poso two or three mornings a week; the fare is 17,500 rp deck class. Buy your ticket at Pos Keamanan Pelabuhan at the port. The ships usually stop off at various ports along the coast.

PALU

On the western seaboard of Sulawesi, it's rather larger but just as dull as Poso.

Information

Bouraq (tel 21195) is at Jalan Mawar 5. Merpati (tel 21295) is at Jalan Sultan Hasanuddin 33. Garuda is at Jalan S Aldjufrie 128. The latter is open weekdays and Saturdays 8 am to 1 pm and 2 to 4 pm, Sundays 8 am to 1 pm.

Places to Stay

The *Hotel Pattimura* (tel 222-311) on Jalan Pattimura is an OK place, though bathrooms could do with a clean. The front rooms are extremely noisy from the traffic! Singles from 4500 rp and doubles from 8000 rp (with attached bathroom). The *Hotel Taurus* (tel 21567) on Jalan Sultan Hasanuddin has small rooms and the mandis and toilets could do with a clean but otherwise it's good at 3500/5000 rp for singles/doubles.

The *Hotel Pasifik* at Jalan Gajah Mada

130 has singles/doubles from 2500/5000 rp. Despite its rough looking frontage this place is quite good inside. *Penginapan Arafah* is near the Hotel Pasifik on a street running off Jalan Gajah Mada near the bridge. Singles/doubles are 2000/3500 rp and it's very basic – but reasonably clean. Rooms are thinly partitioned little cells.

Places to Eat

The *Rainbow Restaurant* at Jalan Sultan Hasanuddin 19 is quite good value – but probably too expensive for most shoestring travellers. Head north along Jalan Wahidden and on the left is a string of rumah makans and warungs. The *Kios Bambuden* at Jalan Wahiden 6 is quite good but on the expensive side. The *Depot Dunia Baru* is a big place on Jalan Danau Linau – large helpings of nasi cap cai for 2000 rp.

There are other little warungs and rumah makans scattered about – such as the *Rumah Makan Phoenix* at Jalan S Aldjufrie 4. In the early evening there are murtabak trolleys set up on Jalan Hasanuddin near the bridge.

Getting There

From Palu (or the nearby ports of Pantoloan or Donggala) you can take a ship across to Kalimantan, to northern Sulawesi, or to Pare Pare in southern Sulawesi. Palu is connected by road to Poso in central Sulawesi and to Gorontalo in northern Sulawesi.

To Gorontalo There is a scungy sort of road all the way from Palu to Gorontalo now. For buses try PO Popula on Jalan Sudirman (near corner with Jalan Sultan Hasanuddin). Palu to Manado is around 30,000 rp. But if the road through central Sulawesi is any indication then you're probably better off flying with Bouraq; Palu to Gorontalo is 43,500 rp and to Manado 80,900 rp.

To Poso & Tanatoraja For colts to Tanatoraja, try CV Alpit Jaya at Jalan Gaja Mada 130 (tel 21168). Palu to

Rantepao is around 20,000 to 25,000 rp and the bus runs via Tentena, boat across Lake Poso to Pendolo, and then by 'road' to Rantepao. There are various agents around for colts to Poso: PO Saba Jaya on Jalan Gaja Mada 69; Marrennu Express (tel 21868) at Jalan Hasanuddin 46.

To Pare Pare Boats to Pare Pare leave either from Wani, Pantoloan (the ports of Palu) or from Donggala. Enquire at the shipping offices down at the waterfront in Wani, and at the harbour master's office at Dongalla and in Pantoloan.

Getting Around
There are colts to Pantoloan and Wani from the junction of Jalan Iman Bonjol and Jalan Gajah Mada in the centre of town. Colts to Pantoloan cost 500 rp and take 30 minutes. Palu to Wani (which is 2½ km past Pantoloan) is 500 rp. Wani to Pantoloan is 150 rp.

The airport is 10 km out of town and probably the best way to get there is to charter a bemo or *bajaj*. A *bajaj* will cost about 1500 rp. Taxis from the airport to centre cost 3000 rp.

DONGGALA
A super boring place, but you can catch a ship to northern or southern Sulawesi. There are some pretty stretches of coastline in the surrounding regions and it's not a bad town to hang around really – definitely preferable to Palu.

Places to Stay & Eat
Stay at the *Wisma Bakti* – an OK place run by a Chinese family. It's quite pleasant with singles/doubles at 3000/4000 rp and triples at 5000 rp. Eat at the *Rumah Makan Gembira* or the *Rumah Makan Dinda*.

Getting There
There are taxis (1000 rp per person) and bemos departing frequently for Donggala from the vicinity of the Bioskop Istana at the junction of Jalan Iman Bonjol and Jalan Gajah Mada in Palu. It takes half an hour by taxi to cover the 34 km along a well surfaced road.

MINAHASA
In the northern peninsula of Sulawesi, Minahasa is a strongly Christian region and was often referred to as the 'twelth province of the Netherlands' because of the closeness of its ties to Holland during the colonial days. Minahasa would also form a good jumping off point for the southern Philippines – if only there was some reliable way of getting across.

Getting There
Gorontalo and Manado are the main towns of Minahasa. They are connected by road and colts go there – fare is 9000 rp and the trip normally takes 12 hours. The vehicles, however, have to ford two rivers, so if they're surging monstrously you'll probably end up being stuck until the water recedes. There are also buses all the way through from Manado and Gorontalo to Palu in central Sulawesi – one company running these buses has an office at Manados terminal to Gorontalo. Fares from Manado to Palu are around 30,000 rp.

Various ships travel the coastal route between Manado (or its port of Bitung), Toli Toli, Kwandang (the port north of Gorontalo) and Donggala (near Palu). These include the Pelni ships *KM Tampomas* and *KM Kerinci* on their loops out of Java around Sulawesi and Kalimantan. There are regular ships between Poso and Gorontalo – usually two or three per week with costs around 15,000 to 17,500 rp deck class. There are fairly regular ships between Manado or Bitung and Ternate in the Moluccas.

Bouraq, Merpati and Garuda all fly into either Manado or Gorontalo. Worth considering is the Bouraq flight from Gorontalo to Manado (37,200 rp) and from Palu to Gorontalo (43,500 rp).

MANADO
Manado is the capital of the province of

North Sulawesi. Unlike Ujung Pandang it's a tidy, more prosperous looking city, though the canals are clogged and filthy – yet only a half-hour motorboat ride away is the crystal-clear water off the island of Bunaken with its brilliant coral reefs. Manado is an interesting place though the 'sights' are to be found in the surrounding areas in short trips out of the city.

Information

The tourist office (Dinas Pariwisata Sulawesi Utara) is off Jalan Eddy Gogola, and is open daily except Sundays from about 8 am. Take an 'E GOGOLA' bemo (125 rp) from Pasar 45 and get off at the Kantor Immigrasi (Immigration Office) – walk up the little road diagonally opposite Kantor Immigrasi – this will take you round (veer right) to the tourist office – a 10 minute walk. Ask for a guy by the name of F F Ticoalu. He speaks quite good English and is *extremely* helpful and informative – he's usually to be found though at Sam Ratulangi Airport. The tourist office has an excellent map of the Minahasa region called the *Handy Tourist Map North Sulawesi Indonesia* and a useful booklet – despite the title – called *Visit Indonesia Guide to North Sulawesi As a New Destination.*

The Bank Expor Impor Indonesia on Jalan Yos Sudarso near the corner with Jalan Sutono changes foreign cash and travellers' cheques. The post office is on Jalan Sam Ratulangi. The approximate opening hours are Monday to Thursday 8 am to 4 pm; Friday 8 to 11 am and 2 to 4 pm; Saturday 8 am to 1 pm; Sunday 8 am to 12 noon.

Garuda is at Jalan Sudirman 2 and is open Monday to Saturday 7 am to 4 pm, and Sunday 10 am to 4 pm. Bouraq (tel 2757) is at Jalan Sarapung 27. Mandala (tel 51324) is on Jalan Sarapung 17. Merpati (tel 4027) is at Jalan Sam Ratulangi 138 and is open Monday to Saturday 8 am to 3 pm, Sundays and holidays 9 am to 12 noon.

Pelni (tel 2844) is at Jalan Sam Ratulangi 3. There are many shipping offices for boat tickets near Manado harbour.

Places to Stay

There's not a great deal of accommodation at the lower end of the price range in Manado. At the bottom of the barrel both in terms of price and standards is the *Penginapan Keluarga* on Jalan Jembatan Singkil near the bridge – a large shed with a floor of thinly-partitioned little boxes. Singles/doubles are 1500/3000 rp. On the credit side it's centrally located and the people here are quite friendly.

Losmen Kotamobagu is a door or two down from Penginapan Keluarga and has singles/doubles for 2500/5000 rp. It always seems to be 'full' but give it a try as it's much better than the Keluarga.

After that there are a couple of places – all pretty similar – in the 5000-rp-a-single and 10,000-rp-a-double bracket. Amongst them the *Hotel Kota* on Jalan Yos Sudarso is a clean, decent place. Singles 5500 rp, doubles 11,000 rp.

The *Wisma Mustika* (tel 51801) at Jalan Hasanuddin 107 has singles for 5000 rp, doubles for 10,000 rp – good place in a good location. Rooms have fans.

The *Ahlan City Hotel* on Jalan Yos Sudarso is basic but clean – singles from 7500 rp, doubles from 10,000 rp plus 10% service and tax.

The *Hotel Minahasa* (tel 2059, 2559) is on Jalan Sam Ratulangi. Of the upper mid-range hotels this is probably the best. Singles from 13,300 rp, and doubles from 17,500 rp.

The *Hotel Mini Cakalele* is on a street running off Jalan Sam Ratulangi, immediately past the post office. Rooms cost from 13,000 rp. It's probably rather overpriced, but the rooms are clean and have a fan and attached mandi.

Places to Eat

There's a string of eating houses all the way along Jalan Sam Ratulangi – generally good and relatively cheap. Try the *Rumah Makan Surya* at No 16 – most dishes are 1250 to 1700 rp. For a hamburger sandwich try the *Sweetsteak* at No 176 – you get all the components of a hamburger laid out on a plate with chips and toast – an excellent meal for 1000 rp.

Some of the cheaper eats can be found in the small rumah makan in the laneway alongside the Manado Cinema – nasi campur for 500 rp. There are more cheap nasi goreng and nasi campur places around the northern boundary of Pasar 45. There's a whole string of somewhat up market places along Jalan Yos Sudarso – all pretty much the same.

Getting Around

Transport around Manado is mainly by Suzuki bemo. Pasar 45 is the central bemo station and fares around Manado are a flat 125 rp. Destinations are shown on a card in the front windscreen, *not* on the side of the van. There are various bus stations around town for destinations outside of Manado. Some important places are:

Calaca Bemo Station is just north of Pasar 45. Take a Lapangan bemo from here to the airport. It costs 225 rp and takes 20 minutes.

Gorontalo Bus Station – for buses to Gorontalo. Take a Sario bemo from Pasar 45 (and tell the driver that you want to go to the bus station because the bemo has to make a detour to do this).

Pasar Paal2 – for colts to Bitung and Airmadidi. To Pasar Paal2 take a Paal2 bemo from Pasar 45. Paal2 is sometimes written as PAL2

Pasar Karombasan – for colts to Tondano and Kawangkoan. To Pasar Karombasan take a Wanea bemo from Pasar 45.

The Wanea and Sario bemos from Pasar 45 will take you straight down Jalan Sam Ratulangi – useful for Merpati, PT Pola Pelita, and the restaurants along this road. There are no becaks in Manado. There are bendis but they're not much good for long distance transport.

AROUND MANADO

Bunaken Island

The first and foremost attraction of Manado are the stunning coral reefs off Bunaken Island which lies close to Manado.

To get a boat to Bunaken go to the *Toko Samudera Jaya* in the Kuala Jengki (the large market near the bridge across the river – over which runs Jalan Sisingamangaraja). Motorboats depart through the day from the Toko Samudera (the shop backs on the river and there are steps leading down to the water where the boats dock). It's 500 rp to Bunaken and you go over in outrigger longboats powered by an outboard motor. Once on Bunaken Island you could ask around for a boat to go to the reefs. Or walk from the village to the long pier close by and climb down the steps into the water – this lands you right on top of the reef.

To see the reef to best advantage you really need your own boat. It's probably easiest to charter a boat at Toko Samudera. You'll be looking at about 20,000 rp for them to take you out to the reef in the morning, paddle around for a few hours and take you back to Manado in the afternoon. There is a village but no losmen or penginapan on Bunaken. Alternatively the travel agency PT Polita Express (tel 52231, 52768) at Jalan Sam Ratulangi 74 organises expensive scuba diving and glass-bottom boat tours to Bunaken Island. Snorkels and masks (and perhaps flippers) can be bought from two shops in Manado; one is the Toko Akbar Ali in Pasar 45. A decent mask here will cost around 16,000 rp and a snorkel 4000 rp.

Airmadidi

At Airmadidi you'll find the 'warugas' – odd little tombs built before the Minhasa region was Christianised. They look like small Chinese temples, and the corpses were buried inside in a squatting position with household articles, gold and porcelain – most have been plundered. There's a whole plantation of these tombs at Airmadidi Bawah, a 15-minute walk from

Airmadidi bemo station. Colts to Airmadidi from Pasar Paal 2 in Manado cost 300 rp.

Kawangkoan

During the Japanese occupation of Indonesia in WW II, caves were built into the hills surrounding Manado to act as air-raid shelters, quarters and storage space for supplies. One group of caves is three km out of Kawangkoan on the road to Kiawa. There are colts to Kawangkoan from Pasar Karombasan (WANEA Terminal) in Manado. A bemo from Kawangkoan to the caves is 100 rp.

Tondano

Some of the more impressive Japanese caves are just outside Tondano on the road to Airmadidi. A bus from Airmadidi to Tondano will get you to the caves in 45 minutes. From the caves you can hitch or walk (takes an hour) to Tondano bemo station and get a colt back to Pasar Karombasan in Manado.

Batu Pinabetengan

This stone, with the vague outline of human figures scratched into it is said to be the place where the chiefs of the Minahasan tribes would hold their meetings. The stone is close to Desa Pinabetengan – take a bemo to Kawangkoan from Manado's WANEA terminal (600 rp, about 1¼ hours). Then take a bendi from Kawangkoan to Desa Pinabetengan (150 rp, half an hour). The bendi will take you as far as the turnoff road that leads to Batu Pina-betengan and then you have to walk the last half hour.

BITUNG

Bitung is the port of Manado and you may have to come here to catch a ship. There are many bemos to Bitung from Pasar Paal2 – 750 rp, takes an hour along a very good road. Pelni (tel 152, 226) is on Jalan Jakarta inside the Bitung harbour compound.

Places to Stay

Penginapan Beringin (tel 240) at Jalan Yos Sudarso 19 has rooms for 5500 rp. *Penginapan Samudra Jaya* (tel 114) is an OK place, basic but clean and rooms with fan and attached mandi and toilet are 7500 rp.

GORONTALO

A quiet town with streets full of Dutch-built villas – a fine example being the Rumah Sakit Umum (Public Hospital), and the Saronde Hotel. On the outskirts of Gorontalo and the port of Kwandang to the north are the ruins of some interesting European-built fortresses (in Bahasa Indonesia, 'benteng' means fort).

Information

There are a couple of places to try for ships out of Gorontalo and Kwandang. Pelni (tel 20-419) is at Jalan 23 Januari 31 and has another office at the port in Kwandang. Gapsu has an office at Jalan Pertiwi 55 in central Gorontalo, and also at Gorontalo Harbour on Jalan Mayor Dullah (tel 198). Other agents to try include Toko Ujung Pandang (tel 157) on Jalan Suprato and Toko Sumber Tahnik at Jalan S Parman 94.

Merpati (tel 143) is at Jalan S Parman 45; Bouraq (tel 70-870) is at Jalan A Yani 34.

Things to See

Otanaha Fortress On a hill at Dembe overlooking Lake Limbote are the three towers of this probably Portuguese-built fortress. Take a bendi (300 rp) to the pathway that leads up the hill from Jalan Belibis. Or take a bemo (150 rp) though these are infrequent on this road. There's a sign at the foot of the pathway pointing the way to the fort.

Fortresses at Kwandang On the outskirts of Kwandang are the remains of two interesting fortresses, possibly Portuguese built. Whilst the town itself is nothing (just a Pelni office and a few warungs) the fortresses are well worth checking out. To get to Kwandang, take a bus from Gorontalo bus station (two hours, 1000 rp). The two fortresses are a short walk off the road leading into Kwandang from Gorontalo – one on either side.

Places to Stay

Penginapan Teluk Kau (tel 785) at Jalan S Parman 42 is one of the most pleasant places in Indonesia. Singles 4000 rp and doubles 8000 rp. Just down the road at No 35 is the *Penginapan Shinta* (tel 461) – an OK place with singles for 4000 rp, doubles 8000 rp.

The *Hotel Saronde* (tel 735) at Jalan Walanda Maramis 17, is comfortable though not luxurious – it's a Dutch-built villa converted into a hotel. Singles and doubles from 6000 rp. The *Wisma Kartini* on Jalan Kartini is a good place, with singles and doubles for 7700 rp.

Places to Eat

The *Rumah Makan Padang* is quite a decent place with a friendly owner. The *Rumah Makan Dirgahayu* serves goat satay dipped in peanut sauce (tersida sate kambing spesial). There's a string of cheap places serving nasi campur, and several Padang places – quite good – up the road leading to the cinema in the middle of town. There are also some very cheap warungs in the large Pasar Central at the northern end of town.

Getting Around

Gorontalo is rather spread out. Getting around is mainly by bendi – 100 rp gets you almost anywhere. For Kwandang and other places around Gorontalo take colts from the bus station across the road from the Pasar Central. A bemo to Gorontalo Harbour is 200 rp – takes 15 minutes. Colts to Kwandang are 1000 rp and take two hours along a roughly surfaced road.

Moluccas

The Moluccas are the fabled spice islands of Indonesia and it was mainly for the spices that grew here and nowhere else that foreign traders – including the Europeans – came to the Indonesian archipelago. The Moluccas – Maluku Province – consist of a scattered series of islands between Sulawesi and Irian Jaya. The largest islands are Halmahera in the north, looking a little like a small scale version of Sulawesi, and Seram in the south. Visitors to the Moluccas usually go to Ambon (a small island near Seram), the Banda Islands to the south-east of Ambon, or Ternate and Tidore (two adjacent small islands just off Halmahera). These days the Moluccas are noted for their fine tropical scenery and for some interesting relics of the early European contact.

Climate Timing a visit to the Moluccas is a bit different from the rest of Indonesia. The dry season in the Moluccas is September to March; the wet season is from the beginning of April to the end of August. There's not much point in visiting the region in the wet season; the rain *pounds* down, which means the islands are not their best, and since the seas are rough there's less inter-island transport.

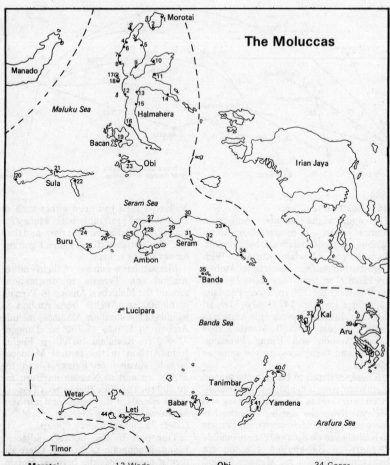

The Moluccas

Morotai	13 Weda	Obi	34 Gesar
1 Berebere	14 Patani	23 Laiwni	**Banda**
2 Daruba	15 Mafa	**Bura**	35 Neira
Halmahera	16 Saketa	24 Airbuaya	**Kai**
3 Galela	17 Ternate	25 Leksula	36 Har
4 Kedi	18 Tidore	26 Namlea	37 Elat
5 Tobela	**Bacan**	**Seram**	38 Tual
6 Tongitisungi	19 Labuha	27 Taniwel	**Aru**
7 Susupu	20 Bobong	28 Pim	39 Dobo
8 Jailolo	21 Dofa	29 Masohi	**Yamdena**
9 Kao	22 Sanana	30 Wahai	40 Larat
10 Lolobata	**Leti**	31 Tehoru	41 Saumlaki
11 Buli	43 Serwaru	32 Werinama	**Babar**
12 Payahe	44 Kisar	33 Bula	42 Tepa

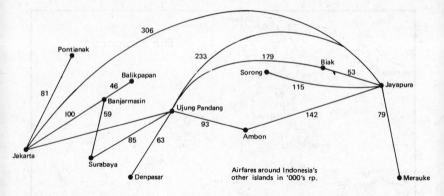

Airfares around Indonesia's other islands in '000's rp.

GETTING THERE

The capital of the province – Ambon on Ambon Island – is connected by air to various parts of Indonesia by Merpati, Garuda and Mandala Airlines. With Garuda, flights from Jakarta to Ambon are 193,800 rp; from Yogyakarta 184,000 rp; Denpasar 135,100 rp; Ujung Pandang 93,000 rp; Jayapura 142,000 rp. Merpati fares are cheaper – for example Ambon to Jakarta is just 164,700 rp. Mandala flies Jakarta-Ambon and Ujung Pandang-Ambon and their fares are the same as Merpati.

There are flights to Ternate, the second main town, from other parts of Indonesia – often with Garuda flying you one leg and Merpati flying the last leg. Bouraq has some interesting connections from Ternate to Kalimantan via Sulawesi; these include Ternate to Balikpapan 136,800 rp, Samarinda 164,200 rp, Manado 39,000 rp, Gorontalo 76,200 rp, Palu 119,900 rp.

There are occasionally ships between Ternate and Manado (or its port of Bitung), and Ternate and Sorong. There are Pelni ships to Ambon with their customary irregularity; fares from Java range from around 40,000 rp deck class – depends on the route taken by the boat.

GETTING AROUND

If you're planning to do a lot of travel in the

Moluccas then you need either time or money – and preferably both! Money for air tickets if you haven't got time, and time and also patience if you haven't got any money for air tickets.

Merpati has a number of flights out of Ambon and Ternate to destinations around the Moluccas. Ambon to Ternate is 63,600 rp. Flights from Ambon to islands of the southern Moluccas include Ambon to Banda 42,300 rp, Langgur 71,400 rp, Saumlaki 75,700 rp. Flights from Ambon to the central Moluccas include Amahai on Seram Island for 27,900 rp and to Namlea on Buru for 30,600 rp. There are flights from Ternate to the islands of the central and northern Moluccas, including Morotai 36,100 rp, Galela 31,200 rp, Kao 23,000 rp.

Transport by sea between adjacent islands is generally fairly easy. There are regular passenger ferries between Ambon, Saparua and Seram, and frequent motorboats every day making the short hop between Ternate and Tidore, as well as regular passenger ships from Ternate to various destinations on Halmahera.

Long distance sea transport around the islands becomes more of a problem. The Pelni ship KM Niaga X makes a regular loop out of Ambon around the southern Moluccan islands, including Bandà, Tual, Saumlaki and various other ports – the whole loop from Ambon and back takes three weeks. It gives you some chance to hop out and look around the ports. Another Pelni ship, the *KM Baruna Bhakti* does a three week trip to Ambon and back, stopping off at various ports in the northern and central Moluccas. Fare from Ternate to Ambon is about 8500 rp deck class.

AMBON

Ambon, the main town on the island of Ambon and the capital of Maluku province, is a big, dirty, noisy city and expensive compared to Bali or Java. The island itself is pretty and has some interesting attractions, including the ruins of European-built fortifications. Also worth checking out are the model boats made entirely of cloves – several shops in the city stock these – try along Jalan A Y Patty and Jalan A J Pattimura. They also sell flower arrangements made out of mother of pearl and fans out of turtle shell.

Information

The immigration office (tel 42128) is at Jalan Batu Capeo 57/5. It's way out in the south-east end of Ambon. There's also an immigration office at the airport where your arrival will probably be registered. You're supposed to register at the immigration office in the city also, though your losmen will probably do this for you – and you're also supposed to register once again at the city office before you leave but it doesn't matter if you don't. Bemos from the city centre will take you straight to the office.

The tourist office is on the ground floor of the governor's office (Kantor Gubernor). It's open Monday to Friday 8 am to 2.30 pm, on Saturday 8 am to 1 pm, closed on Sundays. One of the guys here speaks reasonable English and is quite friendly and helpful.

The post office is on Jalan Raya Pattimura. On the same street is the Bank Expor Impor Indonesia which will change major foreign travellers' cheques so long as they're in US or Australian dollars or

pounds sterling. The bank is open Monday to Friday 8 am to 1 pm, Saturday 8 to 11 am.

Mandala (tel 2444) is at Jalan A Y Patty SK 4/18. Merpati (tel 3480) is on Jalan Anthoni Rhebok and is open Monday to Thursday 8 am to 3 pm, Friday 8 am to 12 noon, Saturday 8 am to 3 pm, Sundays and holidays 10 am to 12 noon. Garuda (tel 2481) is on Jalan Jen A Yani. The Pelni office is at the harbour.

Things to See

War Cemetery This WW II cemetery is in the suburb of Tantui, about two km from the centre of Ambon. The cemetery is for Australian, Dutch and British servicemen killed in Sulawesi and the Moluccas – row upon row of marker stones and plaques. A bemo from the terminal on Jalan Pattimura takes you straight past the cemetery – 100 rp.

Victoria Fortress An old Portuguese fortress located on Jalan Selamat Riady, dating back to 1575. Presently the seaside walls are still standing while other parts have decayed and have been replaced by new buildings used by the military.

Siwalima Museum An interesting museum and definitely worth a visit. Part of the collection includes some 'magic' skulls from a cave in northern Buru and once worshipped by the local people. There are also model boats made of tortoise shell, sago palm and cloves, and ancestor statues of the south-east Moluccas. The museum is located on the Taman Makmur Hills, just off the road leading from Ambon to the the village of Amahusu. To get there take a bemo from the terminal (75 rp) and get off at the Transmigrasi Office – the road leading up to the museum is immediately after the office, and it's a 10-minute walk up to the museum. The museum is closed on Mondays, open Sunday 9 am to 3 pm; Tuesday to Thursday 9 am to 2 pm, Saturday 9 am to 1 pm.

Places to Stay

Accommodation in Ambon city is expensive, with nothing at the bottom end of the budget and little even moderately priced.

The *Hotel Silalou* (tel 3197) at Jalan Sedap Malam 41, is not only one of the cheapest but also one of the best places to stay in Ambon. It's in a good, central location, is run by a friendly elderly couple and has singles/doubles at 6000/12,000 rp.

The *Hotel Transit/Rezfanny* (tel 41692) at Jalan Wim Reawaru 115 has singles from 6500 rp and doubles from 13,000 rp – plus 5% tax and 5% service charge. *Penginapan Beta* (tel 3463) at Jalan Wem Reawaru 114 is a reasonable place run by nice people; singles/doubles are 7500/14,000 rp.

The *Hotel Amboina* (tel 41725) at Jalan Kapitan Ulupaha 5A is several storeys of exceptionally good rooms – singles from 10,000 rp and doubles from 15,000 rp – plus 10% tax and 10% service.

The *Hotel Bahtera* on Jalan Chr M Tiahahu is a very small place but has incredibly nice rooms! Real bath tubs, colour TVs, air-con, piped in music (which you can switch off) – some rooms are equipped with a big double bed. Singles from 12,000 rp and doubles around 30,000 rp.

The *Hotel Eleonoor* (tel 2834) at Jalan Anthoni Rhebok 30 has singles for 14,000 rp and doubles for 20,000 rp. Pleasant people, OK place, but really quite basic for what you're paying.

Places to Eat

There's nothing much to recommend – though there are lots of rumah makans and warungs which serve cheap food – try the stretch of road between Jalan A Y Patty and the harbour. There are a couple more places along Jalan Said Perintah, and some cheap warungs around the corner from the Garuda office. In most of these places you'll get nasi ikan (rice, fish, some veggies) for around 500 to 750 rp.

Getting Around

Get becaks from the Hotel Silalou to the post office for 200 rp, or to Garuda for 300 rp. You can catch bemos around town from the station on Jalan Pattimura – after you've argued your way out of chartering one! For travel further afield around the island, colts depart from along Jalan Yos Sudarso. Or charter a taxi from the stand at the corner of Jalan Pahlawan Revolusi and Jalan A Y Patty – opposite large mosque.

There is a vehicle and passenger ferry from just past Galala village to the other side of the harbour – thus cutting short the circuitous road route – bemos and taxis sometimes use it as a short cut to the airport. Cost is 75 rp per person and 600 rp for a bemo. The ferry runs every day.

Ambon airport is 48 km out of the city. There is a taxi counter at the airport and a taxi to the city will cost 10,000 rp. There are public colts to the city for 600 rp per person. Beware of rip-offs at the airport – taxi drivers will ask for 20,000 rp and colt drivers for 3000 rp! As for getting out to the airport, if you take a public colt from Jalan Yos Sudarso then allow lots of time – its about an hour's drive from Ambon to the airport but take into account the usual Indonesian procrastinations. Alternatively, hire a taxi from the stand across the road from the mosque. Or charter a bemo from the bemo station – I got one for 7000 rp.

AROUND AMBON

Palau Pombo

Pombo is a tiny, attractive island off Ambon with a coral garden where you can go snorkelling. To get there take a colt from the stand on Jalan Yos Sudarso to the village of Tulehu (takes one hour, 400 rp). The colt will drop you off at the wharf and from there you can hire a speedboat to go out to Palau Pombo – a 20 minute ride. There's an OK little beach on Palau Pombo, sheltered by the reef. You could get the boat to drop you off in the morning and pick you up in the afternoon – makes a nice escape. Bring your own food and water – there's a small derelict shelter on the island.

Hila

Hila is a village 42 km from Ambon, noted as the site of a ruined Portuguese-built fortress and an old Christian church. The fortress was originally built of wooden palisades by the Portuguese at the end of the 16th century and was later rebuilt by the Dutch and renamed Fort Amsterdam. The main tower and fragments of the wall remain (the cannons have gone) and the interior of the tower has been taken over by enormous tree roots which have wrapped themselves all over the walls from top to bottom – looks like something out of Tolkien.

The church is just a few minutes walk from the fort. Dating from 1780, it is the oldest building in Ambon – though it has virtually been rebuilt from the stumps up over the years. There's a Dutch-inscribed plaque on the outside wall. Wapauwe is an old mosque near Hila – the original mosque dated back to the early 15th century.

To get to Hila take a colt from Jalan Yos Sudarso (700 rp, and allow 1½ to two hours for the ride).

Other Attractions

At Waai, 31 km from Ambon, is a pool which contains a very large 'holy eel'. The pool at Kawa is a home to 'holy' fish – Kawa can be reached by road and lies a short distance from either Amahai or Masohi.

Natsepa, located 14 km from Ambon, is an OK beach – but avoid going on Sundays when the place gets really crowded. Take a colt from Jalan Yos Sudarso (400 rp, 45 minutes).

Leitimor is the southern peninsula of the island and Hutali, Ema and Naku are interesting villages to walk to along the south coast.

The coastline at Latuhalat and Eman Latu is supposed to have good scuba diving and snorkelling on the coral reefs offshore. To get there take a colt from Jalan Yos Sudarso (275 rp – about 45 minutes – Latuhalat is not far past Eman Latu). Eman Latu is a sort of beach littered with concrete tables and chairs , but if you're going there just for the beach don't bother. On your way down to these places, note the old Japanese blockhouses dotted along the coast, particularly between Amahusu and Eri. There's supposed to be another coral reef off Amahusu.

BANDA ISLANDS

The Bandas consist of a group of seven islands which lie to the south-east of Ambon. If you're looking for somewhere quiet then this is it – there's just a handful of motor vehicles, a fistful of motorcycles, zero televisions. The people are friendly, the scenery is beautiful and the place is unspoilt by tourism. Apart from the scenery, there are several old forts here to scramble around, and some coral gardens where you can go snorkelling and diving.

Information

Buy a copy of Willard Hamilton's *Indonesia Banda* from the museum or the Hotel Raguna in Bandaneira. It gives you a blow by blow description of the history of the Banda Islands over the last several hundred years.

Bandaneira

Bandaneira is the chief centre of the islands – this was the former Dutch settlement, and is today a rambling collection of interesting but deteriorating Dutch mansions. Notable buildings include the Dutch church on Jalan Greja – buried beneath the floor of the church is a procession of people. Nutmeg is processed at the government factory and shipped off to Ambon and then exported to other parts of Indonesia and overseas.

Things to See

The Museum – Rumah Badya The museum is contained in an old Dutch villa which also doubles as a hotel and houses a small collection of cannon, old coins and modern paintings – including one of the massacare of Bandanese by the Dutch in 1621. Also housed here are some traditional feathered headdresses and Portuguese helmets.

Fort Belgica Built by the Dutch East Indies Company in 1611, this fort stands above Bandaneira. The towers of the fort seem to be held together by a copious quantity of grafitti.

Fort Nassau Built by the Dutch in 1609 (on the stone foundations laid by but eventually abandoned by the Portuguese) Fort Nassau is below Fort Belgica. It's very much overgrown – only three walls and a gateway remain and an old cannon lies rotting on the ground.

Fort Hollandia Located on Lontar Island this fort was constructed by the Dutch in 1621. Apparently it was once enormous but an earthquake wrecked it in 1743 and there's not much left – what there is is derelict and overgrown. A long flight of steps leads up to it. Get to Lontar Island by motorboat from Bandaneira Pasar (I chartered one for 3000 rp return, with about half an hour at the fort).

Gunung Api Jutting out of the sea directly in front of Bandaneira, this volcano has some good coral in the shallows approximately opposite Taman Laut and diagonally opposite Bandaneira. It's only a short paddle across to Gunung Api from Naira in a canoe.

Palau Karaka (Palau Sareer) This island lies off Gunung Api; Palau Karaka has some fine coral reefs. Karaka is close enough to paddle from Bandaneira in a dug-out canoe (takes about an hour). There is also a sea garden between Naira and Lontar Island – you can take a canoe out here and snorkel around – but the coral is nowhere near as attractive as Palau Karaka.

Places to Stay

Four hotels have been built to accommodate tourists (all horrendously expensive) and you may find the two cheaper, privately run hotels on the island reluctant to take foreigners. Diving equipment can be rented from the Hotel Complex – flippers for 1000 rp per day; snorkel and mask for 1000 rp; air tank for 10,000 rp; motorboat for 12,000 rp per hour.

The *Penginapan Selecta* is one of the two relatively cheap places in Bandaneira. Singles are 7500 rp without meals and 10,000 rp with three meals; doubles are 15,000 rp without meals and 20,000 rp with meals. A very basic place, but most pleasant and run by very friendly people.

The *Penginapan Delfika* is an old Dutch mansion (now painted a loathsome green, white and purple). It's run by friendly people and has big, basic but clean rooms for 15,000 rp including meals.

The *Hotel Raguna* is the main tourist hotel; single rooms for 35,000 rp and doubles for 60,000 rp (including four meals per day), but bare and basic. The *Hotel Complex* and the *Hotel Mulana* are the same price as the *Raguna*. The fourth one is the *Rumah Badya (Museum Hotel)* – probably the best if you have to choose from the tourist hotels – it's very private, very quiet.

Places to Eat

There are a couple of little rumah makans around, like the very cheap *Rumah Makan Nusantara*. Top off the diet with fruit and fried skewered fish from the market. Nangka and sarsik are both available, but generally you'll get a wider variety of food in port.

Getting Around

The town of Bandaniera is very small and easy to walk around. There are few roads – only one on 'Niera leads to the airport. Trails connect other places on the island – makes for some nice walks. Take motorboats from the pasar to Lontar Island. There are lots of canoes for hire at, say, 2000 rp for the canoe plus 1000 rp for the boatman (if you have one) for a couple of hours. If you hire one to go out and snorkel over the sea gardens it's easy enough to get out of the canoe and into the water, but virtually impossible to get back in without capsizing it. There is probably a way but there were no boy scouts around to tell me how! There don't seem to be any outrigger canoes around either.

Getting There
Merpati flies Ambon to Banda for 42,300 rp, two flights per week. These flights continue on to Langgur in the south-eastern Moluccas. A shop on Jalan Pelabuhan is the agent for Merpati in Bandaneira.

The *KM Niaga X* does a three-week loop out of Ambon and around the southern Moluccas, calling in on Banda on the way out and back. I got back from Banda to Ambon on a ship called the *Nusantara Daya* (which means 'Mighty Archipelago') which – in the best traditions of Pelni boats – was dirty and crowded, and needless to say, the toilets reeked and were filled to the brim. The fare from Banda to Ambon was 3500 rp and the trip took about 13½ hours.

TERNATE
One of the first places the Portuguese and Dutch established themselves in the Moluccas, the island of Ternate is littered with the ruins of old European fortifications. A rather slow and placid town – quite a contrast to Ambon. The peace is occasionally broken by intermittent rumblings of the huge volcano to which the town of Ternate clings.

Information
The Bank Expor Impor Indonesia on the waterfront on Jalan Pahlawan Revolusi, and the Bank Negara Indonesia on the same street, will both change US dollar travellers' cheques. The first is open Monday to Friday 8 to 11 am, Saturday 8 to 9.30 am The post office is also on Jalan Pahlawan Revolusi, near the Bank Negara Indonesia.

Merpati (tel 314) is on Jalan Bosoiri and Garuda also has an agent in the same

building. Bouraq is on Jalan Stadion; open every day from 8 am to 7 pm.

The harbour master's office (tel 21129, 21206 and 21214) is at Jalan A Yani 1. Pelni is on Jalan A Yani by the harbour.

Things to See
Kedaton (Palace) of the Sultan of Ternate
This interesting slab of architecture looks more like a European country mansion than a palace and lies just back from Jalan Baballuh, the road leading to the airport. It's now a museum containing a few Portuguese cannon, Dutch helmets and armour – not much to see, though the ill-kept building itself is worth having a look at. To get to the museum take a bemo from the bemo station on Jalan Pahlawan Revolusi – 100 rp.

Benteng Toloko Take the road from Ternate out towards the airport. A path leads off this road (beyond the Sultan's palace and before the airport) to Dufa Dufa and the Benteng Toloko which is on a rocky hill above the beach. It's a small fort, but in better condition than others.

Fort Orange (Benteng Oranye) This fort dates from 1637 and is a Dutch construction. It's right in the middle of Ternate, opposite the bemo station. Forlorn looking cannons, overgrown and sadly crumbling walls and buildings – but you can get an idea of its importance from its great size. It's an interesting building to walk around.

Benteng Kayuh Merah At the southern end of Ternate is Pelabuhan Bastion where you can catch motorboats to Tidore. A km down the road past Pelabuhan Bastion, and just before you get to Desa Kayuh Merah, is Benteng Kayuh Merah. It's a small fort located right on the beach – the waves splash on its walls.

Benteng Kastelle Continuing around the island in a clockwise direction from Benteng Kayuh Merah you come to Benteng Kastelle – you'd hardly know it was there. The ring road around Ternate cuts straight through what's left of the fort – it's covered in moss and undergrowth and grazed by goats. The roots of trees have wrapped themselves around the ruins of the main tower. A bemo from Ternate to Kastelle will cost you 250 rp.

Batu Angus – the Burnt Corner North of Ternate, the 'Burnt Corner' is a volcanic lava flow caused by an eruption in 1737 of Gunung Api Gamalama – what's left today is a massive river of jagged volcanic rocks. Take a bemo just past Tarau village to see this – like a landscape on another planet. On the subject of volcanic eruptions, there's a display of photos in the airport restaurant of the eruption of the 1721 metre Gunung Api Gamalama in September 1980.

Danau Tolire A large volcanic crater on the northern side of the island now filled with deep green water. The lake is just off the road in the vicinity of Takome – but bemos don't seem to go up here very often.

Places to Stay

One of the best places to stay is the *Wisma Alhilal* (tel 21404) at Jalan Monunutu 2/32. Quite plain but run by a friendly family and it's in a good location. Singles 3500 rp or 7500 rp with three meals; doubles 7000 rp or 15,000 rp with meals. Rooms have a fan and attached mandi and toilet. Excellent meals here – mainly barbecued fish or fried chicken with noodles and rice and a more than liberal dose of chili.

The *Wisma Sejahtera* on Jalan Lawa Mena is a very pleasant place. Singles for 4500 rp or 8000 rp with meals; doubles for 9000 rp or 16,000 rp with meals.

The *Angin Mamiri Hotel* (tel 21245) at Jalan Babullah 17 has singles from 7700 rp and doubles from 10,500 rp. It's quite a pleasant place but too far out to walk to – take a bemo for 100 rp.

The *Hotel Merdeka* on Jalan Monunutu has singles and doubles for 8000 rp (including meals). Big rooms – looks like it must have been Dutch-built. Mandis could be cleaner, but the place is almost palatial.

The *Hotel Indah* (tel 21334) at Jalan Bosouri 3 has singles/doubles from about 8200/13000 rp and triples from 17,000 rp.

There are a couple of places down on the waterfront. The *Hotel Nirwana* (tel 21787) at Jalan Pahlawan Revolusi 58 is quite a decent little place and centrally located. Including meals rooms are 10,000/15,000 rp. On the same street and opposite the entrance to the harbour is the *Penginapan Yamin* with rooms for 3500/7000 rp. The *Penginapan Sentosa*, further up the road from the Yamin, is very basic and reasonably clean – but they may not take foreigners. Singles/doubles are 3000/6000 rp.

Places to Eat

Nothing particularly special. Two OK masakan Padang places are the *Rumah Makan Roda Baru* on Jalan Pahlawan Revolusi which is fairly cheap as masakan Padang places go, and the *Rumah Makan Jaya* on Jalan Bosoiri.

The *Gamalama Restaurant* on Jalan Pahlawan Revolusi is quite a good cheap place – gado gado for 650 rp, udang goreng for 750 rp. Cheapest eats are at the *Rumah Makan Anugerah* on Jalan Bosoir across the road from the bemo station. For fruit juices there's the *Warung Es Bung Tanjung* and the *Rumah Kopi Asano* – both on Jalan Pahlawan Revolusi. Buy sago wafers from the market on this street – 100 rp for 10.

Getting Around

Transport around town and around the island is by Suzuki bemo – there are no becaks here. Bemos are 100 rp flat rate to anywhere around town. One way of seeing all the sights quickly in one go would be to charter a bemo – a surfaced road runs in a ring around the island linking up Ternate township with Batu Angus, Lake Tolire (which lies less than 10 minutes' walk off the main road), Benteng Kastella, Benteng Kayuh Merah, and back to Ternate township. It takes a bit less than two hours to circle around the island in a bemo with short breaks.

The airport is at Tarau, close to Ternate township – charter a bemo for 1500 to 2000 rp. Or walk down to the main road from the airport terminal and pick up a bemo for 100 rp.

TIDORE

This is the island adjacent to Ternate. To get there take a bemo from Ternate township to Pelabuhan Bastion (100 rp). Boats powered by outboard motors depart frequently from the Pasar Impris at Pelabuhan Bastion for Rum on Tidore – takes about half an hour and costs 500 rp. From Rum take a bemo for 500 rp to the main town of Soa Siu (a 45-minute ride). There's a fort above the road as you enter Soa Siu – but you need a local to show you the ill-defined sort of track up to it and there's not much to see. The jungle has just about taken over from the fort and you'd really have to be an enthusiast to get worked up about this place. Apparently there is another fort near Rum.

Irian Jaya

Irian Jaya is the Indonesia side of the island of New Guinea – it was only acquired from the Dutch in 1963. Since it had no racial or historical connection with the other Indonesian islands some interesting arm bending had to be conducted to get the Dutch to hand it over. It was agreed that an 'act of free choice' would later determine if the inhabitants wished to join Indonesia permanently – and by choosing a 'representative' selection of voters a unanimous decision to remain was arrived at! The Indonesians have since followed the Israeli fashion of creating facts by moving lots of settlers in from Java or Sulawesi. The Indonesian occupation has not gone unopposed by the Papuans and since 1963 the Indonesians have had to put down – with military force – several uprisings of rebellious tribes. Meanwhile the independence movement known as the Free Papua Organisation (the OPM) continues a guerrilla war against the Indonesians.

The Indonesian settlements are still largely a fringe thing but things could change dramatically in the next decade or so. West Irian has a total population of some 800,000 Papuans and 220,000 Indonesians – 60,000 of the later having come to the province under the Indonesian governments' transmigration schemes. And between 1984 and 1989 the government plans to move in another 700,000 settlers!

For the moment the interior of the province is still inhabited by tribes who, until a few decades ago, had little or no contact with the outside world. They are the only reason to visit Irian Jaya unless you're simply using the island as a transit point to somewhere else.

Permits

It is no longer necessary to get a special permit to visit Irian Jaya but if you are going inland – to the Baliem Valley for example – you must have a permit (a *surat jalan*) from the police. This is easily obtained at the head police station in Jayapura (on Jalan Jen A Yani) – 1000 rp and four photographs is all it takes, and the permit is issued on the spot. There appears to be no limit as to how long you can stay in the interior, so long as you don't exceed the expiry date of your visa or tourist pass.

Certain parts of the interior are off limits to foreign tourists and you won't get a permit for them. However the situation is likely to be variable so you should check out what's open and what's closed to foreigners when you get to Jayapura; the head police station will tell you where you can and can't go. It may also be possible to get permits for the interior in Biak – but don't count on it.

Visas

Check the introductory section about Indonesian visas – Jayapura is not one of the 'no visa' entry or exit points to Indonesia. If you are arriving from PNG you must have a visa for entry to Indonesia. If you are exiting from Jayapura to PNG you must also have a visa for PNG. There is no PNG diplomatic office in Irian Jaya – the only PNG representation in Indonesia is in Jakarta. And most important – you may not be allowed to exit Indonesia from Jayapura to PNG, regardless of what Indonesian officials in other parts of the country tell you – so be prepared for a long and expensive trek back to Denpasar or Jakarta or some other exit point!

Money

In Jayapura, the Bank Expor Impor Indonesia on Jalan Jendral Ahmad Yani will change American and Australian dollar travellers' cheques and cash – including Bank of America, American Express and Thomas Cook. The Hotel Dofonsoro in Jayapura will also accept some travellers' cheques and foreign currency from guests. The Bank Expor Impor Indonesia in Biak also changes some foreign currency and travellers' cheques. Make sure you change plenty of money before heading into the interior – and stock up on small notes and change.

GETTING THERE

Air and sea are the only ways to enter Irian Jaya. From PNG the only way of getting there is the once weekly flight from Wewak to Jayapura with Air Niugini. They're worried about guerrilla activities in the border area so just strolling across the border is definitely not on. The Merpati office in Jayapura is the agent for Air Nuigini; the weekly flight runs Wewak-Vanimo-Jayapura-Vanimo-Wewak-Port Moresby. Jayapura to Wewak is US$136; Jayapura to Port Moresby US$269; Jayapura to Vanimo US$47.

From other Indonesian islands you can get there by air with Merpati or Garuda or by sea with Pelni. Garuda is generally more expensive, many flights operate via Biak, the island off the north coast of Irian Jaya. Garuda fares are 53,700 rp Jayapura-Biak, 114,900 rp Jayapura-Sorong, 142,000 rp Jayapura-Ambon, 233,300 rp Jayapura-Ujung Pandang and 306,800 rp Jayapura-Jakarta. Merpati flights can be sizeably cheaper than Garuda; Jakarta to Jayapura for example is just 260,800 rp.

For most travellers the usual route by air out of Irian Jaya is Jayapura-Biak-Ujung Pandang then after some time in Sulawesi either across to Kalimantan, Java or (cheapest of all) Denpasar. If you've got no yen to see Jayapura you can fly in from Wewak in the morning and probably be able to fly out the same day.

Pelni ships call at Jayapura with their customary regular irregularity and there are also the odd freighters which ply the West Irian coast calling in at the main ports. From Jakarta Pelni fares to all the main West Irian ports (Sorong, Manokwari, Biak or Jayapura) are pretty much the same. Fares to Sorong are the cheapest starting at 55,000 rp deck class, and to Jayapura starting at 72,000 rp deck class. Routes tend to vary – sometimes by one port, sometimes by another. Trying to exit West Irian by ship you also get treated to customary Pelni vagueness; it's basically just a case of hanging around and seeing what's available. There are also occasionally ships between Sorong and Ternate in the Moluccas.

GETTING AROUND

Unless you're into mounting full scale expeditions and are adept at cutting your way through tropical jungle with a machete, then flying is really the only way to get around West Irian. There are roads in the immediate vicinity of the urban areas – and a good paved one extending westwards along the coast from Jayapura, but apart from these, there's nothing. If you want to go inland then you have to fly; Garuda operates some routes, but Merpati carries the bulk of the traffic with many connections from the major centres to other parts of the coast and to the interior.

A couple of Merpati fares out of Jayapura; Wamena 31,300 rp; Timika 82,100 rp; Oksibil 51,300 rp; Nabire 64,300 rp; Bokondini 39,400 rp. Merpati has a number of flights emanating from Biak to other parts of Irian Jaya – particularly to the western sector of the province and the 'bird's head'. Flights from Biak to other parts of Irian Jaya include Bintuni 44,300 rp; Manokwari 38,200 rp; Timika 53,700 rp; Sorong 54,100 rp; Illaga 69,100 rp; Nabire 39,900 rp.

Various mission groups are strongly represented in Irian Jaya, and maintain a communication network of airstrips, light aircraft, occasionally helicopters. They *will* accept passengers and charters, subject always to their own immediate needs. The air transport organisations of the missions are known by their initials – the MAF (Mission Aviation Fellowship) and the AMA (Associated Missions Aviation). They have set rates for carrying passengers, and both have their offices at Sentani Airport, Jayapura. It's your own responsibility to get permits for the places you're visiting in the interior – otherwise you'll be flown straight back to Jayapura at your own expense. Try and book flights on mission planes as far ahead as possible

– in fact, you'll probably find the missions very booked up, so be prepared to go back to Jayapura or Biak and then fly out to another inland destination with Merpati.

There are also aircraft operated by various mining companies. Both mission and mining company planes occasionally fly down to Australia – you never know, you may be able to get a ride.

JAYAPURA

Since the close of its Dutch days as Hollandia, Jayapura – which means 'victorious city' – has really gone through the name changes – first Kota Bahru then Sukarnapura (one of his Jakarta-style statues in the town square) before its current name was adopted. The hills of Jayapura slope right down to the sea and the town is squeezed onto every available bit of semi-level land. It is a pretty sight from the air at night with the lights of fishing boats winking out on the bay.

This is the usual entry point for Irian Jaya from PNG and capital of the province but of no particular interest other than that. It's quite a dull place, and apart from the hills and the Irianese it looks like any other sizeable Indonesian town – there's no particular reason to come here unless you're heading inland.

Information

Though Jayapura spreads itself up onto the hills and out around the bay, just about everything you'll want – most of the hotels, the shops, head police station, airline offices, the large IMBI movie theatre, are all confined to a very small area in the centre of town down near the waterfront. The two main streets are Jalan Jen A Yani and running parallel to it, Jalan Percetakan.

The Bank Expor Impor Indonesia on Jalan Jendral A Yani will change travellers' cheques and cash. The Immigration Office is on Jalan Percetakan and is open Monday to Thursday 7.30 am to 2.30 pm, Friday 7.30 to 11 am, and on Saturday 7.30 am to 1 pm. The head police station, from which you obtain permits for the interior, is on Jalan Jen A Yani. You can stock up on various types of film at the 'Variant Color Photo Studio' in the IMBI cinema in the centre of town.

Garuda (tel 21220) has its office in the Hotel Dafonsoro at Jalan Percetakan 20-24. It's open Monday to Friday 8 am to 12.30 pm and 1.30 to 4 pm, Saturday 8 am to 1 pm, and closed on Sundays. Merpati (tel 21913, 21810 and 21327) at Jalan Jendral A Yani 15 and is open Monday to Thursday 7 am to 2 pm, Friday 7 to 11 am, Saturday 7 am to 2 pm, and Sundays and holidays 10 am to 12 noon. The MAF office is located at Sentani Airport. It's open every day from 5.30 am to 12 noon and 2 to 4 pm. AMA has its office at Sentani Airport, right next to the MAF terminal. AMA is open Monday to Saturday 5 am to 1 pm and closed on Sundays. The Pelni office is located near the waterfront in the centre of town.

Things to See

Not a great deal. Worth checking out is the suburb of Hamadi, a 10- to 15-minute drive by colt from Jayapura. Apart from its interesting market (the Pasar Sentral) stocked with innumerable varieties of fish, a nearby beach is the site of an American amphibious landing during WW II, with barges and a Sherman tank rusting away on the beach. The first group of rusted landing barges lies near a small monument to the landing with a plaque which reads 'Allied Forces landed here on April 22 1944'. Further down the beach is a group of rather more intact landing barges (one being used for more peaceful purposes – as a toilet and a pig pen) and a Sherman tank with its tracks embedded in the sand. To get to these you have to walk through a navy base – they'll let you in but you have to leave your passport at the office at the entrance and collect it on leaving. Apparently there are some sunken vessels in the water directly in front of the beach. Colts to Hamadi zoom up and down Jalan Jen A Yani or can be caught

from the little street near the Bank Expor Impor Indonesia; fare is 200 rp.

If you want to idle away a few hours then try Base G, so named because somewhere around here was an American military base during WW II. The beach here is pretty dull – white sand covered in broken coral, and lots of broken coral in the water, lots of rocks, and the surf can be strong – real dumpers. There are colts to Base G from the terminal at the end of Jalan Percetakan near the IMBI cinema. It drops you off about a 15-minute walk from the beach and the fare is 200 rp.

There's also a university museum at Abepura on the road in from the airport – supposed to be quite good with lots of interesting but neglected artifacts and photographs.

Places to Stay

Hotel prices in Jayapura are the black hole of your wallet – 'highway robbery' said one letter.

Cheapest is the *Losmen Hamadi Jaya* in Hamadi. Singles for 5000 rp and doubles for 10,000 rp. Rooms are basic and fairly clean, but the mandis and toilets are fairly grotty. The place is noisy at night when things really start to happen in and around the losmen – it appears to be a part-time brothel. It's cheap for Jayapura, but don't go there if you want to sleep though they do bring around a nice breakfast at 5.30 am and pots of tea are readily supplied in the evening, all included in the price. A colt from the airport will cost you 750 rp and it will probably drop you off at the junction of the road leading to the airport and the one leading to Jayapura – from there it's only a 10 minute walk to the losmen. From Jayapura there are colts running all the time to Hamadi – just hang out on Jalan Koti and wave one down – the fare is 200 rp. The ride from Jayapura to Hamadi only takes about 15 minutes and the colt goes straight past the losmen.

Also at Hamadi, near the Pasar Sentral, is the *Wisma Asia* (tel 22277). Basic but quite clean and the rooms have a small attached mandi but the toilets are outside. Singles 8000 rp, doubles 16,000 rp.

Central Jayapura has several places to choose from. *Losmen Irian Indah* didn't look too *indah* (beautiful) nor too interested in taking foreigners. It's located on the 3rd floor of a row of shops on Jalan Jen A Yani. If you want to give it a try it's 8000 rp for a single and 16,000 rp for a double.

At *Losmen Sederhana* (tel 21291 or 22157) on Jalan Halmahera they only speak one word of English – 'full' – but it would at least be worth a try since it's one of the cheaper places around. Rooms from 13,200 rp with meals and 9900 rp without meals.

Nearby is the *Hotel Dafonsoro* (tel 21870 or 22285) on Jalan Percetakan. Singles from 10,000 rp and doubles from 13,000 – plus 21% service and tax. By Jayapura standards it's not such bad value for money – even the cheapest single rooms have a television, fan, and attached toilet and mandi.

Also centrally located is the *Mess GKI* (tel 503) on Jalan Dr Sam Ratulangi. The people here are friendly and it's a fairly pleasant place but unpleasantly expensive, particularly if you're on your own. You pay by the room and that's 15,000 rp per night. Rooms are basic but clean and have a fan; the price includes three meals a day and the food ain't bad. You could possibly try negotiating a price for room without meals and save some money by eating at the local warungs.

Places to Eat

The best places to eat in Jayapura are the warungs. Night foodstalls in front of the Pelni office serve up gado gado, lontong, tahu, bakso sapi, kikil lontong, bubur, – a bowl of tahu lontong with hot peanut sauce will cost just 400 rp. There are also many warungs around the mosque on Jalan Jen A Yani, serving nasi goreng, nasi campur, soto ayam, mee goreng, mee bakso, mee kuah, rawon dan knoro, nasi telur bakso.

There are several more expensive restaurants along Jalan Percetakan, such as the *Restaurant Flamboyan* which has simple rice variants for 1200 to 2000 rp per dish. For stuff like cumi cumi and udang you're looking at 4500 to 5000 rp per person. Similarly priced is the *Rumah Makan Oasis*.

Getting Around

There are colts to destinations around Jayapura depart from the stand on Jalan Percetakan near the waterfront, and from near the Bank Expor Impor Indonesia on Jalan Jen A Yani. There are good paved roads in the vicinity of Jayapura. Jayapura to Abepura is 350 rp; Sentani Airport to Abepura is 400 rp; Sentani Airport to Jayapura 750 rp; Jayapura to Hamadi 200 rp.

Jayapura's Sentani Airport is conveniently located a mere 36 kms out of town. It's 10,000 rp to charter a colt from the airport to central Jayapura and there's a taxi counter in the airport terminal where you can buy a ticket. Alternatively, just walk for 10 minutes down the road directly in front of the terminal to the main road where you can easily pick up a Jayapura-bound public colt for just 750 rp.

The main problem is getting back out to the airport. If you go down to the colt stand the drivers just point you to colts one after the other that you can charter. There never seems to be one heading to Sentani when you want it – they even tell you to charter vehicles that are already half full. The best way to avoid all this is to walk out of town a little distance up the road for the airport and wait for a colt – allow plenty of time. The straight through trip to the airport takes 45 minutes to an hour.

THE BALIEM VALLEY

There are a number of places in the interior worth a visit but top of the list is the Baliem Valley where the Dani people were only discovered in 1938. The Danis have adopted many modern conveniences (like steel axes rather than the traditional stone ones) but here you can still see men wearing penis gourds and little else, and some of their other customs have remained intact or only recently died out.

The Danis maintain their polygamous marriage system – a man may have as many wives as he can afford. Brides have to be paid for in pigs and the man must give five or six pigs to the family of the girl. Girls can also change husbands so long as the new husband pays back the former with pigs. Grass skirts usually indicate that a woman is unmarried – though in some parts of the valley married women also wear them. One of the more bizarre Dani customs involves the amputation of women's fingers when a relative dies; you'll see many of the older women are missing fingers right up to the second joint – a very common sight. Apparently the practice continued until just a few years ago. The fingers were dried and then buried under a banana tree.

Many Danis wear pig fat in their hair and cover their bodies in soot – intended for health and warmth – the hairstyle looks like a cross between a Beatles' mop top and a Rastafarian. As the evening closes in, the men naked except for their penis gourds, stand with their arms folded across their chests to keep warm. The women dangle string bags from their heads to carry food, fuel, even babies.

WAMENA

The main town of the Baliem Valley, Wamena is a neat and rather spread out place. It's a good place to base yourself though there's not much in the town itself. The market is a focal point and the villagers come in every day dressed in grass or string skirts and penis gourds. Accommodation in Wamena is expensive – in fact everything is very expensive compared to the rest of Indonesia – but since everything has to be flown up here that's inevitable. You must report to the police station when you arrive and they're a friendly, helpful bunch.

Information

Near the airstrip is the Bank Rakyat Indonesia which is open Monday to Friday 8 am to 1 pm, and on Saturday 8 to 11 am. Also close by is the post office which is open Monday to Thursday 8 am to 12 noon, Friday 8 to 10 am, and Saturday 8 to 11 am.

Your permit from Jayapura is taken from you at the airport and you then have to collect it on leaving Wamena from the head police station. They also held my passport here until I departed Wamena for Jayapura. The police station in Wamena cannot give you a permit for other parts of West Irian, apart from Soba and Ninia and places in the Wamena region. Places like Illaga, Oksibil, and Enarotali require permits from Jayapura.

There's a map in the office of the Hotel Baliem showing the villages and rivers in the Baliem Valley.

Places to Stay

The *Hotel Baliem Cottage* on Jalan Thamrin is the No 1 hotel of Wamena. Singles 17,500 rp, doubles 25,000 rp and an extra bed is 5500 rp. These prices include breakfast and afternoon snack, 21% tax and service charges. Lunch is an additional 4000 rp, and dinner is an additional 4500 rp. The hotel is made up of grass-roofed, concrete-walled bungalows shaped like Dani huts and each has an attached toilet and bathroom in an open-roofed annex.

The only other hotel is the *Nayak Hotel* on Jalan Angkasa, directly opposite the airport terminal. Rooms including meals and tax are 18,700 rp a single and 37,400 rp a double. Without meals you can have a single for 10,000 rp – which given that the local places to eat are quite cheap doesn't make Wamena as hideously expensive as you would first think. The hotel doesn't look like much more than an army barracks from the outside, but the rooms are clean, quite large and comfortable, and have an attached mandi/toilet. It's also unbelievably quiet!

Whatever you do, bring some mosquito repellant with you! Wamena is infested with them!

Places to Eat

There are a couple of places to eat in the market. The *Warung Sipatuo* has forgettable but palatable food; nasi ikan at 500 rp, fried sweet potatoes with vegetables and rice at 500 rp. Similarly-priced food at the *Warung Mario Marannu* which is probably the best of a mediocre bunch. More expensive is the *Minang Jaya* – memorable for the posters on the wall of Chips, Serpico, Brooke Shields and the inevitable Rolling Stones.

The *Cota Masakan* is mainly a soup place. The *Rumah Makan Mirasa* is also primarily soup, but also has dull ayam goreng, nasi and ikan goreng. There are several small kios scattered around selling sweet doughnuts and snacks.

Things to Buy

There's quite a good souvenir shop right next to the Hotel Nayak; medium-sized string bags for 3000 rp, small penis gourds for 200 rp, stone axes from 1000 to 7000 rp, large black-stone axes for 40,000 to 45,000 rp, black stone axe blades for 15,000 rp, spears 7000 rp. The shop also sells head and arm bands of cowie shells, feathers and bone, containers made of coconuts, wooden combs and grass skirts. Some of these things, like the string bags, are cheaper in the market – 3000 rp for a large bag or 1000 rp for a small one – after bargaining. Other things are more expensive – some of the sellers strike hard bargains so check out prices in both places. The shop is *generally* cheaper than the market.

Getting There

Merpati has flights several days a week between Wamena and Jayapura; the fare is 31,300 rp. Also several flights per week direct to Biak for 81,500 rp. There are a couple of flights per week out of Wamena timed so that you can connect with flights to Surabaya and Ujung Pandang – so you don't have to hang around Jayapura or Biak on the way out of Irian Jaya. Merpati opens its desk at Wamena airstrip a few hours before the planes are due to leave.

The MAF and AMA have offices in Wamena and fly to numerous destinations – but again it's a case of waiting around until there's a plane going where you want to go, and when there's space for you. Be prepared to fly back to Jayapura and fly back to some other place in the interior with Merpati. The AMA has a ticket office at the southern end of the airstrip; Wamena to Enarotali, for example, is around 60,000 rp; Wamena to Illaga is 50,000 rp. The MAF has an office next to the airport building and which is open Monday to Friday 5.30 am to 5 pm, and closed on Saturday and Sunday.

Another airline worth calling on is Airfast; when I was in Wamena there was a plane flying Wamena to Jayapura to Port Moresby to Australia. Inquire at the office of the *Direktorat Jendral Pelabuhan* at the airport – never know, you may be able to catch a ride.

WALKS IN THE BALIEM VALLEY

While there are more dirt and compacted gravel roads leading out of Wamena, essentially the best way to get around is to walk. Trucks sometimes trundle down the roads in the immediate vicinity of Wamena. For places accessible by vehicle, such as Pirimid and Akima, you may be able to charter a vehicle (enquire at the Baliem Hotel) or you may even be able to rent a trail bike.

This is great hiking country – but travel light since the trails are muddy and slippery – you have to clamber over stone fences, maybe cross rivers by dugout canoe or raft, ford streams on rocks or cross trenches and creeks on bridges made of a single rough wooden plank or a slippery log. Rivers are crossed by dugout canoes – and while you crouch in the canoe and wonder if it's going to tip – the locals go across seven or eight at a time (with their bundles) standing up! If there's no canoe there might be a raft made of three logs loosely lashed together and pushed along with a pole. It can also get bloody cold at night up here – bring warm clothes. It also rains a lot – bring an umbrella, and a waterproof tent if you're going to camp out. Apart from camping, you can stay with the missionaries – but don't count on it as they've been flooded out with tourists looking for shelter. Staying in the villages should cost you around 3000 rp per night.

If you can't find a local guide then the Baliem Hotel has them for 15,000 rp per day, and porters for 13,000 rp per day – try bargaining! You *don't* need a guide for some walks – many places have obvious tracks and roads leading to them and sometimes you'll be latched onto by a local who'll show you the way. Some possible destinations include:

Akima a non-descript little village, except that it is where the the 'smoked mummy' is found. The mummy is a weird thing – completely black, decorated with a string mesh cap and cowrie shell beads, and a feather. The penis gourd is still there, though the penis has withered away. The body is bunched up in a sitting position, arms wrapped around knees and clawed fingers draped over feet, with the head tucked down. It is said to be 200 years old. Bargain with the old men who live here (after providing them with a couple of cigarettes) to show you the mummy. They'll ask for at least 5000 rp per person from an individual, but you can knock this down to 3000 rp.

To get to Akima, walk along the road heading north-west from Wamena Pasar and when you get to the T-intersection turn left. Follow the road past the jail to Hom Hom. Turn down the road to the river and cross the modern suspension bridge. Then follow the dirt road leading to Akima – takes about two hours in all from Wamena.

Sinatma is a Protestant mission near Wamena, an hour's walk from Wamena airstrip. Walk past fields of grazing cows near a raging tributary of the Baliem River, forded by two suspension bridges – frail constructions made of wood and vine and a walkway of thin rough wooden slats.

Pyramid A hill so named because of its shape. A motorable road leads from Sinatma all the way to Pyramid via Elegaima. But if you walk to Pyramid it's quicker to take the Wamena-Hom Hom-Musatfak-Miligatmen – Pyramid route. There's a dirt road from Wamena to Musatfak negotiable only by motorcycle. But from Musatfak to Piramid there is a walking-only track.

Hitigima Near the village of Hitigima are the salt water wells; banana stems are beaten dry of fluid and then put in a pool to soak up the brine. The stem is then dried and burned, the ashes collected and used as salt. Saltwells are also found at Jiwika village.

From Wamena it's an easy 2½ to three hour walk to Hitigima – walk past hills with neat chequerboards of stone fences on the slopes enclosing cultivated fields. From Wamena just walk straight down Jalan Jen A Yani – and then over the bridge and follow the road. Two hours' walk from the bridge a track branches off the road (there are several, so time your walk and ask people along the way – you can see Hitigima from the road but there's no sign and it's not obvious. The saltwells are past Hitigima – about another two hours' walk. There is a trail but it's not all that obvious which direction to turn – you should be able to pick up a guide in Hitigima.

BIAK

Not much of a town – just somewhere on the way to somewhere else. If you've got to pass a few hours here the most interesting place is the central Pasar Panir where you can sometimes buy lorikeets and cockatoos. When a Pelni ship goes through half the crew seem to buy one to sell later in Java. And at the end of a flight from Biak to

Jakarta there's the odd glimpse of birds crammed into cages and boxes trundling out on the baggage conveyer belts. You can make a trip out of Biak to Bosnik and Sabul, interesting if you want to make comparisons with PNG.

Information

Like Jayapura, Biak is a fairly compact town. Jalan Prof M Yamin runs from the airport and connects with Jalan Jen A Yani which is Biak's main street and along which you'll find many of the hotels, restaurants and offices. The other main street, Jalan Iman Bonjol, cuts at right angles through Jalan Jen A Yani.

The Bank Expor Impor Indonesia at the corner of Jalan A Yani and Jalan Iman Bonjol, will change a number of foreign currencies and travellers' cheques. The bank is open Monday to Friday 8 am to 2 pm, Saturday 8 to 10 pm, and closed on Sundays.

The post office is on the road coming in from the airport. The head police station is on Jalan Selat Makassar opposite the Pasar Panir – it *might* be possible to get permits for the interior in Biak – but don't count on it. The immigration office is at the corner of Jalan A Yani and Jalan Iman Bonjol.

Garuda is on Jalan Iman Bonjol and is open daily 7 am to 12 noon and 1 to 4 pm, except on holidays when it's open 9 am to 12 noon. Merpati is on Jalan Jen A Yani, near the corner with Jalan Iman Bonjol. Pelni is also on Jalan Jen A Yani, but further down the road from the Merpati office away from the direction of the airport. The entrance to the harbour is near the Pelni office and you could try looking down here for ships to other parts of the province

Places to Stay

The *Losmen Atmelia* (tel 21415) has singles for 4400 rp, doubles for 8800 rp. Basic but most pleasant and run by a friendly woman – it's also quiet. You'll see a sign on the side of Jalan Prof M Yamin coming from the airport pointing the way to the losmen, though it is itself unmarked.

The *Losmen Maju* (tel 21218) on Jalan Imam Bonjol has singles for 6000 rp, and doubles for 12,000 rp. Basic but clean – rooms have fan and an attached mandi/toilet.

The *Hotel Irian* is straight across the road from the airport. Quite basic really, but has a pretty seaside garden and the rooms have attached mandi/toilet. Rooms for 14,000 rp a single and 22,000 rp a double. If you fly Merpati from Jakarta to Jayapura you have to spend one night in Biak – Merpati will put you up free of charge at the Hotel Irian.

The *Hotel Mapia* on Jalan Jen A Yani is definitely the nicest of the upper market hotels – cool rooms, large attached baths and toilets – quite pleasant. Rooms (with fan) start from 12,500 rp a single and 17,000 rp a double – including tax and service.

Places to Eat

Several places around but not a great many of note. Probably the best are the evening foodstalls in front of the Hotal Mapia – a filling gado gado for 1000 rp. There are some cheap places along Jalan A Yani like the *Rumah Makan Anda*, the *Restaurant Megaria* and the *Restaurant Himalaya*.

Getting Around

Much of Biak is easy walking. You can even walk into the city from the airport if you're feeling energetic. From the airport to the Losmen Atmelia is only a 15-minute walk, and another 15 minutes from there into the centre of town. A colt from the airport to the centre is 200 rp – these are regular colts running up and down Jalan Jen A Yani and Jalan Prof M Yamin, so there's no need to charter one to get to the airport.

OTHER TOWNS

Other towns in Irian Jaya are hardly worth the effort. You can fly down to Merauke or

Tanah Merah south of the mountain range – or make your way by air or sea to Fak Fak, Manokwari or Sorong on the 'bird's head' – but why bother. In Sorong stay at Tony Yapen's place. Small passenger ships sail from Biak to Manokwari fairly regularly.

Macau

Sixty km east of Hong Kong, on the other side of the Pearl River's mouth, is the oldest European settlement in the east – the tiny Portuguese territory of Macau. The lure of Macau's casino gaming tables has been so actively promoted that its other attractions are almost forgotten. It's actually one of the most fascinating places in Asia – steeped in history and, with a little effort, quite cheap and comfortable. If you're in Hong Kong, don't miss Macau.

HISTORY
Macau has a far longer history than its younger and brasher sister Hong Kong – and it certainly shows. Portuguese galleons were dropping by here in the early 1500s and in 1557, as a reward for clearing out a few pirates, China ceded the tiny enclave to the Portuguese. For centuries it was the principal meeting point for trade with China – a look around the intriguing old Protestant Cemetery will show just how international this trade was. In the 19th century European and American traders could only operate in Canton, up the Pearl River, during the trading season and would then retreat to Macau during the off-season.

When the opium squabbles erupted between the Chinese and the aggressive (and somewhat unprincipled) British, the Portuguese stood diplomatically to one side and soon found themselves the poor relation of the more dynamic city of Hong Kong. More recently Macau's existence has depended on the Chinese gambling urge that every weekend sends hordes of Hong Kong's more affluent citizens shuttling off to the casinos.

During the cultural revolution Macau suffered worse than Hong Kong, virtually capitulating to Chinese management. It's a nice anomaly today – Portugal and China both disapproving of colonies but neither making any noise about their little joint operation. Curiously, while all the noise has been going on about Hong Kong being handed back in 1997, not a squeak has been heard about what will happen to Macau!

FACTS
Population Macau has about a third of a million people, 98% Chinese, the rest Portuguese and a sprinkling of other western nationalities.

Geography Macau's 15 square km consists of the city itself, which is part of the China mainland, and the islands of Taipa and Coloane, which are joined together by a causeway and linked to Macau city by a bridge.

Economy The spin of the wheel, the toss of the dice.

INFO
The Macau tourist board has offices in Hong Kong and Macau. Pick up a copy of their excellent little *Guide to Macau* with detailed descriptions of many Macau sights. Abroad they are often part of the HKTA's office. In Hong Kong they're at the Macau Tourist Information Bureau (tel 3-677747), 1729 Star House, Salisbury Rd, Kowloon – where they are open from 9 am to 1 pm and 2 to 5 pm on weekdays, 9 am to 1 pm on Saturdays.

The Department of Tourism & Information in Macau is at Travessa do Praia (tel 7218) off the Rua da Praia Grande. It's open 9 am to 1 pm and 3 to 5 pm on weekdays and 9 am to 1 pm on Saturdays.

BOOKS
Hong Kong, Macau & Canton from Lonely Planet has a section on Macau with much more information. Also look for *Discovering*

Macau by John Clemens, an interesting little Hong Kong production.

VISAS

You can get a visa in Hong Kong, but don't bother; they're issued quickly on arrival in Macau and they're cheaper that way. The visa cost has doubled to M$50 but the list of people exempted from visa fees or issued visas for free has been extended. You now enter Macau free if you're a Hong Kong resident or a national of Australia, Belgium, Brazil, Canada, Italy, Japan, Malaysia, New Zealand, Philippines, Portugal, Thailand, the UK or the USA.

One traveller commented that when arriving in Macau from the Peoples' Republic late at night, the Macau bus which picked him up from the Chinese border post sailed right by the Macau entry post. They frowned when he left Macau for Hong Kong, but didn't do anything about his no-visa entry.

MONEY

A$1	= M$5.80
US$1	= M$8.0
£1	= M$8.80
HK$1	= M$1.04

The pataca (M$) is divided into 100 avos and is worth a tiny bit less than the HK$ (there is a permissable variation of up to 10%) so they are quite happy to take your HK$, but don't bother taking their M$ back to Hong Kong. Change it back before you depart, the exchange rate in Hong Kong is very poor. Make sure you arrive with some HK$ because there's no place to change money at the ferry terminal on first arrival and you'd be unable to take a bus into town. The nearest money exchange is at the beginning of Avenida de Almeida Ribeiro and it's open 16 hours a day.

COSTS

Costs are about the same as Hong Kong; cheap places need a bit of hunting out. To really enjoy Macau don't rush in and out – the place is definitely worth a few days' stay and there are places to stay economically. Avoid weekends when hotels are full and costs leap up.

CLIMATE

The climate is just like HK – cool and pleasant in the autumn/winter from October to December, hot with occasional typhoons from April to October.

GETTING THERE

To get to Macau you have to take a boat from Macau's airport – better known as Hong Kong. There are a number of ways of crossing the 60 km of sea to Macau – not counting the mooted helicopter service or going via Canton in China.

Fastest and most expensive is the Boeing Jetfoil. Powered by two jumbo jet engines, they fly (almost literally) across in about 45 minutes. Cost is HK$66 on weekdays, HK$70 on weekends, HK$88

1 Barrier Gate	12 Guia Lighthouse
2 Kun Iam Tong	13 Ferries & Hydrofoils
3 Camoen Gardens & Museum	14 GP Starting Line
4 Old Protestant Cemetery	15 Hotel & Casino Lisboa
5 Floating Casino	16 Bike Hire
6 Grand Hotel	17 St Dominic Church
7 Central Hotel	18 Estrela do Mar Restaurant
8 Ruins of St Paul	19 Tourist Office
9 Old Monte Fortress	20 Taipa Ferry
10 Lou Lim Ieoc Gardens	21 Temple of A Ma
11 Sun Yat Sen House	

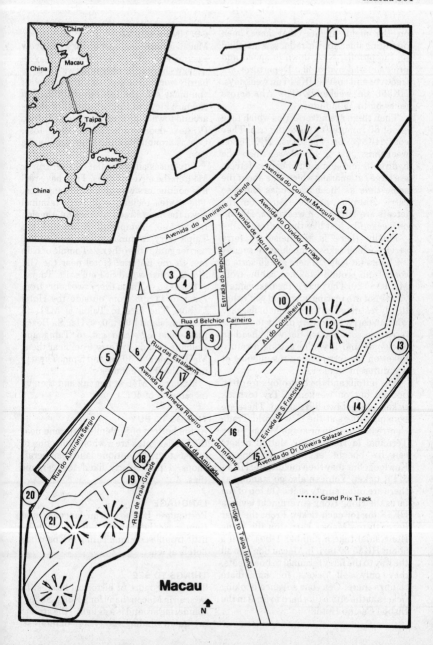

Macau

N

China
China
Macau
Taipa
Coloane
China

Avenida do Almirante Lacerda
Avenida do Coronel Mesquita
Avenida do Ouvidor Arriaga
Avenida de Horta e Costa
Estrada do Repouso
Rua d Belchior Carneiro
Av do Conselheiro
Rua das Estalagens
Avenida de Almeida Ribeiro
Rua do Almirante Sergio
Av do Infante
Av da Amizade
Estrada de S Francisco
Avenida do Dr Oliveira Salazar
Rua de Praia Grande
Bridge to Taipa Island

•••••• Grand Prix Track

on the night 'flights' that have been operating since special radar was installed on the jetfoils. Next down in speed and price are the hydrofoils. Departures are frequent and cost is HK$46 on weekdays, HK$58 on weekends. The trip across takes 65 to 75 minutes.

Then there are hoverferries which take about 80 minutes to make the trip. They cost HK$45 on weekdays, HK$56 on weekends: just a bit slower than the hydrofoils and just a bit cheaper. Jetcats are large catamarans which take about the same time as the hoverferries and also carry 200-plus people. Fares on the jetcats are HK$46 on weekdays, HK$58 on weekends, just like the hydrofoils.

Finally there is the leisurely ferry service which takes a much more seemly 2½ hours (at least). There are all sorts of costs from around M$20 or cabins from M$30 to 120. The ferry is the best value if you're not in a tearing hurry and you're not tightly restricted on the amount of baggage you can carry, as you are on the foils. The ferry also gets booked out well ahead on weekends and if you're getting a return ticket on the ferry it requires queuing at two different windows.

The jetfoils and the hydrofoils are often booked out on weekends. Try to book tickets at least two days ahead. There are booking offices at the New World Trade Centre in Kowloon or at the Macau Ferry Terminal in Hong Kong. Jetfoil tickets can be bought at MTR stations in Kowloon, but they then include the HK$4 MTR ticket. You can also go standby as there are often empty seats. On top of the fares the Hong Kong government levies a HK$8 tax for each ticket. From the Star Ferry to the Macau Ferry (on the Hong Kong side) take a number 1 bus, or it's about HK$5 by taxi. In Macau don't go all the way to the ferry terminal to book seats, they only sell tickets for immediate sailings there. Get your advance booking tickets at the office (it's hard to find) in the Lisboa Casino Hotel.

GETTING AROUND

Macau is fairly compact and it's relatively easy to walk almost everywhere. Bicycle trishaws have to be bargained with and it's hardly worth the effort – if there are two of you make sure the fare covers both. You can hire bicycles from a number of places around town. One is on Avenida de D Joao IV, next door to the Colegio de S Jose. Cost is around M$4 per hour, less by the day.

City buses all cost a flat 50c per trip or M$1 on the air-con buses. They have real live conductors who give you change too. The routes include – 3: ferry terminal down the main street, Avenida de Almeida Rebeiro. 5: Temple of A-Ma and the Taipa ferry terminal at one end to the barrier gate at the other. 2: Temple of Kun Iam to the Estorial Hotel near the Old Monte Fortress and St Paul's. 11: Taipa.

Buses go to Taipa every two hours from 7 am to 11 pm from outside the Hotel Lisboa. The fare to Taipa is M$1, to Coloane island M$1.50, to Hac Sa Beach M$2. You can also get to Taipa and Coloane islands by ferry from near the A Ma Temple at 8.30 am and 5 pm. The trip takes about 25 minutes.

Taxis cost M$3 at flag fall and then by increments of 40c.

THINGS TO BUY

At the bottom of St Paul's steps and near the barrier gates are a whole collection of rather touristy antique and handicraft shops. I particularly liked the ceramic tiles.

LANGUAGE

Portuguese is the official language and Cantonese the real one, but you will have little trouble communicating in English in hotels at least.

THINGS TO SEE

There's far more of historical interest to be seen in Macau than Hong Kong. Simply wandering around is a delight – the streets are quiet, winding, always full of interest.

Old hands say it's now getting speedy like Hong Kong – but you'd hardly notice.

Sao Paulo The ruins of Sao Paulo (St Paul's) are the symbol of Macau – the facade and majestic stairway are all that remain of this old church, considered by many to be the greatest monument to Christianity in the East. It was designed by an Italian Jesuit and built in 1602 by Japanese refugees who had fled anti-Christian persecution in Nagasaki. In 1853 the church was totally burned down during a catastrophic typhoon – the light from the burning church on its hilltop site lit the way for people escaping from the typhoon floods. *Guide to Macau* has an excellent description of the stone carvings on the facade.

WINEGLASS GONG

CYMBAL & GONG

Chinese Priest - MACAO

Monte Fort The Citadel of Sao Paulo do Monte overlooks Sao Paulo and almost all of Macau from its high and central position. It was built by the Jesuits at about the same time as Sao Paulo, but the governor of Macau took it over by the neat trick of coming to dinner and at the close of the meal announcing he was going to stay and his hosts could depart. In 1622 a cannonball fired from the fort conveniently landed in a Dutch gunpowder carrier during an attempted Dutch invasion, demolishing most of their fleet.

Temple of Kun Iam The most historic and interesting temple in the city has a whole host of interesting things to search out. In the temple study are 18 wise men in a glass case – the one with the big nose is said to be Marco Polo. It was here in 1844, that China and the US signed a treaty of 'undying friendship'. So much for R Nixon. The 400 year old temple complex is dedicated to Kun Iam, the Queen of Heaven and Goddess of Mercy.

Old Protestant Cemetery Knock at the door and someone will open it for you; it's the most fascinating place to wander around. The English artist George Chinnery and Lord Churchill (one of Winston's ancestors) are buried here but far more interesting are the varied graves of traders, seamen, missionaries and their families and the often detailed accounts of their lives and deaths. One US ship seemed to have half its crew 'fall from aloft' while in port.

Camoes Museum On the Praca Luis de Camoes, this fine little museum has items from China and a particularly fine collection of paintings, prints and engravings showing Macau in the last two centuries. It's right next door to the cemetery.

Barrier Gate The Portas do Cerco used to be of interest because you could stand a hundred metres from it and say you've seen into China. You might even have seen a bus arriving from China or leaving Macau. Now you can be on the bus yourself so the gate is of little interest.

Leal Senado, or Loyal Senate, looks out

over the main town square and is the main administrative body for municipal affairs. At one time it was offered (and turned down) a total monopoly on all Chinese trade! The building also houses the National Library.

Guia Fortress The highest point in Macau is this fortress overlooking the ferry terminal, with a 17th century chapel and lighthouse built on it. The lighthouse is the oldest on the China coast, first lit up in 1865.

San Domingos Church One of the most beautiful churches in Macau is this 17th century building which has an impressive tiered altar. There is a small museum at the back, full of church regalia, images and paintings.

Lou Lim Loc Gardens These beautiful and peaceful gardens and the ornate mansion with its columns and arches (now the Pui Ching School), once belonged to the wealthy Lou family. The gardens are a mixture of Chinese and European influences with huge shady trees, lotus ponds, pavillions, bamboo groves, grottoes and strange shaped doorways.

A-Ma Temple Macau means the 'City of God' and takes its name from A-Ma-Gau, the Bay of A-Ma. The A-Ma Temple, which dates from the Ming Dynasty, stands at the base of Penha Hill on Barra Point. According to legend A-Ma, goddess of seafarers, was supposed to have been a beautiful young woman whose presence on a Canton-bound ship saved it from disaster. All the other ships of the fleet, whose rich owners had refused to give her passage, were destroyed in a storm. The boat people of Macau come here on a pilgrimage each year in April or May.

The Islands Directly south of the mainland peninsula are the islands of **Taipa** and **Coloane**. In the past these islands were most notable for their pirates, the last raid being as recent as 1910. A bridge connects Taipa Island to the mainland, and another connects Taipa and Coloane.

Gambling Even if gambling has no interest for you it's fun to wander the casinos at night. There are three main arenas for losing money. Largest is the Hotel Lisboa with all the usual games, a special private room for the really high rollers and row upon row of 'hungry tigers' – slot machines. It's gambling Chinese style though, none of the dinner jacket swank of Monte Carlo or the neon gloss of Vegas – at Macau you put your money down, take your chances and to hell with the surroundings. At the other end of the main street is the *Macau Palace* a floating casino (China is visible through the windows) and midway between is the Chinese casino where they play games like *Dai-Siu* (big and small). You can also bet on the games at the Jai-Alai on the waterfront near the ferry terminal.

Festivals

Macau's main festival time is November when the Grand Prix is held – not a good time to go unless you're a racing fan, as the place is packed and prices sky-rocket.

The Chinese in Macau celebrate the same religious festivals as their counterparts in Hong Kong but there are also a number of Catholic festivals and some Portuguese national holidays. Most important is the *Feast of Our Lady of Fatima* when the Fatima image is removed from San Domingo's Church and taken in procession around the city.

The Macau Grand Prix is held in November each year and, as in Monaco, the actual streets of the town make up the raceway. There are in fact two Grand Prix – one for cars and one for motorcycles and the six km circuit attracts contestants from all over the world.

Places to Stay

Cheapest accommodation in Macau is at the *villas* and *hospidaries*, the equivalent of guest houses. Weekends are a bad time to come to Macau; try to make your trip on a weekday. During the quieter midweek time it's worth bargaining a little. There are quite a few *villas* around the back of the Hotel Lisboa; they usually have a sign by the door. The ones very close to the hotel are more pricey, so walk around and check. Some of these places along here don't take westerners, so be prepared to be turned away.

There are others along Praia Grande, before the government palace, such as the *Yat Lou Hotel* at 74 with a good atmosphere and friendly staff. Avenida de D Joao IV, which runs down the side of the Sintra Hotel, also has a number of other places. *Vila Nam Loon* at 30C Rua Dr P J Lobo is a pleasant little place with rooms from around M\$75. *Vila Vai Lei* on Rua de D Jao IV is another similarly priced and good place. *Vila Tak Lei*, a few doors up from the Hotel Matsuya on Estrada Do Sao Francisco, has superb ocean views and air-conditioning. Rooms are M\$65 although they may try to charge more.

If you want a sample of the old colonial Macau, well away from the casino glitter, spend a night at the fine old *Bela Vista* (tel 573821) on Rua Comendador Kouhoneng. This is the Raffles of Macau, an old colonial-style place with rooms from M\$90/120 plus 15% service and tourist tax. Second floor rooms (M\$120-140) even have private balconies. It's popular so getting a room may not be easy. Even if you don't stay there a meal on the verandah terrace is a good investment.

At any hotel it's worth asking for a discount on weekdays. Even the Hyatt cuts prices 40% during the week. If you want a hotel quickly and easily one of the cheapest of the 'approved' ones is the *Grand Hotel* (tel 2741) at 146 Avenida de Almeida Ribeiro, near the floating casino. It's a big old hotel – rooms with and without air-con from around M\$120. In the middle of the same street the *Hotel Central* is at 26-28 near the Leal Senado. Here rooms cost from M\$88 to 136 for singles, M\$104 to 158 for doubles. The Central at one time had a casino with a balcony – reclusive gamblers would lower their bets in small baskets from above.

Hotel Cantao is just back from the Avenida de Almeida Ribeiro, next to the Grand Hotel. It's cheap, pleasant enough and rather noisy. Rooms cost from around M\$40. Other cheaper hotels include the *Hotel Man Va* (tel 88656) at 30-34 Rua de Caldeira with doubles at M\$110 to 140. The *Hotel Ko Wa* (tel 75599 or 75452) is on the 3rd floor at 71 Rua de Felicidade, one block south of the upper end of the Avenida de Almeida Ribeiro. *Hotel London* (tel 83388) is at 4 Praca Ponte E Horte near the floating casino and has singles at M\$80-110, doubles at M\$120-160, all air-con.

Places to Eat

A long, lazy Portuguese meal with a carafe of red to keep it company is one of the most pleasant parts of a Macau visit. The menus are often in Portuguese so a few useful words are *cozido* – stew, *cabrito* – lamb, *carreiro* – mutton, *galinha* – chicken, *caraguejos* – crabs, *carne de vaca*– beef, *peixe* – fish. Apart from carafe wine you can also get Mateus Rose, that best known of Portuguese wines. Another Macau pleasure is to sit back in one of the many little cake shops with a glass of *cha de limao* (lemon tea) and a plate of cakes – very genteel! People eat early in Macau: you can find the chairs being put away and the chef gone home at 9 pm.

Some good places to try include the *Estrela do Mar* (Sea Star) on a little road off the seafront Rua da Praia Grande, right next door to the tourist office. It's become a little more expensive of late but is still good value, probably the cheapest Portuguese place around. *Cafe Safari* on Avenida de Almeida Ribeiro is equally nice.

If you feel like spending up a little then the *Macau Inn* (*Pousada de Macau*) on the Praia Grande is Macau's most famous eating place and is particularly well-known for its African chicken. The superbly old-world *Bella Vista* has a beautiful view from the open terrace to accompany the excellent and not too expensive food. *Cafe Safari* on Avenida de

Almeida Ribeiro has also been recommended.

The *Solamar Restaurant* in the Rua da Praia Grande has high prices and slow service. *Fat Siu Lau* is Portuguese despite the Chinese name. You'll find it on the old red-light street Rua da Felicidade. It's supposed to be the oldest restaurant in Macau, and roast pigeon is a speciality. There are some good and cheap little Chinese places down the same street.

Other places include *Henri's Galley* (good for a burger) on the Avenida do Republica. At 135 Rua Cinco de Outubro, near the Hotel Cantao, the *Cafe Ieng Keng Tsing* does good breakfast specials and reasonably priced meals. There are plenty of Chinese places around and it's often easier to get what you want than in Hong Kong. The *Mfi Nga Cafe* near the Estrela do Mar in Rua Central has excellent food at low prices and is run by three old Chinese ladies. Good dim sum at the *Jade* in Avenida Almeida Ribeiro. The food in the coffee shop of the Casino Lisboa is surprisingly reasonably priced.

For economy minded winelovers Macau is the best bargain in this book. Wine in stores in Macau starts at M$15 for a bottle of the cheaper Portuguese wines. In restaurants half bottles are generally M$16-20, full bottles M$30-45. The Estrela do Mar is cheaper. You can bring a litre of wine or spirits back to Hong Kong. It's all cheaper in Macau.

Malaysia

A country of beautiful scenery, easy and comfortable travel, and friendly people rather than of deep historical or cultural interest. One of the most advanced and well-off countries in Asia, Malaysia offers a wide variety of beaches, mountains and parks for lovers of the outdoors. It also has a fascinating mixture of peoples, from the peninsular Malays and the commercially minded Chinese, to the diverse tribes of Sabah and Sarawak in North Borneo.

HISTORY

Malaysia's history has almost always been an offshoot of other countries. A thousand years ago Buddhist and Hindu empires from Thailand and Indonesia spread their influence over the peninsula. The arrival of Muslim traders turned Melaka (Malacca) into the centre of an Islamic empire, but its conquest by the Portuguese in 1511 once again took the power from Malayan hands. In 1641 the Dutch took over Melaka and in 1795 it went through changes again when the British took control.

For years the British were only interested in Malaya for its seaports and as protection for their trade routes, but the discovery of tin prompted them to move inland and take over the whole peninsula. Meanwhile Charles Brooke, the 'White Rajah', and the North Borneo Company performed similar British takeovers in Sarawak and Sabah respectively. The British, as was their custom, also brought in Chinese and Indians, an action which radically changed the country's racial mix.

After independence from Britain – 'Merdeka' – in 1957, Malaysia had serious problems with Communist guerrilla activities and the 'confrontation' with Indonesia. Sukarno's demise ended 'confrontation' but sporadic outbursts of guerrilla activity still occasionally take place. The building of the east-west road linking Penang with Kota Bahru brought them out of hiding to hamper construction. Singapore withdrew from the Malaysian confederation in 1966 and the elections of 1969 ended with violent intercommunal rioting and the suspension of parliamentary rule. Tension between Malays and Chinese is still a problem, but in general Malaysia is peaceful racially. The 1974 elections resulted in a overwhelming majority for the National Front, which managed to absorb half of its rivals and steam roller the rest. Rocketing rubber and tin prices have kept the Malaysian economy happy of late and the wayward state of Sabah has finally been brought under more effective Kuala Lumpur control.

The old Malay-Chinese rivalries have risen again in the past few years. The Chinese have been feeling that the pro-Malay tilt has gone a little too far and have effectively been withdrawing their expertise (and money) from the economy. For a time the arrival of Vietnamese boat people along the Malaysian east coast (where the population is more heavily Malay than on the west) exacerbated racial relations but that seems to have quietened down. Malaysia has followed, though fortunately at a fairly great distance, the worldwide swing to more fundamental and conservative Islamic rule.

FACTS

Population A confederation of 13 states, mostly with their own Sultans, Malaysia has a population of nearly 14 million split between Malays (who control the government) and Chinese (with their fingers on the economic pulse), with a substantial minority of Indians.

Geography Malaysia covers an area of 330,000 square km, approximately 40% of which is the Malay peninsula, reaching down from the Thai border to Singapore. The other 60% is the northern Borneo states of Sabah and Sarawak. Malaysia is 75% covered by dense forests.

Economy A prosperous and progressive country, Malaysia is a major exporter of tin and rubber – rubber trees seem to cover the whole peninsula. In East Malaysia the economy is based on timber in Sabah, pepper and oil in Sarawak. This healthy economic base contributes to Malaysia's position as one of the wealthiest countries in the region – although still some way behind Singapore or Japan.

Religion The Muslim religion is recognised as the state religion of Malaysia although, naturally, few Chinese pay much attention to it and there are substantial numbers of Christians in Sarawak. As in Indonesia it's a very laid-back brand compared to the religion of the Arab countries.

INFO

There are good tourist offices in the major cities, especially KL and Georgetown, with interesting leaflets and brochures. Road maps available in Malaysia are probably the best and most accurate in South-East Asia. The maps from Shell and Mobil petrol stations are probably the best.

BOOKS

There are many good bookshops, particularly in Penang and KL. Look for Lonely Planet's *Malaysia, Singapore & Brunei – a travel survival kit* for a complete run down on the country. Apa's *Insight Guide Malaysia* is a colourful coffeetable-guidebook with many photos. Look for cartoon books by Malaysian cartoonist Lat, he captures Malay life just right.

Many novelists have set their tales in Malaysia. Anthony Burgess' *The Malayan Trilogy* is one of the best. Somerset Maugham also set many of his classic short stories in Malaya and, more recently, Paul Theroux's *The Consul's File* tells of events in the small town of Ayer Hitam. Blanche d'Alpuget's Australian award winning novel *Turtle Beach* is also insightful.

VISAS

Visas are not necessary for most western nationalities and visitors are now usually given a one-month stay permit on arrival and a further month's extension is quite straightforward. The 'suspected hippy' hassles of Batu Ferringhi in the early '70s are hopefully a thing of the past but there is still an official campaign to keep the country free of pernicious 'hippy' influences. If you might be mistaken for such a creature try to look clean, neat and affluent when dealing with officialdom.

Sabah and Sarawak are treated in some respects separately from the rest of Malaysia and you have to go through another immigration process when entering either state from the peninsula or from each other. Not if returning to the peninsula from East Malaysia, though.

MONEY

A$1 = M$2.04
US$1 = M$2.49
£1 = M$2.79

The Malaysian dollar, known as the ringgit, is divided into 100 cents. It's currently worth about 10% less than the Singapore dollar so while Malaysians are usually quite happy to take Singapore dollars you'll find Malay dollars are not so popular in the city state. In actual practice Singapore currency is not 100% acceptable, but there'll usually be somebody around who'll change notes for you if you're having trouble. Bank rates tend to vary a little with banks and there are lots of money changers, particularly in Georgetown.

COSTS

Like Singapore, Malaysia is more expensive than other South-East Asian countries but you get what you pay for – hotels, restaurants and transport are generally clean, safe and efficient.

CLIMATE

It's fairly warm and fairly damp year-round in Malaysia. In Peninsula Malaysia it tends to be wetter from October to January on the east coast, from September to November on the west. In north Borneo the monsoon brings rain from November to January, especially on the coast. At times during the wet season travel on the east coast can be difficult (even impossible) due to flooding and the road being cut off.

FOOD
The three main racial groups in Malaysia provide distinctive cuisines:

Malay Malay food is closely related to Indonesian with nasi goreng, sate and gado-gado, but Malay restaurants are few in number. The best Malay food you will probably find will be in food stalls, especially the night markets in KL.

Chinese Good Chinese food can be found throughout Malaysia. Particularly popular are chicken rice restaurants – chicken with cucumber, soup and really delicious rice.

Indian Indian food is so good in Malaysia that it is hard to believe it can be so bad in India. For a cheap meal or filling snack ask for roti chanai – a sort of crispy fried pancake served with dahl dip. Murtabak – thin pastry stuffed with egg, vegetables and meat – are also good.

Specials Fruit and drinks are two of the pleasures of a Malaysian visit. See the section on South-East Asian fruit for all the info on fruit. In Malaysia look out particularly for rambutans which are one of my favourites – there are two rambutan seasons which are marked by red rambutan peels scattered in every street. Steel yourself to try an *es kacang* (or ais kacang), a hideous-looking concoction of syrup, crushed ice, jelly cubes and fruit – tastes delicious. Fruit juice is *es buah*. Street stall drinks are very popular, as are fruit slices from street stalls, just like in Singapore. As in Singapore there is a wide variety of soft drinks available, always cold. Plus those fruit juice boxes and, of course, Malaysia's popular Anchor and Tiger Beer although these days it costs around M$2.60 a bottle and Tiger is falling out of favour.

ACCOMMODATION
The usual accommodation in Malaysia is in traditional Chinese hotels. On the peninsula they generally start from around M$10 to 16, rather more expensive in north Borneo. For that you get a bare, but usually clean, room with bed, a couple of chairs and a table, a sink and a gently swishing ceiling fan. The toilets, usually squat style, will be down the corridor along with the showers.

The main catch with these places is that they're often very noisy – first because they often front on to the main streets and second because of the terrible racket the Chinese naturally make. Particularly in the morning when the terrible dawn chorus of coughing, hawking and spitting has to be heard to be believed. It's worse still if you've got a room where the walls don't quite reach the ceiling, but are meshed in at the top for ventilation.

On the other hand Chinese hotels are always good fun and generally have a restaurant directly below them. Throughout Malaysia couples can save some money by asking for a single rather than a double. A single simply means one double bed, not two of them. Other possibilities include youth hostels and YMCAs or YWCAs in some cities and village-style accommodation at certain places like Tanjong Kling near Melaka, Cherating on the east coast, or Tioman Island.

GETTING THERE
From Europe, Australia & North America
See the introductory Getting There section for details on air fares to Malaysia from far afield. The usual gateway to Malaysia is Kuala Lumpur although there are also some international flights into Penang. From London you're looking at £200 for a one-way ticket; from the Australian east coast a bit under A$400.

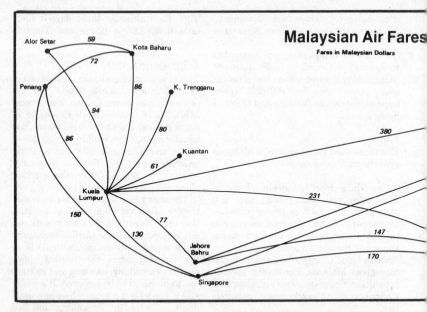

Malaysian Air Fares

Fares in Malaysian Dollars

Alor Setar — 59 — Kota Baharu
72
Penang
86 — K. Trengganu
94
86
80
380
Kuantan
61
Kuala
Lumpur — 231
150
77
130
147
Jahore
Bahru
170
Singapore

From Thailand

There are all sorts of ways of travelling between Thailand and Malaysia although most travellers will probably intend to cross the border by land. Even that offers a number of alternatives. The various possibilities are:

Air You can fly from Bangkok, Phuket or Hat Yai to Penang – note that flying via Phuket or Hat Yai is no more expensive than flying direct from Bangkok, at least on the officially stated fare. In practice you may well find cheaper tickets.

Rail The Singapore-KL-Butterworth railway line continues into Thailand and runs through Hat Yai all the way to Bangkok. There is a three times weekly International Express in each direction Bangkok-Butterworth with connections on to KL and Singapore. There are only 2nd and 1st class carriages on this train and it tends to get delayed quite a long time at the border.

There is also a daily service just between Hat Yai and Butterworth which also has 3rd class – Butterworth-Hat Yai cost is around M$10. The daily train leaves Hat Yai at 11.40 am and arrives at Butterworth at 5.39 pm. From Butterworth it departs at 6.50 am and arrives at Hat Yai at 11.20 am. Recently this service has become sad, slow and grotty.

Road – West Coast The great majority of travellers cross the border between Penang and Hat Yai. The actual border towns are Changlun on the Malaysian side, Sadao on the Thai side. There's a long stretch of no-man's-land between these two border points making border crossing rather difficult as you cannot easily hitch across and there are no buses or taxis just across the border. The usual way is to take the Thai taxis that make daily trips between Georgetown and Hat Yai. They cost around M$20 and are usually much faster than the trains because of the greater speed in getting through the customs and immigration formalities. The taxis are easy to find in hotels in Georgetown.

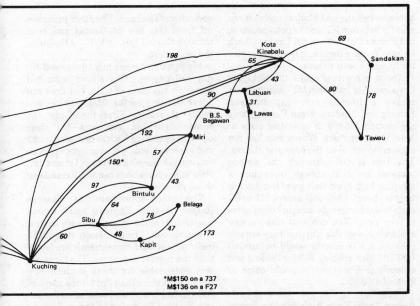

*M$150 on a 737
M$136 on a F27

An easy alternative is to cross the border at Padang Besar, slightly west of Changlun-Sadao. This is the point where the railway crosses the border and here you can easily stroll across, arriving and departing by bus.

Road – East Coast A 29 Bus will take you from Kota Bahru to Rantau Panjang for M$2, taxis cost M$3.5. It's 45 km and takes about 1-1/2 hours. Once there you've just got a 1-1/2 km walk across the border to the station at Sungai Golokis. The border is closed from 6 pm to 6 am, there's no place to stay there so if you arrive too late you'll have to go to Kota Bahru. You can change your last ringgit into baht at the stores by the Malaysian immigration in Rantau Panjang – the rate is better than the banks in Hat Yai. From Sungai Golok trains run to Hat Yai (daily at 10.40 am) and four days a week straight through to Bangkok at 8.30 am.

Sea – West Coast Finally there are some unusual routes on the west coast. From time to time yachts operate between Phuket and Penang, sometimes on a regular basis. Another alternative is to take a boat between Satul in Thailand and Kuala Perlis in Malaysia. Kuala Perlis is the place where you take boats across to Langkawi and there are fairly frequent Thai long-tail boats which make this short hop for around M$3. There are customs and immigration controls at both these places so it's OK, although unusual to cross here.

From Indonesia The usual Malaysia-Indonesia route is the very short flight between Penang and Medan in Sumatra. MAS and Garuda both fly this route and the current fare is about US$50. There are also occasional or regular charter flights between Melaka and Pekanbaru, again in Sumatra.

From India & Elsewhere Although the majority of travellers make the jump from South-East Asia to the sub-continent from Bangkok to either Dacca, Calcutta or Kathmandu there are some interesting alternatives. MAS have regular services between Penang and Madras and you can also fly between KL and various points in India or to Colombo in Sri Lanka. Check Penang for fare details, it is a good centre for finding cheap tickets.

About every two weeks the Shipping Corporation of India ship *MV Chidambaram* makes a four-day crossing between Penang and Madras. From Penang fares are around M$400 in economic class or M$600 in 1st class. Westerners are not allowed to travel on the cheapest classes. The trip is OK although the air-con sections are cold enough to require a sleeping bag. Food isn't great but Anchor beer is cheap. They only accept M$ or S$ and the exchange rate for other currencies is very poor. You can also take cars or motorcycles on this ship but they are not cheap – a VW Kombi would be around US$700 plus another 100 for loading and unloading. A motorcycle would come to around US$200.

Airport Taxes From Malaysia the airport tax is M$3 on domestic flights, M$5 to Singapore or Brunei, M$15 on other international flights.

GETTING AROUND
Air MAS has an extensive domestic network but land travel is so easy on the peninsula that there is little reason to take to the skies. On the other hand if you're going to Sabah and Sarawak you're virtually forced to fly – there are very few ships between Singapore and north Borneo these days. Similarly the roads in north Borneo are still sketchy and at times you'll have to fly, or take lengthy alternative routes. There are some cheap night flights and advance purchase fares available on MAS domestic routes – particularly between the peninsula and Sabah or Sarawak.

Rail Malaysia has a modern, comfortable and economical system although there are basically only two rail lines. One runs from Singapore to Kuala Lumpur, Butterworth and on into Thailand. The other branches off from this line at Gemas and runs through Kuala Lipis up to Kota Bahru on the east coast.

Foreign tourists can buy 10-day and 30-day rail passes. This allows unlimited travel on any class of train, but does not cover sleeping berths. Malaysia has two types of trains. First there are the conventional 1st, 2nd and 3rd class services operating both as ordinary trains and express trains. On overnight services you can get sleeping berths in 1st and 2nd class and reservations can also be made on those classes.

The other trains are the Ekspres Rakyat (Peoples Express) and Ekspres Sinaran. Here the only classes are air-con or non air-con. The trains only stop at the main stations and consequently are faster than the regular expresses. The fares are very reasonable for these modern new trains, a bit more than 3rd for the non air-con carriages, a bit more than 2nd for air-con. Ekspres Rakyat and Ekspres Sinaran only operate Singapore-KL and KL-Butterworth.

Fares on the two Ekspres classes are the same for Singapore-KL or KL-Butterworth – M$28 air-con, M$17 non air-con. On the regular services supplementary charges for sleeping berths are M$6 for a 2nd-class upper berth, M$8 for a lower berth. In 1st class the berths are M$10 or M$20 air-con. Timetables for the main railway services are readily available from railway stations or tourist offices.

There is a daily Ekspres Rakyat train from Singapore in the morning and Ekspres Sinaran in the afternoon, also from KL to Butterworth and vice versa. The trip takes around six hours for either sector. There are also two express trains on each sector in each direction, one by day and one by night. They take rather longer. On the central route Singapore-Tumpat (for Kota Bahru) costs M$25.50 in 3rd, M$41.10 in 2nd, M$91.10 in 1st. From Gemas, where you have to change trains for the central route, the daily train takes over 12 hours.

There is also one stretch of railway line in the north Borneo state of Sabah but it's rapidly disappearing.

Long Distance Taxis These taxis are the great Malaysian travel bargain. In each major (and most minor) town there is a taxi station where you just turn up and announce where you want to go. As soon as there is a full complement of four passengers assembled for that destination, off you go. For most places the wait is never long and the fare is generally about twice the regular bus fare, about the same as 2nd class rail. The taxis are fast, convenient and a little harrowing as the drivers seem to specialise in suicidal overtaking manoeuvres. Closing your eyes at times of high stress certainly helps. You can often arrange a pick-up or drop-off right at your hotel and if you've got a full taxi load you can charter the whole taxi and not worry about waiting at all.

Buses Malaysia also has an excellent bus system with public buses and a whole variety of privately owned ones. In large towns there may be a number of bus stops. Buses are fast, economical and reasonably comfortable and seats can be reserved. On many routes there are also air-con buses costing just a few dollars more than the regular ones, but come prepared for frigid conditions. As one traveller described it: 'Malaysian air-con buses are really meat-lockers on wheels with just two settings – cold and suspended animation'.

Other Transport Malaysia has a reputation for being one of the easiest countries for hitching. If you're ever stuck by a roadside for a few hours you may disagree, but in general it certainly true. The usual hitching rules apply – it's certainly helps to look like the proper sort of traveller, flag on your backpack and so on. At the other end of the scale you can easily hire rental cars in Malaysia. Due to lower licensing and registration costs Malaysian car rental is cheaper than in Singapore.

Local Transport In almost every town there will be taxis and in most cases they will be metered. Large cities also have bus systems, usually a mixture of private and public operators. Bicycle rickshaws may have died out in KL but in many other cities they are still an everyday and very convenient method of getting around – Melaka, Georgetown and Kuala Trengganu are just three places where the bicycle rickshaw is probably the most convenient form of transport.

THINGS TO BUY

Penang's reputation as a semi-free port is somewhat over-rated. There are no great bargains; save your shopping for Singapore. Note that film is particularly expensive anywhere in Malaysia compared to Singapore and Hong Kong. There are lots of shops along Penang Rd and Campbell St in Georgetown, though. Penang also has a number of interesting galleries and print shops both in Georgetown and out at the beaches. Visit the Yahong handicrafts centre at Batu Ferringhi for example. At Telok Bahang there are several batik workshops – Malaysian batik is very different from the Indonesian style.

In Kuala Lumpur you can look at the shops along Jalan Mountbatten or Petaling St. The Saturday night/Sunday Market is also worth exploring.

On the east coast you'll find huge wooden tops, wickerwork, silverwork, beautiful *kain songket* cloth, batik and those fantastic Malaysian kites. Kota Bahru is a centre for the latter and you'll find several good places for them along the road to Pantai Cinta Berahi. Look for the sign *wau bulan*, which means 'moon kite'. Difficult to transport, though.

LANGUAGE

Malay is virtually the same as Indonesian so some effort put into one language will pay off in the other. Although bahasa Malay (often simply referred to as bahasa) is the official language you'll find English is very widely spoken by Malays and Chinese. Although it's nice to be able to speak some bahasa it's much less necessary than in Indonesia. Particularly since so much of your dealings with accommodation or restaurants will be with Chinese who are likely to be more familiar with English than bahasa.

Local additions to English are always fascinating and Malaysia has some intriguing ones apart from the ever-present *bumiputra* – which effectively means a Malay-Malay rather than a Chinese-Malay. Many jobs specify that the applicant must be a *bumiputra*. Other terms that seem to pop up are *jaga keratas* – they're people who operate car parking rackets, pay them to protect your car when it's parked or you'll wish you had. In the Straits Times one day I read of someone being accused of *khalwat*, an Islamic term which means 'close proximity' – suspected fornication by being in a hotel room with someone the culprit wasn't married to!

Peninsular Malaysia

The peninsula, a long finger of land stretching down from the Thai border to Singapore, only 137 km north of the equator, comprises 11 of the 13 states that make up Malaysia. Here you'll find the major cities – oriental Penang, the busy capital Kuala Lumpur, historic Melaka – the shining beaches of the east coast, the restful hill stations and the wild central mountains. Starting from Singapore the description below moves up the west coast to the Thai border, then repeats that pattern on the east coast.

JOHORE BAHRU

The rulers of Melaka retreated here after the Portuguese takeover in 1511. Situated just across the causeway from Singapore, Johore has palace and gardens and the fine Sultan Abu Bakar Mosque. Few travellers pause in Johore, however; it's just a stepping stone to or from Singapore.

Places to Stay

Few people stop for long in Johore Bahru, it's too close to the greater attractions of Singapore. There are plenty of hotels though – a number of Chinese cheapies can be found along Jalan Meldrum, which runs parallel to the main Jalan Tun Abdul Razak, close to the causeway. There are rooms from M$12 in the *Nam Yang* and *Suan Fang*. Slightly more expensive rooms can be found in the *First Hotel* in the Tan Chang Cheng Building on Jalan Station.

Getting There

There is a lot of transport from JB because, it acts as a terminus for Singapore. To get to or from Singapore you can take the 90c 170 bus to Queen St terminus in Singapore or the M$1 Johore Bahru Express to the Rochor Rd terminus, only a stone's throw from the 170 bus destination. Or taxis cost M$4 per person.

From the JB taxi and bus station you can find transport to all major peninsular destinations. Buses are M$18 to KL, M$26 to Ipoh, M$30 to Butterworth. Taxis are M$16 to Melaka, M$28 to KL. JB airport is some distance out of town on the KL road.

MELAKA (Malacca)

Malaysia's oldest and most historic town has had a long and complicated history and there is plenty to see. Originally a Malay kingdom, Melaka was visited in 1409 by Cheng Ho, the 'three jewelled eunuch prince'. The envoy of the Ming Emperor, he formed firm links with China and offered protection from the encroaching Siamese, but in 1511 the

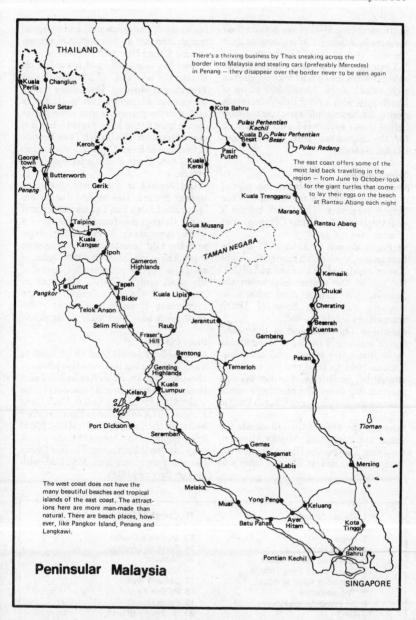

THAILAND

There's a thriving business by Thais sneaking across the
border into Malaysia and stealing cars (preferably Mercedes)
in Penang — they disappear over the border never to be seen again

Kuala
Perlis

Changlun

Alor Setar

Kota Bahru

Pulau Perhentian
Kechil
Kuala D Pulau Perhentian
Besar
Besar Pulau Redang

Keroh

Kuala
Kerai

Pasir
Puteh

George
town

Butterworth

Gerik

The east coast offers some of the
most laid back travelling in the
region — from June to October look
for the giant turtles that come
to lay their eggs on the beach
at Rantau Abang each night

Penang

Kuala Trengganu

Taiping

Gua Musang

Marang

Rantau Abang

Kuala
Kangsar

Ipoh

TAMAN NEGARA

Cameron
Highlands

Kemasik

Lumut

Tapah

Pangkor

Bidor

Kuala Lipis

Chukai

Telok Anson

Cherating

Selim River

Raub

Jerantut

Beserah
Kuantan

Fraser's
Hill

Gambang

Bentong

Genting
Highlands

Temerloh

Pekan

Kelang

Kuala
Lumpur

Tioman

Port Dickson

Seremban

Gemas

Segamat

Labis

Mersing

The west coast does not have the
many beautiful beaches and tropical
islands of the east coast. The attractions here are more man-made than
natural. There are beach places, however, like Pangkor Island, Penang and
Langkawi.

Melaka

Yong Peng

Keluang

Muar

Batu Pahat

Ayer
Hitam

Kota
Tinggi

Peninsular Malaysia

Pontian Kechil

Johor
Bahru

SINGAPORE

Portuguese took Melaka as a port for their spice trade. Alfonse d'Albuquerque raised the massive fortress of A'Famosa.

Then in 1641 Melaka went through changes when the Dutch took over after an eight-month siege. Nearly 200 years of Dutch rule, with a brief British interlude during the Napoleonic wars, was to follow before it was exchanged with the British for the Sumatran port of Bencoolen (Bengkulu today).

Things to See

Porto de Santiago This is the only relic of A'Famosa to survive the Dutch and the British takeovers. The Dutch rebuilt it with the Dutch East India Company coat of arms over the gate.

St Paul's Church Built in 1512 by the Portuguese, this church briefly housed St Xavier's body before it was moved to Goa. On top of the central hill within the fortress, the church now stands in eloquent ruins with beautiful Dutch gravestones inside the walls.

Stadthuys The town hall is the oldest Dutch building in the East, recognisable by its distinctive salmon-pink colouring. Built in 1641 to 1660 and subsequently altered by the British, it is now used as government offices. The Stadthuys stands close by the Dutch Christ Church built in 1713.

Other At the base of the hill stands the small, but interesting, Melaka Museum. On Jalan Tokong the Cheng Hoon Teng Temple is the oldest Chinese temple in

Malaysia. It's an interesting and colourful temple and has an inscription commemorating Cheng Ho's visit to Melaka.

Two km along the road towards Port Dickson is the Sumatran-design Tranquerah Mosque. The Johore Sultan who signed Singapore over to Raffles is buried in the graveyard with some graves dating back to the Ming period – but it is very overgrown. The Po San Teng Temple at the base of Bukit China is dedicated to Cheng Ho. There is also a legendary old well here.

Old Melaka is a fascinating area to wander around. Heeren and Jonker Sts (also called Jalan Tun Tan Cheng Lok and Jalan Gelenggang respectively) have a whole assortment of interesting shops with the odd temple squeezed between them. The small Dutch Fort of St John, or what is left of it, stands on a hilltop east of the town centre. There's not much of interest in the area known as the Portuguese Eurasian settlement – the Portuguese have been gone a long time.

Places to Stay

Melaka Many people head 15 km north to Tanjong Kling but there are also plenty of cheapies in town. *Suan Kee* at 105 Jalan Bunga Raya is a bare and basic doss house with rooms for around M$10. *Hotel Hong Kong* at 154A Jalan Bunga Raya is rather better, or try *Hotel Ng Fook* (tel 06-28055) a few doors down – rooms at these places are just a few dollars more. The *Hoe Chong* has spacious rooms from M$13.20, with air-con they're M$16.

1 Majestic Hotel	11 Church of St. Francis
2 Rex Cinema	12 Stadthuys
3 Regal Hotel	13 St. Paul's Church
4 Wisma Hotel	14 Porta de Santiago
5 Kampong Hulu Mosque	15 Museum
6 Cheng Hoon Teng Temple	16 UE Tea House
7 Kampong Kling Mosque	17 Sultan's Well
8 Tourist Office	18 Po San Teng
9 Sri Pogyatha Vinayagar	19 Palua Hotel
10 GPO	20 St. Peter's Church

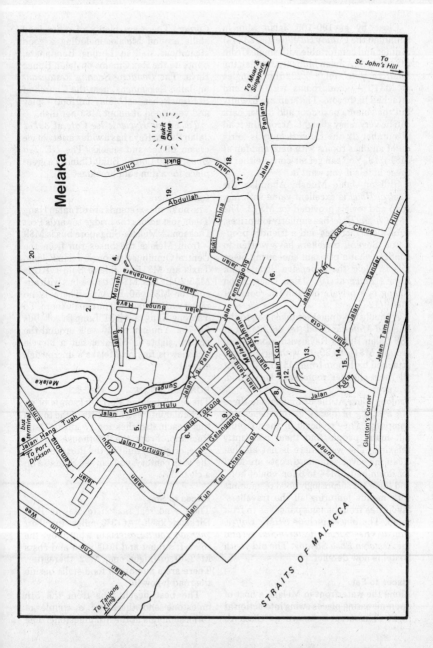

Close by at 100-105 Jalan Munshi Abdullah the *Cathay Hotel* (tel 06-23744) is quiet and comfortable with singles from M$12. At 27A Jalan Munshi Abdullah the *Malacca Hotel* (tel 06-22325) has singles at M$16 – good rooms with fan and attached bathroom. The staff are friendly but the cinema next door and its car park can be very noisy at night. Across the road at number 22 the *Hotel Belangi* is fairly quiet and has rooms with bath and fan at M$14/18. You can get air-con at either of these hotels if you want it.

Still on Jalan Munshi Abdullah the *Central Hotel* is excellent value with fan, soap and towels provided for M$12. The *May Chiang Hotel* has similarly low prices, equivalent facilities and a friendly proprietor. Several travellers have written to confirm what a pleasant shoestring place this is. Near the expensive Straits Inn, *Kane's Place* at 107 Jalan Chan Koon Cheng is a private house with rooms at M$10/12.

A small step upmarket takes you to the fine old *Majestic Hotel* (tel 06-22455) at 188 Jalan Bunga Raya with rooms from around M$15 to 20, or with air-con and attached bathroom from M$30 to 35. Not all their cheaper rooms are very good, however.

Tanjong Kling At the 9th milestone there are a string of places in this beachside kampong. They're basic in the extreme but many people find them pleasantly relaxing. The water here is not all that clean, however. Standard costs are M$2 for dorm beds, M$4 to 6 for 'chalet huts' and there are surprisingly good restaurants with menus featuring all the travellers' favourites from banana pancakes to fruit salad. The places include *SHM's Caffee, Hawaii's Restaurant, Restoren Sun Set* and the *Restoren Rasa Sayang*. The old youth hostel is now derelict.

Places to Eat

Along the waterfront in Melaka a host of open-air eating places swing into action at night. The area is known as *Glutton's Corner*. There are plenty of other food stalls around Melaka including a good steamboat stall in Lorong Bendahara, opposite the Rex Cinema on Jalan Bunga Raya. The *Dondang Sagang Restaurant* on Jalan Laksamana, near the Church of St Francis, has real Malaysian food – spicy and very good at about M$5 per dish.

Tai Chong Hygienic Ice Cafe at 39/72 Jalan Bunga Raya has a wide variety of ice cream dishes and snacks. The *UE Tea House* at 20 Lorong Bukit China is a great place for a dim sum breakfast.

Getting There

The bus and taxi stands are off Jalan Hang Tuah, just across the bridge towards Port Dickson. A Melaka-Singapore bus is M$9 – from Melaka the buses run from the Central Omnibus Station on Jalan Kilang. Taxis are M$15 to Johore Bahru. KL is M$5.20 by bus, M$6.50 for a bus with air-con, or M$10.50 by taxi. There is no railway to Melaka but you can fly there. To Tanjong Kling take a 51 'Long Beach' bus for 75c. You can easily walk around the central sights in Melaka, but a bicycle rickshaw is fine on Melaka's uncrowded streets.

PORT DICKSON

The small town of Port Dickson is of no particular interest, but south of the town a fine beach stretches for 17 km to Cape Rachado. From the lighthouse on the cape, originally built by the Portuguese in the 16th century, you can see Sumatra on a clear day.

Places to Stay

There's no real reason to stay in Port Dickson itself. At 3¾ miles the *Port Dickson Youth Hostel* is on a hill above the road. It's quiet and little used and costs M$2.50 on night one, M$2 thereafter. There are a number of food stalls beside the road below it.

The best beach runs from the 5th milestone and there are a couple of Chinese hotels at the 8th milestone. The

Lido Hotel (tel 06-795237) has rooms for less than M$30, more with air-con. The nearby *Kong Ming Hotel* (tel 06-795239) is slightly less. At the 9th milestone a dirt road leads off to the very pleasant and secluded *Pantai Motel* (tel 06-795265) – rooms from M$30 for a share-bathroom double to M$60 for a more expensive chalet with air-con.

Getting There
By bus it's M$3.30 from Melaka, M$3.70 from KL. A taxi would be about M$6.50 from either town. On Sundays only there is a train-bus excursion from KL, departing at 7.50 am and returning at 5.20 pm. A connecting bus will drop you off at any of the beaches.

PORT DICKSON TO KL
Seremban, the capital of Negri Sembilan, is the centre of the Malaysian Minangkabau area – closely related to the Minangkabau area of Sumatra. The small state museum, in the lake area overlooking the town centre, is a good example of Minangkabau architecture. It's open 9.30 am to 12 noon and 2 to 5.30 pm daily but only to 1 pm on Wednesdays. Kajang, further north towards KL, is supposed to have the best satay in all of Malaysia.

KUALA LUMPUR
When a group of Chinese miners discovered tin near here they landed at the junction of the Kelang and Gombek Rivers and named the spot 'muddy river mouth' – Kuala Lumpur. Later, as tin became more important, the British made KL their Malayan headquarters, the brawling miners were brought into line and KL has never looked back. With independence it became the capital of Malaysia and today it is one of the most progressive, *sky-scrapered*, clover-leafed towns in South-East Asia. For all that, the traffic never reaches Bangkok levels of chaos and there is some interesting stuff to see.

Information & Orientation
KL is relatively easy to get around. The Tourist Information Centre (tel 03-206742) is in the TDC Duty Free Shop in the Bukit Nanas Complex on Jalan Raja Chulan. Immediately south of the river junction which gave the town its name is the crowded Chinatown area.

Two of the most important roads in KL, Jalan Tun Perak and Jalan Tuanku Abdul Rahman, intersect by the central green known as the Padang. Follow Jalan Tun Perak from the Padang across the river and it becomes Jalan Pudu where you'll find the huge Pudu Raya bus and taxi station. Back to the Padang again and north up Jalan Tuanku Abdul Rahman (also known as Batu Rd) will take you to a number of popular restaurants and hotels including the South-East Asia Hotel where the student travel office (MSL Travel) is located. Unfortunately it's a one-way street, the wrong way.

Turn south to get to the Toshiba bus terminal and railway station. Silver Travel Service at 15 Jalan Alor, parallel to Jalan Bukit Bintang, has been recommended for cheap airline tickets. They also have a dorm for penniless travellers about to depart Malaysia. Remember that KL is the capital of Malaysia and all the embassies are located here.

Things to See
Masjid Jame Right at the junction of those muddy rivers stands this fine old red and white mosque. It looks especially good at night from the Benteng street market.
Selangor Club Moorish style similar to the railway station the Federal Secretariat with its clock tower adjoins the old GPO. The nearby Selangor Club looks out over the Padang, where cricket is still played.
Chinatown Just south of the Masjid Jame are the teeming streets of KL's Chinatown. Jalan Petaling is a busy street market at night. Chan See Shu Yuen at the end of Jalan Petaling is a typically ornate Chinese temple. The Sri Mahamariamman temple is Hindu, but also in Chinatown.

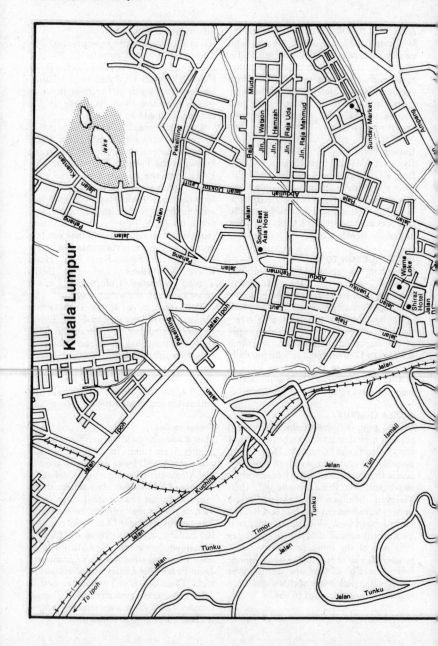

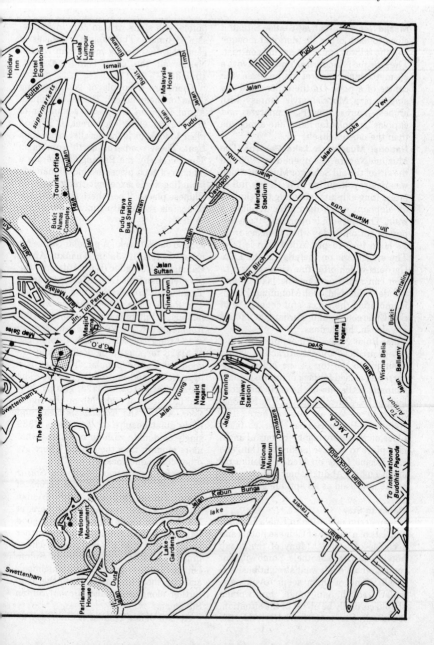

Masjid Negara & Railway Station Situated close to each other the national mosque and the railway station are a fine contrast. The mosque is modern as tomorrow with a 73-metre-high minaret rising from the centre of a pool. On the other hand the station is a Moorish-style fantasy with arches, spires, towers, minarets and cupolas. It looks far more like a mosque than the mosque itself!

National Museum & Lake Gardens The Muzium Negara was opened in 1963, on the site of the old Selangor Museum which was destroyed during WW II. It's full of interesting exhibits including the skull of an elephant which died after derailing a train! The museum is open daily 9 am to 6 pm except on Friday when it closes from 12 noon to 2.45 pm. Admission is free. The museum is on the edge of the Lake Gardens which offer fine views over KL. You can rent boats on the lake or just wander. The National Monument, commemorating the successful conclusion of the Emergency, and Parliament House are also in the gardens.

Other Bukit Nanas, 'Pineapple Hill', is a rather artificial tourist attraction with a chair lift to the top of the hill which is currently closed for lack of interest. Jalan Ampang is the site of the early mansions built by KL's tin millionaires. The National Museum of Art is located here. The Kampong Bahru Sunday Market takes place on Saturday night – colourful and a nice place to wander looking for things to eat. Wisma Loke on Medan Tuanku off Jalan Tuanku Abdul Rahman is a very old house now used as an antique shop.

Places to Stay

Cheap accommodation in Kuala Lumpur consists of a variety of Chinese hotels and a choice of hostels. Many of the cheap hotels in town are brothels. Some will rent rooms, others don't want straight business at all. None of them seem to be particularly rough and tough, but women should certainly be aware of the situation. It's usually easy to tell in a hurry. Also, the hotels with signs written only in Malaysian, 'Rumah Tumpangan', are, as a general rule, offering more than rooms. Nearly all the ones listed here are straight.

There are a couple of good hunting areas for cheap hotels. The Jalan Tuanku Abdul Rahman area, with a number of hotels right along the street, is a good place to look, as is the parallel Jalan Raja Laut. These roads run north from Jalan Tun Perak, by the Padang. There are a number of good places around Chinatown, including some excellent traditional old Chinese places. Then there are a number of hostels scattered mainly south of the centre.

Around Jalan Tuanku A popular centre for cheap hotels is Jalan Tuanku Abdul Rahman (also called Batu Rd) and the parallel Jalan Raja Laut. Moving up Jalan Tuanku etc from its junction with Jalan Tun Perak there's the *Coliseum* with its famous old-planter's restaurant at 100. Rooms are M$18 to 20. At 132 the *Rex* and at 134 the *Tivoli* offer rock-bottom prices of M$18 for singles or doubles and are good values and popular. The Rex is a little better and more friendly, too. The *Paramount* at 154 is M$25, getting dirty and has a sort of nightclub on the eighth floor. At 142 the *Kowloon* is clean and fairly quiet despite its location – M$39 single or double with air-con and rather more modern than the others. There are other cheap ones nearby.

Continuing on you'll find the *Shiraz Hotel* (tel 03-920159) on the corner of Jalan Tuanku etc and Jalan Medan Tuanku. There are 60 rooms here at M$41/46 for singles/doubles and a good Pakistani restaurant downstairs. Further still the *Lai Ann* at 423 is in the dirt-cheap bracket. Nearby at the corner of Sultan Ishmael is the *Hotel Beautiful* which isn't and is a short-time spot. Ditto the *Reno* further along near Jalan Dewan Sultan Sulaiman.

At 285 Jalan Tuanku is the *Dashrun*

Hotel, a modern budget hotel at M$44/50 for singles/doubles. Finally, just off Jalan Tuanku etc at the top end, is the *South-East Asia Hotel* – it's in the middle price bracket, rooms cost from M$72/82, but since it houses the student travel office and offers student discounts it attracts some better-off backpackers.

The story is very similar over on Jalan Raja Laut where there's a string of places between 316 and 340 including the *Sentosa* (tel 03-925644) at 316 with rooms from M$25 to 32 and up with air-con. There's more accommodation across the road although the numbers here are much lower – at 110 the *Cylinman* has rooms at M$20˙ or M$30 with air-con and hot showers. The *Sun Ya* across the street is similar. The *City Hotel* is more expensive. Nearby, the *Great Wall Hotel* looks a bit dubious for more than an hour's stay. Again this is a short-time area – no real problem but single women travellers should be aware of it.

Chinatown Chinatown also has some cheap Chinese hotels like the very rock-bottom *Sai Woo Juan Kee* on the corner of Jalan Sultan and Jalan Panggang. The *Duni* is for business/pleasure only. The more expensive *Lok Ann* on the corner of Jalan Sultan and Jalan Petaling has rooms running from M$35 single or double with bath. Opposite the 'Toshiba' bus stand on Jalan Sultan the *Starlight Hotel* has rooms at similar prices. At 83 Jalan Sultan the *Nanyang Hotel* is a good upmarket cheapie at M$30 cold bath, M$35 hot bath and M$40 double.

The popular *Lee Mun Hotel* on Jalan Sultan close to Jalan Petaling and opposite the Mandarin is a good Chinese cheapie. They are friendly and it costs just M$12 single or double. It's a classic old Chinese hotel with wood panelling, soap, towels, free Chinese tea and huge rooms. Although it's noisy it's also safe and central. At 43 Jalan Sultan is the *Colonial* – the bright yellow place. It's also a good one. Walk through the store and upstairs. The place is big, clean and interesting looking and costs M$15.40 single or double. They also have some cheap air-con rooms.

Not actually in Chinatown, the *Lido Hotel*, just across the street from the YMCA, is a big old place with rooms at M$15 or 22 with bath, single or double. See the YMCA below for how to get there. Also near the YMCA, the *Wing Heng Hotel* is good value with quiet rooms in the back with double beds for M$14. The larger rooms at the front are noisy. All rooms are fan-cooled and have attached toilets and showers, but solo women travellers should beware of the 'night life' in the area.

Other Places For medium-price cheapies Jalan Bukit Bintang used to be a good bet but the prices have escalated out of contention. The medium-priced places here are interspersed with places to eat and also some more expensive hotels. Jalan Bukit Bintang is a short walk from the Pudu Raya bus station. Starting from the Jalan Pudu end of the street at number 4 you'll find the *Weng Hua* where girls come with the rooms. At 16 the *Mey Wah* has rooms at M$40 to 49, but seems half-hearted about renting them. The *Sungi Wang* is at 76 with singles/doubles at M$79/$89, all air-con. Continue to 78 where the *Tai Ichi* is M$42/48 or at 80 the *Park Hotel* is M$39 single, M$48 double.

Along Jalan Pudu from the Pudu Raya bus station, just beyond Jalan Bukit Bintang, there is a string of about 10 brightly painted Chinese hotels through numbers 172 to 190. They are all clean, all about M$20 for one bed, M$30 for two. And all with painted ladies. Most of the places here will rent rooms, and the girls and managers are friendly and not pushy at all.

Hostels Finally there are the hostels. *Wisma Belia* (tel 03-444833) is at 40 Jalan Lornie, (also known as Jalan Syed Putra) a little inconvenient to get to since it's some way out of the centre – take a 52 bus. There are 115 rooms in this government-operated air-con hostel with rooms at M$20/25 without bath, doubles for M$35 with bath. The restaurant is lousy.

Also south of the centre are the YMCA and YWCA. The *YMCA* (tel 03-441439) is at 95 Jalan Kandang Kerbau, just off Jalan Brickfields; get to it on a 12 minibus or a 5, 33, 40, 49, 49A or 243 regular bus and ask for the Lido Cinema. There's a variety of accommodation, from M$7 dorm beds to singles/doubles without private bath at M$15/20; with private bath and air-con costs M$32/40. There's a M$1 temporary membership charge to non-members of the YMCA and women are accepted. The YMCA has a good restaurant with a large menu, not too unreasonable prices and very cheap breakfasts. The small Chinese restaurant across from the YMCA does good cheap meals. Drawbacks of the YMCA are that it is often full and its location is rather depressing, but it's clean and staff are very helpful with travel advice. The *YWCA* (tel 03-283225 or 201623) is at 12 Jalan Davidson and has rooms at M$15/25 for single/doubles but takes women only.

The Youth Hostel (tel 03-672872) is rather a long way out on Jalan Vethavanam, just off Jalan Ipoh. Ask for a bus that goes down Jalan Ipoh (a 66, 146 or 147 from Pudu Raya or a 71 or 143 from Jalan Ampang) and get off at the 3½ milestone or simply tell the conductor you want the YH. For members it costs M$2.50 for the first night, M$2 thereafter. Non-members pay M$4, then M$3. Catches are its distance from the centre and that there's a touch of the 'lights-out' mentality here. Also, at last report the hostel was 'closed for renovations'.

Places to Eat

Night Markets KL has some very good nighttime eating places. The tables set up at dusk at the Medan Pasar car park and nearby Benteng, right across the river from the Masjid Jame, are excellent. *Nasi ayam* is a speciality and the *es campur* here is simply the best anywhere. The mosque looks romantically eastern across the river and if it should rain you can

shelter in the bank frontages. A drink and a meal is about M$4, satay 30c a stick. Unlike in Singapore a lot of sugar is added to fruit drinks here so if you don't want it, say so.

Other night markets with good food include the Sunday market out at Kampong Bahru, and a street off Jalan Tuanku Abdul Rahman close to the South-East Asia Hotel. Both are good places for Malay food. Across the river from the train station is another large food stall area. It's wedged between the river and the edge of Chinatown. There is a big indoor market on Jalan Hang Kasturi near the river between the Masjid Jame and the train station.

Indian Food On Jalan Melayu, near the corner of Jalan Tuanku Abdul Rahman and Jalan Tun Perak, there's the *Ceylon Restaurant* and the *Jai Hind*. Good for Indian snacks and light meals.

Upstairs at 60A Jalan Tuanku etc *Bangles* is an Indian restaurant with a good reputation. Further down the *Shiraz*, on the corner of Jalan Tuanku etc and Jalan Medan Tuanku, is a good Pakistani restaurant. Right across the road from that is the *Akbar* with excellent north Indian food. There are several others here, too. The *Bilal* restaurants – there are two of them at 40 Jalan Ipoh and 33 Jalan Ampang – are other good Indian restaurants. Roti chanai and murtabaks are good here. The *Omar Khayam* is another.

Chinese Food Chinese restaurants can be found all over the place, but particularly around Chinatown and along Jalan Bukit Bintang near the Pudu Raya bus station. There is interesting Chinese vegetarian food in the crowded *Fook Woh Yuen* at the bottom end of Jalan Petaling. Excellent lunchtime dim sums at the expensive *Merlin Hotel*.

A local speciality in KL is *bah kut teh*, supposed to have originated in Kelang. It's pork ribs with white rice and Chinese tea and is a very popular breakfast meal.

Western Food KL has a surprising variety

of western restaurants including, at the bottom of Jalan Tuanku etc, *Colonel Sanders* and *A&W* take-aways. There are several American-style hamburger joints around the bus station including *Wendy's* and, over towards Chinatown, *McDonald's*. There's also an interesting, if expensive, Malay answer to American fast foods here – a take-away satay place. Over on Jalan Bukit Bintang there's also an *Orange Julius* fast food joint. *Uncle Bill's*, in the Tivoli Hotel on Jalan Tuanku etc, is 'plastic but good' reports one traveller.

Not to be missed on the same street is the restaurant in the *Coliseum Hotel* where they have excellent steaks. When they say it's served on a sizzle plate they really mean it; the waiters zip up behind you and whip a bib around your neck to protect your clothes from the sizzle. M$12 buys you a great steak and salad and the place is quite a colonial experience which has scarcely changed over the years.

Down the street the *KK Cafeteria* by the Paramount Hotel has set lunches for M$5.50, soup to tea. The *Ship*, near the Regent Hotel, is also a splash-out steak place. Prior to being closed for extensive renovations the *Station Hotel* did an excellent set dinner for only M$6.50 – worth it just to eat in the station's amazing surroundings. The renovations are complete now and it's once again a superb place for a meal – you can also try the *Corsicana* bar there or the cheap cafeteria actually in the station. At the *New Yorker* on Jalan Bukit Bintang you can get not only a good steak but also wine.

In Chinatown don't miss *English Hotbreads* on Jalan Sultan. They offer all kinds of buns and rolls stuffed with chicken curry or cheeses and fresh from the oven. Also available are pizza, macaroni, fruit tarts and chocolate cakes. Prices are good. There is another similar place across the street and down a bit called the *Angel Cake House*, downstairs from the Nanyang Hotel. The *Brass Rail*, just off Jalan Medan Tuanku, is a British-style pub with cheaper drink prices during the 4 to 7 pm 'happy hour'. Just across the bridge from the GPO is a Chinese bar known to locals as *The Vatican* – it's a popular expat hangout.

Finally *Le Coq d'Or*, a restaurant in a fine turn-of-the-century mansion on Jalan Ampang, is expensive but not quite as expensive as the elegant surroundings might indicate.

Getting There

KL is the main international arrival gateway for air travellers and a central crossroads for travel by bus, rail or taxi. See the introductory rail section for details of railway fares. Buses and taxis mainly operate from the Pudu Raya terminal although there is also the smaller Kelang or 'Toshiba' (from the neon sign on it) terminal. Bus fares include Melaka M$6-8, Johore Bahru M$13-15, Singapore M$15-17, Ipoh M$7-10, Butterworth M$13-15, Cameron Highlands M$7-8. Taxis go from upstairs in the Pudu Raya terminal. Fares include Melaka M$12, Johore Bahru M$30, Ipoh M$15, Butterworth M$30, Kuantan M$20, Kuala Trengganu M$34, Kota Bahru M$40.

Getting Around

Airport Transport Taxis from Kuala Lumpur's international airport operate on a coupon system. You purchase a coupon from a booth at the airport and use this to pay the driver – it's designed to eliminate fare cheating from the airport. Going to the airport is not so simple because the taxi drivers are uncertain about getting a return trip – count on about M$16-18. Or you can go by bus – a 47 bus operates every hour from the Toshiba terminal on Jalan Sultan Mohamed and costs M$1.05. The trip takes 45 minutes and the first departure is at 6 am. There's also a non-direct 61 bus.

Bus There are two bus systems operating in KL. Fare stage buses start from 15c for the first km and go up 5c each two km. City bus companies include Sri Jaya, Len Seng, Lendee, Ampang, Kee Hup and

Toong Foong. There are a number of bus stands around the city including the huge Pudu Raya terminal on Jalan Pudu and the 'Toshiba' terminal on Jalan Sultan Mohamed (so named from the Toshiba sign on top of the multi-storey car park). The faster minibuses operate on a fixed fare of 50c anywhere along their route. Whenever possible have correct change ready when boarding the bus, particularly during rush hours.

Taxis Trishaws have virtually disappeared from KL's heavily trafficked streets but there are plenty of taxis, and fares are quite reasonable. They start from 70c for the first km, then an additional 30c for each extra 0.8 km. Air-con taxis are M$1 then 60c. There's an additional charge of 10c for a third and fourth passenger and from 1 to 6 am there's an additional 50% supplement on top of the meter fare. KL's taxi drivers are not keen on going to the airport or from the station on the meter – in those cases you'll have to bargain your fare. It shouldn't be more than a couple of dollars from the railway station to most places in KL.

AROUND KUALA LUMPUR

Batu Caves A KL sight not to be missed, the Batu Caves are 12 km to the north. A hundred-metre-high limestone hill houses a vast cavern known as the cathedral cave – it's that big. You have to climb 272 steps up to the cave's entrance. The funicular railway beside the steps seems to be shut down permanently.

The adjoining Dark Cave has been closed for a couple of years because quarrying in the hill has made it unsafe. The caves are the site for the annual Thaipusam festival when Hindu devotees carry heavy religious ornaments on steel pins embedded in their flesh. To get to the caves take an 11 minibus (60c) from Jalan Pudu or Jalan Semarang or a Len Seng bus 70 from Jalan Raja Laut/Jalan Ampang.

Other The National Zoo & Aquarium are on the way to Ulu Kelang, about 13 km

from KL. Open daily from 9 am to 6 pm, admission is M$2.50 (only 30c for students). Take a Len Seng bus 170 or a Lenchee 180 from Jalan Leboh Ampang. Or a 17 or 23 minibus. Mimaland, Malaysia in Miniature, is no big deal. It's 18 km from KL on the way to the Genting Highlands. Templer Park, 22 km north on the way to Ipoh, is a 1200 hectare area with jungle walks, swimming lagoons and several waterfalls. Petaling Jaya is a suburb of KL that has become a city in its own right. Port Kelang is KL's port, 30 km to the south-west. You can visit batik factories and see Selangor pewter being made close to KL.

GENTING HIGHLANDS

The Genting Highlands is a modern hill station – casinos instead of jungle walks. Accommodation is expensive (rooms start from around M$40). It's about 50 km from KL and there's a regular M$4.50 bus from the Pudu Raya station or you can get there by taxi for M$7.

FRASER'S HILL

Fraser's Hill is not the easiest hill station to get to, but it's quite a pleasant and relaxing place although not so large and interesting as the Cameron Highlands with its many jungle walks.

Places to Stay & Eat

There's not much by the way of cheap accommodation. The *Puncak Inn* (tel 071-60201) has rooms from M$20 to 50. The cheaper rooms are very small. Prices all go up M$5 in the peak seasons. The *Seri Berkat Rest House* has rooms at M$25 and there are various pleasantly old-fashioned bungalows with rooms at around M$30. They can all be booked through the information centre right across the golf course.

If you need something more reasonably priced try the *Corona Nursery*, a flower nursery about a 25-minute walk from the information centre. It's run by a friendly Indian family. A double with attached bathroom is M$12 and you can use the kitchen and fridge. Beware of the ill-tempered dog belonging to a neighbour.

Adjoining the Puncak Inn is the Chinese *Hill View Restaurant* (quite good food and snacks) and the Malay *Arzed Restaurant* (friendly) or you can splash out at the *Temerloh Steakhouse*, steaks from M$10.

At the bottom of the hill there is the pleasant old *Gap Rest House* with rooms at M$12 and up. In fact this wonderfully old-fashioned place is much nicer than everything up at Fraser's Hill and there are several places to eat near at hand.

Getting There

To get to Fraser's Hill first get to Kuala Kubu Bahru 62 km north of KL, just off the KL-Ipoh road. From there buses run at 8 am and 12 noon to Fraser's Hill and return at 10 am and 2 pm. Fare is M$1.80. The five-mile road from the Gap up to Fraser's Hill operates 40 minutes uphill and 40 minutes downhill with 20 minutes closed in between.

KUALA LUMPUR TO IPOH

The road north from KL is always quite busy. There are turn-offs near Kuala Kubu Bahru (for Fraser's Hill) and further north for Telok Anson and Lumut, for Pangkor Island. Selim River, where a last stand was unsuccessfully made against the Japanese in WW II, has a 'fantastic' *Rest House* with singles/doubles for just M$4/6 – if you can think of a good reason for stopping there!

CAMERON HIGHLANDS

Situated about 60 km off the KL-Ipoh road from Tapah this is the best known and most extensive hill station. The Highlands stand at 1500 metres and the weather is pleasantly cool, not cold. Jungle walks are the thing to do here; the tourist office in Tanah Rata will supply a somewhat inaccurate map of the main walks. Most of them you can stroll in an hour or two but some take rather longer and can be quite tough.

The only wildlife you are likely to see is the fantastic variety of butterflies but it was here that the American Thai silk entrepreneur Jim Thompson (see the Bangkok section) mysteriously disappeared in 1967 – he was never found. The hills around the Highlands are dotted with tea plantations – you can take interesting tours and you might even get a free sample of tea.

Places to Stay

The Highlands can be packed out during the April, August and December holiday seasons. There is no Cameron Highlands centre, it's actually a string of smaller places, starting with Ringlet where there is no real reason to pause. Tanah Rata is the main centre with a lot of places to stay – you'll also find the bus and taxi station here and the tourist info centre. The very clean and well kept *Seah Meng Hotel* at 39 Tanah Rata is a popular place with rooms from M$16. Next door the *Town House Hotel* is similarly priced and clean and well kept. The *Tanah Rata Hotel* at 25 has big rooms and the prices are low but it gets mixed reports from travellers. Or there's the *Hollywood Hotel* but at all these main road places try to avoid the noisy rooms at the front.

Off the main road is the rather more expensive *Garden Hotel* with rooms from M$45. The Tanah Rata *Rest House* is expensive by rest house standards, but pleasant and quiet. Even the ordinary doubles have little sitting rooms as well as attached bathrooms for M$28.

Continuing up towards the golf course you come to the popular *Bala's Holiday Chalets* (tel 05-941660). Prices start from around M$5 per person in basic share rooms, M$10 for doubles but prices tend to vary a bit with demand and season. Bala's a bit of a businessman and if he thinks you can be steered into a M$40 'luxury room' he'll have a go! There's a restaurant but you can also use the cooking facilities to fix your own food. There's a washing machine too and this is

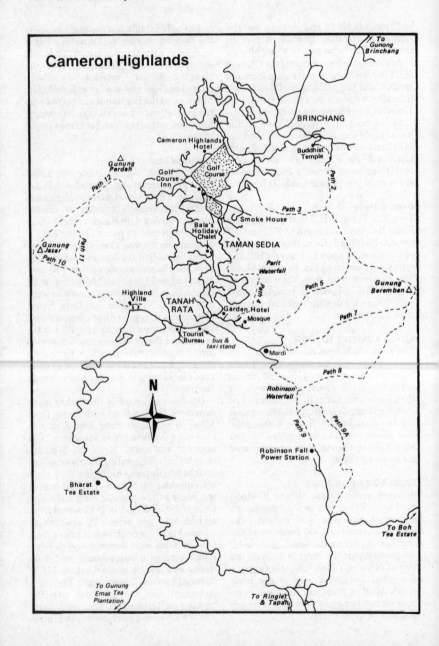

Cameron Highlands

BRINCHANG

Cameron Highlands Hotel

Buddhist Temple

△ Gunung Perdah

Golf Course Inn

Golf Course

Path 12

Path 2

Path 3

Smoke House

Bala's Holiday Chalet

TAMAN SEDIA

△ Gunung Jasar
Path 10

Path 11

Parit Waterfall

Path 5

Gunung Beremban △

Highland Villa

TANAH RATA

Path 4

Garden Hotel

Mosque

Path 7

Tourist Bureau

bus & taxi stand

Mardi

Path 8

Robinson Waterfall

Path 9

Path 9A

N

Robinson Fall Power Station

Bharat Tea Estate

To Gunong Brinchang

To Boh Tea Estate

To Gunung Emas Tea Plantation

To Ringlet & Tapah

a particularly popular meeting place for travellers.

Finally, there's Brinchang up beyond the golf course. There are more cheap Chinese hotels here and the popular *Wong Villa* and *Jolly Villa* where you can get rooms for M$12 or less. Wong Villa has a lovely garden. They're sometimes packed out with noisy parties of Chinese salesmen.

Places to Eat

There's lots of good food in the Highlands; this is one of the best places for cheap Indian food in Malaysia. Try the *Restoran Kumar*, next to the Sri Tanah Rata supermarket in Tanah Rata – the murtabaks and roti chanai are simply 'fantastic'. It used to be known as the Sri Tanah Rata. Nearby is the small, but also very good, *Bunga Raya*. Up at Brinchang there's the low-priced, and excellent, *Sri Sentosa* and the newer *Sri Brinchang*.

There are plenty of Chinese places too, including the *Kowloon* in Brinchang or the really excellent *Hong Kong* down in Tanah Rata – they're rather more expensive though. Steamboat, the Chinese equivalent of a Swiss fondue, is a real Highlands specialty. Try it at the *Garden Hotel* amongst other places. The more people you have for a steamboat the better.

The *Old Smokehouse* is 'ideal for homesick Brits' or you can splash out on a good hamburger at the *Merlin*. If you're fixing your own food at Bala's or elsewhere the vegetables and other food are, reportedly, fresher and cheaper at Brinchang than in Tanah Rata. There's a good bakery on Jalan Sultan and the bar at the *Rest House* is a local social centre.

Getting There

It's a steep climb up from Tapah to the Highlands. The 153 bus runs hourly from Tapah, M$2.75 one way, cheaper for return tickets. A taxi is M$5.50. There's a daily MARA bus to KL for M$8 but for Butterworth you have to get a bus from Tapah. The Town House Hotel will book tickets for the Tapah-Butterworth bus at M$10 to 13 depending on the bus. You have to leave Tanah Rata by 8 am and you get to Butterworth around 2.30 pm.

IPOH

The city of millionaires made its fortune from tin mining. It has a reputation in Malaysia as a bit of a sin city with strip clubs and massage parlours. There are some interesting cave temples on the outskirts of town to the south and north.

Places to Stay

Lots of cheap hotels and restaurants here. The *Beauty Hotel* on Jalan Yang Kalsom is just M$12. On the same road are the similarly priced *Kowloon* at 92 and the *New Nanyang* at 22. At 37 Jalan Chamberlain the *Embassy* is also cheap. Ipoh has a fine old *Station Hotel* (tel 05-512588) at the railway station but rooms are M$40-90.

Places to Eat

Ipoh is renowned for its excellent restaurants. Just ask a local, they all have opinions on what is currently good. Try Jalan Clare for Chinese food. The *Rahman Restaurant* at 78 Chamberlain Rd does superb murtabak, rotis and curries and has great iced lemon drinks. The *Station Hotel* does a great breakfast for M$6.

KUALA KANGSAR

The royal town of Perak has the fine Ubadiah Mosque with its onion dome and the minarets squeezed up against it as if seen in a distorting mirror. This is the place where rubber trees were first grown in Malaysia.

Places to Stay

There's a fine *Rest House* overlooking the Perak River, between the town centre and the mosque, with rooms at M$17.60. The *Double Lion Hotel* at 74 Jalan Kangsar is very cheap at just M$77 but also extremely basic.

TAIPING

The 'town of everlasting peace' was once a raucous mining town. It has a beautiful lake garden and zoo and the oldest museum in Malaysia. Take care with your valuables while looking around the museum. Above the town is the peaceful little Maxwell Hill station. To get there you have to take a government Land-Rover from the station at the foot of the hill, close to the lake gardens. The 40-minute ascent costs M$2 all the way to the top.

Places to Stay

There's an architecturally curious *Rest House* overlooking the lake gardens and a second *Rest House* at around M$10 in the town itself – breakfast on the verandah, very pleasant. Or you could try the *Wee Bah Hotel* also at M$10 (a perfect copy of the Tye Ann in Georgetown). There are many other cheap and clean Chinese hotels, particularly along the main street.

PANGKOR ISLAND

Close to Lumut on the mainland Pangkor has some fine beaches and an interesting round-the-island walking path. There's an old Dutch fort a little south of Pangkor Village and turtles sometimes lay their eggs on the beach north of Pasir Bogak.

Places to Stay & Eat

At the north end of Pasir Bogak *Sam Khoo's Mini Camp* is a collection of thatched-roof huts around a central restaurant area. It's the backpackers' centre with singles, doubles and dorm huts at M$5 for singles, M$8-10 for doubles. It's primitive but popular, particularly on weekends when it can be packed right out. Close by is the *Pangkor' Anchor* with 30 neatly laid-out A-frame huts with simple, mattress-on-the-floor accommodation at M$10 per person per night.

The *Rest House*, also at Pasir Bogak, has a room above the restaurant for M$10 or three bungalows each with two double rooms at M$20. It would be fine were it not

so run down and dismal. There are other more expensive places at Pasir Bogak and at Telok Belanga, at the northern end of the island.

There's reasonably good food at rock-bottom prices at the mini-camp. Or try the *Rest House* and the nearby food stalls. There's a real crowd of restaurants, predominantly Chinese, in Pangkor Village. Lumut has a fine old *Rest House* at M$14, the cheaper *Singa Hotel* and the very good and clean *Phi Lum Hooi Hotel* at just M$7 for a single with fan. Lots of places to eat around Lumut.

Getting There

Boats operate every half hour from Lumut; the fare is around M$1. There are also less frequent connections to Telok Belanga. A taxi across the island to Pasir Bogak (walk in 20 minutes) is around M$2.50. All the way to the mini-camp costs M$3-4, more on weekends. You can easily hire boats to neighbouring islands.

PENANG

The oldest British settlement on the Malay peninsula, Penang (Betelnut) island predates Singapore and Melaka. Captain Francis Light sailed up and took over the virtually uninhabited island in 1786. Founding places must have run in the family; his son later founded Adelaide in Australia. Encouraged by free-trade policies, Georgetown, the city on the island, became a prosperous centre. Unmistakably Chinese, it's one of the most likable cities in South-East Asia. With easygoing kampongs, sandy beaches, warm water, good food and plenty of things to see – who wouldn't like Georgetown and Penang?

Information & Orientation

Don't confuse Georgetown (the town) with Penang (the island). It's Georgetown you arrive at after crossing the narrow straits on the ferries. The attractions of Penang are evenly split between the easygoing charms of Georgetown and the pleasures of the beaches around the island. There's a good tourist office on Jalan Tun Syed Sheh Barakbah. Pick up a copy of the 50c *Penang for the Visitor* booklet here. The GPO and immigration office are close to here. Poste Restante at the GPO is very efficient while the American Express mail service in Georgetown is very inefficient.

Important streets in Georgetown are Leboh Chulia, where you'll find many of the cheap hotels, and Jalan Penang, which Leboh Chulia terminates on. There you'll find many shops and restaurants. Georgetown has a heavy drug scene, take care.

Things to See

Fort Cornwallis The original wooden structure built by Light was rebuilt in stone by convicts from 1808 to 1810. See the nearly 400-year-old Dutch cannon inside the fort.

Khoo Kongsi A kongsi is a Chinese clan house, not really a temple, and the Khoo's kongsi is the finest in Penang. So fine that the day it was completed in 1898 the roof caught on fire. Clan elders took this as a message from above that they were overdoing things and repaired it in marginally-less grandiose style. It's a positive rainbow of dragons, statues, paintings, lamps and carvings.

Goddess of Mercy Temple The oldest and possibly the most popular temple in Penang, Kuan Yin's is the temple for the everyday folk. Outside stand two large burners where you can burn a few million monopoly money, to ensure wealth for the after life.

Mosques On the same street stands the large Kapitan Kling Mosque with its single fine minaret. The Malay Mosque, close by on Acheen St, has an Egyptian-style minaret, unusual in Malaysia.

Hindu Temples The Shiva Temple on Jalan Datu Keramat is hidden behind a high wall – prayers are chanted at sunset. The south Indian Sri Mariamman temple on Queen St has fine carvings over the entrance.

Buddhist Temples The Penang Buddhist Association is quiet and tasteful, and not very interesting. Wat Chayamangkalaram, the Thai Temple, has a big reclining Buddha, more Chinese than Thai.

Around Georgetown There's a pleasant little museum, with gory details of Chinese secret society squabbles, and an art gallery with a statue of Francis Light out front. Next door is the old St George's Church. The Botanical Gardens, better known as the waterfall gardens, have lots of monkeys. Georgetown is a maze of delightful Chinese back alleys and shopping streets. Near the ferry terminal is an old fishing village waterfront.

Kek Lok Si Temple Visit this temple en route to Penang Hill; it's near the Ayer Itam bus stop. It's more a tourist attraction than a temple; well, 'Tiger Balm' Aw Paw had a hand in it. You climb through arcades of souvenir stalls, by a jam-packed turtle-pond and murky fish-pond to the hilltop 'Million Buddhas Precious Pagoda'. You make a voluntary contribution to climb to the summit. Right by the Ayer Itam bus stop are two terrific bakeries.

Penang Hill The top of the 830-metre-high hill offers spectacular views over the island and across to the mainland. The funicular railway was developed by the Swiss – an interesting engineering feat. It trundles up the steep slope to pleasant gardens, a small cafe and a choice of Hindu temple or Moslem mosque perched on top. The excursion is especially good as dusk settles over the island and Georgetown lights up. There are frequent services on the railway from 6.30 am to 9.30 pm. The round trip ascent costs M$3 in the flashy new Swiss railcars – one of the old railcars, replaced a few years back, is on display at the Georgetown museum. On weekends and public holidays the queues can be rather long. The energetic can get to the top by an eight-km hike starting from the Moon Gate at the Botanical Gardens. It takes about two hours, bring a water-bottle along. You can also ride a rented motorcycle to the top.

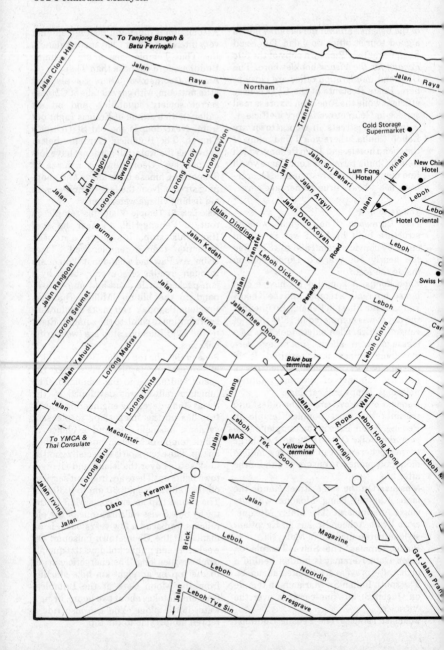

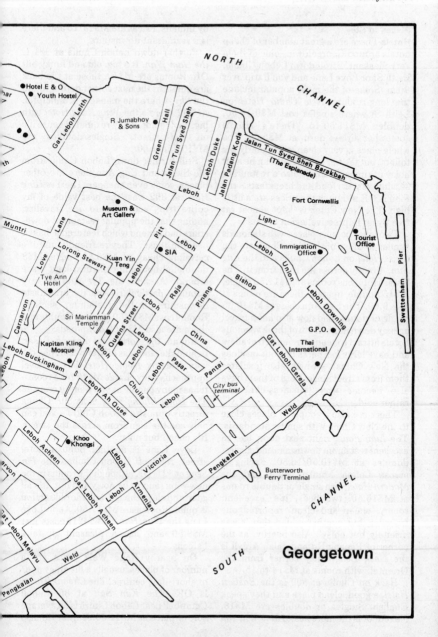

NORTH CHANNEL

Hotel E & O
Youth Hostel

Gat Leboh Leith

Green Hall

Jalan Tun Syed Sheh

Leboh Duke

Jalan Padang Koda

R Jumabhoy
& Sons

Jalan Tun Syed Sheh Barakbah
(The Esplanade)

Leboh

Fort Cornwallis

Museum &
Art Gallery

Pitt

Muntri

Leboh

Light

Lane

Lorong Stewart

SIA

Leboh

Immigration
Office

Tourist
Office

Love

Kuan Yin
Teng

Leboh

Union

Tye Ann
Hotel

Leboh

Raja

Bishop

Pinang

Leboh Downing

Carnarvon

Sri Mariamman
Temple

Queens Street

Leboh

China

G.P.O.

Gat Leboh Gereja

Kapitan Kling
Mosque

Leboh

Pasar

Thai
International

Leboh Buckingham

Leboh

Leboh

Leboh Ah Quee

Chulia

Pantai

Leboh

City bus
terminal

Weld

Swettenham Pier

Khoo
Khongsi

Leboh Acheen

Victoria

Pengkalan

Butterworth
Ferry Terminal

Carnarvon

Gat Leboh Acheen

Leboh Armenian

Gat Leboh Melayu

Weld

SOUTH CHANNEL

Pengkalan

Georgetown

Places to Stay

Hotels There are a great number of cheap hotels around Georgetown, some of them very pleasant. Stroll down Leboh Chulia, Leith St or Love Lane and you'll trip over them. Some of the most popular include the long-running *New China Hotel* on Leith St where singles cost M$9-10.50, doubles M$11.50-15. There's also a somewhat airless dorm at M$5.50. The whole place is very clean, particularly the toilets, but the bar in the back can be a bit noisy at times. There is also a restaurant serving western food and breakfasts – the food is OK although the prices are a little high. The New China is 'kept almost rat free by an impressive legion of cats'.

Two other popular places with standards similar to those of the New China are the *Swiss Hotel* on Leboh Chulia and the *Eng Aun*, directly across the road from it. The Swiss Hotel has rooms at M$11.50 single, M$15 double; upstairs there are rooms at M$19.60. The Eng Aun charges M$10.35 single or double and now also has a travel agency downstairs. Both of these spacious hotels attract a steady stream of travellers and have large car parks in front (as does the New China) – which also insulates them from street noise. Both of them have also become very 'business-like' and rather cold.

There are also a couple of places close to the New China with similar standards. The *Lum Fong*, right next door, has an excellent restaurant downstairs and singles/doubles at M$10.50/16.50. Facing it across Leboh Muntri you'll find the *Modern Hotel* with single or double rooms at M$16.50, two beds. It's 'excellent, roomy, cheap and clean' reported one traveller, but another added that it was 'friendly but noisy'. Also nearby, at the corner of Penang Rd and Jalan Argyll is the *Hock Beng*, kitty corner from the Oriental, with rooms at M$14 to 15.

Back on Chulia at 509 is the *Eastern Hotel*, a good, clean place and they speak English. Singles or doubles are M$16. Next door is the more basic *Han Chow* run

by Indians. Prices are M$14/16 and there is a restaurant downstairs.

Further down Leboh Chulia at 381 is the *Nam Wah*. It's big, old and funky but OK. Rooms are M$10, those at the back are quiet. At the next corner detour round the *Sky*, where the manager is unhelpful. At 392 there's the *Yeng Keng Hotel* with big, cool rooms. They're quiet because it's off the street. Singles/doubles are M$10.35/11.50.

Still further down Leboh Chulia from the Swiss and Eng Aun there are other places, some even cheaper. The *Yee Hing Hotel* at 302 was 'the best value of my entire trip', according to one traveller; adding that the popular restaurant downstairs had a menu which featured a 'baked bean on toast'. They're friendly and it's certainly cheap at M$6.80 single, M$8 double, although not the best-kept place around. At 282 the *Tye Ann* is very popular, particularly for its breakfasts downstairs in the restaurant section. Rooms cost M$10.50 single or double and there are also M$4.50 dorm beds.

Round the corner on Lorong Pasar, behind the Goddess of Mercy Temple, the very friendly *Noble Hotel* has a novel approach. They charge M$12 for a room – for as many people as you want to cram in. The *Hotel Chung King* is at 398 Chulia directly opposite Leboh Cintra – you can only see the sign from across the street. It's cheap but noisy.

Love Lane is another popular hotel street, right off Leboh Chulia. The *Pin Seng* at 82 is OK although the rooms in the new wing tend to be noisy and hot. It's all good and clean though, and the old section is quiet. Rooms are M$11.50. At 35 Love Lane the *Wan Hai* (tel 61421) costs just M$9.50 and has a pleasant upstairs balcony.

On nearby Rope Walk there are a number of places, usually a bit dingy and/ or short-time centres. The *Choong Thean* is OK. The *Kim Sun* at 86 Leboh Campbell near Leboh Cintra is an average sort of place at M$11.50. Burma Rd also has a few hotels like the *Hotel Kim Wah* at 114 where a room with bath and fan costs M$19.80, and is, reported a visitor, 'central, clean, has a restaurant and the short-time ladies are well in evidence'. Another is the *Tong Lok* which is owned by the New China Hotel and sometimes used by them as an overflow place. At 3 Jalan Transfer, a block over from Penang Rd, the *Num Keow* has dorm bes at M$3.50, rooms at M$7/9 and is a clean, spacious, well kept bargain.

There are many, many other hotels around Georgetown. Over on Leboh Light at the corner of King is *Hotel Pathe*, a large place with rooms at M$27 with bath. The *Wen Hai*, between Chulia and Leboh Light, is just M$8.50/11.50 and there's a dorm for M$4.50. It's a quiet place with a travel agency downstairs and small, interesting industrial-type shops next door. Western breakfasts are available across the street. Look around and you'll discover many others.

For a bit of a splurge you can stay at the wonderful-looking *Cathay Hotel*, halfway between the Oriental and the Merlin near the New China Hotel. The lobby nearly equals the exterior. Prices are M$31.20 doubles, M$36 with air-con, M$26.40 singles with attached bath. Also a bit pricier is the *Prince* at 456 Chulia. It's modern, all air-con and the M$40 rooms feature piped-in music. The guy at the desk told me they could find me 'some company to share my room'. Other middle-bracket air-con hotels include the *Federal* on Penang Rd at M$34.50 and the *Hotel Fortuna*, also on Penang Rd, at M$34/38.

In this same price bracket you could try the *Peking Hotel* (tel 04-22455) at 50A Penang Rd or the slightly more expensive *United Hotel* (tel 04-21361) at 101 Macalister Rd. More expensive again, the *Hotel Waterfall* (tel 04-27221) is at 160 Western Rd. At 48F Northam Rd the *Paramount Hotel* (tel 04-63773) has singles at M$20-35, doubles M$25-45. The *Singapore Hotel* at 495H Penang Rd

has large and well-furnished air-con rooms with a shower from around M$20.

The Ys Penang has a conveniently situated, but extremely anonymous, *Youth Hostel* right next door to the gracious old E&O Hotel on Leboh Farquhar. The only clue to its existence is a sign proclaiming 'no visitors'. Periodically it's reported to have closed down completely, but it always seems to reappear. First night cost for a dorm bed is M$2.50, subsequent nights are M$2.20.

The *YMCA* (tel 04-362211) is a little inconveniently situated at 211 Jalan Macalister – get there on a number 7 bus. It is, however, conveniently close to the Thai Embassy, an important Penang address for many travellers. Singles/doubles cost M$17/22 or M$20/26 with air-con. All rooms have attached showers and there are also dorms at M$7 per person. Unfortunately they tend to fill up the noisy dorm rooms in the front before starting on the quieter ones at the back. There's a M$1 temporary membership charge for non-members of the YMCA, but this can be waived if you're a YHA member or have a student card. The YMCA also has a TV lounge and cafeteria. Finally the *YWCA* is much further out at 8A Green Lane and, unlike the YMCA, it's single sex only.

Places to Eat

Penang is another of the region's delightful food trips with a wide variety of restaurants and many local specialities to tempt you. There are two types of soup particularly associated with Penang which are known as *laksa*. *Laksa assam* is a fish soup with a sour taste from the tamarind or assam paste. The soup is served with special white laksa noodles. *Laksa lemak* was originally a Thai dish, but has been adopted by Penang. It's basically similar to laksa assam except coconut milk is substituted for the tamarind. Seafood is, of course, very popular in Penang and there are many restaurants that specialise in fresh fish, crabs and prawns –

particularly along the northern beach fringe.

Despite its Chinese character Penang also has a strong Indian presence and there are some popular specialities to savour. Curry kapitan is a Penang chicken curry which supposedly takes its name from a Dutch sea captain asking his Indonesian mess boy what was on that night. The answer was 'curry kapitan' and it's been on the menu ever since. *Murtabak*, a thin roti chanai pastry stuffed with egg, vegetables and meat, is not a Penang speciality, but it's a dish done with particular flair here.

Indian Food Amongst the most popular Indian restaurants is *Dawood's* at 63 Queen St, opposite the Sri Mariamman Temple. Curry kapitan is just one of the many curry dishes at this popular and reasonably priced restaurant, and is priced at M$2.60. Beer is not available, but the lime juice is excellent and so is the ice cream. Recently, however, Dawood's standards seem to have been sliding downhill. At 166 Campbell St the *Meerah* and at 164A the *Hameediyah* both have good curries and delicious murtabak.

On the corner of King and Bishop Sts you can get a whole selection of curry dishes plus rice and chappatis at *Rio*. The *Taj Mahal Restaurant* on the corner of Jalan Penang and Leboh Chulia is another place for murtabak, but this is also an excellent place for a quick snack of roti chanai with a dahl dip – a cheap and nourishing meal at any time of the day. Near the corner of Leboh Chulia and Jalan Pinang the *Islamik Restaurant* has delicious food, particularly the murtabaks and biriyanis.

At *Poshni's*, on the corner of Leboh Light and Leboh Penang, you can get traditional Malay food. There's a wide selection and it's reasonably cheap. This is one of the few real Malay restaurants in Georgetown. The outdoor restaurants at 62 and 38 Macalister Rd also do good Malaysian food.

Chinese Food There are so many Chinese restaurants in Penang that making any specific recommendations is really rather redundant. On Syed Sheh, behind the library and cultural centre, the *Seaview Restaurant* has good breakfast dim sum. On Leboh Cintra the *Hong Kong Restaurant* is good, cheap and varied and has a menu in English. At the corner of Leboh Cintra and Campbell St the *Restoran Chup Seng* has excellent chicken rice – as do many of Georgetown's 'excellent Hainanese chicken rice' purveyors. The *Sin Kuan Hiwa Cafe*, on the corner of Chulia and Leboh Cintra, is one that specialises in this.

More good Chinese food can be found at *Dragon King* on the corner of Leboh Bishop and Leboh Pitt which specialises in the not-so-easily-found Nonya cuisine. Or try *Sun Hoe Peng* at 25 Leboh Light. The *Wing Lok*, 300 Penang Rd, is more costly but good. They offer a steamboat for four people at M$20. Give them a day's notice.

Breakfasts & Western Food At breakfast time the popular travellers' hangout is the *Tye Ann Hotel* on Leboh Chulia. Every day crowds of people visit this friendly little establishment for its excellent porridge, toast & marmalade and other breakfast favourites. The manager at the front desk is permanently wreathed with that rarest of Chinese sights – a smile. Western breakfasts are also available at the New China, Eng Aun, Swiss and across from the Wan Hai.

The *Super Emporium* on Burma Rd stocks the usual supermarket goodies. *Diner's Bakery*, across from the Meerah restaurant on Campbell St, has great baked goods ranging from cheesecake to wholemeal bread.

There's more good seafood at *Maple Gardens* on Penang Rd. It's a little high priced if economy is on your mind, but the food is good, the servings large and you select your fish straight from the tank. *Kwikie Fast Food* at 276 Penang Rd has also been recommended. Burma Rd has a number of places and quite a few western fast food joints including an Italian fried chicken place.

Night Markets Georgetown has a wide selection of street stalls with nightly gatherings at places like Gurney Drive or along the Esplanade. The latter is particularly good for trying local Penang specialities. The big night market, 7-11 pm, changes venue every two weeks; check at the tourist office as to current location. Cold fruit, cakes, pancakes, noodles, laksa, are all on sale. On Swatow Lane you'll find the stall with the best es kacang in Penang, the guy who produces it gets taken overseas to promote Penang. Medicated tea is a popular item and one Georgetown tea stall has a sign announcing that it will cure everything from 'headache, and stomach ache' to 'malaria, cholera and' (wait for it) 'fartulence'.

Getting There

Air Penang is a major centre for airline tickets and there are a string of places around town selling cheap tickets. See the introductory section on cheap tickets and don't take every word a Georgetown travel agent will tell you as gospel truth. Penang isn't necessarily the cheapest place in the world for tickets, nor are all the agents here necessarily the most honest. Typical fares being quoted out of Penang include Medan M$96, Madras M$570, Hat Yai M$51, Phuket M$106, Bangkok M$257, Hong Kong M$595, USA west coast M$1150, London M$750-1000. There are also interesting return deals offered or tickets from other places – such as Singapore-Los Angeles via the South Pacific for M$1750.

Rail See the introductory rail section for details of trains from Singapore and KL. The station is at Butterworth, right by the ferry terminal for Penang Island. You can make rail reservations by phoning the station (tel 04-347962) or contacting the Railway Booking Station (tel 04-360290) at the Ferry Terminal, Weld Quay in Georgetown. There are good left luggage facilities at Butterworth station.

Bus The bus station is also in Butterworth by the ferry terminal. Typical bus fares are Ipoh M$10, KL M$13-15, Kota Bahru via the new road M$17-20, Singapore M$25-27. To Kuala Perlis for Langkawi the bus fare is M$5, to Lumut for Pangkor it's M$7.

Taxi Yes, the taxi terminus is also in Butterworth by the ferry terminal. Typical long distance taxi fares include Alor Setar for M$7, Ipoh for M$14, KL for M$30, Cameron Highlands for M$30. There are also Thai taxis – big old Chevies – operating to Hat Yai in Thailand. They can usually be booked from the various cheap hotels where they hang out. The usual fare is around M$25.

Sea You can often get rides on yachts from Penang to Phuket in Thailand or even further afield. Notes are often pinned up in the various travellers' hangouts. See the introductory Getting There section for more details on the ship between Penang and Madras in India. The agents are R Jumabhoy & Sons, 39 Green Hall, just off Leboh Light.

Getting Around

Airport Transport Penang's Bayan Lepas Airport, with its new Minangkabau-style terminal, is 18 km south of Georgetown. Between the airport and Georgetown taxis operate on a voucher system – M$15 to Georgetown, M$20 to Batu Ferringhi. Fares should be the same to the airport! You can also get to the airport on a yellow 66 bus for M$1.50.

Ferry The ferry service between Butterworth and Penang operates 24 hours a day. There are passenger ferries and car and truck ferries from adjacent terminals. They operate as frequently as every seven minutes during the day but slow down to once every 30 minutes from 2 to 5.30 am. Vehicular ferries stop from 10 pm to 6.30 am except on Saturdays, Sundays and public holidays when they continue to 1.30 am. Fares are only charged from Penang to the mainland; the other direction is free. Passengers are 40c, cars from M$4 to 6 including the driver. A Butterworth-Georgetown bridge is on the drawing board.

Bus There are a wide variety of buses and bus terminals in Georgetown. City buses (MPPP Buses) all depart from the terminal at Leboh Victoria which is directly in front of the ferry terminal. Fares range from 25 to 55c and the main routes are:

1 Ayer Itam – every five minutes, 55c
2 Bagan Jermal – every 10 minutes, 45c
3 Jelutong – every 5 minutes, 45c
4 Jalan Yeap Chor Ee via Jalan Perak – every 10 minutes, 55c
5 Green Lane via Dhoby Ghaut – every 30 minutes, 55c
6 Green Lane via Jalan Patani – every 15 minutes, 55c
7 Botanical Gardens – every 30 minutes, 50c
8 Penang Hill Railway from Ayer Itam – 30c
9 Green Lane via Caunter Hall Rd – every 15 minutes, 55c
10 Kampung Melayu – every 15 minutes, 55c
11 Aquarium at Bukit Glogor – every 60 minutes, 55c
12 Ayer Itam from Jelutong – every 20 minutes, 30c
13 Bagan Jermal from Jelutong – every 30 minutes, 40c

From Pengkalan Weld, the waterfront road by the ferry terminal, you can take Sri Negara Buses around Georgetown. The other main stand is at Jalan Maxwell where you can take green, blue or yellow buses. These are the buses you take if you want to do a circuit of the island or get out to Batu Ferringhi and the other northern beaches. The green buses run to Ayer Itam like the number 1 MPPP bus. Blue buses run to the northern beaches although a change of bus is required at Tanjong Bungah. Yellow buses run to the south and west of the island including the snake temple, airport and right round to Telok Bahang.

Taxis Penang's taxis officially cost 70c for the first mile and 30c for each additional half mile but in practice they are none too keen on operating on the meter and you may have to bargain fares, particularly for longer trips. Meter fares can be loaded by 50% from 1 to 6 am.

Trishaws Bicycle-rickshaws are ideal on Georgetown's relatively uncrowded streets and cost around 40 or 50c per half mile. The fare table displayed on each trishaw doesn't have too much connection to reality – you must agree the fare before departure. If you come across from Butterworth on the ferry grab a trishaw to the Leboh Chulia cheap hotels area for M$1 to 2 although you can quite easily walk it. The riders will know plenty of other hotels if your selected one should be full.

Bicycles If you want to pedal yourself you can hire bicycles from various places. The Eng Aun Hotel in Georgetown has them for M$5 per day or there are various places at Batu Ferringhi where you can hire them at rather more expensive rates. Motorcycles can also be hired for around M$30 per day.

PENANG – BEACHES

Penang's beaches are somewhat over-rated. They're not as spectacular or as clean as tourist brochures would have you believe and some of them suffer from pollution. They're mainly along the north coast, starting with Tanjong Bungah, then Batu Ferringhi, which is the main tourist centre, and finally Telok Bahang. Batu Ferringhi is a nice long beach but the water is not of the tropically clear variety you might expect and the swimming is not that good. Telok Bahang is still principally a small fishing village, little developed.

Places to Stay & Eat

Tanjong Bungah There's little attraction for swimming here but there are a few hotels and the restaurant at the *Eden Hotel* is renowned for its excellent, though a little expensive, seafood. Rooms at the small *Loke Thean Hotel*, close to the village and bus stop, are M$18. At the *Eden Hotel* they start from around M$10.

Batu Ferringhi This is mainly an 'international resort' and there are a string of

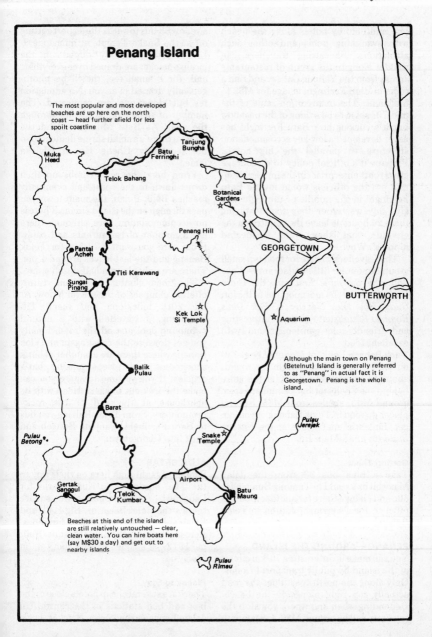

Penang Island

The most popular and most developed beaches are up here on the north coast — head further afield for less spoilt coastline

Muka Head

Batu Ferringhi

Tanjung Bungha

Telok Bahang

Botanical Gardens

Penang Hill

GEORGETOWN

Pantai Acheh

Titi Kerawang

Sungai Pinang

Kek Lok Si Temple

Aquarium

BUTTERWORTH

Although the main town on Penang (Betelnut) Island is generally referred to as "Penang" in actual fact it is Georgetown. Penang is the whole island.

Balik Pulau

Barat

Pulau Betong

Snake Temple

Pulau Jerejak

Gertak Sanggul

Telok Kumbar

Airport

Batu Maung

Beaches at this end of the island are still relatively untouched — clear, clean water. You can hire boats here (say M$30 a day) and get out to nearby islands

Pulau Rimau

big, multi-storey hotels along the beach with swimming pools and other such attractions. Shoestring travellers can wander along to the group of restaurants across from the Yahong Gallery and find a room in Batu Ferringhi village for M$2 to 5 a night. The immigration raids of the mid-70s seem to be a thing of the past now but it's curious how Batu Ferringhi has never developed a low-key accommodation structure to parallel the big hotels. Perhaps it's official policy to discourage grass roots enterprise. In the immigration-raid era the officials would invade Batu Ferringhi in the middle of the night and give any westerner they found staying there 24 hours to leave the country on the grounds that they were 'suspected hippies'. Wow.

The travellers' centre for food is a small group of popular little restaurants – *Yoke Lan*, the *Sunshine Restoran*, the *Guan Guan Cafe* and the most popular of the lot, *Guan Hoe Hin*. Nearby is *Pak Din's Bamboo Restaurant* run by an interesting and friendly old gentleman and with excellent food.

Telok Bahang Look for *Madam Lee* at 130 on the beach road back from the round-about or contact *Miss Loew* at the store behind the Shell station. Dorm beds from around M$3, singles from M$5. Several places do food in Telok Bahang or you can get 'fantastic' murtabaks at the *Kassim Restoran* at 48 Main Rd.

Getting There

Take a blue bus 93 from the Jalan Maxwell bus stand to Tanjong Bungah for 60c and change there for another blue bus (40c) to Batu Ferringhi and on to Telok Bahang.

PENANG – AROUND THE ISLAND

You can make an interesting 70-km circuit of the island by public transport in a day. Only along the north coast does the road actually run right alongside the beach. Depending when and where you stop the total fare will be around M$3-4. Start with

a yellow 66 bus towards the airport getting off at the Snake Temple at milestone 9. Live snakes, suitably doped on the incense smoke, are draped over everything and, for a small fee, they'll be photogenically draped over you. No admission fee but 'donations' are requested. The number of snakes tends to vary through the year. At Batu Muang, behind the airport, there's a small shrine dedicated to the legendary Cheng Ho of Melaka fame.

From here the road climbs up then drops down to the coast and eventually reaches Balik Pulau, the main town you pass through on the island circuit. There is no accommodation here although there are a number of restaurants and cafes. From here you want a 76 bus for Telok Bahang and the last leaves around 4 pm. There are only about a half dozen a day.

The road climbs, twists and turns, offering glimpses of the sea far below. At the 20th milestone you reach Titi Kerawang, a waterfall with a natural swimming pool just off the road. Finally you get down to the coast again at Telok Bahang where there are a number of batik showrooms and places making batik articles. If you've time to spare you can make the trek out to Maka Head with its lighthouse at the end of the rocky promontory. From Telok Bahang you bus to Batu Ferringhi, Tanjong Bungah and back into Georgetown.

ALOR SETAR

People pass through here on their way to the Thai border or to Kuala Perlis for Langkawi. At the open town square there's the Balai Besar or 'Big Hall' and Balai Nobat, both royal palace buildings. Across the road is the Zahir Mosque. Built in 1912, it's one of the largest in Malaysia.

Places to Stay

There are several cheap hotels close to the bus and taxi stations in the centre. On Jalan Langgar the *Swiss Hotel* is basic and, from M$8, cheap. There's a good restaurant downstairs. The equally cheap *Yuan Fang Hotel* is across the road. There are a number of more expensive hotels around town like the *Federal* at 42A Jalan Kancut with rooms from M$25, more with air-con.

Getting There

A bus from Butterworth costs M$2.80, a taxi is M$5.50. Note that the border to Thailand here has a long strip of no-man's land between Changlun in Malaysia and Sadao in Thailand. Although it is very easy to get from Alor Setar to Changlun by bus or taxi and equally easy to get from Sadao into Hat Yai it is very difficult to get across the actual border. An alternative is to cross the border at Padang Besar, where the railway crosses. The border is an easy walk-across there.

KUALA PERLIS

This small port is the jumping-off point to Langkawi. While you wait for a ferry you can wander around the old part of the village, built on stilts over the water, or watch fish being packed in ice at the ice factory. The one and only hotel here is the *Soon Hin* opposite the taxi stand, rooms are M$10. There are direct buses from Butterworth for M$5 which connect (more or less) with the ferry departures. A share-taxi is M$9. Buses from Alor Setar are M$1.70, taxis M$2.80.

From Kuala Perlis you can enter Thailand by a rather unusual route to Satul in Thailand. It's a short hop across the border by Thai long-tailed boat (M$3). There are customs and immigration posts at both ends and you can easily bus from Satul into Hat Yai.

LANGKAWI

Once a haven for pirates, the 99 islands of the Langkawi group are 30 km off the coast from Kuala Perlis. The beaches here are pretty well deserted because Langkawi has never taken off as a tourist destination. Unfortunately they're all rather a long distance from the accommodation centre of Kuah and transport on the island is not easy.

Kuah, the main town, is just one waterside street. Elsewhere around the island there are waterfalls, a rather pathetic hot springs, a legendary tomb and a freshwater lake on an adjacent island. The best-known beaches are Pantai Rhu on the north coast and Pantai Tengah at the south-west corner of the island.

Places to Stay & Eat

There are a number of places in the km or so from the jetty to the main junction in Kuah. First of all there's the spacious *Rest House* with huge doubles at M$18 and a grassy area leading down to the water. Across the road from it the *Youth Chalet* is a youth hostel for large groups only.

Further in towards town you come to the *Asia Hotel* (M$14 or M$26 with air-con), the *Langkawi Hotel* (same price) and the slightly cheaper *Fairwind Hotel*. They're all similar Chinese hotels – clean and tidy with a restaurant down below. Further along the road there are a number of other shopfront cafes and a busy night market area with good roti chanai at some of the Indian places.

Only 15 minutes offshore from Langkawi, the island of Pulau Bumbon has three bungalows which you can rent for M$10; food is an additional M$10 per day per person. There's a pleasant beach nearby and another about 15 minutes' walk over the hill. Look for Pa Wan or Omar to get out there – the yellow boat with 'Bumbon' written on it is a clue!

Getting There

Officially ferry departures from Kuala Perlis are at 10.30 am and 3 pm but in actual fact there are usually several more departures than that and the times tend to be erratic due to tides. Fares depend on the boat and the class – some are air-con, some not; some have economy and first-class sections, some are one class.

Generally fares range from M$3.50 to M$7 and the trip takes two to 2½ hours. There are also air-con express boats which cost M$10. A recent innovation is supposed to be a 10-times-daily hovercraft between Kuala Perlis and the Langkawi resort for M$12.

In mid-84 a daily service commenced between Penang and Langkawi. The boat departs Georgetown at 11 pm and arrives Langkawi at 7 am the next morning. The return trip departs Langkawi at 12 noon and arrives Georgetown at about 6 pm. The one-way fare is M$35.

Getting Around

A taxi from the jetty into town is 50c. Buses are cheap enough around Langkawi, but departures are uncertain so getting to a beach and back again can be difficult. The problem is no better with taxis; you still have to get back. Motorcycles, usually Honda 50 step-thrus, can be hired for M$20 a day with unlimited km. The fit can hire bicycles and (with effort) you can see a fair bit of the island that way. A group can get together and charter a boat across to Pulau Dayang Bunting for around M$70-90.

EAST COAST

The east coast is lazy, easygoing, relaxing and fun. The people are very hospitable and hitching is relatively easy although the traffic is light. Beaches and turtles are the main attractions, plus a sprinkling of truly delightful tropical islands off the coast.

JOHORE BAHRU TO MERSING

The small town of Kota Tinggi, 42 km north of Johore Bahru on the road to Mersing, is not of great interest except for its pleasant waterfalls, 15 km north-east of the town. The falls are a popular weekend escape for Singaporeans but during the week it can be a nice quiet place for a cool swim. Self-contained chalets with cooking facilities are M$40 per day. Phone 073-891146 to book them. In Kota Tinggi itself the *Hotel Kolee*, opposite the bus stand, is large, clean and comfortable. Johore Lama was the Malay capital following the fall of Melaka to the Portuguese. It's 30 km from Kota Tinggi, but there's not much to see and it's rather difficult to get to.

Turn off 13 km north of Kota Tinggi and a rough 24-km road takes you to isolated Jason's Bay. Also reached via Kota Tinggi, Desaru is a new beach resort intended to become a major tourist development. Camping with rented equipment costs M$5 per day but it's rather dull.

MERSING

The east coast road gets to the coast at Mersing, an interesting little fishing port mainly used as a jumping-off point for Tioman, Rawa and other islands.

Places to Stay & Eat

The *Rest House* (tel 072-791103), delightfully situated overlooking the six-hole (yes!) golf course, costs from around M$35 for an air-con double. It's usually full but there's a string of Chinese cheapies down in the town centre.

Several travellers have written to praise the *Mandarin Hotel* in front of the bus station. It's convenient and clean with doubles with shower for M$12, as well as both cheaper smaller room. and more expensive air-con rooms. The excellent *Hotel Embassy* (tel 072-791301) at 2 Jalan Ismail, close to the roundabout, has rooms from M$20 or with air-con from M$30.

Other Chinese hotels include the *Hotel Golden City*, the *East Coast Hotel* and the *Merdeka Hotel*. *Hotel Mersing* on Jalan Dato Timor has rooms from just M$10.50 and similarly cheap rooms are available at the *Syuan Koong* on Jalan Abu Bakar. *Tong Ah Lodgings*, with doubles at M$6 (and on-off water) is even cheaper. The *Tioman Safari* people have a hostel at their office for people going out to the island with them. Nightly cost is M$6 per person.

There are lots of places to eat too. Excellent food in the *Long Fong*, downstairs at the Hotel Embassy. Great roti chanai for breakfast at the *Taj Mahal Restaurant*.

Getting There
Taxis are M$9.20 to JB, M$14 to Kuantan. The JB express bus is M$5.50, the regular bus only M$4.50. There are also buses to and from Singapore for M$8 or a pricey M$15 with air-con. An air-con bus from Rompin, further north, to Singapore is only M$10. The bus and taxi stands are side by side close to the waterfront.

TIOMAN & OTHER ISLANDS
There are a number of delightful islands off the coast from Mersing; the best known and largest is Tioman. It's 19 km long and 12 km wide and was used as the setting for the Hollywood musical *South Pacific*. There are some beautiful beaches and you can walk clear across the island from Tekek to Juara in a couple of hours. Other islands include Rawa, with just one tourist development covering the whole island; and Babi Besar, rather closer to the mainland.

Places to Stay
Tioman The *Merlin Hotel* at Lalang on Tioman starts at around M$90, but just a little north at Tekek there are lots of places to stay – mostly in the M$4 to 7 per person range. Finding a place to stay is pretty simple. Just turn up at Tekek's wharf and somebody will find you! You may well be dropped off north of Tekek, however, since local entrepreneur Nazri has arranged with most of the boats to drop visitors off in front of his place!

Starting in Tekek places include *Roger's Place* at the Lalang end of the beach with rooms at M$12. The *Rest House* costs around M$10 and would be the best value there if it were not so dreadfully rundown and neglected. You can walk on from Tekek for over an hour, passing numerous

other places along the way, eventually arriving at the village of Ayer Batang. A-frame huts have sprung up all along here including *Nazri's* popular collection and the three-room *Tioman Safari* guest house.

Across the island at Juara, *Happy Cafe* is a pleasant little one-room hostelry at M$5 per person. Even if it's full the cheerful owner will find something for you. You can also stay at *Atans* and eat at the *Turtle Cafe*.

Although accommodation, albeit rather basic, is easy enough to find, getting food at Tioman can be very difficult. Bring some with you; there's a real shortage of places to eat although the situation is definitely better now than a couple of years ago. There's not much entertainment here either, when it gets dark you go to bed!

Other Islands On Rawa the *Rawa Island Chalets* cost from M$32 for two. On Besar there are some pleasant huts at M$6 per person and meals can be arranged at M$10 per day, or you can bring your own food.

Getting There
Most boats leave from the jetty a couple of hundred metres downriver from the town centre. Departures are dependent on the tides so there will usually be a number of boats going out at once. The Merlin launch (which can't always get right up the river) costs M$25 per person and will usually take non-guests too. Otherwise the usual price is M$15 per person on other boats. The trip takes 2½ hours on the Merlin boat, four hours on most others. Rawa is only 1¼ hours out and the cost is M$12. Besar is even closer: M$10 and a one-hour trip.

KUANTAN
This is the start of the east coast beach strip and the place where the road from KL reaches the coast. It's a useful travel crossroads although not of great interest in itself. The town is quite interesting to

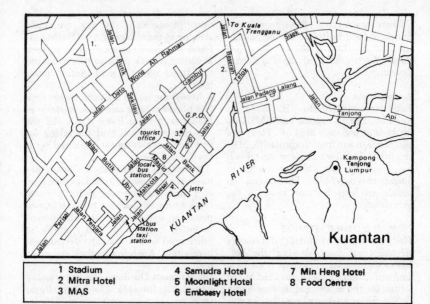

1 Stadium	4 Samudra Hotel	7 Min Heng Hotel
2 Mitra Hotel	5 Moonlight Hotel	8 Food Centre
3 MAS	6 Embassy Hotel	

stroll around and you can boat across the river to see the small fishing kampong of Tanjong Lumpur.

Kuantan's beach resort is Telok Chempedak, four km from the town itself. The Charah Caves, near Sungei Lembing, are similar to the Batu Caves near KL except they're Buddhist. There's a M$1 admission charge to climb up to see the nine-metre-long reclining Buddha. The tourist office in Kuantan is on Jalan Mahkota, near the GPO and MAS office.

Places to Stay

Kuantan Plenty of Chinese cheapies can be found along the two parallel main streets in Kuantan. At 58-60 Telok Sisek the *Embassy Hotel* (tel 095-24884) has rooms from M$11 or there's the marginally more expensive *Moonlight* (tel 095-24277) at 52 and the identically priced *Sin Nam Fong* – all close to one another.

Further down towards the bus station Telok Sisek changes its name to Jalan Besar and there are more cheap hotels like the *Tong Nam Ah* at M$14. A block over at

22 Jalan Mahkota the popular *Min Heng Hotel & Bakery* (tel 095-24885) has rooms at that standard price of around M$10 and is properly old-fashioned. The bathrooms are a bit worn out but the rooms are airy, clean and secure.

Telok Chempedak Many travellers head out to the beach where the spartan but low-priced *Asrama Bendahara* has rooms at M$9 to 12. Nearby is the *Kuantan Hotel* (tel 095-24755) with rooms from M$25 or M$35-60 with air-con.

On the main street to the beach the *Hill View Hotel* has similarly priced air-con and fan-cooled rooms. Behind it there are a number of 'motels', some of them drab and dirty. The *Wady Motel* is cheap and friendly, a good little travellers' centre with small rooms from M$15 to 20. The *Telok Chempedak Rest House* isn't at Telok Chempedak at all; it's midway between there and town and has rooms for M$25.

Places to Eat

There's even a *Colonel Sanders* in

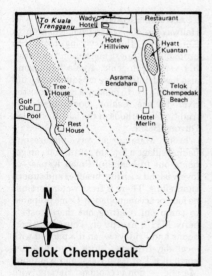

Telok Chempedak

Kuantan but you'll also find a food stall centre between the local bus stand and the tourist office on Jalan Mahkota. There's good Chinese food at the Telok Sisek hotels – try the *Moonlight* for excellent chicken rice and other dishes. *Chandra Vilas* has good roti chanai. It's near the *Min Heng Bakery*, which does indeed have great cakes, baked goods and the like.

At Telok Chempedak you can get cheap food and drinks at the *Asrama Bendahara* or there are a number of open-air restaurants with excellent seafood, for example the *Sea View Restaurant*.

NORTH OF KUANTAN
Only 10 km north of Kuantan the small fishing village of Beserah is a centre for local handicrafts and there is village-level accommodation here. At 45 km the village of Cherating is almost completely devoted to cheap accommodation centres – this is the most popular place on the coast for sampling kampong life. Just round the headland is the big Club Mediterranee. There are more cheap Chinese hotels in Kemaman and Kuala Dungun.

Places to Stay
Jaafar's Place in Beserah (just off the road on the inland side, there's a small sign and bus drivers know it) is a popular shoestring place. Accommodation is strictly basic – mat on the floor, hole-in-the-ground toilets, washing in the river. Daily cost is M$7 including bananas and bread for breakfast and an evening meal. Reactions to Jaafar's are distinctly mixed – some people find it easygoing, relaxed and a pleasant chance to observe kampong life. Others think it's dirty, crowded and very expensive for what it offers. Decide for yourself.

At Cherating, accommodation is also village-level and though it's also basic – water from the well; no electricity – the rooms are generally quite pleasant. At *Hussaien's Bungalows*, for example, you get individual chalets with mosquito-netted beds and a verandah for M$9. Hussaien also runs the *Sea Breeze Restaurant* next door. At other places costs are generally in the M$9 to 14 per person bracket including meals. Popular places are *Mak Dees* (a bit noisy because it's close to the highway but big rooms with mosquito nets), *Mak Long Teh's* (reputed to have the best food, big servings), *Semak binti Awang's* and the *Cherating Beach Village*.

Buses up the coast from Kuantan cost 50c to Beserah, M$2 to Cherating.

RANTAU ABANG
Situated about 160 km north of Kuantan and 60 km south of Kuala Trengganu, Rantau Abang is the premier turtle-watching beach. From May to September each year giant leatherback turtles come to this beach to lay their eggs. It's an amazing spectacle as the huge and ungainly creatures haul themselves up the beach, dig holes and each lay about a hundred ping-pong-ball-sized eggs. Less edifying is the behaviour of some local spectators who prod the turtles, ride on their backs and generally make a spectacle of themselves too.

The beach is very fine here although rather garbage-laden at the height of the turtle season. Finding a turtle is simply a matter of walking up and down the beach until you see the tell-tale tracks — somewhat like tank tracks!

Just north of Rantau Abang is the Visitors' Centre with a handicraft display and turtle museum plus a restaurant and more expensive accommodation. Note that the nearest bank is 22 km away in Kuala Dungun.

Places to Stay

Awang's, Sany's and *Ismail's* are a string of cheap places along the beach. M$10 will get you a basic little wooden shack right on the beach although Awang's has some simple double huts for M$5 per person. There's also reasonable food and cold drinks to pass the day and evening time as you wait for the time for turtle hunting. *Sany's* probably has the best food and certainly the best music.

There's a new place at Rantau Abang which falls between the top and bottom strata here. The *Merantau Inn* (tel 096-841131) is midway between the fancy Tanjong Jara and the Visitors' Centre and has clean two-bed bungalows with bathrooms and fan for M$35.

Getting There

Any bus up the coast goes through Rantau Abang and the bus stop is right by the cheap accommodation centre. Kuala Dungun is M$9 from Kuantan, M$7 from Kuala Trengganu, by taxi.

KUALA TRENGGANU

Halfway up the coast from Kuantan to Kota Bahru this easygoing town has probably the finest market on the coast. It's very photogenic. Kuala Trengganu also has an interesting mosque and an old palace. It's worth making a trip across the river to see fishing boats made by traditional methods at the island of Pulau Duyong Besar.

From Marang, a very picturesque fishing village a few km south, you can get boats out to beautiful Pulau Kapas – a lovely island with fine beaches and superb snorkelling. There is fresh water here but no food or accommodation. Come prepared to camp out. Getting out there costs a hefty M$15, except on Thursday afternoons and Fridays when it's packed with local day-trippers. More good beaches north of KT at Batu Rakit and Kampong Merang – don't confuse Merang with Marang.

Places to Stay

There are lots of cheap hotels along Jalan Paya Bunga, close to the bus stand. Try the *Hotel Tong Nam* (tel 096-21540) at 29B with rooms at M$18, or the rock-bottom *Hotel Lido* (tel 096-21752) at number 62 with rooms at M$12, or the more expensive *Trengganu Hotel* (tel 096-22900) at 12 which has rooms from M$18 up to M$35 with air-con.

Directly opposite the bus station the *Rex Hotel* has doubles with bathroom and fan for M$15. It's fairly quiet despite its location. It's clean, well-kept and there's an open-air restaurant next door. Other places include the *Golden City* or the

1 Tourist Information Office	9 Chinese Temple
2 Pantai Motel	10 Central Market
3 Hotel Warisan	11 Mosque
4 Hoover Hotel	12 Istana Mazia
5 Hotel Tong Nam	13 GPO
6 Hotel Lido	14 Seaview Hotel
7 MAS	15 Dot's Motel
8 Trengganu Hotel	16 Sri Trengganu Hotel

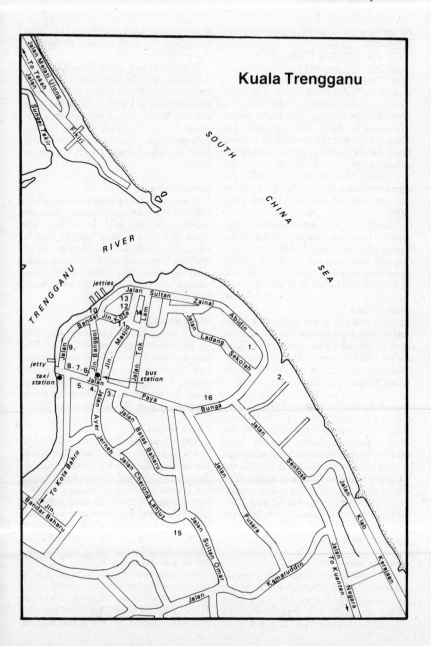

Kuala Trengganu

Bunga Raya on Jalan Banggol beside the bus stand.

Cross to Kampong Dijong, in an island in the river, and you may be able to stay for M$5 at *Awi House* (the 'yellow house'), a sort of unofficial guest house. The little ferry boats shuttle across for 20c. South of town towards Marang, *Ibi's Guest House* has rooms for M$10 and dorm beds for M$4. It's close to the beach, at Kampong Paya, Bandar Marang, at the north of the village. A bus from KT costs 80c. *Zak's* has rooms with fan for M$10, get off at the sign advertising trips to Pulau Kapas, on the right side of the road as you head north.

There are lots of cheap Chinese cafes around town, particularly along Jalan Bunga Raya and Jalan Bandar, but if you feel like splashing out the *Pantai Motel* sometimes puts on a terrific smorgasbord of Malay foods for an all-in M$16.

Getting There

The taxi stand is by the waterfront at the end of Jalan Paya Bunga. The bus stand is back up the road. Fares are M$11 to Kota Bahru (M$6 by bus), M$15 to Kuantan (M$7.50), M$7 for a taxi to Jerteh for Kuala Besut.

KUALA BESUT & PULAU PERHENTIAN

Off the main road between KT and KB the village of Kuala Besut is divided by the river, which has only recently been bridged. On the north side is the amazingly grubby village; on the south side is the pleasant beach and the rest house. The only real reason to come here is to cross to Pulau Perhentian, a beautiful and little-visited island. Out there, 21 km from the coast, there's nothing much to do apart from sun, swim and laze around.

Places to Stay

Kuala Besut's *Rest House* has recently been refurbished. Rooms with bathroom and fan are M$15; some small and basic rooms are M$7. It's friendly but the restaurant is pricey and not too good

although they make excellent tea. Near the bridge the *Banana Leaf Restaurant* has pretty good food.

The *Rest House* on the island has four doubles at M$12 – they must be booked through the District Office in Kampong Raja, a couple of km from Kuala Besut on the rest house side. Otherwise you can camp or stay for around M$5 in huts belonging to the caretaker's father. Bring food and other supplies with you to the island.

Getting There

You can get to Kuala Besut by bus or taxi although you may have to change buses at Jerteh on the main road. To the island the usual fare on a fishing boat is from a minimum of M$5-10, but it's a matter of finding a boat going out (and coming back) since there is no regular service. There are worse places to be stranded! Chartering a boat would be M$50 to 80.

KOTA BAHRU

This is the end of the east coast road and an alternative route into Thailand. It's also a centre for kite flying, top spinning and other traditional Malay crafts and games. The KB Tourist Office is fairly good. It's a stone's throw from the clock tower and a short distance from the GPO.

Places to Stay

At the bottom end of the price scale there is a popular hostel-style place although it has moved since the previous edition. *Hitec* is at 4398 Jalan Pengkalan Chepa, but it's easier to find if you keep in mind that it's right across the road from the Thai Consulate. That's about a km out of town towards the airport; take a number 4 or 9 bus (25c), or it's about M$1 by trishaw. Dorm beds are M$4, rooms about M$10 and there are cooking facilities. There's an excellent travellers' notebook here where visitors write all sorts of useful tips from their trips. 'Mummy', who runs Hitec, is a great talker! A word of caution: Some fast thinker has taken over the old

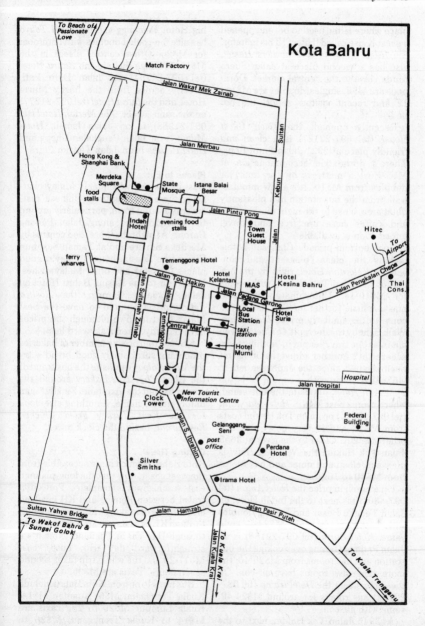

Kota Bahru

To Beach of
Passionate
Love

Match Factory

Jalan Wakaf Mek Zainab

Jalan Merbau

Sultan

Hong Kong &
Shanghai Bank

Merdeka
Square

food
stalls

State
Mosque

Istana Balai
Besar

Kebun

Indah
Hotel

evening food
stalls

Jalan Pintu Pong

Town
Guest
House

Jalan

Hitec

To
Airport

ferry
wharves

Temenggong Hotel

Hotel
Kelantan

MAS

Jalan Padang Garong

Jalan Tok Hakim

Jalan

Jalan Sultanah Zainab

Jalan

Temenggong

Central Market

taxi
station

Local
Bus
Station

Hotel
Kesina Bahru

Hotel
Suria

Jalan Pengkalan Cheps

Thai
Cons.

Hotel
Murni

Hospital

Jalan Hospital

Clock
Tower

New Tourist
Information Centre

Gelanggang
Seni

post
office

Perdana
Hotel

Federal
Building

Jalan S. Ibrahim

Silver
Smiths

Irama Hotel

Sultan Yahya Bridge

To Wakof Bahru &
Sungai Goloki

Jalan Hamzah

Jalan Pasir Puteh

Jalan Kuala Krai

To Kuala Krai

To Kuala Trengganu

place where Hitec used to be, and opened a guest house called 'Hitect'! This imitator, the *Hitect Tourists & Travellers Hostel*, also has a second place at Jalan Suara Muda close to the central market. Dorm beds are M$5, singles/doubles are M$10/12 and recent visitors report it's not bad.

Recently opened, the *Town Guest House* (tel 097-22127) is a clean and friendly place at 2921 Jalan Pintu Pong. There's dorm-style accommodation at M$5 (just a mattress on the floor) or doubles from M$10. It's a few minutes' walk from the bus station in a pleasantly quiet area, close to the night market. Tea and coffee here are free and travel information is available.

Rock-bottom-priced Chinese hotels include the clean, pleasant and convenient *Kelantan Hotel*, right by the bus station on Jalan Tok Hakim, with rooms for M$10-14. Unfortunately it's also noisy. A little further up Tok Hakim you come to the similarly priced *Mee Ching*. Walk right by the decrepit *Ah Chew* – even if it is, as one traveller put it, 'nothing to be sneezed at'! Another added that it 'hasn't been cleaned since the Japanese left in '45'. Also 'basic with a capital B' is the *Tyhe Ann Hotel*, opposite the bus stand, where rooms cost M$10. *Hotel Maryland* (tel 097-22811) on Jalan Tok Hakim costs from M$16 and is very noisy although otherwise OK. Close to the river at 3655 Jalan Tok Hakim, the *New Bali Hotel* is pleasant, clean and quiet and has rooms from M$10 to 16.

Up a notch in price the *Hotel Aman* (tel 097-43049) is next to the Indah Hotel on Jalan Tengku Besar and has big doubles with bathroom for only M$24 – good value. *Hotel Suria* (tel 097-22188) is on Jalan Padang Garong overlooking the bus station and has rooms from M$20-46; the more expensive rooms have air-con. On the same street the *Hotel Irama* (tel 097-22722) has rooms for around M$24-40, some with air-con.

At 3945 Jalan Tok Hakim, next to the big Hotel Temenggong, the *Hotel Tokyo* has nice fan-cooled doubles with bathroom for M$20. Other central places in the M$15-30 range include the *Bahru Hotel* (tel 097-21164) on Jalan Dato Pati, directly across from the flashy Murni Hotel, and the *Intan Hotel* (tel 097-21277) on the same street. The *Meriah Hotel* (tel 097-21388) is on Jalan Ismail, *Hotel Milton* is on Jalan Pengkalan Chepa and *Hotel Berling* is on Jalan Tengku Petra.

Places to Eat

Despite its overwhelmingly Malay character there are plenty of Chinese restaurants around town, particularly around the bus stop and along Jalan Padang Garong. At night there are food centres at Merdeka Square and at Taman Sekebun Bunga (the 'floating house'). They're good places for satay and other Malay dishes. Next door to the Kesina Bahru Hotel on Jalan Padang Garong, the *Rosliza Restaurant* is reputed to have the best Malay food in town although the prices have recently taken a skyward leap.

KB has a surprising number of bakeries producing surprisingly good bread – try the *Maju Bakery* opposite the bus stand or the *Choo Chin Hin Bakery* around the corner behind the taxi stand. Finally for an unforgettable name, if nothing else, look for the *Kent Turkey Fried Chicken Restaurant*, beside the clock tower.

Getting There

Kota Bahru is much more accessible from the west coast, now that the long-planned east-west highway is completed. Previously travel between Penang and KB involved either flying or making a long detour south through KL or a complicated detour north through Hat Yai in Thailand. Now it's a straightforward day trip; buses cost M$17-20 and the whole trip takes around seven hours. Taxis are M$30.

Bus fares to or from Kota Bahru include Kuala Trengganu M$6, Kuantan M$14, Kuala Lumpur M$20 to 28. Taxis are M$14 to Kuala Trengganu, M$26 to

Kuantan. See the introductory Getting Around section for details on rail travel to Kota Bahru. Note that the line does not actually run through Kota Bahru. It's a 40c trip on a 19 or 27 bus from Wakaf Bahru where the line terminates. It makes more sense to get off at Pasir Mas and take a taxi into town – it's the same fare as from Tumpat (M$1.50) and saves an hour of travel to the end of the line. If you're heading for Thailand without pausing in KB then you can go straight from Pasir Mas to the border town of Rantau Panjang (M$2 by taxi).

Getting Around
There are lots of local buses from KB to surrounding places of interest. Take a bus 10 (60c) to Pantai Cinta Berahi (the Beach of Passionate Love) or a 19 or 27 bus to Wakaf Bahru and Tumpat (40c). A taxi to the airport is M$8, share-taxi to Kuala Krai is M$4.50.

AROUND KOTA BAHRU
There are a number of beaches on the coast close to KB. Pantai Cinta Berahi hardly lives up to its exotic name. Pantai Dasar Sabak, just beyond KB's airport, was where the Japanese landed in WW II – an hour and a half before they arrived at Pearl Harbour. Around KB there are also waterfalls, a number of Thai temples including a huge reclining Buddha at Kampong Berok and a number of interesting jungle walks to hides and salt licks. South of KB at Kuala Krai, where the

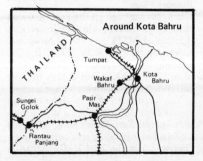
Around Kota Bahru

central road used to end, there's a zoo specialising in local wildlife. You can make a number of river trips from Kota Bahru to villages, caves and more waterfalls.

TAMAN NEGARA
Peninsular Malaysia's great national park sprawls across three states and covers over 4000 square km. Reactions to the park seem to depend on what one sees there. Some people see lots of wildlife and think it's wonderful. Others only seem to see leeches and are not at all impressed! The park headquarters are at Kuala Than and from there you can make a number of jungle walks to hides and salt licks where you may see animals. Going further in requires boat trips up the rivers, which can be expensive. It's a 2½-day walk to Gunung Tahan, the highest mountain in the park, and 2½ days to climb it.

To book accommodation in the park and to arrange to be met by the park boat, contact the Chief Game Warden, Block K20, Government Offices Building, Jalan Duta, Kuala Lumpur. You may be able to make arrangements by phone: call 03-941056 or 941272. There is a M$5 park entrance fee and also camera fees. Only everyday clothing is necessary for the shorter walks around the park HQ, but you'll need heavier-duty gear if you head further afield.

Places to Stay
At Kuala Tahan there is a *Rest House* and four chalets with attached bathrooms at M$15 each – it's usually necessary to book ahead with these. Otherwise dorm beds are M$4. Kuala Tahan has a restaurant with set meals for around M$6 and fried rice for M$3. There's a cheaper restaurant for the staff which others can also use. You can buy provisions from the excellent supermarket near the taxi stand in Jerantut. There are a number of *Visitors' Lodges* and *Fishing Lodges* elsewhere in the park. It costs M$2.50 to stay overnight in the game-viewing hides.

Getting There

The entry point into the park is Kuala Tembeling, near Tembeling Halt on the central railway line. To get there you can take the train north or south and a stop at Tembeling Halt can be arranged if you make a request to the stationmaster upon boarding. If you leave Singapore on the night train, you get to Gemas at 3 am and change to the Tumpat train which departs at 3.30 am. It arrives at Jerantut at 8.19 am or a little later at Tembeling Halt. Very early for the 2 pm park boat!

Travelling south, the day train from Kota Bahru doesn't get to Tembeling Halt until after 6 pm so you might as well continue to Jerantut, arriving at 6.50 pm. Spend the night and morning there before getting to Kuala Tembeling in time for the 2 pm boat.

It's either a short bus trip or a half-hour walk from Tembeling Halt to Kuala Tembeling. Alternatively you can go by bus to Kuala Lipis, then catch the train to Tembeling Halt or go by road direct to Kuala Tembeling. Buses run Jerantut-Tembeling about every 1½ hours. A taxi will be about M$3 per person or M$12 for the whole taxi. Temerloh-Tembeling takes about two hours by bus.

From Tembeling to the park headquarters at Kuala Tahan is a 2½ to 3½-hour river trip depending on the river conditions. The park boat starts at M$10 per person provided you have enough people – the trip can cost more if not enough people are going. The boat doesn't run every day, so it really pays to check by phone or in person with the KL parks office. The boat departs from the park compound a couple of hundred metres beyond the village at around 2 pm. Alternatively, a private boat will cost M$15 to 20 per person, depending on bargaining. The river trip is a high point of a park visit. When leaving the park you can sometimes get a boat right down to Jerantut Ferry, beyond Jerantut.

If you wanted to continue north you'd have to leave the park and stay overnight in Jerantut, then either catch the early morning train coming north from Gemas or the 12 noon local to Kuala Lipis, and overnight there. Travelling south you can catch the train at Tembeling Halt or Jerantut in the evening. It gets to Gemas at 11.45 pm to connect with the midnight train to Singapore, arriving at 5.55 am.

COAST TO COAST

Roads across the peninsula are changing rapidly. The east-west road in the north is now open and a road parallelling the jungle railway is being rapidly pushed through. The east-west road is only open from 6 am to 6 pm – and because of fears of the long-dormant Communist guerrillas in this, their last stronghold, there are many army posts along the road.

The road down through the centre of the peninsula has already reached Gua Musang – Kuala Krai-Gua Musang takes just an hour by car or taxi versus four hours on the antique railway service. The third coast-to-coast route crosses between Kuala Lumpur and Kuantan. A main town on this route is Temerloh, which has a colourful market every Saturday afternoon. Alternatively you can start north from KL on the Ipoh road, turn off to Fraser's Hill, then Raub and eventually Kuala Lipis on the central railway line. Just before Raub you can turn off to rejoin the KL-Kuantan route at Bentong, or turn off at Benta Seberang for Jerantut and the national park.

Places to Stay

Gerik, the junction on the new east-west road, has a pleasant old *Rest House* with doubles at M$12 and the cheaper and more central *Sin Wah Hotel*. In Gua Musang the *Rest House* is decrepit and overpriced at M$14 but is also friendly and convenient. There are other cheapies.

The *Jerantut Hotel* in Jerantut has rooms from M$12. There's also a not-very-special *Rest House* here. At Kuala Lipis make sure they don't try to over-charge you at the *Rest House*; M$16 is tops. The Chinese cheapies here are very basic indeed, and solo women travellers should beware of overly-friendly attention in Kuala Lipis.

In Mentakab, the railway station town just before Temerloh, there's a horde of cheap Chinese hotels, as in Temerloh itself. Temerloh also has a *Rest House*, pleasantly situated overlooking the Pahang River, with rooms from M$12. The *Swiss Hotel* in Temerloh is very good value although the foodstalls downstairs make it noisy.

Sarawak

Sarawak's history reads more like Victorian melodrama than hard fact. In 1838 James Brooke, a British adventurer, arrived in Borneo with his armed sloop to find the Brunei aristocracy facing rebellion from the dissatisfied inland tribes. He quelled the unrest and in gratitude was given power over part of what is today Sarawak. Appointing himself 'Rajah Brooke' he successfully cooled down the fractious tribes and suppressed head hunting, eliminated the dreaded Borneo pirates and founded a dynasty that lasted until after WW II. The Brooke family of 'White Rajahs' gradually brought more and more of Borneo under their power until the Japanese came.

Today Sarawak is a rapidly developing part of Malaysia with major oil exports plus timber, pepper and rubber production. Although Sarawak suffered even more than peninsular Malaysia from communist guerrilla activity, things are relatively peaceful today. For the visitor Sarawak's interest is in its diversity of tribes, especially the land and sea Dyaks with their longhouses. In these a whole village lives under one roof; individual rooms lead on to a common verandah where village activities take place.

GETTING THERE
Singapore & Peninsular Malaysia The regular air fare from Singapore to Kuching is M$170, but from Johore Bahru it's only M$147. To further persuade you to fly from Johore Bahru rather than Singapore MAS have a bus service from their Singapore office direct to the Johore Bahru airport terminal. From KL to Kuching the regular fare is M$162. There are also economy night flights for M$162 and a variety of advance purchase and other discount possibilities.

There are no longer any regular passenger shipping services between Singapore and Sarawak but starting in mid-85 there is supposed to be a weekly car ferry service operating from Kuantan on the east coast of the peninsula to Kuching. Whether it will actually commence operation remains to be seen.

Indonesia There is a weekly flight between Kuching and Pontianak; it continues on to Jakarta. The problem here is that Pontianak is not one of the Indonesian entry points where you can arrive without a visa. And frankly they don't seem to be very enthusiastic about people arriving in Indonesia at Pontianak.

You can physically, but not officially, cross from one side to the other by land. As one traveller described it: 'from Bau you can either go to Sirikan where the immigration post will tell you the border is firmly closed for tourists (not for smugglers though) or you can go right to Kampong Staff and walk to Selias where the Indonesian police arrest you and deport you back to Sarawak!' There may be very occasional boats between Kuching and Pontianak.

THINGS TO BUY
Sarawak has a wide variety of native arts and crafts. A representative selection can be seen at the shop in the new section of the museum in Kuching. Wooden shields

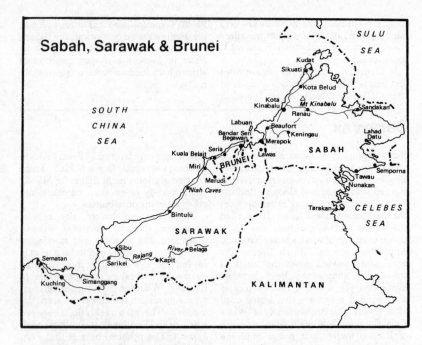

- brightly painted or with traditional carvings – are available full size or in miniature replicas. Borneo pottery is a recently revived craft, there are factories near the airport where all sorts of glazed and unglazed jars, pots and vases are produced. The cheapest ones start at just a few dollars but even in Singapore they are much more expensive. They're very beautiful.

KUCHING

Capital of Sarawak and centre of the White Rajah dynasty, Kuching (cat in Malay) is a green, pleasant, spacious city. The Brooke family influence resulted in far more parks than most Asian towns and an individual touch to the architecture.

Information & Orientation

Kuching is relatively compact and easy to get around. There are a couple of tourist offices. The one on the corner of Temple St and Main Bazaar has maps as well as other information. The national government TDC office is on Song Thian Cheok Rd, not far from Ban Hock Rd. For good maps go to the State Government Complex near the end of Jalan Simpang Tiga and visit the map sales office – Bahagian Katografi. Rex Bookstores at 28 K Hun Yeang St is the best bookshop around.

For information on the National Parks, including advance booking of accommodation and transport, go to the Section Forest Office (tel 24474), Jalan Gertak, near Electra House. Permits to visit the painted cave at Niah are available from the Curator's Office in the museum grounds. The prominently signposted Immigration Office (tel 25661) is off Jalan Song Thian Cheok, off Ban Hock Rd. The Indonesian Consulate (tel 20551) is on Deshun Rd, near the Ban Hock Rd end.

Things to See
Sarawak Museum Styled like a Normandy house by the second Rajah's French valet, this is a museum to satisfy even museum haters. Wallace, Darwin's contemporary, spent two years in Kuching and strongly influenced the concept of the museum. Recently a large new museum building was added across the road. It's linked to the original building by a bridge. Admission to the museum is free, it's open 9.15 am to 5.30 pm Monday to Thursday, 9 am to 6 pm (but closed 12 noon to 1 pm) Saturday, closed all day on Friday. Don't miss it.
Religious Buildings The diversity of Malaysian races is nowhere better illustrated than here. There is the new and not very impressive Masjid Negara Sarawak mosque, the new and very impressive St Joseph's Cathedral and a whole host of interesting Chinese temples including the Tua Pek Kong (or Sia San Tient) temple, the Hong San (or Mt Phoenix) temple and the Temple of Tien Hou (Goddess of Seamen).
Fort Margherita & the Istana Across the river, a 10c boat ride, is the Istana or Astana, the second Rajah's palace. Now the governor's residence, special permission is needed to visit it, but it looks fine from the park across the river. Slightly downstream is the fort named after the second Rajah's wife and placed to guard the entrance to Kuching. Today it houses a police museum with interesting exhibits on opium, illegal gambling and relics of the confrontation. Open 10 am to 6 pm, closed Sunday.
Other The Supreme Court building is another building from early in the White Rajah era. See also the Brooke memorial and the small aquarium behind the museum. Bau, a small lake about half an hour by bus from Kuching, is a good place for a swim. Ask at the tourist office.

Places to Stay
The pleasant *Anglican Cathedral Hostel* in the grounds of the cathedral has singles/doubles for a 'donation' of M$15/20.

They're big, clean rooms with comfortable beds and cane chairs. Look for friendly Pulin Kantul who lives next to the hostel, down a few steps on the left. Use this place discreetly – it would be a shame to spoil it.

On Jalan Temple opposite the Rex Cinema the *Kuching Hotel* (tel 57811) is popular with travellers at M$13/15. The rooms are reasonably clean and the showers and toilets are fairly clean, though somewhat tatty. On India St the *Khian Hin Hotel* (tel 26981) offers similar standards and is also popular with travellers. Rooms are M$15.40.

Two other basic places are the *Ah Chew* at 3 Jawa St and the *Sun Ah* on Market St. Up a bracket in price you could try the *Green Mountain Lodging House* at 1 Jalan Green Hill with simple air-con rooms for M$30. Similar places are the *Kuok Lodging House*, round the corner, or the *Selamat Lodging House*, next door. The area is a little hard to find; it's behind Temple St at the Kuching Hotel and up the small hill. Right at the bottom of the bottom end one traveller suggested the 'grossly undermaintained' M$5 dormitory at the *Rumah Dayak*, near Radio Malaysia.

Places to Eat
On Jalan Tun Haji Openg, opposite the GPO, the *Fook Hoi Restaurant* is the best place to eat for most of the day. The food is good, the quantities more than ample and it's very popular. In the evenings it's rivalled by the *Ho Cafe*, behind the Rex Cinema on Temple and Wayang Sts. It's a collection of popular open air eating stalls with excellent satay. Close by is the *Hua Jang Cafe*, also a good place for a cold beer.

At 53 India St the *Malaya Restaurant* does good Indian food as does the *Jubilee Restaurant* just a couple of doors down at 49. Close to the Fook Hoi the *Supersonic Restaurant* is the place for western food although it's a bit expensive. The *Aurora Hotel* is also quite good for western food or try the still more expensive *San Francisco*

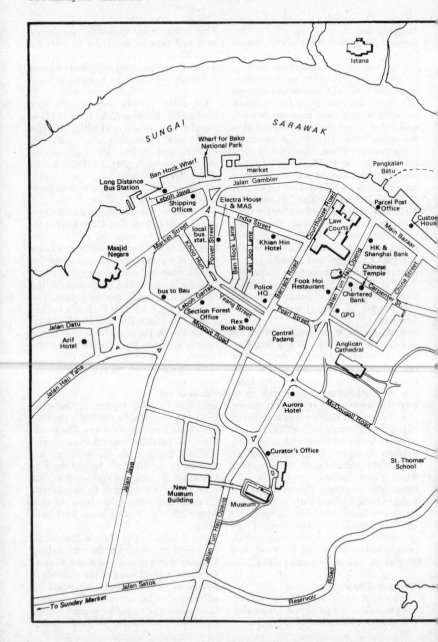

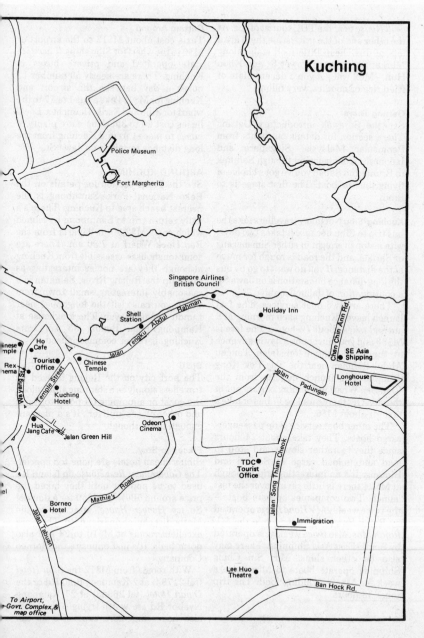

Kuching

Police Museum

Fort Margherita

Singapore Airlines
British Council

Shell
Station

Holiday Inn

Jalan Tengku Abdul Rahman

Chinese
Temple

Ho
Cafe

Chan Chin Ann Rd.

Tourist
Office

Chinese
Temple

SE Asia
Shipping

Rex
Cinema

Weavers St.

Temple Street

Jalan Padungan

Longhouse
Hotel

Kuching
Hotel

Hua
Jang Cafe

Odeon
Cinema

Jalan Green Hill

Mathie's Road

Jalan Song Thian Cheok

Jalan Tabuan

Borneo
Hotel

TDC
Tourist
Office

Immigration

Lee Huo
Theatre

Ban Hock Rd.

To Airport,
Govt. Complex &
map office

Grill House near the TDC tourist office. At the other end of the price scale there are a lots of dirt cheap little food stalls along Market St, between Power St and Khoo Hun – M$2 will get you a decent plate of fried rice or noodles, very filling.

Getting There

See the Sarawak introductory Getting There section for details on flights from Peninsular Malaysia, Singapore and Indonesia. Continuing on through Sarawak to Brunei and Sabah you've got a choice of flying, bus or boat. The first stage is to Sibu.

Kuching-Sibu Not many travellers take the bus trip to Sibu because it takes two days, with a stop overnight in either Simanggang or Sarikei, and the road is rough for much of the distance. If you do want to go by bus the long distance bus station is on Jawa St, a continuation of Jalan Gambier.

There are two boat services. The fast launch leaves Kuching each morning at 8 am and takes about 7½ hours. The fare is M$33 and you must book a day in advance at the Shell Station on Jalan Tengku Abdul Rahman near the Tua Pek Kong Temple. The launch departs from the Chin San Wharf at Pending, six km out of the city. Get there on a 1 or 17 bus or take a taxi for about M$6.

The other boat service is on passenger-cargo boats. They take about 24 hours since they're rather slower and stop to load and unload cargo at Sarikei and Bintang. It's an interesting trip although at M$24 there is little saving over the fast launch. Two companies operate boats – the twice weekly *MV Hong Lee* is operated by Rajah Ramin Shipping while the *MV Rajah Mas*, also twice weekly, is operated by South-East Asia Shipping. There may also be other ships. Miri Sin Ching Shipping operate boats to Miri twice a week for M$40 including food. The trip takes 48 hours.

Getting Around

Taxis cost about M$12 to the airport or M$6 to the wharf for Sibu ships. There are state operated and private buses in Kuching. There are nearly 50 number 12 buses a day between the airport and Kuching for M$1. Take a bus 1 or 17 to the wharf for Sibu and Sarikei launches. Local buses cost 20 to 30c. There are plenty of buses to places around Kuching from the long distance terminus on Jawa St.

AROUND KUCHING

See the Parks section for details on the Bako National Park. Santubong is the nearest beach area to Kuching. There's a daily return trip to Santubong by launch which costs M$2.50. It departs from the Ban Hock Wharf at 7.30 am. There are some longhouses accessible from Kuching although they are not as interesting as those up the Rejang River. Sematan is a reasonably interesting small town from which you can visit the longhouse near Lundu Sungei Kayan. The longhouse at Kampong Segu Benuk, 35 km from Kuching, is rather commercialised.

SIBU

The port city on the Rejang is used by travellers simply as a stepping stone along the coast or a jumping off point to Kapit and other places 'upriver'. It's a pleasant enough town, though.

Places to Stay

Sibu's cheap hotels are none too special. The *Government Rest House* on Island Rd used to be popular until they hiked the price around 500% to M$50 for a double! So try *Hoover House*, attached to the Methodist church on Island Rd. There are excellent rooms at M$10 to 24 and also dorm beds. It's just opposite the Borneo Company.

With rooms from M$12 the *Sibu Hotel* (tel 21784) at 2 Kampong Pulu Rd or the *Dipan Hotel* (tel 26853) at 27 Kampung Nyabor Rd are worth trying – the latter also has some more expensive air-con rooms. Or there's the similar *National Hotel* (tel 22727) at 1 Kampung Pulu Rd. Even cheaper and more basic rooms can be found at the *Sing Hua Hing* and the *Nan Kiew Hotels* off Blacksmith Rd.

More expensive rooms can be found at the pleasant *Miramar Hotel* (tel 22395) at 47 Channel Rd, where pleasant rooms with attached bathroom cost from M$18 or with air-con from M$30. At 32 Cross Rd the similarly priced *Rex Hotel* (tel 21625) is also good value.

Between Kuching and Sibu you can stay in Sarikei at the *Hotel Rejang* or at Simanggang at the *Hoover Hotel* at 125 Club Rd.

Places to Eat

Food in Sibu is chiefly Chinese. Opposite the *Premier Hotel* on Kampung Nyabor Rd there's a place which does good satay or you can get seafood in the restaurant opposite the Palace Cinema on Workshop Rd. The street stalls at night on Jalan Lembangan, opposite the Miramar Hotel, are excellent value or try *Hock Chu Leu* on Blacksmith Rd. There's good food at the more expensive *New Capitol Restaurant* opposite the big Premier Hotel.

Getting There

See Kuching for details of Sibu-Kuching travel. Continuing on from Sibu to Bintulu there is now a road, of sorts, open. It's still pretty rough and ready so transport is irregular and flying is still much easier and very little more expensive. Ships on this route are not too regular either. Although Sibu-Bintulu flights tend to be heavily booked there are a lot of them and if you can't get a confirmed seat you have a good chance on a standby basis. Boats to Bintulu cost about M$35 and take 18 hours.

If you decide to try the road, the stretch between Tatau and Oya was the last to be completed (the last all the way from Kuching to Brunei) and thus the roughest. If you're determined to try it enquire at Hock Lee Travel Service, Sarawak House,

Sibu. They operate a share-taxi which costs M$45 per person. For a very adventurous route to Bintulu see the Further Upriver section below.

Getting Around

Boats to and from Sibu, including the services up the Rejang River, all dock at Delta Wharf which is only a short stroll from the town centre. Take a number 1 bus to or from the airport, the fare is 50c.

UP THE REJANG RIVER

The best longhouses can be seen by travelling upriver on the mighty Rejang from Sibu. Most of Sarawak's timber exports are floated down the Rejang, and up towards the interior the river is dotted with longhouses.

KAPIT

The pleasant, small town of Kapit is the main centre in the interior. There's an old fort (dating from White Rajah days). Known as Fort Sylvia it's by the main jetty. At Kapit you obtain permits to travel further upriver.

Places to Stay

Kapit has a *Methodist Guest House*, a bargain at M$10 per room, or a choice of three hotels. The guest house is by the green-painted church and has just two rooms.

Cheapest of the hotels is the *Hiap Chiong Hotel* at 33 New Bazaar, a friendly, clean place with rooms at M$12 plus a few rooms with air-con from M$25. The *Rejang Hotel* at 9 New Bazaar costs from M$18 and the *Kapit Longhouse Hotel* on Berjaya Rd is more expensive with air-con rooms from M$30.

Places to Eat

There are a couple of reasonable Chinese cafes on the hotel block of New Bazaar or try the popular *Kah Ling Restaurant* near the Methodist Guest House. The places on top of the market hall are also good.

Getting There

The 'Kapit Express' boats leave Sibu six or seven times daily from 7 am to 1 pm – approximately – they often don't depart until full. They are long, narrow boats, steel bottomed to bounce off stray logs and powered by two huge diesel motors. Fast hardly describes them – they are like monster speed boats and churn the 130 km up the river to Kapit in just four or five hours. The fare is M$12 and you make short stops en route at Kanowit and Song. In Kapit the boat stops first at an old, rickety jetty close to the three hotels. If you're going to stay at the Methodist Guest House then continue to the final stop at the main jetty. Downriver departures are at similar times.

FURTHER UPRIVER

Travelling further upriver to Belaga requires a permit, and another permit again if you intend to go beyond Belaga. Go to the Pejabat Am office at the State Government Complex in Kapit to collect forms which have to be stamped at the police headquarters and returned to the government office.

Longhouses can be seen only half an hour or so beyond Kapit but the further upriver you go the more 'authentic' the longhouses become. To visit a longhouse simply front up, smile and you will be invited in for a look. There is no need for an introduction (although it wouldn't hurt) and the people on the boat you take upriver will probably be fairly knowledgeable about which houses to go to. To really get the feel of longhouse living you can stay overnight, or longer, even travel up or downriver from longhouse to longhouse. It is polite to take some small gifts to the longhouse people, a few cans of food won't go astray if you're staying overnight. You can daytrip from Kapit to a longhouse – take an upriver boat, drop off at a longhouse, spend the day and catch an afternoon downriver boat back to Kapit.

Permits for travel beyond Belaga are obtained in Belaga.

Places to Stay

There's a *Government Rest House* in Belaga for M$25 per person. In the big line of shops there's a very clean lodging house with doubles at M$14 or you could try the *Community Hall*.

Getting There

Launches and boats leave daily for Belaga and cost about M$12 for the day-long trip. They can only go when the river is high enough to allow them to cross the several sets of rapids safely. When the river is low you'll have to fly.

A few years ago it was a real adventure to travel overland between Bintulu on the coast and Belaga. In the other direction, between Belaga and Bintulu, it was all but impossible. Now, with new logging roads, it's reasonably straightforward in either direction. From Belaga the locals ask M$30 to 50 up to the logging tract just beyond Long Bangan longhouse although you could do it in sections rather cheaper by yourself. The trip is first by a semi-regular boat from Belaga for M$4 to rapids where you have a 1½ hour walk. A regular canoe then takes you for M$5 to another set of rapids where you have a one-hour walk. There's no regular boat on this next section but you can organise something for around M$10 to 15.

You then have another one-hour walk along the new logging tract to the logging camp and then a short boat trip to Tubau village. The new logging tract has removed the most difficult part of the trip as it is only a few km past Long Bangan longhouse so you no longer have to go up to Long Unan longhouse. In fact there are sufficient travellers making this trip these days that the longhouses are starting to charge for accommodation. From Tubau there's a daily boat to Bintulu, the trip takes all day.

One traveller's report on making this trip, from the Bintulu end:

After taking the boat up to Tubau you can continue on to Belaga via one of the logging camps set up along the Belaga River. They usually maintain daily Land-Cruiser connections with their dumping camps in Tubau. The loggers are friendly and co-operative and you can try to get a ride back to one of the camps with them. Their logging concessions are limited in time and place so the camps tend to move fairly frequently.

Once you get to the Belaga River it is possible to travel down to the town of Belaga, where the Rejang River starts, in one day of river paddling and jungle walking. There are several jungle paths you can choose from but you'll have to use the services of a local boatman at some point or other, either to travel along the river or to cross it. No matter how experienced a jungle walker you may be, you will find it helpful to take along a trustworthy local guide. He can help you bargain with the boatmen along the way. Even for local people there is no fixed price for hiring a boat on a given stretch of the river; the prices vary with the weather, the strength of the currents, the time of the day and willingness of the boatman to leave his farmwork to take you up or down the river. Nevertheless, when foreigners appear on the scene the locals are likely to ask for outrageous fares. And their bargaining position is certainly strong! Just for reference I paid M$100 for two of us to travel from a logging camp all the way down to Belaga. This included three boat rides and the fees for two young Kenyah guides. The whole trip took seven hours. It turned out to be one of the most exciting jungle trips I have ever had, partly due to the Belaga River being rather swollen at the time.

Police permits are still necessary and are partly meant for your own safety. The police may tell you the story of the German guy who ventured on his journey without a permit and disappeared – never to be seen again. Local touts will tell you the same story but stress that the unfortunate German didn't have the good sense to hire a guide! Bureaucratically the river seems to be a sort of one-way road because the permit is apparently easy to obtain in Bintulu for the Tubau-Belaga trek, but not so easy to to get in Kapit for Belaga-Tubau. We did not have a permit and nowhere were we asked to produce one.

I should think it is possible to do it alone, without guides and at the 'local price', even if you don't speak the local language. Make sure, however, that you have a good map, food, water, clothing, possibly a sleeping bag and maybe simple cooking utensils. Mosquito coils would be a good idea and mosquito net still better – Belaga is a bad malaria area. There are three rest houses (read stilted platforms topped by an attap roof) along the Belaga River, conveniently placed before and after the 'impassable' rapids. This is where you are most likely to get stuck if there is no boat or if it's too expensive. If you stay at the rest houses you are likely to meet small parties of travelling Kayans, perhaps families engaged in shifting agriculture or groups of young men who leave their longhouses in the Belaga basin and go to look for work in the logging camps. If they like you they may share their food with you and perhaps the boat they are going to charter next morning too. Be patient and be prepared to wait a few days for a passage which money could buy immediately.

This trip is likely to become easier as the logging roads are slowly pushed further down the river. There's even talk of a government plan for a Bintulu-Kapit road.

BINTULU

Bintulu is simply another stepping stone along the coast. It's got something of a boom town atmosphere (and price levels) due to the oil and timber developments in the region.

Places to Stay & Eat

Hotels here are expensive and often full. Getting a room for less than M$30 a night is quite a feat. Try the *Hock Chuhn Lodging House*, a stone's throw from the Tubau Express pier, where there are pigeonhole-like rooms for M$12.

Otherwise the *Capitol Hotel* at 48 Keppel Rd (not the New Capitol further along the street) has one room under M$30, most are M$50 or more and it's often full. The claustrophobic *Bintulu Hotel* (10 minutes walk out of town), the *Sky Hotel* (right behind the cinema and about 30 seconds stroll from the airport terminal), the *New Capitol* and a bunch of others can also be tried.

The night food stalls beside the taxi ranks are the best places to eat.

Getting There

Between Bintulu and Sibu you can attempt the recently completed road, wait for boats, make the long overland trek via Belaga, or follow the majority of people and fly.

On from Bintulu to Miri there are buses and taxis, but most travellers will make the diversion to the Niah Caves. There are a couple of buses daily which cost M$15 to either Batu Niah junction or Miri. If you're heading to the caves get off at the junction, which is 2½ hours out of Bintulu. The junction is about 12 km from the village of Batu Niah and there are no buses along this stretch so you'll have to hitch (easy) or take one of the occasional taxis which come through. It's advisable to book the bus the night before at the tailors between Yung Kiew Boarding and the Tanjung Kedurong Hotel – a sign announces Bas Suria Sdn Bhd Agent. Straight through to Miri takes about five hours. It's sometimes possible to find boats from Bintulu to Miri.

MIRI

Like Bintulu this is a rapidly expanding boom town with not a lot of interest. Travellers often pause here on their way to or from Brunei or the Niah Caves.

Places to Stay

Monica Lodgings (tel 36611) at 4 Kwang Tung Rd is cheap, for Miri, with rooms from M$18, although rather run down. The management are pleasant, however. *Malaysia Lodging House* (tel 34300) at 1C China St is the next cheapest. The *Tung Foh Hotel* at 7 Brooke Rd, near the corner of China St, has doubles with fan for M$18.

Other hotels are rather more costly – like the *Tai Tung Lodging House* (tel 34072) at 26 China St which costs from M$30 and is really quite pleasant. You can sometimes get a bed in the corridor or lobby for M$6. Other places include the *Hotel Miri*, the *Kheng Nam Lee* and the *Lodging House Yeo Lee*.

Places to Eat

There are lots of good places to eat between Brooke Rd and the waterfront in the new blocks. Near here the *King Hua Restaurant* has excellent Chinese food. *Supreme Fried Chicken* is the place for western fast foods. *The Kitchen* is new, has air-con and serves good dim sum and Korean food. If you're waiting for a bus the *One Cent Cafe*, next to the big Park Hotel, is OK.

Getting There

To Bintulu Buses and taxis run to Miri and to Batu Niah, about midway between Miri and Bintulu. The Syarikat Bas Suria office is across the street from the main bus stand. Book in advance.

To Brunei The Sharikai Berlima Belait bus company (office at the main bus stand) operates four buses daily to Kuala Belait – the first town in Brunei – from 7 am to 1 pm. The fare is M$10 and the trip takes about 2½ hours. The road is sealed from Miri to Kuala Baram where a river crossing is made. You unload everything from the bus here and walk on to the free car ferry or pay M$1 to take a motor boat across. They do this to beat the long line of cars waiting for the Shell car ferry. Small vehicles have priority, something to bear in mind if hitching.

Another bus on the other side of the Baram River takes you on the sand road to the Brunei border. After immigration and minimal customs formalities you board a third bus, a Brunei one, to the car ferry over the Belait River, just before Kuala Belait. The road from the border to Kuala Belait is bad, but if it's low tide you just drive along the beach.

At Kuala Belait you will be dropped at the Belait United Traction Co Ltd bus stand where you take another bus to Seria. There are 28 buses daily and the fare is B$1. The road is sealed all the way and the journey takes 30 to 45 minutes. If you need to change money – they're not very keen on Malaysian dollars – there's a branch of the Hong Kong & Shanghai

Banking Corporation just opposite the bus stand in Kuala Belait. From Seria you must take another bus to Bandar Seri Begawan, the capital of Brunei. Several bus companies do the run and there are many buses daily. The fare is B$4.50 and the journey takes 1½ hours. It's a good sealed road all the way. From Kuala Belait or Seria to BSB it's easy to hitch.

INLAND FROM MIRI

If you're heading to the mountains near the Kalimantan border the first stage will be by road to Kuala Baram and then by river to Marudi. It's an interesting small trading town with really nice people. You can buy Iban spears or blowpipes here and this is an easy place to meet Iban people. From here there are regular launches to Long Lama, further up the Baram River.

Marudi makes an interesting trip and once there you can visit longhouses or carry on further upriver. Further inland Bario is a popular destination and there are interesting longhouses and good walks in this region of the Kelabit people.

Places to Stay

The *Marudi Grand Hotel* is very nice with rooms from M$11/13. They even meet launches with a car to drive you the four or five blocks to the hotel. The new *Mayland Hotel*, over the cinema of the same name, is also good value. There are some even lower-priced Chinese cheapies.

Getting There

The express boats from Kuala Baram to Marudi cost M$10, no extra charge for kung fu videos. Kuala Baram is on the road from Miri to the Brunei border. From Marudi you can continue to Long Lama, up the river, but beyond that point there is no regular transport and you have to negotiate with the tribesmen. It takes about 1-1/2 days for around M$25 to Long Akah from Long Lama. MAS operate a network of flights into the interior. Permits are necessary to visit many places in the mountains.

NIAH CAVES

Sarawak's best known national park is about midway between Bintulu and Miri. Only in the '50s was the archaeological significance of the Niah Caves realised. Here a human skull from 35,000 years ago was found, and traces of habitation from that time until the caves were mysteriously deserted about 1400 AD. The Sarawak Museum in Kuching has an exhibit of finds from the caves and you can get a booklet on the caves from the tourist office.

The caves, the greatest of which was named 'hell' by the excavators, are a source for that most famous Chinese delicacy, birds' nest soup. Countless tiny swifts built their nests in the caves, constructing them out of hardened, sticky saliva. Collecting the nests is a difficult and dangerous occupation – accounting for the hefty price they collect from gourmets. Guano, bird and bat excrement, is also collected from the caves for use as fertiliser. It's quite a sight each evening as the vast population of swifts flock in from the dayshift while the bats leave on the nightshift. If you go into the caves in the evening and find the gate locked on your return, simply lift it off its hinges.

No permit is necessary to visit the Great Cave but you are supposed to have a permit for the Painted Cave. You can get this from the Curator's Office at the Sarawak Museum or at the Forest Office (Pejabat Utan) in Miri. In actual fact if you hire a guide at the park headquarters you're unlikely to be asked for your permit. Guides cost M$30 shared between as big a group as you can muster and they're near-as-damn-it a necessity. It's easy to get lost in the caves. Don't miss the Iban longhouse near the mouth of the cave.

Places to Stay

The *Visitors' Hostel* at Pangkalan Lubang is the place to stay, there are three dormitory rooms with costs of M$2.50 per night for a bed. Cooking facilities are provided, but it's an idea to bring some food with you from Batu Niah, Bintulu or Miri. There's a store across the river from the hostel, but the supplies there are very limited. You can also buy batteries and a torch (flashlight) here for the caves. The hostel is rarely full so you are usually OK if you turn up without prior booking. If you want to make sure then phone the Forest Office in Miri (tel 085-36637).

If for some reason you cannot or do not want to stay at the hostel there are hotels in Batu Niah. The *Niah Caves Hotel* is clean and reasonably cheap at M$18 for a double and has good, basic food in the restaurant downstairs. The *Yung Hur Lodging House* is similarly priced and the *Hock Sen Hotel* has a dormitory.

Getting There

From Bintulu there are no direct buses, you have to get off a Miri bus at Batu Niah junction (midway point) and hitch the 12 km into Batu Niah. There are occasional taxis at M$2 although they will ask for more. From Miri there are two buses daily to Batu Niah which cost M$9, it takes about 2½ hours. Taxis are M$15 per person, slightly more with air-con.

From Batu Niah to Pangkalan Lubang, where the Visitors' Hostel is located, you can walk along the riverside track in 45 minutes to an hour or get a ride on a motor boat for M$2, with haggling. The park department's boat costs M$5 round-trip. By road you can get to within 10-minutes

walk of the hostel at Supopok Kecil Kampong – turn left 2½ km before Batu Niah on the Datuk Sim Kheng Hong Rd, not the road to Niah. Pangkalan Lubang is four km from Batu Niah and from there you have a four km plankwalk to the caves themselves.

OTHER PARKS

There are a number of other parks in Sarawak apart from Niah. The magnificent Gunung Mulu park is still closed to visitors.

Near Kuching at the mouth of the Bako River the Bako National Park has fine beaches and some unspoilt rain forest. There are also a number of interesting marked walks in the park. You can stay at Telok Assam either in the park rest houses (M$22, accommodate up to seven), in the hostel cabins (M$1.10 per person) or in the permanent tents (M$1.10 per tent).

The park is 37 km north of Kuching and can only be reached by boat. One-way fare to Kampong Bako, the nearest village to the park, is only M$2. From there you need another boat for the half-hour trip to the park HQ at Telok Assam. Unfortunately the park boat no longer seems to be running and a private charter may cost M$25 to 30 for a boat big enough for five to 10 people. During the November to March monsoon period the sea may be too rough to get to the park.

Sabah

Once part of the great Brunei empire, Sabah came under the influence of the North Borneo Company after centuries of being avoided due to its unpleasant pirates. At one time Kota Kinabalu was known as Api Api, 'fire, fire', from the pirates' tiresome habit of repeatedly burning it down. Eventually in 1888 North Borneo, along with Brunei and the Brooke family's Sarawak, were brought under British protection.

Today an integral part of Malaysia its economy is based chiefly on timber, with agriculture providing the balance. Only in the past few years have new roads begun to open the vast untouched interior. Sabah never suffered from communist guerrilla activity to the same extent as Sarawak, but relations with the Philippines have been unhappy due to Sabah's unofficial support of the Muslim insurgents in the southern Philippines. For the visitor

Sabah's appeal is chiefly its scenic grandeur and variety of tribes. Unfortunately it is a rather expensive area to visit and the budget traveller should try to make his visits to the towns short and sweet. The Mt Kinabalu National Park deserves all the time you can spare it.

GETTING THERE

Singapore & Peninsula Malaysia The usual route into Sabah is to fly. From Peninsular Malaysia the cheapest flights to Kota Kinabalu are advance purchase (M$256) or economy night flight from Johore Bahru. There are also special discounts available from Kuala Lumpur.

There used to be a variety of shipping services with Straits Shipping to various Sabah ports from Singapore, but they have now virtually all disappeared. These fine old cargo/passenger ships were a delightful way to travel – there were only a handful of cabins so virtually every meal was at the captain's table. The food was excellent and there was plenty of it. A real shame they have gone. There is talk of a new service commencing in '85 between Kuantan on the east coast of the peninsula and Kota Kinabalu.

Brunei There are a number of interesting routes from Brunei into Sabah – see the Brunei section for more details. In brief: you can take a boat to Limbang in Sarawak and another from there to Punang from where share-taxis run to Lawas. Or you can take a launch out to the Sabah island of Labuan and another boat from there to Menumbok on the mainland from where buses and share-taxis run to Beaufort and Kota Kinabalu.

Or you can take a boat to Lawas, another from there along the river to Merapok, from where you can travel to Sipitang and on to KK. The road from KK actually runs all the way to Lawas now, but as of yet there is little traffic. Make sure you clear Sabah immigration at Merapok – it's very easy to miss them and you could then have complications later. As one traveller reported the trip: 'all the way

from Merapok it's a pleasant journey except for Sipitang. During WW II the Japanese probably saw Sipitang and passed right through thinking they had already destroyed it. Rest House was full when I passed through – I can't imagine with whom. I stayed in a dive in the middle of town (the only other place). You can't miss it, just find the mid-point between the two ends and ask'.

As a final alternative you can fly between Bandar Seri Begawan and Kota Kinabalu.

Philippines There are daily flights between Manila and KK with MAS and with Philippine Airlines. The fare is around US$200 and the flight takes two hours. Sabah Air (Air Mindanao) has had a once-weekly flight between Zamboanga and KK and also Zamboanga to Sandakan, but these flights tend to be unreliable and at present are not operating at all.

With Indonesian Kalimantan immediately south of Sabah and the long string of islands in the Sulu archipelago looking like stepping stones to the Philippines you might think it would be very easy to get across from one country to the other. It isn't. In fact there seems to be a real conspiracy to force you to either fly Sabah-Manila (for the Philippines) or backtrack all the way to Singapore and go to Jakarta (for Indonesia)!

In actual fact getting out of Sabah to the Philippines or Indonesia is physically very easy – but you're likely to be barred from entry (at best) or deported (at worst). That is if you're not murdered by pirates in the Sulu archipelago on the way. There are thousands of Filipino refugees around the Semporna area (between Tawau and Lahad Datu). Because Sabah is Muslim, and because of the continuing strife between the Muslim rebels of the Philippines island of Mindanao and the Catholic government, this is a popular area to escape to.

The refugees make frequent trips home and they'll probably be quite happy to take you along, after all they're smuggling stuff into the Philippines on these trips in any case. Once upon a time they used to be running guns into Mindanao, but with relations between the Philippines and Sabah now on a better footing it's more likely to be consumer items from cigarettes to Coca Cola. Unfortunately when you arrive there is no way you will get your passport stamped so the first time some official takes a look at it you'll be given your marching orders. For an interesting description of a recent successful voyage to Zamboanga by this route read *Slow Boats to China* by Gavin Powell.

Coming the other direction most of the Sulu archipelago is off-limits. Of course if you just want to visit the Philippines without actually 'visiting' the Philippines you can make a nice little trip to the islands of Sitangko or Sibutu. The one exception to this no-travel ruling is the on-again, off-again flight between Sandakan and Zamboanga.

Indonesia Much the same story applies for making the border hop between Tawau and Tarakan. There are frequent boats between these two places, via Nunakan, but only Malaysians and Indonesians are allowed to travel on them. There are also regular flights (M\$150) and the no-foreigners rule was recently lifted for the flights so this is a possible entry point to Indonesia. It is not, however, a 'no visa' entry point so make sure you have a visa before setting off.

There is an Indonesian embassy in Kota Kinabalu and in Tawau. If, for any reason, the KK embassy suggests you should get your visa in Tawau, ask them to put it in writing. Otherwise the Tawau embassy may suggest you should go back to KK and get it there!

Hong Kong You can also fly to KK from Hong Kong for about US\$300. The four-hour flight is operated by MAS and by Cathay Pacific.

KOTA KINABALU
The capital of Sabah was destroyed during WW II and changed its name from Jesselton only in 1963. It doesn't have the history or easy going charm of Kuching or the oil-money wackiness of Bandar Seri Begawan and, worse, KK is also rather expensive.

Take a walk up Signal Hill for a view over the town and the China Sea. There's an interesting museum right in the centre of town and a modernistic new mosque en route to the airport. Only a short ride offshore from the city are some pleasant islands in Tunku Abdul Rahman National Park – good swimming and beaches. Tanjong Aru Beach is several km south-west of the city, near the airport. KK also has an interesting night market around Kampong Ayer Square.

Information
The Tourist Office is very helpful as is Hornbill Tours next door and the nearby National Parks Office. You have to visit the latter to book accommodation for Mt Kinabalu.

Places to Stay
Finding a decent budget hotel in KK is not easy. Essentially to get a good room here you have to pay for it. For many years the most popular budget hotel with travellers has been the *Islamic Hotel* (tel 54325) at 8 Jalan Perpaduan. It has 15 rooms at M\$25.50. Rooms are very basic although you get a ceiling fan. The sink in the room likely won't work, nor the one in the toilet, nor the shower. A tap in the bathroom does, so with that and a plastic bucket you've got your shower. The restaurant downstairs serves OK Indian and Pakistani food.

An alternative, diagonally across the street, is the *Pine Bay* (tel 54900), but it's really no better. Singles are M\$28, doubles M\$33, with air-con M\$40/44. Some rooms are OK, some are totally airless holes where 'not even the cock-roaches stay around'. Along the street the hotel is on there are numerous cheap restaurants – mostly Indian and Muslim.

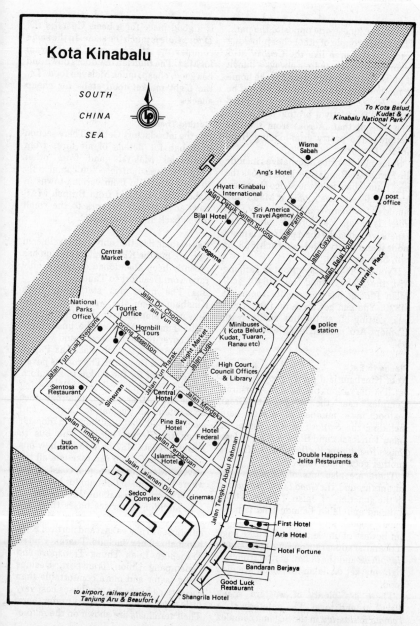

Kota Kinabalu

SOUTH CHINA SEA

To Kota Belud, Kudat & Kinabalu National Park

Wisma Sabah

Ang's Hotel

Hyatt Kinabalu International

Sri America Travel Agency

Jalan Datuk Salleh Sulong

Bilal Hotel

Jalan Pantai

post office

Jalan Gaya

Jalan Balai Polis

Australia Place

Segama

Central Market

National Parks Office

Jalan Dr. Chong Tain Yun

Tourist Office

Jalan Tun Fuad Stephens

Lorong Jessefton

Hornbill Tours

Minibuses (Kota Belud, Kudat, Tuaran, Ranau etc)

police station

Jalan Tugu

Night Market

Jalan Tun Razak

Sinsuran

Sentosa Restaurant

High Court, Council Offices & Library

Central Hotel

Jalan Merdeka

Jalan Timbok

Pine Bay Hotel

bus station

Hotel Federal

Jalan Perpaduan

Islamic Hotel

Double Happiness & Jelita Restaurants

Jalan Laiaman Diki

Jalan Tengku Abdul Rahman

Sedco Complex

cinemas

First Hotel

Aria Hotel

Hotel Fortune

Bandaran Berjaya

Good Luck Restaurant

to airport, railway station, Tanjung Aru & Beaufort

Shangrila Hotel

There's a Chinese one opposite the park. There are a couple of other cheap-looking hotels in this area like the *Central* at 5 Jalan Tugu, where there's always a bunch of people you wouldn't want to take home to mother hanging around the door. The *Long House Hotel* on Jalan Tun Fuad Stephens is strictly a brothel and a very busy one at that. Across from the bus station is the pretty grim-looking *Hotel Golden Dragon*.

Some middle price alternatives include the *Fortune* in Bandar Berjaya, across the large roundabout from the Sedco Complex. It's friendly and has rooms at M$33 with fan, M$41 with air-con. The nearby *First Hotel* is clean, comfortable and more expensive, while the the *Asia Hotel* is more modest and pretty good value at M$33, or with bath at M$39.

If you don't mind staying out at Tanjong Aru, the *Victory Hotel* (tel 52640) at 9 Jalan Pinang has reasonable rooms at M$20. You can get there on the airport bus, getting off at the bus shelter with 'Tanjong Aru' painted in big letters on the wall.

Places to Eat

Kota Kinabalu is a pretty good place to eat. Try the various places in the Sinsuran Complex near the waterfront. Great seafood in a number of places here including the *Sentosa* on the corner of Jalan Tun Razak and Block 5. The *Village House Restaurant* by the tourist office is another good place for seafood.

There are also lots of Chinese restaurants around, the *Good Luck Restaurant* at the junction of Jalan Tengku Abdul Rahman and Jalan Laiman Diki is particularly good. It's a very popular restaurant, but beware of unwanted extras (like bags of peanuts) appearing on your bill. *Double Happiness* and the *Jelita*, across from the night market on Jalan Merdeka, are also good.

There are plenty of western snack places around town. The cafeteria-style *Tomato Restaurant* in the Segama complex is a good place for a beer. Upstairs the *Tidbits Cafe* is much the same. In the same complex the *Ali Restaurant* has biriyani for M$4. The *Bilal* is a few doors down and has good, cheap, quick Malayan food. Try the night market food stalls for cheap snacks.

Getting There

See the introductory Getting There section in Sabah for details of air fares from Peninsular Malaysia and from other neighbouring countries. You can also fly to Kota Kinabalu from various towns in Sabah, Sarawak and from Brunei. MAS have an extensive network to the small towns back in the hinterland.

Rail Sabah has the only railway line in Borneo, but the KK-Beaufort section has recently been abandoned so now it only runs from Beaufort to Tenom.

Bus The main bus station in Kota Kinabalu is on the west side of the Sinsuran complex over the other side of Jalan Timbok. Most of the buses from here cover the routes south and west of Kota Kinabalu to such places as Papar, Kimanis and Beaufort. The road is paved and excellent for the 90 km to Beaufort. Beyond that it's gravel, generally getting worse the further you go. The road does now extend all the way to Lawas – and even beyond that – although it doesn't reach the Brunei border. The bus to Beaufort costs M$7 or M$8 in a new bus with air-con. Or you can take one all the way to Menumbok on the coast (from where boats run to Labuan) for M$14 air-con. The trip takes about three hours.

In addition to service buses there are several companies which operate fleets of minibuses to places east and north of Kota Kinabalu. They include Tuaran United Transport, Luen Thung Transport and Penampang Union Transport. Besides being faster and more comfortable than the service buses the minibuses cost very little more, so most travellers prefer them. Their terminals are shown on the map of

Kota Kinabalu. There's no problem finding the minibus you want as you can hear the drivers shouting their destination from a long way off. They go when full but, for the long hauls, departures are only in the mornings. Because of road improvements and faster times some fares haven't changed much in recent years. Some examples from KK include:

To Kota Belud (77 km), departures up to 2 pm daily, two hours on a road that is sealed nearly all the way for M$8.

To Kudat (22 km), departures up to 8 am, four hours on a road which is partially sealed for M$15.

To Sandakan (400 km), two minibuses daily at 8.30 and 11 am, about 10 hours for M$40. The road is sealed as far as Ranau and then rough most of the way to Sandakan. It's paved in and around Sandakan. Going the other way from Ranau to Tenom, you'll travel on an all-weather gravel road. From KK to Tambunan the road is surfaced.

If you're heading for Kinabalu National Park from KK you can get there by taking either the minibuses for Ranau or Sandakan and getting off at the park HQ, which is right by the side of the road. Ask the driver to drop you off there. It costs M$10 and takes about two hours.

Besides the minibuses there are also share-taxis to most places. Like the minibuses they go when full and their fares are usually about 20-25% higher than the minibuses. Journey times are about the same. There are some routes, however, which can only be covered by Land-Rover or share-taxi. The one you're most likely to come across is the route from KK to Keningau over the Crocker Range. The route first follows the sealed road as far as Papar, where it turns off and heads up into the mountains. From here on it's as rough as hell until you get to Keningau and if you like a degree of comfort then take a share-taxi in preference to a Land-Rover. The fare is M$15

for a Land-Rover and M$20 for a taxi – an expensive ride but then cars don't last too long over this kind of terrain!

Getting Around

A red bus 12 or 13 to the airport cost 60c. A taxi is M$6.20, M$7.70 with air-con. The Kota Kinabalu airport has a surprisingly reasonably priced snack bar, but no place to change money. Getting out to the airport at Tanjong Aru is about the only occasion you'd have to use local transport in KK.

BEAUFORT

This quiet little town is of no real interest although people often stop here on their way between KK and Brunei. Sabah's only railway line runs from Beaufort to Tenom.

Places to Stay

The *Wing Foh Lodging House*, once permanently full of migrant workers is now fairly easy to get into and has spartan doubles at M$20. The *Economy Inn* has rooms from M$19 (for a fan-cooled single) to M$38 (for an air-con double). It's pleasant and clean. The *Padas Hotel* is slightly more expensive.

Places to Eat

The *Padas Hotel* has Beaufort's best eating place although it's a little expensive. The restaurant under the *Economy Inn* is also pretty good and slightly cheaper. There are several noodles-and-little-else Chinese cafes around town.

Getting There

See the introductory Sabah Getting There section for details of transport from Menumbok through Beaufort to Kota Kinabalu. Or see the Kota Kinabalu Getting There section. See Tenom below for details of the Beaufort-Tenom railway.

AROUND BEAUFORT
Tiga Island

Off coastal Kuala Penyu is Tiga Island

which has a good beach and a government rest house. Boat charters to the island are expensive.

Labuan Island

The island of Labuan is off-shore from Brunei and recently became a Federal Territory, governed directly from Kuala Lumpur. It used to be part of Sabah. It is a stepping stone between Brunei and Sabah since there are flights from KK to BSB via Labuan, boats from the Sabah coast to Labuan, and launches between BSB and Labuan. See the Brunei section for transport details.

Labuan was the place where the Japanese forces in Borneo surrendered at the end of WW II and there's an appropriate memorial. Apart from the war cemetery and some beaches there is not much to see or do in Labuan and it's fairly expensive – there are several hotels but finding anything for less than M$50 is not easy. The *Kim Soon Lee* on Jalan Okk Awang Besar or the *Victoria Lodging House* at 147 High St are typical.

The ferry from Menumbok is M$7 and from there buses and share-taxis run to Beaufort and KK.

TENOM

There is nothing to do or see in this pleasant little rural town. It's simply the end point for that interesting railway trip up through the deep jungle along the Padas River Gorge from Beaufort.

Places to Stay

If you can get in, Tenom has a four-room *Government Rest House* (tel 677) at the usual price of M$12 per person or M$5 for government workers. The cheapest hotels – the *Hotel Lam Fong* and the *Ram Tai Hotel* – will almost certainly be full with migrant workers. *Hotel Tenom* (tel 587) only has double rooms; they're fairly spartan but clean and cost from M$33 for a fan-cooled room without bathroom up to M$50 for a room with bathroom and air-con. Downstairs there is a very spartan 'lounge' which serves cold beers; meals can be provided on request.

The next best is the *Sabah Hotel* (tel 534), Jalan Datu Haji Yassim, which has clean doubles with fan and common bathroom for M$22. The third place where you're likely to find a room is the *Hotel Kim San* (tel 611), Jalan Datu Haji Yassim, where rooms start from M$22 (with bargaining), but it's poor value and best used only for emergencies.

Places to Eat

Probably the best place to eat is the *Yun Lee Restaurant*, Jalan Tun Datu Mustapha. It isn't the cheapest place to eat in Tenom, but it does have the best menu, the food is excellent and the staff are very friendly. You'll find everything from sweet & sour pork to nasi goreng. Downstairs in the *Sabah Hotel* there's a good and very reasonably priced Muslim restaurant serving excellent Indian-style food.

For breakfast you should go to the Chinese cafe on the corner of Jalan Datu Haji Yassim and Jalan Tun Datu Mustapha, diagonally opposite the *Yun Lee Restaurant*, where they have their own freshly-baked bread and *hard* boiled eggs. They speak English.

Getting There

The colourful jungle railway trip from Beaufort up to Tenom is well worth making although it's likely this final short section of line may soon cease operation. There are two of the slower diesel trains and one of the faster and more comfortable rail cars daily. On Sunday a second rail car also operates. The 1st class fare is around M$10, economy is M$3.50.

You can continue by road from Tenom up to Keningau and Tambunan. the fare is M$6 and the minibuses and share-taxis operate from the outside the railway station.

KENINGAU

Again there's nothing of great interest in this town serving the timber-cutting activity of this part of Sabah. The trip up over the Crocker Mountains is the main attraction of the place.

Places to Stay

No real bargains here; the cheaper places are generally permanently full and the rooms you can get are expensive. There's a *Government Rest House* with eight rooms which costs the standard M$12 per person.

The cheapest hotel in town is probably the *Tai On*, followed by the *Park*, the *Wing Lee* and the *Ling Ling*. *Hotel Alisan* is very little more expensive although its entrance hall is unbelievably filthy. It's all air-con, and rooms cost from around M$35. Better hotels include the well-maintained *Hotel Hiap Soon* and the *Hotel Ria*, both in the same price bracket.

Getting There

It's a rough trip by share-taxi (M$23) or Land-Rover (M$18) to Kota Kinabalu. The trip takes two to 2½ hours. You can continue to Tambunan and Ranau by taxi or minibus and from Ranau you can go either to Sandakan or to the Kinabalu National Park.

KOTA BELUD

There is nothing of interest in Kota Belud during the week, but each Sunday the *tamu* or market brings the place alive. It's a real Asian market with goods scattered on the ground, betel-chewing grannies, hard bargaining for water buffaloes and cock fights for entertainment. If you are lucky, the colourful Bajau horsemen – the 'cowboys of the east' – might even make an appearance. It's a pleasant trip from KK to Kota Belud with fine views of Mt Kinabalu along the 80 km route.

Places to Stay & Eat

The *Hotel Kota Belud* (tel 576) on the central square costs M$30/35 for singles/doubles with air-con. It's a little pricey but good value as it's clean and well-equipped. Otherwise there's a faint chance of getting in to the *Government Rest House*, or you can try the school near the police station.

There's not much choice of food in Kota Belud and almost everything, including the restaurant in the *Hotel Kota Belud* shuts down very early. A solitary exception is the *Indonesia Restoran* in the car park behind the hotel which stays open until 8 pm.

Getting There

The 1½ hour trip from KK costs M$6; the road is all sealed. There is an amazing amount of traffic on Sunday, market day. To get to the national park from here take a minibus or share-taxi to KK and get off at Tamparuli, about halfway there. From there you can get transport going to Ranau which will drop you off at the park entrance.

AROUND KOTA BELUD

Midway between KK and Kota Belud the small water village of Mengkabong is worth a detour. Further on at the north-east tip of Sabah there are beautiful beaches around Kudat.

Places to Stay

Kudat has three main hotels – cheapest is the *Hasba Hotel* with not very good rooms at M$25/30, next up are the *Kudat Hotel* and *Hotel Sunrise* with rooms from M$35 to 70. There's also a *Government Rest House* at M$12 per person.

Getting There

There's a daily bus along the coast from Kota Belud to Kudat – it departs at 10 am and costs M$10. Bak Bak beach is 11 km from the town and difficult to get to without your own transport. A taxi there would cost M$6 and to be picked up would cost M$12.

MT KINABALU

Sabah's number one attraction is the highest mountain in South-East Asia with views from the top which can stretch all the way to the coast in the north,

Kalimantan in the south and islands of the Philippines in the east. Getting to the top of the 4101 metre peak is not so much a climb as a stiff and steep walk. The walk up is well worth it – fantastic views and some very interesting plant life.

The climb to the top requires an overnight halt on the way so bring plenty of warm clothes and a sleeping bag. You're supposed to have a guide with you and these cost M$25 a day (for one to three people), M$28 (four to six), M$30 (seven to 12), so the more people you have the cheaper it is. A guide is not really necessary and it's fairly easy to avoid having one. There is also a M$10 climbers' permit fee (M$2 for students).

You get almost to the top in a day's walk from the park HQ and there are mountain huts every couple of hours' walk. In the morning you leave very early on the final haul to the top and should have a couple of hours clear before the clouds roll in. Back down to the bottom takes the rest of the day so from park HQ to park HQ takes a day up and a day down with an overnight stop somewhere near the top. You can shorten the walk by taking a truck up to the power station, saving about 500 metres of vertical ascent.

There are some good walking trails around the park HQ, and more at Poring. After you've climbed the mountain you can continue on to the Poring Hot Springs to soak your weary limbs.

Places to Stay

Park HQ There is a variety of accommodation at the park HQ. For M$15 (M$4 for students) in the new building, M$10 (M$3) in the old building, you can get a bunk bed in the *Fellowship Youth Hostel*, but there's an extra charge to rent sheets and pillows. Then there are a variety of cabins, chalets and lodges available, all of them rather expensive. Twin-bed cabins start from M$100! Other range up to lodges for eight which cost M$360 per night.

You can get food at the *Club Canteen* or the slightly more expensive (but really excellent value) *Steak & Coffee House*. The park HQ has free lockers where you can leave your gear while climbing the mountain plus it rents out sleeping bags, backpacks and other useful items – but no rain gear.

On the Mountain Up on the mountain you can get a bunk for M$6 (M$2 if you're a student) at the mountain hut at Panar Laban (3344 metres) or Sayat-Sayat (3800 metres). Bring food and kerosene for cooking and be prepared for a serious lack of utensils for cooking or eating your food. The higher hut does mean you only have a 1½ hour climb (against 2¾) the next morning.

Poring At Poring there's the campground with open-sided bamboo huts for M$2 per person (M$1 for students). The new hostel costs M$8 per person (M$2 for students). The *Old Cabin* has a flat rate of M$100 for up to six people. The *New Cabin* is M$80 for up to four people. Bring food from Ranau, there's a small shop at the entrance to springs but nothing else. You can fix your own food and firewood is provided.

Getting There

It's a three or 3½ hour trip from KK to the park HQ – take a Ranau or Sandakan minibus, the fare is M$11 to the park, M$13 to Ranau. You can also reach the park HQ from Kota Belud via Tamparuli. From the park to KK just go out to the main road and wait for something to come by; minibuses pass by particularly around 8.30 am and 12 noon to 1 pm. If you get tired of waiting you can try hitching – there's plenty of traffic.

To reach Poring go first to Ranau then take a pickup to the hot springs for M$3. On weekdays it may be difficult to find one in the afternoon; you can either overnight in Ranau or charter a taxi for M$15 to 20. There are lots of Land-Rovers available for charter all along this route and between 10 or 12 people it's cheaper than by minibus. From the park you can get minibuses straight through Ranau to Sandakan.

RANAU

This is just a small town on the way from KK to Sandakan, but it's a very friendly place and from here you get to the Poring Hot Springs, 18 km away.

Places to Stay & Eat

The *Ranau Hotel* (tel 351) is the first place you see when you enter the town, opposite the petrol stations. Rooms start from around M$35 for singles. At the *Kheng Lok Hwa Hotel*, above the cafe of the same name, there are spartan rooms from M$20. It looks deserted and it's difficult to find anyone to let you in! The *Government Rest House* is a little out of town and costs M$12.

There's good Chinese food at the place around the corner from the Ranau Hotel. There are other cheap Chinese places around but they all close very early.

Getting There

Minibuses from KK cost M$13. On to Sandakan costs M$25.

SANDAKAN

Once the capital of Sabah this is a major port and a centre for the export of everything from timber and palm-oil to rattan and birds' nests for that famous Chinese delicacy. From Sandakan you can visit the orang-utan sanctuary at Sepilok, the Gomantong Caves across the bay where the birds' nests are collected, and with effort you may be able to visit the turtle sanctuary off-shore. Apart from the waterfront area there's not much to see in Sandakan itself, however.

Take a Sepilok Batu 14 bus for M$1.45 to Sepilok to see the orang-utan. It's best to go in the morning; the 9.30 am bus gets you there for the morning feeding-time. Officially you must have a permission-slip from the National Forests office in Sandakan to visit the sanctuary. Check about the opening times too – they vary

from day to day. Getting to the Gomantong Caves or the turtle sanctuary is either difficult or expensive. Enquire at the National Parks office if their boat is going out to the turtle island.

Places to Stay

The cheapest hotel in Sandakan is the *Hotel Bunga Raya* near the mosque. Rooms cost around M$20. Other base-price places include the empty classrooms of *St Mary's Catholic Church* (ask a taxi to take you there – M$1.50). Here you can sleep free, but look clean and tidy when you turn up, otherwise the old Chinese father may refuse you. Or there's the police station.

If you're not on too tight a budget try the *Cosmo Hotel* (tel 2151) on Jalan Empat. This hotel has three floors of air-con rooms and a top floor of non air-con rooms, and despite the fact that it's cheaper than most it's very good value. Rooms cost from M$30 to M$55 and have their own bathroom although the hot water system seems to be defunct. The disco on the ground floor is very well sound-proofed, but the muezzin in the nearby mosque will wake you up well before dawn with his amplified wailing.

All the middle-range hotels are of a similar standard and there's very little to choose between them. They fill up rapidly so you may have difficulty finding a room late in the day (all the non air-con rooms will certainly have been taken by then).

At the cheaper end of the middle-range the *Mayfair Hotel* (tel 5191-2), on the waterfront opposite the market and local bus stand, has non air-con rooms from M$30. It's often full because the long-distance minibuses park round the corner. *Hotel Paris* at 27 Lorong Dua is similarly priced.

Places to Eat

Sandakan is full of cheap Chinese restaurants and coffee houses serving the standard rice or noodles with fried vegetables. If you'd like a break from this sort of high-carbohydrate fodder then go to the *Silver Star Ice Cream & Cafe* where, in the evenings, you can buy satay at 25c per stick with hot peanut sauce. It's a friendly place, popular with local people.

At a little higher cost try the excellent *Kuala Lumpur Restoran*, first floor, Leboh Tiga, opposite the MAS office – red table cloths, hovering waitresses and very good food. The menu has a bewildering selection of Chinese and Malay food. The helpings are large but bear in mind that the average price of a dish is M$6 to 8. Other places in this range are the *Carnival Restaurant* and the *Restoran Double Happiness*, at the far end of Leboh Tiga from the MAS office. Or the *Yen Yun* at the Hsiang Garden Complex on Jalan Leila.

Getting There

All the long distance minibuses leave from near the waterfront, behind the Mayfair Hotel. There are direct buses to Ranau (M$25) and Kota Kinabalu (M$35). To Tawau you normally have to take a bus to Lahad Datu (M$13) and change there. Sandakan's airport is 11 km out of town, M$2 by regular minibuses.

LAHAD DATU

The main reason for coming here is to take boats out across Darvel Bay to the islands between here and Semporna.

Places to Stay

The *Government Rest House* is at the airport, less than a km from the town centre. Ask the bus driver to stop there if you're coming from Sandakan or Tawau. Overnight cost is M$12 per person.

If you can't stay there, the *Liang Ming Lodging House* at Kampong Sawmill cost from M$22. Middle-range hotels are much more expensive; the *Ocean Hotel* costs from M$45 without air-con.

Places to Eat

Plenty of rice and noodle places again, or try the rather better *Good View Restaurant* on the hill east of town.

Getting There

The minibus stand is next to the Esso station by the market. Buses go to Sandakan (M$13), Semporna (M$13) and Tawau (M$22). The bus to Tunga, east of Lahad Datu, goes past a really fine beach about 20 km out. Boats go to Semporna daily for M$14 and to Kunak for M$7. The trip is worth the effort if you have time. Kunak is a small town with one hotel.

TAWAU

A mini-boom town in the south-east of Sabah and an exit point to Kalimantan.

Places to Stay

Nothing is good value, as usual for Sabah. *Hotel Lido* (tel 74547) on Jalan Stephen Tan, has rooms, all doubles, from M$30 to 50. At the same location *Hotel Foo Guan* is slightly cheaper but it's mainly short time. *Hotel Soon Yee*, on the same street, is a small, clean place at similar prices. *Hotel Tanjung* is also on the same street and again at similar prices, if you haggle.

Middle range hotels include the *Hotel Ambassador* (tel 72700, 72718) at 1872 Jalan Paya Tawau with air-con rooms with bathroom from M$35. Others are the *Hotel Malaysia* and the *Wah Yew Hotel*.

Places to Eat

Cheap rice and noodle places are the usual eating story, or try the reasonably priced *California Cafe* on Jalan Dunlop.

Getting There

Share-taxis to Semporna cost M$12. Between Tawau and Lahad Datu the cost is M$25 for the five hour trip; there's also a M$20 minibus. Boats operate irregularly to and from semporna. A taxi from the airport costs around M$3 but the big hotels will take you on their bus for free.

Tawau is used as a jumping-off point for Tarakan in Kalimantan and currently you are allowed to use this route although Tarakan is not a 'no visa' entry point. See the introductory Sabah Getting There section for more details.

Papua New Guinea

PNG, the eastern half of the island of New Guinea (the western half is the Indonesian province of Irian Jaya), is one of the newest independent countries in the world. It's a strange mixture of remote tribes in untouched regions and modern coastal towns. Wild jungle, wide rivers, beautiful coral seas, idyllic islands are all here. The only catch is that for the budget traveller it's very expensive.

HISTORY

In their frantic search for spice, Portuguese and Spanish explorers were the first to stumble upon the island of New Guinea. When the first Portuguese set foot on the island in the 1500s he named it 'Ilhas dos Papuas' – 'island of the Fuzzy-haired Men'. The name stuck. Later, in 1545, a Spaniard decided 'Neuva Guinea' was more appropriate but for a long time after that all the European powers left the daunting big island strictly alone.

In 1828 the Dutch, who already had most of the neighbouring islands under their thumb, added the western half to their list – then promptly forgot about it for another 60 years. As the century progressed the colonial powers became more energetic in their search for the remaining scraps of unclaimed land and Britain hastily put in a claim for the southern half of the unclaimed eastern portion which became known as Papua. Literally days later the Germans claimed the northern half. During this same period explorers began to penetrate into the unknown interior of the island.

German power was a fleeting thing. They moved from town to town along the north coast – with malaria always in hot pursuit – before settling for the healthier climate of Rabaul. At the start of WW I, Australia, which had taken control of Papua from Britain, also took over the German colony. After the war the discovery of gold and the beautiful and fertile valleys of the Highlands prompted Australian development. The Dutch half of New Guinea, with less than half the Australian side's population and much less agricultural and mineral potential, lagged behind.

During WW II the Japanese invaded the island but never managed to capture Port Moresby although they got very close at one time. As the tide of the war turned the Japanese were pushed back in a long and gruelling fight up the Kokoda trail. Energetic bushwalkers can follow that same trail from the south to the north coast today.

With the Japanese gone the colony drifted on until the anti-colonial spirit finally prompted Australia to grant self-government in 1973, followed by independence, in 1975. The developments on the Dutch half of New Guinea were not so simple; it remained a Dutch colony after Indonesian independence but after Indonesia claimed it in 1962 (the only real basis was the connection of Dutch colonialisation) it was soon handed over –subject to a vote by the inhabitants. To no one's surprise when the vote was held in 1969 they decided to become part of Indonesia – perhaps the useful technique of pre-selecting a 'representative' selection of voters helped.

FACTS

Population The current population is estimated to be about 2-1/2 million, over 90% of which live in the rural areas. Papua New Guinea is still a basically tribal society with an estimated 700 different languages and dialects. Although the level of inter-tribal warfare (and even head hunting) has been fairly drastically reduced, there are still some primitive tribes in the remote regions as yet barely touched by modern society. In addition the smaller islands to the north and west have people with ties to the Pacific islands rather than the New Guinea mainland. There's a distinct cultural difference between the Papuans south of the main mountain range and the New Guineans to the north.

Geography Papua New Guinea's 474,000 square km encompass some incredible variations – from a high central mountain range to endless swampy plains. The highest mountains reach over 4700 metres and along the north coast and out on the island of New Britain there is a chain of active volcanoes. In the mountains are the fertile, hidden, Highland valleys – only discovered in the 1930s when aircraft started to fly over the central ranges. The heavy rainfall over the mountains runs down to form some of the largest rivers in the world including the Fly River running south and the Sepik running north – both are navigable for over 800 km upstream from the sea.

Economy PNG's economy is still largely a subsistence one although there is vast potential for timber production and as yet untapped mineral resources. Tea and copra are both grown commercially and coffee is now a very important crop. The mainstay of the economy is the enormous open-cut copper mine at Panguna. There are other mining projects underway such as that at Ok Tedi, up near the Irian Jaya border.

Religion The missionaries have had a good go at PNG and in many places the mission is still the local centre. Unfortunately the missionaries eradicated much of the precolonial culture but dances, art forms and legends are being resurrected for tourists! Of course there was no overall New Guinean religion prior to colonialisation but fine examples of the *haus tambarans*, the old tribal cult houses, can still be seen in the Sepik region. And of course there's the cargo cult, whose believers await the God who will ship in endless supplies of goodies – like WW II GIs.

INFO

A couple of years ago the PNG government decided that tourism had such a low priority that they disbanded their tourist department. It's supposed to be about to commence operation again but until it does there's no telling how good it might be.

Safety There is much talk about 'safety' in PNG and the country does indeed suffer from a couple of internal problems. In the cities, most particularly Port Moresby, there has been a large increase in muggings, grab-and-run operations, burglaries and the like. Be cautious after dark in Moresby, particularly on heavy drinking nights when PNG's drink problem is all too evident.

The other problem area is the Highlands where there has been a major return to the old days of tribal warfare. Fortunately this is very much tribe versus tribe and highly unlikely to involve visitors – unless you try to get between the two sides!

BOOKS

If you'd like a lot more detail on PNG I've written a much more comprehensive guide titled *Papua New Guinea – a travel survival kit*. It should be fairly readily available in PNG. *Bushwalking in Papua New Guinea* is another Lonely Planet guide with descriptions of the main walks and mountains to be climbed.

There have been an enormous number of books written about PNG including its own subgroup of literature known as 'Patrol Officers' Memoirs'. *The Last Unknown* by Gavin Souter is the book to read if you read nothing else about PNG – enthralling descriptions of the early explorers. *Patrol into Yesterday* by J K McCarthy is one of the most readable of the patrol officers' tales; really exciting reading.

In Papua New Guinea by Christina Dodwell is a recently published book of a wonderfully eccentric Englishwoman's delightful wanderings through the country.

Read it if you're contemplating walking through the jungle or canoeing down the Sepik. If you get a chance to fly on third-level carriers and decide it's a pretty heart-stopping way of getting around, then read *Sepik Pilot* and find out what it was like 30 years ago. There are plenty of other books if those whet your appetite.

Turning to films, rather than books, if you get a chance to see *First Contact* while in PNG don't miss it. The Leahy brothers, who pioneered exploration of the Highlands of New Guinea, had the foresight to bring a movie camera along with them. Recently their footage was turned into an engrossing documentary about that historic 'first contact', interspersed with superb film of Highlanders who can still remember that shattering occasion.

VISAS

The visa situation in PNG has gone through several forwards and reverses in the past couple of years so it's wise to check the current story with a PNG consular office or with Air Niugini before setting out. At present the situation appears to be that provided you have 'adequate' finance and an onward ticket you can arrive without a visa *at Port Moresby airport* and be granted a 30-day stay. This 'easy visa' system only applies to citizens of certain countries – which include Australia, Canada, New Zealand, the USA, most of Papua New Guinea's close Pacific and Asian neighbours, and a number of western European countries.

Visas, on the other hand, are valid for up to two months and cost the equivalent of K5. Since they seem to give you what you ask for it's wise to ask for too long, rather than a shorter period and have to extend it. If you expect to be in PNG for more than a month, or even suspect you might be, then it's wise to get a visa rather than arrive without one. Renewing the 30-day stay permit appears to be rather difficult and in any case the only place you can extend visas in PNG is Port Moresby. In Australia the consulate in Sydney is rather

more efficient at issuing visas than the High Commission in Canberra. There is also a consulate in Brisbane but not in Cairns. In countries where there is no PNG diplomatic representation you can apply to an Australian consular office.

Coming to or from Indonesia requires some special thought. First of all Jayapura in Irian Jaya is not one of the 'no visa' entry points for Indonesia. No matter what you do at the other end you must have an Indonesian visa if you arrive or depart via Jayapura. Secondly the PNG embassy in Indonesia is in Jakarta. There is no PNG consulate in Jayapura and (see the italics above) you must have a PNG visa to arrive in PNG from Jayapura at Wewak. The 'no visa' entry for PNG only applies at Port Moresby airport.

MONEY

A$1   = .77 K
US$1 = .95 K
£1   = 1.06 K

The kina (K, pronounced keenah) is divided into 100 toea (t, pronounced toyah); at first they were directly equivalent to Australian dollars and cents. The one-kina coin is an attractive large coin with a hole in the centre. If you're planning to stay long in PNG a convenient way of handling your money is to open a passbook savings account with Westpac or one of the other banks. They're easy to transfer money to from Australia and you can very easily withdraw money in most PNG towns and get interest on the balance!

COSTS

PNG is easily the most expensive country in this book for the traveller – it's kind of interesting to speculate why. Part of the reason is the difficulties of travel – the still sketchy road network means that a lot of stuff gets moved round by air and is consequently expensive. Furthermore what roads there are are often sufficiently rough to shake the fillings out of your teeth. Add that to the local indifference to

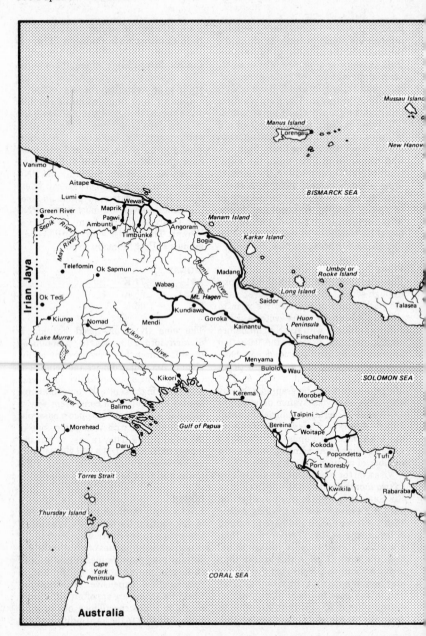

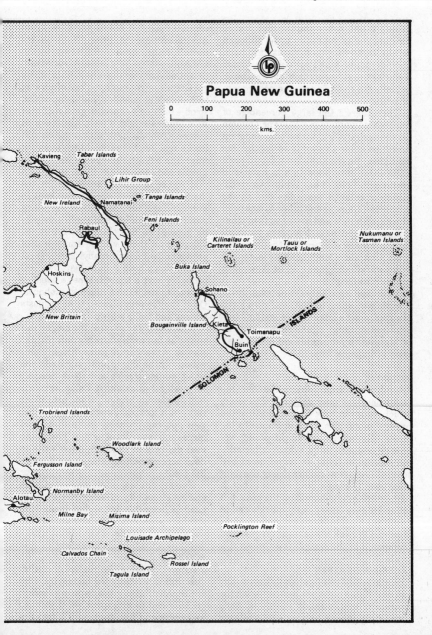

vehicle maintenance and the high cost of fuel and you've got costly travel although recent improvements in roads have been so widespread that PMV (Public Motor Vehicle) travel has actually been static or actually got cheaper over the past couple of years.

Then there's the large percentage of expatriates working in PNG. They're paid on western rates and with accommodation and trips home thrown in so another big hike goes into the local costs. Plus there's little local enterprise in the hotel and restaurant field. The 'White Australia' policy of colonial times has limited the number of Chinese and other Asians (who run cheap hotels and restaurants in other countries) and have left since independence. Finally a lot of stuff is imported from Australia – food, building materials, mechanical equipment; all at Australian prices plus freight.

Of course it isn't always necessarily so. People who come to PNG and do a lot of walking, meet a lot of people and find free accommodation, hitch rides, stay in villages and try the local food, often have a very economical time of it.

CLIMATE

The dry runs from May to October, the wet from December to March. The wet is much wetter in New Guinea, north of the central mountains, than in Papua to the south. Except at the height of the wet you're unlikely to be greatly affected – unless you're trying to travel down bad roads. Temperatures are pretty constant year round – ranging from warm to hot. It can be sticky and humid on the coast but inland it gets cooler fairly quickly and at night the highlands can get really cold. In Lae and Wewak the seasons are inverted compared to the rest of New Guinea.

ACCOMMODATION

Not too good – you'll generally have to pay around K10 a night per person. Again the reason is that there is simply no local supply of places to stay and the only

commercially-run hotels are once again Australian-style in price. So look for hostels, transit houses or flats run by the CWA (Country Women's Association), Salvation Army or the missions. If you've got friends or contacts you can often stay with people at missions, aid agencies and so on – but don't expect to get a roof over your head as a right; it isn't. And if you do stay on a friendly basis with someone who isn't a real longtime friend then pay your way – the pay isn't so special for mission people and their cost of living is high.

If you're in remote areas ask for the 'haus kiap' – these are houses kept in every village for the use of travelling government officials and you'll generally be allowed to use them. In fact at the village level there will be some sort of accommodation almost anywhere you go. If they don't have a haus kiap they will probably have a spare teacher's house, a mission hostel, even a village guest house. Often they're very pleased to have guests staying and make a little extra income.

Where you'll really feel the crunch is if you come to a town where the only place to stay is a very expensive hotel. Since nobody will be able to understand why you won't/wouldn't/can't stay there you may very well get stuck with it. Camping gear is well worthwhile bringing if you plan a long stay – if it looks like reasonably together gear you can probably camp in a lot of places and save a lot of money. There is no mail delivery in PNG so if you write to book accommodation make sure it is to a PO box.

If you're hitching or off the beaten track and get stranded you can often stay at the head policeman's house but make sure you have your own food – and some gift to show your gratitude.

FOOD

Terrible – there is really no other description. PNG for the budget traveller is just Australian greasy-spoon – except greasier and more expensive. If you like meat pies and fish & chips it'll feel like home. There's really no indigenous food unless you get well off the beaten track – in which case you'll have to learn to like a good sago or taro stew for your kaikai. The lack of local food places is the reason for the expense of eating.

There are a few escapes. Many of the places to stay are in the form of self-contained flats or have shared cooking facilities – so you can eat better and cheaper by fixing your own food. The food stores are supermarket style with Australian food at Australian-plus prices so it might be worth bringing a few cans or packages with you. There are also markets of course, with good fresh food (nice sweet corn), although the supply can be somewhat erratic.

Another escape is the expatriates' clubs you can find in all the towns – they are private members' clubs but, with the falling expatriate population, are generally only too happy to sign in 'out-of-town visitors'. They have good, reasonably priced food of the steak & chips variety. Another get-out are the Burns Philp and Steamships department stores – they are in virtually every town and usually have a snack bar with good quality sandwiches available. Of course, if you have money to spare you can eat in the restaurants of the more expensive hotels – the quality and price goes hand in hand.

If beer is required for your continued existence then you'll be happy with PNG; the Aussie beer culture has been accepted wholeheartedly and South Pacific beer is available everywhere. It's good beer but it's a shame it has such a large influence on PNG life.

GETTING THERE

The straightforward way into PNG is to fly into Port Moresby or take the short border-hop flight between Jayapura and Indonesian Irian Jaya and Wewak. There are also some much less usual routes into PNG; some of them are quite an adventure. The airport departure tax in PNG was for a while K20, one of the most expensive in

the world, but recently it has been cut back to K10.

From/To Australia Flying between Australia and Port Moresby is by far the most 'usual' way of entering PNG. Qantas and Air Niugini both have regular flights although Air Niugini, with connections from Sydney, Brisbane and Cairns, has the more comprehensive schedule. The flight from Cairns is the cheapest way out of Australia. Fares to Port Moresby are:

	economy*	apex**
Cairns	A$191	A$280
Brisbane	A$320	A$454
Sydney	A$392	A$555

*one way, **return

Apex tickets must be bought 35 days in advance and there is a 50% cancellation penalty.

There are some other much less 'usual' possibilities. One is to hang around in North Queensland and look for a yacht going across. You'll often find them in Cairns, Cooktown or Thursday Island and may be able to hitch a ride.

From Thursday Island you can easily get fishing boats to Daru in PNG. A catch is that once you've had your passport stamped out of Australia in TI you're not supposed to visit any of the Australian Torres Straits Islands. But the officials in TI admit that there is no way they could find out if you did or not. From Daru you can fly to Port Moresby for K82 or you can go by the ship *Niugini Trader* for K15 deck class.

From/To Indonesia The once-weekly K143 flight between Jayapura in Irian Jaya and Wewak in PNG is the connection with Indonesia. Using this flight you can travel from Australia to Bali via PNG, Irian Jaya and Sulawesi. It's a much more interesting route but with the various cheap fares now available to Jakarta from Australia it's by no means a cheap way of getting there. Note also that from time to time restrictions are placed on visitors in Irian Jaya. They may be limited to the number of days they may stay in the area or may not be allowed to go out of Jayapura.

Periodically relations between PNG and Indonesia go sour due to border incidents and at one time the Indonesian embassy in Port Moresby actually stopped issuing visas. If you arrived in PNG without an Indonesian visa you had to apply back to Australia for it. Note again that there are no consular offices in Jayapura or Wewak.

The Wewak-Jayapura flight sometimes stops in Vanimo so you can fly Vanimo-Jayapura, rather cheaper than Wewak-Jayapura. Although it's really illegal some travellers have travelled from Jayapura to Vanimo by powerboat for just a few dollars. When the mood is good it seems to be possible to get away with this from coming in to PNG, but arriving in Indonesia this way would almost certainly cause the

Indonesian officials to throw a fit . . . and you out of the country!

From/To Solomons The neighbouring Solomon Islands makes an interesting stepping stone between PNG and the South Pacific. See *South Pacific Handbook* by David Stanley (Moon Publications) for the best source of information on travelling on through the Pacific. You can fly directly to Honiara from Port Moresby but more interesting, though no cheaper, is to island hop from the PNG North Solomons province down through the 'slot' of WW II fame. At present, however, this route appears to be out of official favour.

From/To Other Places You can also fly between the Philippines, Hong Kong or New Zealand and PNG but the overwhelming majority of travellers arrive or depart to Australia with Indonesia as the secondary link.

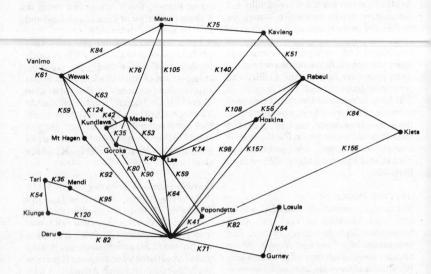

Air Niugini's Domestic Route Network

GETTING AROUND

Air Because roads are still relatively few and far between you're bound to have to do some flying in PNG. Which is often rather fun, but always rather expensive. Air Niugini have an extensive internal network operated with Fokker F27s and F28s and, for the present at least, De havilland Dash 7s. Some of the main routes and fares in kina are shown on the chart.

Air Niugini is supplemented by third-level carriers like Talair, Douglas Airways and a host of others. Some of these flights are quite delightfully hair-raising – strips cut into the sides of mountains, sheer drops, all that sort of stuff. In some places you can fly on the third-level carriers along the same routes as Air Niugini but taking in extra stops on the way.

Student discounts are available on Air Niugini and Talair flights and Air Niugini also has a 25% discount on its internal fares for people who come to PNG on return tickets and stay for less than 25 days. Flights in PNG tend to be heavily booked, especially during the Australian school holidays when many expats bring their children up from Australia. Over Christmas, May and August are the bad times. There is, however, an answer – when they say, 'check in 45 minutes before departure' they really mean it. Once the boom is lowered nobody gets through. So if you can't get a confirmed seat it's often worth turning up at the airport for the earliest flight of the day. There is always a good chance somebody's Melanesian time will have made him miss the flight.

Road It's only since the war that the road network has started to develop in PNG and only in the last few years has town-to-town public transport really arrived. The only extensive road system runs from Lae up into the Highlands with a spur off to Wau and Bulolo and to Madang. The road network is being expanded rapidly and eventually will probably link all PNG's major towns. Hopefully the decreased dependence on air freight will bring costs down.

The Lae-Madang road is now pretty well established and a road is rapidly being pushed through from Mt Hagen to Madang. Only about 20 km is needed to complete the Madang-Wewak link. From Wewak you can travel up to Angoram on the Sepik; eventually you'll be able to cross the Sepik by barge to a point further downriver then drive to Madang. In the Highlands the road from Mt Hagen to Mendi is now in much better condition and extends much further into the western Highlands.

The important road is, of course, a link from Port Moresby in Papua to the towns in New Guinea – it's much talked about but as yet little planned. The romantic road is along the old Kokoda Trail – but highly improbable. More likely is a road broadly following the old wartime Bulldog Trail to Wau and Bulolo or a route heading west from Port Moresby then crossing the mountains to link up with the western Highlands road system.

The main Highlands Highway will soon all be surfaced but elsewhere roads are often pretty rough going. Transport is the ubiquitous PMV or Public Motor Vehicles. At first they were all small pickups or trucks, sometimes with wooden benches in the back, but now they are often regular minibuses. They operate freelance on almost every route in the country. They're frequent, not really as unsafe as some people would make out and their costs have remained remarkably stable over the past few years. They're the real grassroots form of travel in PNG.

Ship PNG has quite an extensive coastal shipping service which could save you quite a bit of money over air fares – so long as you don't have to hang around waiting for it. The best way of finding ships is to just go down to the docks and ask around – local agents aren't likely to know too much. From Port Moresby it's sometimes possible to find ships running around Milne Bay and stopping at places like Tufi or Popondetta en route to Lae. Shipping is much more regular and easier to find on the north coast, however.

Lae is the centre for north coast shipping – big ships from Milford Haven docks, small ones from Voco Point, directly opposite the Hotel Cecil. The Lutheran Shipping Company, office at Voco Point, has a number of ships operating along the coast to Madang, Wewak and Vanimo, just before the Indonesian border. You can also find boats to Finschhafen and the islands off the coast along here. There are also regular services from Lae to Kimbe and Rabaul in New Britain. Also between New Britain and the North Solomons. There are a lot of ships moving around PNG – it's just a matter of hanging around and asking a lot of people!

In the Milne Bay region there are lots of 'workboats' ploughing back and forth between the islands. They're the PMVs of this island area. You can, if you're willing to wait, find a boat from almost anywhere to anywhere else but you can also charter boats from around K40 a day – worth considering between a group of people. Out of Samarai there's a government boat available for charter for K150 a day.

See the relevant sections for specific details on boat travel.

THINGS TO BUY

Artifacts and handicrafts are expensive in PNG, in line with the generally high costs. Strict regulations have, belatedly, been brought to prevent irreplaceable artifacts leaving the country, but there is a thriving industry turning them out for visitors. Every town has a number of artifact shops but the closer to source the better the prices. Town shops may have a wider range than you'll find in the villages so don't count on finding exactly what you want away from the shops.

Look for the intricate and meaningful Sepik River carvings, masks and shields.

The touristy ones generally look smoother and better finished. You can find pretty shell and bead necklaces, bracelets and collars in the markets – Madang is a good place. The crude-looking, primitive pottery is often poorly fired and rather fragile. Pleasantly coarse, woven mats and carpets are made in the Highlands. Get a bilum, the colourful and infinitely expandable string bags that every local seems to carry. In remote regions you can still deal on a barter basis.

LANGUAGE

Papua New Guinea is estimated to have over 700 different languages and dialects, the result of myriad tribes with little contact. Three are of importance for the visitor – English, Motu and Pidgin. English is widely spoken in all the major centres and you'll probably have no need for anything further in a short stay. It's interesting to know a little of the others, though.

Motu is the language of the Moresby and south coast area and as 'Police Motu', the language of the native police force of colonial days, was spread further. You can easily find Motu phrasebooks in Moresby.

Of greater interest is Pidgin English, or more correctly neo-Melanesian, which is widespread through PNG. A very interesting explanation of the language with an English-Pidgin and Pidgin-English dictionary is *The Book of Pidgin English* by John J Murphy which costs about K2.

Pidgin is now a recognised and studied language and its relations to English and to local languages is intriguing. Many words have an interesting descriptive quality — as *wantok* = one-talk, therefore someone who speaks the same language as you, a countryman or a friend. Or *haus kaikai*; since *kaikai* means food or to eat a *haus kaikai* is obviously a restaurant. Some are onomatapoeic, like *frog* = *rokrok*. Other words apply local terms to western objects – a *balus* (pigeon) is also an aircraft. Still others seem to indicate foreign contacts – milk is *susu* as in

Indonesia and Malaysia (although it also means breasts). And some of the slang is really interesting!

Then there are strange uses obviously related to tribal concepts – a man's brother is his *brata* but so is a woman's sister; your *sisa* is of the opposite sex to you whether male or female. If that is initially confusing consider also that holding up fingers to indicate a number is the opposite to our culture – it's how many fingers you don't hold up that counts!

PORT MORESBY

Moresby, as the locals call it, is hardly packed with interesting things to see and do but with a little effort you can pass the time well enough.

Information & Orientation

Port Moresby is initially rather confusing since it's a string of suburbs rather than one town. The old 'Port Moresby' is on a spit of land ending in Paga Hill. Here you'll find the older buildings, the docks and most of the office buildings. Between the airport at Jackson or Seven Mile you pass through first Boroko then either Three Mile Hill or Korobosea (depending on the route) and then Koki before reaching Port Moresby itself. Boroko is the secondary centre with more shops and offices. Koko is where the road reaches the coast and there's a big market here. From Boroko you can turn off to the government centre at Waigani and then the university campus.

PNG's national tourist department has only just been re-established and at the time of writing doesn't seem to have an office. Get excellent maps of PNG from the National Mapping Bureau in Waigani. The best bookshop is the University Bookstore at the university. Otherwise try the Steamships department store in Port Moresby or City News next door.

Remember that Port Moresby is the place where PNG's 'rascal' problem is worst. Take care, especially at night and most especially on payday nights.

Things to See

The 'old town' of Port Moresby has the most 'colonial-Pacific' feel to it although even here much new construction is going on. Just beyond the town centre is the now virtually defunct cultural centre and beyond that is Hanuabada, a stilt village which was the original settlement in this area. It's now very unoriginal and also a place which should only be visited with caution.

Going back from the town centre towards Koki and Boroko the road follows Ela Beach; not a bad beach but the water is shallow and weedy. Near the beach St Mary's Catholic Cathedral has a haus tambaran-style front. At the west end of the beach is the Sea World aquarium with dolphins and sea lions. Admission is K2.50.

Ela Beach ends at Koki with well-known Koki Market and a couple of reasonable crafts shops. From here the road continues to Boroko but most of the remaining places of interest are beyond Boroko at Waigani, the government centre. The PNG parliament moved to its impressive new building at 'Canberra in the tropics' in 1984. The impressive building is in haus tambaran style and cost K22 million. Inside you can watch proceedings, which are simultaneously translated into English, Pidgin and Motu – the three main languages of PNG. Nearby is the National Museum and Art Gallery with excellent displays of crafts and masks. Admission is free but the hours are very limited – Sunday 1 to 5 pm, Tuesday and Thursday from 8.30 am to 3.30 pm. You can get to Waigani by PMV for 30t (and a long walk) or take a taxi to the museum door from Boroko for K4.

Places to Stay

Moresby is not the traveller's dream town – you pay a lot of money for not all that much. Since none of the cheaper places to stay are right in the centre there is no reason to come right into town from the airport. Remember that Moresby is more

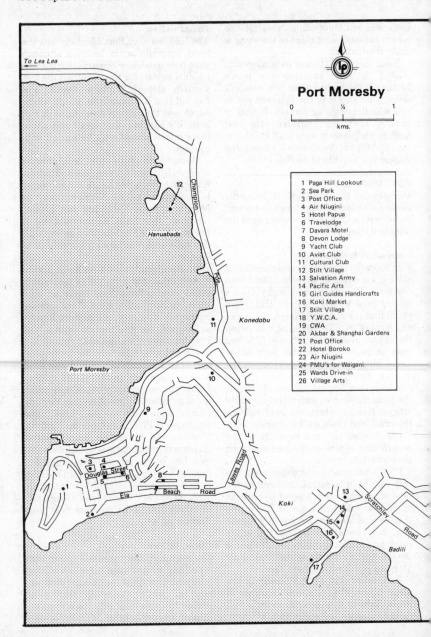

Port Moresby

0   ½   1

kms.

1 Paga Hill Lookout
2 Sea Park
3 Post Office
4 Air Niugini
5 Hotel Papua
6 Travelodge
7 Davara Motel
8 Devon Lodge
9 Yacht Club
10 Aviat Club
11 Cultural Club
12 Stilt Village
13 Salvation Army
14 Pacific Arts
15 Girl Guides Handicrafts
16 Koki Market
17 Stilt Village
18 Y.W.C.A.
19 CWA
20 Akbar & Shanghai Gardens
21 Post Office
22 Hotel Boroko
23 Air Niugini
24 PMU's for Waigani
25 Wards Drive-in
26 Village Arts

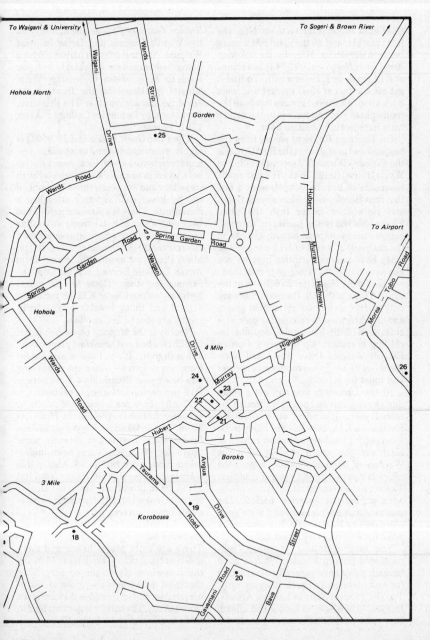

a series of suburbs than a town. Near the Koki market, and on the main PMV route between Boroko and Moresby, the *Salvation Army Koki Hostel* (tel 25 3744) has rooms at K12 single or K20 for a twin. To find it get off the bus at Koki market and walk back about a hundred metres to where the road splits. You can walk into the centre from here in about half an hour.

On Taurama Rd, right across from the hospital and next door to the Red Cross, is the *Country Women's Association* (Jessie Wyatt House) (tel 25 3646). It's just on the town side of Boroko but you want a bus that runs Boroko-Koki-Moresby via Badili and Korobosea rather than the usual Three Mile Hill route. Ladies or 'married' couples only (although nobody checks on the married) at a cost of K12 per person. They have kitchen facilities here so you can save money by fixing your own food.

The *YWCA Hostel* (tel 25 6604) is at the top of Three Mile Hill, Boroko. There are only four rooms for non-permanent guests and it takes women or couples only at a cost of K16/25 for singles/doubles including breakfast. Up at Spring Garden Rd, off Waigani Drive, the small *Kone Hotel* (tel 21 1879) has rooms with shower and toilet for K13/26.

At the *University* you can get a room during vacations and possibly through the school year, depending on availability. Rooms are K14, but they are likely to be less costly if you have a student card or at least say you are a student. See the Warden of Students before 4 pm; the office is upstairs in the central complex. There's a cheap cafeteria but it may not be open during the vacation period. The surroundings are pleasant and it's a good place to meet local people. Try phoning 24 5682 ext 682 or 24 5425 ext 425.

You may also hear of cheap, self-contained flats in Boroko. While a good bargain these have generally been set up for volunteer and church workers only. Try *Dove Travel Flats* in Lakatoi Arcade, Boroko – they have to be booked ahead. One more possibility is staying at the *In-Service Teachers' College* just across from the Ward's Cinema and Drive In, near Waigani. Accommodation here is K6 for a dorm bed including breakfast, but you have to book ahead in writing. Write 'Hostel Bookings' on the front of the envelope and address it to The Principal, Port Moresby In-Service College, PO Box 1791, Boroko.

The *Civic Guest House* (tel 25 5091) is highly recommended and most volunteers and foreign workers on local wages put up here when in town. It's also popular with travellers and can sometimes be booked out by lower civil servants attending a conference. There is a pleasant garden out back with a sort of home-made swimming pool and a pet bird whose squeak is heard intermittently throughout the day. It's on Mairi Place just around the corner from Angau Drive in Boroko, not far from the Steamships store. There are 22 rooms with singles/doubles at K22/38 including a good and filling breakfast. The bathrooms are shared but spotless.

Nearby is the *Mapang Guest House* (tel 25 5251), a bed and breakfast place run by a church group. It's on Lahara, also not far from Angau Drive – turn right after going one block past Steamships. Cost here is K18 per person including breakfast.

Finally there are a couple of hotels to consider. In Boroko the *Boroko Hotel* (tel 25 6677) is on Okari St. It has a reputation for beer and brawls but recently some upgrading of its image has been undertaken. Rooms are K33 to 45. Also in this class is the venerable old *Papua Hotel* (tel 21 2622) in downtown Moresby. During the war General MacArthur used the hotel as his headquarters.

Places to Eat

There are more places to eat and more different types of food available in Moresby than anywhere else in the country. Note that most restaurants are closed except at meal times, and on Sundays they are often closed all day. The better restaurants tend to be in hotels and clubs or are Chinese.

There are a few good and inexpensive restaurants around town for cheap eats and snacks. The *Corinthian* is on the corner opposite Steamships in Boroko. It's a cool, quiet sanctuary done up with posters of Greece and even offers Greek salad and baklava. There are also hamburgers, sandwiches and milkshakes with prices K1-2. Next door is the long-standing *Pinocchio Coffee Shop* which may now have become a take-away joint rather than the comfortable place it was. It's worth checking out as it offers a variety of western snacks and meals.

Upstairs and a few doors closer to the post office in Boroko is the *Oyster Bar* in the Hugo Building. Run by a Filipino family, it offers fish & chips, other seafood plates and hamburgers. K1 to 3 with a view. There's a good, cheap sandwich bar in the walkway between Nambawan Haus and Brian Bell Plaza near Burns Philp in Boroko. It's very busy at lunchtime with prices of K1 to 2.

Fides serves local-style PNG food at rock-bottom prices at two outlets in Moresby. Most convenient is the one on Douglas St, just up the hill from the Papua Hotel, opposite the Steamships store in downtown Moresby. Chicken, fish, meat pies and rice are available for about K1 and it's better than most of the cheap kai houses you'll see all over the country. The other outlet is around at the Gavamani Mall in Boroko, behind the Akbar Restaurant.

Other kai houses serving Australian-style greasy snack foods are scattered around the city. One in Boroko, beside the newsagent and near the Corinthian, is cleaner and better than most. Sandwiches, meat pies and drinks can also be had at the stand-up counter in Steamships and Burns Philp stores all around PNG. The *Papua Hotel*, opposite Burns Philp, has a rather rowdy milk bar and cafe.

Moving up a price notch the restaurant in the *Boroko Hotel* serves good food at reasonable prices in a cool, quiet setting. On Fridays there's a lunchtime smorgasbord. Also popular is the dining room at the *Papua Hotel*, long a favourite with local businessmen. It also has a smorgasbord on Fridays. In the room adjacent is the recently opened *Vienna Cafe*, a very pleasant spot for sandwiches, soups and an incredible array of pastries, cakes and other European treats.

For Chinese the *Green Jade* has a good reputation. It's located in Boroko on Tabari Place and is a little difficult to find. Look about half-way down the block; it's on the ground floor but at the back, down a short, enclosed walkway. Also Chinese is the *Rex*, across from the Boroko Police Station. It's open Monday to Friday for lunch, every day to 10 pm for dinner.

The clubs are also a good source for food. Formerly the RSL, the *ESA Restaurant* on Bava St, Boroko (not far from Taurama Rd) offers both western and Chinese dishes. It's open Monday to Friday, 12 noon to 2 pm, plus Saturday and Sunday from 6 to 10 pm. Prices are from K5 and up. You can try the *Germania Club* on Waigani Drive for lunch with a continental flavour. The *Royal Papua Yacht Club*, in town by the waterfront, serves beer and snacks at the bar and also has a restaurant. You can even get a lunchtime steak or hamburger at the *Car Club*. There's a good open-air curry house at the *University Sports & Social Club*, Monday to Friday from 12 noon to 2 pm.

Getting There

See the introductory Getting There section for details on arriving in PNG at Port Moresby from abroad. Port Moresby has no road connections to the northern town or, for that matter, to any major centres in the south. So when you want to go from Papua (the southern side) to New Guinea (the northern side) about the only way of doing it by land is to walk the Kokoda Trail. The usual route is to fly to the Highlands or Lae.

Getting Around

Airport Moresby's taxis didn't use to bother visiting the airport, but they've become more enterprising. From the airport Boroko will cost about K5, the town about twice that. Alternatively you can take a PMV – they run to and from the airport for the standard fare of 30t. Simply walk out of the terminal, across the car park and by the control tower and you'll find PMVs on the dirt area to your left. It's only a hundred metres. Getting to the airport you want a PMV to 'Jackson' or 'Seven Mile'.

Getting there for an early departure can be difficult since PMVs aren't early starters and taxis are notoriously unreliable – although Moresby residents say they do turn up, far later than you ask but with just sufficient time to get you there before the flight leaves. Maureen and I hitched out there once in a police car! Moresby is not a good place to arrive at night, particularly for solo women travellers. International departure tax is K10; it went up to K20 at one time but has now been cut back.

Local Transport There are plenty of PMVs running around Port Moresby with a standard fare of 30t for any trip, including out to the airport. The PMVs are either minibuses or trucks; ask the destination before hopping on if there is no sign and simply yell 'stop' or thump the driver's window when you want to stop.

AROUND MORESBY

You can get to some of the surrounding points of interest by PMV; go to the stop at Boroko. Lots of PMVS head out to Sogeri, a rubber plantation village. It makes an interesting trip out, then come back stopping off at points along the way. Sogeri has a far more appetising market than Koki if you're hungry for some good fruit and vegetables. You can buy delicious sweet corn already cooked at 10t an ear.

Heading back from Sogeri you'll come to the turnoff to the Kokoda Trail, marked by a monument. Unfortunately you'll have trouble getting transport further down the road to the start of the trail at Ower's Corner. If you can make it you can try the first little bit of the trail, a steep downhill section to the Goldie River, then a long climb up the 'Golden Staircase' to Imita Ridge where the Japanese were finally halted on their almost-successful push for Moresby.

Back on the road you'll pass several hydro-electric power plants before the lookout to the spectacular Rouna Falls. The Hotel Rouna a bit further down is a good place for a cold beer if you've walked down from Sogeri – the food is a cut above Moresby's food and on weekends there's a very good smorgasbord. The turnoff to Varirata National Park leads to a series of interesting bushwalks if you're feeling energetic – plus some good lookout points. Further back towards Moresby you can stop for another beer in the pleasant riverside beer garden of the Bluff Inn. This is a *ples bilong pukpuk* – an animal reserve with a *pukpuk* (crocodile).

There are a series of other routes from Moresby leading to places like Hombrum's Bluff or Brown River but if you've just got a day to spare the Sogeri trip is probably the easiest and most interesting. Close to town the Moitaka Crocodile Farm has plenty of crocodiles and some other native wildlife. It's only open on Friday afternoons from 2 to 4 pm.

Central Ela Beach is Moresby's best known swimming spot but there are plenty of others in the vicinity. You have to get permission to pass through the army barracks to Taurama Beach and when you get there it's shallow and weedy like Ela. There are lots of diving and boating opportunities around Moresby. If you hang around the yacht club on weekends you can often get an opportunity to crew on a boat.

LAE

Lae is the busiest town in the New Guinea part of PNG and the gateway to the Highlands. Prior to the war Lae was just a little missionary settlement (earlier attempts by the Germans to settle here had been set back by malaria), but two events started Lae's growth. The goldfields at Wau and Bulolo required a larger airstrip from which components of the gold dredges could be flown in. Salamua, the old goldfield port, wasn't suitable so Guinea Airways built a new strip at Lae around which the town sprang up.

Then in 1937 the eruptions at Rabaul caused colonial eyes to look elsewhere for a New Guinea capital. Lae was hardly installed in its new position when WW II intervened and the heavy fighting pretty well wiped the town out. Since the war, amalgamation of Papua and New Guinea ended Lae's period as a colonial capital but it has grown to be a very attractive tropical town with lush green parks and flowers blooming everywhere. Furthermore the development of the Highlands, virtually unexplored territory prior to the war, has put the spotlight on Lae as the port with the best road access.

Places to Stay

Lae is better than Moresby for cheap accommodation although still no bargain. *Buablung Haus* (tel 42 4412) on Cassowary St is not too far from the town centre. It's a hostel-style place with small doubles at K7 per person and a reasonably priced restaurant where you can get meals for K1 to 2. It's one of the better places in PNG for the budget traveller.

The *Salvation Army Motel* (tel 42 2487) is on Huon Rd about a km from the centre towards the Botanic Gardens. The number of rooms are limited and cost K15 per person. They have kitchens so you can fix your own food. A little further out on Klinkii Rd, which runs off Huon Rd, the *Klinkii Lodge* (tel 42 1281) is K21/27.50 for singles/doubles including breakfast.

The rickety old *Hotel Cecil* (tel 42 3674) has a nice location near the waterfront and costs K18/28 including breakfast. The *Lutheran Mission* runs a guest house east of the downtown area on the PMV route to Wagan. It's clean, well kept, friendly and

costs K12 including breakfast. The *S I L* missionary group also runs a guest house (tel 42 3214) on Poinseana Rd, off Kivila Rd which runs into Milford Haven opposite the Botanical Gardens. Rooms are K12/20. Further out at the Lae Technical College the *Lae School of Catering* (tel 42 2734) has a few rooms, but only when the school is in session, at K16 per person including breakfast. Finally the *CWA* has a small establishment on 7th St near Buablung Haus.

Places to Eat

There are a variety of places good for a quick snack such as *Togo's Coffee House* on 7th St at Coronation Drive in the Central Arcade. It's cool and pleasant with sandwiches, burgers and milkshakes in the K1 to 2 range. The *Terrace Coffee Lounge* on 2nd St is also good. The *Lae Kai Haus* at the corner of 4th and Huon has decent food for its type. There are also several cheap take-away joints around town.

In the 'real' restaurant category the emphasis is on Chinese but, unfortunately, the two good places are inconveniently situated. The *Taiping Restaurant* is on Butibum Rd, quite a distance beyond the Hotel Cecil. The *Red Rose Restaurant* is similarly inconveniently situated on Mangola Rd, out beyond the market on the other side of the airport.

Much more central is *Jason's* on 2nd with Chinese and other dishes. The unimaginatively named *The Restaurant* is adjacent to the Rotary Club and has a lengthy menu, mainly Chinese. It's quite good value. *Buablung Haus* is popular with travellers for solid, cheap food – nothing to write home about but it fills you up.

Getting There

The usual way to Lae from Port Moresby is to fly. The new and short-lived Nadzab Airport, far out of Lae, is no longer used. Flights are once again operated into the very central Lae city airport. Short of walking the Bulldog Track or the Kokoda Trail there's no way of crossing from south to north by land. On the northern side, however, Lae is the coastal hub for PNG's most extensive road network and also the main centre for shipping.

Road See the Highlands section for details of road travel between the Highlands and Lae. The PMV fare to Goroka is K6. PMVs now run regularly to Madang for K9 and there's a daily 'bus' which costs K15 for the 6½ hour trip. PMVs to Wau cost K4 to 5.

Sea There are a number of services between Lae and Madang, best known of which is the Lutheran Shipping *MV Totol*. This operates Madang-Finschhafen-Lae-Finschhafen-Wasu-Madang one week and Madang-Sialum-Finschhafen-Lae-Finschhafen-Sialum-Madang the next. Fares are K14 deck or K21 cabin class. Cabin class can be uncomfortably hot. The fare to Finschhafen is K11.

Coastal Shipping has a ship on Fridays to Rabaul, also calling at Kelengi and Kimbe. The fare to Rabaul is K25 deck class, K60 cabin. The trip takes 38 hours. Pacific New Guinea Line also has a weekly service which costs K35 with a bunk. Ships also operate eastwards to Popondetta and to Samarai in Milne Bay.

Getting Around

PMVs around Lae cost 25t. Taxis are pretty cheap – a kina or two seems to get you to most places in town. The airport is so central you can walk into the middle of town in a couple of minutes.

WAU & BULOLO

These adjacent towns (Wau is 150 km from Lae) were the site for the New Guinea gold rush of the '20s and '30s. You can still see the rusting, remains of the huge dredges which were flown up, piece by piece, from Lae in the biggest airfreight operation the world had ever seen at that time. The road from Lae is a comparatively recent innovation. Today the area is no

longer mined on a commercial scale although plenty of people still have a fossick.

In Wau the Wau Ecology Institute is a good place to stay and also of scientific interest. You can climb up to Mt Kaindi, towering above Wau and Edie Creek. Beyond here is the start of the WW II Bulldog Trail. There are several crashed WW II aircraft in the vicinity of Wau.

From Bulolo you can take a PMV to Aseki, a tough four-hour trip for K7. There's a guest house at the local mission, and a further four hours takes you to Menyamya (impassable when wet). In both of these places, which are also accessible by air, you see the fierce Kukukuku people. Small and distinctive in their bark capes they are greatly feared by the Highlanders but actually seem quite friendly and curious. At Aseki you can see cliff face caves with smoked, mummified bodies. This is interesting country for walking.

Places to Stay

The *Wau Ecology Institute* (tel 44 6207/41) or WEI, usually referred to as the 'Ecology', is the best place for travellers and one of the best cheaper places in PNG. It's on a hillside overlooking the town, a couple of km out. Try to get a ride up there or ask your PMV to take you to the 'Ecology'. The rooms all have cooking facilities and there's a 10-room hostel with a kitchen and lounge area. Nightly cost is K7 per person.

Otherwise there's the the *Pine Lodge Hotel* (tel 44 5220) in Bulolo which even has a swimming pool – it costs K35/45 for singles/doubles.

Getting There

There are regular Talair flights to Wau (with its amazingly steeply-sloped runway) from Port Moresby or from Lae with Talair plus numerous charter flights. Or you can make the 120 km trip by PMV – a winding road; the trip takes four or five hours and costs K4 or 5. The old gold miners' trail up from Salamua and the WW II Bulldog Track from the south coast are both a hard slog for bushwalkers. Wau is about 25 km beyond Bulolo and 400 metres higher up.

FINSCHHAFEN

On the Huon Peninsula, east of Lae, Finschhafen was the first, unsuccessful base of the German Neu Guinea Kompagnie. Today it's just a quiet little coastal town with few reminders of its colonial past. Offshore are the beautiful Tami Islands where fine wooden bowls are carved.

Places to Stay

The *Dregerhafen Lodge* (tel 44 7050) is run by the local high school and costs K7 per person. You have to bring your own food from Lae and the lodge is five km from the town, at the school site. There is also a *Finschhafen Community Hostel* (tel 44 7046) with cheaper dormitories.

Getting There

The wartime road between Lae and Finschhafen has disappeared although a new road is gradually being built, piece by piece. You can get to Finschhafen either by Talair or on the Lae-Madang shipping service on the *Totol*. The ship takes about eight hours and costs K11. It's quite an interesting walk between Lae and Finschhafen, taking about three days and sometimes following the beach. Ask the headmaster at the Finschhafen high school as students there do the walk regularly.

HIGHLANDS

Until the '30s the Highlands of New Guinea were terra incognita – you can imagine the surprise when those empty hills, thought to be covered only in a tangle of impenetrable jungle, turned out to be a neat patchwork of hundreds of tiny villages. Today the Highlands Highway is the core of the most extensive road system in PNG. They're not always particularly

smooth or comfortable roads but there are plenty of them.

Heading up the highway from Lae to Goroka stop at Zunim, about 130 km out. Traditional unglazed pottery is made in this village and you can see examples of pots and bowls, the clay being beaten out and the pottery turned by hand. Ask for Jessie Bunham, he'll let you stay in the shed for nothing, otherwise accommodation is K2.

Highland Shows

The annual Highland Show is the area's number one attraction. It's a tribal get-together with dances, sing-sings, handicrafts and lots of colour. They were originally organised to show the often warring clans that the people from the other side of the hill weren't really so bad. They take place on even-numbered years in July in Goroka, odd-numbered in Mt Hagen and although they are, unfortunately, not so spectacular as it was in the days prior to independence they are still worth seeing. Admission to the grounds is usually K1 or 2; for K5 you can get right in to the arena for close-up photographs.

Getting There

The road from Lae up into the Highlands is the spine of the only extensive road system in PNG. For over half the distance to Goroka it runs through the wide, flat Markham Valley but once it starts to rise and twist it doesn't stop. Lae to Goroka is about 325 km and it's a further 240 km on to Mt Hagen. The Highlands Highway is gradually being sealed, which apart from reducing the wear and tear on vehicles also considerably reduces the cost of keeping the road in usable condition.

To get up into the Highlands you want a PMV – there are lots of them running along the highway and they have the usual PMV pluses and minuses; when you fall off the road here it's a long, long way down. It's generally a day's travel for each sector Lae-Goroka and Goroka-Mt Hagen and usual fare is K7 for each trip. With an early start and considerable endurance you could do the whole trip in one day, even travel all the way to Mendi, but it would hardly be worth the effort. I did Hagen-Goroka once in a very speedy five hours in a very safe and steady PMV so it's no hassle.

From Lae PMVs normally depart from the market or from the area known as Erico. Similarly in the Highlands the market is the normal starting point. Set off early: the PMV drivers like to arrive well before nightfall so you don't find many vehicles after 9 am.

You can still occasionally get a free trip up to the Highlands by delivering a car or pickup from Lae. Today many of them are delivered by truck but you can still sometimes find one so ask around the car dealers in Lae. If you do take to the road, anywhere in PNG but particularly in the Highlands, drive with caution – running down a Highland tribesman would not be wise. If that sort of thing happens do not hang around to explain about third party insurance – even the PNG Tourist Office advises (in large bold print) that you should 'not stop after an accident'. They advise reporting at the next police station but it may be better to wait until the one after the next police station! An arm for an arm, an eye for an eye seems to be the law of the land after traffic accidents.

Beyond Mt Hagen roads run on to Mendi and Wabag and there are a number of other lesser roads in the Highlands. From Watarais a spur runs off to Madang and this road is now usable for much of the year. You can also fly to the main Highlands towns from Port Moresby, Lae, Madang or Wewak.

GOROKA
Goroka is not a particularly interesting town; it mainly clusters around the end of the airstrip. The J K McCarthy museum by the showground is 'not to be missed', but it's a long walk from the centre so check the opening hours (9 to 12 noon and 1 to 4 pm on weekdays, different hours on weekends, at last report) before setting out. There are many interesting artifacts (check the necklace of human fingers) and crafts here and a new Leahy wing with a fascinating collection of photographs by the Leahy brothers, pioneers of Highland exploration.

The market is also interesting, particularly on Saturdays, with food, vegetables and occasional colourful Highlanders. The Mt Hagen market is much more exotic, however. Be cautious if you plan to visit the lookout above Goroka; it's a hangout for local 'rascals'. Outside Goroka at Kotuni there's a trout farm which is a popular local picnic spot.

The Asaro mudmen are a prime Goroka attraction but strictly for the tourists – unless you're in the Highlands for the Highland Show or some similar big occasion, forget about them. They're known as mudmen because of their fearsome clay helmets and mud-daubed bodies worn to re-enact a traditional victory in battle. A visit to the Bena Bena tobacco factory is much more interesting. You can also arrange visits to one of the coffee plantations in the vicinity.

Places to Stay
The pleasant *Lutheran Guest House* (tel 72 1171) is right in the town centre and costs K11 for bed and breakfast or K16 for

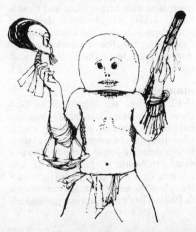

full board. The meals are substantial and it's probably the best value in town but it is somewhat unreliable. Occasionally it shuts down completely or at other times the manageress may be away and you'll only be allowed to use the kitchen to make tea and coffee.

The *Salvation Army Flats* (tel 72 1218) are about a km out of town. They're self-contained with their own well-equipped kitchen and cost K12/24 for singles/doubles – book ahead if possible. The fairly new *National Sports Institute* rarely fills its large accommodation complex so it offers good rooms cheap to visitors. There are 100 rooms, all singles, at K10 per person. Plus good meals are available and you can use the gym and other sporting facilities. It's near the museum and you need to see the accommodation officer between 7.30 am and 4.30 pm, Monday to Friday. Or call 72 2391 or 72 2664 during working hours; 72 2436 or 72 2019 later.

The *Minogere Lodge* (tel 72 1009) has rooms at K26/42 or K33/46 in the more modern motel section. There are other more expensive hotels.

Places to Eat

The Goroka food picture has improved but it's still not very exciting. Good lunchtime food is available at the *Minogere Lodge* or at the rooftop 'Flight Deck' at the expensive *Bird of Paradise Hotel*. The restaurant in the *Lantern Lodge* is quite good; they even have some Indian dishes on the menu.

A new and welcome addition is the *Goroka Coffee Shop* in the Gouna Centre, behind the ANZ Bank. They do breakfast and sandwiches but close at 4 pm. *Aurora's*, run by some Filipinos, is a larger, fancier place. It's a little further down the street towards the Steamships Store. Otherwise there's just the usual Steamships and haus kais.

MT HAGEN

From Goroka the highway continues through the Chimbu (or Simbu) province to Kundiawa and Mt Hagen. There's nothing of great interest in Mt Hagen either (except its very colourful market), but it makes a good base for further trips and you have a good chance of seeing a sing-sing somewhere nearby. Ask in the post office or at the market; the people there often seem to know what is going on. So do the local tour operators.

The first Europeans only reached Mt Hagen in 1933! Outside the Hagen Club, next to the Highland Hotel, you can see the Hagen Eagle which originally (1897) perched on the Madang tomb of Kurt von Hagen, a murdered German administrator after whom the town takes its name (via the nearby mountain). The Western Highlands Cultural Centre, also known as the museum, is small but worth a visit. It's on Hagen Drive beside the newsagent Forster's.

Places to Stay

Kunguma Haus Poroman is a popular new place for travellers. It's in the bush, about seven km out of town, and run by Maggie Wilson who runs the Jara Clothing store (tel 52 1957) in Hagen Plaza in town. You can contact her there during working hours and she'll drive you out in her four-WD. Take a sleeping bag and your own food. Nightly cost is K7 per person.

About 10 minutes' walk from the centre of town on the Goroka side, the *Kimininga Hostel* (tel 52 1865) is the longest-running cheaper place in Hagen. Singles/doubles are K15/30 in the old wing, K20/40 in the new wing, all including breakfast. There's free coffee in the lounge in the evening and good meals are available for K5 at lunch or K8 at dinner. There's also a video TV and if you stay more than one night you can get your laundry done.

Right next door to the Kimininga Hostel is the *Baptist Hostel* (tel 52 1003) which is used mainly by nationals although for-eigners are welcome. You need your own bedding and food although there is a kitchen you can use. Cost is K3 to 4 per night; see Pastor Mapia. The *Mt Hagen Missionary Home* (tel 52 1041) is across from the hospital and is cheap and very good. Rooms are K12 per person with breakfast, another K5 with dinner.

Places to Eat

Apart from the hostels and hotels you can try the *Mt Hagen Coffee Shop* in Hagen Plaza where you can get sandwiches and snacks. The outdoor patio under the umbrellas is a good place to relax. There's a good deli across from here.

Mr Chips, opposite the police station, does take-away hamburgers, hot dogs and french fries which are said to be the best in PNG. There's also a good health food store on Hagen Drive; plus the usual kai joints around town – a couple of decent ones near Steamships for fish & chips.

OTHER HIGHLAND PLACES
Baiyer River

The Baiyer River wildlife sanctuary is 55 km north of Mt Hagen. it has an extensive collection of birds of paradise and other native wildlife. You can daytrip there from Hagen or stay overnight. PMVs K2 or 3 and the trip is quite spectacular. The PMVs normally stop about three km up the road from the sanctuary but you can arrange to be taken right there or be picked up later. Drivers won't go down this road in the later afternoon or at night because of clan battles.

Places to Stay The *Baiyer River Bird Sanctuary Lodge* (tel 52 1482 in Hagen) has rooms at K10 per person (K4 for students). There are cooking facilities but no food is available so bring your own. Costs are K2 higher from 1 July to 31 December. You can camp at the sanctuary for K2 or if you use the lodge facilities for K4.

Mendi

Mendi, 137 km south of Mt Hagen, is in part of the most isolated and primitive country of the Highlands area. It's reached by a spectacular road through the country of the Wigmen, noted for their complex wigs made of human hair – usually their wives'! Mt Giluwe, the second highest mountain in PNG, is near the Hagen-Mendi road.

PMVS now run regularly to Mendi and the fare is K6 from Hagen. The road now continues beyond Mendi to Tari in reasonable condition and on to Lake Kopiago in much worse condition. Beyond that point it's walking only.

Places to Stay The *Menduli Guest House* (tel 59 1158) has rooms at K18 per person including meals. The *Education Resource Centre* (tel 59 1252) offers a place to rest your head at K5 per person and there are cooking facilities. Or you can stay at the *Mendi Hotel* for K32/42 for singles/doubles. There's a hostel that will take travellers at Tari and you may be able to find accommodation at Kopiago.

Wabag

It's a fairly rough road to this town in Enga Province. The town has a nice little museum. You can continue on from here to Laiagam and Mendi although the road (the highest in PNG) is very bad – you may have to walk. Some travellers have walked from Kompiam over the watershed down to Amboin in the East Sepik Province. A PMV from Hagen to Wabag will cost K4

Places to Stay

To get to the *Kaiap Orchid Lodge* (tel 52 2087) take a PMV from Wabag to Sari Village, a couple of km towards Laiagam, then walk 1½ to two hours. It's a pleasant walk with good views but it's sometimes possible to get somebody from the lodge to pick you up in their four-WD. There's great scenery and, of course, orchids when you get there. Nightly cost of K24 per person includes breakfast and dinner. Otherwise there's the *Wabag Lodge* at K27/377 and the *Malya Hostel*, out of town on the road to Hagen, at K12/24.

MADANG

Madang is the nicest towns in PNG – it's green and gardenlike, a little more compact so you don't have to walk so much. There are things to see and do, and terrific swimming and diving. In the centre of town there's a miniature patch of jungle overwhelming the old graveyard – you can even find graves from the German Neu Guinea Kompagnie here. In the late afternoon hordes of fruit bats screech and wheel around the treetops. Directly behind is the Madang market with lots of fruit and vegetables and beautiful shell bracelets and necklaces. The lakes and ponds in Madang's parks have signs around warning you to 'luk aut long pukpuk' although residents say crocodiles are more than slightly rare!

Coastwatcher's Avenue follows the curve of the coastline, shaded by beautiful hibiscus and bougainvillia trees. The Coastwatcher's Monument is a tall column to the men who stayed behind in the New Guinea jungle and kept watch on Japanese troop and ship movements during WW II. Save yourself lots of walking by renting a bike from the Madang Resort Hotel.

Carrying on along the avenue past the golf course you'll reach several pleasant swimming spots and a little park with some rusty WW II relics. The Lions Reserve beach has another 'beware of the crocs' sign – ignore it and swim out to the fantastic coral, thick with brilliant tropical fish only a few stroke from the shore.

Keep on and you'll come to the small museum near Smugglers' Inn. It's open Monday to Friday from 8 am to 12 noon and 1 to 4 pm. Nearby at Tusbab High School there's a small artifacts museum and a collection of birds including two cockatoos. One speaks Australian ('hello cocky'), one Pidgin ('kokky kaikai'). Further from Madang is Yabob village where traditional pottery is produced. If you're energetic you can pedal on to Bilbil village (more pottery) or right round past the airport (some carving places on the way) to Siar Village and Siar island.

Madang has a beautiful harbour dotted with islands and reefs. Take a boat trip to see it – the cheapest harbour tour is the 20t local ferry service from the Lutheran Shipping wharf to Kranket Island (irregular but reasonably frequent). Or you can hire one of the local outrigger canoes to paddle you around. Or check at the Madang Hotel about boat rental. Or lay out K12 for the half-day harbour cruise. Bring your mask and snorkel, the diving is terrific.

Places to Stay

There are several places to try in town or you can find very cheap places to stay on Siar Island in Madang Harbour.

Madang The *Lutheran Guest House* (tel 82 2589) on Coralita St is about midway between the big Madang Resort Hotel and the Coastwatcher's Motel. Each room has its own bathroom and nightly cost is K14 for bed and breakfast; dinner is available for K4.

Very close to the Madang Hotel, the *CWA Cottage* (tel 82 2216) is a little bit closer to the centre and costs K14 per person. There's a fully equipped kitchen so you can shop in the market and save a little money on food. The woman who runs it is only there to check people in between 8 am and 12 noon. Other times call 82 3051.

The expensive *Smugglers' Inn* (tel 82 2744) has a budget bargain – a wing of rooms without air-con at just K10 per person. There are ceiling fans and you can use the swimming pool and so on.

Siar Island The other alternative is to stay on Siar Island. Two people have set up places to stay here and it's a pleasant chance to sample village life although the rivalry between the two men ranges from bitter to hostile!

Saimon Tewa is the originator and you can contact him via the Madang Club. His place is better for the beach and has reasonably 'western' facilities but it's wise to keep an eye on Saimon, and the booze.

Smith Keenan is the imitator and he can be contacted via the CWA. His place is further up the island and there's no electricity there. Either place costs K5 a night including breakfast and a dinner of local food. You may want to bring some of your own food for lunch and to supplement the meals. If you contact Smith or Saimon they'll take you out to the island from Madang for a kina. Or you can take a PMV round to Siar Village and take a boat across to the island although the fare for this very short trip is absurdly high. Siar is a delightful place to stay with good snorkelling in the waters around it and this is a good chance to get into local village life.

Places to Eat

The *Madang Club* offers good, down-to-earth food at reasonable prices. It's officially members-and-their-guests-only, but if you hammer loudly on the door somebody will come and sign you in. They need the business! Everything is under K5; dinner is served at 6.30 to 8 pm but it's closed on Sundays. It's next door to the CWA Cottage and is a good place for a sundowner drink.

Other than that you can get sandwiches and the like at the golf course *Country Club*. The *Coral Seas Snack Bar* next to the cinema stays open in the evening until after the movie interval. Or there's the usual *Steamships* sandwich bar and haus kais.

Getting There

The road to Madang, turning off the Highlands Highway at Watarais, is now open most of the year and is regularly used by PMVs. They run direct from Lae or Goroka to Madang for K9. It's an interesting route with plenty of scenery but there are still some unbridged rivers to cross and these can be impassable during the wet season.

The weekly Lutheran Shipping service, on their ship *Totol*, leaves Lae on Wednesdays goes through Madang to Wewak and back via Madang again to Lae. Fares Lae-Madang or Wewak-Madang are K14 deck or K21 upper class and either sector takes about 24 hours. Those cabins get hot. There are other ships operating this same route.

There are plenty of flights into Madang including a flight from Goroka which hops down over the southern fringe of the Highlands in just a few minutes' flying time.

Walking to Madang

Starting from Gembogl, near the starting point for the Mt Wilhelm climb, you can walk down to Madang in a couple of days. The route ascends to Bundi Gap but from there on it's downhill. The road between Bundi and Brahmin, down towards the coast, is being pushed through rapidly. Brahmin is only about 15 km from the Lae-Madang road.

Getting Around

PMVs around Madang cost a standard 25t. They also venture farther out from town at reasonable fares. Bikes can be hired from the Madang Resort Hotel for K3 a half day or K6 a full day. They're good for jaunts to villages around Madang.

UP THE COAST

You can continue along the coast a considerable distance from Madang and eventually this road will reach all the way to the Sepik, which will be crossed by barge near Angoram. From there a road runs into Wewak. Along this road you can visit the Alexishafen Catholic Mission near which there is a Japanese WW II airstrip with some wrecked aircraft. The *Jais Aben Resort* is a centre for scuba divers, just 12 km out of Madang. Further north are the *Plantation Hotel* and the small *Bogia Hotel*.

You can make interesting trips out to Manam Island, off the coast near Bogia, or to larger Karkar Island. Both of these islands are actively volcanic and boats run to them from Madang. Services to Manam are somewhat irregular although there is a boat to Karkar nearly every day for K5.

WEWAK

There's not a great deal of interest in Wewak itself. It serves mainly as a gateway to the Sepik or as the departure or arrival point for Jayapura in Irian Jaya. To the west of Wewak is Cape Wom where the Japanese made their final surrender to Allied forces in PNG at the close of WW II. From the air the multitude of pockmarks around the Wewak airstrip indicate just how many bombs fell on this area during the final phase of the conflict.

You can visit some of the islands off the coast from Wewak including Kairiru, about two hours to the north. April to November is the best time to visit this island: then the sea is calm and there are plenty of fish. In June they have yam festivals and all-night dances. Boats go from the old small-boat wharf across from the post office. The fare is only about K2 and there are fairly regular departures – the *MV Tauk* is best known but something should go out there or to Mushu Island every day. There's good swimming, mountain walks, hot springs and even an inactive volcano on the island. There's no organised accommodation there but you should be able to stay at the school or local people may offer to put you up.

Places to Stay

Not too far from town is *Ralf Stuttgen's* place (tel 86 2395), an excellent spot for the budget traveller. He has eight beds in two rooms and charges only K5 per night. It's about six km from Wewak on the road to Maprik – turn right when you see a radio tower on top of a mountain. It's then the first house and at 400 metres above the coast it's cool and has good views. A taxi is K4 or a PMV down the road to the turnoff costs 30t. Often Ralf will be able to pick you up in town or from the airport. His wife, Teresa, works at the Windjammer so you might be able to make contact there. Cheap meals are available at the lodge and

Ralf can offer advice on Sepik River trips. There's a good travellers' notebook here.

The *Windjammer Motel* (tel 86 2548), is a km or two round the bay from town towards the airport. It's right on the fine beach – only a couple of steps into the sea from the rooms at the front. It's also a popular local eating place at lunch and dinner times and a particularly good place for a beer and a chance to meet people. There are a variety of rooms, with or without attached bathrooms, fan-cooled or air-con, 35 of them in all. Rooms away from the beach are cheapest. Singles/doubles start from K22/30 for the simplest rooms without facilities and go up to around K70 for an air-con double with attached bath.

There are three mission houses in town – the Swiss Mission, the South Seas Evangelical Mission and the Assembly of God Mission. All three usually take only missionaries and are usually too full even for them. Around K5 if by chance they do have room.

Cape Wom, about 10 km west of Wewak, is a park where it may be possible to camp. Otherwise campers could try the police station.

Places to Eat

The *Windjammer* has reasonably priced food including some Chinese dishes and even some PNG-style food like beef with local spices, cooked with coconut milk and taro. Aside from its regular meals it also offers sandwiches and snacks from the bar.

In town, *Robyn's Nest* is a friendly little cafe with hamburgers, sandwiches and milkshakes. Nothing costs over K2 and it's nice and cool. It's closed Sundays and from noon on Saturday. Down at the Yacht Club, opposite the post office beyond the wharf, you can get decent, basic lunches for about K4.50.

Getting There

Although you can travel by land most of

the distance between Madang and Wewak there is still an uncompleted stretch of road and some wide rivers to contend with before the road link will be completed. Meanwhile you can reach Wewak by coastal ship from Madang or Lae or you can fly from Madang or Mt Hagen in the Highlands. The flight from Wewak on to Jayapura in Irian Jaya operates once a week so it's wise to book well ahead.

THE SEPIK

If you've got the time and the energy the mighty Sepik River is one of PNG's 'not-to-be-missed' features. Getting out on the Sepik is not cheap although you can make it much more attractive if you get a group together to split the cost of hiring a long canoe – they will take six people. The main centres on the river are Ambunti, well upriver, Angoram, well downriver towards the mouth, and Pagwi about midway between the two. Ambunti can only be reached by air or by the river itself but you can reach both Pagwi and Angoram by road. The simplest and cheapest shoe-string way of exploring the Sepik would be to go Pagwi and either wait for a boat coming downriver to Angoram and from there go back by road to Wewak. Many of the most interesting places along the river are on this stretch. Recently a road has also been completed through to the river at Timbunke, between Pagwi and Angoram.

The Sepik River region is famous for the culture and crafts of its tribes – most evident in the haus tambarans. Tambarans are the spirits that inhabit the jungles and mountains. The carvings that represent them are kept in these spirit houses. Although the missions and rich art collectors have taken their toll on the finest carvings (some missions actually burned them down) the haus tambarans still have considerable significance. Women are still totally barred from entering the haus tambarans although western women visitors seem to enjoy honorary male status! Haus tambaran styles vary from village to village although the ornately painted, forward-leaning style found around Maprik is best known.

Interesting places along the Sepik include the Murik Lakes, the swampy area around the river mouth. Marienberg was an important mission station even in the German days. Kambaramba is famous as the 'brothel village'. Tambanum is the 'artifacts factory' of the Sepik. Kanganam has the oldest haus tambaran on the Sepik. Palembai is quite stunningly beautiful and green after the wet season. Don't miss the crocodile farm just out of Pagwi. Ambunti is the major town upriver, the last breath of civilisation before you get into the really wild country up towards the Irian Jaya border. Wherever you go on the Sepik watch out for the mosquitoes, which are legendary for their size and appetite.

River Trips

The only regular boat services on the Sepik are the *Melanesian Explorer* trips operated from Madang. At around K140 a day they're great fun but far outside most budget travellers' budgets! The simplest alternative is to look for people who can arrange a canoe rental. Between a group of people, a big canoe can take six or so and the cost can be fairly reasonable. Charges vary from around K35 to K80 per day depending on the place, local prices, the owner, the river conditions, where you want to go and so on. Take a little care in organising a rental; not all the people on the Sepik are 100% trustworthy. Ask around – that's the best suggestion.

In Angoram start asking at the hotel although this is not the best place to start since the most interesting part of the river is all upstream. You could visit Kombot, off the Sepik on the Keram River, where the beautiful Kombot storyboards are carved. In Timbunke ask at the trade store or look for Jeff. In Pagwi you could try Steven Buku who lives about four km downriver. Pagwi is not a bad place to start from – you can make interesting day trips from there: longer trips to the Chambri Lakes and back, or go all the way downriver to Timbunke or Angoram. At Ambunti the trade stores are good places to ask.

An alternative to hiring a canoe is to buy one and the best way to do that is to start well upstream and travel well downstream. Read Christina Dodwell's wonderful book *In Papua New Guinea* for the full story. Ambunti is a pretty good place but you'll get a better bargain further upstream. Prices for canoes are very variable although they can go as low as K20. Canoes last about three or four years before falling apart. Every village seems to have plenty of cracked, discarded canoes lying around. A volunteer worker at Green River, over 400 km upstream from Ambunti, recommended that as a good starting point. He said you could buy canoes there from K40 and travelling fast could get all the way to Ambunti in eight days. A traveller wrote that he bought a canoe at Iniok, about halfway from Ambunti to Green River, and went downriver all the way to Angoram. Don't forget to buy paddles too! A good map is a necessity too; get *Wewak – The Gateway to the Sepik*, published by Wirui Press in Wewak.

Places to Stay

At Maprik, the main town on the way to Pagwi, there is just the usual hotel/motel place at high prices. You can also try the Maprik High School which may have accommodation – it's two km from Hayfields, the road junction towards Pagwi. In Pagwi you can sleep on the floor of the Council House for K2 per night. Bring your own food from Wewak for either place (indeed for the whole Sepik) since there is little available.

The *Angoram Hotel* in Angoram is rather expensive but it is an excellent information source. There's mattress-on-the-floor accommodation for K5 at the *Ludwig Schuzz crocodile farm* by the river in Angoram. The Timbunke Catholic mission has a guest house but there's absolutely no chance of staying there. You may have better luck at the mission guest house at the Chambri Lakes. There's a local lodge at Kaminabit but it seems to be down for the count. There has been talk of establishing a guest house in the Yentchen cult house.

Upriver at Ambunti the *Ambunti Lodge* is the standard PNG expensive price but again it's a good information source. Try the *Akademi School* for mattress-on-the-floor accommodation.

Getting There

PMVs run regularly to Angoram, Timbunke, Maprik and Pagwi. Angoram is the closest access point to the river. The trip from Wewak is 113 km, takes two or three hours and costs K5. Wewak-Maprik is 132 km and costs K5, it's a further 53 km (rough km too) for K2 to Pagwi on the river. Maprik is actually about eight km off the Wewak-Pagwi road and you can save a kina or so by getting a PMV that's going straight through. Maprik has a hotel and nothing much else apart from trade stores selling tinned meat. Maprik's famous but rather run-down haus tambaran has reportedly burned down recently. There are numerous other haus tambarans in the area and you can enquire about the walking route back to the coast. The road to Timbunke has only recently opened, count on around K6 for a PMV from Wewak.

WEST SEPIK

Few travellers get even further upriver beyond Ambunti although there are interesting and remote places right up to the Irian Jaya border. The development of the huge Ok Tedi mine is focussing interest on this neglected area and there are some interesting walks from places like Telefomin or Oksapmin. Vanimo is a pretty little coastal town quite close to the Irian Jaya border. Aitape is further back towards Wewak and linked with Wewak by road.

NEW IRELAND

The pretty, sleepy little town of Kavieng is at the northern end of the island. The old cemetery has a large monument to the iron-handed German district administrator Boluminski. During his period of rule from 1899 to 1913 he pretty much brought civilisation there single-handed. He established copra plantations and built the first long road in New Guinea ('today you vil build ze Boluminski highway'). Until the 1940s it was still the only long road in PNG! It's relatively easy to hitch or find PMVs between Kavieng and Namatanai – about 250 km apart.

Places to Stay

In Kavieng the *Kavieng Hotel* has rooms from K18/27 and up while the *Kavieng Club* is a local gathering place with rooms at K25 (K5 more with air-con) although you'll quite possible be given the cheaper members' price. In Namatanai Bernie Gash's easygoing *Namatanai Hotel* costs K20/40; it's worth the few kina more than the *Council Accommodation*.

NEW BRITAIN

The island of New Britain, with its beautiful capital of Rabaul, is north-east of Lae, east of Madang and can be reached by air or sea from either. It's got a long and interesting history by PNG standards. After their unsuccessful (due to malaria) efforts to establish themselves on the New Guinea coast the Germans made Rabaul their HQ from 1907 and laid out the town. At the start of WW I the small German command was rapidly overrun by the Aussies and became the capital of the Australian New Guinea colony until WW II.

In 1937 the spectacular eruption of Matupit and Vulcan volcanoes in Rabaul harbour did remarkably little damage to the town (although a native village was wiped out), but the prospect of a further eruption prompted a decision to transfer the New Guinea capital Lae. WW II halted that, the Japanese moved in and con-

verted the town to a near-impregnable fortress. Allied bombing totally levelled the town, but the Japanese had created an underground city, parts of which can still be explored today – complete with docks for their transport barges. The end of the war came while the Allies were still reluctantly considering the cost of a full-scale invasion.

During its German period Rabaul had many Chinese, Filipino, Malay and Ambonese immigrants – their descendants make Rabaul the most cosmopolitan city in PNG. The Gazelle peninsula area around Rabaul has an extensive road network and there are many interesting drives.

An interesting little volcano climb can be made from Rabaul – take a bus round beyond the airport to Matupit Island. Stop just before the village and look for the wrecked Japanese aircraft off the end of the runway: kids will show you where they are. From Matupit Island hire a canoe (K2) across to the base of Matupit Volcano, it's an easy climb to the top and you can scramble back down to the road on the other side and get a PMV back into Rabaul. If the weather is clear you can also climb the Mother Volcano in the early morning. Every Friday there is an excursion with geologists; it's possible to go along. In early 1984 it seemed very likely that Matupit was about to do a repeat performance of 1937, but as the year wore on nothing seemed to happen.

Places to Stay

Rabaul has another of PNG's all too rare accommodation bargains at the corner of Atarr St and Cleland Drive where you'll find the *Rabaul Community Hostel* (tel 92 2325). Nightly cost is K12 all-inclusive but if you've got a student card it's only K6. They even give you a packed lunch of sandwiches. The place is already becoming rather run-down although some rooms are better than others.

Alternatives are the *New Britain Lodge* (tel 92 2247) on the corner of Kamarere St and Kombiu Avenue which costs K14/25 for singles/doubles including breakfast. Also good, but more expensive, is the *New Guinea Club* (tel 92 2325), opposite the War Museum. It's a classic old wooden building with rooms at K18/25. You don't have to be a member to stay there.

Out at Pila Pila, 13 km out of town, the *Kulau Lodge* (tel 92 2115), has simple rooms at K26/34 for single/doubles including breakfast.

Places to Eat

If you decide to venture away from the hostel's bargain price eating you will find that Rabaul has an excellent selection of places to eat. Ah Chee Avenue in Rabaul's depleted Chinatown has the *Taiping* which is supposedly a Chinese club, but anyone is welcome in the restaurant – good food, plain surroundings, slow service. *Chang's* is similar, probably slightly faster and flashier but similarly priced.

Cafe de Paris, in the middle of town, is one of the better non-hotel restaurants in PNG. It's relaxed and quite reasonably priced. Across the road and a little further along Mango Avenue the *Kai Kitchen* is a newish take-away place with food rather better than the majority of PNG's fast-food joints.

Rabaul also has some good clubs where guests are always welcome. The big three are the RSL, the New Guinea Club and the Rabaul Yacht Club. The *Kulau Lodge* at Pila Pila is a popular place for a night out. Generally it's rather expensive (at least K14 a head) but the Sunday smorgasbord is a real bargain at K7.50. The top end hotels do good counter-style lunches but all in all it's very hard to beat the community hostel for rock-bottom bargain eating.

Getting There

There are regular flights to Rabaul from Port Moresby, Lae, Wewak and other centres. For K28 you can make the short hop across from Namatanai in New Ireland. Rabaul is an important shipping centre and there are regular services between Lae and Rabaul with deck class fares from K27. Ships also operate from here to Bougainville or to other ports in New Britain.

Getting Around

There are lots of PMVs around the Gazelle Peninsula from Rabaul. Fares start from the usual 25t and you can get to most places for less than a kina. There are also plenty of taxis – count on K2 to the airport, K3 late at night or early in the morning.

OTHER ISLANDS

The Trobriand Islands are famous for Bronislaw Malinowski's studies which resulted in his series of books including *The Sexual Life of Savages*. The Trobriands are either expensive or time-consuming to get to, though. The 'Trobes' are the best known of the many islands of Milne Bay, which spill out into the Pacific from the eastern end of the main island.

The island of Bougainville is notable for the huge copper mine which substantially underwrites the entire PNG economy. You can island hop from here into the Solomons, but otherwise few people make the effort to get this far. Manus is a small island off to the west of New Ireland. Margaret Mead based some of her anthropological work here but again there are few visitors. There are also interesting islands off the north coast of PNG, particularly around Wewak or Madang.

Three PNG minuses – walking, beer and mosquitoes. PNG's towns aren't so much towns as extended suburbs; every single one of them seems to sprawl for miles. Which means plenty of walking.

One of the unhappiest western influences on PNG has been the wholesale acceptance of the Australian beer culture. It's not a good sight to see people staggering out of the pubs with half a week's pay under their arm in the form of a case of beer. It's even less pleasant if you should be foolish enough to wander the streets of Port

Moresby on weekend nights as crowds of drunks stumble home.

Mosquitoes are part of the scenery – they're strong, healthy and persistent. On the Sepik you'll get the feeling that with just a little bit more development they could pick you right up and cart you off home to be fed on at leisure.

BUSHWALKING

Papua New Guinea is absolutely packed with bushwalking or mountain climbing possibilities. Most of them have been barely touched and, unlike in much of the Himalaya, you can still feel you're really adventuring here. Two of the most popular walks are the hard slog of the Kokoda Trail from Port Moresby to the north coast and the ascent of Mt Wilhelm, the highest mountain in PNG.

Kokoda Trail

During WW II the Japanese marched down the Kokoda Trail from the north coast of PNG and came very close to taking Moresby. Today you can walk that same trail in about a week's hard-going. If you plan to do it make sure you're fit and well equipped and before departing inform the civil defence people so you can be looked for if you don't turn up at the other end.

It's a difficult walk through dense rain-forest but there are many villages along the way. Nearly 20,000 Japanese and Australians lost their lives in the bitter fighting up and down the trail and you'll still see many relics of the war. At Kokoda, the northern end of the trail, you can fly out or take a PMV to Popondetta near the coast.

The Kokoda Trail isn't the only walking route between the south and north coast, there's also the almost equally well known Bulldog Track. Or if you want a shorter walk try the walk from the beautiful village of Tapini to Woitape. It's a good walking track with few snakes and leeches (the bane of PNG walking trips).

Mt Wilhelm

At 4509 metres Mt Wilhelm is the highest peak in PNG, at times snow-covered, and the walk to the top is an unforgettable experience. Start out from Kegusugl, about 57 km from Kundiawa – you can get there by PMV. It's not necessary to have a guide, you can stay at the village at the base of the mountain for K5 (ask for Herman) and get the key for the huts at the Pindaunde Lakes from the ranger at Kegusugl. They're at about 3500 metres, where it can get very chilly – bring warm clothes and food. Next day you make the stiff climb to the top. On a clear day you can see both coasts but it's a long, hard walk and it's probably worth getting some altitude acclimatisation at the lakes before making the final climb.

The Philippines

The Philippines are the forgotten islands of this book – because they're off the regular overland route they've never attracted the travelling hordes in great numbers. So if you make the effort to get there you're in for a pleasant surprise – the food's pretty good, accommodation is easy to find, you've got over 7000 remarkably diverse islands to choose from and if island hopping attracts you the Philippines are the place to go. Boats run everywhere, very frequently, remarkably cheaply, reasonably comfortably. Add that to an incredibly friendly people, many of whom speak Enlgish, and it's hard not to have a good time. In fact many people reckon the Philippines is their favourite country in the whole region.

HISTORY

The Philippines are unique among the countries of South-East Asia both for their varied colonisers and their energetic attempts to cast the colonial yoke aside. The Filipinos are Malay people, closely related to the people of Indonesia and Malaysia. Remarkably little is known about their pre-colonial society, as the Spaniards – who ruled the country for over 300 years – energetically eradicated every trace of what they felt was a 'pagan' culture.

Ferdinand Magellan, a Portuguese who had switched sides to arch-rival Spain, set off from Europe in 1519 with varied instructions to sail round the world, claim anything worth claiming for Spain, and bring back some spices (a very valuable commodity in Europe). Finding a way round the southern tip of South America took nearly a year but finally the small fleet, two of the original four ships, reached the Philippines in 1521.

At the island of Cebu, Magellan claimed the lot for Spain and managed to do a few Christian conversions to boot. Unfortun-ately, Magellan then decided to display Spanish military might to his newly-converted flock by dealing with an unruly tribe on the nearby island of Mactan. Chief Lapu-Lapu managed to kill Magellan; the Cebuans decided their visitors were not so special after all and those remaining scuttled back to Spain, collecting a cargo of spices on the way and arriving in the sole remaining ship in 1522.

The Philippines, named after King Philip II, were more or less left alone from then until 1565 when Miguel de Legaspi stormed the no-longer-friendly island of Cebu and made the first permanent settlement. In 1571 Spanish HQ were moved to Manila and from here Spain gradually took control of the entire region – or more correctly converted the region since Spanish colonial rule was very much tied up with taking the cross to the heathen. The Spanish were far from alone in the area: other European powers and the Japanese and Chinese also made forays into the Philippines and throughout the Spanish period the strongly Muslim regions of Mindanao and the Sulu archipelago were neither converted nor completely conquered.

Spanish power was a fleeting thing; after the defeat of the Spanish Armada by the English in 1588 Spain entered a long period of decline and its rule over this colony was never fully exploited. The Philippines were generally treated as a subsidiary of Spain's colony in New Spain – Mexico. When the Pope divided the world up between the two great Catholic powers in 1494, Spain was forced to approach the region by sailing west while the Portuguese sailed east. Not until long after this demarcation had lapsed did the Spanish wake up to the fact that they could save much time and expense by travelling in the opposite direction. The tight Spanish restrictions on trade (only trade with Spain was permitted and only via the Mexican colony) limited development and made the colony a continual drain on the Spanish treasury until the introduction of tobacco in 1782 started to make it profitable.

From 1762, as a result of the Seven Years' War in Europe, the British took control of Manila for over a year, but never extended their rule far into the country. Internal events were more serious and it is estimated that over 100 revolts against Spanish power were organised. Finally the Spanish sealed their fate by executing Jose Rizal in 1896. A brilliant scholar, doctor and writer, Rizal had preferred to work for independence by peaceful means, but his execution (on trumped-up charges) sparked off the worst revolt to that time.

Finally chucking the Spanish out required the Americans, however. The Spanish-American war in 1898 soon spread from Cuba to the Philippines and Spanish power was no match for the US. Unhappily for the Philippines, American liberation was only from the Spanish – after victory in Manila Bay, Admiral Dewey sent back the message, 'Have captured Philippines; what shall we do with them?' The reply (which according to President McKinley came via his direct line to God) was to annex them in order to ensure America's duty 'to Christianise them .... ' So colonial power number one was replaced by colonial power number two and once the inevitable Filipino revolt had been stamped out the Americans set out to convert the country to the American way of life – no doubt suitably amazed to discover it had already been Christianised.

The American colonial period (or 'tutelage', as they preferred to call it) was abruptly ended by WW II, but at the close of the war independence was granted – as it had been promised in 1935 for 10 years later. The American colonial period was considerably more enlightened than that of the Spanish, but it left equally deep impressions, particularly on the economy, since American companies had firmly

entrenched themselves in the country during their period of control. In addition, Filipino democracy was to be modelled on the American pattern and events were to prove that a system wide open to vote-buying in its home environment could spawn spectacular abuses in Asia. So in the '50s and '60s the Philippines bounced from one party to another (generally remarkably similar) party until Ferdinand Marcos took power in 1966.

Following his re-election in 1970 (a feat previously unmanaged), Marcos decided to declare martial law in 1972, ostensibly to cut down the anarchy reigning in the country which would inevitably have become worse as the 1974 election approached; but also, no doubt, because he liked being in control and under the constitution could not run for a third term. Martial law, as is its wont, soon become total control and so the situation remains today. On the brighter side random violence has been dramatically cut (the Americans left their love of guns too and at times Manila was like an Asian version of Chicago in the '30s), and some political abuses are now much decreased. On the darker side the often lurid Filipino press has been stifled and the economy has become one of the weakest in an otherwise booming region.

Even President Marcos and his lovely lady are no longer doing quite so well because the assassination of Marcos' opponent Benito Aquino has pushed opposition to Marcos to new heights and has further shaken the tottering economy. Just how long Marcos can last is an open question; he undoubtedly still enjoys strong, though reluctant, US support because the huge US bases in the Philippines are so important and some of the possible alternatives to Marcos are, in the eyes of US policy makers, too horrible to contemplate.

FACTS
Population The population of the Philippines is estimated to be about 50 million

and growing too fast for comfort. The people are mainly of the Malay race although there is the usual Chinese minority and a fair number of mestizos – Filipino-Spanish or Filipino-American. There are still some remote pockets of pre-Malay people living in the hills – including the stone-age Tasaday who were discovered in a remote Mindanao valley as recently as 1972.

Geography The official statistics state that the Philippines is comprised of over 7000 islands – but what is an island and what is a rock that occasionally appears above water level? Together they make a land area of about 299,000 square km, 94% of which is on the 11 largest islands. The Philippines can be conveniently divided into four areas: 1 – the largest island of Luzon (site of the capital, Manila) and the nearby island of Mindoro; 2 – the Visayas, the scattered group of seven islands south of Luzon; 3 – Mindanao, the Muslim trouble centre in the south, second largest island in the country and with a string of islands in the Sulu archipelago like stepping stones to Borneo; 4 – the island of Palawan, nearly 400 km long but averaging only 30 km wide.

Economy The economy is principally agricultural – like several other countries in the region the Philippines is potentially self-sufficient in rice and other important foods but due to poor yields and the continued evils of absentee landlordism in a peasant society it generally ends up having to import rice along with fish and meat. All of this could conceivably be produced locally. Slow or non-existant progress towards much-needed land reform has been a problem in the Philippines ever since independence. Copra, sugar and abaca (a fibre from a relative of the banana plant) are the principal agricultural exports. Timber and some gold and silver mining are other important economic activities.

Religion The Philippines are unique for being the only Christian country in Asia; over 90% of the population claims to be Christian, over 80% Roman Catholic. The Spanish did a thorough job! Largest of the minority religions are the Muslims who are chiefly on the island of Mindanao and along the Sulu archipelago. When the Spanish arrived, toting their cross, the Muslims were just getting a toehold on the region. In the northern islands the toehold was only a small one and easily displaced, but in the south the people had been firmly converted and Christianity was never able to make a strong impression.

INFO

The Ministry of Tourism (MOT) office in Manila could be more aptly called the Temple of Tourism. It is so vast and has so many employees it is hardly surprising that facts are hard to find. The information is all there – it's just that nobody knows where! Nevertheless, get a city and country map from them and ask what else they have. The regional MOT offices can be quite different – often very knowledgeable, all the facts at their fingertips and best of all ready at hand with useful information sheets on their localities. Philippine Airlines has an info-leaflet on every city they fly to – get these at their tourist promotion office near the domestic terminal.

The Philippines have rip-offs like anywhere else, but recently they've had more of them. Beware of people who claim to have met you before. 'I was the immigration officer at the airport when you came through' is one often-used line. Don't accept invitations to parties or meals from people who accost you in the street. Drugged coffee is a favourite. Beware of pickpockets in crowded areas of Manila.

BOOKS

If you want a lot more information on travelling in the Philippines, then look for *The Philippines – a travel survival kit*, another in the Lonely Planet series. Apa Productions in Singapore publish *Insight Philippines*, part of their coffee-table guidebook series.

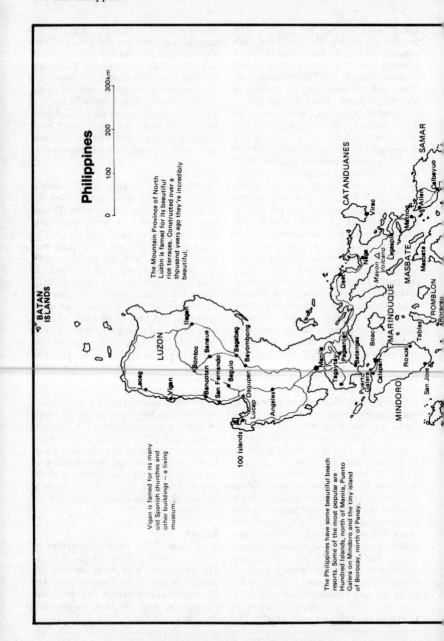

Philippines

The Mountain Province of North Luzón is famed for its beautiful rice terraces. Constructed over a thousand years ago they're incredibly beautiful.

Vigan is famed for its many old Spanish churches and other buildings – a living museum.

The Philippines have some beautiful beach resorts. Some of the most popular are Hundred Islands, north of Manila, Puerto Galera on Mindoro and the tiny island of Borocay, north of Panay.

BATAN ISLANDS

LUZON

Laoag
Vigan
Ilagan
Bontoc
Banaue
Bangued
Bangued
San Fernando
Bayombong
Baguio
Dagupan
Manila
Angeles
Lucap
Tagaytay
Batangas
100 islands
Pagsanjan
Puerto Galera
Calapan
Roxas
Boac
MINDORO
Tablas
San Jose
ROMBLON
MARINDUQUE
MASBATE
Masbate
Daet
Naga
Mayon Volcano
Legaspi
Matnog
Allen
CATANDUANES
Virac
SAMAR
Calbayuo

0   100   200   300km

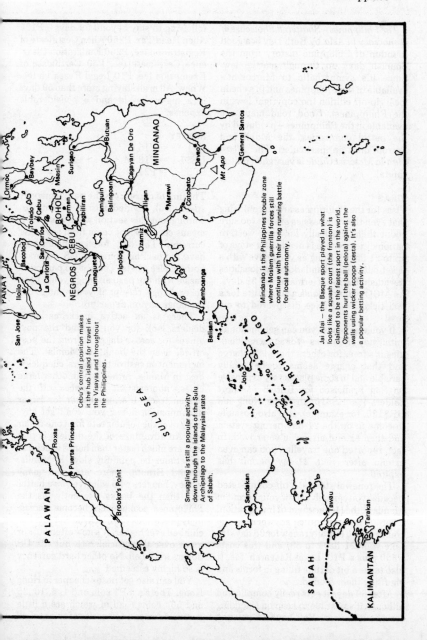

Cebu's central position makes it the hub island for travel in the Visayas and throughout the Philippines.

Smuggling is still a popular activity down through the islands of the Sulu Archipelago to the Malaysian state of Sabah.

Mindanao is the Philippines trouble zone where Moslem guerrilla forces still continue with their long running battle for local autonomy.

Jai Alai — the Basque sport played in what looks like a squash court (the fronton) is claimed to be the fastest sport in the world. Opponents hurl the ball (pelota) against the walls using wicker scoops (cesta). It's also a popular betting activity.

The Philippines – Shattered Showcase of Democracy in Asia by Beth Day is a good roundup of Philippine history from the Spanish days up through martial law. Since it's sympathetic to Marcos it's available in the Philippines and in a cheap local rip-off edition (no copyright laws in the Philippines). Good road maps are available in the Philippines – produced by the petrol companies, the Mobil and Petron ones in particular. The *Metro Manila Motorist Guide* is very good for the capital.

VISAS

Visas for the Philippines are so confusing that even their embassies are not too sure about them. Basically for most western nationalities no visa is needed for stays of up to 21 days so long as you arrive with a ticket-out in your hand. Some nationalities (Swedish, Danish, Germans) get 59 days. An MCO will not do as a substitute for a real ticket, as I once discovered to my cost!

If you want a visa you can get one for an initial stay of 59 days – for some nationalities it's free, for others there is a charge and that charge seems to be totally variable and in some places very expensive (in San Francisco for British passport holders it's US$15, in Hong Kong it's HK$130, for example). It is also possible to come in on the 21-day permit system and then extend after you've arrived. In fact, reported one traveller, you can even extend after your 21-day permit has expired.

The renewal story is a bit complicated because you can only renew your permit in Manila at the Department of Immigration. There is no other office anywhere in the country. You initially renew for 38 days (to take your 21 days to 59) and this costs P300 plus a P10 'Legal Research' fee. It also takes a bit of time filling in forms and shuffling them around.

After 59 days it gets really complicated although it's possible to keep on extending for about a year. You have to pay the following to stay beyond 59 days – P125 Alien Head Tax, P250 Alien Certificate of Registration fee, P250 Emigration Clearance Certificate fee, P50 Certificate of Exemption fee, P10 Legal Research fee. Whew! All in all staying more than 59 days is a major hassle and a considerable expense.

MONEY

A$1	= P15.3
US$1	= P18.78
£1	= P21.1

The unit of currency is the peso (correctly spelt piso), divided into 100 centavos. Throughout this section when it says c it means centavos not cents from any other currency. The only foreign currency to have in the Philippines is US dollars – nothing else exists! There is no particular hassle with the peso although you'll need an exchange receipt if you want to re-exchange any on departure.

There is an active black market – dealers look for you around the post offices (or across the river from the post office, near the banks in Manila). The increment on cash or travellers' cheques is best in Manila, rather less in other large cities, non-existant in places off the beaten track. It's also better for larger denomination notes; you won't get anything over the regular rate for a one dollar bill. An advantage of the dealers is that they are much faster than banks which can sometimes be painfully slow. In Manila, around Ermita, there are also many moneychangers who will give you a better rate than the banks. Recently, as the Philippines' economy has become increasingly precarious the black market rate has climbed ever higher. It's now often 50% or more over the official rate but it's US dollars above all. No other hard currency is so highly esteemed.

You can also get pesos cheaper in Hong Kong. There's a P1 coin and 1, 5, 10, 25 and 50c coins – all of which are a little confusing since a new series of coins are all slightly smaller than the old series which still circulates.

COSTS

Inflation is currently very high in the Philippines, but at the same time the peso has been falling rapidly in value, particularly on the black market. So overall the Philippines remains about the cheapest country to visit in the region. Costs in the Philippines used to be pretty much in line with other neighbouring Asian countries. Now they're decidedly cheaper. Some things seem amazingly cheap, though – local transport and beer are two good examples. Air fares within the Philippines are also very good value, particularly in free-market pesos. Because of the rapidly changing currency values and high inflation, prices quoted in this section are more likely to be incorrect than those in other parts of the book.

CLIMATE

The Philippines are typically tropical – hot 'n' humid year round. Although the actual climate map of the country is fairly complex, it can be roughly divided into a January-to-June dry and a July to December wet. January, February and March are probably the best months for a visit as it starts to get hotter after March, peaking in May. In some places it seems to rain year round and in others it rarely rains at all. From May to November there may be typhoons.

ACCOMMODATION

Finding cheap hotels is no problem. The exception may be Manila, where cheap accommodation is mainly in hostels although even in Manila you'll find a wide selection of medium-priced hotels. There are quite a few youth hostels or YH associated places around the country, so a YH card (student cards are also generally acceptable) is worth having. Even in Manila you can get dorm-style accommodation for P20 and away from the big cities rooms often cost P25 or less. In the Mountain Province and at some of the beach resorts the places will be pretty basic – no electricity for example.

Maintenance in many hotels is a little lackadaisical so it's worth checking if the electricity and water are working before you sign in. Places in North Luzon tend to be cheaper than in the southern islands or elsewhere. Beware of fires in cheap hotels – Filipino hotels don't close down, they burn down. Check fire escapes and make sure windows will open. Finally it's often worth asking for a discount, or bargaining a little on prices – they'll often come down.

FOOD

The Filipinos have taken on American fast-foods wholeheartedly, so there are plenty of hamburgers and hot dogs. Chinese food is also widely available and is actually one of the few reminders of Spain – a lot of menus are a Spanish-English mixture in Chinese restaurants. Local Filipino food, usually called 'native' food, is a bit like Indonesian Nasi Padang in that all the food is laid out on view – and often to western palates it would taste a lot better if it were hot. Some popular dishes:

mongos – chick peas, similar to Lebanese humus.
adobo – stewed chicken and pork pieces.
lechon – a feast dish, roast baby pig with liver sauce.
crispy pata – crisp-skinned pork knuckle, another delicacy or feast dish.
mami – noodle soup, like mee soup in Malaysia or Indonesia.
pangsit – dumplings.
lumpia shanghai – spring rolls.
gulay – vegetable dish simmered in coconut milk, particularly gabi leaves.
pinangat – Bicol vegetable dish laced with very hot peppers – 'the Bicol Express'.
balut – a popular streetside snack, boiled duck egg containing a partially formed duck embryo – yuck.

There are also a number of Filipino drinks worth sampling (apart from Coke, which they must consume faster than any country apart from the US):

tuba – coconut wine, can be very strong.
iced buko – buko is young coconut.
kalamansi juice – tiny lemons, also served with tea, thought to have amazing curative effects.
San Mig – San Miguel beer must be the cheapest beer in the world; it's very good too.
halo halo – an ice cream, fruit, ice, coconut milk and so on mixture; similar to an es buah in Malaysia.

Food words in Tagalog:

food	*pagka-in*
restaurant	*restoran*
water	*tubig*
milk	*gatas*
coffee	*kape*
sugar	*asukal*
snack	*merienda*

GETTING THERE

Apart from occasional boats from Hong Kong or Taiwan and illegal smuggling routes from Sabah through the Sulu Archipelago, the only way to the Philippines is to fly. Manila is virtually the only international gateway so for probably 99% of visitors to the Philippines, Manila is their first experience of the country.

From Australia the one-way apex fares from Sydney or Melbourne vary from A$502 to 608 depending on the season. From London, one-way fares to Manila are in the £200 to 250 range depending on the agent. Hong Kong is very much the gateway to the Philippines and most cheap deals to Manila will be via Hong Kong, even if it means over-flying the Philippines to start with. From Hong Kong it's about US$120 for tickets to Manila. You can also look for cheap fares from Singapore or Bangkok.

There is very little alternative to Manila as a gateway although Air Mindanao/Air Sabah have an on-again, off-again weekly service between Kota Kinabalu and Sandakan in Sabah to Zamboanga on the southern island of Mindanao. It's much more reliable to fly between Kota Kinabalu and Manila where there are flights daily. There is no interesting air connection between Indonesia and the Philippines – no flights from north Sulawesi or from Kalimantan to Mindanao, for example.

GETTING AROUND

Air PAL (Philippine Airlines) runs a frequent and remarkably economical service to most parts of the country. The only thing that can really be said against it is that there are often flights from Manila to town A, B or C but rarely flights between towns A, B and C. After a couple of hijacks (including one that eventually ended in Libya and goes down as the longest hijack ever as it took over a week!) they're very security conscious. Expect to be pretty thoroughly frisked and to pay security tax on every departure – this goes to pay for your friskings.

If you fly to Manila with PAL you are entitled to a 50% discount on any domestic flights. You must show your international ticket and coupon when buying the tickets and you must buy all your tickets in one go – if you later decide to fly somewhere else you will have to pay the full fare, However, the tickets can be open-dated and they are refundable. This is a very good deal! Student card holders are eligible for a 30% discount on domestic flights. There are also the curiously named 'Mr & Mrs' flights. On some routes there are cheaper flights at night or there may be lower 'prop' (rather than 'jet') fares.

Ships Getting around by boat is much easier than in Indonesia – it's not a matter of 'will there be a boat this week?' but 'will there be a boat this day?' – often 'this morning!' And they're cheap, comfortable and pretty fast too. Of course they do sink occasionally, but you can't have everything I

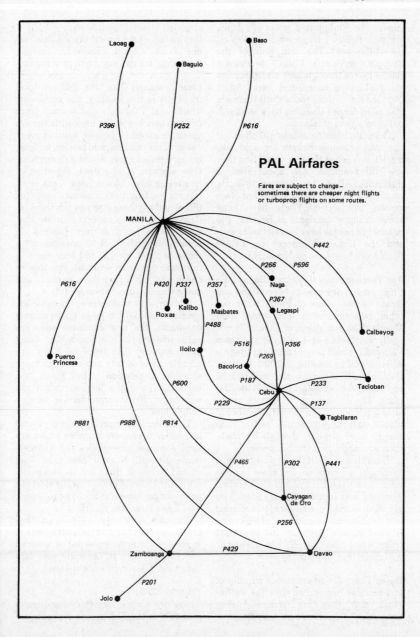

PAL Airfares

Fares are subject to change — sometimes there are cheaper night flights or turboprop flights on some routes.

Laoag
Baso
Baguio
P396
P252
P616
MANILA
P442
P266 P596
Naga
P616
P420 P337 P357
P367
Roxas Kalibo Masbates
Legaspi
P488
Calbayog
P516
P356
Iloilo
P269
Bacolod
P600
P187
P233
Tacloban
Cebu
P137
Puerto Princesa
P229
Tagbilaran
P881 P988 P814
P465 P302 P441
Cayagan de Oro
P256
Zamboanga P429 Davao
P201
Jolo

guess. The Philippines' mass of islands are very tightly packed which makes all the difference. The real hub of the shopping services is Cebu – everything seems to run through here and there are many shipping companies here. Apart from the inter-island route ships there are also many ferries shuttling back and forth between adjacent islands.

The main booking offices will often tell you that economy tickets are sold out, when if you ask at the pier you'll find they are still available. Ask about student discounts. Aboitz Liner gives 30%. Be cautious with local boats which are often grossly overloaded. There have been some unhappy incidents at Boracay (no deaths but people have lost all their gear), and the Roxas (Mindoro) to Tablas (Romblon) boats are particularly bad.

Rail There are only three train lines in the Philippines – one runs between Iloilo and Roxas on the island of Panay while the other two run north and south from Manila. The run north of Manila is not really worthwhile as it terminates at San Fernando, which is not really anywhere – whether you're heading to 100 Islands or Baguio you'll still have to continue by bus, so you might as well start by bus in the first place. The southern route is more useful although if you intend to visit a number of places on your way south, rather than simply head straight through by train, then you might find the bus better.

Third class on PNR (Philippine National Railways) is much like 3rd class in most Asian countries, but the 2nd class (called Tourist Class) is generally very good. You get clean carriages, well-padded reclining seats and an amazing amount of leg-room. A good night's sleep on the overnight trains is no problem at all – which is just as well since they're painfully slow.

Buses There are an enormous number of bus services running all over the Philippines and they are generally very economical. Departures are very frequent

although buses sometimes leave early if they're full – take care if there's only one bus a day! Main companies include Pantranco, Dargwa and Philippine Rabbit.

Local Transport The true Filipino local transport is the jeepney, the recipe for which was: Take one ex-US-army jeep, put two benches in the back with enough space for about 12 people, paint in every colour of the rainbow, add tassles, badges, horns, lights, aerials, about a dozen rear-view mirrors, a tape deck, selection of Beatles' golden oldies (Bee Gees now, reports one traveller), a chrome horse (or three) and anything else you can think of. (Unhappily, recent reports indicate that music in jeepneys is now banned. Is nothing sacred?) Stuff 20 passengers on those benches for 12, add four more in front and drive like a maniac. But they're cheap and you'll find them in cities and doing shorter runs between centres.

Of course the true jeepney is a declining species – the old US jeeps are becoming unreliable, the new Japanese ones are expensive and the new South-East Asian utility vehicles (like the Ford Fiera) are manufactured locally and are a far more sensible proposition – but much less colourful. To stop a jeepney (when you want to get off) the correct term is 'para' or simply hiss.

The other local transport, mainly found in smaller towns, are tricycles which are small Japanese motorcycles with a crudely made sidecar. Normal passenger load should be two or three but six and seven are not unknown! Fares generally start at a peso – longer distances are by negotiation. You'll see some bicycle trishaws.

Taxis are all metered in Manila and they are almost the cheapest taxis in the world. In smaller towns taxis may not be metered and you will have to negotiate your fare beforehand – tricycles are cheaper.

THINGS TO BUY

There are a wide variety of handicrafts available in the Philippines and you will find examples of most crafts on sale in Manila. See the various Manila, Luzon and islands sections for more details.

LANGUAGE

As in Indonesia there is one nominal national language and a large number of local languages and dialects. It takes 10 languages to cover 90% of the population! English and Spanish are still official languages although the use of Spanish is now quite rare. English is also not as widespread as in the American days although the English-speaking visitor will not have any trouble communicating – it remains the language of secondary school education and to say someone 'doesn't even speak English' means they've not gone beyond primary school.

Tagalog, the local language of Manila and parts of Luzon, is now being pushed as the national language. It sounds remarkably like Indonesian; listen to them roll their rrrrs. The following words are in Tagalog, also called Filipino:

Greetings

hello	*kamusta*
goodbye	*pa-alam*
welcome or farewell	*mabuhay*
good morning	*magandang umaga po*
good evening	*magandang gabi po*

Communicating

yes	*oo*
no	*hindi*
good	*mabuti*
bad *masama*	
how much?	*magkano*
how many?	*ilan?*
price	*halaga*
too expensive	*mahal*
that one	*iyon*
where is?	*saan ang?*

Things

cheap hotel	*murang hotel*
train station	*tutuban*
water	*tubig*
boat	*barko*
bank	*bangko*

Numbers

1	*isa*
2	*dalawa*
3	*tatio*
4	*apat*
5	*lima*
6	*anim*
7	*pito*
8	*walo*
9	*siyam*
10	*sampu*

Manila

The capital of the Philippines and far away the largest city, Manila has a population of over four million. Although it sprawls for a great distance along Manila Bay the main places of interest are fairly central. Manila is not a city of great interest in itself, it's really just an arrival and departure point for the rest of the Philippines. Once you've seen the Spanish remains in Intramuros you've pretty much seen all Manila has to offer in an historic sense.

The other Manila attraction, however, is entertainment – there are countless reasonably priced restaurants, pubs, folk music clubs, girlie bars, pick-up joints and anything else you could care to ask for. President Marcos' egotistical and pompous first lady is supposedly in charge of Manila and much effort and money has been spent on cosmetic improvements to Metro Manila. Unfortunately for the worse-off local residents a lot of Manila's progressive image has been achieved by

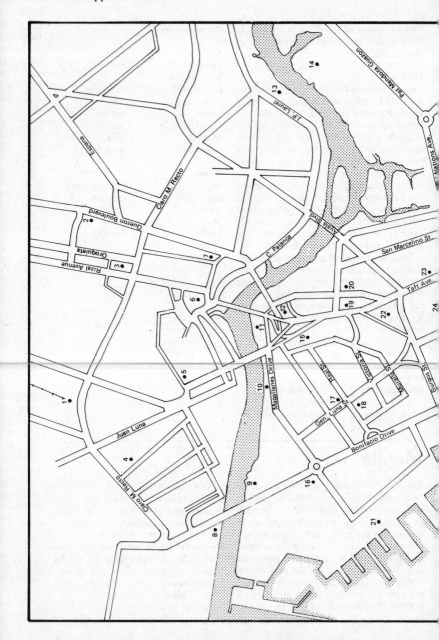

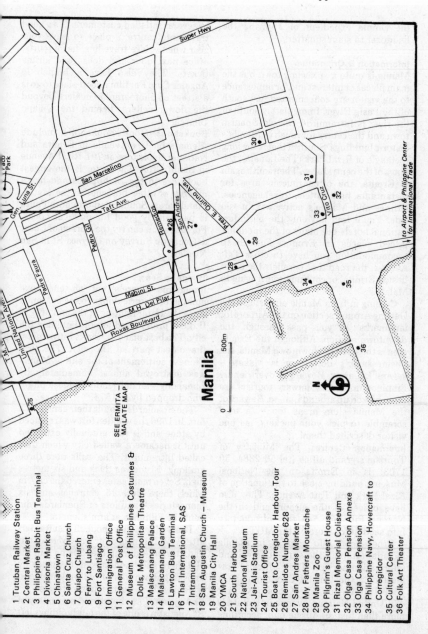

1 Tutuban Railway Station
2 Central Market
3 Philippine Rabbit Bus Terminal
4 Divisoria Market
5 Chinatown
6 Santa Cruz Church
7 Quiapo Church
8 Ferry to Lubang
9 Fort Santiago
10 Immigration Office
11 General Post Office
12 Museum of Philippines Costumes &
   Dolls, Metropolitan Theatre
13 Malacanang Palace
14 Malacanang Garden
15 Lawton Bus Terminal
16 Thai International, SAS
17 Intramuros
18 San Augustin Church – Museum
19 Manila City Hall
20 YMCA
21 South Harbour
22 National Museum
23 Jai-Alai Stadium
24 Tourist Office
25 Boat to Corregidor, Harbour Tour
26 Remidos Number 628
27 San Andres Market
28 My Fathers Moustache
29 Manila Zoo
30 Pilgrim's Guest House
31 Rizal Memorial Coliseum
32 Olga Casa Pension Annexe
33 Olga Casa Pension
34 Philippine Navy, Hovercraft to
   Corregidor
35 Cultural Center
36 Folk Art Theater

Manila

the simple expedient of applying the bulldozer to slum squatters.

Information & Orientation

Manila is quite a sprawling town but the main places of interest and/or importance to the visitor are concentrated just south of the Pasig River. Immediately south of the river is Intramuros, the old Spanish town and the centre for much of Manila's historic buildings. South of that is the long rectangle of Rizal Park (The Luneta), the lungs of the central area. Then south again is Ermita, the often raucous area for restaurants, bars, hotels, travel agencies, airlines and Manila's active sex 'n' sin side. You'll find not only the big international hotels but many of the medium-priced places in Ermita. For cheap accommodation you have to cross Taft Avenue, the road that parallels the coast beside Ermita, or continue south again to Malate.

Coming in from Manila airport see the Getting Around section on the Airport for landmarks as you pass through the downtown section. Although the Ermita area is the visitors' downtown Manila, the businessman's downtown is Makati – several km away. Beware of overfriendly Filipinos in Manila: unwary tourists are often picked up around Luneta. Beware of the Manila slum areas too – 'a mad scramble to pick your pockets,' as one visitor described them!

Information Centres The Ministry of Tourism's grand office (tel 50 2384, 50 1703) is in Ermita in the National Museum building close to the junction of Rizal Park and Taft Avenue. They also have offices at the airport and in the Nayong Pilipino. See the introductory Info section for more on the MOT.

Other good info sources in Manila include Ystaphil, the student travel and information service. Their office is now located in the Unland Condominium at 1656 Taft Avenue. The Kangaroo Club at 476 United Nations Avenue in Ermita is more than just an Aussie pub, according to several satisfied customers. It's a good travel info centre, a place to leave your gear when you're travelling, has a tourist office next door and does good airline tickets. They also have a branch in Angeles City. For film a good place to go is a street of photographic dealers beyond the flower sellers, behind the Quiapo Church.

Bookshops Good bookshops include Alemars on UN Avenue in Ermita and National Bookstore at 701 Rizal Avenue in Santa Cruz. The latter is the largest bookstore in the Philippines and has a number of other branches in the Metro-Manila area. Solidaridad on Padre Faura is particularly good for political books. For maps you can try the Bureau of Coast & Geodetic Survey on Barraca St in San Nicolas.

Things to See

Intramuros There's not an enormous number of historic things to see in Manila since the bitter fighting at the end of WW II did a pretty good job of flattening the city. The best place to start is Intramuros, the oldest part of the city. The first Chinese settlement at the site of Manila was destroyed almost immediately by Limahong – an unfriendly Chinese pirate who dropped by in 1574.

The Spaniards rebuilt their centre as a fort. In 1590 the wooden fort was replaced by stone and it was gradually extended until it became a walled city which they called Intramuros. The walls were three km long, 13 metres thick and six metres high. Seven main gates entered the city, in which there were 15 churches and six monasteries – and lots of Spaniards who kept the Filipinos at arm's length.

The walls are just about all that was left after WW II finished off what MacArthur had started – during the '30s he had his HQ there and 'modernised' the place by knocking down lots of old buildings and widening those nasty narrow streets.

St Augustin The church and monastery of St Augustin is one of the few buildings left from the earliest construction. It was here in 1898 that the last Spanish governor of Manila surrendered to the Filipinos. There is a museum inside which is open daily from 8 am to 5 pm; admission is charged.

Cathedral The Roman Catholic Cathedral is also in Intramuros and has a history that reads like that of a lot of Spanish-built churches in the Philippines. Built 1581, damaged (typhoon) 1582, destroyed (fire) 1583, rebuilt 1592, partially destroyed (earthquake) 1600, rebuilt 1614, destroyed (earthquake) 1645, rebuilt 1654-1671, destroyed (earthquake) 1863, rebuilt 1870-1879, destroyed (WW II) 1945, rebuilt 1954-1958. On that average an earthquake should knock it down again in 2006.

Fort Santiago The ruins of the old Spanish fort – at one time connected to Intramuros – stand just north of the cathedral. They are now used as a pleasant park – see the collection of the Presidents' cars (rusting) and climb up top for the view over the Pasig River. Most interesting part of the fort is the Rizal museum with many items used or made by the Filipino martyr. The room in which he was imprisoned before his execution can be seen.

Fort Santiago's darkest days took place during WW II when it was used as a prison by the Japanese. During the closing days of the war they went on an orgy of killing and in one small cell the bodies of 600 Filipinos and Americans were discovered. It's open daily from 6 am to 10 pm and there is a small admission fee.

The Luneta Intramuros is separated from Ermita, the tourist centre, by the Rizal Memorial Park, better known as the Luneta. It's a meeting and entertainment place for all of Manila – particularly on Sundays when it's packed with people, ice cream and balloon sellers and all kinds of activities. At the bay end of the park is the Rizal Memorial. Two guards stand rather lazily in front of it. Rizal's execution spot is close by.

A Japanese and a Chinese garden flank the planetarium – favourite meeting spots for young couples although it's a little difficult to hide behind a miniature Japanese tree for a passionate clinch. There's a small admission fee to each of these parks. Further up there are fountains, a roller skating circuit, children's amusement park and one amusing construction whose designer deserves to be shot. It's a gigantic pond supposed to represent a 3D map of the Philippines. Try looking at a map edge-on to get the effect; the three-metre-high viewing platform is no help at all. In any case the water level is often too high resulting in half of the islands being totally submerged!

Ermita This is the touristic area although the Hilton is the only major hotel within it. There are lots of restaurants, girlie bars, prostitutes, nightclubs, souvenir shops and non-stop activity. Feminists would love it – every other place has a sign announcing 'attractive' hostess or waitress needed and another sign announcing that unaccompanied women will 'definitely' not be admitted. Ah, it's a male world in Ermita.

Other Nayong Pilipino is the Filipino edition of 'the whole country in miniature'. It's out by the international airport and it has lots of handicraft shops as well as a good little folk museum with some incredible photographs of the forgotten Tasaday tribe.

Manila has lots of museums including the National Museum in the Executive Building, across from the tourist office, beside the Luneta. Admission is free and it's open from 9 am to 12 noon and 1 to 5 pm daily. The Ayala Museum on Makati Avenue is open daily except Mondays from 9 am to 6 pm. It has a series of dioramas illustrating events in the Philippines' history and admission is P10.

There is a Cultural Center Museum in the bay-front cultural center which is open 9 am to 6 pm. At 1786 Mabina St the Carfel Museum of Seashells has an excellent collection of colourful seashells

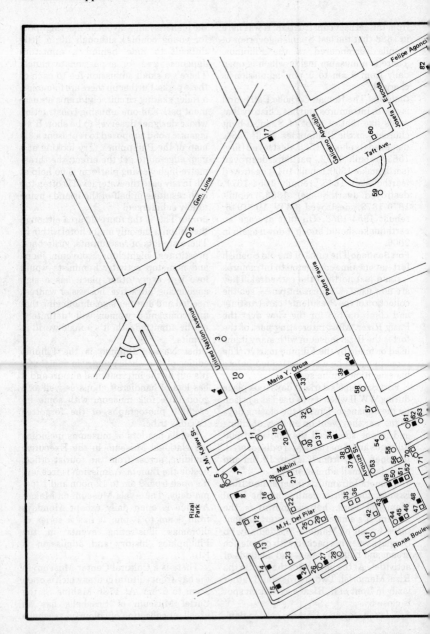

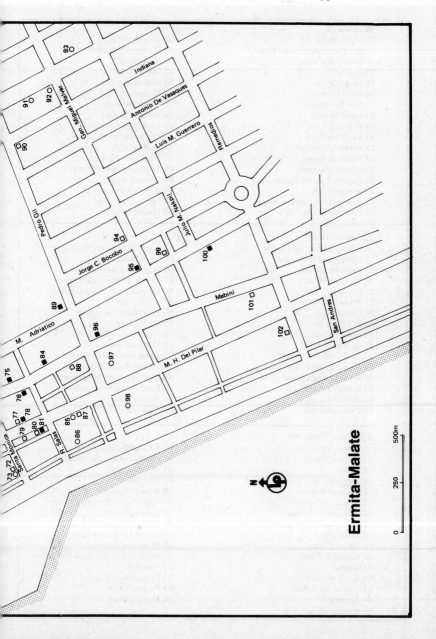

Ermita-Malate

■ Hotels

4 Hilton Hotel	48 Aurelio Hotel
7 San Carlos Apartment Hotel	49 Diamond Executive Inn
8 Mabini Mansion	50 Iseya Hotel
12 Carnes Inn	62 Tower Hotel
14 Luneta Hotel	64 Mabini Pension
15 Otani Hotel	66 Tourist Inn
17 Manda Pension	75 Hotel Mabuhay
20 Hotel Sorinte	76 Pension Conula
24 The Dutch Inn	78 Casa Olga Pension
27 Bay View Plaza	81 Congress Family Hotel
33 Pension Filipinas	82 Youth Hotel
34 Tempura House	83 Travellers' Pension
37 Yasmin Pension	84 Santos Pension House
39 Ryokan Pension House	89 Ramada Hotel
40 Midtown Inn	95 Dakota Mansion
43 Commodore Pension House	96 Las Palmas Hotel
45 Euro House Inn	100 Malate Pension

□ Places to Eat

9 Savory Restaurant Luneta	47 Crab's & Lobsters Restaurant
13 Hong Kong Restaurant	52 Iseya Restaurant
16 Pancake House	56 Espanola's Beer Garden
18 Kangaroo Club	57 Savory, Kashmir Restaurant
21 Club 2	60 Shepards's Inn Restaurant
22 Tahanan Restaurant	67 Suri Inn Bar
23 Daktari Club	68 Guernica's Restaurant
29 St Moritz Bar	69 Lili Marleen
30 Kings Cross Club	70 Padre Fauna Fast Food
31 Bodega Pub	80 Riverboat Bar
32 Barrio Fiesta	87 Swiss Matterhorn Restaurant
35 Myrna's Restaurant	88 Mabini House Restaurant
36 Fortress Restaurant	90 Sun View Cafe & Restaurant
38 Shakey's Pizza	94 Food Fiesta Restaurant
42 Stolt Milanie Bar	101 Hobbit House
46 Casa Esponola	102 Shakey's Pizza

○ Shops, Offices, etc

1 Tourist Office	58 Solidaridad Bookshop
2 Medical Center	59 Philippine General Hospital
3 Police	61 PIT Telegram
5 Singapore Airlines	63 Post Office
6 Pakistan Airlines	65 Money Changer
10 American Express	71 Padre Faura Shopping Center
11 Alemars Bookshop	73 Cathay Pacific
19 International Supermarket	74 Midland Plaza, Robinsons
25 Telex Office	85 Martin's Products Bakery
26 Japan Airlines	86 Philippine Airlines
28 Korean Airlines	91 PLTD – Long Distance Telephone
41 Qantas	92 Ystaphil
44 Egypt Airlines	93 Philippine Airlines
53 Mabini Art Center	97 Pistang Filipino
54 Bookmark	98 Flea Market
55 Mercury Drug Store	

from Filipino waters. It's open from 8 am to 7 pm daily. Other museums include the Central Bank Money Museum, the Metropolitan Museum of Manila, the Museo Ng Buhay Pilipino, the Museum of Traditional Philippine Culture at the Nayong Pilipino and the San Augustin Museum in the Augustine monastery at the San Augustin Church in Intramuros.

Malacanang Palace, home to the Marcoses, is across the Pasig River – it's an impressive place which was built by a Spanish aristocrat. Tours can be arranged for groups. Chinatown, also across the river, is also interesting to wander through.

There are daily one-hour cruises on Manila Bay from Gate A, South Boulevard, Rizal Park, but only for a few months of the year. The Makati Commercial Center is the Philippines at its shiniest, newest and most American. There are good fast-food places and a cinema complex here. Quiapo, an older and more traditional part of Manila, has the Quiapo Church by Quezon Bridge. The wooden statue of Christ known as the 'Black Nazarene' can be seen here.

Places to Stay

There is a wide variety of accommodation possibilities in Manila, many of them close to the central Ermita area. Cheapest are the hostel and Y places but there are also many cheap hotels and pensions.

Hostels One of Manila's most popular hostel-style places is the big YMCA (tel 45 5033). The office is at 1068 Cenception St but there is another entrance around at 350 Arroceros St. There are all sorts of rooms although the best value places tend to be reserved well ahead. They include dorms at P38, rooms with fan from P45, with air-con from P72. Couples can stay here too but the cheaper rooms are male only and the dorm is only for permanent guests. The YMCA also has a good restaurant and a cafeteria with reasonable food. It's beside the city hall, a large yellow building with a clock tower.

The *Youth Hostel Philipinnes* (tel 50 9970) at 1572 Leon Guinto St has dorm beds in fan-cooled rooms at P26, with a YHA card P2 less. There are also rooms from P50 but although the doors shut at 12.30 am it's very noisy and hot. If you're heading up country you can store baggage here for a small charge. *Remedios* at 628 Remedios St is a simple private guest house with a relaxed atmosphere and singles from P30.

The *Pilgrims Guest House* (tel 50 7227) at 2456 Taft Avenue, opposite the De La Salle University, used to be the popular Ystaphil Hostel. It has a billiard table, cafeteria, TV and even a gym room. Beds in the fan-cooled dorm are P35, rooms with fan are P55.

Hotels & Guest Houses The *Traveller's Pension* at 934 Pedro Gil is a notch down in price and standards (a big notch in the latter, according to some travellers) from the pensions in Ermita. Singles are P35, doubles P45 to 55 and very dirty although they have some nicer rooms upstairs. The *Manda Pension House* (tel 59 0607) at 1387 F Agoncillo St (corner of Padre Faura, Ermita) is a simple place (shared bathrooms) but clean and cheap from P60. The *Commodore Pension House* (tel 59 6864) at 422 Arquiza St is similarly priced.

Moving up a little in price the *Casa Pension* (tel 58 7647) at 1406 M H Del Pilar St has singles/doubles from P70/80 and is pleasantly run. There are three other 'Casa Pensions'. The *New Casa Pension* is at 1602 Leon Guinto St; the *Olga Casa Pension Annex* (tel 59 6265) is at 640 Vito Cruz, Malate; the *Olga Casa Pension* (tel 59 3113) is at 1647 Mabini St.

There are lots of other up-a-notch pensions and small guest houses around Ermita, a conveniently central place to stay. They include the *Congress Family Hotel* (tel 59 5482) at 1427 M H Del Pilar St. Not many singles but it's a well-run and clean place which offers good value. Singles/doubles are P75/105 or with air-con from P135 – all the rooms have attached bathrooms. Some of the rooms are very noisy.

Malate Pension at 1771 Adriatico St (tel 59 3489) is off the main road and therefore quieter. This friendly and helpful place has rooms from P75 or with air-con from P100. *Santos Pension House* (59 5628) at 1540 Mabini St, close to Kowloon House, also has a pleasant atmosphere and gives discounts to peace corps workers. It's something of a peace corps hangout although other people also stay there. Rooms are all air-con and rather expensive from P140/180 but there are also some small dorm-like rooms at around P50 a bed. The *Kangaroo Club* in Ermita also has good, clean air-con rooms with bathroom for P300 double.

Others to try include the *Midtown Pension* (tel 50 8780) at 551 Padre Faura St, run by friendly Mrs Mendoza. Or the *Mabini Pension* (tel 59 4853) at 1337 Mabini St – clean and neat, P110 or with air-con rooms P150. Or *Pension Conula* (tel 58 2334) at 1445 Mabini St, close to the Mabuhay Hotel, has rooms from P770/120 to around P150 with air-con. The *Ryokan Pension House* (tel 59 8956) is at 1250 J Bocobo St – large beds, clean rooms and prices very similar to the Conula. The airport hotel desk can book you into most of these places.

Places to Eat

Manila is full of places to eat – all types of food and at all types of prices. The tourist ghetto of Ermita is a good hunting ground. Although you'll pay more here than in other parts of the Philippines you'll still find good and reasonably priced food of all types.

Start on popular M H Del Pilar St where *Myrna's* is popular and crowded. On the corner with UN Avenue the *Tahanan Restaurant* does Filipino food and has a pleasant beer garden where you can watch the passing scene.

On the corner of Malvar and Jorge Bocobo St the *Food Fiesta Restaurant* does Filipino and Japanese food and again you can eat outside. *Barrio Fiesta* at 110 Jorge Bocobo S is a popular place for real Filipino food. Try crispy pata or kare-kare here; the menu is extensive but the prices are rather more expensive than ordinary restaurants.

Despite its name the *Aristocrat*, on the corner of Roxas Boulevard and San Andres St, is amazingly good value. It's a big and very popular Filipino restaurant. Try lapu lapu fish or the fish soup here. Next door, *Josephine's* is a little more expensive but the seafood is superb.

There are a lot of fast-food places around, and international food centres with a whole selection of regional food possibilities under one roof. The *Fast Food Center* on M H Del Pilar is a popular travellers' centre with good food and beer, particularly at *Inglewood*. Or on Padre Faura there's *Fast Food* and the *Restaurant Center*. On Mabini St *Shakey's Pizza* does pretty good pizza. *Shepard's Inn* on Taft Avenue, near the youth hostel, is a friendly place with good cheap food.

Try *United House* on Desmaralda St in Binondo, the Chinatown area north of the Pasig River, for good Chinese food. On Adriatico St, *India House* is good value if you need a curry. The *Iseya Restaurant* on the corner of M H Del Pilar and Padre Faura has Japanese food. *Eddie's Steakhouse* on Santa Monica St has a fixed-price complete menu which is excellent value.

Entertainment

There is plenty to do after-hours in Manila. Try a jai-alai game any evening in the fronton on Taft Avenue across from the Luneta. Admission is just P2 to 5 to see one of the fastest games in the world and one that attracts heavy betting. Jai-alai is something like a cross between squash and lacrosse.

Around Ermita you'll find good folk music, jazz or rock in the bars – all it costs is a beer at a peso or two above normal rates in most places. Check out *Espanola* on Padre Faura as one typical example, if it hasn't shifted to the *Casino Espanola* on Roxas Boulevard. The folk clubs often have amazing 'replicas' of Dylan, Simon & Garfunkel or other western stars. Try the popular *Hobbit* (P10 cover charge) where the waiters are indeed hobbit-sized. It's at 1801 Mabini St. Or there's *My Father's Moustache* on M H Del Pilar St in Malate, *El Bodegon* at 1537 M H Del Pilar or *Guernica's* at 1826 M H Del Pilar.

There are plenty of bars too like the *Kangaroo Club* at 476 UN Avenue, *Lili Marleen's* at 1323B M H Del Pilar, Or the *Old English Pub* on Padre Faura near the junction with Adriatico. Every nationality is catered to!

Getting There

Manila is virtually the only entry point to the Philippines. See the introductory Getting There section for details on flying to the Philippines. Manila is also the centre for the truncated Luzon railway system – trains run north from Manila to San Fernando and south to Legaspi; see North Luzon and South Luzon for more information. Plus Manila is the centre for bus travel to the north and south and for ships from Luzon to the other islands of the Philippines.

Bus Understanding the long-distance buses is slightly complicated by the fact that there are often two bus stations for the various companies. Thus northbound Pantranco Tours operates from 325 Quezon Avenue, Quezon City out towards the airport. From here you get buses to 100 Islands and other beach resorts in the north and to Baguio and Banaue. Southbound Pantranco Tours is at E de los Santos Avenue in Pasay City and buses depart from there to the Bicol region.

Philippine Rabbit Bus Lines is at 819 Oroquieta St in Santa Cruz. The entrance is on Rizal Avenue. This station is known as 'Avenida' and if you're coming from the north take a Philippine Rabbit bus marked 'Avenida via Dau'. It takes the Dau Expressway from Angeles and is much faster. Avoid 'Avenida via Caloocan' buses. Philippine Rabbit has buses to Baguio, Vigan and other places in the north. Their San Fernando La Union, Vigan and Laoag buses go from their second station at the junction of Rizal Avenue Extension and 2nd Ave, Grace Park, Caloocan.

BLTB, which stands for Batangas-Laguna-Tayabas Bus Company, operates to the places south of Manila including Pagsanjan. They're at E de los Santos Avenue in Pasay City. Victory Liner operate northbound from 713 Rizal Avenue Extension, Caloocan to Mariveles, Olongapo and Alaminos. To Zambales, Baguio and also to Olongapo they operate from 651 E de los Santos Avenue, Pasay City.

PNR is Philippines National Railways Motor Service and they operate from Tutuban Station, 943 Claro M Recto Avenue both to the Mountain Province and to the Bicol region.

Ship The shipping companies generally advertise departures in the Manila English-language dailies. Cebu, in the Visayas, is the main hub of Filipino shipping, but there are plenty of departures from Manila. Some of the main companies include Sulpico Lines who have a booking office beside the YMCA and operate to Cebu, Zamboanga, Davao and Tacloban. There are other Sulpico booking offices around town.

Sweet Lines have offices at Pier 6, North Harbour and at 416 Padre Faura in Ermita. Their services are similar to Sulpico. Negros Navigation is particularly good for ships to Negros, find them at Pier 2, North Harbour. William Lines is at Pier 14 and there's an office at 609 San Marcelino St on the corner of Concepcion St in Ermita. They cover all the Visayas and Mindanao ports. There are quite a few other shipping companies in Manila, many of them with offices at North Harbour.

Getting Around

Airport Airport departure tax is P100 for international flights. Domestic and international flights go from the same airport. Security is tight in the Philippines, they're very hijack conscious. Manila International Airport (MIA) is only 12 km from the city centre and since taxi fares are very low it's pretty cheap to get between the airport and the centre. On the meter it should be about P25 but they'll ask you for P40 or more. All Manila's cabs are metered. Beware of people impersonating tourist officers at the airport. They'll try to steer you into pirate taxis where you'll be severely overcharged. The taxi drivers will ask for US$50 if you give them a chance.

Reportedly an airport shuttle bus service has just been started. It costs P26 and goes to all the main hotels and guest houses in Manila, door-to-door service.

If you are really intent on pinching pennies you can also get into the centre by bus. Come out of the terminal and turn left, walk about 100 metres and there should be a bus stop sign. Ignore the taxi drivers who will tell you there is no bus or the last one has already gone. Every 10 or 15 minutes a yellow bus with destination sign 'Santa Cruz, Monumento' should come by. The fare into Manila is P1.

You'll want to get off well before the end of the line so watch out for some landmarks as you come down Taft Avenue into the city. First landmark is La Salle College on your left – careful of street numbers down Taft Avenue: they repeat. Further down on your left you'll be passing the Ermita area and the highest building is the Hilton Hotel. Get off shortly before it for the YH or the Ermita pensions or abreast of it for the YWCA. Next landmark is the Coca Cola/Jai Alai neon sign on your right and almost immediately you're at the City Hall. This is only about 200 metres past the Hilton and you've now got to leap off for the YMCA. If you cross the river you've missed everything and will have to turn back.

If you get stuck at Manila airport overnight try the lobby of the Village Hotel behind the airport. You can leave your luggage at the casino counter and see the unbalanced wealth of the Philippines being recklessly lost and won at the roulette tables. Not many hassles during the night – I just told them I had a friend in the casino who kept on winning and that I was waiting for him (it's open 24 hours). The mosquitoes are bad, though.

Tom Channell

City Transport For areas around Manila, buses depart from the station across Taft Avenue from the City Hall – beside the Intramuros walls. There are countless metered taxis (make sure the meter is on), very reasonably priced jeepneys with fares from P1 and a comprehensive bus system around Manila. It's a little difficult to find your way around on jeepneys or buses until you've got some idea of Manila's geography and can recognise the destination names. Jeepneys are still so cheap that it's no great loss to get on the wrong one occasionally. A useful jeepney route is from Santa Cruz down M H Del Pilar to Harrison and Taft near the airport to Buendia. That covers most of visitors' Manila.

Buses are much the same. There are a lot of different companies. Metromanila buses are more modern, blue in colour and somewhat easier to find your way with. Standard fares are from P1 or P6.50 on the 'Love Buses'. Buses and jeepneys generally display their destinations on a board in front. Some popular routes include MIA-Santa Cruz-Monumento (MIA is Manila International Airport). This bus runs right down Taft Avenue from the airport, crosses the river for Santa Cruz and returns to the airport along E de los Santos Avenue and Cubao. Ayala-Buenida-Monumento runs from the Makati Commercial Center down Ayala Boulevard, on to Buendia then Taft across the bridge to Rizal Avenue and along that street to Monumento. Quiapo-Buendia goes from Quiapo along Taft Avenue to Buendia (Pasay City) then south on Ayala Boulevard to the Makati Commercial Center. UP-Balara-Quiapo starts at the University of the Philippines and goes along Quezon Boulevard (passing the Pantranco North Station) to Quiapo, it loops around South Harbour and Rizal Park and then returns. Monumento-Baclaran travels along E de los Santos Avenue via the Farmers' Market in Cubao and the Makati Commercial Center on Ayala Boulevard.

Things to Buy

The Philippines are a great handicraft centre and you can find all sorts of interesting things around Manila although, not surprisingly, you'll find them even cheaper out in the country. There are many handicraft shops and centres around Manila, check out the handicrafts bazaar between M H Del Pilar and Roxas Boulevard and the variety of handicraft places at the Nayong Pilipino – demonstrations there on Mondays. The Shoe Mart department store at the Makati Commercial Center is good for souvenirs if you can't get around the country. Prices are fixed and competitive.

Good buys include canework, carvings, shell hanging-lamps and clothes. It's hard not to look like a caricature of Marcos in a Barong Tagalog but the short-sleeved version, Barong Polo is cool and fashionable – authentic ones are made of pina, a fabric woven from pineapple fibre. Bargaining is not done as much in the Philippines as in other South-East Asian countries but you should still do a little haggling.

LUZON

Luzon is the largest island in the Philippines and has a lot to offer apart from Manila itself. North of the capital are the famous rice terraces of Banaue, the cool summer-capital of Baguio, the historic old town of Vigan, the beaches of the China Sea coast and the swimming and diving opportunities at 100 Islands.

South of Manila are the Pagsanjan rapids and the Taal Volcano – both within day-trip distance from Manila. Further south is the Bicol region – site of the Mayon Volcano (climb it for an unforgettable experience), the Tiwi hot springs and the islands of Masbate and Catanduanes. West of Luzon, but close enough to be easily reached, are the islands of Mindoro and Marinduque – with unspoilt beaches and aboriginal people on the former, the colourful Moriones festival at Easter on the latter.

Around Manila

There are quite a few places within day trip distance of Manila – some of then can conveniently be included en route to other places. If you are heading south to Legaspi it's worth stopping off at Taal or Pagsanjan on the way, for example.

CORREGIDOR

The small island at the mouth of Manila Bay was the American-Filipino last stand after the Japanese invaded. It certainly wasn't as impregnable as planned but it did hold out for a long time. Today it's a national shrine where you can look around the underground bunkers and inspect the rusty relics of the fortress armaments.

The Philippine army runs the place today and there's a friendly captain who may be happy to show you some of the less accessible places. There's lots of WW II junk lying around, plus the shattered remains of MacArthur's pre-war HQ and a museum of the war with a good 3D map. There are stunning views and sunsets from the summit of the highest hill and a soft drink stand which sells Coke and San Mig beer.

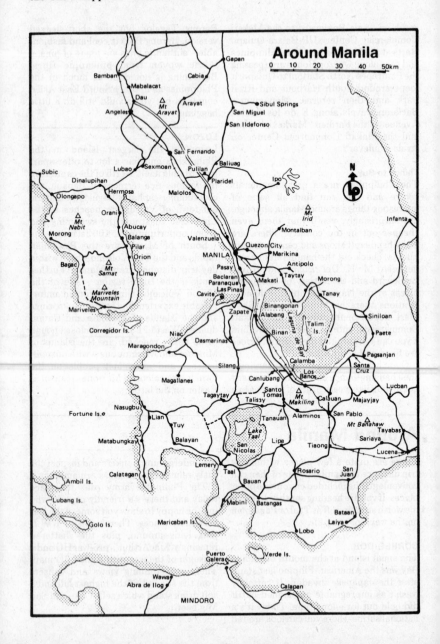

Around Manila

0 10 20 30 40 50km

N

Gapan
Cabiao
Bamban
Mabalacat
Dau
Arayat
Mt Arayat
Angeles
Sibul Springs
San Miguel
San Ildefonso
San Fernando
Baliuag
Subic
Lubao
Sexmoan
Pulilan
Dinalupihan
Hermosa
Plaridel
Ipo
Olongapo
Malolos
Orani
Mt Nabit
Abucay
Morong
Balanga
Pilar
Valenzuela
Mt Irid
Infanta
Orion
Montalban
Quezon City
Bagac
Mt Samat
Limay
Marikina
Antipolo
Pasay
Baclaran
Taytay
Morong
Mariveles Mountain
Paranaque
Makati
Tanay
Mariveles
Las Pinas
Cavite
Binangonan
Talim Is.
Siniloan
Corregidor Is.
Zapate
Alabang
Laguna de Bay
Paete
Niac
Binan
Maragondon
Dasmarinas
Pagsanjan
Calamba
Santa Cruz
Silang
Los Banos
Lucban
Magallanes
Canlubang
Tagaytay
Santo Tomas
Mt Makiling
Calauan
Majayjay
Talisay
Fortune Is.
Nasugbu
Tanauan
Alaminos
San Pablo
Mt Banahaw
Lian
Tuy
Lipe
Tiaong
Sariaya
Matabungkay
Balayan
Lake Taal
Tayabas
San Nicolas
Lucena
Calatagan
Lemery
Rosario
San Juan
Ambil Is.
Taal
Bauan
Lubang Is.
Mabini
Batangas
Bataan
Golo Is.
Maricaban Is.
Laiya
Lobo
Verde Is.
Puerto Galera
Wawa
Abra de Ilog
Calapan
MINDORO

Getting There

Daily, except Mondays, there's a hovercraft from the Philippine Navy Headquarters, Roxas Boulevard. It makes the 45 km trip to 'the rock' in 50 minutes and costs, including a tour during your two hours on the island, a hefty P280. Departures are at 7.30 am and 12.30 pm.

During the summer there are Friday, Saturday and Sunday day trips from Rizal Park organised by Arpan Tourist Industries (tel 50 1532 or 50 1571). It leaves at 8 am and returns at 6 pm and costs P80.

There's also a more adventurous alternative. First of all take a bus to Mariveles on the Bataan Peninsula – one change on the way. This is where the US forces evacuated to Corregidor and from there when they started the Bataan Death March after it fell. From here hire an outrigger banca for the 13 km trip out to the island – perhaps P100 roundtrip with a bit of bargaining. A rather noisy and wet ride over. If you bring your own food and sleep on the beach the only expense on the island will be a P3 'upkeep charge'. There is also a rest house on Corregidor. Get the banca to come back for you the next day and don't pay until you get back to the mainland.

When the tourists leave, the island is quiet, eerie and has a real sense of history. You can imagine MacArthur stomping around shouting, 'I will return,' while the bombs and shells land all around.

OLONGAPO

Situated north of Manila, this town has a US Navy base and its principal activities have been described as 'beer and prostitution'. A good raunchy, honkytonk place! There are lots of bars but also some so-so beaches around Subic. San Miguel, slightly north of Subic Bay, is better than any of the beaches between Olongapo and Subic.

Places to Stay

On Rizal Avenue the *Bayside Hotel* (tel 5042) has rooms at P35/60 for singles/doubles. The *MGM Hotel* on Maysaysay Drive is good and clean. There are other over-priced and non-descript hotels along Rizal Avenue. Along the coast from Olongapo to Subic there are several resorts with rooms from P50 to 100.

Getting There

It's a three-hour bus ride from the Victory Liner Station in Manila, quite an adventurous trip up and over the mountains. From Baguio buses depart hourly and the trip takes six hours.

ANGELES CITY

This is another major American base city with lots of noisy night life and thousands of 'hospitality' girls. Take care, though; as one traveller reported: 'I was picked up by the police after 'buying dope' from a jeepney driver. It cost me a US$40 bribe and US$20 stolen from me to get out. All the officers in the night station in that suburb are corrupt. Very frightening, but the only laugh was when they put me into the wooden cage at the back of the station – the door jammed and they asked me to kick it. I'd got thongs on so I put my shoulder to it. Unfortunately the door opened inwards not outwards and I broke the hinge off. Fortunately they didn't charge me for that! But be careful, they hold all the cards – if you're going to complain save it for Hong Kong.'

Places to Stay

The *Liberty Inn* on MacArthur Highway, Balibago has rooms from P80. Diagonally opposite in a small sidestreet is the *Far Eastern Hotel*, which is cheaper with rooms with fan and bath from P45.

Getting There

Pantranco or PNR buses go to Angeles from Baguio. From Manila Philippine Rabbit buses go from Rizal Avenue, PNR buses from Tutuban Station, Pantranco North Express buses from Quezon Boulevard. They operate through Angeles and on to Baguio.

PAGSANJAN

Situated 70 km south-east of Manila in the Laguna province, this is the place for an exciting go at shooting the rapids. For P41 per person (no more than two to a boat), plus P5 'entry' you will be taken upriver to the falls (good place for a swim) then come rushing down the rapids – getting kind of wet on the way. Note that there are two sets of falls and only the second has a grotto. You'll probably get hassled for extra money; plenty of rich tourists come here and toss pesos around.

The water level is highest and the rapids are at their best in August and September. The best time is early morning before the tourist hordes arrive, so spend the night in the Pagsanjan YH. The hostel people will arrange the boats for you. The weekends are terribly crowded. The final scenes of *Apocalypse Now* were shot here.

Places to Stay

Willy Flores, the postman at 788 Garcia St, behind the post office, has a few rooms at P40. Everybody knows him but find your own way there or a guide will be taking a commission at your expense. Miss Estella y Umale's *Riverside Bungalow*, also on Garcia St, has two bungalows with rooms with fan and bath for P90 single, P130 double. It's just two houses from Willy Flores and she's a good cook.

At 237 General Luna St the *Pagsanjan Youth Hostel* is clean and tidy, the hosts helpful and very friendly. Nightly costs are P25 in dorm. Regular rooms are P50/70 with fan and bath. A double with fan in the 'Bamboo House' is P50. The hostel can be a little tricky to find. The *Camino Real Hotel* at 39 Rizal St has dorm beds at P50, rooms from P70/100 with fan right up to P180/200 with air-con and bath.

Up market, there's the *Pagsanjan Falls Lodge* at P150 to 200 a double. They also have cheaper cabins. The lodge is beautifully situated on the river bank.

The youth hostel will recommend good places to eat, like the *D&C Luncheonette* on National Rd towards the Falls Lodge or the *Dura-Fe Restaurant* on General Jaina St.

Getting There

Take a bus to Santa Cruz from the Laguna Bus Station or from Taft Avenue in Manila. BLTB buses also operate there. The trip takes about three hours and costs P12, when you get to Santa Cruz ignore the tricycle riders and take a jeepney to Pagsanjan. As an alternative you can continue around the lesser-used route on the north side of Laguna de Bay back to Manila. It's more scenic, the roads are paved and buses and jeepneys operate on this route – it's only slightly further.

From Santa Cruz you can continue south through Lucena to the Bicol region in the south or you can head across to Batangas for the ferry to Mindoro.

TAGAYTAY (Taal Volcano)

The volcanic lake of Taal is a pleasant excursion from Manila. The Taal volcano has a lake inside from which emerges a smaller volcano, inside of which is another lake. There's a pretty incredible view from up on Tagaytay Ridge. If you phone up beforehand you can get a boat out to the cone and climb to the top – arranged by the Vulcanology Commission in Quezon City (tel 60 3803). It's not necessary to obtain permission to climb the volcano, especially if you go from Talisay instead of Tagaytay. There are plenty of boats to the volcano from Talisay for about P150. Talisay is much more convenient for Batangas and Pagsanjan.

On the way to Taal a lot of people stop at a jeepney factory and at Las Pinas to see the small church which is famous for its pipe organ utilising 950 bamboo pipes. It was originally built in 1794 and after a recent restoration it still sounds good.

Places to Stay

The *Taal Vista Lodge* is expensive but you can rent tents in the grounds for P75 a double plus P15 for mattress and sheets. If you ask in the restaurant you should be able to get fairly cheap accommodation in private homes. Alternatively, about three km before the Taal Vista Lodge and just after the roundabout, look for the sign 'room to rent'. A double without bath here is P35, with bath from P75.

Villa Adelaida is a nice place with bungalows at P125/145. Coming from Manila instead of turning right to Tagaytay you have to turn left. It's near the road going down to the lake towards Talisay. In Talisay the *Volcano Village* has bamboo huts for P80.

Getting There

Take a BLTB bus from Manila to Nasugbu; the trip takes 1½ hours. If you're also going to Pagsanjan you can combine the two by continuing from Tagaytay to Zapote and from there continuing in a jeepney to Alabang and another bus to Santa Cruz. Finally another jeepney will get you to Pagsanjan. It sounds complicated but in actual fact it's quite fast and simple.

There's also an interesting back-roads route from Batangas to Lake Taal. Take a jeepney from Batangas to Lemery; it's a dusty 1½ hour ride. From there take a jeepney to San Nicolas on the south-western shore of the lake.

To get to Talisay from Pagsanjan take a jeepney to Santa Cruz, a bus towards Manila, get off at the roundabout in Colombo and take a jeepney to Taunan. From Taunan walk to the far side of the market (about half a km) and take a jeepney to Talisay. The whole trip takes about two hours.

SAN PABLO

There are a wide variety of hikes possible around this town. It's an easy hour's stroll around the Sampalok Lake in an extinct volcano cone. Or you can make the longer half-day trip to the twin lakes of Pandin and Yambo. There are some interesting and historic towns in the area and you can return to Manila via Los Banos, home of the International Rice Research Institute

(IRRI) where the rice varieties that prompted the Asian 'green revolution' were developed. Near here at Alaminos, Hidden Valley is a private park with natural springs and the chance of a swim – but admission is a hefty P70 including lunch. There are hot springs at Pansol, also in the Los Banos area.

Places to Stay

On Schetelig Avenue in Efarca Subdivision, the *Sampaloc Lake Youth Hostel* has good food and costs P25 to 35. The *Lakeview Health Resort* has rooms from P120.

Getting There

Buses run direct to San Pablo from Manila. You can get to Hidden Springs by a jeepney to Alaminos, then a tricycle or jeepney to Hidden Valley. Arrange to be picked up again later in the day.

BATANGAS

The only reason for coming here is to take the ferry service across to the island of Mindoro.

Places to Stay

On the outskirts of town the *Alpha Hotel* (tel 725 2213) has rooms from P70 or P120 with air-con. The *City Hotel* in the centre is simpler and cheaper and the *Lodging House* is good even though it is a short-time place. Rooms are P50 with fan, complete with horizontal mirrors by the beds. The *Batangas Pensione House* (tel 725 3703) on P Herera St is clean and has good doubles from P40 to 60.

The *New Grand Plaza Restaurant* on Evangelist is very clean and pleasant.

Getting There

Always ask for 'Batangas City' to avoid confusion with the general Batangas area. Get there reasonably early if you want to get the Puerto Galera boats at 12.30 pm. It's a 2½ hour trip costing P15. Beware of pickpockets on these buses and be prepared for the Puerto Galera accommodation touts when you arrive at the pier. BLTB has air-con buses which are only a few pesos more expensive but they terminate at Batangas City rather than at the pier. You can then get a jeepney to the pier.

LUCENA CITY

The capital of Quezon Province, Lucena City is the departure point for boats to Marinduque. About four km out of the city is the popular Dalahican Beach and about 18 km out are the Mainit Hot Springs. Take along water and food if you intend to go hiking in the Quezon National Park, one of the largest wildlife reserves in Luzon.

Places to Stay

Cheap hotels are generally in the Barrio Ayam area of the city; get there on a jeepney or tricycle. Places to try include the *Tourist Hotel* from P30 up to P80 for a double with air-con and bath. Or there's the *Fresh Air* which is slightly more expensive. The *Sunrise Lodging House* opposite the BLTB bus terminal is very cheap.

The *Casa Arias Garden Restaurant*, near the BLTB bus station in the centre, is good.

Getting There

It's only four hours by bus to Lucena from Manila. From here you can continue south to Naga in about eight hours. Buses also run to Lucena from San Pablo and Pagsanjan.

North Luzon

After a spell on the beaches at 100 Islands most travellers continue north to the famed rice terraces in the Mountain Provinces. The Igorot and Ifugao villages around Banaue and their superb rice terraces have been dubbed the 'eighth wonder of the world'. The north Luzon area also has the popular summer capital of Baguio and the interesting old town of Vigan with its many reminders of the Spanish period.

THINGS TO BUY

In north Luzon look for wood carvings by the Ifugao tribespeople and also for interesting hand-woven fabrics. The cottons are produced in such limited quantities that they rarely even reach Manila. They're much cheaper in Bontoc or Banaue than in Baguio. Baskets and woven salad bowls are remarkably cheap, but a little bulky to carry home.

WEST COAST BEACHES

There is a string of beaches along the west coast of North Luzon. Best known of these resort areas is 100 Islands, a scattering of tiny islands off Lucap. November and May are the best beach months. If you've not got snorkelling equipment you can rent it or, more cheaply, rent or buy it in Manila.

Getting There

Pantranco North buses run regularly from Manila to Alaminos – a five-hour trip costing around P25. From Alaminos it's just a short P1-1.50 tricycle ride to Lucap, the town for 100 Islands. Dagupan is on the Manila-San Fernando railway line and buses also run here. From Alaminos it's about an hour to Dagupan for P14 and there are more frequent minibuses as well as the larger Pantranco buses. If you're continuing north from Dagupan to San Fernando you have to change buses here and the trip takes about two hours.

Philippines Rabbit buses go from Manila to San Fernando and Bauang. It's a six-hour trip from Manila. San Fernando to Bauang is a short jeepney ride. Don't confuse San Fernando La Union, on the coast here, with the other San Fernando further south between Manila and Angeles. Further north to Vigan takes four hours and costs P40 on a Time Transport bus – a big clock on the front. The Baguio-San Fernando trip only takes an hour.

HUNDRED ISLANDS

Actually there are more than 100 islands, all of them uninhabited, but if clear water, snorkelling, swimming or just lazing around and collecting the sun is your thing then this is a good place. Lucap, just three km from Alaminos, is the main accommodation centre for the islands. From here you can hire boats to get out to the islands. There are no beaches except on the islands and only a few of the islands actually have beaches, but there are plenty of hidden caves and coral reefs.

It's still remarkably untouristed so be prepared to fend for yourself. There is a tourist office on the pier which has a map of the islands and arranges boats. A day trip costs P120 for up to six people. That gives you about six hours on the islands – quite enough. Quezon, the largest island, is being developed as a large tourist resort. Other popular islands for snorkelling include Cathedral, Parde and Panaca. Lucap has a marine Biological Museum and a fishery research centre.

Places to Stay

In Lucap the *Ocean View Lodge & Restaurant* is clean and has a good restaurant, plus rooms from P80/90 for the simplest singles/doubles. They will help you plan trips out to the islands. The *Park View Lodge* is similarly priced but can be bargained down a bit.

Opposite the Ocean View *Gloria's Cottages* are P50/75 for singles/doubles with fan or P60/80 with bath as well. It's quite pleasant and prices are definitely negotiable. The *R&E* (Relax & Enjoy) has rooms at P45/60 or a cottage with fan and bath for P180. It's a good, well-kept place with a restaurant. Still in Lucap there's *Maxine's by the Sea* with rooms with fan

and bath from P80/140. The *Youth Hostel* at Kilometre One (a km from Lucap, as the location suggests) is P35/50 for the cheapest rooms, P40/60 with fan – a student card or YHA card will get you a discount. Dorm beds cost P25.

In Alaminos the *Alaminos Hotel* is a good clean place with rooms at P40/50 or with fan and bath at P80/100. Lucap is a quiet place at night. If you need a beer, hop on a tricycle to nearby Alaminos where the *Plaza Restaurant* usually has a folk singer, or there's the *Imperial Restaurant*.

DAGUPAN

Dagupan is mainly a transport change point but there are also some good beaches in the vicinity. Between Longayen and Dagupan you can try Lingayen Beach (15 km from Dagupan), Blue Beach (three km away at Bonuan) while White Beach is 15 km north-east at San Fabian. White Beach is really brownish-grey.

Places to Stay

The *Villa Milagrosa Youth Hostel* on Zamora St is run by an enthusiastically Catholic lady – 'she'll try to convert you,' reported one traveller. Dorm beds are P30 or there are singles/doubles with a fan and bath for P40/55.

Other places to stay include the *Lucky Lodge & Restaurant* on M H Del Pilar St where rooms cost P30/40 on up to nearly P100 with air-con and attached bathroom. The *Vicar Hotel* on A B Fernandez Avenue has rooms from P30 for a simple fan-cooled single up to P90 for doubles with air-con and bath. On the same street the *Victoria Hotel* is rather more expensive, starting from P100/110 for rooms with fan and bath. There are plenty of restaurants in Dagupan.

In San Fabian the *White Sand Beach Resort* has cottages from P75 to 100 and a restaurant. The family that runs this place also has cheap accommodation in their large, comfortable family home – the *Residenz (Patty) Meija*.

BAUANG & SAN FERNANDO

Further north on the coast Bauang has a
pleasant and long stretch of beach with
many resort hotels. There are better
beaches in the Philippines, but Bauang is
only an hour or two's travel from Baguio in
the hills which accounts in part for its
popularity. San Fernando is only six km
north of Bauang and the beach area is
between the two – about two km north of
Bauang, four km south of San Fernanado.
Lots of jeepneys shuttle back and forth.

Places to Stay

Bauang's resort hotels tend to be expensive
although you can certainly bargain a little.
The *Leo-Mar Beach Resort* has clean
doubles with bath for P150. The similarly
priced *Mark Teresa Apartments* are also
worth trying. These are situated in the
main street, not along the beach front.

For P200 and up you can get a non air-
con double at the *Long Beach Resort Hotel*
or at the *Bali-Hai*. These hotels offer boat
rentals, wind surfing and other entertainment possibilities. Other places include
the *Lourdes Beach Resort* and the cheaper
Fermina's Beach Cottages next door.

On Quezon Avenue in San Fernando
the *Hotel Plaza* has rooms at P50/80 with
fan, P80/105 with bath as well, P135/160
with bath and air-con. On Rizal St the
Casa Blanca Hotel has basic singles/
doubles at similar prices. It's a beautiful,
large house with simple rooms. Buses stop
right outside the *Mandarin House*, which
has rooms for just P40 and up.

Places to Eat

Food in the resort hotels tends to be
expensive – eat in San Fernando. The
Mandarin Restaurant has reasonably
priced food and there are lots of cheap
snack places around. A number of them
offer complete fixed-price meals at P12 to
15. Places to try include the *New Society
Restaurant* opposite the market and the
Mid-Town Food Palace on Quezon Avenue.

Getting There

From Baguio buses take two hours and
cost P10. It's a nice trip down the winding
road to the coast. Try to sit on the left side
for the best views. From Manila direct
buses take six hours and you can also get
there by train although it takes a bit
longer. From Alaminos buses go via
Lingayen and Dagupan. You can take a big
Pantranco bus or a minibus; you have to
change buses at Dagupan. The whole trip
takes about three hours.

BAGUIO

At an altitude of about 1500 metres,
Baguio is much cooler than Manila and for
this reason it once served as a summer
capital. It's still popular as an escape from
the lowlands' heat. It's a laze-around
place with plenty of parks and an interesting market, also good for buying
handicrafts although you have to bargain
aggressively in order to get a good price.

In La Trinidad, the province capital just
to the north of the city, visit the governor's
offices and see the Kabayan mummies.
These remarkably well-preserved mummified bodies were brought from burial
caves in the north. Baguio is also famed for
its 'faith healers' to whom many people
flock each year. To most travellers,
however, Baguio's main role is as a
gateway to the Mountain Province and the
rice terraces.

Places to Stay

Out of town near the Easter School on
Easter Rd *St Mary's Pension House* has a
P35 dorm (P28 for YHA members) and
rooms at P95/120 (P45/85 for YHA
members). The *Patria de Baguio* on
Session Rd also has a dorm at P22 plus
rooms with bath at P75/95. At 36 General
Luna Rd the *Emerald Inn* (tel 6115) has
small rooms at P20 but the toilets are not
very clean.

A little uphill on the same road the
Silvertone Branch Inn is run by pleasant
people and has reasonable but small
rooms from P35/50 up to P100 for a

double with bath. The neat and clean *Happiness Restaurant* is also here. Behind the big Hilltop Hotel at 17 Hilltop St is the *Silvertone Lodge* with tidy rooms with big beds for P40/50.

The *Travellers' Lodge* (tel 5444) at 60 Lakandula St has rooms at P35 per person and is quite good. There are other similar lodges on the same street. Near the Philippine Rabbit bus station on Lapu Lapu St the *Baguio Garden Inn* has rooms at P40/60 or with bath at P90/130. Also near the bus station is the *Leisure Lodge* on Magsaysay Avenue with clean doubles for P50. Nearly opposite the terminal is the *Hotel Linda* with good rooms at P25/50 with bath.

The *Diamond Inn* (tel 2339) on E Jacinto St has dorm beds at P32, regular rooms at P70 for singles, from P90 for doubles. The rooms with bath are expensive. On Session Rd the *Mido Hotel* (tel 2575) is a good, clean place with rooms at P50/80 or with bath a double is P120. The *Everlasting Hotel* on the corner of Magsaysay Avenue and Session Rd has clean singles/doubles from P60/75.

The *Colorado Inn* (tel 4941) on Prefecta St is a bit dark and gloomy and has rooms from P70. On Harrison Rd the *Greenland Hotel* (tel 4080) has regular rooms from P70 to 100, with bath from P130 to 100. Rooms near the reception desk tend to be noisy and overall it is only so-so. Centrally located at 90 Albanao St the *Attic Inn* (tel 5139) is more expensive with big rooms for four at P200.

Places to Eat

The *Kayang Restaurant* on Magsaysay St changes its menu daily. On Session Rd the *Shakey's Pizza Parlour* has an entrance which is easy to miss. At the *Ganza Steak & Chicken House* at the Solibao in Burnham Park you can eat outside.

There are various other restaurants along Session Rd, Baguio's main street. The *456 Restaurant* is pretty good in most respects although prices are cheaper for locals, in the front, than tourists, in the back. Opposite the PAL office the *Fili Deli Restaurant* has good sandwiches. At the other end of Session Rd is the rather expensive *Amapola Cafe*.

Still on Session Rd there's *Mario's Restaurant* and the *Star Cafeteria* (good for hearty breakfasts). *Munchies Paradise* has pizzas, ice cream and cheap beer. Opposite the market *Lucky's Bake House & Restaurant* is clean and quite cheap. *Kem's* on General Luna Rd has good food and cheap beer. On Mabini St, one block from Session St, *Rickham's* is a new place with good food at reasonable prices.

Nightlife

Try the *Ginger Bread Man* and the *Fire Place* for folk music. Or the *Cosy Nook Folk House* opposite the Fire Place.

Getting There

Manila-Baguio costs around P35; PNR, Pantranco and Dagwa all have good services on this route. The trip takes about five or six hours and there are buses every half hour or so plus air-con buses (P70) several times a day. You can also reach Baguio from San Fernando, only an hour away on the coast. Pantranco buses drop you on the outskirts of town while Dangwa buses run right into the centre.

MOUNTAIN PROVINCES

Starting 100 km north-east of Baguio the mountain provinces are famed for their interesting tribes and the spectacular rice terraces. If you've spent much time in South-East Asia going to a place just to see more rice terraces seems a little weird, but these are something else. Some 2000 to 3000 years ago the Ifugao tribespeople carved terraces out of the mountainsides around Banaue which are as perfect today as they were then. They run like stepping stones to the sky – up to 1500 metres high – and if stretched end to end would extend over 20,000 km. The Ifugao people are still, in the more remote areas, quite primitive, although headhunting is no longer a hobby!

Getting There

You can approach the Mountain Province from two directions. The more spectacular route is by the rough winding mountain road that climbs up from Baguio to Bontoc, the main town in the region. From there you can make a variety of side trips to places like Sagada or continue on to Banaue, the main town for rice terraces.

The faster alternative route is direct from Manila via the Nueva Viscaya province – on good roads the bus trip only takes seven to eight hours. From Baguio it's a similar distance to Bontoc and another three or four hours to Banaue. The Baguio-Bontoc-Banaue road is often cut during the wet season; but it's far more interesting so you should try to make the trip in at least one direction by this route.

July-August is the wettest period. The road reaches a height of 2000 metres, the highest road in the Philippines. Dangwa is the main bus operator for services north of Baguio.

BONTOC

Bontoc is the first major town you come to from Baguio and the main town of the area. It's possible to walk from here to the villages of the Igorot people – they built their rice terraces with stone dykes, unlike the earth terraces of Banaue. Take food and water for yourself and dried fish or gifts for the villagers. The village of Maligcong is a two or three-hour walk into the mountains. You have to follow a narrow creek for about 200 metres before you reach the footpath leading to the village. It's not a bad idea to take a guide with you. Always ask permission before taking photographs of the people here.

Bontoc has an excellent museum run by the local Catholic mission. The Belgian nun who came out here in 1925 and was a local expert on the hill tribes died recently but her replacement is equally enthusiastic. The museum includes a typical village of native huts – Bontoc as it was prior to the American period. Plus many headhunting relics and Chinese vases – a P5 donation is all it costs. Bontoc is a good place to buy locally woven materials, woodcarvings and other handicrafts of the Mountain Provinces.

Places to Stay

Bontoc seems to have suffered even more than most from the traditional Filipino hotel fate – fire. The *Bus Stop Lodge* and *Mountain Hotel*, both popular cheapies, have been burnt out! The *Mountain Hotel* is back in operation in a new concrete (fireproof?) building and has rooms at P25. The popular *Happy Home*, opposite the bus stop, has good accommodation at P20 per person. It's a stone building with pleasant rooms and the knowledgeable young couple who run it provide good food.

The *Bontoc Hotel* has rooms in the same price bracket. It's clean, has good food and is near the bus stop. The *Chico River Inn Hotel* has singles/doubles at P25/45 and is also run by helpful people. The *Pines Kitchenette & Inn* is more expensive but there are a variety of rooms and you can bargain. A single without bath can go for as low as P60 although rooms are normally P120 or more. There's also a good, although slightly pricey, restaurant here and it's about five minutes' walk from the bus stop.

Food is pretty good in Bontoc – try the great cinnamon rolls in the local bakery. Bontoc is also a centre for the Filipino passion for dog meat – about which there has been much controversy in the west of late. 'Cheap and not bad,' reported one dog-loving traveller.

Getting There

There are four or fives buses daily between Baguio and Bontoc, generally departing in the early morning from the Baguio bus station. The fare is P85 and the 150 km trip takes seven or eight hours. On from Bontoc to Banaue there is usually a bus every day but here, as elsewhere in the Mountain Provinces, transport is somewhat unreliable. Departure of this bus is usually at 8 am; between 11 am and 12.30 pm there may be another. The trip takes two or three hours and costs P38. If you can't find a bus you can charter a jeepney for around P140.

SAGADA

Only 18 km from Bontoc the village of Sagada is famed for its burial caves. Take a 10 am bus there one day and the 1 pm bus back the next. The local people are friendly and it's also a good place to buy local weaving. The cliff-face burial caves here are somewhat similar to those of the Toraja people of Sulawesi in Indonesia. You'll probably need a local guide and some sort of light to explore the caves.

Places to Stay

The places to stay in this popular little town all seem to follow a standard charging policy – P20 per person. *Julias' Guest House* is very popular – 'quaint, charming, cosy and rustic', was how one traveller described it and many others have gone on in a similar vein. There's also great vegetarian food here for P15, including as much tea or coffee as you want. There are even flowers on the tables!

Other places include the *St Joseph Guest House*, across from the hospital where the bus stops. It's also friendly and well kept and the food is superb value. *Sagada Pension*, about a km up the hill from Sagada itself, is new, clean and has hot water. Or there's the *Sagada Guest House*, formerly Daoa's Lodging, run by the local schoolteacher, which once again is a pleasant place and does good meals, particularly breakfast.

You can also eat at the convent, close to the church. The *Shamrock Cafe* and the *Moonhouse Cafe* are other good places. The food at the latter is very good and the bar is the 'in' place to spend the evening. Banana cake is a Sagada speciality which all the places serve.

Getting There

Skyland Motor Express has daily buses direct from Baguio to Sagada. The trip takes seven hours and costs P60. It's difficult to day trip from Bontoc to Sagada, even though it's only an hour away, because the number of buses is limited. The fare is P10.

BANAUE

From Bontoc the road turns south and runs through incredibly spectacular countryside to Banaue, the heart of the terrace country. It's a narrow, rough and slow road – but what a view. Take the right side of the bus to appreciate it best.

There are many hiking trails in the vicinity of Banaue – details from the youth hostel. Batad is one of the best viewpoints and takes two hours to walk to after an 11 km jeepney ride from the town – around P250 return. There are a number of small places to stay in Batad but it's still rather touristy. Near Batad there's a delightful waterfall with good swimming. The Ifugao villages and the handicraft centres in Banaue are also worth visiting.

Places to Stay & Eat

Banaue There are plenty of small places to stay here, mainly in the P15 to 30 range. The town also appears to have suffered from fires although the popular *Wonder Lodge* is back in operation with rooms at P15 to 25 per person and a new extension. Right at the bottom of the price scale the *Adespa Lodge* is dirt simple, but good value.

Near the market the *Val Greg Hotel* costs from P30 for a single, P50 for a double with bathroom. The *Half-Way Inn* is P20 per person and is a well-kept, orderly place with a very good restaurant. It's right in the village, down the hill from the Val Greg, and just a few metres away is the very pleasant *Stairway Lodge* where the rooms have balconies. It's a new place with doubles around P60. The *Traveller's Inn* is P15 per person including the use of cooking facilities.

Behind the city hall the *Banaue Youth Hostel* is dorm style at P25 for members (a student card will do) or P48 for non-members. There are hot showers here and it's very clean, but food is expensive. Other places include the *You & I Lodge*, *Vegas Lodge* and the *Family Hotel* in the Commercial Center. The *Folkhouse* has good folk music and there's excellent, though slightly upmarket, food in the *Terrace Restaurant*, overlooking the terraces.

Batad The *Hillside Inn* costs P10 per person; other places, such as *Jubilyn's* in the village itself, are a bit cheaper.

Getting There

Manila-Banaue direct costs P95 with Pantraco or Dangwa and takes seven or eight hours. The Pantranco bus operates from Quezon City. If you miss the direct bus take a bus to Cagayan Valley – about five hours to Solano from where jeepneys run to Banaue in another two or three hours.

There is a direct daily bus between Baguio and Banaue via Bayombong. It leaves at 5 to 5.30 am and takes seven to eight hours (only four hours according to some travellers). Either way it's much faster than the long and arduous, though interesting, Baguio-Bontoc-Banaue trip.

ILOCOS

On the northern part of the west coast there are some more pleasant beaches and the interesting town of Vigan. You can continue north from Vigan to Laoag, Claveria and Aparri and even loop right around the north coast via Tuguegarao.

Getting There

Philippine Rabbit buses from Manila for Laoag go through Vigan. The trip takes six to eight hours and costs P50. You can also reach Vigan from Baguio via San Fernando or by the coast from 100 Islands and Dagupan, again via San Fernando.

VIGAN

North of San Fernando, this interesting old town was second only to Manila during the Spanish era. If you're interested in old Spanish architecture and ancient-looking churches this region of Ilocos North is prime hunting ground. The Jose Burgos Museum behind the capitol building has lots of old antiques, paintings, photographs and the curator is delighted to tell tourists' of the history of the area. The Sequirino Museum on Quirino St is the old house of former President Quirino.

It's fascinating just wandering around the town, taking in the narrow streets, listening to the clip-clop of horse-drawn caleasas. 'Vigan,' according to one traveller, 'is the only town in the Philippines with a population of 10,000 or more without a single disco. Local teenagers sit around the cathedral and discuss theology.' Puerto Beach is a pleasant fishing village just out of Vigan.

Places to Stay

There are lots of places in Vigan like the *Village Inn* on the corner of Bonifacio and Plaridel St with rooms with fan at P35/50 or with fan and bath at P60/100. It's a beautiful old Spanish house with a view of a neighbouring haunted house from the balcony!

Two hundred metres down Bonifacio St is *Grandpa's Inn* with rooms from P30/60 (for a bare, fanless room) up to P100 and 150 for better rooms. It's a nice place run by friendly people. The *Cordillera Inn* is on the corner of Mena Crislogo St and General Luna St and has rooms with fan for P40, with air-con and bath for around P100 to 120.

The *Vigan Hotel* on Burgos St has rooms with fan at P60/100, more expensive with air-con. The cheaper *Venus Inn* on Quezon Avenue is P35/45 for rooms with fan, P95/110 with air-con. On General Luna St the simple *Luzon Hotel* has rooms with fan at P25/50. The *Plaza Inn* is similarly priced but not very clean.

Places to Eat

The *Tower Cafe* on Burgos St (corner of the main plaza, opposite the cathedral) has excellent sandwiches and superb barbecued pork satay and at very reasonable prices. There's great ice cream at the *Vigan Plaza Restaurant* in Florentino St.

The *Venus Inn* has a large restaurant or try the *Victory Restaurant* on Quezon Avenue and the lovely open-air restaurant behind the Vigan Hotel on Quirino Boulevard. On Quezon Avenue *Cheryl's Snack Bar* is a large Vigan pub and is open till after 9 pm.

South Luzon

The Bicol region is composed of four provinces and two islands (Catanduanes and Masbate). Plenty of buses and trains run here from Manila and you can fly. The number one attraction of the Bicol region is the majestic Mayon volcano, claimed to be the most perfectly symmetrical volcano cone in the world.

Getting There

You can get south to the Bicol region from Manila by bus or rail. Buses to Legaspi all pass through Naga. Pantranco buses depart from the terminal on Taft Avenue in Pasay and the trip takes nine to 11 hours. There are also air-con buses at night, leaving at 7 and 8 pm. The fare to Legaspi ranges from P100 to 150 depending on the bus.

Trains south depart from the Paco Station on Quirino Avenue – take a Santa Ana jeepney from the Ermita area. There are a variety of trains but the 4 pm Mayon

Limited or the 7 pm Mayon Limited Special are the fastest and most comfortable. Like the buses they run through Naga (11 hours) but the trains do not actually terminate in Legaspi. In the mid-70s a flood from the volcano cut the line and it has never been reopened. The trains, therefore, terminate at Camalig from where you continue the last few km into Legaspi. If you're heading straight through to Legaspi get a train ticket that includes the final bus trip. You can then step right off the train into a PNR bus. Train fares on these faster services vary from around P50 to over P100 for the more expensive air-con sleepers. Get tickets early in the day or book well ahead.

If you're continuing south from the Laguna area, below Manila, you'll probably find it easier to travel by bus rather than train. There are more services and ticketing is easier.

Getting Around

There are a lot of bus and jeepney services around the Bicol region. For Tiwi take a Tabaco bus from Quezon Avenue in Legaspi and then a jeepney to Tiwi. Finally a tricycle to the hot springs area. The ferry to Virac in Catanduanes departs Tabaco each day at noon, the crossing takes four hours.

Continuing south to Sorsogon there are JB buses every half hour and the trip takes 1½ hours. Jeepneys continue to Matnog in one hour. There are also direct Pantranco buses from Legaspi to Matnog, but these

tend to be booked out as they come straight through from Manila.

THINGS TO BUY

In south Luzon, abaca products are the main craft. Abaca is a fibre produced from a relative of the banana tree. It's best-known end-product was the rope known as Manila hemp (as opposed to Indian hemp, produced from fibre from the marijuana plant!) but today it's made into all manner of woven products including bags or place mats. Pili nuts are a popular favourite of the Bicol region. Around Daraga you can find oddities like marble eggs from Romblon or whole suites of furniture made from used car tyres! Interesting pottery can be found in Tiwi.

NAGA

The otherwise uninteresting town of Naga is the site for the late-September Penafrancia festival, a huge and colourful procession down the river through the town.

Places to Stay

The *Fiesta Lodge* on Paganiban St, close to the town centre by the middle bridge, has straightforward rooms at P20/40 or with bath at P35/50. On the same street the *Emerald Resthouse* is P25/30, but it also has a short-time clientele.

The *Naga Guest House* (tel 2503) on B Burgos St has rooms from P30 right up to P100 for the best rooms with air-con and attached bathroom. The *Fiesta Hotel* (tel 2760) on Padian St is also a good, simple place with rooms starting from P25/40 and going up towards P100 for the best rooms with air-con. The *Crown Hotel* is right in the same price bracket. It's in the town centre on Plaza Martinez, over-looking the Martyrs' Square, the San Francisco Church and Pantranco bus terminal.

Out at the station, which is a tricycle ride from the centre, there are a string of cheapies (turn left as you leave the station) like the extremely basic (but very

cheap) *PNR Lodging*. More expensive places include the *Lindez Hotel* (tel 2414) on Burgos St with rooms from P35/50 or at P90/100 with air-con. The *Plaza Holiday Hotel* on Plaza Martinez is similarly priced.

Places to Eat

Under the Crown Hotel the *Crown Restaurant* offers air-con comfort or you could try the clean and comfortable *Graceland* at 58 Elias Angeles St. *Peppermill Restaurant* specialises in seafood and steaks while spaghetti at *Mama's Steakhouse* is also good value. The *Naga Restaurant* is good too.

SAN MIGUEL BAY

There is an interesting detour on the route south which takes you by some good beaches around San Miguel Bay. First you travel to Daet (buses run there from Manila), then take a jeepney to Mercedes from where a boat departs every morning at 11 for the other side of the bay.

You've got a short walk from Takal to Siruma and from there you can take another boat to Bagacay, the harbour for Naga. There are good beaches at Mercedes and on Old Siruma Island, just off Siruma.

Places to Stay

In Daet the *Alegre Hotel* on Justo Lukban St has rooms from P35/50. On Wincon Avenue the *Mines Hotel* is slightly more expensive. On the same street the *Karigalan Hotel* has rooms at P45/65, more expensive with air-con. There's also the *Sampaguita* and a variety of restaurants.

IRIGA & LAKE BUHI

About mid-way between Naga and Legaspi, Iraga is the jumping off point for visits to Lake Buhi where the smallest food-fish in the world are netted (with tiny mesh nets!). There's a danger of the lake being overfished.

Places to Stay

Just as you come into town from Naga, the *Lemar Hotel* (tel 594) on San Nicolas St has rooms from P40. Other basic cheapies include the *Crown Hotel, Pearl Hotel* and *Gem Hotel*. The *Bayanihan Hotel* (tel 556), on the street where the jeepneys stop, close to the railway line, has air-con rooms but also some cheaper ones from P50.

The flashy *Ibalon Hotel*, below the grotto on the hill, has a hostel but it's not great value. While in Iriga or Buhi try the 'omelette of a thousand fishes' made with the tiny sinarapan or taybos, the minute fish caught in nearby Lake Buhi. You can have a 1000-fish omelette in the Ibalon Hotel for breakfast.

MAYON

Derived from the word 'beautiful' in the local dialect, Mayon is claimed to be the world's most perfect volcano cone. You can best appreciate it from the ruins of Cagsawa church. In 1814 Mayon erupted disastrously, killing 1200 people including those who took shelter in the church. To get to Cagsawa take a jeepney bound for Camalig and alight at the Cagsawa sign, from where it's a few minutes' walk. Mayon is said to erupt every 10 years and recently it's been doing even better than that. The spectacular eruption in 1968 was followed by another in 1978 and then another in late 1984. Thousands of people were evacuated from around the volcano during the 1984 eruption.

If you want to appreciate Mayon from closer up you can climb it in a couple of days – the tourist office in Legaspi will fix you up. Usual cost for two people inlcuding a guide, porter and tent is US$50. Provisions are extra. You can also try hiring your own guides and porters in Buyuhan for a standard daily charge of P25 to 35. I climbed Mayon once with Ricardo Dey, who has been up it many times since his first ascent in 1951.

The first day's climb takes you up through the forest to the start of the lava area. Day two is a hard scramble through loose lava to the top – don't stay too long, the fumes are powerful – then a rapid descent back down. You can climb from the Legaspi side (safer and more interesting, but a lower-level starting point) or from the northern side, starting at the Mayon Rest House (higher starting point but difficult to get to).

If you can't climb the volcano the Mayon Rest House is a good view point, 800 metres up the 2450-metre volcano. There's also a small volcanology musum here and a fantastic view, but the rest house is semi-derelict and you must bring your own bedding and food if you intend to stay. To get there take a Naga-bound bus from Tabaco to the turn-off. Then walk or hitch the eight km to the rest house. Or hire a jeepney from Tabaco.

LEGASPI

The main city of the Bicol region hugs the waterfront in the shadow of Mayon. See the memorial to the Filipinos who died opposing the American invasion in 1900. The 'headless monument' to those who died at the hands of the Japanese in WW II is sadly neglected. In the St Raphael Church on Aguinaldo St (across from the Rex Hotel), the altar is a 10-tonne volcanic rock from Mayon. Legaspi is actually divided into two parts. Inland from the port area is the Albay area of the town. Here you will find the tourist office beside Penaranda Park and near the cathedral. The two areas are linked by Rizal Avenue.

Places to Stay

There are plenty of cheap hotels around Legaspi but none of them are going to win any prizes for high accommodation standards. On Magallanes St, close to the centre of town, the *Ideal Hotel* has rooms at P30 per person, but you can bargain a little. The rooms are not all that clean, as with quite a few other Legaspi places. On Mabini St the *Legazpi Lodging House* has rooms from P25 but is also not very special.

There is quite a choice along Penaranda St, parallel to the waterfront. Right next to the railway station the *Ritz Pension House* is fairly typical – illuminated Jesus dioramas, sacred hearts and even full-length horizontal mirrors by the beds. All for P35-100 depending on the room. Other places along the street include the *Hotel Xandra* with rooms from P40 to 120. At the junction with Rizal St the *Mayon Hotel* is more expensive.

Next-door to the post office on Quezon Avenue is the rock-bottom-priced *Rolit Rest House*. Across the road from the Rex Theatre, but on E Aguinaldo St, is the *Rex* with rooms from P50 to 150. It's a good place with rooms with bathrooms, with and without air-con. One of Legaspi's best bargains, even though it is a bit more expensive, is the *Albay Hotel* further up Penaranda St. For P85 you can have a single with fan, shower, toilet, hot water and even a balcony with views of Mayon! It bridges the gap to Legaspi's top end hotels and has rooms all the way up to P150 for an air-con double.

Outside of Legaspi at Camalig, where the train stops, the *Villagomar Resort* is a great place to stay with a good outdoor pool, a restaurant and rooms from P40. It's booked out in the summer but empty in the winter.

Places to Eat

Legaspi offers a wide choice of places to eat – like *Wah Foo Chan*, almost next-door to the Rex Theatre, the *Peking* a couple of doors down and the *New Legaspi*, across Penaranda St. All are clean-looking places offering all-inclusive meals. The food is basically Chinese with some Filipino dishes. Try the *New Legaspi's* pineapple pie for a special treat. The *New Shangai* looks much more expensive than it turns out to be.

The *Family's Bakery*, near the Ritz, has good and reasonably cheap Filipino food and also does great pan de sal bread rolls in the morning. Try the *Filipino Restaurant* on Penaranda St; it has a special rep-

utation locally for Filipino food. Watch out for the 'Bicol express' here; dishes with red-hot peppers that get you running for relief at express speed.

Others to try include the *Hongkong Dimsum & Tea House* on Penaranda St or the *Shangrila Restaurant* on the same street. Finally the *Great Wall Palace* on Magallanes St is the place for all sorts of ice cream treats including a far-out halo halo. It's also the only ice cream parlour I've ever seen with an armed guard at the door!

AROUND LEGASPI

After the destruction of Cagsawa the church was rebuilt in an ornate baroque style at nearby Daraga – sensibly placed high up on a hill. It's just a short jeepney ride from Legaspi. There are some other ruins at Budia, about two km from Cagsawa, not so interesting and many of them have now been washed away. The interesting Hoyohoyopan Caves are about 10 km from Camalig – hire a tricycle there and back or take a jeepney. In Camalig the church has artifacts that were excavated from the caves in 1972.

TIWI

The hot springs at Tiwi are a bit of a letdown. They've been commercialised in very bad taste. Also the development of geothermal power plants in the area has pretty well dried up the hot springs. The hostel here is still a very pleasant place to stay while you explore the area – beaches, bubbling pools of hot mud, steam issuing from the ground, the geothermal plant and some interesting old church ruins in the town of Tiwi.

Places to Stay

About three km beyond the town of Tiwi you'll find the *Tiwi Youth Hostel*, actually at the hot springs – it's less than P1 by tricycle. This place is in quite a different league from the usual youth hostel. There are rooms at P100 plus cheaper new cottages in the gardens from P40. Costs are lower with a YHA or student card. The hostel also has a spring-fed swimming pool and hot spring fed bath downstairs. Plus there's a casually run restaurant with fairly uninspiring food. Alternatively you can try the more expensive *Tiwi Hot Springs Resort Hotel*, near the youth hostel.

CATANDUANES
This island, east of Legaspi, can be reached by ferry from Tabaco or by air from Legaspi. There are some excellent beaches, good snorkelling and pleasant waterfalls, but very few tourists come this way. The main town and accommodation centre is Virac.

Places to Stay
In the main town of the Catanduanes Islands you can stay at the very cheap *Cherry Don*, right on the central town square, with rooms from P20 per person. Or there's the more expensive *Catanduanes Hotel* on San Jose St with rooms with fan at P60/90.

Eat at the *Appetizer*, just around the corner from the central town square.

SORSOGONON
This is the southernmost province of Luzon and is really just a transit region to the Visayan islands. You can visit volcanic Lake Bulusan or the long stretch of unexciting Rizal Beach at Gubat. Or take the ferry across to Samar from Matnog or to Masbate from Bulan.

Places to Stay
The *Dalisay Hotel* in Sorsogonon is simple and clean with rooms from P40 to 100. The *Al-Mon Lodge* is similar. At the *Rizal Beach Resort Hotel* there are rooms from P55 and also private cottages.

In Bulusan you can stay in the *Lodging House* behind the town hall where rooms cost about P40.

Getting There
Buses from Legaspi to Irosin and Matnog go via Sorsogon. The trip takes 1½ hours.

MATNOG
Right at the southern tip of Luzon, this is the departure point for boats to Allen on Samar.

Places to Stay
The *Seaside Eatery* and *Villa's Inn* both have very simple rooms for P15. The dock is only a few steps away.

Getting There
Buses run to Irosin from Legaspi, from where you continue by jeepney. You can do the trip with all connections in 3½ hours. There are also direct Pantranco buses, but the bus comes straight through from Manila and it can be difficult to get a seat. Coming from Allen there are usually jeepneys waiting to meet the ferry.

Other Islands

Although Luzon is the main island and offers a lot of things to see and do, that is only the start – there are still nearly 7000 islands left to explore. The majority of these 'other islands' are in the group known as the Visayas. This tightly-packed scattering of islands lies between Luzon to the north and Mindanao to the south. The main Visayan islands are Samar, Leyte, Bohol, Cebu, Negros, Panay and Romblon. It is in these islands that you can really come to grips with Filipino island-hopping. With so many islands, so many ferries and boats and such relatively short distances, the possibilities are immense.

Cebu, the central Visayan island, is the

travel centre of the group and the capital, Cebu City, is one of the most historic and interesting cities in the Philippines, as well as being second in size only to Manila. It was here that Magellan landed on his epic circumnavigation of the world and here that the Spaniards first claimed the Philippines.

At the extreme south of the Philippines is the large island of Mindanao. This is the second largest of the Philippine islands and the centre for much of the Philippines' unrest. The predominantly Muslim Mindanaoans have campaigned long and hard for separation from the rest of the country. Then there is Palawan, the long, narrow island that almost looks like a bridge from Luzon to the Malaysian state of Sabah. It has been described as the last frontier of the Philippines. Very close to Luzon and easily reached from that island, Mindoro has become a very popular escape area due to its beautiful beaches and laid-back accommodation possibilities. Finally, sandwiched between Mindoro and Luzon, is the smaller island of Marinduque.

THINGS TO BUY
In Cebu you'll find lots of shell jewellery and guitars. Making guitars is a big business on Mactan Island near Cebu City. They vary widely in price and quality. In Cebu City the guitar alley is Lincoln St where you will also find cheaper ukeleles.

Iloilo is also known for its shellcraft and for fabrics, particularly the pina fabric used to make barong shirts. This is also a good town in which to look for 'santos', antique statues of the saints. Other Visayan buys include baskets in Bohol, ceramics in Bacolod and marble items from Romblon.

In Mindanao the barter trade market in Zamboanga is somewhat overrated. Because the smuggling instinct was so ingrained the government gave up fighting and legalised it in this one market only. There you will find everything from Indonesian

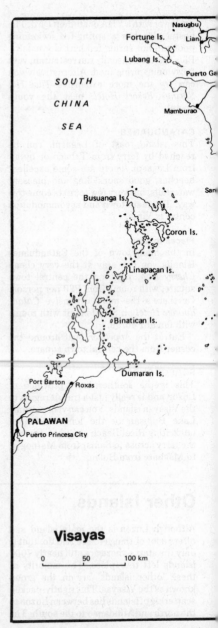

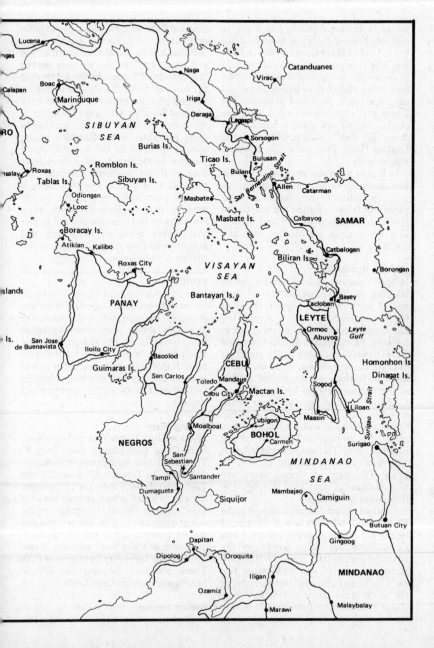

batiks to Japanese radios. But if you've recently been to Yogya in Indonesia (for the batiks) or Hong Kong (for the radios), you'll be unimpressed. For local crafts go to the neighbouring central market – some interesting stalls can be found in amongst the vegetables, meat and produce. The Rocan shell shop is worth a look if you like shells. Badjao sea gypsies bob up and down in their outriggers beside the Lantaka Hotel. They sell shells, coral and ship models.

In Davao, once you've checked out the brassware, jewellery and handicrafts, devote your time to sampling the amazing variety of fruits – durian are the Davao speciality. Cagayan de Oro and Marawi City are centres for Moslem arts and crafts.

ISLAND HOPPING

In the Visayas, possibilities for island hopping in the Philippines are at their best. A possible island-hopping circuit of the Visayas could take you to most of the places of interest with minimal backtracking. Starting from Manila you could travel down to the Bicol region and from Matnog at the southern tip of the island there are ferries every day across to Allen at the northern end of Samar. The new road down the west coast of Samar means it is now a quick and relatively easy trip through Calbayog and Catbalogan then across the bridge to Tacloban on the island of Leyte. This was where MacArthur 'returned' towards the end of WW II. From Tacloban or Ormoc there are regular ships to Cebu City or less regularly from Maasin to Bohol.

Cebu was where Magellan arrived in the Philippines and there are a number of reminders of the Spanish period. From Cebu there are daily ferries to the island of Bohol. Its 'Chocolate Hills' are strangely rounded and look rather like daily between Cebu and Negros, either in the south of the island to Dumaguete or closer to Cebu City from Toledo to San Carlos. You can then continue by bus to

Bacolod from where ferries cross to Iloilo on Panay.

Panay has the usual assortment of bus and jeepney routes plus the only railway line outside of Luzon. At the north-west tip you can make the short crossing by outrigger to the beautiful and laid back island of Boracay. After a spell of lazing on the beach there you can find another to cross to Tablas in the Romblon group, usually to Looc in the south. Take a jeepney to Odiongan and a boat from there to Roxas in Mindoro. Another bus ride will take you to Puerto Galera, a popular travellers' beach centre. Finally there are daily ferries to Batangas, only a few hours by bus from Manila. Altogether that makes quite an interesting and adventurous loop taking in most of the islands of the Visayas.

BOHOL

It's a short ferry trip from Cebu City to the island of Bohol. It's 'Chocolate Hills' are strangely rounded and look rather like chocolate drops when the vegetation turns brown in the dry season. They are about 60 km from Tagbilaran, the main town. Bohol is an easygoing, quiet sort of place with some fine beaches, relatively untouched forests and interesting old churches.

Getting There

There are PAL flights several days a week from Cebu City plus a daily ferry to Tagbilaran (four hours) and a three-times-daily ferry to Tubigon (2½ hours). From Tagbilaran the ferry leaves at 12 midnight; it's wise to board at least an hour ahead of time. Also you can only buy tickets on the day of departure and the office closes at 5 pm! Fare is around P30 and you can sleep on board in Cebu until morning. From Tubigon the fares vary from around P20. There are less frequent services to Mindanao, Camiguin and Leyte.

Getting Around

Several buses daily make the 1½-hour trip

between Tagbilaran and Tubigon. Carmen, the town for the Chocolate Hills, is 58 km from Tagbilaran – everybody on the bus will assume you're going there so there is no chance of missing the place where you get off. There is a bus every 30 to 60 minutes; the fare is P14. It's about two hours by bus between the Chocolate Hills and Tubigon.

TAGBILARAN

You can make day trips from Tagbilaran, the capital and main port, to Bikini Beach on nearby Panglao Island. It's difficult to get to by jeepney, better to hire a tricycle. Alona Beach on the same island is also good. There's a cave lake in the Hinagdanan Cave at Dauis, but the cave is full of bats so the water is not all that clean for swimming. Hire a tricycle for P15 for the 14 km trip there or take a JG jeepney for Panglao. Baclayon, six km from Tagbilaran, has the oldest stone church in the Philippines, dating from 1595.

Places to Stay

There are rooms with fan at P25 per person at the *New Life Hotel*. On Lesage Street the *Vista Lodge* is good value with rooms from P30, more with bath or aircon. The *Executive Inn* is cheap and very basic, ditto for the *Clifftop Hotel*. The *Gie Garden Hotel* is nice but rooms are over P100. Great food there, especially the calamari. The *La Roca Hotel* on Graham Avenue is excellent value at P125/160, and there's even a swimming pool.

The *Majestique Restaurant* is opposite the community hospital and has excellent hamburgers. The *Bistro de Paris*, next to the Plaza, does 'French hamburgers', whatever they might be. Good food also at the *Horizon Restaurant* at the bus station.

CHOCOLATE HILLS

Legends relate that the Chocolate Hills are either the teardrops of a heartbroken giant or the debris from a battle between two giants, but the scientific explanation for these curiously similarly shaped hills is more mundane. They're the result of volcanic eruptions at the time when this area was submerged. The hills (there are about 50 in all) are around 30 metres high and hiking in the area is best in the December-May dry season. At this time they are also most 'chocolate-like' since the vegetation has turned brown.

Places to Stay

The *Chocolate Hills Complex* is right in amongst the hills, about 53 km from Tagbilaran. It's a km off the main road on the top of the highest hill. Cottages (doubles) are P80, the hostel dorm is P20. There's also a swimming pool and a quite good restaurant.

CAMIGUIN

Located off the north coast of Mindanao this is an idyllic little get-away-from-it-all sort of place. The name is pronounced 'come again!'. The tiny island actually has seven volcanoes, best known of which is Hibok-Hibok which last erupted in 1951. The beaches are nothing special, but the people are great.

Getting There

There may be occasional ships from other islands, but the usual route is from Balingoang in Mindanao to Binone on Camiguin. A ferry crosses three times daily and the trip takes about two hours for P6. Leaving Cebu one evening you can reach Cagayan de Oro in 10 hours for P45 in 2nd class, make the 1½-hour bus ride for P13 to Balingoan and then ferry across to Camiguin, arriving mid-afternoon. There are less frequent ships direct from Cagayan de Oro to Binone. Once weekly there are direct ships Bohol-Camiguin and Cebu City-Camiguin.

Getting Around

You can make the 65 km circuit of the island in about eight hours – it's best to go clockwise and start early for the best connections. Mambajao-Binone is made by jeepney as is Binone-Catarman, take a tricyle Catarman-Bonbon. Then a four-km walk and a short tricycle ride from Yumbing to Mambajao. The whole trip costs about P15, but there's only one jeepney a day between Catarman and Mambajao although there are several connections Mambajao-Binone-Catarman.

MAMBAJAO

The capital and main town on the island has most of the accommodation and a bank where you can change travellers' cheques.

Places to Stay

The *Tia Lodging House*, near the Municipal Hall, has rooms for P18 per person. *Julie Jean's* near the church is also cheap. For P25 per person the *Camiguin Travellers' Lodge* is rather noisy in the morning, but still a delightful place – you even get soap and a towel – and the manager is a fund of local information.

Out of town between Agoho and Bugong there are several beach bungalows, some with kitchens, for less than P20 per person. The *Caves Lodging House* has cheap rooms and a restaurant but be careful what they charge you, keep an eye on the bill. Half a km east of Caves is *Yasmin* (there's a sign on the road), with four huts with toilet and shower for P60 double. There's a nice cozy restaurant too. Just a five-minute walk from the town proper at Cabua-an Beach there is *Gue's Cottage* which is clean, quiet and costs P30 for two. There's also accommodation at Binone and Yumbing.

OTHER PLACES

The 1800-metre Hibok-Hibok volcano can be climbed in the dry season – enquire at the tourist department in the Capitol Building, Mambajao. A guide is a good idea because the weather on the mountain is very changeable and it's easy to get lost.

The Katibasan Waterfalls, with good swimming, are three km from Pandan, which in turn is only two km from Mambajao. The small White Island is three km off Yumbing – just a sand spar so there is no shade, but great diving. Count on P40 to 50 to rent a boat for the round trip, arrange a definite time to be picked up.

There are hot springs at Tangub, about three km south-west of Yumbing. Bonbon has some interesting church ruins and a cemetery which is submerged in the sea and only visible at low tide.

CEBU

The most visited of the Visayan islands, Cebu is also the shipping hub of the Philippines. The number of shipping companies and agents in Cebu City and the number of ships at the dock is quite incredible. This is also the place where Magellan first landed in the Philippines so it also has the longest history of European contact.

Getting There

Bohol There are several departures daily between Cebu City and Tagbilaran and Tubigon on Bohol. The crossing takes 2½ hours to Tubigon (P20) and four hours to Tagbilaran (about P30). There is now plenty of transport between Tubigon and the Chocolate Hills so there's no reason to prefer one route over the other.

Camiguin The usual route is Cebu-Cagayan de Oro in Mindanao, then a bus to Balingoan from where ferries run across to Binone three times daily.

Leyte A variety of ships operate between Cebu City and Baybay, Maasin, Ormoc or Tacloban.

Luzon You can fly between Cebu City and Manila or Legaspi. Lots of ships operate between Cebu and Manila; the trip takes about 20 to 24 hours.

Mindanao There are an enormous number of ships operating between Cebu and Mindanao. It takes 10 to 12 hours between Cebu City and Butuan, Cagayan de Oro, Dipolog, Iligan, Ozamis or Surigao. Zamboanga is about 16 hours away, Davao about 24. There are also flights between Cebu City and all those ports.

Negros There are several departures daily between Toledo on Cebu and San Carlos on Negros. the trip takes two or three hours and there are connecting buses between San Carlos and Bacolod. There is also a reasonably regular daily ferry service between San Sebastian and San Jose. This trip only takes an hour. Santander-Tampi and Moalboal-La Libertad are other routes between these narrowly separated islands.

Getting Around

There are several buses daily from the Southern Bus Terminal for the 1½-hour, P8 trip from Cebu City to Toledo on the other coast. You also find buses at the Southern Bus Terminal for Santander and Moalboal, other departure points for Negros. Closer to Cebu City there are jeepneys to Mactan Island, where the airport is located, P2 to Lapu-Lapu on the island. A tricycle to Marigondon Beach costs around P15 to 20.

A taxi from city to airport should be around P25 to 30 including the bridge toll, but negotiate first. There is also an airport bus which costs P5 and runs between PAL's office at Fuente Osmena and the airport. The office is rather inconvenient for anything apart from the YMCA in Cebu City. Jeepneys around Cebu City cost from 65c. PUVs, the local taxi-trucks, are a flat P3. The Southern Bus Terminal in Cebu City is on Rizal Avenue, the Northern Bus Terminal is on MacArthur Boulevard.

CEBU CITY

The capital and main city on the island of Cebu, Cebu City is not all that interesting although it does have Colon St, claimed to be the oldest street in the Philippines. It's quite an easygoing city and there are plenty of places to stay and eat.

Information

The Ministry of Tourism Office is inside Fort San Pedro – explain that you're going into the office and you shouldn't have to pay the fort admission charge. Around the city there are lots of jeepneys and PUVs (Public Utility Vehicles). Colon St is the main street in the town, where you will find most of the restaurants, hotels and travel agencies. If you are arriving or leaving by ship take great care with your valuables – pickpockets are notorious around the dock area of Cebu and it's easy to lose things in the crush. Main offices of the major shipping lines include:

Aboitiz Lines	Juan Luna St
Escana Lines	Pier 4
George & Peter Lines	D Jakosalem St
Sweet Lines	Arellano Blvd
Sulpico Lines	Pier 4, Gothong Bldg
William Lines	Gotiaco Bldg

Things to See

Fort San Pedro The oldest Spanish fort in the country – it was originally built in 1565 by Legaspi to keep out the marauding pirates with whom the Spanish were having more than a little trouble. Today it is gradually being restored and the main entrance is very impressive. The MOT have their office here.

Cross of Magellan A small circular building, opposite the town hall, houses a cross which is said to contain fragments of the actual cross brought here by Magellan and used in the first conversions.

Basilica of San Augustin Opposite the Magellan kiosk is the only basilica in the Far East. The *Santa Nino*, an image of Jesus as a child, was said to have been given by Magellan to Queen Juana on her baptism in 1521. It's the oldest religious relic in the country.

Other There's an interesting small museum in the University of San Carlos and another exhibition with portraits made out of butterfly wings. Overlooking the town in the ritzy Beverley Hills residential area is a gaudy Taoist temple. To get to the temple take a Lahug jeepney and ask to stop at Beverley Hills – you've then got a 1½ km walk (uphill of course). Or take a taxi! Colon St in Cebu is said to be the oldest street in the Philippines but you'd never know it. The interesting Carbon market is at the end of M C Briones St.

Places to Stay

At 61 Jones Avenue, about halfway from Fuenta Osmenta (where the airport bus stops) to the city centre, the *YMCA* (tel 9 2013) has good dormitory accommodation at P30 through to rooms with fan for P32/60. Couples are accepted and it's P5 less if you're a YMCA member. Only about 100 metres away the *Town & Country* (tel 7 8190) is also on Jones Avenue and is reasonably plush and modern. Sometimes known as the Town House, it has singles/doubles for P36/55.

In the same area, down a side street between these two places, is the popular little *Arbel's Pension Hotel* (tel 6 2393) with singles/doubles at P40/48. The address is 57E Jones Avenue. At 165 J Urgello St, about a half km from the Town & Country, the *Royal Pension House* (tel 9 3890) is clean and pleasant with rooms at P50-100.

The *Ruftan Pensione & Cafe* (tel 7 9138) at the corner of Legaspi and Manalili Sts, much closer to the centre, is related to Arbel's. It's a good, clean place, popular with Peace Corps workers, and has simple rooms at P30/60.

In the centre, on P Burgos St opposite the Cebu Cathedral, is the *Patria Cebu* with rooms from P30 to 60 but it's rather grubby. The peaceful *Cebu Mayflower Hotel* (tel 9 1939) is near the Capitol and has rooms from P55 on up to P100 or more with air-con. *Lovena's Inn* (tel 9 9212) on Juan Luna St is nicely central and has rooms from P50/70 with fan up towards P100 with air-con, all with bathroom.

The *Consulate Hotel* (tel 9 6753) on Sikatuna St is a little more expensive with fan-cooled rooms from P55/80. It's a typically lazily decrepit Filipino place, but not bad value. *Elicon House* (tel 7 3653) is on the corner of P del Rosario and General Junquera Sts and has rooms with air-con

1 Tung Yan Restaurant	24 House of Men, Mutya
2 Magellan Hotel, St Moritz Bar & Apartments	25 Tagalog Hotel
	26 Pete's Kitchen
3 Jumalon Museum	27 Jercy's Kitchenette
4 Binamira's Antiques	28 Mercedes Hotel
5 Casa Vasca	29 Cathay Hotel
6 Club 68	30 Snow Sheen Restaurant
7 Iglesia Ni Cristo (Church)	31 Snow Sheen Restaurant
8 Great American, Tuxedo Junction	32 Consulate Hotel
9 Shakey's Pizza	33 Queen's Inn
10 Lawiswis Kawayan	34 Rajah Humabon Hotel
11 Kan Irag Hotel, Bachelors Too Bar	35 Lovena's Inn
12 PAL Office, Airport Bus, Rajah Hotel, Avis Office	36 Ruftan Pensione & Cafe
	37 Ngo Hiong House (Angela's)
13 Barbecue Stalls, Beer Garden	38 Sky Vue Hotel
14 Playgirl, Pow Disco	39 PAL Office
15 Andy's Folkhouse, Before & After Six	40 Patria de Cebu
	41 Carbon Market
16 Town & Country Hotel	42 Basilica Minore Del Santo Nino
17 Arbel's Pension House	43 Magellan's Cross
18 YMCA, American Consulate	44 Eddie's Log Cabin
19 Royal Pension House	45 Plaza Independenzia
20 Elicon House	46 Eddie's Log Cabin
21 Triton Hotel	47 Fort San Pedro, Tourist Office
22 San Carlos University	48 Post Office
23 Our Place	

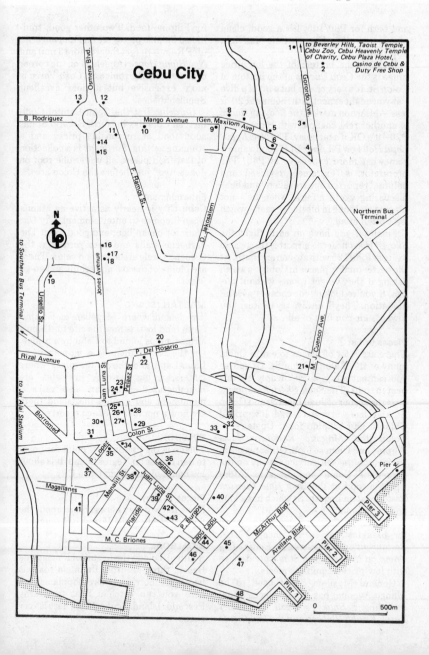

Cebu City

to Beverley Hills, Taoist Temple,
Cebu Zoo, Cebu Heavenly Temple
of Charity, Cebu Plaza Hotel,
Casino de Cebu &
Duty Free Shop

N

0   500m

and bath for P80/105. It's a good, clean place and the Elicon Cafe is right downstairs.

Right at the bottom of the low price range is the *Cebu Queens* at the bottom of Colon St. It's very cheap but a bit of a dive – as you might expect with rooms at P20 or less. At Carbon market the *Lodging House* is another real cheapie with rooms from P20 – it's OK if a bit noisy. The *New Lapu-Lapu Hotel* on P Lopez St is good value if somewhat more expensive at P45. The proprietor is 'extremely civilised and helpful,' reported one traveller, 'and likes discussing world affairs, when he's not playing mahjong in his underwear – which isn't often at all.'

Finally if you have an early flight the *Silayen Hotel* near the airport is reasonable value at P90/125 with air-con and bath. At the better quality places in Cebu it's worth asking if they've got rooms without air-con, if you're looking for cheaper accommodation. They'll always try to steer you towards air-con first of all.

Places to Eat

There are a lot of places to eat in Cebu, many of them along Colon St. Of course you can eat much more cheaply off this beaten track. The *Snow Sheen Restaurant* is on the corner of Juan Luna St and Colon St and has very good and low-priced Chinese and Filipino food. Upstairs on Colon the *Majestic Restaurant* has Filipino and Chinese food. Other places to try include the self-service *Colony* on the corner of Colon and Legaspi. More Chinese food at the *Ding How Dimsum Restaurant* on Legaspi St which has a long and varied menu.

The *Ruftan Cafe* on Legaspi St is good for breakfast, as is the cheap *YMCA Restaurant* on Jones Avenue. *Eddie's Log Cabin* on M C Briones St is a good place with low-priced complete meals.

General Maxilom St (it used to be Mango Avenue) has lots of places to eat including a *Shakey's Pizza*, the *Dairy Farm*, *Kalilili Chicken* and the *Lighthouse*

for Filipino food. Two other good, traditional Filipino places are *La Pampanguena* off F Ramos St (get there before 8 pm) and *Ngo Hiong House* (Angela's) on the corner of Lopez and Borromeo St. *Casa Vasca* is more expensive but it does excellent Spanish dishes.

Gardenia's at the Cebu Capitol Commercial Complex in North Escario St has good food at reasonable prices and a stunning setting. *Fastfoods* is a collection of fast-food places all under one roof on Jones Ave., just before the Colon area.

Entertainment

Cebu City is nearly as active as Manila when it comes to entertainment. Try *Our Place* for cheap beer and good food. The barbecue stalls and beer garden at the Osmena Circle are also good value. There are plenty of discos, nightclubs and go-go joints.

MACTAN ISLAND

The island where Magellan met Lapu-Lapu (and lost) is now the site for Cebu's airport and is joined to Cebu by a bridge. On the island there is a monument to Lapu-Lapu and this is the place where guitars, a big industry in Cebu, are manufactured. Magellan also rates a monument and around the island there are now a number of beach resorts.

TOLEDO

Toledo is the jumping-off point for boats to San Carlos on Negros Island. It is about 1½ hours by bus from Cebu City.

Places to Stay

If you have to stay here enquire about the *Lodging House* at the *Vizcayno Restaurant*.

MOALBOAL

South of Toledo the beautiful Panagsama Beach, three km from the main road, is becoming more and more popular. From here you can catch a boat to nearby Pescador Island. Scuba diving here is very cheap.

Places to Stay

You can stay in town – enquire at the *People's Bakery* – but it's better to rent a cottage on the beach from P15 per person. Try *Pacita's Nipa Hut, Evie's Mabuhay Lodge & Cold Inn, Analou's Cottage, Norma's Travellers' Rest House, Doto's Place* or others. The food's good at *Evie's*.

Getting There

Several buses daily make the 90 km, three-hour trip from Cebu City. A friendly bus driver may even take you right down to the beach; it's worth asking. Otherwise take a tricycle from Moalboal.

Transport between Moalboal and Toledo is tricky and may require several bus changes. Buses run regularly to San Sebastian at the southern of the island, from where ships make the short crossing to Negros.

LEYTE

As is the case with Samar, few westerners get to Leyte, so you can expect to be stared at a lot. Although there are some outstanding national parks and an impressive mountain region there is little tourist development on Leyte. It's notable for being the island where MacArthur fulfilled his promise to return to the Philippines. Towards the end of WW II Allied forces landed here and commenced to push the Japanese out.

Getting There

Between Leyte and Cebu you can fly Tacloban-Cebu City with PAL. Ships operate between Cebu City and Tacloban, Ormoc or Baybay. There are often outriggers between Ubay on Bohol and Maasin on Leyte. Ships also operate between other Bohol and Leyte ports. There are ships between Tacloban and Cagayan de Oro in Mindanao or between Maasin and Surigao or Butuan. A bridge connects Leyte with Samar and there are about 10 buses daily from Tacloban to Catbalogan, Calbayog and all the way to Allen for a fare of P40.

Getting Around

Buses go hourly between Tacloban and Ormoc; the trip takes four to five hours. Ormoc-Baybay and Tacloban-Baybay-Maasin also have regular bus services.

TACLOBAN

The capital of Leyte (and hometown for Mrs Marcos), Tacloban is a small port. There are a variety of shops along Justice Romualdez St which sell local handicrafts. Seven km out of town Red Beach (it isn't red; that was just a WW II code name) is the exact place where MacArthur fulfilled his 'I will return' pledge in October 1944. There's a memorial statue showing MacArthur wading ashore. Take a jeepney there but return by getting another jeepney in the same direction; it loops back via Palo. For a short period Tacloban served as the capital of the Philippines until Manila was liberated. The Tourist Office (MOT) is in the Children's Park near the waterfront.

Places to Stay

There is quite a variety of places to stay in Tacloban. The *Central Lodging House* on the corner of M H Del Pilar and Justice Romualdez Sts is pretty basic and simple, rooms cost from P25/50. *San Juanico Travel Lodge* at 104 Justice Romualdez St has singles/doubles at P30/40 or P40/60 with bath. It's hard to find (no sign) and gets mixed reports – 'clean and friendly' report some travellers, 'a dump,' say others.

The new *Grand Hotel* is good value although more expensive. At 119 Zamora St the *Christian Hostel* is clean, has good facilities and costs from P30, but no sharing rooms if you're not married! *Cecilia's Lodging House* at 178 Paterno St is good and clean, but badly signposted. Rooms cost from P35/50, more expensive with air-con. On Justice Romualdez St again (it's a popular street for cheap hotels), the *Imperial Lodging House* is a simple hotel with rooms from P30 to over P100. Solo male travellers are likely to find themselves introduced, soon after arrival, to a female 'student'.

More expensive places include the *Primerose Hotel* on the corner of Zamora St and Salazar St – rooms range from P75 to 150 with air-con. The *Village Inn* on Imelda Avenue has air-con rooms from P120 to 200. It can get pretty hot in Tacloban – air-con can be worth having. So can running water – the city's water supply is pretty erratic.

Places to Eat

Try the *Moongold Restaurant* on M H Del Pilar St for good and generous servings of Chinese and Filipino food. Other places with the familiar Chinese/Filipino combination are the *Asiatic Restaurant* or the *Savory Steak House*, both on Zamora St. *Felisa's Cafe* on Justice Romualdez St is good for breakfast. *Sergeant Pepper's Pizzeria* is a friendly student place, good for a beer. Try the local speciality, 'binagol', in any bakery.

ORMOC

Just the jumping-off point for boats to Cebu. Near Ormoc is the start of the 50 km 'Leyte Nature Trail' which crosses right over the island from Lake Imelda to Lake Mahagnao.

Places to Stay

Eddie's Inn is 250 metres from the bus terminal and has simple rooms at around P20 on up to P50 for a double with fan. On Bonifacio St the *Hotel Don Felipe* has rooms from P40/65, more expensive with air-con. On the same street the *Pongos Hotel* is virtually identically priced.

OTHER PLACES

From Barauen (bus there from Tacloban) you can visit the magnificent Mahagnao Volcano National Park with a number of walking trails. You can camp near the Lake Imelda National Park where there is a very deep and large crater lake – get there from Ormoc. There are some good diving possibilities around Leyte but they

have not been developed much as yet. You can soak in the Tungonan Hot Springs, just north of Ormoc, but the area has been desecrated by a geothermal project.

Higitagan Island can be reached by taking a bus from Tacloban to Naval. At Naval you can stay at the *LM Lodge* on Vicillento St and from there take a boat out to the island – it's undeveloped and has great snorkelling.

MARINDUQUE

The small island of Marinduque is sandwiched between Mindoro and Luzon. It's noted for its Easter Moriones Festivals. On good Friday, 'antipos' (self-flagellants) engage in a little religious masochism as they flog themselves with bamboo sticks. On Easter Sunday at Mogpos, Gasan and Boac one of the most colourful religious ceremonies in the Philippines takes place. Dressed as Roman centurions wearing large carved masks, the participants capture Longinus, the centurion who was converted after he had stabbed Christ in the side with his spear. The festival ends with a mock beheading or *pugutan* of the hapless Longinus.

Getting There

There are usually one or two boats daily from Lucena City in Luzon to Balanacan. There are also ships to Mindoro several times a week.

Places to Stay

In Boac there are three main travellers' hotels along Neponuceno St. The *Boac* starts at P40 for a single with fan, *Ruby Lodging* is marginally more expensive and has a good restaurant while *Lagio's Resting House*, opposite the Ruby, is also fairly good.

MASBATE

The small island of Masbate is between Luzon and the main Visayan group. It's noted for its large cattle herds.

Getting There
There are a couple of ships a week from
Cebu and a daily boat from Bulan in South
Luzon.

Places to Stay
Doubles cost P30 at the *Hotel Dalisay* and
Hotel La Cabana in Masbate. The *St
Anthony Hotel* is more expensive. In the
port area *Peking House* has good food, or
try the *Petit Restaurant* opposite the St
Anthony Hotel.

MINDANAO
The island of Mindanao, second largest in
the country, is the Philippines' trouble
spot. Mindanao has a large Muslim
population and they have long chafed at
Christian rule. Armed by Libya's fervent
(and oil-rich) Qadafi the Mindanao guerrilla
force (the Moro National Liberation
Front) has staged a long-running battle
with the government forces. It is wise to
enquire carefully and think twice before
travelling through troubled areas. Mindanao certainly isn't new as a trouble spot –
it was the one area of the Philippines
where the Muslim religion had gained a
toehold when the Spanish arrived. Throughout the Spanish era it varied from outright
rebellion to uneasy truce.

Getting There
You can fly to Mindanao from Cebu or
Manila. There are flights to a number of
major cities in Mindanao including Zam-
boanga, Davao, Cagayan de Oro and
Surigao. There are several ships weekly
from Cebu to various Mindanao ports and
also from Leyte, Negros and Panay. From
Manila there's a weekly service departing
Manila on Sunday and arriving in
Zamboanga 31 hours later.

Getting Around
It is wise to be careful when travelling by
bus in Mindanao – guerrilla shoot-ups do
occur and bus travel is none too safe in any
case. The MOT will advise you on which
routes are safe and which ones to forget

about. From Zamboanga there are buses
to Pagadian and Dipolog. From Pagadian
you can continue to Iligan from where
another bus ride will take you to Cagayan
de Oro; if you're adventurous you can
head south to Marawi. Davao can be
reached from Cagayan de Oro or Iligan.

SURIGAO
There are a number of beautiful small
islands around Surigao on the northeast
tip of Mindanao. They can be reached
from General Luna on the island of
Siargao. The trip out to the island passes
through beautiful scenery with many
small islands. It's a five-to-six hour trip
out to Siargao Island and you can stay in
Dapa or General Luna if you ask around.

Places to Stay
On Borromeo St the *Fredden Hotel* is P35
for a single with large bed. The *Litang
Hotel* on the same street is about the same.
On San Nicolas St the *Garcia Hotel* is a
good place with rooms at P35/70, more
expensive with air-con. Back on Borromeo
St the *Tavern Hotel* costs P65/75 for
rooms with fan, more with air-con. It's a
pleasant place with a seaside restaurant.

BUTUAN
Just a junction town south of Surigao,
three hours by bus.

Places to Stay
Near the bus terminal the *A&Z Lowcost
Lodge* is very cheap or the *Canton Lodge*
on R D Calo St is similar – both P20 or less
for singles. On Burgos St the *Butuan New
Society Hotel* is a bit better at P35 and up.
More expensive hotels include the *Elite
Hotel* at the corner of San Jose St and
Conception St or the *Imperial Hotel* on
San Francisco St – both start from around
P40 but go up to P100 or more.

BALINGOAN
Midway between Butuan and Cagayan de
Oro, this is the port for ferries to beautiful
Camiguin Island.

Places to Stay

Try *Lingaya's Restaurant & Lodge* with rooms for P25 or the hotel directly opposite.

CAGAYAN DE ORO

On the north coast Cagayan de Oro is an industrial town and the centre of the Philippines' pineapple industry. The Xavier University Folk Museum is worth a visit, but otherwise there's not much to see here.

Places to Stay

On the corner of Pacana and Capistrano Sts the *Palace Lodge* has basic rooms from just P18. The *Red Star Lodge* on D A Velez St is a simple Chinese hotel with rooms with fan for P35. The *New Golden Star Inn* on J R Borja St is another straightforward, but good, hotel. Rooms cost from P40 with fan. On the same street the *Casa Filipina Lodge* has rooms from P25; again it's pretty basic although there are also more expensive air-con rooms.

The *Tropicana Hotel* on D A Velez St and Yacapin St is P55/70. The *Sampaguita Hotel* on J R Borja St costs from P45/55 with fan, again there are more expensive rooms with air-con. The *Mabini Lodge* at 113 Mabini St on the corner of D A Velez St is fairly new and has clean rooms from P40.

Places to Eat

The *Imperial Palace Restaurant* has good meals and the menu changes daily. Opposite is the *Ice Cream Palace* which does a tasty although rather expensive chop suey. Try *The Bungalow* for typical Filipino food, or *Thrive's Chicken House* on the same street. On Velez St you can get big, cheap meals at the *Bagon Lipunen Restaurant*. Try the pancakes at the *White Elephant Restaurant*.

ILIGAN

Iligan is a major industrial city but there is not much of interest here either although you can visit the Maria Christina Falls,

nine km from the city. Iligan is the jumping-off point for visits to Marawi and the Lake Lanao area, 33 km south. This is a centre of guerrilla activity so make enquiries first before setting out. The route through from there to Cotabato is all a trouble zone. The Aga Khan Museum in Marawi is noted for its exhibits of the Mindanao Muslim culture. You can find some local handicrafts here too.

Places to Stay

The *Jiddy Lodge* on Sabayle Avenue has simple rooms from P15 per person. On Quezon Avenue there's the clean and well-run *Maxim Inn* with rooms from P35/40. Near the pier on Tomas Cabili Avenue the *Altoro Hotel* is rather more expensive – rooms with fan and bath are P70/120.

At Marawi you can stay in the expensive *Marawi Resort Hotel* or you may be able to use the Mindanao State University (MSU) guest house, although it's mainly used for students.

Places to Eat

Iligan has a surprising variety of restaurants, but they tend to close early. The *Canton Restaurant* does Chinese food, or go to the *Lions Restaurant* for a good sandwich. The *Bar-B-Q* on the plaza is great for an evening meal, and for evening entertainment you can make your way to the *Sugbakilan Beer Garden*.

DAPITAN

Close to the city of Dipolog, Dapitan is the site of Jose Rizal's period of exile from 1892 to 1896. The city waterworks and a grass-covered relief map of Mindanao, in the town square, were made by Rizal. A few km away from the city is the place he stayed with a dam he built to create a swimming pool. Other attractions in the area include a fruit bat roosting place and some good swimming areas.

ZAMBOANGA

The most visited city in Mindanao, Zamboanga acts as the gateway to the

Sulu Islands. Fort Pilar is a rather run down old Spanish fort on the waterfront south of the city. From its battlements you get a good view to Rio Hondo, the Muslim village on stilts a little further down the coast. A lot of new government financed housing is going up at Rio Hondo. It's not very interesting.

Pasonanca Park is a large park in the hills a little beyond the airport – main attraction here is the famous tree house. Ten minutes across the bay by banca is Santa Cruz island, with good swimming, skin diving and a beautiful beach. It costs around P70 to rent a boat for the round trip; you can rent snorkeling equipment at the waterfront Lantaka Hotel.

The barter trade market isn't as incredible as Zamboangans like to make out. There are several interesting Muslim villages a short bus ride from Zamboanga and if they'll let you go you can visit the island of Basilan about a two-hour boat ride away. It's the centre for the colourful Yakan tribespeople. The MOT office is in the Lantaka Hotel.

Places to Stay
On Corcuera St the *Bel-Air Hotel* (tel 3598) is right at the bottom of the price scale and very simple, even primitive. Rooms with fan go from P25/40. On L Magno St the *Old Astoria Hotel* (tel 3231) has rooms from P35 per person with fan. On the same street the *New Zamboanga Hotel* (tel 2425) has rooms with fan from P40/80, more with air-con. It's a good, clean place with a reasonably priced dining room.

On Pura Brilliantes St the *Imperial Hotel* (tel 3548) is good value – there are other cheaper places around Zamboanga but things actually work at the Imperial. Toilets flush, taps turn, water flows. Singles/doubles are P40/80 with fan. The *Pasonanca Hotel* (tel 4579) on the corner of Almonte and Tomas Claudio Sts has rooms from P40 up to over P100 with air-con. The rooms are clean but small and there's a good restaurant.

On Guardia Nacional the *New Astoria Hotel* is nice and clean but pricier; rooms with fan cost from P72. The *New Sultana Hotel* (tel 5531), corner of Governor Lim Avenue and Pilar St is also pleasant and costs from P75/100 with fan and bath.

Places to Eat
Zamboanga has lots of places to eat around the centre. Try the *Hover Restaurant* on the corner of Guardia Nacional and Pura Brilliantes for good Chinese Food. The *Bread & Butter* on Valderosa, almost next-door to the city hall, is clean and cool. Ditto for the *Shop-o-Rama Snack* on Pedro Reyes.

Upstairs in the *Hotel Zamboanga* there's a restaurant with fixed-price meals – also at the *New Astoria*. The *Swiss Bar & Restaurant* has European food and about 30 reasonably priced dishes on the menu. Along Justice R T Lim Boulevard there are a string of bayside places, good for open-air dining at sunset. Spend up with an expensive beer at the *Lantaka's* pleasant waterfront bar.

Getting Around
PUV's (Public Utility Vehicles) run between the airport and the centre. There are lots of jeepneys to places around Zamboanga.

SULU ARCHIPELAGO
The string of islands that dribble from Zamboanga to Sabah in north Borneo are home for some of the most fervently Muslim people in the country. The Spanish never conquered them, the Americans also had serious problems and things still aren't totally together. Jolo is the main town and island; the old walled city with its gate and watchtowers is worth seeing. The people of the archipelago are great seafarers – many live on houseboats or in houses built on stilts over the water; particularly the Badjao or 'sea gypsies'. Smuggling and piracy are popular activities in the area – some of the practitioners are reputed to be very well equipped and armed.

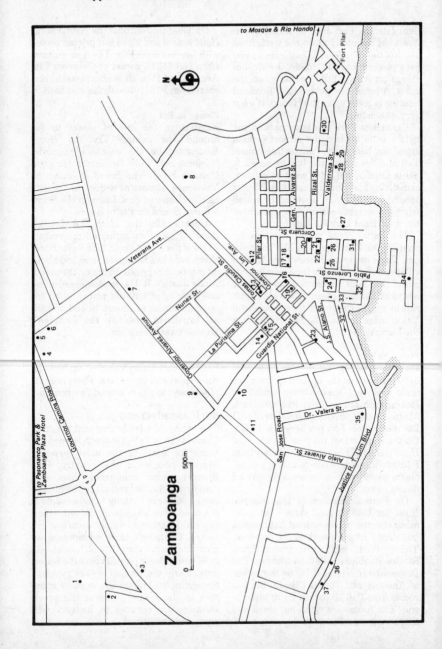

to Mosque & Rio Hondo

Fort Pilar

N

Zamboanga

to Pasonanco Park &
Zamboanga Plaza Hotel

Governor Camins Road

Veterans Ave.

Governor Alvarez Avenue

La Purisima St.

Nunez St.

Tomas Claudio St.

Lim Ave.

Pilar St.

Governor

Gen. V. Alvarez St.

Corcuera St.

Rizal St.

Valderroza St.

Pablo Lorenzo St.

Guardia National St.

J.S. Alano St.

San Jose Road

Dr. Valera St.

Alejo Alvarez St.

Justice R. T. Lim Blvd.

0   500m

DAVAO

On the south coast of Mindanao this cosmopolitan city is the fastest growing in the Philippines after Manila. Settlers have come here from all over the country and the population is now approaching one million. There is an MOT office in the Apo View Hotel on J Camus St.

Things to See

City Sights Davao has a large Buddhist temple with the 'Buddha with 1000 hands', a Chinatown, the Shrine of the Holy Infant Jesus of Prague and some pleasant parks. The city is renowned for its wide variety of tropical fruits – particularly the durian for which there is even a durian monument! The fruitstalls are colourful and tasty places, lots of them along Poncicno Reyes St.

Beaches & Islands There are a variety of good beaches around the city like Talomo (eight km south), Santa Cruz (41 km south) and Digos (59 km south). Get a motorized banca for the 45-minute ride to Palma Gil Island which has good skin diving. Samal Island is also 45 minutes away, bancas only run here on weekends,

which is also the only time the Aguinaldo Pearl Farm on the island is open. Recently renamed the Agro-Seafoods Corporation, this is one of Davao's big attractions and the boat leaves from the Santa Ana Pier at 8 am and costs P20, returns at 3 pm. The island also has an aquarium, marine zoo, good snorkelling, a lousy beach and caves used by local tribes for burials.

Mt Apo The highest mountain in the Philippines overlooks Davao and can be climbed in four or five days. On your way to the top you'll pass waterfalls, hot springs, pools of boiling mud and you might even spot the rare monkey-eating eagle. No special equipment is needed for the climb, March to May are the driest (hence best) climbing months and the tourist office can offer advice and can fix up guides.

Places to Stay

The *Tourist Lodge* (tel 78760) at 55 MacArthur Highway is P25/50 for singles/doubles with fan – clean, well-kept and has a restaurant but it's some distance out. The *Sunya Lodge* (tel 76183) on San Pedro St is much more central. A straight-

1 Airport	20 SKT Shipping Corporation
2 J's Pad, New Elvida Bar	21 George & Peter Lines
3 Zambayan Hotel	22 Sunflower Restaurant
4 Atin Atin Restaurant	23 Buses to Ayala & San Ramon
5 New Market	24 Philippines National Bank
6 Buses to Cagayan de Oro, Iligan & Dipolog	25 City Hall
7 Disco Inferno	26 Sweet Lines, Basilan Lines
8 Zamboanga General Hospital	27 Bel Air Hotel, Post Office (opposite)
9 Fil-Er Beer Garden	28 PAL Office
10 New Astoria Hotel & Restaurant	29 Tourist Office, Lantaka Hotel
11 Small Bars	30 Barter Trade Market
12 New Sultana Hotel	31 Post Office
13 Pasonanca Hotel	32 Market
14 Imperial Hotel	33 Jeepneys to Pasonanca Park & Taluksangay
15 Preciosa Tours	34 Wharf
16 Old Astoria Hotel	35 Alavar's House of Seafoods
17 Swiss Bar & Restaurant, Aristocats	36 Sunview Cocktail Lounge, Boulevard by the sea
18 Sulpicio Lines	37 Bachelor's
19 New Zamboanga Hotel & Restaurant	

forward place with rooms at P20/35 or with bath at P40 and up.

On Claro M Recto Avenue the *Davao Hotel* (tel 78911) costs P20/30 or P55/65 for rooms with air-con and bath. The *El Gusto Family Lodge* (tel 4463) on A Pichon St (Magellanes St) is P25/45 while air-con rooms go up to P100. The *Davao Bay Inn* (tel 78859) on Magsaysay Avenue has rooms at P35/45 and up. It's a good, clean, simple hotel near the wharf. Ditto for the *Davao Pension House* (tel 76263) on Pelayo St with rooms for P45/75.

On San Pedro the *Men Seng Hotel* (tel 75185) is fairly good value. The rooms have big beds and cost from P45/65, more with air-con. There are other real cheapies along San Pedro St. More expensive places include the *Imperial Hotel* on Claro M Recto Avenue.

Places to Eat

Good food at the *Golden Dragon* or the *International Restaurant* on San Pedro St. Yes, there's a *Shakey's Pizza*; it's near the Indonesian consulate. Other popular restaurants include the *Lotus Garden* on Claro M Recto Avenue or the *Davao Famous Restaurant* on Magsaysay Avenue. The *Merco Restaurant* on San Pedro St has good ice cream or at *Lirah's Store* near the city hall you can get fruit shakes. Don't forget to sample Davao's famous durians if they are in season.

Getting Around

Davao's jeepneys are not so organised as in other towns. They don't ply specific routes but just shunt around at random. Call out where you want to go; if it interests the drivers they may stop. Or take the mini-car taxis which cost P3 anywhere in town.

GENERAL SANTOS CITY (Dadiangas)

Not a great deal of interest in this city in the south-west of Mindanao.

Places to Stay

The straightforward *Family Country Home* is some distance outside the town on the Lagao Road Highway at the junction with Mateo Rd and has rooms from P40/60 with fan. Or there's the *Golden City Hotel* on Cagampang St with rooms from P25/40 and up. The *Matutum Hotel* is on P Acharon Boulevard and costs from P70/120 with fan and bath.

MINDORO

The relatively undeveloped island of Mindoro is the nearest last frontier to Manila – the Philippines have quite a few last frontiers. You can get there very easily from Manila and many travellers make the trip to try the beautiful beaches – in fact it's a toss-up if this isn't a better place for lazing on the beach than 100 Islands. Mindoro's population is concentrated along the coastal strip, inland is mainly dense jungle and mountains.

Getting There

The usual route to Mindoro is from the Luzon port of Batangas to Calapan. You can get buses directly to Batangas from Manila for P16 but beware of pickpockets who work overtime on this route. There are three ferry departures a day in each direction and the fare is P13. There's also one Batangos-Puerto Galera service a day for P12. You have to leave Manila as early as possible in the morning in order to get to Mindoro the same day.

From Mindoro you can continue on to Marinduque, Panay or Romblon. It's becoming quite a popular route from Mindoro to Tablas then to Boracay – combining the two resorts of Puerto Galera and Boracay. Boats operate fairly regularly from Roxas (Mindoro) to Tablas, but be careful – some of them are rusty, leaky buckets. It takes about four hours and costs P30. Táblas-Boracay you can usually find a boat (perhaps P25 per person) or charter a whole boat for P100 to 150 from Santa Fe.

Getting Around

It takes about two hours and costs P10 by

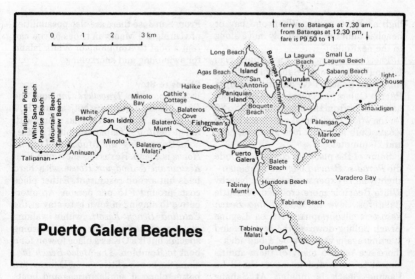

Puerto Galera Beaches

ferry to Batangas at 7.30 am,
from Batangas at 12.30 pm,
fare is P9.50 to 11

jeepney from Calapan to Puerto Galera, the main beach centre at the northern end of the east coast road. Southwards buses run down the coast to Bongabong and Roxas, a seven-hour trip although a good bus can do it in an hour or two (even three on an express bus) faster. Celapan-Roxas is P20-25. Instead of travelling straight through you can go just to Bongabong and take a minibus on the final stretch. You can continue on south to Bulalacao by jeepney but to continue around the southern end of the island to San Jose you have to take a boat. A road is under construction from Mansalay to San Jose.

PUERTO GALERA

The fine beaches and excellent snorkelling around Puerto Galera have been attracting travellers for some time. There are lots of little coves and bays, some of which you need a boat to get to – get a group of travellers together and split the cost. There are also some pleasant walks but the whole area is starting to become very popular – there are lots of places to stay not only in the town but also out at the various beaches. The beaches include La Laguna, White Beach at San Isidro (seven km out of town), Sabang Beach, Balete Beach, Long Beach, Mountain Beach and Santo Nino. Note that the bank in Puerto Galera won't, yet, change travellers' cheques. For that matter there are no telephones in Puerto Galera either.

Places to Stay

Places in Puerto Galera itself are generally around P20 to 30 per person. You can try the *Puerto Galera Lodge* at Balete Beach in town, or *Montiel's Nipa Hut*, or the friendly atmosphere of *Malou's Hilltop Inn* or *Apple's Huts*. If you want something a little less basic try the *Hotel El Canonera Marivelis* with rooms with fan and bath from P35/45. The *Villa Margarita White House* and the *Outrigger Hotel* are more expensive again. *Melxa's Greenhills Hotel & Beach Huts* have a small hotel in Puerto Galera and nipa huts about two km out of town on the way to White Beach.

You're liable to be hassled by touts for the beach cottages all the way from Batangas. Some even start on you on the bus from Manila. Out at the beach there are lots of cottages from around P30 to as high as P100 a day. When one bay or beach is built out they simply move along to the next one.

The beaches include La Laguna, San Isidro (White Beach), Sabang Beach and Mountain Beach. Take an outrigger from Puerto Galera to Sabang, it takes about half an hour from the pier, costs P15 to 30 for the whole boat. Or take the track by the Koala Club and walk it in about an hour and 20 minutes.

Some of the places to consider include the *Paradise Beach Lodge* at Talipanan – slightly more expensive but good. Nearby White Beach is more crowded. At Little Balateros Cove the *Santo Nino Beach Resort* is also popular. At La Laguna Beach pulling down all the cottages and starting again wouldn't be a bad idea – there are far too many of them andit's almost too crowded to move. Small La Laguna Beach is quieter. At Sabang Beach, *Green Hills* and *Cartillo Lodge* are friendly but measure the distance from the noisy disco. You can walk around the coast from here to La Laguna; it's better for sunning and snorkelling.

Mountain Beach, a P3 jeepney ride, 1½ km beyond White Beach, is fairly quiet. You can walk to Santo Nino Bay from the pier, it's only a km from town towards white Beach. *Fisherman's Cove* there is very cheap and has a good info board with maps detailing walks in the vicinity.

Getting Around
From Puerto Galera jeepneys and bancas run to the various beaches. For example it's P5 per person for a jeepney to Sabang or P30 for a banca. To La Laguna a banca costs P20 or 25.

OTHER PLACES
Calapan is just a jumping-off point for Luzon. In the south you can get boats for Romblon from Bongabong or Roxas. From Mansalay, further south from Roxas, you can walk to the villages of the Mangyan tribes. Or you can continue around the coast to San Jose by boat.

From San Jose there are also possibilities of visiting the Mangyan tribes or you can rent a boat to Ambulong or White Island for swimming and snorkelling.

Places to Stay
In Calapan the *Travellers' Inn* and the *Casa Blanca Annexe* are both around P30 per person. The *Eric Hotel* has rooms with fan at P40/50. Calapan is a bit of a dive.

In Bongabong the *Mabuhay Lodging House* is cheap. Roxas has the *Santo Nino Restaurant & Lodging House* with hard beds but a good restaurant. Either place costs around P15 per person. An alternative to staying in town is to stay at the *Catalina Beach Resort*, within walking distance of the town. The beach is nothing special, but it's OK as a place to wait for a boat to Romblon. The *Melco Beach Inn*, along the beach a little way at Dangay, is a better place at similar prices and boats also go across from here to Romblon and direct to Boracay.

In San Jose the *Kapit Bahay Mini Hotel* has rooms for P25/40. *Mosquera's Hotel* is a bit cheaper, the *Executive Inn* is cheaper still. More expensive places include *Roda's Hotel* with rooms with fan from P40/60.

NEGROS
Sandwiched between Cebu and Panay, and easily connected by ferry services in both directions, this is the sugar island of the Philippines.

Getting There
There are several departures a day from Toledo in Cebu to San Carlos in Negros, and the crossing takes two hours. There are also several services daily from San Sebastian in Cebu to San Jose, the crossing takes one hour. There are a variety of other crossing points plus longer-distance services from Cebu City. PAL fly Cebu City-Bacolod three times daily.

Between Iloilo on Panay and Bacolod there are two ferry services daily. The crossing takes an hour and a half. Allow an hour to get from Bacolod to the Banago wharf.

Getting Around
It's 313 km between Bacolod and Dumaguete which are at opposite ends of the island. The trip takes 7½ hours and it's wise to take an express bus as it avoids the many small village stops. Bacolod-San Carlos takes two or three hours.

BACOLOD
Bacolod is a typical Filipino city of no great interest. You can visit the huge Victoria Milling Company Central, one of the world's largest sugar refineries, in the north of the city. Bacolod is also a major ceramics centre for the Philippines.

Places to Stay
On Burgos St the *YMCA* (tel 2 6919) has dorm beds at P18 (P16 if you're a member) and is a good clean place. There are also singles from P30, P40 with fan and bath. *Ted Canada* has pleasant private accommodation at P25 per person at 30 Libertad St, across from the school.

On Lacson St the *Gabina Yanson Lodge* has very simple rooms from P30. The *New Pacific Lodging House* (tel 2 4142) on North Drive has rooms with fan and bath for P40, with air-con for P55. There are also some cheaper rooms in this straight-forward hotel.

The *Standard Lodging House* (tel 2 8351), on the corner of San Sebastian and Gatuslao St, is a simple place with a variety of rooms from P30 to P100 or more. Ditto for the *Friendship Inn* (tel 2 3312) on Bonifacio St. This is no hotel for late-risers – it's noisy in the morning. *Las Rocas Hotel* (tel 2 1373) at 13 Gatuslao St is also in this same price range with rooms starting from around P45 for a single with fan and bath and going up to P150-plus for air-con doubles.

Moving up a notch in price you could try the newish *Halili Inn* (tel 8 1548) on Locsin Avenue, or the *Mandarin Hotel* (tel 2 1721) on Gatuslao St, or the *Bascon I Hotel* (tel 2 1005) on the same street. The Bascon I is a well-kept place and quite good value. There's also a pricier *Bascon II Hotel* on Gonzaga St.

Places to Eat
Good Chinese and Filipino food at the *Mardi Gras Luncheonette* on Ballesteros St or the *International Restaurant* on Gonzaga St. *Barrio Fiesta* on Araneta St does Filipino food while on San Juan St there is yet another of the Philippines' many *Shakey's Pizza Parlours*. At *Jumbo's Food Circus* in the City Plaza on the waterfront you can get hamburgers or spaghetti. The *Food Park* on Rizal St has a variety of restaurants.

DUMAGUETE
Dumaguete is a very pleasant little town which centres around the large Silliman University Campus. There's a small anthropological museum here and a cheap cafeteria. There are many good beaches around Dumaguete including Kawayan to the south, El Oriente and Wuthering Heights (!) to the north. Silliman Beach, close to the town, is not very good. Camp Look Out, 14 km west of the city, provides fine views over Dumaguete and across to Cebu and Bohol.

Places to Stay
Opena's Hotel & Restaurant on Katada St has rooms from P40 for a fan-cooled single up to 150 for an air-con double. It's a clean and pleasant place in a new building. On Real St the *Hotel El Oriente* is also pleasant and has rooms with fan and bath for P70/110. On the corner of Rizal Avenue and San Juan St the *Al Mar Hotel* has similarly priced rooms.

On Silliman Avenue the *Insular Hotel* is a good place near the university, but more expensive with rooms with fan starting at P120. Right at the rock bottom on the same street you can get rooms for P20 a the *Lodging Inn*, across from the main university entrance. *Jo's Lodging* is similarly priced. The rather run-down *Victory Lodge* is even cheaper. These Silliman Avenue places are all within walking distance of the wharf.

Near the Silliman Marine Laboratory on Silliman Beach the *South Sea Resort Hotel* (tel 2857) is the best place around there with rooms from around P150.

Places to Eat
You can eat well and cheaply at *Opena's Restaurant* or in the *Self-Service University Cafeteria*. The *South Sea Beach Restaurant* at Silliman Beach is open-air and breezy. Students like the *Kamagong Restaurant*, and *Jo's Bake House* on Alfonso St is also a student hangout. Near the market on Legaspi St, *Savoury's Restaurant* is cheap and very good.

OTHER PLACES
Mambucal, just a P4 jeepney from Libertad St in Bacolod, has hot springs and cottages you can rent from P30. It's a pleasant resort from where you can climb the Canlaon Volcano in three days – guides cost around P25 a day and you need a good sleeping bag. From the town of Canlaon you can climb it in two days.

San Carlos, jumping-off point for Cebu, is nothing special but you can take little speedboats across to nearby Sipaway Island for 75c. It's a pleasant and quiet place with some good beaches but bring your own food and water. In San Carlos cheap places to stay include *Van's Lodging House*, *Papal's Lodge* or the *San Carlos Lodging House*. The *Coco Grove Hotel* on Ylagan St is better.

Malabatay and Zamboanguita is the best area near Dumaguete for beaches and snorkelling. You can charter a boat from here to get to popular offshore Apo Island. A day-trip shouldn't cost more than P100 to 120.

PALAWAN
Located off to the west of the Visayas, Palawan is the long thin island stretching down to the Malaysian north Borneo state of Sabah. Things to do and see here are mainly natural – islands, skin diving, caves with underground rivers and wildlife.

Getting There
There are ships once weekly between Manila and Puerto Princesa; the trip takes three days. Alternatively there are daily flights with PAL.

Getting Around
Puerto Princesa, the capital, is roughly half-way down the island. Buses and jeepneys run up and down the island, as far as Brooke's Point, seven-to-nine-hours' drive south, or Roxas (P50) and Port Barton (another P25) to the north.

PUERTO PRINCESA
The capital of the island is a small town with a population of only about 10,000. It's simply a place to use as a base for excursions elsewhere on the island. Tricycles around town cost P1, out to the airport is P2.50.

Places to Stay
Try *Mrs Abordo* at 36 Sand Oval St – she rents out rooms with fans to students and travellers for P50/80. Cheap and good food there too. Or there is the pleasant *Duchess Pension House* on Valencia St with rooms from P25 per person.

Yayen's Pension on Manalo Extension is also pleasantly run and has rooms from P40/70 with fan to around P180 for an aircon double. *Civen's Inn* on Mendoza St has rooms from P55/75 but it's only OK.

More expensive places include the *Circon Lodge & Restaurant* at Mendoza Park on the corner of Rizal St and Valencia St. Singles/doubles are P80/100 with fan and bath, more with air-con. On Rizal St near the airport the *Badjao Inn* is a clean, well-kept place with rooms with bath and fan at P100/180.

Places to Eat

There are a number of restaurants along Rizal St such as the *Golden Horse Restaurant* which does Chinese and Filipino food. On the same street the *Kamayan Restaurant* is pleasant but rather expensive. Other Rizal St places include the *Bahay Kamayan* for Filipino food or the *Badjao Steak House*, popular with oil-workers.

On Valencia St *Edwin's Food Palace* does good value Chinese food. The *Ignacio Restaurant* on Quezon St is a simple restaurant with good Filipino food. On Saturdays the *Hyatt* puts on a big buffet by the swimming pool. The *Bulakenia Beer Garden* on the other side of the street is also popular.

OTHER PLACES

There is good diving at the coral island just off San Raphael and a beautiful beach at Port Barton. Bird watchers will find uninhabited Ursula Island, near Brooke's Point, interesting. The ancient burial caves at Tabon are about half an hour by boat from Quezon. At Anabag, 69 km north of Puerto Princesa, the *Duchess Beach House* is run by the same people as the Duchess Pension House in Puerto Princesa. Cost is P25 per person, good meals are available at reasonable prices. It's right on a beautiful beach and there's good coral nearby.

PANAY

The large, triangular Visayan island of Panay has a number of decaying forts and watchtowers – relics from the days of the Moro pirates – plus some interesting Spanish churches. The south coast stretch from Iloilo around the southern promontory at Amini-y to San Jose has many fine beaches and resorts. There are two major annual festivals in Panay, the Ati-Atihan festival in Kalibo and the Binirayan festival in San Jose. Last, but far from least, off the north-west tip of the island is the delightful little island of Boracay, another traveller's centre.

Getting There

There are a variety of flights and shipping services to Panay from Manila, Cebu City and other major centres. Shortest crossing is the 1½-hour trip from Bacolod in Negros to Iloilo. The trip costs P10 to 14 and there is at least one boat a day. It's possible (with some difficulty) to get across from Boracay to Mindoro, via Tablas to Roxas. Check the boats carefully, some are leaky buckets.

Getting Around

Panay has the only railway in the Philippines, outside of Luzon. It's a good one for railway enthusiasts. There are seven trains daily between Roxas and Iloilo. The trip takes three to 4½ hours depending on the train. Buses also take 4½ hours and depart hourly in the morning. Roxas-Kalibo is 2½ to three hours by bus.

ILOILO

The capital city of Panay, Iloilo, is a large and interesting town which was very important during the Spanish era. There's the small and interesting Museo Iloilo in the city plus the Molo church. Iloilo is noted for its jusi (raw silk) and pina (pineapple fibre) weaving. You can see weaving in the Arevalo district of the city.

You can make a pleasant day trip from Iloilo to nearby Guimaras Island. There are good swimming beaches in Nueva Valencia and the walk to the Daliran Cave from Buenavista is pleasant.

Places to Stay

The *YMCA* on Iznart St costs P23 for dorm beds (P18 to members) and is no big deal. There are also rooms. On J M Basa St the *International House* (tel 7 4786) has rooms at P30 for a single, P75/90 for rooms with air-con but it's not all that special either.

Across the road on Aldeguer St is the *Iloilo Lodging House*, which is simple and clean but has very small rooms from P50/80. *D'House* at 127 Quezon St has large, airy rooms with fans from P35 per person. The *Family Pension House* on General Luna St is clean and pleasant with rooms with fan from P55/70, more with air-con. This popular place has had a number of travellers' recommendations and also has a tree house snack bar.

The *Centercon Hotel* (tel 7 3431) on a lane off J M Basa St where it meets Iznart St, is clean, quiet, central, run by helpful people and has rooms with air-con from P85/110.

Places to Eat

There's good although rather expensive Chinese and Filipino food in the *Summer House* on J M Basa St. Ditto for the *Mansion House Restaurant* and the *Hong Kee Restaurant*, both on J M Basa St. There's also yet another *Shakey's Pizza Parlour* on the same street. The *Tree House Restaurant* has good food, excellent service and a great atmosphere.

On Valeria St the *Oak Barrel* is one of a number of Batchoy restaurants on this block. The nearby *Iloilo Supermart*, on the corner of Delgado St and Varleria St, is also a good place for cheap food. Finally *Ganeco Fast Foods*, back on J M Basa, is clean and modern and popular.

There are plenty of pubs around town, like the *Bodga Pub* on J M Basa which has good folk music on the weekends. Other places for a beer include the *Swan Restaurant*, the *Open Air Restaurant* on Fort San Pedro Drive or the comfortable *Kings Head Pub*.

THE SOUTH COAST

The south coast, from Iloilo to Amini-y on the southern tip of Panay and around to San Jose on the opposite coast, is full of interest. At Guimbal, 28 km south, is an old Spanish watchtower – from this cone-shaped, now moss-covered, building smoke signals were once sent up to warn of pirate attacks. The Miagao Church is 11 km further; it was originally built as a fort as well as a religious centre – hence the two sturdy sandstone towers. See the relief

sculpture of St Christopher surrounded by coconut and papaya trees.

The Church of San Joaquin, 15 km further again, was built of white coral in 1869 and its facade is carved as a sculpture of the Spanish victory at the battle of Tetuan in Morocco, 10 years earlier. All along the coast between Arevalo and San Joaquin there are beach resorts with cottages you can rent. It's a very attractive coastal road and at Amini-y and San Jose there are good sites for skin diving.

ROXAS

Roxas is nothing special, just a stop on the way to or from Manila, Romblon or Boracay.

Places to Stay

On Roxas Avenue the *Beehive Inn* (tel 418) has rooms with fan at P30/40 or more expensive rooms with attached bathrooms and air-con. There's also a restaurant and swimming pool and the manager is helpful and informative. Also on Roxas Avenue *Halaran House* (tel 615) is reasonable value with rooms from P50/75.

Right at the bottom of the price scale rooms are very cheap, but very basic, at *Nino's Restaurant & Lodging House* or the *A&B Lodge*. Outside at Punta Tabok the *Capiz Hotel* is a resort complex with rooms from P85/110 and up.

You can eat at the *Beehive Restaurant* or the pleasant *China Rose Restaurant*.

KALIBO

The only real interest here is the annual Ati-Atihan festival in January. A smaller version of this popular festival takes place at the same time in Cebu City and a week later at Iloilo.

Places to Stay

The *High Chapparal Restaurant & Hotel* is good value at P20 per person. On R Pastrana St the *Everlasting Hotel* is also good value at P25/40. On the same street the *Iris Lodge* is another simple, cheap

place. Ditto for the *Kalibo Lodge* on C
Laserna St.

In the *Kalibo Youth Hostel* on Bankaya
Avenue, dorm beds are P20. The
Glowmoon Hotel on San Martelino St has
singles/doubles with fan at P35/60. At the
Hotel Ati-Atihan on Old Busuang rooms
with fan and bath cost from P40/80. It's a
tricycle ride out of town. The Glowmoon
and the Ati-Atihan both have more
expensive rooms with air-con.

Prices in Kalibo increase astronomically
during the Ati-Atihan Festival. If you can
get a room at all it may cost P300 or more.
A piece of floor in a private house may cost
P25. Special ships run here from Cebu
and Manila at the time of the festival.

Places to Eat

Eat at the *D C Kitchenette*, on R Pastrana
St near the Everlasting Hotel, or the
Glowmoon Restaurant.

BORACAY

This superb little island off the north-west
tip of Panay has beautiful clear water and
superb beaches. You can walk right across
the island in just 15 minutes. Places to
stay are springing up like wildfire as more
and more travellers discover what a fine
escape this still relatively untouched
paradise is. There is no place to change
money in Boracay and there's a real
shortage of small change – be warned.
Take care of your valuables too, Boracay
has had a rash of robberies.

Places to Stay

There are three little villages connected
by walking tracks – Yapak, Balabag and
Manoc-Manoc. Most places to stay charge
a standard P50 for a double although
there are also some more expensive
places. Most of these cottages are located
on White Beach, between Balabag and
Angol. Some say Angol is cheaper.

Popular places include the early arrivals
like *Williams Place*, *Happy Home* or the
White Beach Guesthouse and newer places
like *Yap's Rest House* and *Ome's Beach*

Boracay

House. There are lots of others. There's a
feeling somewhat like Lake Toba in these
small places.

Places to Eat

You have to order food in advance at the
guest houses. There are a number of
restaurants around, particularly in
Mangayad. The *Villacelo* is particularly
good for spaghetti. Next door is a good
bakery. *Happy Home* does fantastic pancakes while *Aqua Blue* is good for
Chinese-style food. *Starfire* has frequently
changing specials and the *Travellers Place*
is popular for an after-dinner drink. The
Jolly Sailor is a local information centre
and gathering place with good food. You
can use it as a mailing address.

Getting There

There are several ways of getting to Boracay. The large outrigger *MB Jem* goes directly between Kalibo and Boracay. The three-hour trip to White Beach costs P30. Alternatively you can take a 1½ hour, P15 jeepney ride from Kalibo to Caticlan and in good weather there will be boats crossing regularly to the island. It only takes 15 minutes across to the island at a fare of P8. Take care, they tend to grossly overload the boats; more than one traveller has lost his gear from a capsized boat.

If you want to get back from White Beach to Caticlan just wave a boat down, the standard fare will apply. To continue to Looc on Romblon check at Roger's or at the Jolly Sailor. There are boats Manila-Looc (Thursday), Manila-Kalibo and Batangas-Odiongan. Williams Line has a ship between Manila and Malay, near Boracay. Pacific Air and Boracay Air fly direct to Caticlan from Manila, the fare is around P815 one-way. Alternatively you can fly from Manila to Tablas and then go by jeepney to Looc and cross from there by boat.

ROMBLON

This scattering of small islands is in the middle of the area bordered by south Luzon, Masbate, Panay and Mindoro. It's noted for its marble and much marble carving and souvenirs are produced. There are some good beaches and the town of Romblon has a notable cathedral. The three main islands of the group are Romblon and the larger Sibuyan and Tablas.

Romblon is particularly useful as a stepping stone from the beach resort of Puerto Galera on Mindoro to the resort island of Boracay, just off Panay and directly south of Tablas.

Getting There

There are regular boats between Romblon and Luzon and between Romblon and Mindoro. Services to or from Mindoro include Romblon (Romblon) to Carmen

(Tablas) to Bongabong (Mindoro). Or you can travel between Looc or Odiongan (Tablas) and Roxas (Mindoro) for P45. The trip takes about four hours. The *MB Jem* connects with the Roxas-Looc service so you can connect straight through to Boracay. Looc-Boracay costs P35-50 depending on the number of passengers. A jeepney between Odiongan and Looc is P12.

There's a weekly ship from Manila which goes via Romblon and on to Roxas City on Panay. There are also connections to Kalibo on Panay. There are now regular services between Looc on Tablas and Boracay Island off Panay. The crossing takes two to three hours by motor launch at a fare of around P35. The *MB Jem* is one of the boats that operate this trip.

Places to Stay

In Romblon try the *Sea Side Hotel* on the harbour with rooms at P20 per person. A few km south-west at Agnay you can stay at the superb *Selangga Tree House* for a similar cost. A little further south at Mapula there's the very friendly and cheap *Tumamon Inn*.

In Odiongan there's the *Anita Fernandez Lodge* while Looc has *Pador's Guesthouse* on the Plaza or the cheap and very clean *Tablas Pension*. Pador's also has excellent food.

SAMAR

The large Visayan island of Samar acts as a stepping stone from Luzon to Leyte. There is a regular ferry service from Matnog at the southern end of Luzon to Allen at the northern end of Samar, while at the other end a bridge connects Samar with Leyte. Samar is relatively undeveloped so transport can be hard going and it is also the scene for some guerrilla activity from anti-government forces.

Getting There

There are a number of ferries daily between Matnog and Allen. The crossing takes two hours and costs P16. It's four to five hours by bus from Catbalogan to Tacloban in Leyte. The buses depart at least twice daily.

Getting Around

With improvements in the Pan-Philippine Highway across Samar, transport is now much easier. Allen to Tacloban takes six or seven hours by bus. The new coastal road runs from Allen to Calbayog, Catbalogan and Tacloban. The old road took a longer and bumpier route from Allen to Calbayog via Catarman. You can also skip around the coast by banca.

ALLEN

This is simply a port town for the ferry service to Luzon.

Places to Stay

There are a number of cheap hotels around P15 per person. They include *La Suerta* (nice people), *Bicolana Lodging House* and *El Canto Lodging House*.

CATARAMAN

A university town with the Tamburosan Beach four km away.

Places to Stay

The *Sanitary Lodging House* (great name) is on Bonifacio St and costs P20 per person. On Jacinto St the *Rendezvous*

Lodging House is P20. Others include the more expensive *Island Hotel* where rooms cost P35 per person.

CALBAYOG

Just another 'through' town although the Barsodos Waterfalls are nearby.

Places to Stay

Try the *Calbayog Hotel & Restaurant* at P30 per person for a room with fan or the *Hyacinth Lodge House* at P20. The *San Joaquin Inn* on Nijaga St is better with rooms from P30 all the way to P150.

CATBALOGAN

There are beaches around Catbalogan, but once again it's just a stepping stone to more interesting places.

Places to Stay

The *Town Hotel* on San Bartolome St is cheap (P15) and simple while the *De Luxe Hotel* is anything but deluxe! On Del Rosario St the *Fortune Hotel* has rooms all the way from P25 to P150 and has a good restaurant. On the same street *Tony's Hotel* or on Curry Avenue *Kikay's Hotel* have rooms with a similar spread of prices.

Eat in the *Fortune Hotel's* good restaurant or at *Tony's Hotel*.

Singapore

Singapore is a small island at the tip of the Malaysian peninsula; it thrives on trade and through a combination of hard work and clever government has become the most affluent country in Asia after Japan. It's a travel crossroads with a wide variety of places to visit, things to buy and some of the best food in Asia. Singapore – with its cleanliness and orderliness – can be a pleasant break from the more hectic travelling you find elsewhere in Asia. It's also becoming more and more antiseptic and dull – just another big city with numerous huge hotels and air-conditioned shopping centres.

HISTORY

Singapore's improbable name, it means 'Lion City', came from a Sumatran prince who thought he saw a lion where they have probably never been. It would have drifted on as a quiet fishing village if Sir Stamford Raffles had not decided, in 1819, that it was just the port he needed. Under the British it became a great trading port and a military and naval base. This didn't save it from the Japanese in 1942.

In 1959 Singapore became internally self governing; in 1963 it joined Malaysia, and in 1965 changed its mind and pulled out. The reason behind this was a basic conflict of interests between 'Malaysia for the Malays' and Singapore's predominantly Chinese population. Under Prime Minister Lee Kuan Yew, Singapore made the best of independence and trade, tourism and industrialisation soon made up for the loss of British military bases.

Mr Lee's somewhat iron-handed government also turned Singapore into a green, tidy garden city where no one dares litter the streets, or even carelessly drop cigarette ash. Birth control programmes are pushed hard, the water is drinkable from the taps, smoking in public places is forbidden; even big cars are being taxed off the streets. Unfortunately these progressive attitudes have another side; speaking out against the government is not a recommended activity – the elected opposition to Lee Kuan Yew's People's Action Party consists of just two people. Nevertheless Singapore's government is democratic, although the press is kept under a fairly tight rein.

FACTS

Population Singapore's polyglot population of 2.3 million is made up of 76% Chinese, 15% Malay, 7% Indian and the remaining 2% of any and every nationality you can imagine.

Geography The population squeezes itself into a low-lying 616 square km island at the tip of the Malaysian peninsula, not much more than 100 km north of the equator. A 1000-metre long causeway connects Singapore with Johore Bahru in Malaysia.

Economy The economy is based on trade, shipping, banking and tourism with a growing programme of light industrialisation. Ship building and maintenance is also an important industry.

INFO

The Singapore Tourist Promotion Board office on Tanglin Rd is open from 8 am to 5 pm from Monday to Saturday and has a variety of leaflets, brochures and useful information. Pick up a copy of the *Singapore Weekly Guide* at the airport – it has a good fold-out map as well as much other useful information.

Student Travel have an office in the Ming Court Hotel on the corner of Tanglin Rd and Orchard Rd. The GPO, with its efficient poste restante, is on Raffles Quay beside the Singapore River. The Immigration Office is just across the river on Empress Place. Singapore's anti-litter laws really mean it – you can be fined on the spot for dropping so much as a cigarette butt, although in practice it rarely happens.

Singapore Notes

Visas Singapore is generally a good place to get visas. It's the best place in the region for Indonesian visas although visas are only now required if you're going to enter by some really odd route. The Thai embassy, on Orchard Rd, is also reasonably fast and efficient. Round the corner on Tanglin Rd the Burmese embassy is quite OK but not as fast as the embassy in Bangkok.

Health You've not got to worry about health too much in Singapore but if you need to renew vaccinations head for the Health Centre, 5th floor, Office Tower Block, Tanjung Pagar Complex, 280 Tanjung Pagar Rd, Singapore 0208.

Communications Singapore is a good place for international phone calls if you have to contact home. There are several telecom centres, like the ones on Hill St or Robinson Rd, where you can make calls charged by the time used, not for three-minute blocks.

Chinese New Year The new year falls in late January or February and can be quite a hassle. It's more a stay-at-home holiday then anything to see and hotels will be packed out, taxis scarce, restaurants often closed, prices temporarily higher. This goes on for a week and many Chinese hotels raise their prices at that time.

BOOKS

The Lonely Planet guidebook *Malaysia, Singapore & Brunei – a travel survival kit* is about the most detailed book you can find on Singapore and its neighbours. Apa Productions' *Insight Guide Singapore* is an attractive photo-guide to the city state. There are lots of history books and a number of novels about Singapore to read. Try *The Singapore Grip* for an enthralling novel based on the fall of Singapore in WW II.

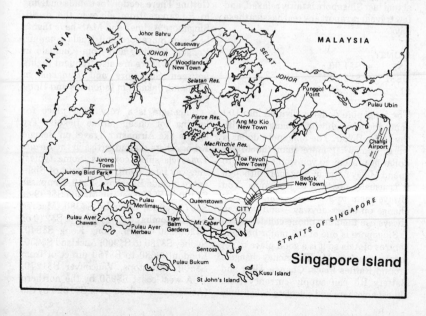
Singapore Island

Singapore probably has the best bookshops in South-East Asia. The main MPH shop on Stamford Rd is excellent, but there are numerous other good bookshops around the city.

VISAS

For most western nationalities visas are not required and you are granted an initial two weeks on entry. Officially this can be extended at the immigration department at Empress Place, but without a local sponsor you will find extending it extremely difficult. The government seems to feel that two weeks is long enough for anybody to do their duty free shopping.

Singapore used to be very sticky about 'hippies', and long hair or scruffy clothes could cause you all sorts of problems. Furthermore, evidence of your financial soundness or possession of a ticket to far away places was required before you could enter the country. Although the letter of the law still insists that people with long hair will have a hard time, in actual fact Singapore is fairly relaxed, and few travellers report any real hassles these days.

MONEY

A$1	= S$1.90
US$1	= S$2.15
£1	= S$2.45

The Singapore dollar is divided into 100 cents and is roughly interchangeable with the Malay dollar. The Singapore dollar is worth somewhat more than the Malay dollar at present so you won't be able to spend Malay notes in Singapore although it is usually possible to use coins. You always seem to get Malay coins in your change on buses anyway – and you can always use them for phone calls!

Singapore is one of the major banking centres of Asia so it is a good place to get money transferred to. The money changers around Raffles Place, Change Alley and Battery Rd can supply currency from almost anywhere and calculate delightfully complicated double exchanges – if you want to change Thai bahts into Indonesian rupiah for example. They are generally better than the banks for changing cash. If you're watching every cent it is worth shopping around the banks a bit – exchange rates tend to vary and many banks also make a service charge on a per-transaction or per-cheque basis.

CLIMATE

Situated so close to the equator Singapore is hot and humid year round although it does get better at night and the weather never seems to be quite as damp as Bangkok, 1500 km to the north. November to January tend to be the wettest months – it can rain every afternoon for weeks on ends.

GETTING THERE
Air

Singapore is a major travel crossroads and flights operate in and out of Changi Airport at all hours. See the introductory Getting There section for details on flying to Singapore from all over the world. Singapore Airlines and MAS have flights between Singapore and Kuala Lumpur, Penang, Kuching and Kota Kinabalu in Malaysia. There are also frequent flights between Singapore and Bangkok in Thailand, Jakarta in Indonesia and Hong Kong.

Singapore is a very good place for looking for cheap airline tickets. Try agents like Airmaster Travel on Selegie Rd or others that advertise in the *Straits Times* classified columns. Some typical one-way fares being quoted out of Singapore include Bangkok S$240, Denpasar S$400 or S$590 return, Manila S$699 or S$971 return, Colombo S$380, Madras S$555, Bombay S$671, Jakarta S$210 or S$260-280 return, Hong Kong S$840, Sydney S$780 to S$900, Auckland S$950, London S$680 to S$750 direct or from S$800 with stops, Vancouver S$1270, USA west coast S$950 by the northern (Asian) route with stops or S$1620 by the southern (Pacific) route, Seattle S$1050, Perth or Darwin via Bali and Jakarta S$658. STA (Student Travel Australia) (tel 734 5681) in the Ming Court Hotel is another reliable place for airline tickets.

Rail

Singapore is the southern termination point for the Malaysian railway system, although Singapore has no real system of its own. Leaving Singapore you clear immigration and customs at the station so there is no further delay at the causeway when crossing into Malaysia. See the Malaysia transport section for full details on the rail system from Singapore right through Malaysia and into Thailand.

Road

Although there is a great variety of bus services operating from Singapore the choice is much greater in Johore Bahru where there is also a wide variety of taxi services. To get to Johore Bahru you can take the 170 bus from Queen St for 80c. Or for S$1 you can take the direct bus which departs every 10 minutes from the nearby Rochor Rd Terminus. It's a red and grey bus and leaves from Albert St across from the food centre. Don't be worried if the bus departs while you're clearing immigration and customs for Malaysia – you can just hop on the next one that comes along. Take it all the way to the Johore Bahru terminus though – don't abandon the bus at Malaysian immigration.

In the same locality in Singapore you will find taxis operating to Johore Bahru at S$4 per person or S$16 for a full car. Foreigners are likely to have to pay slightly more since they take longer to clear the border than Singaporeans or Malaysians.

You can get taxis into Malaysia right from Singapore and don't need to bother getting to Johore Bahru first. Try Malaysia Taxi Service (tel 298 3831) at 290 Jalan Besar, for all points in Malaysia. Another is Kuala Lumpur Taxi Service (tel 223 1889), 191 New Bridge Rd.

To Melaka buses operate from 579 New Bridge Rd (tel 223 8868), nearly opposite the main bus station. Buses leave at 8 am, 9.30 am, 11 am, 2 pm and 3 pm and the cost is S$11; with air-con it's S$16. Most other buses operate from the New Bridge Rd Fringe Car Park Terminus. Some fares and times:

air-con

Kuala Lumpur	9 am or 9 pm	S$17
Ipoh	7 pm	S$25
Butterworth	7 pm	S$30
Kuantan	9 am or 10 pm	S$11
Kuala Trengganu	8 pm	S$23
Kota Bahru	7.30 pm	S$31

non air-con

Kuantan	10 am	S$8.50
Kuala Trengganu	8 am	S$19
Kota Bahru	7.30 pm	S$26

There is a money changer at the bus depot – if you don't see him ask at the desk and they will point him out to you. Last visit he was giving 8% extra on the Singapore over the Malaysian dollar.

Many of the air-con Kuala Lumpur buses are really flashy – new, immaculate, with radio, TV and toilet. The trip takes about eight hours, mainly because the road is very busy in both directions. Parts of it are now divided with toll booths (!), but this widening project will not be completed for a while yet. There's also a lunch and snack break on the way. If you want to hitch into Malaysia get yourself to Johore Bahru before starting.

Sea

There used to be lots of shipping services out of Singapore, but very few still operate – it's all airlines today. The only passage available today is the five-day service to Tawau in Sabah which costs about S$400. For details, check with Mansfield Travel behind the Ocean Building on Collyer Quay. They are also the people to see for details on ships to Fremantle in Western Australia.

To Indonesia Curiously there is no direct shipping service between Indonesia and near neighbour Singapore. You can, however, travel by sea between Singapore and Indonesia via Tanjung Pinang – the Indonesian island south of Singapore in the Riau Archipelago.

This service has, however, gone through quite an upheaval recently and is no longer nearly as convenient. There is no regular service from Jakarta, but there may be one soon. See Getting There in the Java section.

Coming from Jakarta you take a hydrofoil from Tanjung Pinang to Singapore for 21,000 rp. There's an additional 1000 rp port charge at Tanjung Pinang (only 100 rp for locals!) and you stop at Batam to clear Indonesian immigration. From Singapore ferries to Tanjung Pinang depart daily from Finger Pier and cost S$45 for the 2½ hour fast ferry or S$26 for the five to six hour slow ferry. Make sure if you pay the fast fare it really is a fast ferry. Finger Pier is on Prince Edward Rd, which is reached by a large number of bus services. The usual ferry departure time is from around 11 am. Beware of pickpockets during the mad stampede at Tanjung Priok port in Jakarta.

Fares between Jakarta and Tanjung Pinang start from around US$20 for deck class, then go up to about US$35 for a 3rd class cabin. For US$40 you can get an aircon cabin with private facilities and travel in some comfort. Deck class includes nothing – you have to provide your own sleeping bag, even your own plate and eating utensils if you want to eat the *Tampomas'* infamous rice-and-a-fish-head food. Toilet facilities are nothing to write home about either. Four-berth cabins utilise the same facilities too. It's a wise idea to bring some food with you and drinks too, since they tend to be expensive on the *Tampomas*. One advantage the *Tampomas* does have is the 'nightclub' that operates at night; (all passenger classes permitted) and beers are reasonably priced. Note that cabins tend to be booked out some time ahead, though deck class are always available on the boat.

If you want to take the ship to Medan then each Wednesday at 6 am it departs Tanjung Pinang travelling north and arrives at Belawan (the port for Medan) on Thursday afternoon. It is also possible to find ships from Tanjung Pinang to Pekanbaru in Sumatra.

GETTING AROUND

A fairly extensive subway system is being put in, but is not due to start operating for a couple of years. Its construction adds a good deal to the general turmoil and noise of the downtown redevelopment, but should in future ease traffic and the overworked bus system.

Singapore Airport Singapore's ultramodern new Changi International Airport is vast, efficient, organised and was built in record time. At the airport there are banking and money-changing facilities, two post offices, a free hotel reservation service from 7 am to 11 pm, left-luggage facilities, a variety of shops in the boarding area, and a supermarket in the basement. The reservation service will not call or book a room to the *cheap* hotels.

There are plenty of places to eat at the airport (this is Singapore after all, food capital of South-East Asia), including a *Swensen's* ice cream bar upstairs, a Chinese restaurant, a Japanese restaurant and a cafeteria-style restaurant. If you are one of the millions of air travellers fed up with over-priced and terrible food at airports, then Changi Airport has the answer to that too – there is a *McDonald's* at one end of the arrival hall and a *Church's Texas Fried Chicken* at the other end. Both at normal prices. To find even cheaper food just take the elevator beside McDonald's on the arrival level and press the button marked 'staff cafeteria' one floor below. There you'll find a kind of hawkers' centre with Chinese and Malay food.

Airport tax from Singapore is S$5 to Malaysia and Brunei, S$12 further afield.

Airport Transport Singapore's Changi International Airport is at the extreme eastern end of the island, about 20 km from the city. A new expressway has been built along reclaimed land to the city and with fast bus services it is no problem getting into the city.

You've got a choice of a very convenient public bus or taxis. For the public buses follow the signs in the airport terminal to the basement bus stop. You can take a 392 bus to Somapah for 50c; Somapah is an interchange for other bus services around Singapore. Or you can take a 394 bus to Batu Interchange for 80c.

For budget travellers heading for the Bencoolen St-Beach Rd-Middle Rd cheap accommodation enclave, by far the best bus service is the 390, which also costs 80c. You must have exact change for this bus so when you first change money on arrival make sure you get some coins. This drops you off right in Bencoolen St, in the heart of the cheap hotel area. The 390 bus departs frequently and takes about half an hour to the city. From the city, near Bencoolen, catch the 390 from the Peace Centre at the corner of Selegie and Middle Rds or from the side of Rochor Centre opposite its arrival point. From Orchard Rd take a 7 bus to Bedok Interchange and from there you can take the 390 or 347.

Taxis from the airport are subject to a S$3 supplementary charge on top of the meter fare, which will probably be S$7 to 10 to most places. Note that this only applies from the airport, not from the city. At the airport, pick up a free taxi guide, which lists many fares around town.

Bus Singapore has a high frequency and comprehensive bus network. You rarely have to wait more than a few minutes for a bus and they will get you almost anywhere you want to go. If you intend to do much travelling by bus in Singapore, a copy of the bus guide, which also includes a bus route map, is a vital investment. They cost 70c at bookshops, but shoestring travellers may well find their hotel has a supply left behind by departing visitors.

The buses follow the same route into and out of the city. Fares start from 40c and go up in 10c increments to a maximum of 80c. There are also OMO (One Man Operated) buses which charge a flat fare – you must have the exact change as none is given. There are two types of OMO bus – one charges a flat 80c (like the 390 airport bus) while the other operates a step-fare system where you pay 80, 60 or 40c depending on where you board. A sign in the front of the bus indicates the fare to be paid. For information on how to reach a certain point call 284 8866 during business hours.

Taxis Singapore has plenty of taxis, all metered. Flag fall is S$1.20 (there are still some non air-con taxis which cost S$1, but they're mainly air-con now) for the first 1.5 km then 10c for each additional 375 metres. A third and fourth passenger adds 10c each to the cost as does each piece of luggage other than hand luggage. From 1 am to 6 am there is a 50% surcharge over the meter fare. Note the surcharge from the airport and the CBD regulations. You can also book taxis by calling 293 3111 for an extra 40c.

Other Singapore's Central Business District (CBD) regulations prohibit cars from entering the centre between 7.30 and 10.15 am unless they have four people on board or pay for a special CBD licence. This applies to taxis too so unless you're willing to pay for the day licence you'll find taxis into the centre hard to find during that time.

Bicycle rickshaws are disappearing although you still see quite a few in Chinatown and other older sections of town. They're having a modest revival for tourist night tours. You can easily rent cars in Singapore although rates are higher than in Malaysia. Check the what to see section for details on the ferries out to the various islands. Walking is hot work but no hassle in Singapore – just watch out for those open storm drains.

THINGS TO BUY

Shopping is a big attraction in Singapore. There are plenty of bargains to be had although a few ground rules should be followed if you want to get your money's worth. First of all don't buy anything unless you really want it and don't buy anything unless you know the savings are worth the hassles of carting it back home. There are lots of discount houses in the west whose prices may be pretty competitive, for many items, with Singapore.

Prices & Bargaining Apart from in big department stores you have to bargain, so first of all find out what to bargain from. The prices in those big department stores will give you some idea of reality. After all it's no feat to knock 160 dollars down to 140 if a fixed price place has it for 120 all along. Maintain some disinterest when bargaining (not hard, there are plenty of other shops) but remember when you've made an offer you're committed.

Guarantees Make sure a guarantee is an international one. It's no good having to bring it back to Singapore for repair.

Where to Shop Almost anywhere is one answer, but some good places include People's Park, a huge and not so tourist-oriented shopping centre where you'll find clothes, watches, electronic gear, cameras and so on. Plus there's a Chinese emporium here. There are many ultra-modern centres, particularly down Orchard Rd and peripheral areas. For oddities try Arab St, Thieves Market in the same area or Chinatown. For regional handicrafts check the Singapore Handicrafts Centre on Tanglin Rd. For luxury goods it's Tanglin Rd again or Orchard Rd.

What to Buy Almost anything – Levis or other brand name jeans at cheap prices, cameras and film (cheaper by the dozen), tape recorders, radios, typewriters, calculators, watches (cheap ones for Indonesia, expensive ones for India if you want to resell), even Persian carpets. Chinese emporiums and some night markets have good money belts and other Chinese stuff.

LANGUAGE

English is widely spoken, plus Malay, Tamil and a number of Chinese dialects. After a spell in Singapore you may come to the conclusion that Chinese is not a language to be whispered or even spoken. It is a language to be howled, yowled, shrieked and screamed. Any Chinese restaurant will show you how.

THINGS TO SEE

Start at Raffles Place, the trading centre of a city that lives from trade. The banks, offices, shipping companies cluster around and here is Change Alley, which has a little bit of everything, not just money changers. From Clifford Pier you can get a good view over the teeming harbour, then walk along what used to be the waterfront to Merlion Park, where the symbol of Singapore spouts water over the Singapore River. Recently Singapore River has been cleaned up and the picturesque view of the crowded bum boats, backed by towering office blocks, is another part of Singapore consigned to the history books.

Chinatown It seems strange to have a Chinatown in a Chinese town, but the area north of the city centre as far as New Bridge Rd is just that. It's a maze of streets, shops and stalls with overhanging windows from which poke flagpoles of laundry. Unfortunately this area, the most picturesque in Singapore, is being ploughed under by new development and cleaned up at the same time. There's still little pockets of interest but you'd better visit them soon.

Temples There's a whole dictionary of religions in Singapore so you find a lot of temples. Sri Mariamman on South Bridge Rd is a technicolour Hindu shrine – brilliant statuary on the tower over the entrance. Several times a year there are fire-walking ceremonies inside – the firewalkers usually start at a slow ceremonial pace but soon break into a sprint! Also in Chinatown, the Thian Hock Keng Temple on Telok Ayer St was imported in

pieces from China in 1840 and is the most important Hokkien temple.

The Sultan Mosque on North Bridge Rd is the biggest mosque in Singapore. The Temple of 1000 Lights on Race Course Rd has a fine 15-metre-high seated Buddha, illuminated for a small fee by the promised 1000 lights. There is also a mother of pearl replica of the Buddha's footprint. There is a new and impressive Hindu temple on Serangoon Rd near the 1000 lights temple.

Around Town See it all in one go at Instant Asia, a 45 minute S$5 show at the Cultural Theatre behind the Rasa Singapura food centre. There is also a 45 minute S$5 multi-screen 'Singapore Experience' several times daily at this same location.

On Stamford Rd the National Museum traces its ancestry back to Sir Stamford Raffles himself and includes many items related to Singapore's early history plus an art gallery and the Haw Par jade collection. It's open 10.30 am to 7 pm daily and admission is free.

The Van Kleef Aquarium has a good (but not brilliant) collection of tropical sea life. It's open 9.30 am to 9 pm daily and costs 60c. On Science Centre Rd in Jurong the Jurong Science Centre has handles to crank, buttons to push and levers to pull – all in the interest of making science come alive. It's open 10 am to 6 pm from Tuesdays to Sundays and admission is S$1. Get there on a 143 or 158 bus.

Don't miss the Raffles Hotel, more an institution than simply a luxurious hotel; it's even finer now than it was in Kipling's day. Invest in a cup of tea on the lawn or a beer in the Writer's Bar. On the Singapore River, near the Empress Place food centre, a statue of Raffles marks where he first set foot on the island.

Wander the streets of 'little India' around Serangoon Rd – just follow your nose from one curry and rice aroma to another. Arab St is the Malay and Muslim centre of the city – lots of cane products on sale. Or see crocodiles (bound for an afterlife as handbags) at the crocodile farms. Or simply follow that favourite Singaporean pastime – eating.

Parks, Gardens & Birds There are lots of parks and gardens in Singapore including the fine Botanic Gardens on Cluny and Holland Rds, not far from Tanglin Rd and the Tourist Office. Or you can climb Mt Faber or Bukit Timah, about as high as you can get in Singapore.

There is also a zoo (admission S$3.50) and out at Jurong there's the Chinese and Japanese Gardens. The Jurong Bird Park is interesting, even if you're not a feathered friend freak. There's even a two hectare walk-in aviary which alone contains 3000 birds. Admission is S$3.50.

The Sunday morning bird-singing sessions are one of Singapore's real pleasures. At these bird lovers get together to let their caged birds have a communal sing-song while they have a cup of coffee. There's one of these gathering places off behind the Palace Hotel on Jalan Besar and another at the junction of Tiong Bahru Rd and Seng Poh Rd, It's all very organised – tall pointy birds go in tall pointy cages, little fat ones in little fat cages.

Tiger Balm Gardens A monument to inspired bad taste. Haw Par Villa, financed by the fortune Aw Boon Haw made from that miracle cure-all Tiger

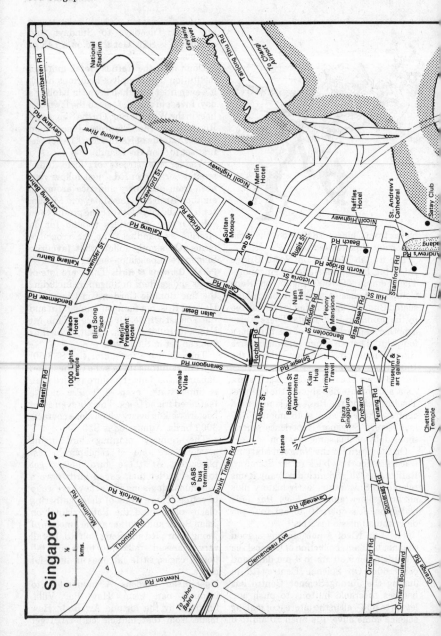

Singapore

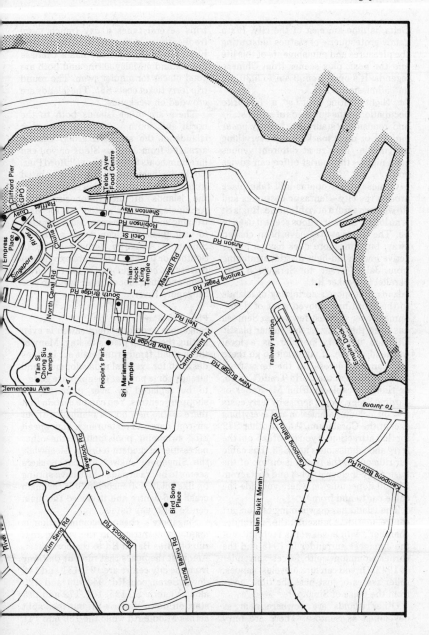

Balm, is nine km east of the city. It's a gaudy grotesquerie of statues illustrating the pleasures and punishments of this life and the next, plus scenes from Chinese legends. It's open from 9 am to 5.30 pm and admission is free.

At Night Eating out is a favourite occupation at the hundreds of street stalls and roadside restaurants. Nightly *pasar malams* or night markets sell everything imaginable. They're at different venues each night – the tourist office can advise you.

Chinese street operas still take place around the city – fantastic costumes and (to western ears) a horrible noise. Bugis St is no longer the marvellous scene it used to be. The transvestites have been chased away, but Singapore does have a highly active lowlife red-light district stretching from Jalan Besar to Serangoon Rd, parallel to Desker Rd.

Islands Singapore's sprinkling of islands to the south has enjoyed a lot of development over the past few years. Sentosa has been the major push – rather plastic although it's very popular as a local weekend escape. If you want to go there you can hop across on the ferry from Jardine Steps at the World Trade Centre, or ride the cablecar from Mt Faber or Jardine Steps. Going across by ferry costs S$5.50 including admission and everything except the Coralarium. Add another S$2 for that attraction. If you go after 5 pm the ferry and admission is just S$3. The cable car ride out to the island is on top of the basic ferry-inclusive ticket and costs from S$3.50 depending on where you ride the cable car to and from.

The island has a swimming lagoon, art centre, maritime museum, the 'surrender chamber', with a waxworks recreation of the Japanese surrender in 1945 and the earlier Commonwealth forces surrender of 1942. Or you can hire bicycles, canoes, roller skates or just pass the time, away from the noise of Singapore.

Other islands are nowhere near as developed as Sentosa. There are ferry trips several times a day (much more frequently on weekends) to St John's and Kusu Islands. Tiny Kusu has a Chinese temple and a Malay shrine and both are good places for a quiet swim. The round trip ferry ticket costs S$5. The islands are crowded on weekends.

There are other islands both to the north and south – boats to the other islands of the southern group can be arranged from Jardine Steps or you can hire bum boats from there or Clifford Pier. To the northern islands boats can be hired from Ponggol Point. Further south still are the islands of the Indonesian Riau Archipelago – they're too far for day-tripping and an Indonesian visa is required to visit them. You can go on a Port of Singapore Authority harbour cruise to Sentosa or flashier (and more expensive) private harbour cruises. Or you can hire a boat and just mooch your way up the Singapore River.

Places to Stay

Singapore's rapid modernisation is even hitting the cheap places to stay. Many of these small, family-run hotels are in areas destined for eventual redevelopment and already some popular cheapies are gone – to be replaced by ever more air-con shopping centres. You can be certain that there are no new hotels planned without air-con, bars and restaurants, high-speed lifts, swimming pools and all the other necessities of modern tourism. Meanwhile the Singapore answer for backpackers seems to be crash pads which have sprung up like wildfire. Bencoolen St is the main crash pad centre and it is also the main centre for cheap hotels.

Singapore's cheap accommodation is mainly concentrated in the streets that run off Bras Basah Rd to the north-east. Amongst the buses that run out that way from the city centre are 101, 131 and 146 down Serangoon Rd; 94, 100 and 120 along Victoria St; 125, 161, 172 and 175 start off down Victoria St, but then split across Middle Rd while the 130 and 141 continue further down before turning off across Jalan Besar. Jalan Besar, which becomes Bencoolen St at Rochor Rd, runs one way – the wrong way if you're coming from the city centre, the docks or the railway station.

Coming in from the airport the public bus will drop you at the Queen St terminus, conveniently close to most of the Bencoolen St and Beach Rd hotels.

Crash Pads Singapore's crash pads are all mildly illegal since they're just residential flats which have been broken up into dormitories and cubicle-like rooms. But then this is Singapore and free enterprise is what counts! The trouble with them is that the jam-packed crowds tend to overstretch the limited facilities and the rooms really are small. Plus everybody else there will be another traveller, just like yourself. On the other hand they're good information sources and good places to meet people – since so many other travellers stay there – and you won't find any cheaper accommodation in Singapore.

Almost down at the Bras Basah end of Bencoolen St you'll find the *Peony Mansions* crash pad, longest running of these places. It's at 46-52 Bencoolen St, on top of a Mazda (at last count, it's also been a BMW and a Holden) showroom. There's no sign at all – go around back and take the lift to the 5th floor and knock on the door at 50E. Like all the crash pads it's rather anonymous. Inside you can stay for S$8 a night; simple dormitory-style accommodation, but it's quite OK. As in nearly all the crash pads some private rooms are also available. Here they are S$20-24. There are other flats in the block, but also run from 50E. This very popular place is often full – people in the building have taken to offering any spare room or bed they might have. You may get such an invitation if one of the tenants sees you in the hall or elevator.

Across the road and up a bit at 173/175 is another centre for crash pads. They are in the newish Hong Guan Building nearly

opposite the *Nam Hai Hotel*. There are no outside signs here either, again go around back and up the elevator by the parking lot. The *Bencoolen St Service Apartments*, also known as *Goh's Homestay*, has a reception desk at the 5th floor, but also has rooms on the 6th. In their dorm you get a mattress on the floor and a locker for S$7. Shared rooms are S$9 each and private rooms go for S$24. They've got a good noticeboard with bus guides.

On the third floor is *Philip Choo's*. Here the foam mattress dorm is S$8, rooms S$22. Again the dorm has lockers and there's a noticeboard. There may be other places in the building as well – they come and go.

Bencoolen House Home Stay (tel 338 1206 or 292 6000) is on the 7th and 8th floors at 27 Bencoolen St near Middle Rd. It's very good, clean and pretty quiet and there's a kitchen you can use. The dorm costs S$7, rooms are S$22 single, S$24 double, three people S$26. A bit extra for air-con rooms.

Another of these central crash pads is *Airmaster Travel Centre* (tel 338 9720) at 36G Prinsep St, a block over from Bencoolen and down towards Bras Basah Rd. Here there are dorm beds at S$7 and a washing machine and TV available for your use. Travellers report this is a friendly, convenient place and there's an excellent noticeboard. Airmaster Travel is a popular travel agent for cheap tickets to almost anywhere and you enter through their office. A last minute letter said that Airmaster have moved – it may be true.

Not too far away is *Sim's Rest House* (tel 336 4957 or 336 0176) at 114A Mackenzie Rd. Mackenzie Rd becomes Albert St across Serangoon. It's a bit of a walk from Serangoon along the sort of industrial/factory-lined Mackenzie Rd. The owner is a friendly guy with dorms for S$7 (lockers available) and real rooms for S$20. If you phone him up from the bus terminus he'll pick you up.

There are a couple of others too, in a different area of town. The *Friendly Rest*

House (tel 294 0847) is just that and is found at 357A Serangoon Rd just past Kitchener Rd. The door is actually around the corner from Serangoon on Perumal Rd. Look for Fong Tat Auto – it's below the guest house which is one floor up. It's well run and helpful and has dorm beds for S$6, double rooms at S$23 with attached bathroom. A bus 390 from the airport gets you in the general area, then a bus 131 or 140 will take you down Serangoon Rd. A bus 146 from the train station will get you practically to the door.

Sandy's Place (tel 292 6720) nearby at 28B Rangoon Rd, has a S$6 mattress on the floor dorm; S$8 with a bed. They also ask a S$10 deposit which you get back when leaving. It's clean and the management are friendly. Rangoon Rd runs off Serangoon Rd by the New World Amusement Park and can be a bit noisy. The stairs for Sandy's Place are beside the Swiss Bar.

Other crash pad possibilities to investigate include *Traveller's Lodge* at 16 Penhaus St off Lavender St at the far end of Jalan Besar. This is a slightly run-down industrial area. Rooms with fan cost S$14 to 17. *Sunseeker's Rest House* is next to the Neptune Building on the 2nd floor of 20 South Quay. Or there's *New Handy Place* right in the heart of Orchard Rd at 3A Angullia Park. Dorm beds are S$8, doubles S$20 and you can get there on a 490 bus from the airport.

Chinese Hotels – Bras Basah Rd to Rochor Canal Rd Many travellers would prefer to spend a few dollars more for the cheap Chinese hotels. Your money will get you a fairly spartan room with a bare floor, a few pieces of furniture, a sink and a fan. Toilets are usually shared, but you might even get hot water in the showers. Couples should always ask for a single room – a single usually means just one double bed, whereas a double would have two. As for the crash pads, Bencoolen St is a good place to start looking.

The *Nam Hai* (tel 337 5395) at 166 is pretty well an institution and usually full

every night. The two old Cantonese women who used to run it have retired and gone back to China and the place is now run by a small family. They're friendly, the man in particular can tell a funny story or two and they don't watch the TV late at night! This new owner figures that his place and others on Bencoolen don't have many years left before the ball hits them. Singles/doubles are S$22/24 and there's cold water in the fridge. A bit further up towards Bras Basah Rd at 81 is the *Kian Hua* (tel 338 3492) with rooms from S$20 single, S$28 double. It's another fairly typical old Chinese hotel.

Other places around Bencoolen St include the rather more expensive *San Wah* (tel 336 2428) at 36 Bencoolen St with singles at S$30 and doubles S$32, S$35 with air-con. Almost at the end at 12 Bencoolen St is the clean *Hotel Ben* with singles from S$24 and doubles from S$30. Rooms with bathroom or air-con cost more. These latter two are both a little upmarket from the cheapest Chinese hotels. Round on Prinsep St (next one over) is the *Tiong Hoa* (tel 338 4522) at number 4. Rooms in this very pleasantly run air-con hotel are S$20 single, S$30 double, S$36 air-con.

The Park is around the corner from the Nam Hai at 239B Victoria at the corner where Albert becomes Bugis St. It's the freshly painted white place with blue shutters. Inside it's very clean with lots of tilework and has singles for S$27, doubles for S$30 to 34. The *South-East Asia Hotel* (tel 338 2394) at 190 Waterloo St, directly behind the Nam Hai, is a bit more costly, but if you really need a rest it has air-con, and is quiet and modern with singles/doubles at S$34/41. Also on Waterloo St the *Waterloo Hotel* is good value for a middle range hotel at S$45/57.50.

Beach Rd, a few blocks over towards the (ever-receding) waterfront, is another centre for cheap hotels although some of them have already fallen prey to redevelopment. If you aspire to the Raffles, but can't afford to stay there, at least you can stay close at these places! The *Shang Onn* (tel 338 4153) at 37 Beach Rd, on the corner of Purvis St, has singles at S$26, doubles at S$30 and is clean and friendly. Another one hanging on despite construction all around is the *Hai Hin* (tel 336 3739) at 97. Rooms, single or double, cost S$30.

If you follow Middle Rd from Beach Rd back towards Bencoolen St you'd find a few more cheapies like the rather inconspicuous *Soon Seng Long* (tel 337 6318) at 26 Middle Rd where rooms are also around S$20. Big rooms, if you can wake the proprietor up from his slumbers, or pry him loose from that mah-jong table.

Others on Middle Rd include the *Lido* (tel 337 1872) at 54 with singles/doubles at S$24/28. Nearly back at Bencoolen is the *Tai Loke* (tel 337 6209), at 151. There are big, airy rooms with fine old furniture for S$30 single or double. By that time you're almost back at Bencoolen St. Continuing up Middle Rd near the corner of Selegie at number 260 and 262 is the clean and very nice *Sun Sun Hotel* (tel 338 4911). It's a little more expensive with singles/doubles at S$30/35 and there's a bar and restaurant downstairs.

Rochor Rd also runs from Beach Rd to Bencoolen St, parallel to Middle Rd. At 228/229 the *New 7th Storey Hotel* (tel 337 0251-4) is an upmarket cheapie with singles/doubles at S$49/59 or with bath S$65/75.

Chinese Hotels – Rochor Canal Rd to Lavender St Another batch of cheap hotels is across Rochor Rd down to Lavender St on and around Jalan Besar. Going down Jalan Besar from Bencoolen at 315 Jalan Besar there's the *Singapore Island Hotel* (tel 258 3337) with reasonable rooms S$22/25 or S$30 with air-con. Across the road the *International* (tel 258 3347) at 290 costs S$30 single, S$35 double, S$40 double with bath.

Further down Jalan Besar at 383 is the *Kam Leng* (tel 258 2289). It's upstairs and has good, clean rooms at S$22 single or double and also an excellent restaurant

with an English menu and fish tanks where you select your fish while it's still swimming. Right down at the end of the street near Lavender is the *Palace Hotel* (tel 258 3108) where singles/doubles are S$22. The Palace is spotlessly clean and a favourite touch here is the free coke you're always presented with when you make your hot and sweaty arrival. The front rooms are very noisy, however, due to the round-the-clock traffic along Jalan Besar. Traffic noise is quite a problem in most of these central hotels though.

There are quite a few other ones in this area, too; many about halfway down Jalan Besar around Kitchener Rd. The *Siong Cheong* (tel 294 7147) is at 18 Verdun, near the big President Merlin Hotel. Verdun runs parallel to Serangoon Rd and Jalan Besar – midway between them. It's a quiet street and pleasant rooms cost S$20 single or double, S$28 with air-con. The owners' brother also runs a small hotel (tel 258 4883), clean but maybe not as nice, nearby at 330A Serangoon Rd. Here rooms are S$18 single, S$20 double with fan, more with air-con.

The *Hong Kong Hotel* (tel 293 1145) at 16 Burmah Rd, on the corner with Race Course Rd, is a pleasantly clean place with rooms at S$30 single or double, S$40 with air-con. It's fairly quiet too since it is not on a busy main road. The *Tai Nam* at 187-189 Serangoon Rd charges S$28 single or double, but is a bit grubby.

Chinese Hotels – Other Places Oddly, there are no hotels to speak of in Chinatown – nearly all are in the areas mentioned above, east of Bras Basah Rd. One exception of note is the *Majestic Hotel* (tel 222 3377) at 31 Bukit Pasoh Rd near Chinatown. Bukit Pasoh runs between New bridge Rd and Neil Rd. It's a quiet street lined with traditional houses and buildings, but all well maintained, in good condition and brightly painted. There's a pleasant park nearby and in the morning and evening people do tai chi and tai kuan do exercises there. The hotel is immaculate and rooms are pleasant, some with a balcony. Singles/doubles are S$25/32 without bath, S$24/44 with bath.

Not far away is the *New Asia*, once a large colonial place but now with just a portion of the rooms open and apparently dying a slow death. Fan-cooled singles/doubles are S$18/24. It's on Maxwell Rd at Peck Seah, a couple of blocks up from Robinson Rd.

At Chinese New Year it can be very difficult to find a room in Singapore and some places are prone to sudden price increases. Student Travel, who have their office in the Ming Court Hotel, offer substantial discounts at some of Singapore's 'International Standard' hotels – which means they will still cost something like S$70 and up for a single.

The Ys & Camping Singapore has a number of YMCAs and YWCAs, although the cheap old YMCA Katong has now been redeveloped. The *YMCA* (tel 222 4666) is at 70 Palmer Rd and has rooms from S$25 single without bath up to S$40 double with bath. The Stevens Rd *Metropolitan YMCA* (tel 737 7755) at 60 Stevens Rd is rather more expensive at S$55 single, S$60 double with private bath, TV and air-con. They take men or couples only.

There is a large new YMCA under construction which should be open in 1985. It's located on Bras Basah Rd at Prinsep, opposite the big Cathay movie theatre. The *YWCA Hostel* (tel 336 1212) at 6-8 Fort Canning costs S$42 for a private room or S$50 for a double. Nice dorm rooms are available, for women, at S$13. They take women or couples only and this has been recommended by solo women travellers as a safe and secure place.

Singapore is probably overdue to get a real YHA youth hostel – there's no sign of one yet. You can, however, camp at the good *East Coast Campsite* on East Coast Parkway, at the five km marker. Unfortunately there are no buses stopping on this expressway so you have to get off at the bus stop in Upper East Coast Rd and

then walk 15 minutes; from the end of Bedok Rd a walking track leads under the expressway right to the camp. The site has a clean, well-lit reading and TV room and there are a few shops and a hawkers' centre nearby. The site is deserted during the week but very busy on weekends and school holidays. A four-person tent costs S$5 a night Monday to Friday, S$6 on weekends and holidays.

Places to Eat

In Singapore you find every kind of Asian food, and even western food if you must. For its combination of wide variety, high quality and low prices Singapore has to be the food capital of Asia. Best of all it's accessible – there are no problems with understanding menus, searching out places, getting what you want across. Some places to try:

Hawkers' Food Hawkers are the mobile food stalls – pushcarts which set their tables and stools up around them and sell their food right on the streets. This is the base line for Singapore food, the place where it all starts, where the prices are lowest and the eating quite possibly the most interesting.

Real, mobile, on-the-street hawkers are a disappearing species, but they've been replaced by hawkers' centres where a large number of non-mobile hawkers can all be found under the one roof. Scattered amongst them are tables and stools and you can sit and eat at any one you choose – none of them belong to a specific stall. Indeed a group of you can sit at one table and all eat from different stalls, and at the same time have drinks from another.

It's one of the wonders of food-centre-eating how the various operators keep track of their plates and utensils – and manage to chase you up with the bill. The real joy of food centres is the sheer variety; while you're having Chinese food your companion can be eating a biriyani and across the table somebody else can be trying the satay. As a rough guide most one-dish meals cost from S$1.20-3. Higher for more elaborate dishes.

There are hawkers' centres all over Singapore and more are being built as areas are redeveloped and the hawkers moved off the streets. In the business centre one of the best is *Telok Ayer*, built in an old Victorian market building between Robinson Rd and Shenton Way. The two other business centre places – *Empress Place*, beside the Singapore River, and *Boat Quay*, directly across the river, have recently been demolished. *Telok Ayer* and others in the business district are very busy at lunch, but tend to be quiet or closed in the evenings, apart from the ones by the river.

The once popular and still well-known *Satay Club* area by the waterfront at the foot of Stamford Rd seems to have fallen on hard times. It's still there, but never busy. There's demolition and construction all over the place at this end of town and with less housing in the area few people bother coming to eat I suppose. Still, it is near the river and Raffles Quay – a pleasant strolling area in the evening.

Right beside the Handicraft Centre on Tanglin Rd is the *Rasa Singapura* centre where the hawkers were all selected in a special competition to find the best stalls for each individual dish. This centre is promoted heavily for tourists although all the food centres are perfectly safe and healthy – you really can eat anywhere in Singapore. As a result prices are a bit higher than at other centres and some people say the food is not really any better – decide for yourself.

Continue down Orchard Rd and there's another popular centre upstairs in the *Cuppage Street* centre. The downstairs section is a vegetable and produce market, but the upstairs food stalls section includes many of the operators relocated from the famous old Orchard Rd car park (Gluttons' Square) when it was redeveloped. The *Newton Circus* centre, at the traffic circle at the end of Scotts Rd, is particularly popular at night as it stays

open later than usual. There are other centres on Serangoon Rd just beyond Rochor Rd; on Jalan Besar just before Kitchener St; in the Peoples' Park complex near Chinatown; and in the high-rise block on the corner of Waterloo and Rochor Rds. Bugis St still has a number of traditional hawkers' stalls.

Near Bugis St, at the corner of Waterloo or Queen and Albert Sts there is a very busy, very popular and very good centre with all types of food at low prices. It's conveniently close to the Bencoolen area hotels. Also along the alleys off Bugis St there are stalls. Some people now set up a dozen tables or so with white tablecloths, napkins, wine glasses – the whole bit. The prices are a bit higher, of course.

In Chinatown, there's a hawkers' centre alongside the *Tanjong Market* not far from the train station. There's also the *Amory St Food Centre*, where Amory meets Telok Ayer, in Chinatown.

On Kitchener Rd, across from the big President Merlin Hotel near Serangoon Rd is an outdoor food stall area that has steamboats – as does the Satay Club – one of the few that seems to offer it as standard fare.

Chinese Food Singapore has plenty of restaurants serving everything from a south Indian thali to an all-American hamburger, but naturally it's Chinese restaurants that predominate. They range all the way from streetside hawkers' stalls to fancy five-star hotel restaurants with a whole gamut of possibilities in between.

One very popular place that has now fallen on hard times is *Albert St*. A couple of years ago half the street disappeared to make way for a multistorey car park. Now the government has put another nail in the coffin by preventing the restaurants from spilling out into the street. And if you can't eat out on the street in Albert St, why, most people seem to think, eat there at all? So *Fatty's* (Wing Seong) at 184 Albert St may still be turning out great Cantonese food, but the crowds aren't like they used to be. If eating in Albert St – because you certainly can still eat there and the food is still superb – be certain to agree beforehand on a price for the meal.

The *Manhill* at 99 Pasir Panjang Rd and its companion the *Hillman* at 159 Cantonment Rd are two more traditional-style Cantonese restaurants with moderate prices in straightforward surroundings. The *Mayflower Peking* at the International Building on Orchard Rd (beside the Thai Embassy) and the *Mayflower* at the DBS Building on Shenton Way are the opposite end of the scale in size and setting. They're huge Hong Kong-style dim sum specialists, but surprisingly reasonably priced for all the carpeting and air-conditioning. Dim sum starts from around S$1 per plate. Remember that dim sum is a lunchtime or Sunday breakfast dish.

At 147-153 Kitchener Rd, between Jalan Besar and Serangoon Rd, the *Fut Sai Kai* (which translates as 'monk's world') is another spartan old coffee shop where the speciality is vegetarian cooking. Prices are not low, but it offers a good chance to sample a slightly unusual variation of Chinese cuisine. Ditto for the *Lok Woh Yuen* at Jalan Tanjung Pagar 25. Or try the old-fashioned *Majestic* on Bukit Pasoh Rd near Chinatown.

Chicken rice is a common, but popular, dish all over town and *Swee Kee* on the 4th floor of the Fortuna Centre at the corner of Middle Rd and Bencoolen St is a long-running specialist with a high reputation. Chicken and rice is S$3.30 served with chili, ginger and thick soya sauce. They also do steamboats; a S$20 version has a stock enriched by various Chinese herbs and Mao Tai wine. The menu includes mostly Cantonese dishes, mainly seafood – S$5 for a basic, S$10 for a varied meal. They used to be at 51 Middle Rd too – without air-con, simpler and a bit cheaper – but that branch seems to be closed now. The *Rasa Singapura* chicken rice stall also does a good job of it – they even offer the chicken as 'regular' or boneless'.

Although Cantonese is the most readily available Chinese cuisine in Singapore you can also find most of the regional variations although they often tend to be more expensive than the common, everyday Cantonese restaurants. If you've got a yen to try Peking duck then the *Eastern Palace* on the 4th floor of Supreme House is one of the best Peking restaurants. Szechuan restaurants are relatively common. They include the reasonably priced *Omei* in the Hotel Grand Centre. In the old Mayfair Hotel on Armenian St the *Great Shanghai* is the place to go for Shanghainese food like drunken chicken.

Hokkien food is not all that popular a cuisine despite the large number of Hokkiens in Singapore, but *Beng Hiang* at 20 Murray St is renowned for its Hokkien food. Teochew food is a relatively widely available cuisine – you could try *Guan Hin* at 1 Bendemeer Rd where steamboat is also very popular. Or the traditional *Chui Wah Lin* at 49 Mosque St. At several of these places there may be no menu, but a request for suggestions and prices will be readily answered. Finally there's Taiwanese food – try the *May Garden* at 101 Orchard Towers or the reasonably priced *Goldleaf* at 185 Orchard Rd.

Singapore has another delicious local variation on Chinese food. Seafood in Singapore is simply superb, whether it's prawns or abalone, fish-head curry or chilli crabs. Most of the better seafood specialists are some distance out from the city centre, but the travelling is worthwhile. Upper East Coast Rd is one of the best areas where you will find places like *Seaview* at 779A. Or try the *Chin Wah Heng* at 785 Upper East Coast Rd, at about the 14½ km marker – moderately priced, but with the usual glass tanks containing crabs, eels, prawns and fish all ready to head for the wok. Others include the *Choon Seng* at 892 Ponggol Rd at Ponggol Point right up at the north of the island. Or the *Chin Lee* at 18C Jalan Tuas in the small fishing village of Tuas, way out beyond Jurong at the western tip of the island, 30 km from the city. The trip out to Ponggol Point, on an 82 or 83 bus, is quite an experience in itself; you pass miles of cemeteries and then chicken and pig farms, surprisingly rural for Singapore.

Indian Food As with everything else some of the best Indian food is in the hawkers' centres. This particularly applies to biriyani dishes – in virtually any of the centres, but particularly Telok Ayer – you can have a superb chicken biriyani for just S$2.50.

If you want to sample eat-with-your-fingers south Indian vegetarian food then the place to go is the famous and very popular *Komala Vilas* at 76 Serangoon Rd. Established soon after the war, Komala Vilas has an open downstairs area where you have masala dosa (S$2.25) and other snacks, while upstairs, which is now all air-conditioned, S$3.50 buys you their eat-all-you-can rice meal. Remember to wash your hands before you start, to use only your right hand and to ask for eating utensils only if you really have to! On your way out try an Indian sweet from the showcase at the back of the downstairs section. Another rice plate specialist is *Sri Krishna Vilas* at 229 Selegie Rd.

For north Indian food *Jubilee* at 771 North Bridge Rd, near the Sultan Mosque and Arab St, is an even more venerable establishment – it has been in operation since before the war. It's a great place for a biriyani or other north Indian dishes and again is absurdly cheap. A few doors down at 791-793 the *Islamic* is very similar.

Much pricier, but with a great reputation for high-quality food, is *Omar Khayyam* at 55 Hill St, virtually opposite the American Embassy. Here the food is Kashmiri, a subtle variation on normal north Indian food, but the tandoori dishes are the highlight. There's a small, basic north Indian place called the *Muslim Restaurant* or something similar on Bencoolen St near Middle Rd, across from the Fortuna Centre. They have very good food and specialise in fish dishes, including fish-head curry, but have chicken and vegetable items too. Cost is S$3 to 4. There are plenty of modest Indian places in little India along Serangoon Rd.

Malay, Thai, Indonesian & Nonya Food You won't find a great deal of Malay or Nonya food in Singapore although there are one or two Nonya specialists in the food centres – particularly *Telok Ayer*. Satay, of course, is available in many centres – you'll find good satay in the *Rasa Singapura* and, of course, at the *Satay Club* on Elizabeth Walk, where the stalls all specialise in satay.

There are a number of Sumatran nasi padang specialists, one of the best known being *Rendezvous* at 4-5 Bras Basah Rd, at the junction with Prinsep St. At lunchtime only *Nasi Padang* at 24 Tanglin Rd, across from the Tanglin Centre, is equally good.

For Thai food try *Siamese's Chef Snack Bar* on the 3rd floor of the Fortuna Centre, corner of Bencoolen St and Middle Rd. It's open 11 am to 3.30 pm only, closed Sundays. Sliced beef and duck Kway Teow soup costs S$2; most dishes are just S$1.50 to 2. A lunch of curry vegetables and rice is S$2.50. Various cheap desserts are also offered. Although the restaurant is tucked away in a corner, most of the food is sold out by 2 pm.

Western Food Yes, you can get western food in Singapore too – including *McDonald's* at a string of places such as Orchard Rd near Scotts Rd, Peoples' Park and Changi Airport. There are also *A&W Root Beer* and *Kentucky Fried Chicken* outlets and you can even try eat-all-you-can pizzas, spaghetti or other meals at *Shakey's Pizza* in the City Plaza Shopping Complex in Geylang.

The *Pavilion Steak House*, next door to the Specialists Centre on Orchard Rd, is a curious colonial hangover; a Singapore equivalent to the *Coliseum* in Kuala Lumpur. Unfortunately their prices, drinks in particular, have got very high of late. Or try *The Beefeater* at 417 River Valley Rd where you can sip a pint in the air-conditioned comfort and forget how close you are to the equator.

For upscale western food, but at bargain prices, there is the *Restaurant*

Shatec (tel 235 9533), the Singapore Hotel Association's Training and Educational Centre. Now open to the public, the place is really a training centre for hotel dining room food preparation and presentation. They offer set, five-course meals at lunch and dinner as well as an a la carte menu in a fairly elegant setting. Lunch is S$9.50, dinner S$12.50 with items such as escargot, Scottish salmon and duck a l'orange.

Odds & Ends Naturally Singapore has a lot of personal favourites and obscure odds and ends. If you want a light snack at any time of the day there are quite a few Chinese coffee bars selling interesting cakes which go just nicely with a cup of coffee or teh-o. Try the *Dong Log Wee Cake House* at 235 Orchard Rd.

There are several places worth trying for breakfast around the Bencoolen St cheap hotel area. *Bakers Cafeteria*, at the corner of Bras Basah and Victoria, has complete breakfasts for S$3.80. Set western lunches go for S$5.20. The little

Chinese coffee shop beside the Nam Hai Hotel where the city buses stop serves two eggs, toast and tea or coffee – watch out for that sweetened milk – for S$2. They're basic, but they try, and might even lend you an English paper to read while you eat. Others in the area can give you toast and jam if you can make yourself understood. A few doors down Middle Rd there's an Indian place that does great breakfast roti chanai.

The *Cafe de Coral*, in the Far East Plaza on Scotts Rd opposite the Holiday Inn, does orange juice, eggs, bacon, toast and coffee for a bargain S$4.

Towards the back of the Empress Place food centre *Neuborne's* is a great place for fish and chips, believe it or not. There are plenty of supermarkets in Singapore with everything from French wine to Australian beer, yoghurt to muesli, cheese to ice cream. A pot of tea on the lawn at the Raffles Hotel is a fine investment and a chance to relive the Singapore of an earlier era.

Thailand

There is probably more historical evidence of past cultures to be seen in Thailand than in any other South-East Asian country. If you've got the slightest interest in ruins, deserted cities and Buddhas, Thailand is the place to go. It's a remarkably fertile country and a major agricultural exporter, but very much one big city and a lot of countryside – Chiang Mai, the second city, is a village compared to Bangkok. Easy travel, excellent and economic accommodation, some fine beach centres and an interesting (but very hot!) cuisine make Thailand a very good country for a visit.

HISTORY

Thailand's history often seems fantastically complicated – so many peoples, kings, kingdoms and cultures have had a hand in it. The earliest civilisation in Thailand was probably that of the Mons who brought a Buddhist culture from the Indian subcontinent. The rise of the Davaravati Kingdoms in central Thailand was ended by the westward movement of the energetic Khmers. Their great Cambodian capital of Angkor is currently out of bounds, but Khmer influence can be seen in Thailand at Phimai and Lopburi. At the same time in southern Thailand the Sumatran-based Srivijaya empire extended up through Malaya and into Thailand.

Kublai Khan's expansionist movements in China speeded up the southern migration of the Thai people, and in 1220 Thai princes took over Sukhothai, their first Siamese capital. Other Thai peoples migrated to Laos and the Shan states of Burma forming ethnically-related populations. Another Thai kingdom, under King Mengrai, formed in Chiang Rai in North Thailand and later moved to Chiang Mai. In 1350 the Prince of U Thong founded still another Thai capital in Ayuthaya and eventually over-shadowed Sukhothai. For two centuries Ayuthaya was unsurpassed, pushing the Khmers right out of Siam; their capital of Angkor was abandoned to the jungles, which would hide it almost to this century.

In the 16th century the Burmese – archrivals of the Thais who had been disunited by Kublai Khan's sack of Pagan – regrouped and caused further havoc. Chiang Mai, which Ayuthaya had never absorbed, was captured by the Burmese in 1556 and in 1569 Ayuthaya too fell before them. Their success was short-lived; in 1595 the Thais recaptured Chiang Mai. During the next century European influences first appeared in Thailand, but the execution of the Greek Phaulkoun, emissary of the French, ended that little episode.

In the 18th century the Burmese attacked again and in 1767, after a prolonged siege, took and utterly destroyed Ayuthaya. The Siamese soon regrouped and expelled the Burmese, but Ayuthaya was never reconstructed. In 1782 the new capital at Thonburi was moved across the river to its present site of Bangkok and the continuing Chakri dynasty was founded under King Rama I. In the 19th century – while all the rest of South-East Asia was being colonised by the French, Dutch and British – Siam managed to remain independent. By deftly playing off one European power against another, King Mongkut (Rama IV) and Chulalongkorn (Rama V) also managed to obtain many of the material benefits of colonialism.

In 1932 a peaceful coup converted the country into a constitutional monarchy and in 1939 the name was changed from Siam to Thailand. During WW II the Thais opened their borders to Japan and as a reward took Cambodia and Laos, sovereignty of which they had relinquished to the French. At the end of the war, these policies were repudiated and the whole

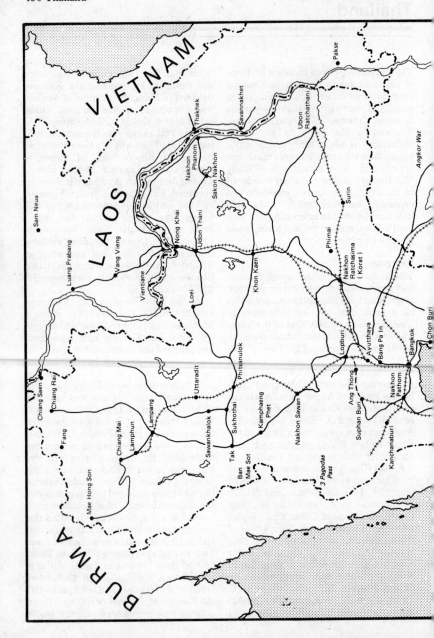

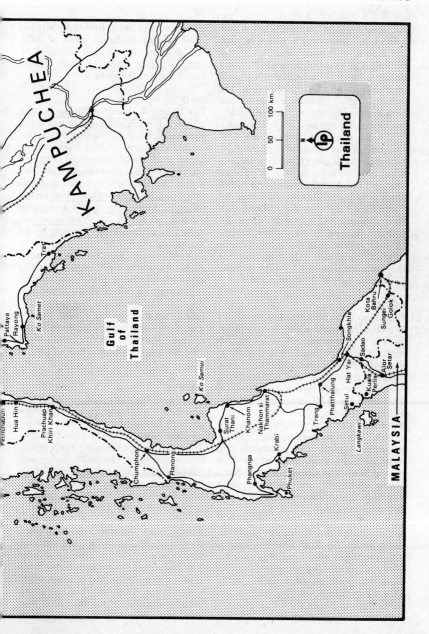

matter forgotten by the allies. The wartime collaborator came back to power in 1948 and for years Thailand was run by the military. The next two premiers followed similar policies of dictatorial power, self enrichment, and blind obedience to US policy. In 1973 Thanom was given the boot in an unprecedented student revolt, and democracy was restored in Thailand.

It was a short-lived experiment. The government was continually plagued by factionalism and party squabbles and was never able to come to firm grips with Thailand's problems – made worse by the upsurge of border dangers following the Communist takeovers in Cambodia and Laos. Nobody was surprised when the military stepped in once more in late 1976. Despite an abortive counter-coup in early 1977, elections in 1979 and another abortive counter-coup in 1981 the generals seem to be back in firm command.

FACTS

Population Thailand's population is about 35 million. Although basically homogeneous there are interesting hill tribes in the northern area and some Malay people in the south. There are also a large number of refugees from Laos and Cambodia in festering camps in the border areas and Thailand too has suffered from the Vietnam refugee problem.

Geography The country occupies an area of 508,000 square km and apart from its southern border with Malaysia its neighbours are none too friendly. The central area is composed of flat, damp plains, ideal for rice growing. In the north and down the narrow southern isthmus it becomes quite hilly.

Economy Tin mining and rubber production are major export activities, but rice is the mainstay of the Thai economy and is widely exported to surrounding countries. There is some mining being developed in the south. Some people would say sex & sin is a very marketable Thai commodity, particularly in Bangkok.

Religion Buddhism is prevalent – orange-robed monks and Buddhas sitting, standing and reclining; made of gold, marble, stone or whatever – they're all common sights. There's a small Muslim minority in the far south.

INFO

The Tourist Authority of Thailand has an office at the airport, another in central Bangkok and quite a few regional centres around the country. They have a lot of useful brochures, booklets and maps and will probably have an information sheet on almost any Thai subject that interests you. The TAT is probably the best tourist office in South-East Asia for the production of useful information sheets rather than (often useless) pretty colour brochures.

They also put out an accommodation guide covering the whole country, including quite cheap places, plus more detailed regional accommodation sheets. In Bangkok they sell the invaluable bus map which lists all the Bangkok bus routes. The flip side of the bus map has a pretty good map of Thailand with Thai script as well. Make sure any map has names on it in Thai as well as English.

SAFETY

There has been a lot of talk about safety in Thailand – what with insurgent groups, guerrilla forces, muggings, robberies and who-knows-what getting wide publicity. The internal opposition forces are mainly communist or, in the south, Malay separatists, and in general they stick to harassing government forces. There is little likelihood of visitors coming into contact with them.

Robberies and hold ups, despite their publicity, are relatively infrequent but if there is a rule of thumb it's that the hold-up gangs seem to concentrate more on the tour buses then the ordinary buses or the trains, assuming that the pickings will be richer there. Theft in Thailand is still usually a matter of stealth rather than strength. You're more likely to be pickpocketed than mugged. Take care of your valuables, don't carry too much cash around with you, watch out for razor artists (they slit bags open in crowded quarters) and the snatch-and-run experts in Bangkok. Don't trust hotel rooms, particularly in the beach-hut places like Phuket and Koh Samui. Try not to have your bag on the roof of buses or in the underfloor luggage compartments. And don't worry – it probably won't happen to you!

BOOKS

Hardly surprisingly there's a Lonely Planet guide to Thailand. Written by Joe Cummings, a young American who speaks Thai and was a peace corps worker in the country. *Thailand – a travel survival kit* provides much more detail than I can squeeze in here. With so many interesting archaeological sites, temples, buildings, and other attractions a good guide book is essential and *Discovering Thailand* by Clarac and Smithies is excellent for the cultural, architectural and archaeological points of interest. *Insight Guide Thailand* is another Apa coffee-table guidebook.

VISAS

You've got a variety of choices in the visa game for Thailand. First of all you can enter Thailand without any visa and be granted a 15-day stay permit. Officially you must have an outward ticket, but in practice this does not seem to be rigidly enforced. The major catch with the 15-day permit is that no extension is possible – 15 days is your lot.

Next up are one-month transit visas which cost US$5 and (like the 15-day permit) cannot be extended. From the traveller's point of view the best deal is a two-month tourist visa which costs approximately US$10. They are issued quickly and fuss-free. Singapore, Penang, Kota Bahru and Kathmandu are all good places to get Thai visas. Extensions to your visa are possible although recent reports indicate that they are currently not extending tourist or transit visas. If they are extending them, there are immigration offices in Hat Yai, Bangkok and Chiang Mai and the extension only costs 1B.

If you are leaving Thailand then returning (going to Burma for a week for example) you can get a re-entry visa, but this costs a hefty 300B. The immigration office in Bangkok for these visas is on Soi San Phlu. If you can provide a good reason for getting one, non-immigrant visas are also available – these cost US$15 and are valid for 90 days.

Other Visas Bangkok is a popular place for getting visas for onward travel, particularly for people heading on to west Asia. Visas are required for Burma for all nationalities and they take 24 hours to issue. The embassy is at 132 Sathorn Neua Rd and is only open from 10 am to 12 noon daily. Visas for Bangladesh are required for some nationalities and the embassy is on Soi Chareohmitr off Ekamai Rd.

Following the upheavals in the Punjab, visas are now required for most nationalities visiting India and the embassy is at 46 Soi Prasarnmitr off Sukhumvit Rd. Reportedly this embassy is a real shambles at the moment and getting visas there is a major hassle. In Chiang Mai, however, there is an efficient Indian consulate and visas are no problem at all.

Visas are not required in advance for Nepal; they can be issued on arrival at the airport or at the land borders. This 'on arrival' visa is only valid for seven days, however, and extending it is such a time-consuming hassle that it's well worthwhile obtaining a visa in advance if you have the time. The Nepalese embassy is at 189 Soi Puengsuk (Soi 71), a long way down Sukhumvit Rd.

MONEY

A$1	= 22.4B
US$1	= 27.4B
£1	= 30.7B

The baht (B) is divided into 100 stang

although 25 and 50 stang coins are the only ones you generally see. There are also 1B and 5B coins and a variety of paper denominations. Changing a larger note than 100B can be difficult up-country. The baht is aligned with the US dollar and is stable – there is no black market, and banks or money changers give the best rates. Bangkok is, however, a good centre for buying other currencies. In markets you may hear prices referred to in saleng – a saleng is equal to 25 stang.

COSTS

Thailand is an economical country to visit and it offers excellent value for your money. Transport is very reasonably priced, comfortable and reliable. Finding a place to stay is never difficult and again costs are low and you get good value for your money. So long as you can stand a little spice the food is also very good, and once again, it's cheap.

Bangkok is, of course, more expensive then elsewhere in the country, but in part that's because there are lots of luxuries available in Bangkok which you simple won't be tempted with up-country. In the last few years so many cheap guest houses have sprung up in the Banglamphu area of the city that accommodation needn't necessarily be any more expensive in Bangkok than elsewhere in the country. Of course the Bangkok hassles – noise and pollution being the big two – also drive you to look for extra comfort here. Air-con becomes a very nice idea.

CLIMATE

Thailand is tropical and sticky year round – especially in Bangkok –although it's the north-east plains where you get the highest temperatures. The three seasons are hot – March to May, rainy – June to October, cool – November to February. Towards the end of the hot season Chiang Mai can get even hotter than Bangkok but it's a drier heat. In the cool season the north can almost get 'cold'.

The rainy season rarely brings things to

a complete halt, and it's not a reason to put off visiting Thailand. Towards the end of the season, when the ground is completely saturated, Bangkok is often flooded. This is in large part due to poor planning since more and more canals are being filled in, indiscriminate drilling of wells has lowered the water table, and the whole place is sinking anyway!

ACCOMMODATION

For sheer, consistent good value the cheap Thai hotels are amongst the best in the region. Almost anywhere in Thailand, even Bangkok, you can get a double for 60B or less. In fact Bangkok has had such a proliferation of small guest houses in the past few years that it's actually become easier to find rooms in that rock-bottom price category.

There can often be an amazing variance in prices in the same hotel – you'll find fancy air-con rooms at over 200B and straightforward fan-cooled rooms at a quarter of that price. Even the smallest towns will have a choice of hotels although 'hotel' will often be the only word on them in our script. Finding a specific place in some smaller towns can be a problem if you don't speak Thai.

A typical Thai 60B room will be plain and spartan, but will include an attached toilet and shower and a ceiling fan. At the beach centres on Koh Samui and Phuket you'll find pleasant individual beach cottages at 60B and less. As in Malaysia many of the hotels are Chinese-run and couples can often save money by asking for a single – a single means one double bed, a double means two.

FOOD

Thai food is like Chinese with a sting – it can be fiery. The problem with eating Thai style is knowing what to get, how to get it, and finally how to get it for a reasonable price. Outside of the tourist areas few places have a menu in English and as for having prices on a menu . . . . To make matters worse your mangled attempts at asking for something in Thai are unlikely to be understood. Make the effort for there are some delicious foods to be tried. *Eating in Thailand* is a useful leaflet from the tourist office with English descriptions and the equivalent Thai script.

Most Thai restaurants are actually Chinese serving a few of the main Thai dishes amongst the Chinese or some Thai-ised Chinese ones. In the south look for delicious seafood, in the north various local specialities centred around 'sticky' rice.

Soft drinks are cheaper than almost anywhere in South-East Asia, which is just as well since the Thais make terrible tea and coffee. It manages to taste like the two have been mixed together and left to stew for a month. They also have a penchant for putting salt in fruit drinks. More dairy products are available in Thailand then anywhere else in Asia including very good yoghurt.

Beer is good and reasonably priced; Singha is the most popular brand – 20B for a small bottle, 35B for a large. There is a variety of local firewater including the famous Mekong whisky which is about half the strength of scotch and drunk in enormous quantities. The most common drink at corner restaurants is often iced coffee which is invariably known by its Chinese name as 'oh-lee-ang' (rhymes with bung). Cheap and nasty.

Some Thai foods with approximate pronunciations:

fried rice	khow phat
with chicken	khow phat kai
with pork	khow phat moo
with prawns	khow phat gung
spicy lemon soup	tom yam
Thai curry	kaeng kari
and again	gang ped
fried noodles	mi grob
sweet & sour vegetables	phat pree oh whan
beef in oyster sauce	nua phat nummunn hoy
chicken with lemon in coconut milk	tom kha khai
fried fish with ginger	pla pad ging
curried chicken	ghaeng kari khai
grilled fish in banana leaves	pla pow haw bai tong
clear fine noodle salad	yum woon sen
pork, chicken or prawn soup	kaeng clud
fried eggs	khai dao
scrambled eggs	khai khon
omelette	khai gee oh
toast	khnompang bing

Drinks

lemon drink	nam man now
black coffee	gafae dum ron
white coffee	gafae ron
black tea	nam cha ron
white tea	cha ron

Khow phat is the served-every-day national dish – a close cousin to Chinese fried rice or Indonesian nasi goreng. It usually comes with sliced cucumber, a fried egg on top and some super hot peppers to catch the unwary. Beef in oyster sauce, a popular Chinese dish, is another favourite of mine. A Thai dish I developed a real liking for is sour hot beef, *neua yum*, a very spicy and hot concoction of ground beef with salad. *Pad thai* is fried noodles, beansprouts, nuts, eggs, chilis and often mussels and prawns – good value at any street stall.

GETTING THERE

Except for people coming from Malaysia almost all visitors arrive by air. There are plenty of land crossing points between Thailand and Burma, Laos or Kampuchea, but very few border crossings are made. Officially at least! By air, however, Bangkok is a major arrival point with flights from all over the world.

Air

See the introductory section on getting to South-East Asia for information on air fares to Bangkok from Europe, Australia or the USA. You can also fly to Bangkok from various other Asian cities such as Hong Kong, Manila, Singapore, Kuala Lumpur, Penang, Colombo, Rangoon,

Dacca, Calcutta and Kathmandu. Bangkok is a major access point for Burma (Rangoon) and Nepal. Although Bangkok is the main entry point for Thailand you can also fly into Thailand at Chiang Mai from Hong Kong or at Hat Yai from Penang.

Bangkok is a popular place for buying airline tickets, although it's no longer the number one bargain of the region. Some typical fares available from Bangkok include Bangkok-Singapore 2420B, Hong Kong 3415B, Kuala Lumpur 2300B, Calcutta 3220B, Kathmandu 4320B, Colombo 4130B, New Delhi 4490B.

Over the years we have had a lot of letters complaining about various travel agencies in Bangkok – and a few saying what a good deal they got. Remember nothing is free so if you get quoted a price way below other agencies be suspicious. In smaller agencies insist on getting the ticket before handing over the cash. Don't sign anything either. A favourite game has been getting clients to sign a disclaimer that they will not request a refund under any circumstances. Then they pick their ticket up and find it is only valid for one week or something similar – not very good when you're not planning to leave for a month or two yet. Alternatively the ticket may only be valid within certain dates, or other limitations may be placed upon it. Another catch is you may be told it's confirmed ('OK') only to find on closer inspection the ticket is only on request ('RQ') or merely open. So read everything carefully and remember – *caveat emptor*. One agency which seems to have collected a particularly large number of complaints over the years is J Travel.

From Malaysia
Entering Thailand from Malaysia or departing to Malaysia there are a variety of ways of crossing the border. You can fly, bus, train or taxi and there are border crossings at several places both on the east and west coast. There's even one place you can cross the border by boat.

Air Simplest and fastest is to fly between Penang and Hat Yai – the fare is around M$55 or 710B. On flights that continue on to Phuket you can leave the beach at Penang in the morning and be on the beach in Phuket in the afternoon. You can also, of course, fly straight through from Penang or Kuala Lumpur to Bangkok, but note that it is cheaper to fly Penang-Bangkok via Hat Yai or Phuket than flying direct! Of course Penang-Bangkok is a route where you can usually find discounted tickets – expect to pay around M$250 in Penang. The Hat Yai-Penang flights are made by MAS and by Thai Airways.

Rail The International Express will take you straight through from Singapore to Kuala Lumpur, Butterworth (Penang), Hat Yai and Bangkok without changing train. The train only has 1st and 2nd class, but there is also a daily train operating just between Hat Yai and Penang. The trouble with the train is that it tends to spend a long time sitting at the border while everybody is cleared through immigration and customs. Travellers have reported that the International Express can be rather worse than the regular train, and the wait at the border can extend to several hours. It's for this reason that many travellers prefer to cross the border by road.

The International Express departs Bangkok on Monday, Wednesday and Saturday at 4.10 pm, arrives Hat Yai at 10.43 am next day, and Butterworth at 5.53 pm that evening. From Malaysia it's Butterworth at 7.55 am, Hat Yai at 12.32 pm and Bangkok at 6.45 am the next day. Fares Butterworth-Hat Yai are M$10.60 for 2nd class, M$22.10 for 1st. Butterworth-Bangkok is M$39.30 and M$82.20 respectively. From Bangkok the fares to Butterworth are 203B in 3rd, 397B in 2nd.

The ordinary daily train departs Hat Yai at 11.40 am and arrives Butterworth at 5.39 pm, while from Butterworth it departs at 6.50 am and arrives at 11.20

am. The Butterworth-Hat Yai fare is around M$8 in 3rd. There is an additional express surcharge on the International Express and the berth costs vary from around M$6 to M$25 depending on the class and the berth.

Road – West Coast The basic land route between Penang and Hat Yai is by taxi – fast and convenient, and for around M$20 or 200B, not even too expensive. The taxis that operate this route are generally big old Chevrolets, all Thai-registered. From Penang you'll find the taxis at the various travellers' hotels around Georgetown. In Hat Yai they'll be at the railway station or along Niphat Uthit 2. This is the fastest way of travelling by land between the two countries and you cross the border with the minimum of fuss.

On the map it looks pretty easy to travel between Malaysia and Thailand by local transport, but in actual fact the long stretch of no-man's land between Changlun, the Malaysian border post, and Sadao, the Thai equivalent, makes crossing the border rather difficult. It's quite easy to get to either side by local bus or taxi, but finding a ride across the actual border is not easy at all. There is no bus or taxi service across the border. I've hitched across on three occasions, once getting a ride on a Thai fish truck and arriving at the other end smelling a little odd! However there is not exactly a steady flow of vehicles across the the border and they're unwilling to pick up hitch-hikers. If, however, you go a few km west to Padang Besar, where the railway line crosses the border, you can easily just walk across the border. Buses run there from either side.

Road – East Coast From Kota Bahru you take a 29 bus to Rantau Panjang – 45 km for about M$2. It's then just a half km (maybe nearer a km) stroll across the border to the town of Sungai Golok. From here trains run to Hat Yai and Bangkok. The actual border used to be very inconspicuous and it was easy to miss the immigration authorities as you entered

Malaysia, which caused lots of problems when you came to extend your stay or depart. It's now much more visible but is still only open from 6 am to 6 pm.

Unusual Routes There are also some unusual routes between Malaysia and Thailand. One of the most unusual is to go to Kuala Perlis (jumping off point for Langkawi Island) and take a long-tail boat for about M$3 to Satun (or Satul), just across the border in Thailand. These are legal entry and exit points with immigration and custom posts. It costs about 10B for the three km ride from the docks to immigration. From Satun you can then bus into Hat Yai. Again make sure you get your passport properly stamped.

Another possibility is to take a yacht between Penang and Phuket. From time to time there have been people running yachts back and forth on a regular basis. The yacht *Gypsy* operated by Encounter Overland may no longer be there but *Szygie* may still be in operation. Ask around and scan the noticeboards in travellers' centres. 'Good winds, easy seas, no sharks and only a few pirates,' reported the skipper of the *Szygie*! Costs between Penang and Phuket were generally around US$100 to 200 depending on the route and length of voyage. Those boats apart, there are quite often regular yachties just passing through and willing to take on paying crew.

GETTING AROUND

Air Thai Airways have a useful little flight network around Thailand – the chart shows the main routes and fares. It's not much used by budget travellers because ground level transport is generally so good. Thai Airways have propjet and 737s.

The internal fares are generally firmly fixed but it's quite possible that you'll be able to find cheaper tickets for the international sectors like Bangkok-Penang. Nevertheless Bangkok-Penang direct is 3065B while Bangkok-Hat Yai-Penang is only 2240B or Bangkok-Phuket-Penang is only 2290B.

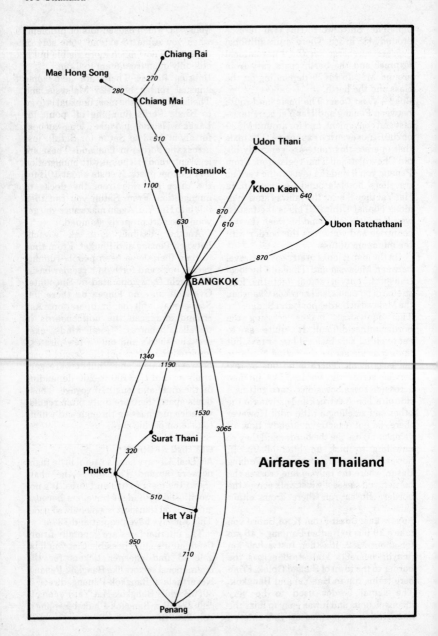

Airfares in Thailand

Rail The trains in Thailand are comfortable, frequent, punctual, cheap and rather slow. On comparable routes the buses can often be twice as fast, but the relatively low speed means you can often leave at a convenient hour in the evening and arrive at your destination at a pleasant hour in the morning. Even with a sleeping berth the prices are still comparable with buses. The trains have a further advantage over the buses in that they're far safer. Plus the food on board is really very good. All in all, Thailand's railways are a fine way to travel.

There are four main railway lines plus a few minor side routes. The main ones are the northern to Chiang Mai; the southern to Hat Yai with lines going from there to Malaysia on the west cost and to Sungai Golok on the east coast; the eastern to Ubon Ratchathani; and the north-eastern to Nong Khai.

Unfortunately the trains are often heavily booked so it's wise to book ahead. At the Hualamphong station in Bangkok you can book trains on any route in Thailand. There is a 30B surcharge for express trains and a 20B surcharge for rapid trains – the greater speed is mainly through fewer stops. There may be a 40B surcharge for air-con in 2nd class. The charge for 2nd class sleeping berths is 70B for an upper berth and 100B for a lower berth. The lower berths are cooler since they have a window; upper do not. Sleepers are only available in 1st and 2nd class, but that apart 3rd class is not too bad.

Fares are roughly double for 2nd over 3rd, double again for 1st over 2nd. Count on around 170B for a 500 km trip in 2nd. You can break a trip for two days for each 200 km travelled but the ticket must be endorsed by the stationmaster, cost is 1B. Pick up a copy of the very useful condensed railway timetables available in English.

Bus The Thai bus service is widespread and phenomenally fast – terrifyingly fast much of the time in fact. Nothing would get me to sit in the front seats of a Thai bus – some drivers have a definite Kamikaze streak. There are usually air-con buses as well as the normal ones and on major routes there are also private, air-con tour buses. The air-con buses are set so cold that blankets are handed out as a matter of routine and the service is so good as to be embarrassing. You often get free drinks, pillows, free meals and other luxuries like 'in-flight movies' on some routes! There are often a number of bus stations in a town – usually public bus stations for travel in different directions, plus private stations.

Hitching Although hitching is not the same relatively easy proposition it is in Malaysia you can hitch through Thailand. In places traffic will be relatively light and the wait for a ride can be quite long. It is certainly done though.

Boat There are lots of opportunities to travel by river or sea in Thailand. You can take boats out to many off-shore islands and there are many riverboats operating on Thailand's large number of waterways. The traditional Thai run-about for these river trips is the 'long-tail boat', so called because the engine operates the propeller via a long open tailshaft. The engines are often regular car engines with the whole thing mounted on gimbals – the engine is swivelled to steer the boat.

Local Transport There is a wide variety of local transport available in Thailand. In the big cities you'll find taxis – generally unmetered or with meters that will not be used. Always negotiate your fare before departure. Then there are *samlors*, Thai for three-wheels. There are regular bicycle *samlors* (ie cycle rickshaws) and also motorised *samlors* which are usually known as *tuk-tuks* from the nasty put-put noise their woefully silenced two-stroke engines make. You'll find bicycle *samlors* in all the smaller towns through Thailand.

Tuk-tuks will be found in all the larger towns as well as in Bangkok. Both of these systems of transport require bargaining and agreement on a fare before departure, but in many towns there is more or less a fixed fare for *tuk-tuks* anywhere in town.

Songthaew literally means 'two-rows' and these small pickups with a row of seats down each side also serve a purpose rather like *tuk-tuks* or minibuses. In some cities certain routes are run on a regular basis by *songthaews* or minibuses.

Finally there are regular buses with services in certain big cities. Usually in Thailand fares are fixed for any route up to a certain length – in Bangkok up to 10 km. Of course there are all sorts of unusual means of getting around – horse drawn carriages in some smaller towns, ferries and river boats in many places. In some of the more touristed centres you can also rent motorcycles or bicycles.

LANGUAGE

Although Thai is a rather complicated language with its own unique alphabet it's fun to try at least a few words. *Thailand Phrasebook* is one of the Lonely Planet language survival kits and gives a handy basic introduction to the language. The main complication with Thai is that it is tonal; the same word could be pronounced with a rising, falling, high, low or level tone and could, therefore, theoretically have five meanings! Do you wonder why they can't understand you?

hello	*sawat dee*
please	*khaw tord*
thank you	*khop khoon*
yes (female)	*kha*
yes (male)	*khrap*
no	*my*
excuse me	*khaw thoad*
so it goes	*mai pen rai*
you are joking	*kun poot len*

where?	*tee nai?*
when?	*meua rai?*
today	*wan nee*
tomorrow	*meua wan nee*
yesterday	*wan nee*
how much?	*taow rai?*
too much	*paeng pai*
what is this in Thai?	*pasa Thai riak wah ari?*
do not understand	*mai kao jai*
toilet	*hagnam* or *suka*

Numbers

1	*neung*
2	*song*
3	*sam*
4	*see*
5	*ha*
6	*hok*
7	*jet*
8	*paet*
9	*gow*
10	*sip*
11	*sip et*
12	*sip song*
20	*yee sip*
21	*yee sip et*
30	*sam sip*
100	*neung roi*

The use of the word *chun* for I is dangerous since it is only used when speaking to persons of inferior status. Therefore it's better to simply say 'don't understand' rather than 'I don't understand' and risk offending an immigration official or somebody similarly important! The rules for which form of 'I' to use are very complicated.

Mai pen rai actually has far more meanings than simply 'so it goes'. It can mean 'don't bother' or 'forget it' or 'leave it alone' or 'take no notice' or even 'that's enough'. A very useful phrase

Bangkok

Thailand's coronary-inducing capital is surprisingly full of quiet escapes if you make your way out of the busy streets. Before you get out you will have to put up with some of the worst traffic jams in Asia, noise, pollution, annual floods and sticky weather. It's hardly surprising that many people develop an instant dislike for the place, but beneath the surface Bangkok has plenty to offer. There are lots of sights, cheap accommodation and some excellent food.

Bangkok, or Krung Thep as it is locally known, has been the capital of Thailand since the Burmese sacked Ayuthaya in 1767. At first the Siamese capital was shifted to Thonburi, across the river from Bangkok, but in 1782 it was moved to its present site.

Information

There are tourist offices at the airport and in Bangkok city – the Thai tourist office is very good for detailed leaflets and information sheets (which are generally far more useful than the average pretty colour brochure). You'll find the city office of the Tourist Authority of Thailand at 4 Ratchadamnoen Nok Avenue (tel 282 1143-7). One thing to buy from them (or elsewhere) as quickly as possible is a Bangkok bus map (30 or 40B). It's very easy to follow and is an absolute necessity for coping with Bangkok's frenetic bus system. *Nancy Chandler's Map of Bangkok* is a colourful map of Bangkok's unusual attractions. It has all the Chao Phya Express river taxi stops in Thai script. Cost is 40B.

The Thai Student Travel Office is in the Viengtai Hotel in Banglamphu. Apart from airline tickets they also have some good local tours. The Malaysia Hotel's famous noticeboard is but a pale shadow of its former glory. The GPO is on New Rd (Charoen Krung Rd) and has a very efficient poste restante service open from 8 am to 8 pm on weekdays, 8 am to 1 pm on Saturdays and Sundays. Every single letter is recorded in a large book and you're charged 25 stang for each one. They also have a packing service here if you want to send parcels home. After the GPO is shut you can send letters from the adjacent Central Telegraph Office. Close to the GPO there are a number of money changers along New Rd, good if you want to buy other Asian currency, such as Burmese kyats.

Bookshops The best bookshops in Bangkok, and hence in Thailand, include Chalermnit at 108 Sukhumvit 53. There are often some interesting second-hand books on sale here as well as the new ones. Asia Books at Soi 15-17 Sukhumvit also has an excellent selection of books as does DK (Duang Kamol) Bookstore in Siam Square. The Bookseller at 81 Patphong Rd, right in the middle of Bangkok's sex & sin centre, is also very good. There's a good book department in the Central Department store at 306 Silom Rd and you can find books in the bookshops of many of the better hotels.

Orientation

The Chao Phya River divides Bangkok from Thonburi. Almost the only reason to cross to Thonburi (apart from the Thonburi Railway Station) is to see the Temple of the Dawn.

The main Bangkok railway line virtually cuts off a loop of the river and within that loop is the older part of the city including most of the interesting temples and the Chinatown area. The popular Banglamphu travellers' centre is also in this area.

East of the railway line is the new area of the city where most of the modern hotels are located. One of the most important roads is Rama IV Rd which runs right in front of the Sri Hualamphong Railway Station and eventually gets you to the

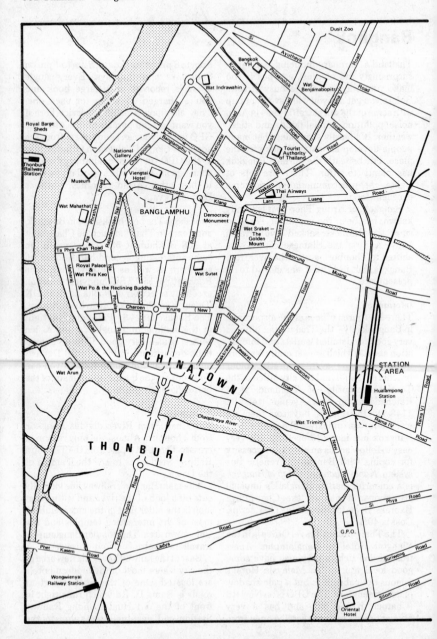

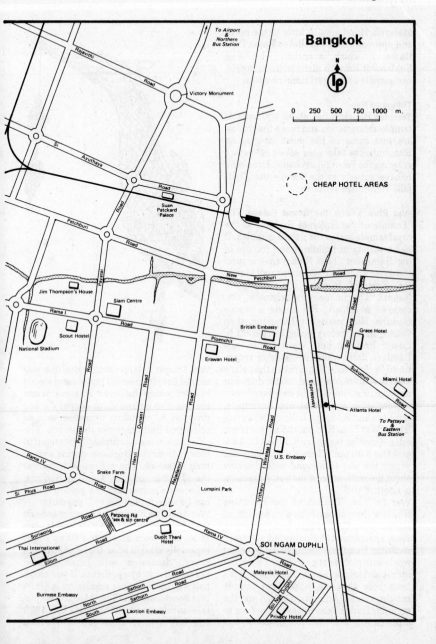

Malaysia Hotel area. A little to the north and approximately parallel to Rama IV is Rama I which eventually becomes Sukhumvit Rd with many popular hotels, restaurants and entertainment spots.

Things to See

Temples Bangkok has about 400 *wats* or temple-monasteries and those that follow are just some of the most interesting. Remember to take your shoes off before entering the *bot* or main chapel. Dress and behave soberly in the wats – the Thais take Buddhism seriously.

Wat Phra Keo & the Grand Palace The 'Temple of the Emerald Buddha' is the royal temple within the palace complex. It has a variety of buildings and frescos of the Ramakien (Thai Ramayana) around the outer walls. In the main chapel stands the Emerald Buddha (he's made of jasper). The image was originally discovered in Chiang Rai inside a stucco Buddha, later moved to Lampang, then Chiang Mai – before being carried off to Luang Prabang and Vientiane by the Laotians, from where it was later recaptured by the Thais. Entrance to the palace used to require coats and ties for men, but dress regulations have been relaxed.

Admission is 60B except Saturdays, Sundays and Buddhist holidays when it is free to Wat Phra Keo but the palace is not open. Opening hours are 8.30 to 11.30 am and 1 to 3.30 pm. There's also a museum within the wat compound with displays about the restoration of the wat. Admission is another 10B.

Wat Po The 'Temple of the Reclining Buddha' has an extensive collection of panels, bas reliefs, chedis, and statuary to view, apart from the celebrated 45-metre reclining Buddha, looking like a beached whale with mother of pearl feet. This is the oldest and largest wat in Bangkok and it's from here that all those Thai temple rubbings come. Admission is 10B and the reclining Buddha can be seen from 8 am to 5 pm daily.

Wat Traimit A large stucco Buddha was moved here from an old temple and stored in a temporary shelter for 20 years. When moving it to a permanent chapel a crane dropped it, revealing over five tons of solid-gold Buddha under the stucco. The stucco covering was probably intended to hide it from the Burmese during one of their invasions. The wat is now known as the Temple of the Golden Buddha. Admission is free and the golden image can be seen from 9 am to 5 pm daily.

Wat Arun The Temple of Dawn stands on the Thonburi side of the river and is seen at its best from across the Chao Phya, especially at night when the 82-metre high prang, decorated with ceramics and porcelain, is lit by spotlights. If you climb half way up the tower admission is 5B.

Wat Benchamabophit The 'Marble Temple' is relatively new, built by Rama V in 1899 and has a huge collection of Buddha images from all periods of Thai Buddhist art. There is a pond full of turtles beside the temple. Admission is free.

Wat Saket The Golden Mount is a most unbeautiful lump of masonry topping an artificial hill. Since Bangkok is pancake-flat it provides a fine view from the top. Admission is free, but 1B to the top terrace.

Other Temples Wat Rajanadda is across Mahachai Rd from Wat Saket, and is in an unusual Burmese-influenced style. There's a popular market here selling amulets and charms. Wat Bowonniwet is on Phra Sumen Rd and is the headquarters for a minority Buddhist sect. Wat Indrawihan, just north of Banglamphu on Wisut Kasat Rd (near its junction with Samsen Rd), has an enormous standing Buddha image. The 'giant swing', Sao Ching-Cha, used to be the centre for a spectacular festival, but it is no longer held. Interesting temples on the Thonburi side of the river include Wat Kanlayanimit and Wat Phailom.

National Museum Supposedly the largest museum in South-East Asia, this is a good place to get into Thai art and culture before you start exploring the former Thai capitals. All the periods and styles of Thai history and art are shown here. The museum is open 9 am to 12 noon and 1 to 4 pm, but is closed on Mondays and Fridays. Admission is free on weekends, 5B on other days. There are free tours of the museum in English on Tuesdays (Thai culture), Wednesdays (Buddhism) and Thursdays (Thai art), all beginning at 9.30 am. These tours are excellent value and highly recommended.

Jim Thompson's House On Soi Kasem San 2, Rama I Rd, this is the beautiful house of the American Thai silk entrepreneur Jim Thompson, who disappeared without trace back in 1967 in the Cameron Highlands in Malaysia. His house, built from parts of a number of traditional wooden Thai houses and furnished with an absolutely superb collection of Thai art

and furnishings, is simply delightful. Pleasantly sited on a small klong, the house is open Monday to Friday from 9 am to 5 pm. Admission is 50B but students under 25 only pay 30B. The gardens are open any time and for free.

Floating Market The Thonburi floating market is really a tourist trap – although there are still plenty of produce-boats there are often even more tourist-boats. It's picturesque but with all the tourist shops, snake farms and the like it all looks a bit artificial. Tours cost around a hefty 120B and generally depart from the Oriental Hotel's pier, where a group can also hire their own boat. The various travel agencies around the Malaysia Hotel book tours and they're generally OK.

An alternative and far less touristed floating market can be seen at Klong Damnoen Saduak, 104 km from Bangkok, beyond Nakhon Pathom. If you want to go there you'll probably have to stay in Nakhon Pathom and take an early morning bus to Samut Songkhram, getting off at Damnoen Saduak. An interesting canal tour in Bangkok can be made by taking a Chao Phya River taxi from Soi Klongsung (lots of buses go there) as far north as Nonburi. This is an interesting three-hour 10B trip with plenty to be seen along the way. The Klong Bangkok Noi canal taxi route from Tha Phra Chan, next to Thammasat University, only costs a few baht and takes you along an interesting route seemingly far from Bangkok.

Other All sorts of oddities can be found at the enormous Weekend Market which has recently been shifted to opposite the Northern Bus Terminal – take an air-con bus 3, 9, 10 or 13. It's open all day on Saturday and Sunday and you can find almost anything here from opium pipes to unusual posters. There's also lots of other activity to watch at the market. There are a number of other interesting markets around Bangkok.

At the Pasteur Institute on Rama IV Rd snakes are milked of their venom every morning at 11 am; admission is 10B.

Bangkok has a Chinatown with a thieves' market and an Indian district on its periphery. Thai boxing, where they kick as well as punch, is quite a scene. There are stadiums at Lumpini (Rama IV Rd) and Ratchadamnoen (by the TAT office). Admission prices start from around 100B and go up to 500B for ringside seats. The out-of-the-ring activity is even more frenzied and entertaining than within the ring.

The National Theatre gives dance performances by the Chulalongkorn University Dance Club. At 11 am on Thursday and Sunday there's a dance/martial arts performance (the Kodak Siam show) at the historic Oriental Hotel. The Oriental is an attraction in its own right, the Raffles of Bangkok only in better shape.

There are a couple of artificial tourist attractions out of town – TIMland (Thailand in Miniature) and Ancient City. Admission to Ancient City is 50B and you can get there on a 25 bus from Sukhumvit Rd to Pak Num and then a small local bus. Ancient City is 33 km out of Bangkok and spreads over 80 hectares. There is also a Crocodile Farm in the same area and the Rose Garden Country Resort south of Bangkok.

Some Patphong Rd bars are good places for whiling away an afternoon watching video movies. About 15 km out of the city there's an excellent swimming pool complex at Siam Park; a 27 bus will get you there although not every 27 goes to Siam Park. Entry cost is 60B, which ensures it is very uncrowded.

Oddities At the shrine outside the Erawan Hotel people come to seek help for some wish they want granted – like their girlfriend to marry them. The person promises that if the grant is made they will pay for something to be done – a favourite is to pay for 20 minutes dancing by the Thai dancers who are always ready and waiting for such commissions. There's a similar shrine by the Narai Hotel.

In the British Embassy grounds (access difficult) a statue of Queen Vic is prayed to by women without children since the good Queen is reputed to be very helpful in providing pregnancies. At the southern and northern bus terminals there are amazing family planning supermarkets run by the enterprising Mr Metchai who revolutionised and popularised family planning and contraception in Thailand.

Sex & Sin Bangkok is, of course, sin-city and hordes of (male) package tourists descend upon the city simply to sample its free-wheeling delights. Patphong Rd, just off Silom Rd, is the centre for the city's spectator sports while massage parlours are found at many hotels and in the tourist ghettos like Sukhumvit or, of course, on Patphong. In Thailand a 'body massage' means the masseuse' not yours. As one traveller told it in Burma: 'and then she took all her clothes off, and then she took all my clothes off, and then I missed my flight to Burma.' Or there are the coffee bar pick-up joints like the infamous Grace Hotel at Soi 5, Sukhumvit, or the Thermal Coffee House or many others.

Last – but far from least – many Bangkok visitors find that indulgence in the pleasures of sin-city can easily lead to social diseases. For some people drinking the water isn't the only health hazard in Asia! Careless males should be aware, if they are travelling west, that getting plugged full of penicillin is much easier to arrange in Bangkok than anywhere further west. Less physical problems also occasionally befall Bangkok revellers – wallets have disappeared while peoples' pants were down.

Bangkok can be one of the noisiest, most traffic-polluted and congested cities in the east, but it's also full of delightful escapes from the hassles. Step out of the street noise and into the calm of a wat for example. The Chao Phya River is totally refreshing compared to the anarchy of the streets and a visit to Jim Thompson's house will show you how delightful the klongs once were and occasionally still are.

Places to Stay

There are all sorts of places to stay in all sorts of price categories in Bangkok. Generally you can pick your accommodation by area since there are a number of definite 'areas' to search in.

In the last few years there's been a wholesale shift as Soi Ngam Duphli, once the main travellers' centre, has become more and more expensive and Banglamphu has gradually become the backpackers' favourite. Then there's the Sukhumvit Rd area with some travellers' hotels amongst the more expensive places. Much more central there's the noisy Hualamphong Station and Chinatown area, or the Siam Square area.

Competition in Banglamphu is so fierce that you can get a room in Bangkok for scarcely more than it was 10 years ago. Cheapest rooms start around 40B for a single, say 70B for a double – you'll find rooms around that price in the Banglamphu and Hualamphong areas. The air-con places in Soi Ngam Duphli and along Sukhumvit are now 200 or 300B. Some hotels give student discounts if you ask. There's a hotel booking desk at the airport which can book you into many of the cheaper (but not rock bottom) hotels.

Banglamphu This area is over towards the river, near the Democracy Monument and on the route towards the airport. At 42 Tanee Rd (a street back from Khao San Rd) the *Viengtai* is the Student Travel Australia HQ in Bangkok. They have a special student price here and the Thai student travel office is across the road from it. But even with discount this is an expensive hotel – it's mainly useful as a landmark! Two similar student travel places are the *Liberty* at 215 Sapan Kwai Pradipat and the *Royal* at 2 Ratchadamnoen Avenue – the latter will also give student discounts.

The Banglamphu area is pleasantly central, particularly for the various wats. There are now a large (and growing) number of very cheap hotels and guest houses here and although some are very basic many are excellent value. The standard Banglamphu price is 40B per person. Popular guest houses include the *VS Guest House* at 136 Tanao Rd with rooms at 40B per person, not one of the best around. Close by is the small *ET Guest House*. Over on Khao San Rd the *Bonny Guest House* costs the standard 40B and is friendly and fairly clean. Next door is the *Tum (Toom) Guest House*, owned by the same family.

The *New Sri Phranakhon Hotel* at 139 Khao San Rd is Chinese-owned and costs from 120B for a room with fan, bath and the obligatory 'short time' horizontal mirror. Next door is the popular *Nit Jaroen Suke* (or Nith Charoen Suke) (tel 281 9872) which has excellent doubles for 120B with fan and bathroom. Still on Khao San Rd the *VIP Guest House* has a restaurant in front, a 40B dorm and rooms at 60/80B. Other Khao San Rd places include the *Ponderosa Guest House* at 66, the *PB Guest House* at 74, the *160 Guest House* at 160 and so on.

Just off Tanao Rd (at the end of Khao San), look for the rather inconspicuous sign for the *Central Guest House* (tel 282 0667) which is clean, quiet, well-kept and good value even if it is somewhat spartan. It's the regular 40B per person price and pleasantly quiet since it's back off the main road. Beware of theft; don't leave valuables in your room. Other places which have been recommended are the *Chuanpis Guest House* (tel 282 9948) at 86 Chakrapong Rd, behind the police station at the end of Khao San Rd. Or the *Chusri Guest House* at 61/1 Soi Rambutri off Chakrapong Rd.

Around Banglamphu More guest houses have started to pop up around the Banglamphu area. There are several along Trok Rong Mai (*trok* means alley) opposite the UNICEF building and closer to the river. The *Apple Guest House* at 10/1 Trok Rong Mai is friendly and very popular at 40B per person. There's a good notice-board and a pleasant garden to sit out in.

The *Ngam Pit* is at 28/2. At 28/6 the *Roof Garden Guest House* has box-like and bare rooms but the staff try to please and from the roof you get a fine view over the river and Bangkok. Prices are the standard 40B per person once again.

Turn right from Khao San Rd and head up Chakrapong and then Samsen Rd (it changes names) and turn right again into Soi Phra Sawat (walking distance) where the new *TV Guest House* (tel 282 7451) is at number 7. There are dorm beds at 40B and good, clean doubles at 80B. Another km or so along, just before the National Library, Phitsanulok Rd dead-ends on Samsen and Si Ayuthaya Rd crosses it. At 71 Si Ayuthaya Rd, on the river side of Samsen Rd, is the very popular *Sawatdee* (Hello!) guest house (tel 281 0757). It's very basic, but clean and well kept and the family who run it are unbelievably friendly and helpful. It's got a great atmosphere, is pleasantly quiet and it's conveniently close to a terrific market and a Chao Phya Express stop on the river.

Close by is, at last, the *Bangkok International Youth Hostel* (tel 282-0950) at 25/2 Phitsanulok Rd. It opened in late '84 and has a dormitory at 30B and singles/doubles with toilet and shower at 50/100B if you have a youth hostel card, 10B more without.

Soi Ngam Duphli Just off Rama IV Rd this was for many years Bangkok's travellers' centre. Today the places here are not the best value in Bangkok and it's no longer the only centre. Get there on a 4, 13, 14, 22, 27, 46, 47 ur 74 bus; getting off just after the roundabout on Rama IV Rd.

Once upon a time the prime attraction here was the *Malaysia* – back in the Vietnam days this was one of the hotels quickly thrown together for the R&R trade. It's multi-storey, air-con, swimming pool and all that sort of thing. Then Vietnam ended and they would have had an empty hotel had they not decided to cut prices to the bone and fill it with the travellers who were invading the region at that time. Of course in the intervening years the prices crept higher and higher and were prevented from going through the roof by simply doing no maintenance at all. The Malaysia was a sort of working test on how long a building could hang together with much abuse and no care.

In the last few years the *Malaysia* has been cleaned up and is now just another middle-bracket hotel. A backpack now looks quite out of place in the lobby (now filled with video machines) and the famous noticeboard is just a memory. The *Malaysia* (tel 286 3582) is at 54 Soi Ngam Duphli, There are 120 rooms, all with air-con and attached bathroom. A double costs 318B, a deluxe double 362B, a single 282B.

Right across the road is the Tung-mahamek or *Privacy Hotel* (tel 286 2339) which acts as an overflow centre for the Malaysia. It's probably a bit quieter. Rooms, all air-con, are around 200B for a double. The third big Soi Ngam Duphli place is just off that road on Soi Si Bamphen. The *Boston Inn* is probably the best value of the bunch. The rooms are well kept and the staff are friendly. Rooms cost 120/140B for singles/doubles with fan; 150/190B with air-con. It's even got a pretty good noticeboard.

Smaller places around Soi Ngam Duphli include the *Love Guest House* with dorm beds at 40B, rooms at 60/90B or at 160B with air-con. Or the *Freddy Guest House* at 100 to 120B, the *Kitchen Top Guest House* and the *D Guest House*. Apart from the hotels there are also lots of travel agencies, restaurants, bars and all manner of 'services' in the area. Once upon a time it was also a prime target for the Bangkok dope squad and although those days have passed there are still occasional raids.

Sukhumvit Rd North of Rama IV Rd and running out from the centre, much like Rama IV, this is a major tourist centre. Take a bus 2, 25, 40, 48 or 71. The hotels here are not Bangkok's top-notch places although most of them are out of the travellers' price range. There are a few worthwhile places scattered in amongst them, however. All the small lanes running off Sukhumvit are called *Soi*, and then a number – so the bigger the number the further up Sukhumvit. All even numbers are to the south, odd to the north.

Starting at the Rama I end (Rama I changes into Sukhumvit) you'll find the *Atlanta* at 78 Soi 2. At one time (before the Malaysia rose to the top) this was the number one travellers' hotel, but then for a while there were so many dope raids nobody could get any sleep and the popularity plummeted. Now it's reasonably popular once again and has rooms at 150/200B with fan but shared bath, up to 250/300B with air-con. There are some smaller, cheaper singles and there's a restaurant and swimming pool.

Further up at Soi 13 the *Miami* (tel 252 5140-2) is one of the cheaper tourist hotels. There are a few doubles with fan for around 220B but most rooms are air-con at 300B and up. The Miami is comfortable, clean and well kept and has a good central swimming pool – with a memorable noticeboard warning you that leaping into the pool from the upper storeys is entirely at your own risk!

Further still the *Crown* at Soi 25 is also clean, efficient and well kept – and again it has a pool. Doubles are again 300B plus. The *Golden Palace Hotel* at 15 Soi 1 is similarly equipped and costs from 300B. There are others.

Chinatown-Hualamphong Station This is one of the cheapest areas in Bangkok but also one of the noisiest. The traffic along Rama IV Rd has to be heard to be believed. Since the last edition the Thai Song Greet, Bangkok's original budget travel hotel (I read a book about travelling in Bangkok in the early '50s which mentioned it) has disappeared but there are numerous others.

Across Rama IV, near Wat Traimit, the *Empire Hotel* at 572 Yaowarat Rd has doubles from 120B (up to 300) and is kind of noisy but in a good Chinatown location. It's near the intersection of Yaowarat and New Rd (Charoen Krung Rd). The *Burapha*, at the intersection of Chakraphat and Charoen Krung on the edge of Chinatown is similar. There are a number of other Chinatown hotels around, but most don't have signs in English.

There are several hotels right alongside the station such as the *Sri Hualamphong Hotel* (tel 2142610) at 445 Rong Muang Rd. This is one of the better ones at 80/140B for rooms with fan. The *Sahakit Hotel* is a few doors down towards Rama IV Rd and has rooms from 90B. Between the two is the rather basic *Jeep Sweng* which has none-too-clean rooms from 70B. The *No Name Hotel* doesn't have any sign outside to indicate it's a hotel; it's down at the far end of Rong Muang and is also rather primitive and costs just 70B. Frankly these station area cheapies are no bargain compared to the even cheaper places over in Banglamphu.

An exception is the relatively new *TT Guest House* (tel 235 8006), about a 10-minute walk from the station at 138 Soi Watmahaphruttharam, Sipraya Manakorn Rd. Turn left out of the station along Rama IV Rd and look for signs. It's a little difficult to find but well worth the effort. A number of travellers have written to recommend the 60/80B rooms here.

There are numerous good cheap eating places right around the station. A word of caution at Hualamphong – some of Bangkok's best pickpockets and razor artists work the station area. And a second warning – while checking out the hotels for this update I got arrested for jaywalking right outside the station! *Jaywalking!!* In Bangkok! It cost me 40B.

Siam Square Near the National Stadium on Rama I Rd there are more places including the *National Scout Hotel* (Sala Vajiravudh) which is probably the cheapest place in Bangkok. You'll find it on the 4th floor of the National Scout Executive Committee Building near the National Stadium. There are five dorms, each with 12 beds at 30B each. Women can stay (there's no need to be a boy scout) and it's not a bad place although the traffic is a little noisy. Bring a padlock for your cupboard though. Buses 11, 15, 29, 47, 48, 73 or 76 will get you there. The 29 airport bus goes right by it.

Nearby there are a couple of places which are good value – like the *Star Hotel* at 36/1 Soi Kasem San 1, off Rama I Rd. Rooms are air-con and cost 150 to 200B. Right on the corner of that Soi and Rama I Rd is the *Muangphol Building* which offers very good standard rooms for 300B – similar to the Miami, Viengtai or Liberty, but with a better location and lower prices.

Places to Eat

Banglamphu & Around There are lots of cheap eating places around the Banglamphu guest houses including the *Hello Restaurant* on Khao San Rd.

Phra Athit Rd, over towards the river where you find the Trok Rong Mai guest houses, has many good, inexpensive restaurants and food stalls. *Taew*, across from the alley entrance is good. There are a number of good restaurants around the Democracy Monument area.

Soi Ngam Duphli There are several travellers' centre restaurants here like the *Lisboa* and the *Blue Fox*. Cheaper food can be found at the open-air restaurants on Soi Si Bamphen, near the Boston Inn. The curry shops out on Rama IV Rd are good value or in the daily market across Rama IV Rd.

Hualamphong & Siam Square Lots of good cheap restaurants can be found along Rong Muang Rd by the station. The alleys between Siam Square sois also have plenty of good places. Try the big noodle restaurant *Co-Co* on the last soi, facing Henri Dunant Rd. On Soi Lang Suan, off Rama I Rd more or less equi-distant from the Siam Centre, Sukhumvit and Silom Rd, is the *Whole Earth Restaurant* which does good Thai and vegetarian food.

Sukhumvit The *Yong Lee Restaurant* at Soi 15 near Asia Books does great Thai and Chinese food. *Laikhram*, way down at Soi 49, and then way down Soi 49 with several twists and turns, has superb Thai food at not too outrageous prices. It's so far down Soi 49 you may want to take a tuk-tuk from Sukhumvit.

Sukhumvit has some restaurants aimed squarely at the tourist trade with reasonable food at average prices. The *Number One Restaurant* near the Miami Hotel is a good example. There's also a *Crown Pizza*, round the corner from the Crown Hotel, between Soi 29 and 31.

Patphong & Silom Rd On Patphong the *Thai Room* has Thai-Chinese-Mexican food and is pretty reasonable. Try *Bobby's Arms* for a good Aussie-Brit pub. Great Thai food at the *Talaad Nam Restaurant* on Silom. Down at the end of Silom, across from the Narai Hotel, you can get good Indian snacks near the Tamil temple. Around the corner on New Rd is the *Muslim Restaurant*, a travellers' standby for curries. The *Royal India* at 392/1 Chakraphat Rd in Pahurat is probably better. The *Moti Mahal Restaurant*, near the post office and the Swan Hotel, is also good.

Other There are several *Sala Foremost Ice Cream* shops in Bangkok – one at Siam Square, one on Ploenchit Rd, a couple on Charoen Krung, one on Ratchaprarop Rd in Pratunam. They're not bad and keep springing up. *PanPan* also has good ice cream and other delicacies. There's one at Soi 33, Sukhumvit and another near the Siam Society.

Getting There

Bangkok is the central travel focus in Thailand. Unless you enter by crossing the border in the south from Malaysia this is the place where you are most likely to arrive in Thailand. It's also the centre from where travel routes fan out across the country. See the various South, North, North-East and Around Bangkok sections for travel to these areas by bus, rail or aircraft.

Rail There are two main railway stations. The big Hualamphong Station on Rama

IV Rd handles services to the north, north-east and some of the services to the south. The Thonburi or Bangkok Noi Station handles some services to the south. If you're heading south make certain which station your train departs from.

Bus The Bangkok bus terminals are:

North
    Northern Route Terminal, Pahaholyothin Rd (tel 279 6621-5)
East
    Eastern Route Terminal, Soi 40, Sukhumvit Rd (tel 392 2391)
South
    Southern Route Terminal, Charan Sanitwong Rd, Thonburi (tel 411 4978-9)

The northern terminal is on the road out to the airport. Go there for buses to Ayuthaya, Sukhothai, Chiang Mai and Chiang Rai plus the towns in the north-east. The southern terminal is across the river and there you will get buses for Nakhon Pathom, Kanchanaburi, Hua Hin, Surat Thani, Phuket and Hat Yai. The eastern terminal has buses for Pattaya and Ancient City. The North and East Bus Stations (South too?) have good left luggage facilities.

Air Bangkok is a major centre for international ticket discounting. Check the introductory section for various warnings about discounted tickets. It's also the centre for Thai Airways' domestic flight schedules.

Getting Around

Airport The Bangkok airport, Don Muang, is 25 km north of the city centre and there are a variety of ways of getting from there to your hotel on arrival. Bangkok taxis are unmetered (or rather they are metered but won't use them) so you have to bargain your fare. With some effort you can knock them down below 150B, even down towards 100B – which means between two or more people it's as cheap as the airport bus and rather more convenient. You can also flag down taxis on the highway just

outside the airport and they will be cheaper. Thai International's airport limousine is just a glorified air-con taxi service costing a flat 280B.

Thai International also has a minibus which goes to most major hotels (and some minor ones if the driver's in the mood) for 80B per person. There are air-con buses direct to Pattaya from the airport at 11 am and 9 pm for 160B.

There's a road straight into the city just a few steps outside the airport. Walk out there and you can get an air-con public bus No 4 into the city for just 15B; less if you get off in north Bangkok but you've got to sort this out before you pay. The No 4 goes down Mitthaphap Rd to Ratchaprarop/ Ratachadamri Rd, crosses Phetburi, Rama I, Ploenchit and Rama IV Rds, then down Silom, left on Charoen Krung and across the river to Thonburi. Alternatively the No 13 from the airport goes down Pahaholyothin Rd, turns left at the Victory Monument to Ratchaprarop then south to Ploenchit and east out Sukhumvit all the way to Bang Na. Air-con bus No 10 also goes by the airport.

If half a dollar is all-important you can take a No 29 (possibly recently renumbered as 59?) which is the regular non air-con public bus and follows a similar route to the 13 but continuing beyond Sukhumvit to Rama IV Rd (get off for the Soi Ngam Duphli hotels) and then turning right to the Hualamphong Station area. Fare is just 3B. Or you could walk over the pedestrian bridge from the airport, turn left (south) and after several hundred metres you'll come to the railway station, right in front of the big Airport Hotel. Trains will take you straight in to the Hualamphong Station for 6B.

If you really want to save money the public bus or the train is fine – except you may have real trouble getting your gear on board the bus. The public bus is also good, of course, if you're going to Hualamphong Station. But then the train is even better. The air-con buses are great, usually not crowded at all and no great financial burden. You just have to know where you're going and when to get off. So overall, if it's your first time in Bangkok I'd suggest bargaining for a good taxi fare. Particularly if there are several of you to split the cost.

Bangkok airport is quite OK – not the most modern in Asia but a new international terminal is under construction. There's a good value restaurant/snack-bar upstairs. The domestic terminal is a tiny affair about a hundred metres right (north) out of the main terminal. Right across the road from the terminal (take the pedestrian bridge) there's the Don Muang town area with lots of little shops, a market, many small restaurants and food stalls, even a wat. But no cheap hotel.

Departure tax on international flights is 120B. You're exempted from paying it if you're only in transit and have not left the airport building.

Bus The Bangkok bus service is frequent and frantic and a bus map is an absolute necessity. Get one from the tourist office or from bookshops and newsstands for 30 to 40B. The buses are all numbered and the bus map is remarkably easy to follow. Don't expect it to be 100% correct though – routes change regularly. For any journey under 10 km the fare is 1.5B; over 10 km – like the airport – it jumps to 3B.

There are also a number of public air-con buses with numbers that may cause confusion with the regular buses. They cost 5B, jump to 15B on the long trips. Take care when hopping on a bus that it's not the air-con one if you're economising. Apart from the cool comfort the air-con buses are uncrowded, especially in comparison to the mayhem on the regular buses. At peak hours an unofficial and mildly illegal shadow service of private bus-trucks operates on the same routes and with the same numbers as the public buses. They're necessary, which is why no attempt is made to control them. The number 17 bus does a useful circuit of the city attractions and terminates near the National Museum and Emerald Buddha.

Taxis & Samlors You must fix fares in advance on taxis or the hideously noisy little three-wheeler *samlors*. The *samlors* must be one of the prime causes of Bangkok's pollution. *Samlors* (also known as *tuk-tuks*) are really only useful for shorter trips. When the distances get longer they often become more expensive than regular taxis. Plus you need real endurance to withstand a long *samlor* trip and half the time the drivers don't know their way around Bangkok anyway. Around central Bangkok taxi fares should generally be 35B or less – fares jump 5 or 10B late at night or with heavy traffic. You have to bargain, but since there are plenty of taxis it doesn't require much effort.

Boat River travel through and around Bangkok is not only much more interesting and peaceful than fighting your way through town in a bus or taxi, it is also much faster. The water buses run all over and you can manage a bargain price floating market tour with a little effort. The problem for visitors is that they always think you want to charter the whole boat – it's a good idea to get a Thai to write a note saying something like 'I don't want a charter, I want the regular boat service'.

There are a number of regular services along the Chao Phya River through Bangkok and on the associated klongs. Boats also buzz back and forth across the river from numerous points on one side to the other. Easiest to use and understand is the Chao Phya Express that runs up and down the river although it only stops at certain landing stages, like the Oriental Hotel. This river-bus service costs 3, 5 or 7B depending on the distance you travel. You buy your ticket on the boat. The Chao Phya Express is a big, long boat with a number on the roof.

Bangkok still has quite a few canals (klongs) but it's no longer the 'Venice of the East'. More and more of the canals are filled in to become roads for Bangkok's ever-growing traffic jams. Periodic floodings in the city are in part due to the loss of drainage the canals used to provide. Places you can go to include the klong behind Sukhumvit Rd, along which long-tailed boats run. Pratunam market is a good place to eat and even has a unique floating red light district – the name means 'watergate'! In Thonburi the floating market is now thoroughly spoilt but there are others – and other interesting river trips elsewhere in Thailand.

THINGS TO BUY

Anything you can buy out in the country you can also get in Bangkok – sometimes the prices may even be lower. Silom Rd and New Rd (Charoen Krung Rd) are two good shopping areas. Things to look for include:

Cotton & Silk Lengths of cotton and the beautifully coloured and textured Thai silk can be made into clothes or household articles. There are some good shops along Silom Rd.

Temple Rubbings Charcoal on rice paper or coloured on cotton, these rubbings are made from temple bas reliefs – or they were once upon a time, today they're made from moulds taken from the temple reliefs. Wat Po is a favourite place with a very wide choice, but check prices at shops in town before buying at Wat Po as they often ask too much.

Clothes The Thais are very fashion conscious and you can get stylish clothes ready made or made to measure at attractive prices. You'll find trendy tailor shops in all the small towns too, often cheaper than in Bangkok.

Other Silver, bronze and nielloware items include a variety of jewellery, plates, bowls and ornaments. Nielloware is silver inlaid with black enamel. Antiques are widely available but you'd better know what you're looking for. Temple bells and carved wooden cow bells are nice souvenirs. There is a string of art galleries along New Rd (Charoen Krung Rd) from the GPO where you will find those attractive little leaf paintings – nicely framed and small enough to make handy little presents.

The Weekend Market is, of course, a great place to look for almost any oddity although it has moved out from the centre to near the Northern Bus Terminal. The Thai Hill Crafts Foundation, Scapathum Palace, behind the Siam Centre on Ploenchit Rd, has a lot of interesting crafts. Behind the Chalerm Thai Theatre there's an amulet market where you can buy an amulet to protect you against almost anything. Bangkok is a great place to buy student cards – some fine fakes are produced here, but make sure you give them a good university name or you'll end up with something like 'University of Australia'.

Around Bangkok

There are a number of interesting places within day trip distance of Bangkok – some of them also make interesting stepping stones on your way north, east or south. You can stop off at Ayuthaya on your way north for example, or Nakhon Pathom on your way south.

AYUTHAYA

Until its destruction by the Burmese in 1767 this was the capital of Thailand; it stands 86 km north of Bangkok. Built at the junction of three rivers, an artificial channel has converted the town into an island. To find your way around get a copy of the excellent guidebook and map available from the museum either here or in Bangkok. Places to see are either 'on the island' or 'off the island'. There's a small 2B admission charge to some of the ruins.

Things to See

National Museum The main museum here

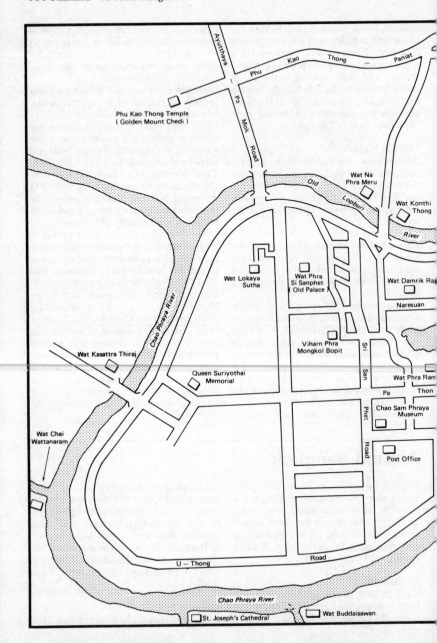

Phu Kao Thong Temple
(Golden Mount Chedi)

Wat Na
Phra Meru

Wat Konthi
Thong

Wat Damrik Raj

Wat Lokaya
Sutha

Wat Phra
Si Sanphet
(Old Palace)

Naresuan

Viharn Phra
Mongkol Bopit

Wat Phra Ram

Wat Kasattra Thiraj

Queen Suriyothai
Memorial

Chao Sam Phraya
Museum

Wat Chai
Wattanaram

Post Office

St. Joseph's Cathedral

Wat Buddaisawan

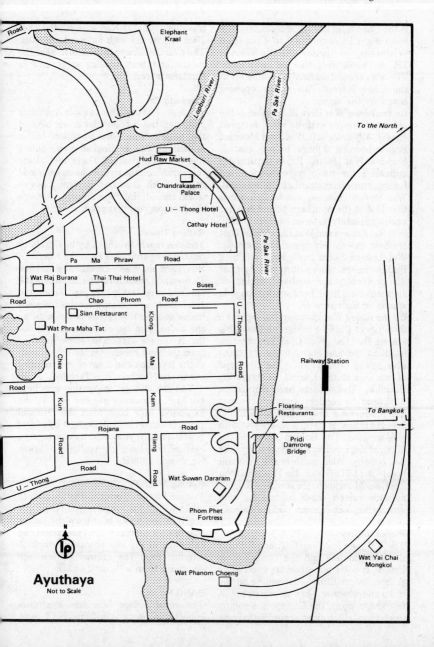

Ayuthaya
Not to Scale

Elephant Kraal

Lopburi River

Pa Sak River

To the North

Hud Raw Market

Chandrakasem Palace

U – Thong Hotel

Cathay Hotel

Pa Ma Phraw Road

Wat Raj Burana

Thai Thai Hotel

Buses

Chao Phrom Road

Sian Restaurant

Wat Phra Maha Tat

Klong Ma Kam Rieng Road

Chee

Kun

Road

Rojana Road

Railway Station

Floating Restaurants

Pridi Damrong Bridge

To Bangkok

U – Thong Road

Wat Suwan Dararam

Phom Phet Fortress

Wat Yai Chai Mongkol

Wat Phanom Choeng

N

is the Chao Sam Phraya Museum and it's open 9 am 12 noon and 1 to 4 pm from Wednesday to Sunday and admission is 2B on weekdays; free on weekends. There's a second national museum here at the Chan Kasem Palace; the opening hours are the same.

On the Island Wat Phra Si Sanphet is the old royal temple with its three restored chedis. Adjoining it is Wat Phra Mongkol Bopitr housing a huge bronze seated-Buddha. Wat Damrik Raj is particularly appealing for its overgrown, deserted feeling; stone lions guard a toppling chedi. Wat Suwan Dararam was built towards the close of the Ayuthaya period and has been completely restored – very colourful. Wat Raj Burana and Wat Phra Maha That are both extensively ruined but majestic. Wat Lokaya Sutha has a huge reclining Buddha image. Queen Suriyothai lost her life protecting her husband during an elephant-back duel; her memorial pagoda stands on the riverside.

Off the Island Wat Phanam Choeng was a favourite of Chinese traders and has a big seated Buddha. Wat Chai Wattanaram used to be one of Ayuthaya's most overgrown, evocative-of-a-lost-city type of ruin with stately lines of disintegrating Buddhas. Today some hard restoration work (and the wonders of modern cement) has produced a row of look-alike brand new Buddhas! It's still a lovely wat with nice gardens. The Golden Mount to the north of the city has a wide view over the flat country. Also north is the elephant kraal – the last of its kind in Thailand. Wat Yai Chai Mongkol to the south-east, has a massive ruined chedi contrasting with surrounding contemporary Buddha statues.

Places to Stay
The *U Thong Hotel*, on U Thong Rd near the boat landing and the Chan Kasem Palace, is noisy but otherwise good value at from 60 to 120B – depending on the room and whether it has air-con or not. A few shops down the *Cathay* is similarly priced and 'much nicer' according to some

travellers. At 13/1 Naresuan Rd the *Thai Thai* has rooms with air-con from 80B. The *Chandrakasem Hotel* is also near the palace and boat landing stage and is similarly priced.

Places to Eat
There are lots of places to eat in Ayuthaya including the market just down beyond the palace. The *Chandrakasem* has a restaurant with an English menu plus a fine view from the roof. There are floating restaurants on the river – one on each side of the Pridi Damrong Bridge. They're worth considering for a splurge although the food isn't all that good.

Getting There
You can reach Ayuthaya by bus, train or boat. There are buses from the Northern Bus Terminal every 10 minutes and the 1½ hour trip costs 20B. The first bus is at 5 am and the last at 7 pm. From the Hualamphong station there are frequent trains and the travel time is the same as the buses. The 3rd class fare is 14B but the Ayuthaya station is some distance from the town centre. On the other hand, at the Bangkok end it saves you trekking out to the Northern Bus Terminal.

You can also get to Ayuthaya by boat but the only really regular way is the expensive tour boat from the Oriental Hotel (around US$30). Doing it by a local boat isn't easy; you could try chartering a long-tail boat Bangkok-Ayuthaya-Bangkok for around 1200B.

Getting Around
You can hire a taxi or *samlor* by the hour to explore the ruins. Or get a group of people together and hire a boat from the palace pier to do a circular tour of the island and see some of the less accessible ruins. A minibus from the railway station into Ayuthaya town will cost 2 to 3B.

BANG PA IN
The royal palace here has a strange collection of baroque buildings in Chinese,

Italian and even Gothic style. Plus a Thai-style pavilion in a small lake. It's not all that interesting, but does make a pleasant riverboat trip from Ayuthaya, only 20 km north. Note that the palace is closed on Mondays and Fridays. Across the river from the palace is an unusual church-like wat reached by a trolley-like cable car across the river – the crossing is free.

Getting There
From Bangkok there are buses to Bang Pa In every half hour from 6 am to 6 pm and the fare is 14B. There are minibuses (or large *songthaew* trucks) between Bang Pa In and Ayuthaya every 15 minutes. The short trip costs 10B.

LOPBURI
Situated 154 km north of Bangkok this ruined city of the Davaravati period shows strong Hindu and Khmer influence in its architecture. Most important is the Phra Prang Sam Yod or 'sacred three spires pagoda' which was originally built as a Hindu shrine and is reckoned to be the finest Khmer structure in the region. Prang Khaek and Wat Phra Sri Ratana Mahathat are also notable. Phaulkon's House, the home of the Greek adviser to Ayuthaya during its heyday, is also in Lopburi. You can get a good map from the tourist office.

Places to Stay & Eat
You can day-trip to Lopburi from Ayuthaya but if you want to stay the *Thai Sawat* on Na Kala Rd, close to the railway station, is about the cheapest around at 40B. Also on Na Kala, opposite Wat Nakhon Kosa, the *Indra* costs 70B for passable rooms with fan and bath. On the same road, but closer to the railway station, is the *Julathip* which doesn't have an English sign. Rooms with fan and bath are 60B, but ask to see them first.

Still on Na Kala, the *Suparaphong* is not far from Wat Phra Sri Ratana Mahathat and the railway station. It's similar in price and standard to the Julathip and the

Indra. Overlooking King Narai's palace, the *Asia Lopburi* is on the corner of Sorasak and Phra Yam Jamkat Rds. It's clean and comfortable and has two Chinese restaurants downstairs. Rooms with fan and bath are 100B. *Muang Thong*, across from Prang Sam Yot, has noisy but adequate rooms for 70B with fan and bath plus some cheaper rooms without bath for 50B.

There are several Chinese restaurants along Na Kala Rd, parallel to the railway line. They tend to be a bit pricey; the places on the side streets of Ratchadamnoen and Phra Yam Jamkat can be better value.

Getting There
There are buses about every 10 minutes from Ayuthaya or from Bangkok about every 20 minutes – a three hour trip costing 32B. You can also reach Lopburi from Bangkok by train for 26B in 3rd, 55B in 2nd. *Samlors* go anywhere in Lopburi for 5B.

One way of visiting Lopburi on the way north is to take the train from Ayuthaya (or Bangkok) early in the morning, leave your gear at the station for the day while you look around and then continue north on the night train. From Kanchanaburi you can loop around Bangkok to Lopburi via Suphanburi and Singhburi.

SARABURI
There's nothing of interest in Saraburi itself, but between here and Lopburi you can turn off to the Phra Buddhabat. This small and delicately-beautiful shrine houses a revered Buddha footprint. Like all genuine Buddha footprints it is massive and identified by its 108 auspicious distinguishing marks.

Places to Stay
Try the *Tanin* at Amphoe Phra Buddhabat or the *Keaw Un* on Pahalyothin Rd with rooms from 100B. Other hotels include the slightly cheaper *Saraburi* opposite the bus stand.

ANG THONG

Between Lopburi and Suphanburi, outside this small town, Wat Pa Mok has a 22-metre long reclining Buddha.

Places to Stay

Rooms cost from 80B in the *Bua Luang* on Ayuthaya Rd.

SUPHANBURI

This very old Thai city has some noteworthy Ayuthaya-period chedis and one Khmer prang. Wat Phra Si Ratana Mahathat (is there a more popular name for a wat in Thailand?) is set back off Malimaen Rd close to the centre. A staircase inside its Lopburi-style Khmer prang leads to the top.

Places to Stay

The *King Pho Sai* at 678 Nane Kaew Rd has rooms from 80B. The *KAT* at 433 Phra Phan-va-sar and the *Suk San* at 1145 Nang Pim Rd are similarly priced.

NAKHON PATHOM

The gigantic orange-tiled Phra Pathom Chedi is the tallest Buddhist monument in the world. It was begun in 1853 to cover the original chedi of the same name. Nakhon Pathom is regarded as the oldest city in Thailand; it was conquered by Angkor in the early 11th century and in 1057 was sacked by Anawrahta of Pagan in Burma. There is a museum near the ched, and outside the town is the pleasant park of Sanam Chan – the grounds of the palace of Rama VI. Nakhon Pathom is 56 km west of Bangkok.

From Nakhon Pathom you can make an excursion to the floating market at Klong Damnoen Saduak. This has become a popular, less-touristed alternative to the over-commercial atmosphere of the Bangkok floating market.

Places to Stay & Eat

On Lungphra Rd, near the railway station, the *Mitsamphan Hotel* has rooms from 80B, some with air-con. The *Mittaowan*, on the right as you walk towards the chedi from the train station, has rooms at 90B with fan and bath.

The *Mitphaisan* (its English sign says 'Mitfaaisal') is further down the alley to the right from the Mittaowan and has rooms from 100B. All three 'Mit' hotels are owned by the same family. The Mittaowan is probably the best.

There's an excellent fruit market along the road between the train station and the Phra Pathom Chedi. The excellent *Ha Seng* Chinese restaurant is on the south side of the road which intersects the road from the train station to the chedi. Turn right if walking from the chedi and walk about 20 metres.

Getting There

Every weekend there's a special rail trip to Nakhon Pathom and on to Kanchanaburi. Otherwise you can get here by bus from the Southern Bus Terminal or by rail. Buses leave every 10 minutes and cost 12B for the one-hour trip. Rail fare is 13B in 3rd class.

KANCHANABURI

During WW II the infamous bridge over the River Kwai was built here, 130 km west of Bangkok. The bridge that still stands today is not the one constructed during the war – that was destroyed by Allied air raids. The graves of thousands of Allied soldiers can be seen here. You can train across the bridge and continue further west where there are caves, waterfalls and a neolithic burial site.

In Kanchanaburi the interesting JEATH museum is run by monks – it's set up just like a POW camp and on the actual spot in Kawchow where the camp was during the war. Entry is 20B and it's worth seeing. The town was originally founded by Rama I as protection against Burmese invasion over the Three Pagodas Pass, which is still a major smuggling route into Burma. There's a good tourist information office near the bus station.

The Erawan waterfalls are an interesting

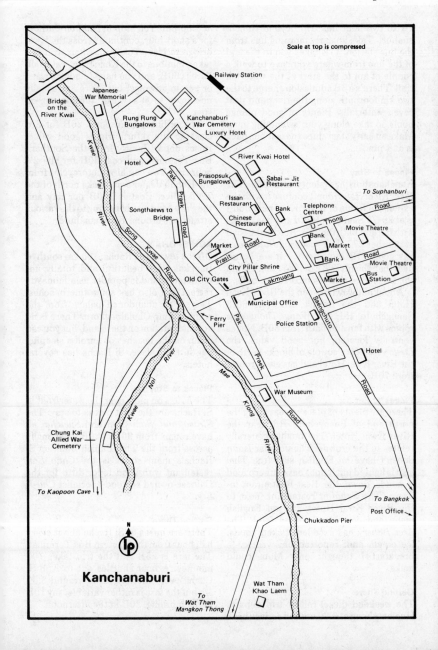

Scale at top is compressed

Railway Station

Japanese War Memorial

Bridge on the River Kwai

Rung Rung Bungalows

Kanchanaburi War Cemetery

Luxury Hotel

River Kwai Hotel

Hotel

Prasopsuk Bungalows

Sabai – Jit Restaurant

To Suphanburi

Kwae Yai River

Pak Praek Road

Issan Restaurant

Bank

Telephone Centre

U – Thong Road

Songthaews to Bridge

Song Kwae Road

Prasit Road

Chinese Restaurant

Road

Bank

Movie Theatre

Bank

Market

Movie Theatre

Market

City Pillar Shrine

Bank

Market

Bus Station

Old City Gates

Lakmuang

Municipal Office

Pak

Saengchuto Road

Ferry Pier

Police Station

Hotel

Kwae Noi River

Chung Kai Allied War Cemetery

Mae Klong River

War Museum

Praek Road

To Kaopoon Cave

To Bangkok

Post Office

Chukkadon Pier

N

lp

Kanchanaburi

To Wat Tham Mangkon Thong

Wat Tham Khao Laem

1½ to two hour bus trip beyond Kanchanaburi. Take an early morning bus from the bus station, 17B takes you to the end of the line from where you have to walk a couple of km to the start of the waterfall trail. There's a 3B admission charge to the two km footpath along the river and past seven waterfalls. Plenty of good plunge pools so take along your swimming gear. Make an early start since the last bus back is at 4 pm.

Places to Stay

Kanchanaburi has plenty of hotels. The *River Kwai Hotel* (don't confuse it with the expensive Rama of River Kwai next door) is at 284/3 Saengchuto Rd and has rooms with fan and bath for 90B. Across the road at number 277 the *Prasopsuk Bungalows* has good 90B bungalows – it's a better deal than the *River Kwai* if you don't mind the horizontal mirrors next to the beds.

About midway between the River Kwai Hotel and the tourist office at 60/3 Saengchuto Rd the *Wang Thong* has rooms with fan and bath from 80B. Not as centrally located, but good value, the *Luxury Hotel* is a couple of blocks north of the River Kwai Hotel and has clean rooms from 70B.

Places to Eat

There are plenty of places to eat along the north end of Saengchuto Rd near the River Kwai Hotel. The quality generally relates to the crowds! The popular *Isaan* doesn't have an English sign (the Thai sign is lighted but it does have superb food – hands down the Best-Restaurant-in-Town. The *Sabai-jit* restaurant, next to the River Kwai Hotel, has an English menu and consistently good food. The *Aree Bakery* has excellent baked goods, ice cream and, reported one visitor, 'a breakfast I thought only Mom could make.'

Getting There

The weekend diesel railcar trip departs Hualamphong at 6.30 am and arrives back

at 7.30 pm. You stop in Nakhon Pathom for a short tour, continue across the Kwai bridge to Nam Tok from where you can take a minibus to the Khao Pang waterfall. Fare is 60B, and you have to book a week or two in advance, but there are usually no-shows so it's worth turning up on spec.

The ordinary train costs 26B for 3rd class so the return trip is good value. Buses depart hourly from the Southern Bus Terminal and cost 30B for the 2½ hour trip. You can hire motorcycles from the Honda dealer two blocks north of the TAT office. Cost is 100B per day and they're a good way of getting to the various attractions around Kanchanaburi.

KOH SI CHANG

Off the town of Si Racha, 105 km south of Bangkok, this beautiful and totally untouristed island is popular as a monastic retreat and also has some fine beaches. There's an abandoned palace from the reign of King Chulalongkorn. There is no accommodation on the island, but you can camp on the beaches or unroll a sleeping bag in the palace. Si Racha has several hotels.

Places to Stay

The hotels on piers over the waterfront in Si Racha are the best places to stay. The *Siriwattana, Sam Chai* and *Siwichai* all have rooms from 90 to 120B. Diagonally across from the Thai Panich Bank on Si Racha's main street is the *Chao Ban* restaurant with good food; ditto for the Chinese-owned seafood-specialist *Chu-A Lee*.

Getting There

There are buses to Si Racha about every half hour from the Eastern Bus Terminal. The fare is 25B and the trip takes 100 minutes. A boat shuttles out to Koh Si Chang every morning from around 8.30 am but the fare is rather variable; say 10B in the morning, 20B in the afternoon.

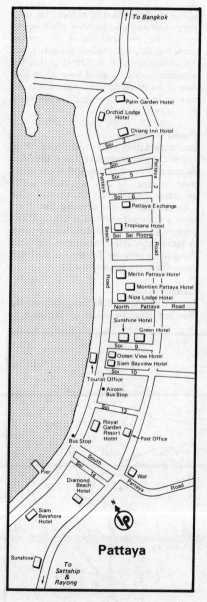

Pattaya

PATTAYA

Thailand's biggest and most popular beach resort is a long way from being its nicest. Situated 154 km south of Bangkok, a fourth 'S' (for sex) has been added to the Sun-Sea-Sand group in this gaudy and raucous resort. Pattaya is designed mainly to appeal to European package tourists and there are plenty of snack bars along the beach strip proclaiming that 'bratwurst mit brot' is more readily available than 'khow phat'.

Pattaya consists of a long beach strip of mainly expensive hotels. The beach is drab and dismal and if you venture into Pattaya's equally uninviting water you run the risk of being mowed down by a ski-boat lunatic, an out-of-control boat-cycle (or whatever they call them) or simply dropped on from above by a para-skier. Pattaya is not my idea of fun. Its one real attraction is the rather beautiful offshore islands where the snorkelling is good.

Places to Stay & Eat

Although Pattaya is basically a package tourist, big hotel deal there are a handful of cheaper places squeezed in the small Sois, back off the main beach road. Cheap in Pattaya would be expensive just about anywhere else in Thailand; this is not Koh Samui or Phuket.

The *Bonanza Lodge* at Soi 15, Pattaya Beach Rd has rooms from 60/80B and is not so clean and rather noisy but it is liveable. The *Siam Guest House* on Soi 13 is a lot better than many at 100B for a clean double with toilet and shower. *Pattaya 12* on Soi 12 has very clean and comfortable double rooms with fan on the second floor for 150B. It's about the best accommodation value in Pattaya.

Most food in Pattaya is expensive – cheap eating here means *Pizza Hut* or *Mr Donut*! Shops along the back street, away from the beach, Pattaya No 2 Rd, have good Thai food. Look for cheap rooms to rent back here, too.

Getting There

There are departures every half hour from the Eastern Bus Terminal for the 2½ hour, 29B trip to Pattaya. Air-con buses are 50B. There are also all sorts of air-con tour buses to Pattaya from a number of tour companies. At 11 am and 9 pm there are buses direct from the airport for 160B one-way.

RAYONG

There's a pleasant beach here, at this 'real' Thai resort beyond Pattaya.

Places to Stay & Eat

On Tha Pradu the *Rayong Hotel* has rooms from 80B while the *Rayong-O-Thani* at 169 Sukhumvit Rd costs from 100B and up. There's good cheap eats at the market near the Thetsabanteung movie theatres, and beside the river there's a very good open-air restaurant belonging to the Fishermen's Association

KOH SAMET

Further on beyond Rayong this small island is off the coast from Ban Phe. It's a very quiet and un-touristed place but no competitor to Koh Samui for natural attraction although the beaches are superb. An advantage of Koh Samet is that the weather is usually good here when Koh Samui is getting its worst rain. There are no cars, motor bikes or shops on the island so it is very peaceful.

Places to Stay

Accommodation goes from 50 to 150B, rather more expensive than the Koh Samui or Phuket norm, and it's nowhere near as nice. In fact it's really pretty primitive. The island is also short of water – there's enough for drinking but if you want a shower it's off to the well.... The picture seems to be improving, however. A last minute letter recommended *Naga Bungalows* between Tubtim and Sai Kaew (near the concrete mermaid!).

Getting There

It's a three hour, 69B bus ride from the Eastern Bus Terminal in Bangkok to

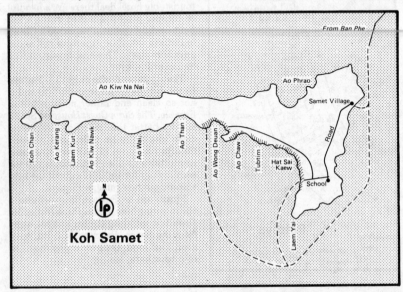

Rayong, then a 10B bus to Ban Phe (the touts will find you). For just 1B more, however, you can get a direct Bangkok-Ban Phe bus so why bother with Rayong?

From Ban Phe, a fishing boat will take you out to Koh Samet for around 20B, 25B tops.

Northern Thailand

The northern area was the region where Thai kingdoms first developed so it is full of interesting ruins such as those at Sukhothai. For the modern visitor it's equally interesting for the easy-going and interesting northern capital Chiang Mai. From here you can make treks which pass through the country of Thailand's many colourful hill tribes. This too is the region of the infamous Golden Triangle where Thailand, Laos and Burma meet and from where much of the world's opium comes.

GETTING THERE

The straightforward way of getting to the north is simply to head directly from Bangkok to Chiang Mai either by bus, train or air. Fortunately there are also some more unusual routes although the old 'Laotian Loop' – which took you from Bangkok to Vientiane, Luang Prabang and Ban Houei Sai, then back into Thailand to Chiang Rai and eventually Chiang Mai – has been short-circuited by the change of government in Laos. You can still make an interesting northern loop from Bangkok to Chiang Mai and back through north-east Thailand.

Starting north you could visit the ancient capitals of Ayuthaya, Lopburi and Sukhothai on your way to Chiang Mai. If you visit these ancient cities southbound rather than northbound you'll hit them in chronological order. Or you could take a longer and less 'beaten track' route by first heading west to Nakhon Pathom and Kanchanaburi and then back-tracking to Nong Pladuk and travelling north-east by bus to Suphanburi and Ang Thong en route to Ayuthaya. From Chiang Mai you then head north to Fang, take the daily riverboat down the Mekong (well a tributary of the Mekong, the Mekok) to Chiang Rai.

From there you head back towards Chiang Mai but get off at Lampang and either bus via Tak to Sukhothai or take the train to Phitsanuloke. From there it's bus to Lom Sak and then Loei and Udon Thani. There is also a new road between Lom Sak and Khon Kaen. Udon Thani and Khon Kaen are both on the rail and bus routes back to Bangkok but there are a number of other places worth exploring in the north-east before heading back to the capital.

THINGS TO BUY There are a lot of things to attract your money in the northern capital, but basically Chiang Mai is a very commercial and touristy place and a lot of junk is churned out for the undiscerning. So buy carefully. The night market in Chiang Mai, near the expensive hotels, is a good place to look for almost anything, but you have to bargain hard. The jet-setters don't – and push the prices up. The Hilltribe Products Foundation, near the Vegetarian Restaurant, or Thai Tribal Crafts, on Bumangrat near McCormick Hospital, are excellent places for their crafts. Their prices are often much lower than the night market.

Cotton & Silk Very attractive lengths of material can be made into all sorts of things. Go to Pasang, south of Lamphun, for cotton. For Thai silk, with its lush colours and pleasantly rough texture, try San Kamphaeng. It's cheaper up here than in Bangkok.

Ceramics Thai Celadon, about six km

north of Chiang Mai, turns out ceramic-ware modelled on the Sawankhaloke pottery that used to be made at Sukhothai and exported all over the region hundreds of years ago. With their deep, cracked, glazed finish some pieces are very beautiful and they are cheaper than in Bangkok. Other ceramics can be seen close to the Old Chiang Mai centre.

Woodcarving All sorts of carvings are available including countless elephants – but who would want a half-life size wooden elephant anyway? Teak salad bowls are good and very cheap.

Antiques You'll see lots of these around, including opium weights – the little animal-shaped weights used to measure out opium in the Golden Triangle. Check out prices in Bangkok first as Chiang Mai's shops are not always so cheap.

Lacquerware Decorated plates, containers, utensils and other items are made by building up layers of lacquer over a wooden or woven bamboo base. You'll also see Burmese lacquerware in the north and I must admit I prefer the Burmese stuff although the quality is higher here – and higher still in Japan.

Silverwork A number of silverwork shops are located close to the south moat gate. The hill tribe jewellery is very nice.

Clothes All sorts of shirts, blouses and dresses, plain and embroidered, are available at very low prices – but check the quality carefully.

Umbrellas Take a bus out to Baw Sang, the umbrella village, where beautiful paper umbrellas are hand-painted. A huge garden one is around 350B, but post and packing would add a fair bit more. Leaf paintings – framed – are also made here and are very attractive.

CHIANG MAI

Thailand's second city is a bit of a tourist trap – full of noisy motorcycles and souvenir shops – but it offers interesting contrasts with the rest of the country and there is plenty to see. It's also an excellent base for trips further afield.

At one time Chiang Mai was an independent kingdom, much given to warring with Burma and Laos as well as Sukhothai to the south. You can still see the moat that encircled the city at that time, but the remaining fragments of the city wall are mainly reconstructions. Originally founded in 1296, Chiang Mai fell to the Burmese in 1556, but was recaptured in 1775.

Information & Orientation

Finding your way around Chiang Mai is fairly simple although a copy of Nancy Chandler's *Map Guide to Chiang Mai* is worth its 50B price. Chiang Mai has a tourist office on Tha Phae Rd. The old city of Chiang Mai is a neat square bounded by moats. Moon Muang Rd, along the east moat, is one of the main centres for cheap accommodation and places to eat. Tha Phae Rd runs straight out from the middle of this side and crosses the Ping River where it changes name to Charoen Muang Rd. The railway station and the GPO are both further down Charoen Muang Rd, a fair distance from the centre. Beware of drug busts in Chiang Mai; some guest houses have been known to supply you with dope and then turn you in.

Things to See

Wat Chiang Man This is the oldest wat within the city walls and was founded by King Mengrai, Chiang Mai's founder, in 1296. Two famous Buddha images are kept here in the abbot's quarters and can be seen on request. One is the Crystal Buddha which, like Bangkok's Emerald Buddha, was once shuttled back and forth between Siam and Laos.

Wat Phra Singh In the centre of town, this well kept wat was founded in 1345. There are a number of interesting buildings here but the supposedly 1500-year-old Phra Singh Buddha image is subject to some doubt and its exact history is vague.

Wat Chedi Luang Originally constructed in 1411 this wat contains ruins of a huge chedi which collapsed in a 1545 earthquake.

Other Wats Wat Jet Yod has seven (jet) spires and was damaged by the Burmese in 1566. It's near the Chiang Mai Museum and is modelled (imperfectly) after the Mahabodhi Temple in Bodh Gaya, India where the Buddha attained enlightenment. Wat Koo Tao has a peculiar chedi like a pile of diminishing spheres. Wat Suan Dawk was originally built in 1383 and contains a 500-year-old bronze Buddha image and colourful Jataka murals showing scenes from the Buddha's lives. Wat U Mong also dates from Mengrai's rule and has a fine image of the fasting Buddha.

National Museum The National Museum has a good display of Buddha images and is open from 9 am to 12 noon and 1 to 4 pm from Wednesday to Sunday. Admission is 2B on Saturday and Sunday, free on other days.

Other The Tribal Research Centre at the Chiang Mai University has a good small museum of hill tribe artifacts. Head out towards Wat Suan Dawk – it's two blocks north once you get to the university. Old Chiang Mai is a touristy 'instant hill tribes' centre. There are Thai and hill tribe dance performances here every night. The rather kitsch Laddaland also puts on a dance performance every morning.

The annual dry-season water festival takes place in mid-April with particular fervour in Chiang Mai. The late-December to early-January Winter Fair is also a great scene with all sorts of activities and lots of colourful visitors from the hills. You'll often see local hill tribespeople in Chiang Mai – check the night market just off Tha Phae Rd. There are lots of handicrafts on sale in Chiang Mai. In the centre of town, Chiang Mai's jail has a large resident farang population – those without enough money to buy their way off drug busts.

Places to Stay

In Chiang Mai travellers' accommodation is usually in the guest houses. There are plenty of them with prices mainly in the 40 to 80B bracket. The guest house definition is a rather loose one, some cheap hotels have changed their name in English to 'guest house' while retaining the word 'hotel' in Thai. It's simply a convenient buzz word. Many of the guest houses are along Moon Muang Rd on the inside of the east moat. Others can be found along Charoen Rat, on the east side of the Ping River, or on Charoen Prathet, on the west side of the river. The latter streets are some distance from the centre, but convenient for the railway station and Chiang Rai buses.

Guest houses typically cost 60B for a double. Popular ones include *Lek House* at 22 Chaiyaphum Rd, near the Chang Moi Rd intersection on the Soi to Wat Chompoo. It's clean, quiet and has a nice garden. Rooms with fan and bath are 60/80B. There's a good restaurant, breakfast is 15B.

Chiang Moi House at 29 Chang Moi Kao Rd is behind the New Chiang Mai Hotel and is good value at 60/70B. There are only five clean and comfortable rooms. *Chiang Mai International Youth Hostel* (tel 212863) is at 31 Pra Pokklao Rd, Lane 3 and has a dorm at 25B per person, singles from 40B, doubles from 50B with a student or YHA card, 10B more without. It has recently moved to this new, more central location.

Chumpol Guest House (tel 234526), 89 Charoen Prathet Rd, has rooms from 70 to 120B. Next door is the popular *Chiang Mai Guest House* (tel 236501) at number 91 with rooms from 100 to 200B.

Gemini House at 22 Ratchadamnoen Rd is an old teak house with dorm beds at 15 to 20B or rooms from 50 to 80B. Near Wat Chiang Man the *Chiang Man Guest House* at Soi 9, 46/1 Moon Muang Rd costs 40/60B for singles/doubles with shared bathroom and is a friendly, pleasant place to stay.

The *Je T'aime Guest House* (tel 234912) at 247 Charoen Rat Rd is a long-running favourite in a peaceful and relaxed garden-like setting. It's rather far from the centre, but that doesn't seem to bother people. Rooms all have fan and private

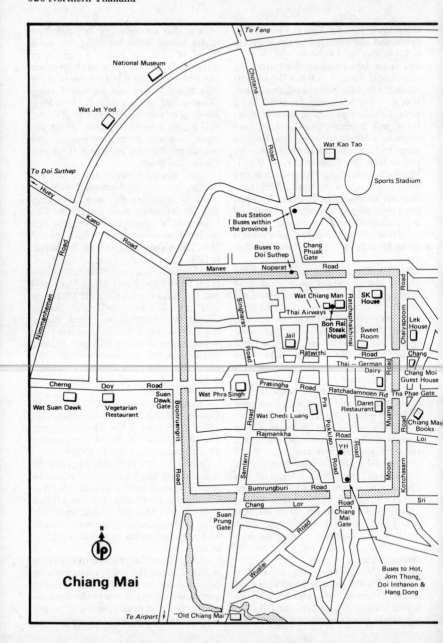

Chiang Mai

To Fang

National Museum

Wat Jet Yod

To Doi Suthep

Chotana Road

Wat Kao Tao

Sports Stadium

Huey Road

Kaeo Road

Nimmanhemen Road

Bus Station
(Buses within
the province)

Buses to
Doi Suthep

Chang
Phuak
Gate

Manee

Noparat

Road

Singharat Road

Wat Chiang Man

Thai Airways

Bon Rai
Steak
House

SK
House

Ratchaphakhinai

Sweet
Room

Chaiyapoom Road

Lek
House

Jail

Ratwithi

Road

Chang

Chang Moi
Guest House

Thai — German
Dairy

Cherng Road

Doy Road

Suan
Dawk
Gate

Wat Phra Singh

Prasingha

Road

Ratchadamnoen Rd

Tha Phae Gate

Wat Suan Dawk

Vegetarian
Restaurant

Wat Chedi Luang

Pra Pokklao Road

Daret
Restaurant

Muang Road

Chiang Mai
Books

Boonruangrit Road

Rajmankha

YH

Moon Road

Loi

Samlarn Road

Bumrungburi

Road

Kotchasarn Road

Sri

Suan
Prung
Gate

Chang

Lor

Road

Chang Mai
Gate

Wualai Road

Suan
Prung
Gate

N

LP

To Airport

"Old Chiang Mai"

Buses to Hot,
Jom Thong,
Doi Inthanon &
Hang Dong

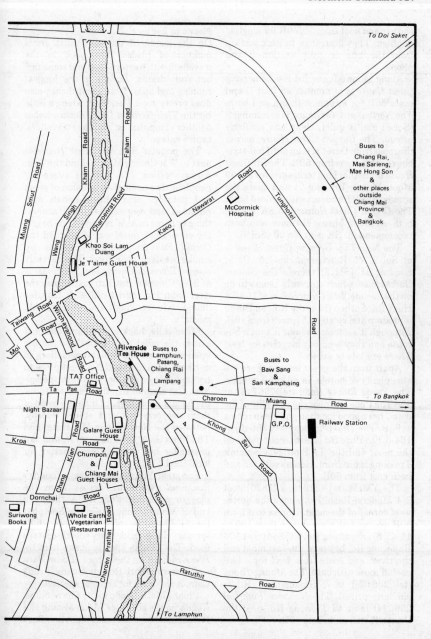

shower and cost from 50/60B for singles/doubles. They'll arrange to pick you up from the bus or train station if you phone.

Along Moon Muang Rd the *Lamchang Guest House* is at number 28 (Soi 7) and costs 60B for a room with fan and bath. The *North Bed & Breakfast* is at number 9 (Soi 8) and is quiet, clean and similarly priced. The *Garden Guest House*, across the moat from Daret's, is an old Thai-style house with rooms from 50B. The *PK Guest House* is another long term survivor at 109 Moon Muang Rd (Soi 7) and costs the standard 60B for rooms with fan and bath. The *Orchid Guest House* and *SK House*, both on Moon Muang Rd have also been recommended. SK is at No 30 (Soi 9).

The *New Thai-German Guest House* is at Soi 2, 25 Ratchamankha Rd. Or at number 21 (Soi 2) there's the *Saitum Guest House* which currently seems to be on the decline. *Isra Guest House* at 109/24 Huey Rd, Suthep (near the Rincon Hotel) is modern and clean with prices from 40B. Although it's a long way out it's on a bus route but they lend out bicycles for free. There are lots of others.

Apart from the guest houses there are also plenty of hotels, in all price ranges. The *Roong Ruang Hotel* (tel 236746) at 398 Tha Phae Rd, near the east side of the moat, has a good location and clean rooms at 90B. The *Thai Charoen* (tel 236640) at 164-6 Tha Phae Rd is further out between the moat and the TAT office – Summit Trekking is out front. Rooms with fan and bath cost from 60B.

The *YMCA* (tel 221819, 221820) is at 2/4 Mengrai-Rasni Rd, above the northwest corner of the moat. Dorms cost from 50B, rooms with shared bath from 100 to 160B. *Sri Rajawong* (tel 235864) is at 103 Rajawong Rd, between the east moat and the river, and costs from 60B for a fan-cooled room with bath. The *Muang Thong* (tel 236438) at 5 Rajamankha Rd is similarly priced. The *Nakhorn Ping* (tel 236024) is at 43 Taiwang Rd, near the Prince Hotel, and costs 80B.

Places to Eat

On the inside of the east moat are a number of places that pack in the travellers with western food and some far-out fruit drinks. *Daret's* is the longest running and apart from great drinks also does pretty good Thai food. Along a little bit the *Thai-German Dairy Restaurant* is another long-runner in the travellers' centre category.

The popular *Ban Rai Steak House* is next to Wat Chiang Man, behind the Thai Airways office. It's just the place for people in dire need of an infusion of steak and potatoes or a sheesh-kebab with potatoes and vegetables. The 'nearest thing to home in Asia' reported one happy traveller. Back on Moon Muang Rd the *Orchid Pub & Steakhouse* serves up similar western-style food. The recently opened *Riverside Chiang Mai Tea House* is at 9-11 Charoen Rat Rd, just across the river from the tourist office. It features 'home-style cooking' and country/folk music.

Meanwhile, back in Thailand and just across the moat from Daret's is the big open-air *Aroon Rai* which specialises in northern Thai food and is a great place to try sticky rice and other northern specialities. Get a group together in order to try the maximum number of dishes – some of them are *very* hot and spicy. Nearby, between the New Chiang Mai Hotel and Tha Phae Gate, the *Thanarm Restaurant* is smaller but possibly even better for local food.

For great Yunnanese Chinese food try *Ruam-mit Phochana*, across from the playground on Sithiwong Rd. At the north end of Moon Muang Rd in the Somphet (or Si Phum) market there are stalls serving cheap and tasty north-eastern food. The Singha beer is cheap here to. *Phu Kradung*, on the corner of Sam Larn and Bamrungburi Rds at Suang Prung Gate, is also good for regional specialities.

Chiang Mai is famed for its fine noodles. *Kolian* on the corner of Moon Muang and Ratchamankha does great 'boat noodles'.

Khao soi, a concoction of spicy curried chicken with flat wheat noodles, is the true Chiang Mai speciality. *Khao Soi Lam Duang* on Charoen Rat Rd, not far from the Je T'aime Guest House, is particularly good and their noodles cost just 8B a bowl. Even the king has tried their noodles.

Chiang Mai has several vegetarian places such as the very cheap *Vegetarian Restaurant* (Raan Ahaan Mangsawirat) beside the road on the way out to Wat Suan Dawk. Too bad they're only open for lunch. *Ngam Nit* at 107/1 Chang Moi Tat Mai, off Chang Moi Rd just after it crosses the canal, is another vegetarian place. Or try *Whole Earth*, which is run by the local TM folk and is a little more expensive. It's out Si Dornchai Rd, past the Chang Klan intersection, and has Thai and Indian vegetarian fare. There's also a vegetarian place right by Daret's.

Getting There

There are lots of buses from the Northern Bus Terminal in Bangkok and the trip north takes eight hours and cost about 150B; air-con buses are 250B. There is also a variety of tour buses making the Bangkok-Chiang Mai trip. The Boston Inn in Bangkok operates a particularly cheap tour bus. If you're intending to hop from town to town on your way north, Chiang Mai buses operate via Phitsanuloke, Sukhothai, Lampang and Uttaradit.

The trains to Chiang Mai from Bangkok are rather slower although there is no problem on the overnight service since it gives you a night's sleep if you have a sleeper. There's an express at 6 pm arriving at 7.30 am and a rapid at 3 pm arriving at 5.20 am. On the express you can get 2nd class tickets for 242B plus express surcharge and sleeper cost. Third class tickets are only available on the rapid trains and cost 136B plus surcharges. Bus or train you should book in advance if possible.

You can also fly to Chiang Mai three or four times daily from Bangkok. The flight takes an hour and the fare is 1100B. There are also flights between Chiang Mai and other towns in the north including Chiang Rai. You can also enter Thailand at Chiang Mai since there is a regular Thai International service between Hong Kong and Chiang Mai.

Getting Around

You can rent bicycles (20 to 25B a day) or motorcycles to explore around Chiang Mai – check with your guest house or the offices near the moat. There are plenty of *songthaews* around the city with standard fares of 5B. City buses cost 2B – get a bus route map from the tourist office. A taxi from the airport should be less than 50B; a *songthaew* will be less again. The airport is only two or three km from the city centre. Hordes of *songthaew* jockeys meet incoming buses and trains at Chiang Mai – they wave signs for the various guest houses, and if the one you want pops up you can have a free ride there.

AROUND CHIANG MAI
Doi Suthep

From the hill-top temple of Wat Phra That there are superb views out over Chiang Mai. Choose a clear day to make the 16 km, hairpinned ascent to the temple. A long flight of steps, lined by ceramic-tailed *nagas* (dragons) leads up to the temple from the car park.

Phu Bing palace is five km beyond the temple; you can wander the gardens on Fridays, Saturdays and Sundays. Just before the palace car park a turn to the left will lead you to a Meo village. It's somewhat touristed as it is so near to Chiang Mai, but it's still worth seeing. The last couple of km to the village is for jeep, motorcycle or feet only.

Getting There Minibuses to Doi Suthep leave from the Elephant Gate and cost around 35B; downhill it's 20B. For another 5B you can take a bicycle up with you and zoom back downhill.

Baw Sang – San Kamphaeng

The 'umbrella village' is nine km east of Chiang Mai. It's quite a picturesque spot and engages in just about every type of northern Thai handicraft. Four or five km further down Highway 1006 is San Kamphaeng which engages in cotton and silk weaving. Pasang, see below, is probably better for cotton, though.

Getting There Buses to Baw Sang (sometimes spelled Bo Sang or Bor Sang) leave from the north side of Charoen Muang Rd, towards the GPO. The fare is 4B to Baw Sang, 5B to San Kamphaeng.

Elephants

A daily 'elephants at work' show takes place near the 58-km marker on the Fang road. Arrive around 9 am or earlier to see bath-time in the river. It's really just a tourist trap, but probably worth the admission price. Once the spectators have gone the logs are all put back in place for tomorrow's show! It's a good idea to take a picture of an elephant to show the bus conductor or 'elephant' may be interpreted as 'fang', the town further north. There's a northern Thailand elephant meeting in November raising local prices.

Another place to see elephants is the Elephant Training School (really) on the Chiang Rai-Lampang road. From Lampang it's about 10B on a bumpy old bus. A big sign on the roadside in Thai and English (on the other side) indicates the location. You have to walk a couple of km up and down hills to get to the well-hidden school – you might be able to find an elephant to follow! The place is set up for tourists and has seats and even toilets, but nobody seems to know about it. When the trainer feels like it, sometime between 8 am and 12 noon, the show begins and you'll see them put through their paces. The elephants appreciate a few pieces of fruit – 'feels like feeding a vacuum cleaner with a wet nozzle' reported one visitor. Any bus on the main road will take you on to Lampang or Chiang Rai.

Lamphun

Only 26 km south of Chiang Mai there are two interesting wats in this town. Wat Phra That Haripunchai has a small museum and a very old chedi, variously dated at 897 or 1157 AD. There are some other fine buildings in the compound. Wat Chama Thevi, popularly known as Wat Kukut, has an unusual chedi with 60 Buddha images set in niches. There's a third old and interesting wat in Lamphun too.

Getting There Buses depart Chiang Mai regularly from the south side of Nawarat Bridge on Lamphun Rd – fare is 6B or 8B by minibus. A minibus straight through to Pasang will cost 12B.

Pasang

Only a short *songthaew* ride south of Lamphun, Pasang is a centre for cotton-weaving and is also reputed to have the most beautiful girls in the north. The Nantha Khwang shop has good locally made cotton goods.

Hill Tribe Treks

One of the most popular activities from Chiang Mai is to take a trek through the tribal areas in the hills in the north. There are six distinct tribes in the north and they are one of the most interesting facets of the area. The tribal groups are also found across the border in Burma and Laos, and to them political lines on the maps have little meaning. Although pressure is being applied to turn them to more acceptable types of agriculture, opium is still a favourite crop up here and ganja grows wild. The best known tribes are the Meos with their bright costumes and jewellery, the Karens (both red and white), the Lisus, the Lahu, the Yao and the Akha.

Unfortunately the treks have really become a little too popular over the last 10 years and a little care is needed to ensure a good experience. Some areas are simply over-trekked. A constant stream of camera-waving visitors, often accompanied by guides who cannot speak English let alone the hill tribe languages, is hardly a ticket to an interesting trip. Finding a good tour guide is probably the key to having a good trek, but it's also important to check out your fellow trekkers. Try to organise a meeting before departure. The best guides will be conversant with the tribes and their languages, have good contacts and easy relations with them and will know areas which are relatively untouristed. The best way of finding a good operator is simply to ask other travellers in Chiang Mai. People just back from a trek will be able to give you the low-down on how their trek went.

Some recommended operators include Summit Tribal Treks at 164-166 Tha Phae Rd which has a particularly good reputation. SUA Trekking operates out of Daret's Restaurant. Orbit Trekking was very popular for a while, then seemed to go downhill, but may be re-established out of the Thai-German Guest House. Northern Thailand Trekking is next to the Thai-German Dairy Restaurant. Folkways Trekking operate out of the Chiang Moi Guest House or from 1 Prapokklao Rd. There are lots of others; recent writers have recommended YHA Treks and Poppy's.

Treks normally last four days and three nights and the usual cost is 650B although longer treks are also available. Bring a water bottle, medicines and money for lunch on the first and last day and for odd purchases. Don't bring too much money or other valuables with you – there has been the odd 'hold up' of trekking parties. You can leave your gear behind in Chiang Mai with your hotel or trek operator. A useful list of questions to ask would be:

1. How many people in the group? 'Six is a good maximum', reported one traveller, although others have said that 10 is equally OK.
2. Can they guarantee no other tourists will visit the same village on the same day, especially overnight?

3. Can the guide speak the language of each village to be visited? Can he speak English too?
4. Exactly when does the tour begin and end? The three-day treks of some companies turn out to be less than 48 hours.
5. Do they provide transport before and after the trek or is it just by public bus – often with long waits?

You can also just head off on your own or hire a guide or porter by yourself, but the treks are not that expensive and there are some areas where it is unwise to go. If you've got to bring gifts for the villagers, make it band-aids and disinfectant rather than cigarettes and candy. It may be more for show but it doesn't do any harm. 'Toothpaste and soap', suggested another clean-minded traveller.

Most people who go on these treks have a thoroughly good time and reckon they're great value. Some comments include 'the best experience of my life . . . I hope we left the villages as we found them' (an Orbit trek). 'The guide gave us detailed information on each village, on the history, customs, even told us which drugs were of high quality and if the price was right.' 'The area we covered was only recently opened for trekking and the guides were some of the nicest people I have ever met' (a Summit trek). Note, however, that there have been a number of incidents of hold-ups and robbery over the years. This area of Thailand is relatively un-policed, somewhat 'wild west'. Enquire round that everything is OK before setting blithely off into the wilds.

NAKHON SAWAN

At this fairly large town on the way north there are good views from the hilltop Wat Com Kiri Nak Phrot and interesting boat trips can be made from the jetty.

Places to Stay

If you stay here the *New White House* at 2 Matulee Rd and the *Irawan* at 1-5

Matulee Rd have reasonably priced rooms; the Irawan also has some with air-con. Or there's the *Nakhon Sawan* at Tambol Pak Nam Po. The *Wang Mai*, at the market on the waterfront, is a good place with doubles with bath at 90B and a good restaurant downstairs.

KAMPHAENG PHET

Only a couple of km off the Bangkok-Chiang Mai road there are a number of relics within the old city and very fine remains of the long city wall. Outside can be seen Wat Phra Si Iriyabot, with the shattered remains of standing, sitting, walking and reclining Buddha images. Wat Chang Rob or 'temple surrounded by elephants' is just that – a temple with an elephant-buttressed wall. Take care at the more remote ruins outside of town here.

Places to Stay

It can be a little difficult to find places here since few signs are in English script. *Nitaya Pratapa* at 118/1 Tesa Rd is a little squalid and has rooms from 70B. It's on the main road leading to the river bridge. There are foodstalls opposite at night and the main ruins are around the corner beyond the foodstalls – further down the road away from the bridge towards Sukhothai. The *Chong Sawasdee* at 108 Tesa Rd is also hard to locate while the *Rajdamnoen* at 892 Rajdamnoen Rd is more expensive at 70 to 90B and has air-con rooms. Or there's the *Gor Choke Chai Hotel* at 80B.

TAK

This is nothing more than a junction town for Sukhothai on the way north to Chiang Mai. It's pronounced 'Tark' not 'Tack'. From here you can visit the Lan Sang National Park; it's a good base from which to visit Mae Sot.

Places to Stay

If you have to stay here then try the *Tak* at 18/10 Mahadtai Bamrung Rd or the *Thavisak* at 561 on the same road. The

Sanguan Thai at 619 Taksin Rd has rooms from 90B or from 130B with air-con. A traveller who made a lengthy pause here, and liked the place, recommended the *Meaping* opposite the food market on Mahadtai Bamrung Rd, the main street. Rooms here were 40 to 60B and there was a good coffee bar downstairs.

PHITSANULOKE

There's not a great deal of interest in this town, which is mainly used as a stepping stone to other places. It's on the rail line between Bangkok and Chiang Mai and it's here you get off for Sukhothai. Wat Phra Sri Ratana Mahathat (known locally as Wat Yai) is an interesting old wat, however, and it contains one of the most revered Buddha images in Thailand.

Places to Stay

If you come straight out of the railway station and turn left by the expensive *Amarin Nakhon Hotel* on the first and second right turns you'll find some cheaper hotels. The *Hor Fah* at 73 Phyalithai Rd and the *Unhachak* both have rooms from 100B. The *Phitsanulok* is similar.

There are several cheap restaurants in the vicinity or for a real treat try the restaurant at the expensive *Amarin Nakhorn* at 3/1 Chao Phaya Rd which has excellent western food. At Phetchabun, south of Phitsanuloke, the *Had Chao* on Tambol Had Chao is cheap.

Getting There

Buses for Sukhothai go from close to the centre, but the stations for buses to the east or north are on the other side of the railway tracks, on the outskirts of town. From Chiang Mai or Bangkok you can reach Phitsanuloke by bus or rail. Buses from Bangkok cost 110B or 200B with air-con. You can also fly there from Bangkok. Grey buses run between the town centre and the airport or bus station for 2B. The big hotels also run free buses to and from the airport or a *songthaew* costs 5B.

SUKHOTHAI

Sukhothai was Thailand's first capital but its period of glory was short. From its foundation as a capital in 1257 it only lasted a little over a hundred years to 1379 before being superseded by Ayuthaya. Nevertheless its achievements in art, literature, language and law, apart from the more visible evidence of great buildings, were enormous. In many ways the ruins visible today at Sukhothai and the other cities of the kingdom, like Kamphaeng Phet and Si Satchanalai, are more appealing than Ayuthaya because they are less commercial, more off the beaten track.

Orientation

Old Sukhothai, known as Muang Kao, is spread over quite an area. You can hire bicycles to get around. The old town is about 12 km from the uninteresting (although the market is good) new town of Sukhothai. It's 55 km east of the Bangkok-Chiang Mai road from Tak. Unfortunately the area around the ruins is somewhat bandit infested and it's not wise to visit the more remote sites without brave protection. At Wat Sri Chum there's a sign warning you to report to the police station before exploring remote ruins. One traveller reported tht when he did this he got a police escort to some of the ruins and a ride on the back of the policeman's motorcycle. A 15B guidebook and map is essential for exploring the scattered ruins.

Things to See

National Museum The fine museum has a model of the old city which is good for planning your exploration. They also sell guides to the ruins here. It's open from 9 am to 12 noon and 1 to 4 pm from Wednesday to Sunday and admission is 2B on weekends, free on weekdays. There is also a 2B admission charge to some ruins.

Wat Mahathat This vast assemblage, largest in the city, once contained 185 chedis – apart from various chapels and sanctuaries. Some of the original Buddha images still remain, including a big one amongst the broken columns. The large ornamented pond provides fine reflections.

Wat Sri Chum In this open, walled building a massive seated Buddha figure is tightly squeezed. A narrow tunnel inside the wall leads to views over the Buddha's shoulders and to the top. Candle-clutching kids will guide you up and point out the 'Buddha foot' on the way.

Other Wat Srisawai, with its three prangs and its moat, was originally intended to be a Hindu temple. It's just south of Wat Mahathat. Wat Sra Sri is a classically-simple Sukhothai-style wat set on an island. Wat Trapang Thong is next to the museum and is reached by a footbridge crossing its pond. It is still in use. Somewhat isolated to the north of the city, Wat Phra Pai Luang is similar in style to Wat Srisawai. Wat Chang Lom is to the south and the chedi is surrounded by 36 elephants. Unfortunately, Wat Saphan Hin – with a large standing Buddha looking back to Sukhothai from the hillside to the west – is not safe to visit.

Places to Stay & Eat

Rebuilt after a major fire, new Sukhothai is a clinical and dull town although there are some good hotels and restaurants. Near the town centre, the *Sukhothai Hotel* at 15/5 Singhawat Rd has a sign in English, Thai and Chinese. The rooms are in the 60 to 80B range and it's run by pleasant people. 'Too friendly' said a solo female traveller about unwelcome advances.

At 8 Singhawat Rd the *Rung Fa* is near the Yom River but can be a little difficult to find. It's similar in price and quality to the Sukhothai. Get a room in the back away from the traffic. Other places include the *Sawastipong* at 56/2 Singhawat which has rooms at 70B and isn't bad. The *Chinawat Hotel* has singles for 60B – large rooms with double bed, ceiling fan and attached bathroom. It is also possible to

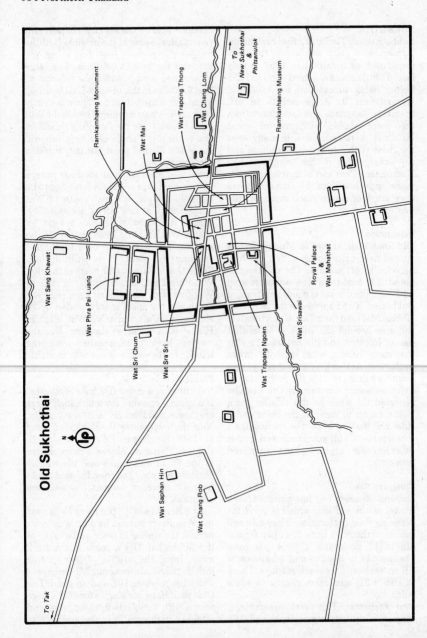

Old Sukhothai

N

To Tak

To New Sukhothai & Phitsanulok

Ramkamhaeng Monument

Wat Mai

Wat Trapong Thong

Wat Chang Lom

Ramkanhaeng Museum

Wat Sang Khawat

Wat Phra Pai Luang

Royal Palace & Wat Mahathat

Wat Srisawai

Wat Sri Chum

Wat Sra Sri

Wat Trapang Ngoen

Wat Saphan Hin

Wat Chang Rob

stay in the old town – places are available opposite the museum in a small village where the bus stops. Mr Vitoon has rooms at 40B but they're kind of noisy.

There are good places to eat both in the night market and the municipal market near the town centre. The *Sukhothai Hotel's* restaurant is also pretty good. *Kho Joeng Hong* is a good, inexpensive restaurant on the road by the Yom River. The expensive-looking outdoor restaurant between the road and Wat Chang Lom, near the old city, is actually quite reasonable.

Getting There

Air-con buses between Chiang Mai and Sukhothai cost 75B; from Bangkok 90B or 170B with air-con. Most services go via Phitsanuloke. From Phitsanuloke (Phit), buses to Sukhothai depart regularly, cost 15B and the trip takes about an hour. Phit is also the nearest point on the Bangkok-Chiang Mai railway line. Alternatively, you can approach Sukhothai from Tak – the fare is also 15B. Buses to Chiang Rai go by a new, more direct route and take about six hours.

Buses to Sawankhaloke and Si Satchanalai leave regularly from the intersection across from the Sukhothai Hotel. It's 3 or 4B for a *songthaew* between the new town and the old ruins. They leave from across the bridge and along a bit on the righthand side, a fair distance from where the other buses depart in the hotel and shopping area. In old Sukhothai you can hire bicycles from opposite the museum. They cost 20B a day and tend to be brakeless and shakey but they're OK for the tracks between the ruins. Alternatively, you can hire a *tuk-tuk* and driver by the hour for 20 to 50B if you want to save your feet.

AROUND SUKHOTHAI
Si Satchanalai

Even more attractive and isolated than the Sukhothai ruins, these stand 56 km to the north of new Sukhothai. Climb to the top of the 'Golden Mountain' for a view over the city and river. Wat Chedi Jet Thaew has a group of stupas. Wat Chang Lom has a chedi surrounded by Buddha statues in niches and guarded by the fine remains of elephant buttresses. Walk along the riverside two km or go back down the main road and cross the river to Wat Phra Si Ratana Mahathat, a very impressive temple with a well-preserved prang and a variety of seated and standing Buddhas.

Sawankhaloke Pottery Sukhothai was famous for its beautiful pottery, much of which was exported. Particularly fine specimens can be seen in the National Museum in Jakarta as the Indonesians of that time were keen collectors. Much of the pottery was made in Si Satchanalai. Rejects – buried in the fields – are still being found. Shops have misfired, broken, warped and fused pieces at Sukhothai and Si Satchanalai. Thai Celadon in Chiang Mai is a modern interpretation of the old craft.

Getting There Take a bus to Sawankhaloke and then change to a Si Satchanalai bus. The ruins are 11 km before the new town – tell the bus conductor 'praht prang' – it's easier than trying to explain where. Look for a big corn-cob shaped 'prang'. The river is less than a km off the road and there is now a suspension bridge across it. The last bus back leaves around 4 pm.

Uttaradit

You could continue north from Si Satchanalai and Sawankhaloke to Uttaradit on the railway line. Places to stay include *Pher Vanich 2* by the river at 1 Sri Uttara Rd, within walking distance of the railway station. The *Uttaradit* at 22 Tambol Tait and the *Thanothai* at 149-153 Kasemraj are also reasonably priced.

LAMPANG

South-east of Chiang Rai, this town was another former home for the Emerald

Buddha. There are a number of fine wats in this old town including Wat Phra Saeng and Wat Phra Keo on the banks of the Wang River to the north of the town. In the village of Koh Kha, 10 km south-east of Lampang, Wat Lampang Luang was originally constructed in the Haripunchai period and restored in the 16th century. It's an amazing temple with walls like a huge medieval castle. Getting there is a little difficult so start out early in the day.

Places to Stay & Eat

The *Lampang Hotel* on Tambol Suandoke has rooms from 80B, suitably luxurious with shower and toilet. On the corner of the same lane, at 213-215 Boonyawat Rd, the *Sri Sanga* has large rooms with fan and bathroom for 70B – a friendly place. There are a number of other hotels along Boonyawat Rd. Good Thai food in the place next to the large ice-cream parlour on Thanon Robwiang or there are several good foodstalls near the railway station.

Getting There

There are regular buses between Lampang and Chiang Mai, Chiang Rai, Phitsanuloke or Bangkok. The bus station in Lampang is some way out of town – a couple of baht by *samlor*, more if you arrive late at night. You can get air-con buses to Bangkok or Chiang Mai from Lampang. The air-con buses have offices in town; you don't have to go out to the bus station.

DOI INTHANON

Thailand's highest peak (2595 metres), Doi Inthanon can be visited as a day-trip from Chiang Mai. There are some impressive waterfalls and pleasant picnic spots here. Between Chiang Mai and Doi Inthanon the small town of Chom Thong has a fine Burmese-style temple, Wat Phra That Si Chom Thong.

Getting There

Buses run regularly from Chiang Mai to Chom Thong for 12B; from there you take a *songthaew* the few km to Mae Klang for about 3B and another to Doi Inthanon for 25 to 30B.

MAE HONG SON

North-west of Chiang Mai – 368 km away by road and close to the burmese border – this is a crossroads for Burmese visitors, opium traders and local hill tribes. There's a Burmese-built wat and a fine view from the hill by the town. It's a peaceful, quiet little place.

Places to Stay

All the hotels are on the two main streets. *Mitniyom* at 90 Khunlum Praphat and *Methi* at 55 on the same street are pretty good at 90B for a room with fan and bath. On Singhanat Rd the *Sanguan Sin* and *Suk Somchai* are cheaper but not so good. The *Siam Hotel*, next to the bus stop, has good doubles at 100B.

In Mae Sariang the *Inthira* restaurant, on the outskirts on the Chiang Mai side, is said to have some of the best chicken in holy basil in Thailand. They also do batter-fried frogs!

Getting There

Mae Hong Son must be getting more on the map – there are now daily flights from Chiang Mai. By bus it's nine hours from Chiang Mai; there are about five departures a day. The trip costs 100B or 150B in an air-con bus. Coming back you can take the 'shorter' route through Pai and Mae Taeng on Route 1095. Although this route is not yet all paved and requires a change of bus in Pai it also takes about nine hours. The scenery is quite spectacular in parts and you can break the trip by overnighting in Pai, which is an interesting, well off-the-beaten-track kind of place.

FANG

North of Chiang Mai this town was also founded by Mengrai in 1268, but there is little of interest today apart from the earth ramparts of his old city. Fang is, however, a good base for hill tribe visits or for the downriver ride to Chiang Rai. Fang is 152 km north of Chiang Mai and there are some points of interest along the way apart from the elephant camp mentioned in Around Chiang Mai. The Chiang Dao caves are five km off the road, 72 km north of Chiang Mai. The Mae Sae cascades are seven km off the road at Mae Rim, a further 13 km north.

Places to Stay

If you must stay in Fang then the *Fang Hotel* has rooms from 70B. Alternatives are the cheaper *Si Sukit* or the *Metta*. It's probably better not to stay in Fang itself but at Tha Ton, from where the boats run downriver to Chiang Rai. You can stay at the *Karen Coffee Shop* (Phanga's House) whose manager is also good for information on visiting the local hill tribes. Per person cost is 30 to 40B. 'Great rat stew and fried cicadas there,' reported one travelling gourmet.

Getting There

It takes three hours from Chiang Mai to Fang. Fare is 32B by ordinary bus, 40B by minibus. The buses go from the new bus station north of White Elephant (Chang Puak) Gate. It's 5B from Fang to Tha Ton.

AROUND FANG

Trekking in the immediate vicinity of Fang isn't all that interesting as most of the villages are either Shan or Chinese (not hill tribe at all) or Lahu. In this area the Lahu no longer wear their traditional costume. Further north, towards the Burmese border, there are some interesting trekking areas and there are fewer tourists and you also find Karen, Lisu and Akha villages. From across the river from Tha Ton you can get taxis east to the villages. Go at least to Ban Mai (10B), a quiet, neat, untouristed Shan village on the river. Another four or five km takes you to Mueng Ngarm, a Karen village. Accommodation may be available in Sulithai, a KMT Chinese village to the east, and in Laota, a Lisu village.

RIVER TRIP TO CHIANG RAI

The downriver trip from Fang to Chiang Rai is a bit of a tourist-trap these days – the villages along the way sell Coke and there are lots of TV aerials. But it's still fun. The boat departs Tha Ton at around 11.30 am to 12.30 pm; to catch it straight from Chiang Mai you'd have to leave at 7 or 7.30 am at the latest and make no stops on the way. The 6 am bus is the best bet. The fare on the boat is an expensive 160B and the trip takes about three to five hours. The length of time depends on the height of the river.

You get an armed guard on the boat, but he seems to spend most of the time asleep with his machine gun in a plastic sack. You'll finish making your trip just in time to catch a bus back to Chiang Mai so it can really be a day trip from Chiang Mai – but it's better to stay in Fang, then Chiang Rai or Chiang Saen and travelling on. You may sometimes have to get off and walk and it's also possible to make the trip (much more slowly) upriver, despite the rapids.

CHIANG RAI

Although this town was once the home of the Emerald Buddha it's of no real interest – just a stepping stone for other places like Fang, Chian Saen and Mae Sai. It is, however, an alternative starting point for hill tribe treks. Chiang Rai is 105 km from Chiang Mai.

Places to Stay

The *Chiang Rai Guest House* at 717/2 Srikerd Rd, near the main bus station, is good value at from 50B for a double. It's got mosquito nets and hot water and is well run (some visitors disagree) and friendly. The rather basic *Pongpun Guest House* at 176 Ngammuang Rd is even cheaper.

At 503 Ratanaket Rd, opposite the court house, the *Porn Guest House* is 'cheap and friendly' but flimsily partitioned. The beds now have mosquito nets and there's a dorm or rooms from 30B. Near the Kok River boat pier for boats from Tha Ton, at 445 Singhakai Rd, the *Mae Kok Villa* also has dorm accommodation plus rooms up to more than 100B. *Chat House*, right off the boat landing, is small, comfortable and cheap at 25/50B and has hot showers and good music. The *Thub Thim Thong Hotel* near the railway station has good, clean doubles with bath from 50B.

At 331/4 Traimit Rd, in the centre of town, a couple of blocks from the clock tower, the more expensive *Rama Hotel* has clean rooms from 180B and up. Also near the clock tower and district government buildings on Suksathit Rd, the *Chiang Rai Hotel* has rooms from 90B. Around the corner from the Chiang Rai Hotel at 424/1 Bunpakarn Rd the *Sukniran* is 120B and up for air-con rooms.

Places to Eat

The *Haw Naliga* or 'clock tower' restaurant has good Thai-Chinese food at reasonable prices and is very popular in Chiang Rai. It's near the clock tower in the centre of town. The *Wiang Hotel* is expensive but has a good (although also somewhat pricey) coffee shop. Next door to the Caltex service station near the clock tower is 'the best dessert shop in all of Thailand' – bananas in custard and coconut cream, soya beans in the same, caramel egg custard – they're all delicious. In February you can get good strawberries in Chiang Rai.

CHIANG KHONG

Right across the river from Ban Houei Sai in Laos this was the place where you started or finished the old 'Laotian Loop'. There's no real reason to go there now, but there are a number of cheap hotels along the main street.

CHIANG SAEN

Only 31 km north of Chiang Rai this interesting little town on the banks of the Mekong River has numerous ruins of temples, wats, chedis and other remains from the Chiang Saen period. There is

also a small museum. Across the river from Chiang Saen is Laos while 11 km further north, at the point where the Sop Ruak River meets the Mekong, is the official top of the Golden Triangle. This is where Burma, Laos and Thailand meet.

There's a bus a day from Chiang Saen to Sop Ruak, in the early morning, but you can also hitch. Mae Sai, north again from Chiang Saen, is the northernmost town in Thailand and is a good place to buy Burmese lacquerware and other crafts from Burma and Laos.

Places to Stay

Sop Ruak The *Golden Hut* is perched right on the Golden Triangle. It's a bit primitive (no electricity or running water) but good fun. You can sit out front watching the sun set over the Mekong while you have dinner and dream about your decidedly exotic location. There's also the relatively new *Golden Triangle Guest House* with clean bungalows at 30B. Or the *Triangle Lodge*.

Chiang Saen Run by the same family as the Golden Hut in Sop Ruak, the *Chiang Saen Guest House* is on the Sop Ruak road in Chiang Saen and costs 30/60B for singles/doubles. Otherwise there's the bright blue (the only sign in English says 'hotel') *Poonsuk Hotel*, a decrepit looking place towards the end of Chiang Saen's main street towards the river. Doubles are 50B.

Behind the post office is the small *Suree Guest House* with doubles at 50B and dorm beds at 20B. They also hire out good bicycles. Between Chiang Saen and Mae Sai is the *Thammachat Village Centre* with accommodation at 30B per person.

Good food is available at the *Sala Thai Restaurant*, sweets from the stall near the bus stop.

Getting There

It's a 40 minute to two hour (very variable!) trip from Chiang Rai to Chiang Saen for 15B. A bus up to Mae Sai from Chiang Saen is 15B. Take a *tuk-tuk* from Chiang Saen to Sop Ruak if you can find

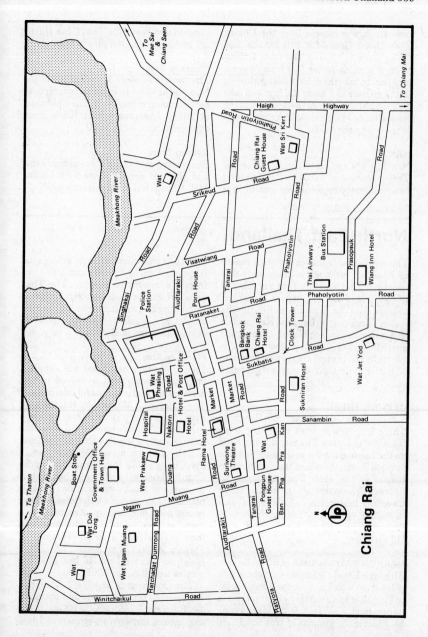

Chiang Rai

one. Or hire a bicycle from the Chiang Saen Guest House for 25B for the day. Going back to Chiang Mai from Chiang Saen it's much faster (4½ hours versus nine) not to take the direct Chiang Mai bus but to go back to Chiang Rai first and take a Chiang Mai bus from there. The Chiang Saen-Chiang Mai buses take a roundabout route over poor roads.

NAN

Nan has opened up recently, since the Thai government brought this formerly bandit-infested region under control. Wat Phumin and Wat Phra That Chae Haeng are two important temples in Nan.

Places to Stay

The *Amorin Si* at 97 Mahayod Rd or the *Nan Fah* at 438-440 Samundhevaraj both have rooms at around 60B. The *Sukkasem* at 29/31 Anantavoraritdet Rd is more expensive from 90 to 160B.

Getting There

Buses run from Chiang Mai and Sukhothai and you can also fly there from Chiang Mai, Chiang Rai and Phitsanuloke.

North-East Thailand

The north-east is the least visited region of Thailand, although in many ways it is the most 'Thai' and there are a number of places here of interest. In part, the lack of tourists can be accounted for by the region's proximity to Laos and Kampuchea and tales of hold-ups and Communist guerrilla actions, but in fact travel is generally OK in most areas and if anything is better now than it was a few years ago.

GETTING THERE

You can fly to Udorn Thani from Bangkok. There are railway lines operating from Bangkok to Udorn Thani and Nong Khai on the Laotian border in the north-east or to Ubon Ratchathani, near the Kampuchean border in the east. You can make an interesting loop through the north-east by travelling first north to Chiang Mai and the other centres in the north then to Phitsanuloke, Khon Kaen, Loei and Udorn Thani.

NAKHON RATCHASIMA (KHORAT)

Although Khorat is mainly thought of as a place from which to visit the Khmer ruins of Phimai, it has a number of attractions in its own right. They include the Mahawirong Museum in the grounds of Wat Sutchinda

with a fine collection of Khmer art objects. It's open 9 am to 12 noon and 1 to 4 pm from Wednesday to Sunday. The Thao Suranari Shrine is a popular shrine to Khun Ying Mo, a heroine who led the local inhabitants against Laotian invaders during the reign of Rama III.

Places to Stay

The TAT office in Khorat will supply a map of the city and a list of hotels, restaurants, and other useful information. The office is on Mitthaphap Rd, the west edge of town, beyond the railway station.

At 68-70 Mukkhamontri Rd, near the railway station, the *Fah Sang* is clean and friendly with rooms at 75B per person. *Poh Thong* at 179 Poh Klang Rd is in the 60 to 80B bracket and is noisy but livable. A couple of blocks west the *Siri Hotel* is pleasantly located in a quiet area and has rooms from 60B and up. According to a traveller there's also 'incredible American food in the hotel's *VFW (Veterans of Foreign Wars) Coffee Shop*.' The *Tokyo Hotel* on Sureerathani Rd has good big singles with bath for 100B.

The *Damrongrak* at 1674/1 Chumpon Rd is inside the city moats and costs 70/100B for singles/doubles. Also inside the city moats, the *Thai Pokaphan* at 104-6

Atsadang Rd is similarly priced. There are lots of good places to eat especially around the western gates to the centre, near the Thao Suranari Shrine. There are also good stalls and curry shops across from the railway station.

Getting There
There are two expresses daily from Bangkok's Hualamphong station but they arrive at ungodly hours in the morning. The trip passes through some fine scenery. By bus there are departures every 20 minutes to half an hour from the Northern Bus Terminal and the fare is 55B. The trip takes 3½ to four hours. Buses to or from Khon Kaen cost 40B.

AROUND KHORAT
Pakthongchai
This is a silk weaving centre 28 km south of Khorat. There are buses there every 30 minutes for 7B.

Phimai
This 12th-century Khmer shrine was once directly connected by road with Angkor in Cambodia. It has been described as the Angkor Wat of Thailand. The main shrine has been restored and is a beautiful and impressive piece of work. There is also a ruined palace and an open-air museum. Admission to the complex is 2B. Phimai itself is nothing special but it's a pleasant enough place to stay.

Places to Stay There's just one hotel, the clean and comfortable *Phimai Hotel* with rooms from 80B without bath right up to 260B for an air-con double with bath. There's a good restaurant next door.

Getting There There are buses every half hour from Khorat's main bus station behind the Erawan Hospital on Suranari Rd. The trip takes one to 1½ hours and costs 14B.

Prasat Phanomwan
Mid-way between Khorat and Phimai, this is another impressive Khmer ruin. To get there, get off the Khorat-Phimai bus at Ban Long Thong from where it's six km via Ban Makha to Prasat Phanomwan.

KHON KAEN
The mid-point between Khorat and Udorn Thani, Khon Kaen is also the gateway to the north-east from Phitsanuloke. The branch of the national museum here has an excellent collection and there is an interesting old wat on the banks of the lake. Khon Kaen also happens to be the centre for the production of Buddha sticks.

Places to Stay
There are plenty of hotels in Khon Kaen but not all of them have their names up in English script. On Srichan Rd the *Khon Kaen Bungalows* are good value from 60 to 120B without air-con. They're near the fancy Kosa Hotel so ask directions for that. The *Roma Hotel* at 50/2 Klang Muang Rd has rooms, all with air-con, from 150B.

The *Ban Phai* is 40 km away at Ban Phai. It's at 396 Chan Prasit Rd and has rooms from 40 to 120B. Ban Phai is noted for a local delicacy – *mooyong*, shredded pork.

Getting There
You can fly or bus from Phitsanuloke to Khon Kaen. From Khorat it's 2½ hours to Khon Kaen by bus. The fare is 39B. You can also do the trip by rail since Khon Kaen is on the Bangkok-Khorat-Udorn Thani rail line. It requires a change of bus to get from Khon Kaen to Phimai. Thai Airways fly to Khon Kaen from Bangkok.

UDORN THANI
This was one of the biggest USAF bases in Thailand – one of those places from where they flew out to drop millions of tons of bombs into the jungle in the hope that somebody might be standing under one of the trees. It's got nothing much to offer apart from massage parlours and ice

cream parlours. Ban Chiang, 50 km east, has some interesting archaeological digs – the excavations at Wat Pho Si Nai are open to the public and there's a recently constructed museum.

Places to Stay

The *Queen Hotel*, at 6-8 Udorn-dutsadi Rd, has rooms with fan and bath from 60B. In the centre of town the *Tokyo*, at 147 Prachak Rd, has similar rooms at similar prices and more expensive rooms with air-con. At 123 Prachak Rd the *Srisawat* has cheaper rooms in the old building from 50B.

The *Thailand* at 4/5 Surakorn Rd, just round the corner from the bus station, has clean rooms from 70B. The *Saiwong*, at 39 Adulyadet Rd, off Udorn-dutsadi Rd near the Chinese temple, is a small wooden Chinese hotel with clean rooms for 40B.

Places to Eat

Udorn Thani has plenty of restaurants – many with western food – but you can also find places that specialise in the ahaan isaan food of the north-east region. Try the *Rung Thong* at the west side of the clock tower. On Prachak Rd, *Rama Pastry* is air-con and has good pastries and coffee.

Six km north of Udorn *Suan Kaset Rang San* has good and inexpensive northern-style seafood. Udorn also has some interesting night-spots including the *Charoen Hotel* for '60s style psychedelia!

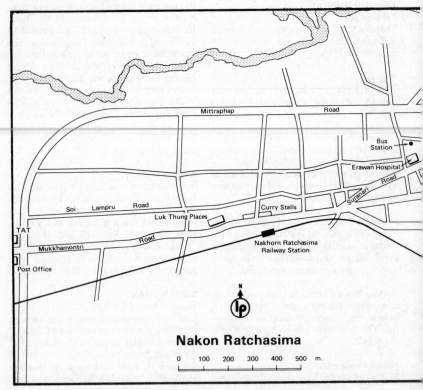

Nakon Ratchasima

0   100   200   300   400   500   m.

Or the *Tibet Club*. Try the north's own Thai beer, *Khun Phaen*, in Udorn too.

Getting There

There's a daily express from Bangkok costing 189B in 2nd, 90B in 3rd and taking 11 hours overnight. Take a sleeper – it's worthwhile on this long trip. Buses from Bangkok depart frequently and cost 110B – the trip also takes 11 to 12 hours. There are also regular flights.

Khorat to Udorn Thani is 35B and takes 3½ hours by bus. To get to Ban Chiang first take a *samlor* or *songthaew* to the north-east market (5B) from where it's a one to 1½ hour *songthaew* trip (10B) to Ban Chiang. There are also regular buses Udorn-Ban Chiang.

NONG KHAI

Right on the Mekong River, this was the old crossing point for Vientiane in Laos. It's 624 km from Bangkok and only 55 km north of Udorn Thani. There's little reason for going there now – unless you can manage to get a visa so that you can take the ferry across to Tha Deua, from where taxis used to run into Vientiane.

There are some places of interest outside Nong Khai including Wat Phra That Bang Phuan 12 km south, one of the most sacred temple sites in the northeast. Wat Hin Maak Peng, 60 km northwest, is a quiet and peaceful place on the banks of the Mekong. Phutthamamakasamakhom (thank God it's normally referred to as Wat Khaek) is a strange,

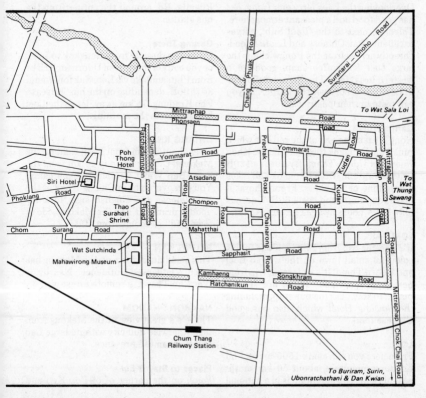

new Hindu-Buddhist temple. It's only four or five km out of town.

Places to Stay

The *Prajak Bungalows* at 1178 Prajak Rd have rooms with fan from 80B; more expensive rooms with air-con and a cheap restaurant in front. The *Poonsup Hotel* (English sign says 'Pool Sub'!) is on Meechai Rd and has reasonable rooms with fan and bath for 70B.

The *Sukhaphan Hotel* on Bamtoengjit Rd is a rickety old wooden Chinese hotel, but cheap at 40B. *Pongwichit* at 723 Bamtoengjit is right across the street and has clean 70B rooms with fan and bath.

Places to Eat

Overlooking the Laos ferry pier *Udom Rot* has good food and a pleasant atmosphere. *Thiparot*, next to the 'Pool Sub', serves excellent Thai, Chinese and Laotian food. Directly across from the Pongwichit is the large *Loet Rot* coffee shop, good for a western breakfast. The French influence in Laos has crept over the border, as you can taste in their pastries.

Getting There

Nong Khai is the end of the rail line which runs from Bangkok through Khorat, Khon Kaen and Udorn Thani. By bus it's 120B (without air-con) from Bangkok and takes a long nine or 10 hours. From Khorat it takes four hours and costs 60B. Udorn is only 1-1/4 hours away. The fare is 20B.

LOM SAK

It's a scenic trip from Phitsanuloke to this colourful small town on the way to Loei and Udorn Thani. It's a pleasant trip from here to Khon Kaen. There are several places to stay near the bus stop, including the *Sawang Hotel* which also has good Chinese food.

LOEI

From here you can climb 1500-metre Phu Kradung mountain, about 50 km south-east of Loei. The mountain is in a national park with trails and cabins available if you want to stay.

Places to Stay & Eat

The *Sarai Thong* on Ruamjit Rd has rooms from 50B to 125B, all with fan and bath. It's off the street, quiet and clean. The *Srisawat*, nearby on Ruamjit, is similar in price and facilities. *Thai Wanit (Vanich)* is at 55 Charoen Rat Rd, near the market, and costs from 100B.

The market at the intersection of Ruamjai and Charoen Rat has cheap eats including some local specialities. Near the Bangkok Bank on Charoen Rat, the *Chuan Lee* and the *Loei Ocha* are two pastry-coffee shops. Good cheap food at the *Nawng Neung* on the west side of Ruamjai Rd, around the corner from the bus station.

Getting There

Buses run directly from Bangkok to Loei, or you can get there from Udorn for 31B or from Phitsanuloke via Lom Sak for around 80 to 90B, depending on the bus. Buses to Phu Kradung, 75 km away, leave the Loei bus station in the morning.

CHIANG KHAN

Only about 50 km from Loei, right on the Mekong, Chiang Khan is 40 km from the large Ban Winai Laotian refugee camp. You can overnight in Chiang Khan at the *Suksamboon* (no English sign, look for 'food & drink'). It's on the Mekong side of town and has rooms from 40B.

BEUNG KAN

This small dusty town on the Mekong has much Vietnamese influence. Nearby is Wat Phu Thawk, a remote forest wat.

NAKHON PHANOM

There's a great view of the Mekong from this otherwise dull city with its large Lao and Vietnamese presence.

Places to Stay & Eat

Pong, on the corner of of Pon Keo and

Bamrung Muang, has rooms at 50B, but it's run down and not very clean. *Charoensuk* at 692/45 Bamrung Muang is adequate at 60B for a room with fan and bath. The *Si Thep* at 708/11 Si Thep Rd costs from 60B up to around 200B for fancier air-con rooms.

The *First Hotel* at 370 Si Thep is a good place with clean rooms with fan and bath for 60B and up. The *Windsor Hotel* at 692/19 Bamrung Muang Rd has very nice rooms at similar prices to the First, but it's not so quiet. Behind the Windsor, on the corner of Si Thep and Ruamjit, is the *Grand* with similar rooms for 60B.

Along Bamrung Muang Rd near the Windsor Hotel there are several good and inexpensive restaurants. Try the *Tatiya Club* on the corner of Fuang Nakhon and Bamrung Muang for a glittery Thai night out.

Getting There

There are regular buses from Nong Khai to Nakhon Phanom through Sakon Nakhon for 50B.

THAT PHANOM

This remote north-east town, on the banks of the Mekong, has the famous Wat That Phanom similar in style to Wat That Luang in Vientiane, Laos. There's also some interesting French-Chinese architecture around the town, again showing the Laotian influence.

Places to Stay

Sang Thong is just off Phanom Panarak Rd near the Lao-style arch of victory in the old town. Adequate rooms cost 60B in this colourful place. The *Chai Won* is similar in style and price and on the opposite side of Phanom Panarak Rd.

Getting There

Songthaews from Nakhon Phanom cost 25B and take about 1½ hours. Stay on until you see the chedi on the right. Sakon Nakhon is three hours by bus at a cost of 45B.

YASOTHORN

Although it's difficult to get to, the two-hour bus trip from Ubon is worth making to catch the annual 8-10 May rocket festival. This popular north-east rain-and-fertility festival is celebrated with particular fervour in Yasothorn.

Places to Stay

The *Udomporn* at 169 Uthairamrit Rd has rooms from 50 to 80B. Or try the air-con *Surawit* at 128/1 Changsanit Rd at 50 to 120B. The *Yothnakhorn* at 169 Uthairamrit is 70 to 150B, again with air-con.

Getting There

A bus to Yasothorn from Ubon should cost 25 to 30B.

UBON (UBOL) RATCHATHANI

This was another major USAF base during Vietnam days. The Wat Ba Pong monastery at nearby Warin Chamrap has a large foreign contingent studying there. Ask for 'wat farang'! Wat Thung Sri Muang in the centre of town and Wat Phra That Nong Bua on the outskirts are also interesting. The latter has a good copy of the Mahabodhi stupa in Bodh Gaya, India.

Places to Stay

There are all sorts of places to stay in Ubon including the *Ubon Hotel* at 929 Kheun Thani Rd. It's the biggest hotel in town, with rooms from 120B. The *Racha Hotel* at 149/21 Chayangkun Rd, north of the centre, has clean rooms with fan and bath from 100B. The *99 Hotel (Ubon Rat)* at 224/5 Chayangkun has rooms, all air-con and with bath, from 120B. Ask for a discount.

Places to Eat

The *ASEAN Women's Development & Service Centre*, across from the Ubon Hotel on Kheun Thani Rd, has great Thai vegetarian food (better than any in Chiang Mai). Near the Racha Hotel at 147/13 Chayangkun Rd, the *Loet Rot* has excellent noodle dishes. The *Raan Khao Tom Hung Thong*, on Kheun Thani Rd near the Ubon Hotel, has a huge selection of Thai-Chinese dishes. On Pha Daeng Rd near the provincial offices, the *Sakhon* restaurant is noted for its northern specialities.

Getting There
There is an express and two rapid trains daily from Bangkok with fares of 91B in 3rd, 191B in 2nd. By bus there are frequent departures daily with fares of 135B in the regular (non air-con) buses. Buses from Nakhon Phanom takes six to seven hours and cost 60B. There are also more expensive and faster tour buses.

SURIN
There's no reason to visit Surin any time of year except in late-November when the elephant round-up is held here with elephant races, fights, tug-of-wars and anything else you can think of to do with a couple of hundred elephants. If you've ever had an urge to see a lot of elephants at one time this is a chance to get it out of your system! There are a lot of day or overnight trips from Bangkok during this time.

Places to Stay
Hotel prices soar during round-up time but normally the *Krung Si* on Krung Si Rd is 70 to 90B. The *New Hotel* at 22 Tanasarn Rd costs 60 to 160B and has some more expensive air-con rooms.

Getting There
Regular buses from the Northern Bus Terminal in Bangkok cost 90B. There are many special tour buses at round-up time. You can also get there on the Ubon Ratchathani express and rapid trains with fares of 84B in 3rd, 161B in 2nd. Book seats well in advance in November.

Southern Thailand

The south of Thailand offers some of the most spectacular scenery in the country plus beautiful beaches, good snorkelling, fine seafood and a good selection of things to see. The old road along the west coast has now been supplanted by the new east coast road, which runs close to the railway line. The south is very different from the rest of Thailand in both its scenery and its people. Here the rice paddies of the central area give way to the rubber plantations which you also see right down through Malaysia. Many of the people are also related to the Malays both in their culture and their religion. This 'difference' has long promoted secessionist rumblings and the Thai government still has to grapple with occasional outbreaks of violence in the south. The guerilla forces melt away across the border into Malaysia when pursued.

The two main attractions of the south are the beautiful islands of Phuket and Koh Samui. They're both real travellers' centres with lots of cheap accommodation and some truly superb beaches. In fact either island makes Pattaya look like a bad dream. Other attractions of the south include the awesome limestone outcroppings which erupt from the green jungle and even straight from the sea between Phangnga and Krabi, beyond Phuket. Chaiya has some archaeologically interesting remains while right in the south is Hat Yai, a rapidly growing modern city with a colourful reputation as a weekend getaway from Malaysia.

Getting There
You can travel south from Bangkok by air, bus or rail. The road south runs down the east coast as far as Chumphon where you have a choice of climbing over the narrow mountain range and continuing down the

west coast (for Phuket) or continuing south on the east coast (for Koh Samui). The railway line also follows the east coast route and the two routes, east and west, meet again at the southern town of Hat Yai. From Hat Yai you can continue on the western side into Malaysia to Alor Setar and then Penang. Or you can head off to the eastern coast and cross the border from Sungai Golok to Kota Bahru. If you take the road on the west coast there's a small shrine at the top of the mountain pass near Chumphon. Truckies beep their horns as they pass it.

RATCHABURI

Just a town on the way south from Nakhon Pathom, well before you get to the coast and Hua Hin. The *Zin Zin Hotel* on Railway Rd is cheap.

PETCHABURI

One hundred and sixty km south of Bangkok, this city has a number of interesting old temples. You can make a walking tour of six or seven of them in two or three hours. They include the old Khmer site of Wat Kamphaeng Laeng, the late-Ayuthaya Wat Mahathat and others.

Places to Stay

The *Chom Klao* is on the east side of Chomrut Bridge and has rooms at 50 and 60B. The *Nam Chai* is a block further east and is similarly priced but not such good value. The *Phetburi* is on the next street north of Chomrut, behind the Chom Klao, and has rooms at 60B with fan and bath. For a meal try the *Khao Wang Restaurant* in front of the *Khao Wang Hotel*, the best hotel in town.

HUA HIN

This is the oldest Thai seaside resort. It's 230 km south of Bangkok. Hua Hin is still a popular weekend getaway although it's a quiet, conservative and dignified place compared with raucous Pattaya. The beach is not all that good. Hua Hin has an interesting market and the pier area,

where the local fishing fleet lands its catch, is always colourful and full of activity. Rama VII had a summer residence here and the royal family still uses it. The Hua Hin Hotel is surrounded by trees and shrubs trimmed into such shapes as roosters, ducks, women opening umbrellas, giraffes and snakes.

Places to Stay

If you can afford it, the *Railway Hotel* is a fine experience. It's a delightfully old-fashioned place just off the beach on Damnoen Kasem Rd. The rooms are big, the ceilings are high, and the restaurant even has tablecloths! Most rooms now cost from 160B although there are a few cheaper ones. Movie fans may recognise it as the Hotel Le Phnom from the film *Killing Fields*.

Cheaper places include the pleasant *Hua Hin Ralug (Raluk)* at 16 Damnoen Kasem with rooms with fan and bath from 100B and up. Around Phetkasem Rd there's the *Chaat Chai* at 59/1 from 100B or the *Damrong* at 46 with similar prices. The *Suphanmit*, just off Phetkasem behind the bank, is also 100B plus.

The *Meechai*, across from the Damrong, is a little cheaper, starting at 80B. On the corner of Phetkasem and Chonsin Rd the *New Hotel* has rooms in the old building from 60B, from 80B in the new.

Hua Hin is noted for its seafood – available on the beach or at the market. There's a big restaurant under the *Chaat Chai* while the *Railway Hotel* also serves western food in its restaurant.

Getting There

Buses run from the Southern Bus Terminal in Bangkok. There are frequent departures for the four-hour trip and the cost is 41B for ordinary, 70B air-con. Trains en route to Hat Yai in the south also stop in Hua Hin. The trip takes around 4½ hours and costs 42B in 3rd class, 88B in 2nd. On the three daily rapid trains the fare is the same but the supplement is only 20B, versus 30B for the express.

PRACHUAP KHIRI KHAN

Further south from Hua Hin there are a row of bungalows on the seafront. Some fine seafood can be found here.

Places to Stay

The *Indira Hotel* has rooms in the 50 to 80B bracket.

RANONG

Only the Chan River separates Thailand from Kawthaung (Victoria Point) in Burma at this point. There's a busy trade back and forth, supplying Burmese needs. Ranong is 600 km south of Bangkok, 300 km north of Phuket.

Places to Stay

The expensive *Thara Hotel*, up on the main road, has good rooms from 100 to 175B with fan, more with air-con. Down in the town there are a number of cheaper places including the *Asia, Sin Ranong* and the *Suriyanon* along Ruangrat Rd.

CHAIYA

Just north of Surat Thani and 640 km south of Bangkok this is one of the oldest cities in Thailand with intriguing remains from the Sumatran-based Srivijaya empire. Indeed one local scholar believes this was the real centre of the empire, not Palembang. The restored Borom That Chaiya stupa is very similar in design to the *candis* of central Java. The modern Wat Suanmoke is a complete contrast, a modern centre established by Thailand's most famous Buddhist monk.

Places to Stay

There are guest quarters in Wat Suanmoke ('with vast numbers of mosquitoes,' reported a visitor) but most visitors make it a day-trip from nearby Surat.

Getting There

Chaiya is on the railway line only a short distance north of Surat so you can get here by rail bus or even taxi. The distance is about 20 km. Wat Suanmoke is about seven km out of Chaiya; buses run there directly from Surat Thani bus station so it isn't necessary to go right into Chaiya.

SURAT THANI

This busy little port is of interest for most travellers only as a jumping-off point for the islands of Koh Samui, 30 km off the coast. Ban Don is the port for the island and there are lots of interesting shops and a fine fruit market to wander around in while you wait for a boat.

Places to Stay & Eat

A lot of Surat Thani's hotels are short-time specialists so you're quite likely to sleep better on the night ferry, without all the nocturnal disturbances as customers come and go.

There are quite a few places along Na Muang Rd, not far from Ban Don. At 428 the *Muang Thong* is clean and comfortable although somewhat expensive – a double with fan and bath costs 120B. Nearby, but off Na Muang on Chon Kasem Rd, the *Surat* is OK, though rather dirty, at 70 to 120B.

Other cheaper places along Na Muang Rd include the *Ban Don* (enter through the Chinese restaurant) with rooms with fan and bath at 75B. It's one of the best bargains in Surat Thani. The *Surasor* has big, comfortable doubles with attached bathroom for 80B. The *Lipa Guest House* is a brand new place at the bus station with rooms for 80B.

The market near the bus station has good cheap food, or in Ban Don try the places on the waterfront. The 3rd floor restaurant in the Muang Thong has good breakfast food or for a minor splurge try the *Pailin Restaurant* in the Tapee Hotel where the seafood is excellent.

Getting There & Around

Surat Thani is on the main railway and bus route from Bangkok to Hat Yai. Bangkok-Surat Thani costs 102B in 3rd class, 214B in 2nd. The Surat Thani train station is, however, 14 km out of town at Phun Phin.

If you're heading south to Hat Yai you may decide it is easier to take a bus rather than go to the station only to find there are no seats left.

From the Southern Bus Terminal in Bangkok the trip to Surat Thani takes 11 hours and costs 125B or 210B for an aircon bus. Private tour buses cost 200B and up. Departures are usually in the early morning or in the evening. From Surat Thani buses run to Songkhla, Hat Yai or Phuket.

From the railway station to the Ban Don pier, for Koh Samui boats, buses leave every five minutes and cost 5B. If there are enough tourists on board buses sometimes go straight to the pier. Otherwise you'll have to walk from the bus station. From the Phun Phin train station there are usually buses every five minutes but if you arrive at a time when the buses aren't running, a taxi to Ban Don costs about 60 to 80B.

KOH SAMUI

This beautiful island off the east coast is very much a travellers' centre yet also still relatively untouched. The reasons why are simple – you can't fly there, you can't even drive there (as you can to Phuket). Since getting there entails a long bus or train trip from Bangkok, followed by a boat trip lasting several hours, it's likely to remain a little remote and untouristed. But if they ever get around to building that much-discussed airport . . . .

Koh Samui is the largest island on the east coast and the third largest in Thailand. It's about 25 km long by 21 km wide and surrounded by 80 other islands, all except six of them uninhabited. The main town is Na Thawn and most of the population is concentrated there or at a handful of other towns scattered around the coast. Coconut plantations are still the main source of income and visitors go relatively unnoticed.

The beaches are beautiful and they, naturally, are the main draw, but Koh Samui also has a number of scenic waterfalls – particularly Hin Lad, three

km from Na Thawn, and Na Muang, 10 km away in the centre of the island. Hin Lad is only 500 metres off the main road and you can easily walk to it from Na Thawn, but Na Muang is the more scenic. Near the village of Bang Kao there's an interesting old chedi at Wat Laem Saw while the 'Big Buddha' temple, with its 12-metre-high Buddha image, is at the north-eastern end of the island on a small rocky islet joined to the main island by a causeway. Go well-dressed if you visit the island, although the monks are pleased to have visitors.

An hour's boat ride north of Koh Samui is the island of Koh Pangan, nearly as big, but very quiet and tranquil. Again there are beautiful beaches and the Tran Sadet waterfall. There are also some places to stay here.

Information

The best time to visit Koh Samui is from February to late-June. July to late-October is very wet and from then until January it can be very windy. The water is not as clear on the west coast as the east.

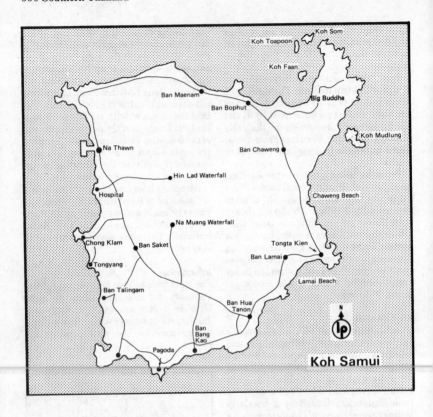

Koh Samui

Be cautious with local agents for train and bus bookings back on the mainland – these don't always get made, or are not for the class you paid for. Several travellers have written to complain of rip-offs here. Get mail sent to poste restante at the GPO, Na Thawn.

Places to Stay & Eat

There are plenty of places to stay at the beaches, and they're all remarkably similar in cost and standards. Curiously, a handful of families owns the majority of the bungalow groups. Chaweng (the largest beach with probably the best water) and Lamai are the two most popular. Both have beautiful sand and clear, sparkling water. Lamai also has a good coral reef and a small island opposite.

Bo Phut and Big Buddha are both on the bay which encloses Koh Faan, the big Buddha island, and these are rather quieter. Thong Yang is also very quiet while Ang Thong, just north of Na Thawn, is rocky but has some colourful fishing boats to watch. Or you can get right away from it all on neighbouring Koh Pangan.

Na Thawn If you want to stay in the town there are nine hotels to choose from. The *Chao Koh Hotel* is the most expensive with rooms from 200B, the *Jinta Hotel* costs from 150B. Most of the others cost from 40 or 50B and they include the *Seaview*

Hotel, Sri Samui Bungalow & Hotel and the *Seaside Hotel*. Na Thawn is also often spelt Na Thon.

Chaweng There are about a dozen bungalow 'villages' strung along the island's longest beach and more are under construction. They are all much the same and cost from 40B a night for a small bungalow – knock it down a bit for a longer stay. *Chaweng Guest House Bungalows*, the first at the southern end of the beach, and the restaurants there are good places to eat but this area of the beach is noisier.

Places currently in favour include *Seaside, Visa* and *Tawee. Joy Bungalow* is comfortable and quiet. *Liberty Bungalows* are cheap, clean and friendly too. *Sak's Bungalows* are good and they loan out books, games and snorkelling equipment for free. *Moon Bungalows* is another new place with pleasant bungalows at 50B with attached toilet and shower, cheaper for shared ones. *Montien*, the last place down the beach, has good food and pleasant people. The *Mellow* also has good cottages. Great food at the *Best Beach Cafe* and the *Vew Star*.

Some more luxurious bungalows at up to 100B are starting to spring up. Maria, a French woman who has been living here for several years, runs the handy little Je T'aime Library & Book Exchange at Chaweng.

Lamai There are nearly as many bungalows at Lamai as at Chaweng with very similar prices. *Palm Beach Bungalows* is another clean and friendly place with solid bamboo huts with verandahs. Or there's *White Sand, Palm Beach* and *Anika Bungalows*.

Big Buddha *Big Buddha Bungalow* is very pleasant with small bungalows at 30B, larger ones at 40 or 50B. Excellent food too.

Bo Phut The *Peace Bungalows* are good; *Chaihaat* and *Neet* are similarly priced. *World Bungalows* are clean and friendly too. This beach is becoming increasingly popular as a place to get away from it all.

Others At Tong Yah there's only the *Seagarden*, with prices from 40B. At Haat Mae Nam, 14 km from Na Thawn, the *Friendly* is cheap and clean. This is the latest place to spring up.

Getting There

From Ban Don There are daily express boats at about 12.30 pm and at a variable time which of late has been 9 am. They take 2-1/2 to three hours and cost 50B; the upper deck is more interesting although there aren't any seats. Take your shoes off on the highly polished deck.

There's also a slow nightboat leaving at 11 pm and taking six hours to cross. It costs 40B on the upper deck, 80B on the lower deck and although the boat looks rickety you may sleep better on board than you would in a noisy Surat Thani hotel.

Travelling in either direction you can get combined train-bus to the pier-ferry tickets which are good value. Coming from Koh Samui the regular ferry departure is at 12 noon but it doesn't connect with anything much.

Car Ferry There is also a big car ferry that operates three times daily from Khanom, almost directly south of Koh Samui and 75 km from Surat Thani. This can be a convenient alternative if you're coming from points south but no big deal if you're coming from Bangkok as it's a 90-minute minibus trip from Surat Thani. The ferry costs 30B for pedestrians and there are four crossings daily, taking 1½ hours. There are now direct buses Koh Samui-Bangkok (270 to 300B) and Koh Samui-Hat Yai (150B) using this ferry service. Leaving Na Thawn at 2.30 pm you take the 3 pm ferry to Khanom, arrive there around 5 pm, get to Surat Thani at 6.30 pm, have dinner there and leave at 8 pm, finally arriving in Bangkok at 6 am. Or for 50B you can take a minibus at the same time which gets you to the Surat Thani train station in time to catch the 6.30 pm express to Bangkok.

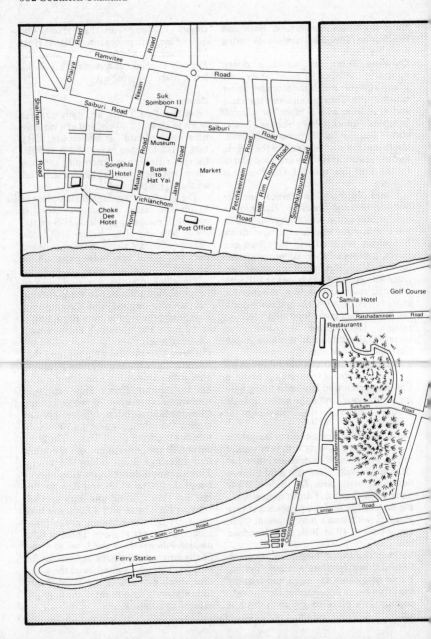

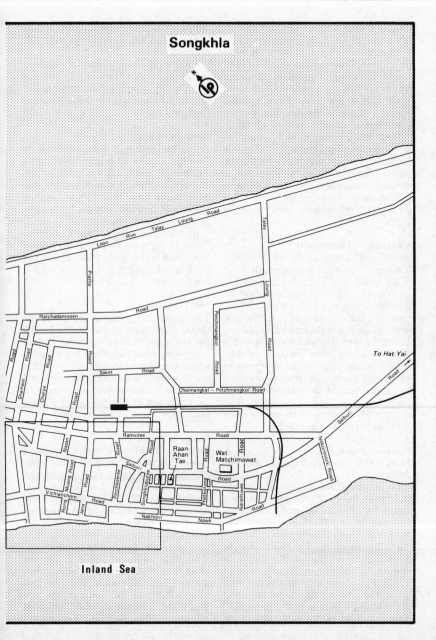

Getting Around

It's about 19 km from Na Thawn to Bo Phut on the west coast, 23 km to Chaweng on the east. There are now minibuses and *songthaews* all day. Official fares from Na Thawn are 10B to Lamai, Mae Nam or Bo Phut; 15B to Big Buddha or Chaweng. From Na Thawn boats go to Koh Pangan every day; the crossing takes 45 minutes.

Often you'll be met in Na Thawn (even on the ferry at Ban Don) and offered free transport if you stay at the place doing the offering. You can rent motorcycles on Koh Samui; these are better value at Na Thawn than at the beaches. Smaller 80 cc bikes go from 200B a day, larger ones at 250B.

NAKHON SI THAMMARAT

Situated 814 km south of Bangkok, Nakhon Si Thammarat has the oldest wat in the south, Wat Mahathat. Reputed to be over a thousand years old and reconstructed in the mid-13th century, its 78-metre-high chedi is topped by a solid gold spire. There is also the interesting Nakhon Si Thammarat National Museum with a good 'Art of Southern Thailand' exhibit.

NST is also noted for its nielloware (a silver and black alloy-enamel jewellery technique) and for the making of leather shadow puppets and dance masks. The town is also supposed to produce the 'best' gangsters in Thailand!

Places to Stay & Eat

Most hotels are near the train and bus stations.

On Yomaraj Rd, across from the railway station, is the *Si Thong* with adequate rooms for 75B with fan and bath. Or try the *Nakhon* at 1477/5 Yomaraj or the *Yaowarat*, both similarly priced.

On Jamroenwithi Rd (walk straight down Neramit Rd opposite the station for two blocks and turn right), the *Siam* at 1407/17 is a large hotel with rooms with fan and bath from 80B. Across the street is the *Muang Thong* at 1459/7 from 75B. Near the Siam, on the same side of the street, is the *Thai Fa* which is good value as the rooms are equally good and 10B cheaper.

Two very good and inexpensive Chinese restaurants, located between the Neramit and Thai Fa hotels on Jamroenwithi Rd, are the *Bo Seng* and the *Yong Seng* (no English signs).

Getting There

From the Southern Bus Terminal in Bangkok it takes 12 hours to Nakhon Si Thammarat and the fare is around 150B or 200B by air-con bus. There are also daily buses from Surat Thani, costing about 65B. You can also get buses to or from Songkhla or Hat Yai.

By train you have to get off at Khao Chum Thong since NST is off the railway line, about 30 km to the west. The fare is 127B in 3rd, 266B in 2nd. From there you can continue by bus or taxi.

PHATTALUNG

The major rice-growing centre in the south, Phattalung is also noted for its shadow puppets. The town has a couple of interesting wats; Lam Pang is a pleasant eating and relaxing spot beside the inland sea on which Phattalung is situated, and the Thale Noi Waterbird Sanctuary is 32 km north-east of Phattalung. The Tham Malai cave is just outside the town.

Places to Stay & Eat

Most of Phattalung's hotels are along Ramet Rd, the main drag. The dingy *Phattalung* at 43 Ramet Rd costs 50B with fan and bath. The *Sakon* (English sign reads 'Universal Hotel') is a little west and has adequate rooms at 65B. Across from the Grant Cinema on the corner of Charoentham the *Ging Fah* is similar to the Universal and slightly more expensive.

Sai Thip, on Ramet Rd, is cleaner and airier than most cheap Phattalung restaurants. The well-known *Hong Thong* on Pracha Bamrung Rd, just past the new Thai Hotel, is Phattalung's best restaurant and has excellent seafood. There's some good takeaways at the market off Poh-Saat Rd.

Getting There

Buses to Nakhon Si Thammarat take 1½ hours and cost 30B. Ditto to Hat Yai.

SONGKHLA

This not-particularly-exciting beach resort is about 30 km from Hat Yai – plenty of buses and share taxis operate between the two towns. The town is on a peninsula between the 'inland sea' and the South China Sea. Offshore are two islands known as 'cat' and 'mouse'. Although the beach is not very interesting, Songkhla has an active waterfront with brightly painted fishing boats, an interesting National Museum (admission free), an old chedi at the top of Khao Noi hill and Wat Matchimawat with frescoes, an old marble Buddha image and a small museum. The National Museum is open from 9 am to 12 noon and 1 to 4 pm Wednesdays to Sundays and has a collection of Burmese Buddhas and various Srivijaya artifacts. The building is an old Thai-Chinese palace.

On Koh Yaw, an island on the inland sea, you can see local cotton-weaving work. Boat taxis to the island cost 4B and there are quite a few early in the morning between 7 and 8 am. On the last Saturday and Sunday of each month there are bullfights at 10.30 am. Songkhla has been a popular arrival point for Vietnamese boat people.

Places to Stay

The *Suk Somboon II* (there's also a Suk Somboon I, but it's more expensive) is fairly popular with travellers although it's not that special. It's at 18 Saiburi Rd, a block from the clock tower and close to the museum. A double is 70B and they're just wooden rooms, off a large central area. The *Sansabay* on Petchkiri Rd, just a block before you arrive at the clock tower, is very similar in price but somewhat seedier. The *Choke Dee* at 14/19

Vichianchom Rd is about 10B more expensive and you get an attached bathroom, but it can be a little noisy.

Also on Vichianchom Rd the *Songkhla Hotel* is across from the fishing station and it's excellent value from 90B; from 120B with bath – clean, comfortable rooms with towels and drinking water supplied. At 12/2 Chai Khao Rd the *Narai Hotel* is a long walk from the bus station (take a trishaw) and somewhat more expensive, but it's a pleasant and friendly place.

Places to Eat

As you might expect Songkhla has a reputation for seafood and there are a string of beachfront seafood specialists. None of them are particularly cheap and eating here is mainly a lunchtime activity. Try curried crab claws or fried squid. At night the food scene shifts to Vichianchom Rd in front of the market where there is a line of food and fruit stalls. *Raan Ahaan Tae* on Tang Ngam Rd (off Songkhlaburi Rd and parallel to Saiburi Rd) has the best seafood around, according to the locals.

Getting There

Surat Thani to Songkhla costs 150B. Air-con buses from Bangkok take 19 hours and cost 250B; non air-con buses are 185B, a few baht more to Hat Yai. By train you have to go to Hat Yai first. There are regular buses and share taxis from Hat Yai to Songkhla – 7B by bus, 12B by taxi. Samlors around Songkhla cost 3B, 4B at night.

Although the usual route north from Songkhla is to backtrack to Hat Yai and then take the road to Phattalung and Trang, you can also take an interesting back-road route. First there's a bus trip to Ranot, 63 km north at the end of the Thale Luang lake. Further buses connect to Hua Sai (32 km) and then Nakhon Si Thammarat (56 km).

HAT YAI

A busy crossroads town, Hat Yai is 1298 km south of Bangkok. It's where the east

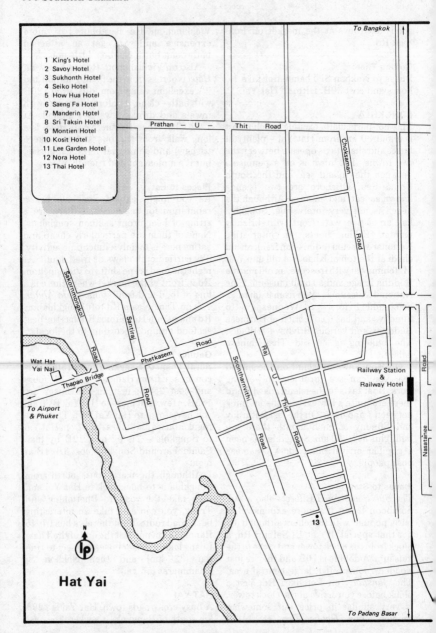

1 King's Hotel
2 Savoy Hotel
3 Sukhonth Hotel
4 Seiko Hotel
5 How Hua Hotel
6 Saeng Fa Hotel
7 Manderin Hotel
8 Sri Taksin Hotel
9 Montien Hotel
10 Kosit Hotel
11 Lee Garden Hotel
12 Nora Hotel
13 Thai Hotel

To Bangkok

Prathan — U — Thit Road

Choksaman Road

Sakornmongkol Road

Santirat Road

Phetkasem Road

Road

Road

Soontharnvithi Road

Rai — U — Thit Road

Nasatanee Road

Wat Hat
Yai Nai

Thapao Bridge

To Airport
& Phuket

Railway Station
&
Railway Hotel

13

N

Hat Yai

To Padang Basar

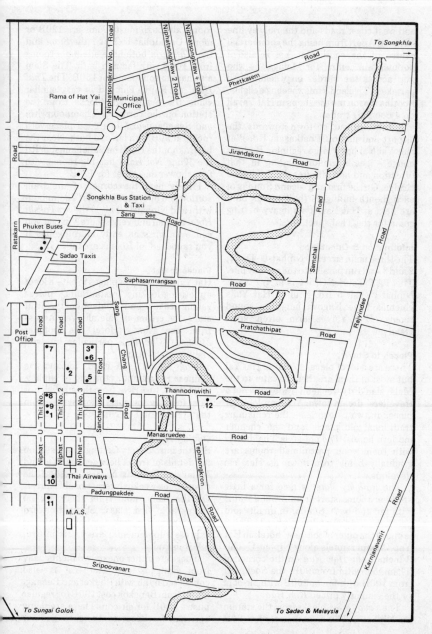

Rama of Hat Yai

Municipal Office

Niphatsongkraw No. 1 Road

Niphatsongkraw 2 Road

Niphatsongkraw + Road

Phetkasem Road

To Songkhla

Jirandakorr Road

Samchai Road

Rajyindee Road

Road

Ratakarn Road

Songkhla Bus Station & Taxi

Sang See Road

Phuket Buses

Sadao Taxis

Suphasarnrangsan Road

Sang Road

Pratchathipat Road

Post Office

Road

Road

Road

Chang Road

Sanchanusorn Road

•7

3• •6

•2 •5

•8
•9
•1

Niphat – U – Thit No. 1

Niphat – U – Thit No. 2

Niphat – U – Thit No. 3

•4

Thannoonwithi Road

•12

Manasruedee Road

Tephsongkron Road

•10

Thai Airways

Padungpakdee Road

•11

M.A.S.

Sripoovanart Road

Karnjanavanit Road

To Sungai Golok

To Sadao & Malaysia

and west coast roads and the railway line all meet. Apart from being the commercial centre of the south Hat Yai is also a popular 'sin centre' for Malaysians who pop across the border on weekends to partake in Thailand's freewheeling delights. For this reason too the shops in Hat Yai all do a booming trade.

A few km out of town towards the airport and just off Phetkasem Rd, Wat Hat Yai Nai has a large reclining Buddha image – get a samlor heading in that direction and hop off after the U Thapao Bridge. On the first and second Sunday of each month bullfights (bull versus bull) are held at Hat Yai. It's a heavy betting game for the Thai spectators.

Information & Orientation
The three main streets – Niphat-U-Thit 1, 2 and 3 – all run parallel to the railway line. The TAT Tourist Office is at 1/1 Soi 2 Niphat-U-Thit 3 Rd. Four of Hat Yai's cinemas have English language sound rooms. Hat Yai is also often spelt Haadyai.

Places to Stay
There are a lot of places to stay in Hat Yai but most of them are there to cater to the Malaysian dirty weekend trade – it's not a travellers' dream town. You can look for places in two categories – the remaining traditional old places and the cheaper modern hotels. The old-style Thai hotels with their wood partitioned rooms are gradually being torn down as Hat Yai develops.

The *Railway Hotel* is nice for a little splurge; rooms start from around 150B with fan and bath. Similar in quality and price, the *King's Hotel* on Niphat-U-Thit 3 is one of the older of the 'new' hotels in Hat Yai. Cheaper hotels along Niphat-U-Thit 3 include the *How Hua* on the corner of Thamnoonwithi from 90B; the *Saeng Fa* from 100B with fan or 200B with air-con; or the similarly priced *Kim Hua*.

The *Savoy* is 3½ blocks from the station on Niphat-U-Thit 2 and has good 80B rooms although most rooms are 120B or more. On Niphat-U-Thit 1 the *Siam* and the *Mandarin* both have adequate rooms from 100B with fan and bath. The Siam also has air-con rooms for 150B. The *Thai Hotel* on Raj-U-Thit Rd is very similar while the *Seiko*, five blocks from the station on the corner of Thamnoonwithi and Sanchanusorn, is a good place with rooms at 90B with fan and bath. Near the big Sukhontha Hotel on Sanehanusom Rd the *Wang Noi Hotel* has big rooms with fan, shower and toilet for 120B.

Finally near the corner of the train station and bus station roads (Thamnoonwithi and Niphat-U-Thit 1) the *Sri Taksin Hotel* is clean and very secure – in fact you can even miss an early morning bus if you're locked in! Rooms are 50 to 75B.

Places to Eat
Hat Yai has plenty of places to eat – a lot of appetising-looking restaurants, places selling cakes and confectionery, fruit stalls, ice cream on sale all over. Across from the King's Hotel the popular *Muslim-O-Cha* is a particular hit with visiting Malaysians.

Jeng Nguan is a good, inexpensive Chinese restaurant at the end of Niphat-U-Thit Rd, turn right from the station. For Thai food try the curry shop across from the Metro Hotel on Niphat-U-Thit 2.

Getting There
See the introductory Getting There section for details of travel between Hat Yai and Malaysia. There is no 3rd class on the three-times-weekly International Express. On the daily rapid train there are no sleepers in 3rd class. Straightforward fares from Bangkok (without rapid or express supplements) are 142B in 3rd, 298B in 2nd.

There are either one or two flights daily from Bangkok and Hat Yai is also connected by air with Phuket and Penang. Buses from Bangkok cost 190B for regular buses, 250B for air-con. There are many agencies for buses to Bangkok and for taxis to Penang along Niphat-U-Thit 2 towards the Thai Airways and MAS offices, or around the railway station.

Getting Around

Songthaews cost 4B anywhere around town. The bus station for most departures is on Phetkasem Highway, a couple of hundred metres from Thamnoonwithi, which is the 'main road' from the railway station. There is no bus service to the airport, 11 km out of town. Count on about 60 to 100B for a taxi, about 50 or 60B for a *songthaew*.

PHUKET

Phuket is barely an island, since it's joined to the mainland by a bridge – yet conversely it's more than just an island since it's surrounded by countless other smaller islands, some of them just swimming distance from the shore. Phuket has been a major tin mining centre, but these days it's the rapidly expanding resort role that is most important. The town of Phuket is pleasant enough but it's the beautiful beaches and the offshore islands which are the main pull – there are plenty of them. Virtually all transport radiates from Phuket and the popular beaches are scattered all over the island – there is no single 'centre'. Phuket island is very hilly, often the hills drop right into the sea except where there are beaches.

Information

The TAT Tourist Office is on Phuket Rd and has a list of standard *songthaew* charges to the various beaches. Thai Airways is on Ranong Rd; the post office is on Montri Rd.

Warning Nothing has ever happened to me in Phuket but there are a lot of tales of theft and muggings. Several places have had suspicious cases of theft from rooms – like the manager lets himself in, you know? Take care. At night you're advised not to go wandering off in unlit areas far from the crowds. Be cautious in the water too; there

have been a number of drownings at Phuket beaches.

Phuket Beaches

Patong All the development in Phuket has taken place in the last few years – the first time I came here Ao Patong (Ao means beach, Koh means island) had just one little restaurant where you could lay your sleeping bag on the floor. Now there are more than a dozen hotels and guest houses and innumerable restaurants. Ao Patong is still very pleasant and has more of a variety of accommodation than most of the other beaches although food is a little more expensive than at Ao Kata. There's also more going on at night here than at the other beaches. The beach itself is long, white, clean and lapped by the proper picture-postcard clear waters. Ao Patong is 15 km from Phuket town.

Karon & Kata Only a little south of Ao Patong is Ao Karon, 20 km from Phuket. This is really a triple beach: there's the long golden sweep of Ao Karon, then a smaller headland separates it from the smaller but equally beautiful sweep of Ao Kata . . . . or more correctly Ao Kata Yai. Another small headland divides it from Ao Kata Noi where you'll find good snorkelling. Offshore there's the small island of Koh Pu.

Most of the development is centred around the two Kata beaches, plus the southern end of Karon beach, but already places are springing up a few km away at the northern end of Ao Karon. A road is being built along the beach, and no doubt there'll soon be a strip of hotels and guest houses like Ao Patong. Ao Karon and the two Ao Katas are beautiful beaches with that delightfully squeaky-feeling sand.

Nai Harn South again from Ao Kata is Hat Nai Harn, a pleasant small beach with just a few guest houses – secluded and off the beaten track if you want to avoid the 'scene'. You can walk along a coastal track from Ao Karon to Hat Nai Harn in about two hours. In fact you could probably walk right around the island on coastal tracks

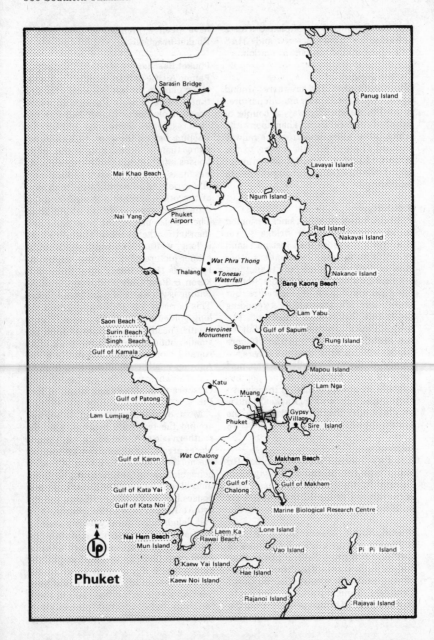

Phuket

although the roads radiate out from Phuket town and you have to backtrack into town and out again to get from one beach to another by road – even though they are just a couple of km apart along the coast. Ao Sane is a pleasant little place between Kata and Nai Harn.

Rawai You turn round the southern end of the island from Hat Nai Harn and come to Hat Rawai, another tourist development. Again these are mostly more expensive places here and the beach is not so special. At low tide there's a long, long expanse of mud exposed before you get to the sea. People staying at Rawai often travel out to other beaches to swim. Rawai is a good place to get boats out to the islands dotted south of Phuket – good snorkelling at Koh Hae.

Other Between Rawai and Phuket town there are more places to stay dotted along the nicely beached south-east stretch of coast – generally more expensive places, though. Ao Chalong, close to the turnoff of the Ao Kata road from the Rawai road, has a few places. There are other places to stay or just to laze dotted round the island. A little north of Ao Patong is Hat Surin, a long beach, less sheltered and with a little rougher water than the normal Phuket calm. Ao Kamala – a wide calm bay, but not so good a beach – is just a km or so south of Hat Surin. Between the two there's an absurdly beautiful little beach: Laem Singha – the very image of a tropical paradise.

If the attraction of beaches starts to pall, Phuket also has a number of waterfalls and other novelties. The Thai-Danish Marine Biological Research Centre has an interesting fish collection. It's open from 8 am to noon and from 2 to 4 pm. Take a *songthaew* to Ao Makham. There is good snorkelling at many points around Phuket; Koh Hae is said to be particularly good and you can get boats out to the island for around 100B from the Rawai Seaside Hotel.

There are many tours operated from Phuket. One of the most popular and (according to some people) good value is the 'James Bond' Tour to Phangnga. You're looking at around 250B for the all-day tour including lunch, the bus trip both ways, the boat trip and a stop to see an interesting reclining Buddha on the way back. The Koh Phi Phi trip, around 400B, is also interesting. There are also a variety of skin diving trips and local island visits. At Mai Khao, Airport Beach, turtles come ashore to lay their eggs from late-October to February. They can be elusive, though. Mai Khao is an hour's walk from Nai Yang.

Phuket's main drawback is that a lot of the development seems to be carried out with total disregard for aesthetics or planning. The beach bungalows at Ao Karon are comfortable, cheap and ugly. More and more of them are being scattered haphazardly up the slopes among the palm trees. Already the local cowboys are zooming up and down the beach on their motorcycles. As usual the problems of water supply – and more importantly water pollution – have not been thought of. A lot of places in Phuket have all the makings of an instant tourist slum. There's also the usual nude bathing problems although those who feel like flaunting the royal decree banning it have only to stroll down the beach a little way in most places to get right away from it all.

Places to Stay – Phuket Town

Most people head straight out to the beaches but should you want to stay in town – on arrival or departure night for example – there are some pleasant places. The *Sin Thavee* at 89 Phangnga Rd is a vast, rambling, rabbit warren of a place, but quite pleasant. There are rooms from 100B and rather better ones with attached bathrooms at higher prices. There is a good, although slightly expensive, restaurant next door.

The *Laem Thong* is central at 13 Soi Rommani, off Thalang Rd, and is cheap at 50B for a room with fan. The *Charoensuk* at 136 Thalang Rd has singles at 40B, doubles at 50B; it's an interesting place to stay. At 19 Phangnga Rd the *On On* has rooms from around 60B.

Other places include the *Koh Sawan* at 19/8 Poonpol Rd, near the waterfront, with rooms from 80B. *Thara* on Thep Kasatri Rd has rooms with fan/bath for 70B.

The nameless Chinese place across the street from the Siam Cinema has very good food. *Kan Aeng*, by the boat pier just past Wat Chalong, has great seafood.

Places to Stay – Phuket Beaches

The two main centres for travellers are Ao Patong and Ao Kata. Ao Patong is more developed and more expensive, Ao Kata is more the real travellers' scene. It's initially a little confusing since some of the Kata places are actually at Karon – the Kata name seems to encompass places at both the Kata beaches and the south end of Karon. There are numerous other beaches of course, some of them very quiet and peaceful.

Ao Patong This was the original beach development but from a single 'sleeping bag on the floor' place in the early '70s it has expanded into a whole beach full of hotels, restaurants, snack bars, motorcycle hire places, wind surfing shops and all manner of things to do. If you want a little more nighttime activity, more to do after dark, then Ao Patong may appeal to you more than the other, sleepier places. Although the accent here is on the more expensive places there are also a number of cheapies, but the costs are a bit higher than elsewhere.

The *Sea Dragon* with bungalows from 100B is among the cheaper places. The *Patong Tropicana* has various standards right up to 250B. Others in the 150 to 200B range include the *Patong Seaside, Patong Bayshore* and *Patong Inn*. The *Seven Seas* and the *Sala Thai* have a few cheap huts. Food also is a little more expensive here. You pay a baht or two more for anything from a Coke or fruit drink to a complete meal.

Ao Kata/Karon Although bungalow rates have soared (there are now places here for up to 300B a night), there are still plenty of places in the 50 to 80B range. They're all fairly similar, pleasant little wooden bungalows with your own toilet, shower and a verandah out front. Popular places include the *Tropicana Beach Bungalows* or right next to it the *Kata Villa* – very similar or even a little nicer. They're both right at the south end of Karon. Then there's *Kata Guest House, Kata Beach Bungalows, Kata Shangri-La* and many others. Along Karon there are a number of places springing up with prices in the 200B and up bracket.

The accommodation area is backed up with a whole collection of very similar beach restaurants featuring the usual travellers' dishes from porridge or pancakes to fruit drinks and banana fritters. Prices for accommodation and food go hand in hand at Phuket – so since Kata is cheaper than Patong for accommodation, so are the food prices. Further south on Ao Kata Noi there are cheaper places without electricity. This is very much the big travellers' centre.

Hat Nai Harn South of Kata and north of Rawai this is a get-away-from-it-all beach which is a bit more off the beaten track and does not have so many places. *Bungalow Nai Harn, Ao Sane Beach* and *Pin* are all around 40B a night. *Johnnies* is even cheaper. *Grandpa Bungalow* is one of the better bungalow complexes and they serve great food. Cheaper bungalows are 40B, up to 100 and 120B for the best ones. Nai Harn is a popular place for the local mushroom omelettes, when they're in season.

Rawai This beach is, like Patong, more expensive, but *Pornmae Bungalows* are only 50B and *P Hut* costs 80B and up. There are a number of restaurants dotted along the beach.

Other Beaches Not all the beaches have accommodation but if you do want to get away from it all you can certainly find other, more remote places. Nai Yang,

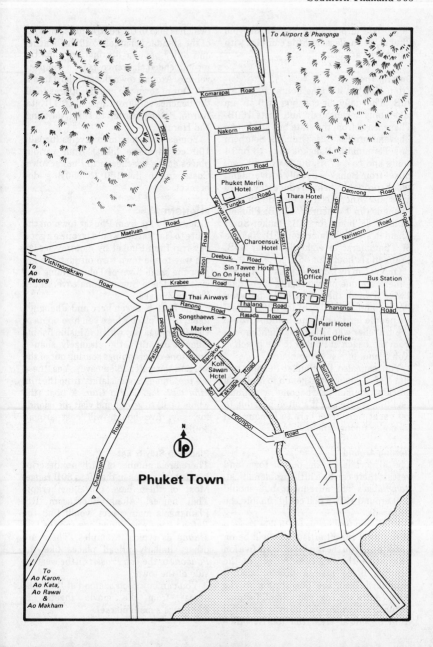

Phuket Town

close to the airport and a good 30 km from Phuket, has a pleasant little complex with bungalows at 50B.

Getting There

From Hat Yai it's nine hours by bus for 90B. The daily air-con bus at 9.45 am takes only seven hours and costs 160B. These leave from the state bus station on Chevanusorn Rd. Buses from the Southern Bus Terminal in Bangkok take 13 or 14 hours and cost 175B, 300B with air-con. Buses from Bangkok usually go overnight, which probably helps reduce the scare quotient. Other bus trips include Phuket-Phangnga in 1¾ hours for 28B; Phuket-Krabi in 3½ hours for 45B; Phuket-Surat Thani in six to 7½ hours for 65B; Nakhon Si Thammarat in eight hours for 80B; Trang in six hours for 65B.

Or you can fly from Bangkok or Hat Yai – there are one or two flights every day. Twice a week there is a flight between Phuket and Surat Thani for 320B. Ideal for people terrified of bus holdups, wrote one traveller who using this flight moved from the beach in Phuket to the beach in Koh Samui in just seven hours.

You can also fly Phuket-Penang (via Hat Yai) if you want to get on to Malaysia quickly. Phuket has become a popular yachting centre and it's often possible to get yacht rides from here to Penang, Sri Lanka or further afield.

Getting Around

The airport is 11 km out of town and getting there can be a little problematical. *Songthaews* are infrequent but should cost around 12B; a taxi could run into the hundreds.

When you first arrive in Phuket beware of the local rip-off artists who will be on hand to tell you the tourist office is five km away, that the only way to get to the beaches is to take a taxi or that a *songthaew* from the bus station to the town centre will cost you a small fortune. Actually *songthaews* run all over the island from a central area, the tourist office (which is also in the centre) puts out a list of the standard charges to all the beaches and other popular destinations plus the recommended charter costs for a complete vehicle. Around town the standard fare is 5B. Out of town the standard fares to all the beaches vary from around 10B (Kata, Karon, Patong, Rawai) to 15B (Nai Yang, Nai Harn).

You can also hire motorcycles (usually 100 cc Japanese bikes) from various places at the beaches or in Phuket town. Costs are in the 150 to 250B a day bracket.

PHANGNGA

Situated 94 km from Phuket town on the route to Hat Yai this would be quite a good day trip from Phuket by motorcycle. On the way to the town turn off just five km past the small town of Takua Thung and visit the Tham Suwan Kuha cave, full of Buddha images.

Tha Don, between here and Phangnga itself, is the place where you hire boats to visit Phangnga Bay with its Muslim fishing villages on stilts, the strangely shaped limestone outcroppings soaring out of the sea and the water-filled caves. Yes, these are the 'James Bond islands' from the film *Man with the Golden Gun*. A boat (the whole boat) to go out and visit the islands for, say, five hours, will cost around 350B.

Places to Stay & Eat

There are a number of fairly nondescript hotels with rooms in the 40 to 80B range. Most of them have un-rememberable Thai names! Along Phetkasem Rd, Phangnga's main street, you'll find the *Ratana Pong, Pak Phang-nga* and the *Lak Muang* as typical examples. There are other similarly priced places like the *Padoong* or the *Tan Prasert* on the western side of the town.

You can buy good seafood at the stalls across from the movie theatre in Phangnga's main market.

KRABI

This small fishing village offers similar offshore excursions to Phangnga. Koh Phi Phi, four hours south by boat, has untouched beaches, skindiving and a huge cavern where the nests for birds' nest soup are collected. Get a ride out on a fishing boat and stay with the very friendly villagers until a boat goes back – at least you *could* do that, today commercialism is starting to catch up with Koh Phi Phi and there are frequent tours from Phuket.

Places to Stay & Eat

The *New Hotel* on Uttarakit Rd and the *Kittisook* on Phangnga Rd both have rooms in the 50 to 80B range. The *Thai* at 3 Adisom Rd and the *Krabi* on Uttarakit Rd are nicer at 80 to 100B. The *Vieng Thong* is the nicest place in town but more expensive. The *Coffee Shop* has an English-language menu.

TRANG

The town of Trang is just another bustling little place between Krabi and Hat Yai.

Places to Stay & Eat

There are a number of places on the main street running down from the clock tower. The *Koh Teng* has rooms from 100B and good Thai food. The *Wattana* is on the same stretch and is a little more expensive. The cheap *Saha Thai* is only labelled as 'hotel' in English. Moving up market, the *Queen's Hotel* is great value at 130B for a big room with fan and a shower with hot water!

Adjacent to the Queen's Hotel the *Fan Foremost* has good, if a little pricey, food.

SUNGAI GOLOK

This small town in the south-east is a jumping-off point for the east coast of Malaysia – it's function is much like Hat Yai's for the busier west coast.

Places to Stay

There are no English signs in this border town to the Malaysian east coast, but in the centre of town there are a number of places to stay – although even the grotty ones cost 100B and up.

Cheapies include the *Savoy Hotel* and the *Thailieng Hotel* next door. The new *555 Hotel* is pretty good value at 100B or double that with air-con. The town is just a 10B rickshaw ride from the border or a five-minute walk straight ahead from the railway station. There are lots of cheap restaurants – for a cheap and delicious breakfast very early in the morning try coffee and doughnuts at the station buffet.

Getting There

Trains from Bangkok cost 172B in 3rd class, 360B in 2nd.

The Other South-East Asia

The end of the long and debilitating Indo-China War in 1975 was the first step towards bringing relative peace to this corner of Asia, so long out of reach of the traveller. Nevertheless it's been far from smooth sailing as Vietnam has been torn by conflicts with neighbouring China while Kampuchea has gone through its own monstrous internal upheavals.

Today, under pro-Soviet governments, the countries of Indo-China make a striking contrast to their ASEAN neighbours as a consequence of the destructive effects of the long war and the nature of their new administrations. All three have a great deal of interest to see and although they're hardly countries where you can wander around at will it is possible to visit Vietnam, Laos or Kampuchea.

VIETNAM

Travel to Vietnam is only possible on a pre-arranged basis with hotels, meals and transport made available through Vietnam Tourism, the state's tourist authority. Although the prices are not at 'shoestring' level, the quality and character of the grand old French-built hotels and the excellent food makes travel reasonable value for money.

Visiting Vietnam

Visas must be obtained via the office of Vietnam Tourism, 54 Nguyen Du St, Hanoi. As they have to refer your application to the Vietnamese Ministry of Foreign Affairs you can expect the visa procedure to take about six weeks before approval is obtained. Yóu then collect the visa from a Vietnamese diplomatic mission abroad. All arrangements are made for you by Vietnam Tourism and as an independent traveller you may have difficulty trying to go outside of Hanoi and Ho Chi Minh City.

Inclusive tours to Vietnam are operated from Britain by Regent Holidays, 13 Small St, Bristol BS1 1DE who have 15 day trips to the country. From Australia Orbitours (tel 02 233-3288), Box 3484, GPO, Sydney 2001 operates similar trips. Their one-week 'Saigon Experience' tour can be joined either in Australia or Bangkok. Diethelm Travel, 544 Ploenchit Rd, Bangkok (tel 252 4041) operates tours weekly, but remember to allow four weeks for visa formalities to be completed. Forget it if you're a US passport holder or a journalist.

Accommodation

Vietnam Tourism makes all the arrangements and they don't charge more than US$30 a night. All hotels will expect you to eat western food even though they are much better at the Vietnamese variety. It's like a spicier version of Chinese food, always served with the fermented fish sauce known as *nuoc mam*.

Getting There

Visitors to Vietnam must arrive by air, and Bangkok or Vientiane are the usual places to fly from. Air Vietnam, Lao Aviation and Thai Airways make these flights. Flights are normally full so ensure that your reservations are confirmed for the return journey. The Vietnam Tourism desk at Noi Bai airport will arrange a taxi to take you into town.

Air France also flies weekly from Paris to Ho Chi Minh City via Bangkok. Aeroflot flies weekly from Moscow via Rangoon to Vientiane in Laos and Ho Chi Minh City. Domestic flights link Ho Chi Minh City with Danang and Hanoi.

Getting Around

Travel is expensive if you are alone as you will be expected to fly. Hanoi to Ho Chi Minh City costs US$151! There are train and bus services which are invariably uncomfortable (not air-conditioned and with seats designed for midgets), but they're a good way of meeting the people if you have the patience and persistence to handle Vietnam Tourism. If you're lucky you may be allowed to tag along with a package tour from Romania or wherever. The 'reunification train' between Hanoi and Ho Chi Minh City takes at the very least 72 hours to cover the 1730 km so the average speed is less than 30 kph. Take plenty of supplies with you and don't expect any catering or sleepers – they don't exist.

Ho Chi Minh City

Still often called Saigon, the former southern capital is an extremely attractive city on the banks of the Saigon River. The centre is compact and ideal for strolling; interesting places to visit are the markets, cathedral, river-port, former American Embassy (now home of the State Petroleum Authority), Presidential Palace (perfectly preserved for some inscrutable reason) and the nearby park which also houses a museum of Vietnamese History and Culture and a small zoo.

Tours usually visit the Chinese sector of Cholon (many interesting temples), orphanages, various types of rehabilitation centres and, inevitably, the Museum of American War Crimes, appropriately housed in the ex-US Information Service Building. There are also quite a few interesting antique shops.

In the centre of town are a few privately operated cafes where you may meet the local people informally. Ho Chi Minh City is in many ways more cosmopolitan and hedonistic than the capital, Hanoi. The city may not be very attractive but it has something in the way of style and atmosphere. There is still a dance once a week with hostesses, and even a bar! Lots of films are made here and the restaurants are good – ask for Madame Dai's; her French cooking is better than anything you will get in the hotels. A nuisance to avoid is the persistent attention of prostitutes who clamour around you at every opportunity. As a reminder of the war Vietnam has an appallingly high rate of syphilis sufferers, some strains of which are unresponsive to conventional treatment with antibiotics.

Around Ho Chi Minh City

An excellent day tour from Saigon is to Cu Chi in Tay Ninh Province. This is an area where extremely heavy fighting took place and is notable as an example of the skill of the Viet Cong at building tunnels. Approximately 200 km of underground tunnels link arms caches and primitive hospitals with villages (most of which no longer exist). An ex-VC cadre explains the extraordinary history of the war in the region. This was a heavily defoliated area and the barren plains are decorated with rusting American tanks and artillery.

A New Economic Zone about 30 km from the city is another popular excursion and gives some insight into the difficult problems associated with the restoration of agriculture in a devastated countryside.

Central Vietnam

The area around Danang is notable for the Cham people, a group with Indian origins and culture. Many of their temples are around a thousand years old and still functioning, and there is a justly famous museum of Cham art in Danang. Concerts of traditional Vietnamese music are often given by a local group.

Danang also boasts the Marble Mountain, a complex of marble-faced caves and temples within a mountain; and an excellent beach dotted with overweight Soviet advisers and their equally massive wives on holiday. Hue, with its interesting citadel and royal palace, can sometimes be visited by air. Up the 'perfume river' 10 km from Hue are the old Imperial tombs.

Hanoi

Hanoi is largely restored since the bombing and is a quiet and attractive city of tree-lined boulevards, bicycle traffic and a complex of beautiful lakes in the city centre. The tomb of Ho Chi Minh in the main square can be visited as can also, sometimes, his humble residence nearby in the grounds of the Governor's Palace. Hanoi also has a number of pagodas worth looking at and a number of museums.

Shopping is fun in the markets and shops, of which two deserve special mention. The Souvenir du Vietnam shop has good traditional handicrafts but for a really stunning purchase go to the foreign book exporters, Xunhasaba, at 32 Rue Hai Ba Trung. You must telephone for an appointment (tel 2257, 2313, 2860 or 4067). They have for sale – complete with export licence – fine Vietnamese paintings, lacquerware and, best of all, superb porcelain.

An interesting excursion is via Haiphong to Ha Long Bay where it is possible to cruise by motorboat, arranged by Vietnam Tourism, around a bay studded with surrealistic limestone outcrops and populated by picturesque fishing junks. Ha Long is 164 km from Hanoi and reached by road.

LAOS

After the fall of Saigon the writing was on the wall for the old Royalist faction in Laos. They simply departed and left the country to the Pathet Lao.

Visiting Laos

To visit Laos you must obtain permission and make arrangements through the Lao Tourism Office (tel 2998 or 3254), Rue Samsenthai, Vientiane. In practice this means that you tell the tourist office your plans and they either approve them or not. If you want to travel outside Vientiane you must inform them at that stage. After obtaining your 'invitation' you should find it easy to pick up a Lao visa in Bangkok, Delhi or Hanoi. The visas cost around US$5 and take 48 hours to issue. At last report Lao embassies only gave five-day transit visas, normally for people travelling between Bangkok and Hanoi. Some can be cajoled into granting it for transit between Bangkok and Rangoon if you use the direct Aeroflot flight Vientiane-Rangoon.

The Lao bureaucracy has a better knowledge of French than any other foreign tongue and letters in French are more likely to be responded to. Note that you need permission from the Ministries of Foreign Affairs and Interior to travel more than 15 km outside of Vientiane and that you will have to pay for an escort provided by the Lao government.

Getting There

There are frequent flights to Vientiane from Bangkok and Hanoi plus weekly flights to Ho Chi Minh City and Rangoon. Domestic services operate to Luang Prabang and Pakse.

If possible avoid arriving in Laos by air. Customs seem so bored that they can think of nothing better to do than minutely search your luggage. It's also staggeringly expensive to get into town as the airport taxis require payment in dollars and charge US$1 a km! The other way to Vientiane is to take a train or bus from Bangkok to Nong Khai and from there a samlor to the customs and immigration office on the Mekong. This should cost 10B and it then costs 30B to cross the river by ferry to the Lao town of Tha Deua. Once you're through customs and immigration take a taxi to Vientiane, a 30 km journey which will cost 50 or 60B. The border posts on both sides of the Mekong are open 8 to 11 am and 2 to 4 pm only. They are also likely to charge you a 20B 'processing fee'. This trip is an exception to the limitation that you cannot go further than 15 km from the capital.

Orbitours in Sydney and Diethelm in Bangkok (see the Vietnam section) operate tours to Laos.

Vientiane

The capital continues to be a dusty and torpid provincial town masquerading as a capital city and sleeping on the banks of the Mekong. The Lao people are as warm and friendly as ever although the sort of overnight friendliness that flourished previously is no more. There's virtually no traffic and almost no tourist rip-offs.

Vientiane is now an 8 am to 8 pm city and most people are in bed by 9. Apart from the disappearance of the nightlife, not much seems to have changed. Such institutions as the Morning Market have survived. The markets are the most Lao thing about Vientiane. Obvious items to look for are Pakse silk and hand-made and tailored Lao shirts which are very good. Silver jewellery is also good and cheap. If you're hankering after an expensive bottle of western liquor or other 'luxury' goods then go to the Magasin d'Approvisionnement Pour les Missions Estrangeres on Rue Samsenthai.

Most of Vientiane's monuments are Buddhist wats although it's a town of bizarre curiosities including two war memorials, one for each side, and a Revolutionary Museum (of course). In the middle of town the Monument des Morts is a curious baroque version of Paris' Arc de Triomphe. The Peoples' Assembly buildings are also worth visiting. That Luang is a pyramid three km north-east of the city, further afield you can visit the stone garden of Xieng Khuane (a kind of Lao Tiger Balm Gardens) 25 km from Vientiane.

There is a tourist office on Sam Sen Thai Rd. Visits to places outside Vientiane are limited by shortages both of transport and visa time! Lao festivals are great.

Places to Stay There is only one reliable hotel in Vientiane, the *Lanexang*, where even a suite costs only US$25! Doubles are US$22 and the Lanexang only accepts payment in US dollars. The French cuisine is both cheap and excellent at the Lanexang.

Two other hotels accept foreigners, the *Vieng Vilay* and the *Imperial* – rooms cost from US$10 to 15. The tourist office was planning to open the *Peace* and *Inter* hotels to foreigners too; these hotels have good restaurants.

For the best coffee and croissants in the far east go to *Santisouk*, near the national stadium. Cost is about 35c (US) or 12 new kip. For Lao food you will have to resort to market stalls where balls of sticky rice and paddek (a sort of fermented fish) and barbecued chicken await the adventurous. Lao lao, the local variant of sake, is good and powerful! There are also undistinguished Chinese and Vietnamese restaurants.

KAMPUCHEA

Kampuchea, with its all-too-well-known and tragic history is the most difficult of these countries to visit although the administration installed by the Vietnamese (the Peoples' Republic of Kampuchea) in 1979 is much more receptive to foreign contact than that of the Khmer Rouge (Democratic Kampuchea), which they overthrew.

Although a number of people have visited Kampuchea since 1979, continued insecurity in the countryside, the absence of regular transport links, except with Vietnam, and the shortage of internal transport and facilities present problems – though not insurmountable ones.

Phnom Penh is reportedly an interesting place to visit, having somewhat recovered from its ghost town status when almost the whole population was forcibly dispersed to the countryside. Among the new attractions is the museum of some of the Khmer Rouge's more mind-boggling atrocities.

The country's most famous attraction is the vast complex of temples at Angkor Wat in the north-west of the country. It's one of the great archaeological and cultural sites of Asia but it lies a long and somewhat insecure drive away from Phnom Penh. It is apparently mostly intact in spite of reports of damage, neglect and vandalism and hopefully it will become more accessible in the future, perhaps by an air service to nearby Siem Reap.

Getting There
Orbitours may have further information. There are missions in Hanoi and Ho Chi Minh City, also in Delhi and Moscow. Most other Kampuchean missions (eg in the ASEAN capitals and Peking) represent the ousted regime and are definitely not the ones to try!

There are flights to Phnom Penh from Hanoi, Ho Chi Minh City and Vientiane. Road travel between Ho Chi Minh City and Phnom Penh is theoretically possible, but the Thai border remains closed for obvious reasons.

ONWARD TRAVEL
South-East Asia can be a trip in itself or some part of a longer journey. Of course the region's various cheap ticket specialists are ready to jet you off to destinations far away, but you can also keep on travelling closer to ground level.

If you're heading west from South-East Asia it's only a short flight from Rangoon in Burma to Dacca in Bangladesh, Calcutta in India or Kathmandu in Nepal. Then the whole sub-continent is spread out before you and if you're in the mood (and the Ayatollah doesn't dislike your nationality) you could keep on heading west through Iran and Turkey all the way to Europe. See *West Asia on a Shoestring* for the full story.

Eastbound Hong Kong is the last stepping stone in this book, but our long-delayed third Asia shoestring guide, *North-East Asia on a Shoestring* will take you into China (now wide open for independent budget travellers) or to Korea, Taiwan and Japan.

Index

Thanks

To all of you many, many people my grateful thanks. If I've missed you out my apologies; if your name is wrong, it's either your handwriting, my handwriting, somebody else's handwriting or a typo.

Rob Mitchell (UK), Jenny Reid (UK), Cliff Cob (US), Babs Macleod & Neil Blake (M), Michel Mons (P), Chris Guin (UK), Candace Lowe (US), Klaas Bisschop (Nl), Robert Storey (US), Richard Evans (UK), Robert Armstrong (UK), A R Snyder (Aus), Michael Heney (NZ), Jennette (UK), Christine Hoyle & Roger Pawling (UK), John de Bresser (Nl), Heidi Gerber (CH), Mike Mundy (UK), Garry Allen & Grant Soosalu (Aus), Eric Grist (UK), Dick Rigby (UK), Jim Waltor (UK), Ralph Mclintock (Aus), John Vickers (NZ), Brent Mander (NZ), Neil Taylor (Aus), Iris Chang (HK), Michael Nixon (NZ), Vlado Oravsky (Dk), David Yost (Aus), Franz Huber (D), Rosemary Jackson-Hunter (UK), Carine Faweade (F), Jurgen Pohlenz (D), Nola Hayes & Gary Bond (Aus), Nenehe Lim (M), Alan Bonsteel (Id), H Keith Pierce (US), Carrie Warder (US), Mike Wheeler (UK), Hans-Jurgen Frundt (D), Roger Baleh (Aus), Diane Countryman (Sin), Patrick Creedon (T), Ian MacDonell (C), Mark L Roelopser (Aus), Margaret & David Lyddiord Aus), David Pinkerton (US), George R Walther US), John R Edwards (Aus), Helen & Colin Goodwin (Aus), Craig Emmoth (Aus), Bill Costello & Wendy Krakauer (US), Bernd-Michael Schauer (D), Hendrik Trepp (S), Asa Ottossan & Las Kalbtrand (S), Jerry Stein & Nick Stephens (US), Finn Frus Lauszus (Dk), Rob Lindsay (NZ), Mary Lippens (B), Peter Norfolk (Aus), Emil Adel (Nl), Ann Douglas & Mark Bryant (UK), Gote Gustappson (S), John Dickinson (UK), Ian Rowland & Yvonne Holmes, Noga & Steve Murdoch, Efrat Elron (Isr), Roger Fredriksson (S), Bjarne Stig Hansen (Aus), John Thornhill (Aus), Harry Golding (US), Dennis Heozle (T), K Brophy (Aus), Simon Hunter (Aus), Brigitta & David Gilbert (Aus), Philip Graham (Aus), Helen Stockley & Lucy Holden (UK), Rakimatsah Amat (M), Ole Winther Nielsen (Dk), John Nettleship (UK), P J Ricketts (In), Angela Dew (NZ), Charles Pollard & Seval Keltell (UK), Peter van der Baan (Nl), Gilles Rubens (Nl), Leon McDonald, (Aus), Franziska Planzer (Tw), Ken Waller (C), Martin Ellison, Richard Waye (UK), ? Cambell (Aus), Chris Tollast (UK), Kathleen Clerle-Pomarede & Patrick Pomarede (F), John Benson (NZ), Fabian Pedrazzini (CH), Tom Eggert (US), Pam Olink & Leicester Cooper (Aus), Tom Hariman & Jan King (US), Bonnie Baskin (US), Val Jones & Chris Watters (T), Johnny Clerke (UK), Bill Harvey (NZ), Chris Zimm (Aus), Hine Alestine (US), Ned & Robert Hall (Aus), Maxine Kilner (US), Mandy Adams (UK), Fred Dong (US), Dorte Verner (Dk), Kohn Kleeman (UK), Tom Hariman & Jan King (US), Michael Green (T), Gill Whybrow (UK), Jay (UK), Jennifer S Maylan (In), Glenn Strachan (US), Steve Sharp & Angie Finnery (UK), Jim Priest (US), Dawsn Polley & Sandy Ross (C), Kevin Dwyer (US), Paul Creamer (Aus), Paul Sukler (US), Caroline Wigram (UK), Jan Hamilton (Aus), Nicola King (NZ), Felise Bisterbosek (Nl), Richard Haverkamp & Linda Lilburne (NZ), Jack Carling (Aus), Mark Voskamp (Nl) Denise Newton (Aus), Peter Gray (Aus), Chris Tyler (UK), Norman Sheppard (UK), Trevor Akerman & Julie Hardcastle (UK), Anthony J Percy (UK), Brian Threlkeld (US), Richard & Carolyn Salisbury (Sin), Michael Woodhouse (Aus), Cathy & Anne Doherty (Aus), Jill & Godfrey Whitehouse (NZ), Neil Taylor (Aus), Kerry & Michele Snyde (HK), John Nania (US), J Walder (Sin), N Richards (UK), Jerome & Regima Pauwels (B), Stephen Currie (UK), Bruce T Singer (US), Andrew Bartram (UK), Carol Collins Wendouree (Aus), Helga Schmidbraver (D), Thomase Hesse (D), Darren Russell (Aus), Stanley Wong (M), Bruce & Lynda Kennedy (C), Garry Neil Watson (NZ), Michael Reeve, Mark & Katrina Harris (UK), Peter C Jackson (UK), Craig Bullock (UK), Laura Liebesman (Tw), Simon & Geraldine Harris (Aus), Geoffrey Bewley (Aus), Bruce & Singa (US).

A – Austria, Aus – Australia, B – Belgium, C – Canada, CH – Switzerland, D – Germany, Dk – Denmark, F – France, HK – Hong Kong, I – Italy, Id – India, In – Indonesia, Isr – Isreal, J – Japan, M – Malaysia, Nl – Netherlands, NZ – New Zealand, P – Philippines, PNG – Papua New Guinea, S – Sweden, Sin – Singapore, T – Thailand, Tw – Taiwan, UK – United Kingdom, US – USA